THE CONTINENTAL AESTHETICS READER

'. . . an extremely impressive selection'.
Malcom Barnard, *University of Derby*

'I fully endorse *The Continental Aesthetics Reader* and believe that for the foreseeable future it will be required reading for all those who "think" about art.'
Gary Peters, *University of West of England*

'*The Continental Aesthetics Reader* is a rich and intellectually uncompromising anthology. It fills an important gap in the literature.'
Timothy R. Quigley, *New School for Social Research, New York*

'Cazeaux's brief introductions to the selections are insightful and cogent. This volume will serve as a much-needed source for considering the range and depth of modern aesthetic theory.'
Tom Huhn, *Wesleyan University*

'This much-needed reader will provide a very valuable resource for teaching, and is an excellent introduction for the general reader interested in the field.'
Michael Newman, *Central Saint Martins College of Art and Design*

The Continental Aesthetics Reader is the first comprehensive anthology of classic writings on art and aesthetics from the major figures in Continental thought. The reader is clearly divided into six sections: Nineteenth-Century German Aesthetics • Phenomenology and Hermeneutics • Marxism and Critical Theory • Modernism • Poststructuralism and Postmodernism • Psychoanalysis and Feminism. Each section is clearly placed in its historical and philosophical context by Clive Cazeaux.

Ideal for introductory courses in aesthetics, Continental philosophy, art, and visual studies, *The Continental Aesthetics Reader* provides a thorough introduction to some of the most influential writings on art and aesthetics from Kant to Derrida.

Clive Cazeaux is Senior Lecturer in Aesthetics at the University of Wales Institute, Cardiff.

THE CONTINENTAL AESTHETICS READER

Edited by Clive Cazeaux

LONDON AND NEW YORK

First published 2000
by Routledge
2 Park Square, Milton Park, Abingdon, Oxon, OX14 4RN

Simultaneously published in the USA and Canada
by Routledge
270 Madison Ave, New York, NY 10016

Reprinted 2005, 2006, (twice), 2007 (twice)

Transferred to Digital Printing 2008

Routledge is an imprint of the Taylor & Francis Group, an informa business

© 2000 Selection and editorial matter, Clive Cazeaux

Typeset in Times by
RefineCatch Limited, Bungay, Suffolk
Printed and bound in Great Britain by
TJI Digital, Padstow, Cornwall

All rights reserved. No part of this book may be reprinted or reproduced or utilised in any form or by any electronic, mechanical, or other means, now known or hereafter invented, including photocopying and recording, or in any information storage or retrieval system, without permission in writing from the publishers.

British Library Cataloguing in Publication Data
A catalogue record for this book is available from the British Library

Library of Congress Cataloging in Publication Data
The continental aesthetics reader / edited by Clive Cazeaux.
p. cm.
Includes bibliographical references and index.
1. Aesthetics, Modern – 20th century. 2. Aesthetics, Modern – 19th century. 3.
Philosophy, European. I. Cazeaux, Clive.
BH201 .C59 2000
111′.85′094 – dc21 00–032177

ISBN10: 0–415–20053–9 (hbk)
ISBN10: 0–415–20054–7 (pbk)

ISBN13: 978–0–415–20053–0 (hbk)
ISBN13: 978–0–415–20054–7 (pbk)

CANISIUS COLLEGE LIBRARY
BUFFALO, NY

CONTENTS

ACKNOWLEDGEMENTS

I am grateful to the following copyright holders for granting permission to reproduce material in this book:

Immanuel Kant, extracts from 'Analytic of Aesthetic Judgment' and 'Dialectic of Aesthetic Judgment', *Critique of Judgment*, trans. Werner S. Pluhar, Indianapolis, Hackett, 1987, §§ 32–38, 44–46, 49, 56–57; pp. 145–56, 172–76, 181–86, 210–17. © Hackett Publishing Company.

G.W.F. Hegel, 'Concept of the Beauty of Art' and 'Division of the Subject', *Aesthetics: Lectures on Fine Art*, trans. T.M. Knox, Oxford, Oxford University Press, 1975, pp. 1–3, 22–25, 69–90. © Oxford University Press.

Friedrich Nietzsche, 'On Truth and Lie in an Extra-Moral Sense', *Philosophy and Truth: Selections from Nietzsche's Notebooks of the Early 1870s*, ed. Daniel Breazeale, Atlantic Highlands, New Jersey, Humanities Press, 1994, pp. 79–91. © Prometheus Publishers.

Martin Heidegger, 'The Origin of the Work of Art', *Poetry, Language, Thought*, trans. Albert Hofstadter, New York, Harper and Row, 1971, pp. 17–22, 26–37, 41–57, 69–70, 72–78. © Harper and Row.

Jean-Paul Sartre, 'What is Writing?', *What is Literature?*, London, Routledge, 1997, pp. 1–25. © Routledge.

Emmanuel Levinas, 'Reality and its Shadow', *Collected Philosophical Papers*, trans. Alphonso Lingis, *The Levinas Reader*, ed. Séan Hand, Oxford, Blackwell, 1996, pp. 130–43. © Martinus Nijhoff.

Mikel Dufrenne, 'The World of the Aesthetic Object', *The Phenomenology of Aesthetic Experience*, trans. E.S. Casey, Evanston, Northwestern University Press, 1966, pp. 166–98. © Northwestern University Press.

Gaston Bachelard, 'The Dialectics of Outside and Inside', *The Poetics of Space*, trans. Maria Jolas, Boston, Beacon Press, 1994, pp. 211–31. © Penguin Putnam.

Maurice Merleau-Ponty, 'The Intertwining – The Chiasm', *The Visible and the Invisible*, ed. Claude Lefort, trans. Alphonso Lingis, Evanston, Northwestern University Press, 1968, pp. 130–55. © Northwestern University Press.

Hans-Georg Gadamer, 'Aesthetics and Hermeneutics', *Philosophical Hermeneutics*, trans. and ed. David E. Linge, Berkeley, University of California Press, 1977, pp. 95–104. © University of California Press.

Gianni Vattimo, 'The Death or Decline of Art', *The End of Modernity*, trans. Jon R. Snyder, Cambridge, Polity Press, 1988, pp. 51–64. © Blackwell.

Karl Marx, 'Private Property and Communism', *Early Writings*, trans. Rodney Livingstone and Gregor Benton, London, Penguin, 1992, pp. 345–58.

Georg Lukács, 'Specific Particularity as the Central Category of Aesthetics', *Über die Besonderheit als Kategorie der Aesthetik*, Berlin, Aufbau, 1985, pp. 136–54. © Artisjus. Budapest.

Theodor W. Adorno, extracts from *Minima Moralia: Reflections from Damaged Life*, trans. E.F.N. Jephcott, London, Verso, 1978, pp. 138–52, 212–31. © Verso.

Herbert Marcuse, 'Nature and Revolution', *Counterrevolution and Revolt*, Boston, Beacon Press, 1972, pp. 59–78. © Beacon Press.

Jürgen Habermas, 'Modernity versus Postmodernity', *New German Critique*, 1981, vol. 22, pp. 3–14. © Telos Press.

Jürgen Habermas, 'Questions and Counterquestions', *Praxis International*, 1984, vol. 4, pp. 234–38, 248. © Blackwell.

Fredric Jameson, 'Postmodernism and Consumer Society', *The Cultural Turn: Selected Writings on the Postmodern, 1983–1998*, London, Verso, 1998, pp. 1–20. © Verso.

Georg Simmel, 'Value and Money', *The Philosophy of Money*, trans. David Frisby, London, Routledge, 1990, pp. 59–79. © Routledge.

Walter Benjamin, 'The Work of Art in the Age of Mechanical Reproduction', *Illuminations*, trans. Harry Zohn, London, Jonathan Cape, 1970, pp. 219–53. © Harcourt, Brace and Company.

Maurice Blanchot, 'The Original Experience', *The Space of Literature*, trans. Ann Smock, Lincoln, University of Nebraska Press, 1982, pp. 234–47. © University of Nebraska Press.

Ernst Bloch, 'Artistic Illusion as Visible Anticipatory Illumination', *The Utopian Function of Art and Literature*, trans. Jack Zipes and Frank Mecklenburg, Cambridge, Massachusetts, MIT Press, 1996, pp. 141–55. © Massachusetts Institute of Technology Press.

Georges Bataille, 'Sanctity, Eroticism and Solitude', *Erotism*, trans. Mary Dalwood, San Francisco, City Lights, 1986, pp. 252–64.

Roland Barthes, 'The Plates of the *Encyclopedia*', *New Critical Essays*, trans. Richard Howard, New York, Hill and Wang, 1980. © Farrar, Straus, and Giroux, Inc.

Michel Foucault, 'Las Meninas', *The Order of Things*, London, Routledge, 1970, pp. 3–16. © Routledge.

Jacques Derrida, 'The Parergon', *The Truth in Painting*, trans. Geoff Bennington and

Ian McLeod, Chicago, University of Chicago Press, 1987, pp. 37–43, 50–67, 77–79. © University of Chicago Press.

Paul de Man, 'The Resistance to Theory', *Yale French Studies*, New Haven, Connecticut, Yale University Press, 1982, pp. 355–71. © Yale University Press.

Jean Baudrillard, 'The Evil Demon of Images', *The Evil Demon of Images*, trans. Paul Patton and Paul Foss, Sydney, Power Institute of Fine Arts, 1987, pp. 13–34.

Jean-François Lyotard, 'The Sublime and the Avant-Garde', *The Lyotard Reader*, ed. Andrew Benjamin, Oxford, Blackwell, 1989, pp. 196–211. © Edinburgh University Press.

Gilles Deleuze and Félix Guattari, 'Percept, Affect, and Concept', *What is Philosophy?*, trans. Hugh Tomlinson and Graham Burchell, London, Verso, 1994, pp. 163–99. © Verso.

Sigmund Freud, 'The Unconscious', *Standard Edition of the Complete Psychological Works of Sigmund Freud, vol. XIV: Papers on Metapsychology*, ed. James Strachey, London, Hogarth Press, 1974, pp. 166–76, 196–204. © Random House, © W.W. Norton and Company.

Jacques Lacan, 'Of the Gaze as *Objet Petit a*', *The Four Fundamental Concepts of Psychoanalysis*, trans. Alan Sheridan, London, Vintage, 1998, pp. 79–89, 91–103, 105–16. © Random House.

Julia Kristeva, 'Approaching Abjection', *Powers of Horror*, trans. Leon S. Roudiez, New York, Columbia University Press, 1982, pp. 1–31. © Columbia University Press.

Luce Irigaray, 'The Invisible of the Flesh: A Reading of Merleau-Ponty, "The Intertwining – The Chiasm"', *An Ethics of Sexual Difference*, trans. Carolyn Burke and Gillian C. Gill, New York, Cornell University Press, and London, Athlone Press, 1993, pp. 151–84. © Cornell University Press, and © Athlone Press.

Hélène Cixous, 'The Last Painting or the Portrait of God', *Coming to Writing and Other Essays*, ed. Deborah Benson, Cambridge, Massachusetts, Harvard University Press, 1991, pp. 104–31. © Harvard University Press.

Diego Rodríguez de Silva y Velázquez, *Las Meninas*.

Lucas Cranach, *Lucretia*.

Hans Holbein, *The Ambassadors*.

While reasonable effort has been put into obtaining permissions prior to publication, there are some cases where it has been impossible to trace the copyright holder or to secure a reply. The editor and publishers apologize for any errors and omissions and, if notified, the publisher will endeavour to rectify these at the earliest opportunity.

The support and advice of friends and colleagues has been invaluable. I would like to thank: Keith Ansell Pearson, Catherine Belsey, Fred Botting, Gideon Calder, Andrew Edgar, Kevin Edge, Judith Fritz, Mark Harris, Karin Hiscock, Martin Gaughan, Christopher Norris, and Christopher Short. Special thanks goes to Nicholas Walker for his translation of Lukács' article, to Ruth Dineen for her feedback on the cover, and to Tony Bruce at Routledge for his guidance throughout. I am also especially grateful to the Fine Art Research Committee at the University of Wales Institute, Cardiff, who sped things along enormously by granting me extra research leave.

Cardiff, December 1999

INTRODUCTION

Aesthetics has undergone a radical transformation in the last hundred years. Traditionally, the subject has always occupied the margins of philosophy, for the simple reason that it deals with those aspects of experience which are the least amenable to categorization, i.e., art, beauty, emotion, and the ever-changing delights of the senses. However, the divisions imposed on reality by modern reason and changes brought about by the industrialization of experience have necessitated a rethinking of the relationship between the individual and reality. Gone are notions of a distinct self in receipt of a mind-independent world and, in their place, are theses to the effect that consciousness and reality are interconnected at a fundamental level. One consequence of this shift is that aesthetic experience is redefined. Far from being a mere adjunct to everyday perception, it is shown to be vital to an understanding of the relationship between mind and world. The aesthetic, formerly exiled from mainstream attention, assumes centre-stage as the region to which we can turn for new cognitive possibilities and a sensibility that is critical of the divisions exercised by modern thought.

This book makes available for the first time in one volume key texts by leading thinkers in modern aesthetics. Thirty-five authors are represented altogether and in nearly all cases their writings are complete and unabridged. One essay is also appearing in English for the first time: Georg Lukács' 'Specific Particularity as the Central Category of Aesthetics'. The selection charts the development of ideas from the nineteenth century and the defining texts of the tradition to recent debates within the major intellectual movements of the twentieth century. The essays are organized into sections, and each section opens with an introductory essay by the editor, giving background information on the individual authors and outlining the principal arguments. There are six sections: (1) Nineteenth-Century German Aesthetics, (2) Phenomenology and Hermeneutics, (3) Marxism and Critical Theory, (4) Modernism, (5) Poststructuralism and Postmodernism, and (6) Psychoanalysis and Feminism.

While this sectioning of material acknowledges certain shared interests and methods, it is not meant to signify the existence of separate, uniform lines of enquiry. There are several instances when an author included in one category could have easily been placed in another. Essays and arguments gain their critical edge by being part of a continuous, evolving body of ideas and, in respect of this, *The Continental Aesthetics Reader* sets out to place its essays in a constellational relationship. Once individual items are placed side by side, connections materialize which transform all the participants. Proximities and distances emerge which let the reader see how the various positions speak to one another, where the claims of one are reinforced by the claims of a second, or are subject to re-evaluation by the criticisms of a third. Just how thought is organized and just how categories relate to their subject matter are in fact prominent themes in contemporary aesthetics, and are explored below by, among others, Kant, Nietzsche, Bachelard, Adorno, and Habermas.

With regard to the communication that occurs between essays, aesthetics is in a particularly unique position. As a subject in its own right, its arguments and counter-arguments achieve the level of specialized focus necessary to bring new possibilities into view yet, because of the scope of the subject, these possibilities have implications which reach beyond aesthetics to theoretical enquiry across the full range of the humanities. For example, poststructuralism's and feminism's interest in the process of writing makes us consider the contingent, constructed properties of thought, and the work done within hermeneutics and critical theory on art and understanding brings to wider attention the need for an ethics of communication. Thus, focusing on the eddies and currents which make up contemporary aesthetic debate lets us witness the flow of ideas within modern European thought as a whole.

The extent to which articles talk to one another has influenced the selection process. On a number of occasions, the first and seemingly obvious choice for inclusion was replaced by an article that participated with others in a dialogue. For example, 'Eye and Mind' is one of Merleau-Ponty's most well-known essays on aesthetics but instead of this I have chosen 'The Intertwining – The Chiasm'. As well as being an important piece in its own right, it is also the subject for discussion in Lacan's 'Of the Gaze as *Objet Petit a*' and Irigaray's 'The Invisible of the Flesh'. Similarly, Marcuse's main work on aesthetics is *The Aesthetic Dimension* but rather than take a chapter from here, I have opted for the lesser-known 'Nature and Revolution', from *Counter-revolution and Revolt*. Not only does it anticipate Marcuse's thesis in *The Aesthetic Dimension* but it also offers critical commentary on Marx's 'Private Property and Communism' and shows how critical theory supports radical feminism.

The decision to make complete and unabridged essays a priority came from my dissatisfaction with anthologies that offer heavily filleted versions of original works. A series of excerpts or selected passages often cannot do justice to the broader argument in which the individual claims are set. In any analysis of a text, certain passages will be highlighted and emphasized at the expense of others, and any process which limits the freedom of the reader to make their own comparisons within the body of an essay is an unwelcome intervention. However, there are some cases where complete works could not be reproduced. The texts from Marx and Adorno are, by their nature, fragmentary and, in a book of this kind, the epoch-defining systems of Kant and Hegel can only be represented in extract form. Where cuts have been made because of length, for example, with Heidegger, Derrida, and Freud, I have excised passages whose removal I felt detracted the least from the overall argument.

I have also considered the different forms of artwork – literature, music, the visual arts – that are discussed in the essays, mindful that too much attention paid to one category might alienate readers from other areas or that by attempting to cover a bit of everything, I end up diluting the whole enterprise. Fortunately, the pattern of debate within mainstream Continental aesthetics is such that it seldom manifests itself as the philosophy of any one particular artform, and so there is little opportunity for bias to arise. Instead, themes emerge which draw on relationships between all the arts. 'Art' is regularly broached as a category *in general*: an artefact – be it a painting, a piece of music, or a performance – which, by being the sensuous embodiment of conscious enquiry, invites us to reassess our understanding of the way we interact with other objects and minds. The body and the five senses represent other areas of common interest. Bodily sensation roots us in existence, and the interventions which art and philosophy make in our appreciation of the senses affect how we view our position in the world. Merleau-Ponty, Marx, Lacan, and Irigaray all show how the textures of sensation are linked to wider debates regarding the structure of thought and the creation of social values.

Another very important development is that, in many respects, art and philosophy have become fused. This is primarily a result of interest in the philosophical and artistic significance of metaphor. Metaphor creates associations between concepts by describing one thing in terms of another, where the two terms literally or seemingly have nothing to do with one another, for example, 'love is *blind*', 'the *fabric* of reality', and 'Pollock's paintings *dance* before your eyes'. Accepted boundaries between concepts are disregarded and, in the newly found intervening space, novel and often insightful perspectives are brought into being. With metaphor, it is the region in between established concepts that becomes significant, for example, the synaesthetic relationships between different artforms, and the question of a middle-ground between art and philosophy. Several authors in this book, for example, Adorno, Blanchot, Bloch, Derrida, Irigaray, Deleuze and Guattari, write their philosophy *as art*, treating language not so much as a linear conveyor of ideas but as a medium which, through transgression and manipulation, can let us witness the creation and construction of thought.

As words with a particular philosophical currency, 'Continental' and 'aesthetics' deserve some explanation. 'Aesthetic' has a number of different though related meanings. There are, I suggest, three senses of the term. (1) In ancient Greek philosophy, in the texts of the pre-Socratics, Plato, and Aristotle, *aisthesis* refers to lived, felt experience, knowledge as it is obtained through the senses, in contrast to *eidos*, knowledge derived from reason and intellection, from which we get the word 'idea'. The distinction remains with us today and underlies much contemporary thought. The seventeenth-century rationalist philosopher René Descartes is one figure who can be singled out as reasserting the distinction. He is generally regarded as the founder of modern philosophy on the grounds that he demonstrates the independence of human rationality from God. However, the argument upon which his entire system rests, the *cogito* – 'I think, therefore, I am' – (from the *Discourse on Method* (1637)) is also an argument for the primacy of thought over sense perception.

(2) Perhaps the most familiar sense of the term is aesthetics as the study of beauty and, in particular, the beautiful in art. This understanding originates in the eighteenth century with the appearance of the 'modern (Cartesian) individual' and the upsurge of interest in harmonious form which accompanied the changes in western society's economic structure. The transition from feudalism to capitalism initiated the move from the 'absolute law' of the aristocracy to the 'subjective freedom' of the new bourgeoisie who instituted beauty and the fine arts as expressions of their new class identity. Allied with this was the emergence of romantic theories of beauty in opposition to the classical tradition. Whereas classicism explained beauty in terms of set relational or mathematical properties, romanticism claimed for the artist a unique, holistic relationship with nature which meant that artistic expression and quality transcended rules or prescriptive criteria. This ensured an excess of individual, subjective autonomy in which to locate bourgeois identity.

(3) Contemporary aesthetics has its roots in the third sense of the term. It appears as a reaction to the previous 'appreciation of beauty' concept, and is articulated in the work of the eighteenth-century German philosopher Immanuel Kant. He saw the interests of subjective experience and objective knowledge becoming increasingly polarized and, in response, constructed a system of thought in which subjective experience and the condition of belonging to a world were shown to be interrelated. Tradition had placed the aesthetic beyond words and Kant's ingenious move was to take its property of being resistant to conceptualization and make it the arena in which the interaction between consciousness and reality is worked out. For the first time, what exists beyond description is not placed beyond understanding or in opposition to everyday experience but argued to be the dynamic state of conceptual reappraisal that is constitutive of our attempts to deal with any new situation. What had been theorized as a narrow and isolated band of experience is seen to arch across all the 'hard', world-confronting regions of thought, e.g., epistemology, ethics, ontology. Occasions when we are coming to terms with an artwork or enjoying a moment of heightened sensation become vital to an understanding of our cognitive and moral contact with the world.

Why 'Continental' aesthetics? In the western tradition, it is often claimed that there are two styles or ways of doing philosophy: the *Continental*, characterized primarily by the work of French and German philosophers, and the *analytic*, dominant in most American and British philosophy departments. Generally speaking, Continental philosophy pays greater attention to the historically rooted and culturally constructed nature of ideas; philosophy is recognized as something which is made and written and, therefore, as something which cannot be divorced from the contingencies of language and tradition. In contrast, analytic philosophy, with its roots in British empiricism and logical positivism, is committed to the belief that a problem can be clarified or brought out into the open through the careful and rigorous analysis of concepts as we understand them today. In response to the question 'what is art?', an analytic philosopher might attempt to devise a checklist of properties that an object must have in order to count as a work of art (a set of necessary and sufficient conditions), whereas the Continental philosopher might take the question less *on its own terms* and suggest instead that it exists as part of a broader sweep of enquiry where the greater interest lies in what it means to be indefinable. In no way are the two approaches antitheses or opposites: the Continental and the analytic share many problems and debates. However, differences in style and other, institutional forces can sometimes mean that communication between the two is not as frequent as it could be.

Of the two, it is Continental aesthetics that has had the greater impact on our understanding of modern art and experience. This, I suggest, is mainly due to the fact that the climate within Continental thought has been more favourable to the propagation of new branches of enquiry from nineteenth-century German aesthetics. Although Kant and Hegel sit quite happily on both analytic and Continental curricula, it is only the latter which has seriously addressed the need to rethink how the world appears to us and how it is made manifest to us in the light of their metaphysics. Phenomenology, hermeneutics, critical theory, and psychoanalysis are all, at decisive moments, extensions of the premise – running through Kant, Hegel, and Nietzsche – that subjectivity and objectivity are abstractions from a much more fundamental and complex dynamic. One consequence of German aesthetics' interweaving of the mental and the physical has been the twentieth century's 'linguistification' of experience: the suggestion that experience does not come to us pure but is shaped and organized into recognizable units by the language we speak. Again, this thesis has been explored in detail by both traditions. However, its more radical implications for the status of aesthetics, the nature of meaning, and the texture of experience are to be found in Continental philosophy, in particular, poststructuralism and feminism. They emphasize the material properties of language and draw attention to the way in which its web-like network of relationships allows unexpected connections to frustrate our attempts at direct or self-evident meaning.

The Continental aesthetic tradition offers some of the most stimulating and innovative thinking on art and aesthetic experience in the modern era. Discussions about art and human sensibility are shown to hold valuable insights for the way we apportion meaning and value in our lives. Cartesian thought and capitalism divide fundamental relationships into isolated things, setting subjective experience apart from the objective world and installing a model of truth where the former is subordinate to the latter. Against this, Continental aesthetics asks us to consider the phenomenal and social textures which implicate us in the world, for within them we find the perceptual possibilities and dynamics of interpretation that generate new models of understanding. In the absence of truth, there is only art. The following essays demonstrate this.

Part 1

NINETEENTH-CENTURY GERMAN AESTHETICS

INTRODUCTION

Immanuel Kant	Extracts from 'Analytic of Aesthetic Judgment' and 'Dialectic of Aesthetic Judgment', *Critique of Judgment*, §§32–38, 44–46, 49, 56–57.
G.W.F. Hegel	Extracts from *Aesthetics: Lectures on Fine Art*, §§1, 2, 5, and 8.
Friedrich Nietzsche	On Truth and Lie in an Extra-Moral Sense

Immanuel Kant

Aesthetic experience has, for the greater part of the history of western philosophy, been regarded as subordinate to rational enquiry. Traditionally, sensory or aesthetic experience is dismissed as a means to truth either because it can be confused or indistinct or because it is not amenable to conceptual analysis; both Plato and Descartes offer arguments along these lines. This changes in the eighteenth century when two German thinkers make aesthetics central to philosophy: Alexander Baumgarten (1714–62) and Immanuel Kant (1724–1804). Baumgarten addresses the charge of confusion. His *Metaphysica* (1739) reconfigures aesthetic confusion as a synthesis ('confusion's field' or *campus confusionis*) and, therefore, as a positive epistemological notion.[1] Whereas rational judgement divides the world into subjects and predicates, aesthetic experience, Baumgarten avers, allows us to perceive these moments as a unified whole.

Kant's writing, however, has overshadowed Baumgarten's contribution. The reason for this, I suggest, is that Kant radically alters the modern European philosophical landscape. The major shift in thought he makes is to acknowledge the finitude of human experience. That is to say, he asserts that human consciousness is not detached from the world but rooted in and actively engaged with it. This is Kant's 'Copernican Revolution'. The comparison with Copernicus is made by Kant himself. Just as Copernicus tries to remove the anomalies affecting sixteenth-century astronomy by adopting a new model of the cosmos, so Kant proposes to resolve the problems of metaphysics by offering a new model of the relation between mind and reality:

> Hitherto it has been assumed that all our knowledge must conform to objects. But all attempts to extend our knowledge of objects by establishing something in regard to them a priori, by means of concepts, have, on this assumption, ended in failure. We must therefore make trial whether we may not have more success in the tasks of metaphysics, if we suppose that objects must conform to our knowledge.[2]

The human subject is made the origin of experience and, from this premise, the conditions of possibility of subjectivity are shown to be, at one and the same time, the conditions of possibility of objectivity. In other words, the structure of my experience and the structure of the world (the fact that it is occupied by perceptually graspable things) are two sides of the same coin. This is Kant's Transcendental Deduction, the central argument of the *Critique of Pure Reason.*

Kant's philosophy is 'critical' in a particular sense. His use of the term is allied to his assertion of human finitude. 'Critique', for Kant, refers to an examination of the scope and limits of our cognitive powers; in particular, a demonstration of both the possibility of knowledge within experience and the impossibility of knowledge beyond the limits of experience. As such, it is a reply to the scepticism characteristic of empiricist philosophy and to the dogmatic metaphysics of rationalism. Philosophy, as Kant found it, was polarized between the rationalism of Descartes, Leibniz, and Baumgarten on the Continent and the empiricism of Locke and Hume in Britain. The presuppositions of both systems, he observed, ultimately worked to undermine them and prevent them from offering coherent theories of knowledge and action. For example, Descartes fails in the *Meditations* (1641) to guarantee clear and distinct ideas and Hume realizes in the *Treatise of Human Nature* (1740) that an empiricist model of knowledge cannot account for abstract, structural concepts such as causality, number, and the self. Critical philosophy seeks to avoid these problems. Human finitude means that our concepts necessarily open onto the world as it is received by us through sensibility (what Kant calls *die Anschauung* or 'intuition'): 'thoughts without content are empty, intuitions without concepts are blind'.[3] This necessary interrelationship disarms Hume's doubt regarding the justification of our concepts and demonstrates to the rationalist that our categories are not abstractions which can be detached from experience and used to construct dogmatic metaphysical schemes.

Kant's main task is to argue for this interrelationship between mind and reality and, in particular, to explain how objectivity is possible given that the subject has been made the basis of experience. This project occupies all three of the books which make up Kant's critical system. The *Critique of Pure Reason* (1781, revised 1787) lays the foundations and considers the application of our cognitive powers (or 'reason' (*die Vernunft*) in Kant's broad sense of the term) to experience. The consequences of finitude for morality are considered in the *Critique of Practical Reason* (1788). Here, Kant faces the question of how a universal moral imperative supplied by reason in advance of experience can serve as a principle for showing us how we ought to act in particular situations.

The *Critique of Judgment* (1790) completes the critical trilogy not just because it is the third and final volume but, more importantly, because it explores those aspects of experience which allow the fullest exposition of the interrelationship between subject and object: art, beauty, and the appearance of design in nature. Aesthetics is not treated in isolation but made central to Kant's entire project, and shown to be directly relevant to moral and epistemological issues. Furthermore, it can be argued that Kant's accounts of the mediation between category and experience in the first two *Critiques* ultimately lie unresolved, and it is the job of the third book to give his thesis its full and final expression. For example, in the *Critique of Pure Reason,* Kant surrenders the operation of the mind which brings pure concepts into relation with empirical intuition as 'an art concealed in the depths of the human soul, whose real modes of activity nature is hardly likely ever to allow us to discover'.[4]

The main question which Kant asks in the third *Critique* is how a *subjective*, aesthetic judgement, a judgement of taste, can claim *universal* assent. Aesthetic judgements are those utterances where we describe something as beautiful or as having special significance, e.g., 'This is a beautiful landscape', 'This is a powerful work of art'. The problem he finds with these judgements is that, although in one sense they are a description of a personal feeling, they nevertheless appear to make a claim about the object concerned, a claim (about its beauty or aesthetic strength) which *arguably* should hold for everyone. Kant refers to this as the antinomy of taste. How can the contradictory aspects of subjectivity and objectivity be reconciled?

In order to overcome the antinomy, Kant distinguishes between determinative and reflective judgement. This distinction is vital. 'Judgement in general', he writes, 'is the ability to think the particular under the universal' (*CJ* 179).[5] Determinative judgements, on the one hand, subsume a particular under a universal or, in a more Kantian idiom, an intuition under a concept, and determine an object to be a certain kind of thing, for example, 'This is a tomato'. Reflective judgements, on the other, do not identify or assign properties to an object. Judgements of taste are reflective: to describe a landscape as 'beautiful' or a piece of music as 'sad' is not to ascribe empirically determinate qualities to the objects. No determination is made by these judgements, Kant maintains, for the simple reason that no definite concept is available to them. (Resistance to conceptualization, we can recall, is the traditional charge made against aesthetic experience by philosophy.) Instead, he argues, our cognitive powers have to *look* for a concept.

Reflective judgement then needs a concept for, in Kantian terms, all experience requires concepts and intuitions, but not a determinate concept. To meet this need, the imagination supplies the *indeterminate* concept of nature's subjective purposiveness, the idea that the world appears to us *as if* it had been designed for our awareness:

> Someone who feels pleasure in the mere reflection on the form of an object . . . rightly lays claim to everyone's assent, even though this judgement is empirical and a singular judgement. For the basis of this pleasure is found in the universal, though subjective, condition of [aesthetic] reflective judgements, namely, the purposive harmony of an object (whether the product of nature or of art) with the mutual relation of the cognitive powers . . . *that are required for every empirical cognition.*
>
> (*CJ* 191, emphasis added)

We experience beauty or aesthetic delight, Kant declares, when we recognize that the order we perceive in the world is a reflection of the order we require for meaningful, intelligible experience. In other words, moments of beauty, for Kant, are moments when we glimpse the conditions of the possibility of experience.

Isn't this simply a restatement of the premise that there is a necessary interrelationship between mind and nature? The only way a philosophy which starts from the point of view of the subject can explain objectivity, it would seem, is to make the rather grand assumption that mind and nature simply interlock. Kant is not guilty of this, though. To rely on the indeterminate concept of nature's subjective purposiveness, he avers, is not to assume that the laws of nature are the laws of our understanding, 'for it is only reflective [as opposed to determinative] judgement that uses this idea as a principle . . . In using this principle, judgement gives a law only to itself, not to nature' (*CJ*

180). Kant is *not* asserting that nature has been designed for our awareness, not arguing for the presence of *a particular order* in nature. This distinguishes him from the Enlightenment belief that our categories cut reality at the joints and deliver to us conceptually all that the world can be. Instead, Kant is arguing for the possibility of order, the state of affairs upon which any experiential, intelligible purchase on the world is conditional. Without this, empirical differences 'might still be so great that it would be impossible for our understanding . . . to divide nature's products into genera and species' (*CJ* 185). Purposiveness, he writes, is

> a principle by which judgement prescribes, not to nature (which would be autonomy) but to itself (which is heautonomy), a law for its reflection on nature . . . We must think nature, as regards its merely empirical laws, as containing the possibility of an endless diversity of empirical laws that [despite being laws] are nonetheless contingent as far as we can see . . . And yet we must necessarily presuppose and assume this unity, since otherwise our empirical cognition could not thoroughly cohere to [form] a whole of experience.
>
> (*CJ* 183–86)

By transforming the determinate notion of 'purpose' (*Zweck*) into the indeterminate notion of 'purposiveness' (*Zweckmässigkeit*), Kant is reconciling another pair of philosophical opposites. Eighteenth-century science was trying to accommodate two world-views: Aristotelian teleology and Renaissance empiricism. Teleology is the study of purpose in nature. It derives from Aristotle's concept of 'final cause' or *telos*. Every inanimate object or organism, Aristotle argues, has a 'natural place' or 'state' and all motion or growth can be explained in terms of transition towards this final state. For example, objects fall to the ground, Aristotle suggests, because the earth is their 'natural state'. The Renaissance, though, brought the recognition that knowledge could be generated simply by detecting regularity through observation, and much of the evidence of the senses was found to conflict with Aristotle's system, e.g., his theory of the celestial spheres. As a result, Aristotle's influence waned. However, deriving mechanical laws from observed regularities cannot explain the sense of organization found in organisms where parts interact in the interests of the greater whole. Thus the Aristotelian notion of purpose was still a necessary explanatory component. In Kant's system, purposiveness (or the appearance of a purpose) becomes the transcendental principle which explains how the apprehension of regularity in experience is possible.

The critical trilogy is a very elaborate structure, and its overall coherence as a unified system continues to be the subject of contemporary scholarship. The importance it holds for aesthetics is immense, since it positions the aesthetic as that realm of human experience where we appraise the relationship between the world and our conceptual understanding of it. We enjoy art, literature, and music because they move us subjectively to offer objective judgement, and it is this tension or interplay between subjectivity and objectivity, Kant affirms, which we find in moral reasoning, the construction of knowledge, and, in fact, every waking moment. Thus, the demands made by an artwork on us to find the right words to describe its effect or significance are paradigms for the conceptual or interpretative decisions which have to be made in moral and epistemological judgements. This would cover aesthetic moments in scientific research: 'we rejoice . . . when, just as if it were a lucky chance favouring our aim, we do find such systematic unity among merely empirical laws' (*CJ* 184).

In making my selections from the *Critique of Judgment*, I have chosen extracts which fit together to demonstrate, in a concise and coherent fashion, the relationship between the first and third *Critiques*. The sections show how the problems posed by aesthetic judgement and the experience of beauty lead to the concept of purposiveness and, more especially, purposiveness as it is displayed in art. Purposiveness, as the 'feeling of freedom in the play of our cognitive powers' (*CJ* 306), is the basis of *the relationship between* mind and nature which *allows us* to bring nature under concepts. It is therefore the term which completes Kant's explanation of finitude, the necessarily interwoven nature of concept and intuition. There are sections from the 'Analytic of Aesthetic Judgment' and the 'Dialectic of Aesthetic Judgment'. The analytic–dialectic structure is common to all three *Critiques*: 'analytic', in this context, refers to what can be said about judgement (bringing an intuition under a concept) *as it applies to experience*, whereas 'dialectic' refers to the transcendental reasoning *beyond experience* Kant undertakes in order to resolve the antinomies of metaphysics. The 'Analytic' sections outline the significance Kant attaches to fine art, and the contradictory aspects of aesthetic judgements (subjective statements making objective claims) which define the antinomy of taste. Reproduced from the 'Dialectic of Aesthetic Judgment' is the solution to the antinomy.

Fine art, for Kant, is the product of genius. The concept of 'genius' belongs to the Romantic era in the history of ideas and denotes the capacity of an artist to produce work which transcends the established rules of composition. In Kantian terms, the genius is an artist who can give phenomenal form to 'aesthetic ideas'. An 'aesthetic idea' is 'a presentation of the imagination which prompts much thought, but to which no determinate thought whatsoever, i.e., no [determinate] concept, can be adequate, so that no language can express it completely and allow us to grasp it' (*CJ* 314). The indeterminate concept of nature's subjective purposiveness belongs to this category:

> in [dealing with] a product of fine art we must become conscious that it is art rather than nature, and yet the purposiveness [the appearance of design or purpose] in its form must seem as free from all constraint of chosen rules as if it were a product of mere nature.
>
> (*CJ* 306)

The appearance of art 'as if it were a product of mere nature' would seem to suggest that Kant confines fine art to *mimesis*. This is not the case. While it is true that much eighteenth-century painting sought to define or perfect beauty in nature, it is important to remember that Kant makes beauty a function of the interplay between our cognitive faculties and the world. Fine art then, for Kant, is first and foremost an activity through which we explore the nature of our moral and perceptual contact with the world. For example, Kant's interest in the possibility of finding new alignments between concept and intuition lends interpretative support to the revolutions in representation generated by modernism, e.g., impressionism, fauvism, cubism. Furthermore, recent research shows that Pollock's drip paintings exhibit elements of pattern and symmetry congruent with fractal images. Given the relation between fractals and chaos theory (the impossibility of a complete description of any particular event or situation), there is some interesting work to be done here on the Kantian notion that art displays nature's purposiveness.

G.W.F. Hegel

Hegel's ambition is the same as Kant's: to reconcile the millennia-old philosophical oppositions of mind and reality, thought and substance. Kant ultimately fails in this, Hegel thinks, because he surrenders metaphysics, knowledge of things as they are in themselves, in contrast to things as they appear to empirical consciousness. Kant's philosophy, for Hegel, is a form of subjectivism: Kant limits our knowledge to appearances, and places noumena or things-in-themselves beyond our grasp. This restriction is arguably present in Kant's admissions, in the first *Critique*, that we can *think* noumena but cannot *know* them and, in the third, that 'judgement gives a law only to itself, not to nature'.

Hegel is arguably the last system-building metaphysician in the history of western philosophy, the last figure to offer a scheme which embraces all aspects of reality, including our aspirations to truth and justice. The simple but far-reaching move he makes in response to Kant is to assert that knowledge and reality are in fact one. All the individual perceptions and experiences we have belong to a procession of thought that is moving towards the end of history. This ultimate and final unity Hegel terms 'Absolute Knowledge' or 'Absolute Spirit'. The basis for this metaphysics is the conceptual point that a unity, to be a unity, must be a unity of parts. In his *Aesthetics: Lectures on Fine Art*, Hegel avows that it is the task of the philosophy 'to show how the Idea in logic has, in accordance with its own Concept, to transpose itself into natural existence and then, out of this externality, into spirit; and finally to free itself from the finitude of spirit again to become spirit in its eternity and truth' (*AI* 94).[6]

Organicism is intrinsic to Hegel's theory: one thing can generate out of itself a network of interrelated parts which work towards achieving unity again; the Idea, in accordance with its own Concept, transposes itself into natural existence. ('Idea' is the term Hegel uses to denote the ultimate unity between a concept and its object.) This is in keeping with the use of 'organism' in nineteenth-century Romanticism as a metaphor for the creative process. In Romantic aesthetics, following Kant, a harmony is held to exist between artistic intuition and nature, and the artist generates insight, the theory has it, in virtue of the holistic nature of her practice. However, for Hegel, there is also a Platonic influence, to the extent that his ideas, in many respects, might be regarded as a revised, dynamic Platonism. In Plato's *Republic*, abstract, transcendental Forms *give shape and determination* to physical, sensory reality: our everyday world displays order and regular appearance, Plato maintains, because each individual thing (for example, a tree, a bicycle, happiness, justice) has been given its being by an original template. To explain how this determination takes place, Plato draws on the metaphor of nourishment:

> The sun [Socrates explains to Glaucon] not only makes the things we see visible, but causes the processes of generation, growth and nourishment, without itself being such a process . . . The [form of the] good therefore may be said to be the source not only of the intelligibility of the objects of knowledge, but also of their being and reality.[7]

Herein lies the basis of Hegel's part–whole idealism: what makes the objects of knowledge intelligible also nourishes them or brings them into being; perception, in some sense, creates its own object. As he writes in the *Logic* (1817), it is 'organic life' that corresponds to the development of the Idea:

> the plant is developed from its germ. The germ virtually involves the whole plant, but does so only ideally or in thought . . . The truth of the hypothesis . . . lies in its perceiving that in the process of development the notion keeps to itself and only gives rise to alteration of form, without making any addition in point of content.[8]

Knowledge is the unfolding of experiences and possibilities that are already implicit in original conscious awareness.

The relationship between thought and substance, for Hegel, is dynamic: a dialectic of subjectivity and objectivity through which human consciousness approaches the realization that mind and reality are one. The dialectic is first considered in Hegel's lectures at the university of Jena (1801–07) but receives its full, systematic exposition in the *Phenomenology of Spirit* (1807). The unfolding of consciousness, he argues, is a cyclic, three-stage process of 'thesis', 'antithesis', and 'synthesis'. Uttering one judgement about an object (the thesis) makes the speaker aware that there is more to the object than her statement allows (the antithesis). A previously unrecognized or unconsidered aspect of the thing is brought to light, and so a revised judgement is made (a synthesis, which becomes the new thesis). As Hegel writes in the *Phenomenology*:

> Consciousness recognizes that it is the *untruth* occurring in perception that falls within it. But by this very recognition it is able at once to supersede this untruth; it distinguishes its apprehension of the truth from the untruth of its perception, [and] corrects this untruth.[9]

Here, then, is another answer to Kant's problem of how subjective mind can offer objective judgement. Judgement, considered dynamically, necessarily includes within itself an awareness of its own partiality or contingency: producing a description or a representation records an aspect of the object and, in so doing, also draws attention to features which have not been taken into consideration. Whereas subjective appearance is traditionally thought to be of a different order from that of objective fact, with Hegel, subjectivity is precisely that which allows objectivity to come into being.

Art plays a significant role in Hegel's system. Hegel gave periodic lecture courses on the philosophy of art during the 1820s when he was professor of philosophy at Berlin, and his *Aesthetics: Lectures on Fine Art* is a reconstruction, made after his death, from student transcripts and his own lecture notes. The extract I have selected is from the 'Introduction' to the work, and outlines his threefold division of the subject: symbolic, classical, and romantic.

Art's ultimate role in Hegel's system is to be the antithesis of thought: a representation which takes shape as an independent object *opposite* consciousness, and which consciousness recognizes as being both of itself and other than itself. This, though, does not mean that Hegel has a negative view of art. In the dialectical unfolding of consciousness, there is the necessary antithetical moment when the mind becomes aware that what is immediately before it is not entirely true or adequate, and so it is motivated to utter a further judgement. Art is the stimulation of enquiry through material estrangement:

> In the products of art, the spirit has to do solely with its own. And even if works of art are not thought or the Concept, but a development of the Concept out of itself, a shift of

> the Concept from its own ground to that of sense, still the power of the thinking spirit lies in being able not only to grasp itself in its proper form as thinking, but to know itself again just as much when it has surrendered its proper form to feeling and sense, to comprehend itself in its opposite, because it changes into thoughts what has been estranged and so reverts to itself . . . For the Concept is the universal which maintains itself in its particularizations, overreaches itself and its opposite, and so it is also the power and activity of cancelling again the estrangement in which it gets involved.
>
> (*AI* 12–13)

For Hegel, the artwork is the sensuous display of mind's relationship with external reality; it is material substance that has been imbued with mind. His threefold division of the arts – symbolic, classical, and romantic – maps the relation between ideal or spiritual content and material form, and makes the former inversely proportionate to the latter. The subject of *symbolic* art, e.g., architecture, 'is matter itself in its immediate externality'; the shape is arbitrary and the reality presented 'remains opposed to the Idea, because it is something external not penetrated by the Idea' (*AI* 84). In *classical* art, material form is 'peculiarly appropriate to the Idea itself in its essential nature', e.g., sculpture depicting the human form. This is because the artist is recreating natural forms, shapes which she *finds* in nature, 'invented . . . for concrete spirit' by the original Concept (*AI* 77–78). However, even though Idea and sensuous form are in complete harmony, this is spirit 'which is still particular and therefore burdened with an abstraction' (*AI* 301). *Romantic* art, Hegel's highest classification, acknowledges that external representation is inadequate to the demands of thought and seeks to free itself from the burden of particularity. The category is represented by those forms which (he thinks) aspire to deny their materiality: painting liberates art from 'the *complete* sensuous spatiality of material things by being restricted to the dimensions of a *plane* surface' (*AI* 87); music is pure sound, and poetry (the highest) consists of 'sound as the mere indication of inner intuitions and ideas' (*AI* 86).

In what sense, though, is physical nature opposed to or antithetical to mind? Despite his claim that all moments in the development of consciousness are equally important and are only making explicit what is already implicit, Hegel nevertheless seems to follow the traditional philosophical practice of placing the mental higher than the physical. The beauty we perceive in art, Hegel argues, is higher than the beauty we see in nature for it is 'beauty born of the spirit', 'a shift of the Concept from its own ground to that of sense' (*AI* 2, 12). The torch-thistle 'withers in the wilds of the southern forests without having been admired'; the work of art, though, 'is not so naively self-centred': 'it is essentially a question, an address to the responsive breast, a call to the mind of the spirit' (*AI* 71). Nature is often described by him as 'spiritless' (*AI* 12) or 'soulless' (*AI* 116).

'Higher', though, as Hegel admits, is 'a quite vague expression' (*AI* 2). He defines his application of the term: spirit or mind is higher because 'spirit is alone the *true*, comprehending everything in itself, so that everything beautiful is truly beautiful only as sharing in this higher sphere and generated by it' (*AI* 2). The diverse and 'spiritless' particularities of nature approach ideality when they are perceived as belonging to a conceptual unity. He gives, as an example, the solar system:

> The suns, comets, moons, and planets appear, on the one hand, as heavenly bodies independent and different from one another; but, on the other hand, they are what they are only because of the determinate place they occupy in a total system of bodies.
> (*AI* 117)

Hegel suggests other instances of physical particulars 'sharing' concepts: 'we must regard the body and its members as the existence of the systematic articulation of the Concept itself' (*AI* 119), and 'shape, whereby . . . content is made visible and imaginable, has the purpose of existing solely for our mind and spirit' (*AI* 71).

The tension arises from having to give a *linear*, dialectic account of what is also claimed to be a *self-present* unity. On the one hand, Hegel needs the *ontological* claim (concerning the nature of reality) that all particulars belong to a unity yet, on the other, he is articulating the *epistemological* claim (concerning our perception of reality) that the awareness of this unity unfolds with time. Again, on the one hand, Hegel argues that particulars articulate or emerge from universals (an ontological thesis) yet, on the other, he asserts that the time will come when we know the world conceptually and no longer have to look (an epistemological thesis). If Hegel can be accused of maintaining the Cartesian divide between the mental and the physical, it is because language makes it impossible to describe something as a whole without first dividing it into components, one of which must come before the other, e.g., 'subject' and 'predicate', thereby creating a hierarchy. Although it is often visualized in terms of clear and crystalline purity, any writer, mathematician, or theorist will tell you that concepts have a materiality of their own. It is a delicious irony that Hegel's appeals to ascension are made necessary by the recalcitrance of thought.

The artist, on Hegel's account, is always destined to be a martyr, to lay down her life in the interests of spirit's progress. For romanticism in Hegel marks the 'death of art', when it 'passes over into higher forms of consciousness' (*AI* 102). Realizing that truth cannot reside in matter, thought turns to religion – 'removed from the objectivity of art into the inwardness of the subject' (*AI* 103) – and, finally, to the pure conceptuality of philosophy. I think, though, we miss Hegel's point if we take this to be the assertion that art's value is limited or finite. We ignore the demands he is making on our understanding of concepts and objects if we take 'passing over into higher forms' to mean the abrupt cessation of a life. The importance of art for Hegel resides in its being the *substantial* expression of ideas: matter presents a recalcitrance which makes thought tangible to consciousness. Hegel's theory of art offers valuable insights into the way the world resists or opposes our ideas.

Hegel can perhaps be criticized for reducing the history of art to a general, linear scheme and excluding properties of art which do not conform to it. His framework assumes, without warrant, that the ontological nature of the *content* of a work should correspond to the ontological nature of its *form*. Architecture, he reasons, can only speak of earth and matter, whereas poetry deals with the inner and the spiritual. This is not the case; neither was it the case in Hegel's time. A building can stimulate thought just as much as a poem can emphasize embodiment. Nevertheless, he does anticipate modern western art. Since the invention of photography, the various revolutions in art have gradually peeled away the layers of art's physicality: from the impressionists painting light instead of objects, through the performative, non-representational project of abstraction, to conceptual art's simple sentences on gallery walls.

Friedrich Nietzsche

Whereas representation and reality, for Kant and Hegel, are elements whose interaction has to be explained, Nietzsche takes the decisive step of removing the distinction altogether. Although there are times during his career when he falls back on the model of representations concealing reality, the general direction of his thought is guided by the thesis that *the world is constructed through representation*, that reality and representation are not in fact separate but are mutually defining aspects of the same process. This makes Nietzsche a crucial figure in the development of aesthetics. Removing the distinction between appearance and reality means that the sensory material with which we come into immediate contact *is* reality. Art, no longer confined to surface impressions, becomes the process through which we shape the world.

Kant and Arthur Schopenhauer (1788–1860) are two key influences. Kant proposes that the mind organizes experience but, as noted above, his system raises the problem of the noumenon or the thing-in-itself: concepts transform intuition and thereby determine the way things *appear to us*, but they do not have access to things as they are in themselves *behind appearances*. Much post-Kantian philosophy tries to overcome this divide, and various attempts are made to reconcile or equate the two realms. Hegel offers one reply, as we have seen, and Schopenhauer provides another.

What is novel about Schopenhauer's proposal, and the aspect of his thought which feeds most directly into Nietzsche, is the suggestion that perception is, by definition, through its own activity, apprehension of the noumenal. As cognitive beings in the world, he argues, our faculties are already part of that which we are wanting to know. Experience comes to us through our bodies. The body is not just a casing or a means of mobility but that which locates us as sensory, sentient beings in the world. Instead of the binary model of appearance and thing-in-itself, Schopenhauer introduces the singular notion of the 'will': reality conceived as a dynamic within which our acts and representations are enfolded. An explanation of how subjective experience can be identified with objective reality, he writes,

> could never be found if the investigator himself were nothing more than the purely knowing subject (a winged cherub without a body). But he himself is rooted in that world; and thus he finds himself in it as an *individual*, in other words, his knowledge, which is the conditional supporter of the whole world as representation, is nevertheless given entirely through the medium of a body, and the affections of this body are, as we have shown, the starting-point for the understanding in its perception of this world . . . To the subject of knowing, who appears as an individual only through his identity with the body, this body is given in two entirely different ways. It is given in intelligent perception as representation, as an object among objects, liable to the laws of these objects. But it is also given in quite a different way, namely as what is known immediately to everyone, and is denoted by the word *will*. Every true act of his will is also at once and inevitably a movement of his body; he cannot actually will the act without at the same time being aware that it appears as a movement of the body. The act of will and the action of the body are not two different states objectively known, connected by the bond of causality; they do not stand in the relation of cause and effect, but are one and the same thing, though given in two entirely different ways,

> first quite directly, and then in perception for the understanding. The action of the body is nothing but the act of will objectified, i.e., translated into perception.[10]

Perhaps the most intriguing feature of this shift in thought is that, on the one hand, we are asked to treat what is normally regarded as separate – conscious experience and reality – as arising out of one thing, the will, and yet, on the other hand, a philosophy of experience, to be coherent or, at least, applicable, needs to be able to explain the fact that experience definitely has a binary nature: it involves counter-pressure; the world resists our expectations. Equating mind and reality solves one problem (Kant's noumenon) but raises another: how we account for the textures and pressures of experience. Both Schopenhauer and Nietzsche, in their individual ways, attempt to explain identity and difference through notions of dynamism, tension, and force. After this, the question of how one thing can give rise to two becomes a central concern of twentieth-century phenomenology. The necessity which impels us to divide continuous experience into subjects and objects is examined by Heidegger in *Being and Time* (1928) and, later, the role which binary oppositions play in structuring (and undermining) intentions is targeted by deconstruction.

Nietzsche's aim, roughly put, is to bring philosophy 'back to life', to make it 'life-affirming' once again. In his view, philosophy, from Plato, through Christianity, to rationalism, has identified knowledge and virtue with the orderly, sombre, life-denying aspects of existence, at the expense of its more intoxicating, chaotic, dream-like moments. In reply, Nietzsche does not advocate a swing to all-out hedonism but, rather, proposes a model of being based on the interplay between order and chaos. These two principles are represented throughout his writing by the Greek gods Apollo and Dionysus. They are introduced in his first book, *The Birth of Tragedy* (1872): a return to the pre-Socratic dynamics of Greek theatre made in order to restore the moral and epistemological significance of tragic drama, stripped from it by Plato's idealist metaphysics.[11] The Dionysian principle brings frenzy, celebration, and loss of self, whereas the Apollonian gives shape, form, and 'necessary illusion' to these drives. It is in the arts, Nietzsche claims, that we can see this play being acted out, for the artist has to mediate between inner, chaotic impulse and outer, organized form.

'On Truth and Lie in an Extra-Moral Sense', written in 1873, a year after *The Birth of Tragedy*, could be regarded as Nietzschean philosophy in tablet form. With impressive clarity, admirable concision, and delightful images, Nietzsche articulates the nihilism that defines his work on aesthetics, epistemology, and morality. Nihilism is the denial of all orthodox values and beliefs and, more specifically, the rejection of the view that values and beliefs derive from or are bestowed upon us by an external, other-worldly source. Religion and metaphysical schemas which identify the possibility of ordered experience with the existence of a supersensible or noumenal realm, e.g., Plato's Forms, Kant's things-in-themselves, are the principal targets. Nihilism, however, is not an anything-goes pessimism but a drawing-attention-to the responsibilities we have for defining in our own terms what counts as truth and order. Nietzsche's arguments in 'On Truth and Lie' challenge the traditional philosophical model of truth as a relation between concepts and an external, mind-independent world. The notions of 'a concept' and 'reality-in-itself' are linked. We form concepts or general ideas, he claims, by subtracting all that is particular or distinctive from individuals:

> A word becomes a concept insofar as it simultaneously has to fit countless more or less similar cases – which means, purely and simply, cases which are never equal and thus altogether unequal. Just as it is certain that one leaf is never totally the same as another, so it is certain that the concept 'leaf' is formed by arbitrarily discarding these individual differences and by forgetting the distinguishing aspects. This awakens the idea that, in addition to the leaves, there exists in nature the 'leaf': the original model according to which all the leaves were perhaps woven, sketched, measured, coloured, curled, and painted – but by incompetent hands, so that no specimen has turned out to be a correct, trustworthy, and faithful likeness of the original model.

This original template, this thing-in-itself, however, is not to be found. It is, Nietzsche asserts, mere anthropomorphism: treating something human or subjective as if it had existence independent of and prior to ourselves. Nature, he avows, 'is acquainted with no forms and no concepts, and likewise with no species, but only with an X which remains inaccessible and indefinable for us'. We delude ourselves into thinking that, because we have a single word for something, there must be a corresponding original essence behind it.

Concepts, Nietzsche announces, rather than being the entities which map out for us the order of things-in-themselves, are in fact metaphors, the products of our own creativity. Perception cannot involve a correspondence relation between concept and thing because there is no original thing. All there is is a mute, indefinable X which is *transformed* by our worldly, sensory faculties into experience and perception. It is the transformational nature of perception which makes it metaphorical. Just as a metaphor consists of the pairing of unrelated terms, e.g., 'life is a box of chocolates', so perception involves the move from one domain – nerve stimulation – to another – an image or sound – where there is no relation of similarity or correspondence between them. This is not just the point that abstract and everyday phrases have metaphorical, imagistic origins, such as 'grasp the idea', 'shed light on the problem', 'the wing of the building', 'kick-start the economy', but also the much more devastating assertion that *what we see, what we hear, what we feel* are events that have the qualities they do *not because they have been given to them by an external source* but because they exist as *creative transformational interactions between our faculties and the wider domain of being* – Nietzsche's indefinable X or Schopenhauer's 'will' – of which our faculties are a part.

In the history of philosophy, aesthetic experience has been maligned for not being reducible to conceptual description or not being readily quantifiable. With Nietzsche, however, it becomes a theory of being: 'a painter without hands who wished to express in song the picture before his mind would, by means of this substitution of spheres, still reveal more about the essence of things than does the empirical world'. Gone is the conventional notion of truth as the 'correct' representation, the one which best corresponds to reality, since knowledge here is no longer understood as a binary relation between representation and object. Instead, perception and understanding are akin to the creation and appreciation of art. In the absence of an external source, value and truth *have to be made*; they become our own creations, and questions of right and wrong become questions of interpretation. However, although the binary relation between appearance and reality has been removed, a coherent theory of experience, as noted above, still has to account for the 'binary feel' of experience, the counter-pressure the world throws up against consciousness. This,

Nietzsche claims, we find in aesthetic, metaphorical transformation, for example, the expression of a mood in sound or a face in charcoal. It is to these 'leaps' in artistic creativity (from one domain to another) and the demands they impose on interpretation, he urges us, that we should look for our understanding of the tensions and resistances which constitute the individual's experience of the world.

Notes

1 Alexander Baumgarten, *Metaphysica*, Halle, 1739. Dual Latin and German extracts from this text appear in *Texte zur Grundlegung der Aesthetik*, ed. H.R. Schweizer, Hamburg, Felix Meiner Verlag, 1983.
2 Immanuel Kant, *Critique of Pure Reason*, trans. Norman Kemp Smith, London, Macmillan, 1990, Bxvi. Numbers refer to the pagination of the original Akadamie edition, included in the margin of this translation. 'A' denotes the first edition *Critique* (1781), 'B' the second (1787).
3 Ibid., A51, B75, p. 93.
4 Ibid., A141, B180–81, pp. 82–83.
5 Immanuel Kant, *Critique of Judgment*, trans. Werner S. Pluhar, Indianapolis, Hackett, 1987. Numbers refer to the pagination of the original Akadamie edition, included in the margin of this translation.
6 G.W.F. Hegel, *Aesthetics: Lectures on Fine Art* vols I and II, trans. T.M. Knox, Oxford, Clarendon Press, 1975. Page numbers refer to the first volume and appear in the main text, prefixed by '*AI*'.
7 Plato, *Republic*, trans. Desmond Lee, London, Penguin, 1987, 509b.
8 G.W.F. Hegel, *Logic*, trans. William Wallace, Oxford, Clarendon Press, 1975, pp. 224–25.
9 G.W.F. Hegel, *Phenomenology of Spirit*, trans. A.V. Miller, Oxford, Oxford University Press, 1977, p. 72.
10 Arthur Schopenhauer, *The World as Will and Representation* vol. I (1819), vol. II (1844), trans. E.F.J. Payne, New York, Dover, 1969, I, pp. 99–100.
11 Friedrich Nietzsche, *The Birth of Tragedy*, trans. Walter Kaufmann, New York, Vintage, 1967.

1

EXTRACTS FROM 'ANALYTIC OF AESTHETIC JUDGMENT' AND 'DIALECTIC OF AESTHETIC JUDGMENT', *CRITIQUE OF JUDGMENT*

Immanuel Kant

§ 32 First peculiarity of a judgment of taste

A judgment of taste determines its object in respect of our liking (beauty) [but] makes a claim to *everyone's* assent, as if it were an objective judgment.

To say, This flower is beautiful, is tantamount to a mere repetition of the flower's
282 own claim to everyone's liking. The agreeableness of its smell, on the other hand, gives it no claim whatever: its smell delights [*ergötzen*] one person, it makes another dizzy. In view of this [difference], must we not suppose that beauty has to be considered a property of the flower itself, which does not adapt itself to differences in people's heads and all their senses, but to which they must adapt themselves if they wish to pass judgment on it? Yet beauty is not a property of the flower itself. For a judgment of taste consists precisely in this, that it calls a thing beautiful only by virtue of that characteristic in which it adapts itself to the way we apprehend it.

Moreover, whenever a subject offers a judgment as proof of his taste [concerning some object], we demand that he judge for himself: he should not have to grope about among other people's judgments by means of experience, to gain instruction in advance from whether they like or dislike that object; so we demand that he pronounce his judgment a priori, that he not make it [by way of] imitation, (say) on the ground that a thing is actually liked universally. One would think, however, that an a priori judgment must contain a concept of the object, this concept containing the principle for cognizing the object. But a judgment of taste is not based on concepts at all, and is not at all a cognition but only an aesthetic judgment.

That is why a young poet cannot be brought to abandon his persuasion that his poem is beautiful, neither by the judgment of his audience nor by that of his friends; and if he listens to them, it is not because he now judges the poem differently, but because, even if (at least with regard to him) the whole audience were to have wrong taste, his desire for approval still causes him to accommodate himself (even against his judgment) to the common delusion. Only later on, when his power of judgment has been sharpened by practice, will he voluntarily depart from his earlier judgment, just as he does with those of his judgments which rest wholly on reason. Taste lays claim merely to autonomy; but to make other people's judgments the basis determining one's own would be heteronomy.

It is true that we extol, and rightly so, the works of the ancients as models, and call their authors classical, as if they form a certain noble class among writers which gives laws to people by the precedent it sets. This seems to point to a posteriori sources of taste and to refute the autonomy of every subject's taste. But we might just as well say:
the fact that the ancient mathematicians are to this day considered to be virtually 283
indispensable models of supreme thoroughness and elegance in the synthetic method[1] proves that our reason [only] imitates and is unable on its own to produce rigorous and highly intuitive proofs by constructing concepts.[2] The same holds for all uses, no matter how free, of our powers, including even reason (which must draw all its judgments from the common a priori source): if each subject always had to start from nothing but the crude predisposition given him by nature, [many] of his attempts would fail, if other people before him had not failed in theirs; they did not make these attempts in order to turn their successors into mere imitators, but so that, by their procedure, they might put others on a track whereby they could search for the principles within themselves and so adopt their own and often better course. In religion, everyone must surely find the rule for his conduct within himself, since he is also the one who remains responsible for his conduct and cannot put the blame for his offenses on others on the ground that they were his teachers and predecessors; yet even here an example of virtue and holiness will always accomplish more than any universal precepts we have received from priests or philosophers, or for that matter found within ourselves. Such an example, set for us in history, does not make dispensable the autonomy of virtue that arises from our own and original (a priori) idea of morality, nor does it transform this idea into a mechanism of imitation. *Following* by reference to a precedent, rather than imitating, is the right term for any influence that products of an exemplary author may have on others; and this means no more than drawing on the same sources from which the predecessor himself drew, and learning from him only how to go about doing so. Among all our abilities and talents, taste is precisely what stands most in need of examples regarding what has enjoyed the longest-lasting approval in the course of cultural progress, in order that it will not become uncouth again and relapse into the crudeness of its first attempts; and taste needs this because its judgment cannot be determined by concepts and precepts.

§ 33 Second peculiarity of a judgment of taste 284

A judgment of taste, just as if it were merely *subjective*, cannot be determined by bases of proof.

If someone does not find a building, a view, or a poem beautiful, then, *first*, he will refuse to let even a hundred voices, all praising it highly, prod him into approving of it inwardly. He may of course act as if he liked it too, so that people will not think that he lacks taste. He may even begin to doubt whether he has in fact done enough to mold his taste, by familiarizing himself with a sufficient number of objects of a certain kind (just as someone who thinks he recognizes a forest in some distant object that everyone else regards as a town will doubt the judgment of his own eyes). And yet he realizes clearly that other people's approval in no way provides him with a valid proof by which to judge beauty; even though others may perhaps see and observe for him, and even though what many have seen the same way may serve him, who believes he saw it differently, as a sufficient basis of proof for a theoretical and hence logical judgment, yet the fact that others have liked something can never serve him as a basis for an aesthetic judgment. If others make a judgment that is unfavorable to us, this may rightly make us wonder about our own judgment, but it can never convince us that ours is incorrect. Hence there is no empirical *basis of proof* that could compel anyone to make [some] judgment of taste.

Second, still less can a judgment about beauty be determined by an a priori proof, in accordance with determinate rules. If someone reads me his poem, or takes me to a play that in the end I simply cannot find to my taste, then let him adduce *Batteux* or *Lessing*[3] to prove that his poem is beautiful, or [bring in] still older and more famous critics of taste with all the rules they have laid down; moreover, let certain passages that I happen to dislike conform quite well to rules of beauty (as laid down by these critics and universally recognized): I shall stop my ears, shall refuse to listen to reasons and arguments, and shall sooner assume that those rules of the critics are false, or at least do not apply in the present case, than allow my judgment to be determined by a
285 priori bases of proof; for it is meant to be a judgment of taste, and not one of the understanding or of reason.

It seems that this is one of the main reasons why this aesthetic power of judging was given that very name: taste. For even if someone lists all the ingredients of a dish, pointing out that I have always found each of them agreeable, and goes on to praise this food – and rightly so – as wholesome, I shall be deaf to all these reasons: I shall try the dish on *my* tongue and palate, and thereby (and not by universal principles) make my judgment.

It is a fact that any judgment of taste we make is always a singular judgment about the object. The understanding can, by comparing the object with other people's judgment about their liking of it, make a universal judgment, e.g.: All tulips are beautiful. But such a judgment is then not a judgment of taste; it is a logical judgment, which turns an object's reference to taste into a predicate of things of a certain general kind. Only a judgment by which I find a singular given tulip beautiful, i.e., in which I find that my liking for the tulip is universally valid, is a judgment of taste. Its peculiarity, however, consists in the fact that, even though it has merely subjective validity, it yet extends its claim to *all* subjects, just as it always could if it were an objective judgment that rested on cognitive bases and that [we] could be compelled [to make] by a proof.

§ 34 An objective principle of taste is impossible

By a principle of taste would be meant a principle under which, as condition, we could subsume the concept of an object and then infer that the object is beautiful. That, however, is absolutely impossible. For I must feel the pleasure directly in my presentation of the object, and I cannot be talked into that pleasure by means of any bases of proof. Hence, although, as *Hume* says, critics can reason more plausibly than cooks,[4] they still share the same fate. They cannot expect the determining basis of their judgment [to come] from the force of the bases of proof, but only from the subject's reflection on his own state (of pleasure or displeasure), all precepts and rules being rejected. 286

There is, however, something about which critics nonetheless can and should reason, since doing so may serve to correct and broaden our judgments of taste. I do not mean that they should set forth the determining basis of this kind of aesthetic judgments in a universal formula that we could [then] use. What they should do is investigate our cognitive powers and what task these powers perform in these judgments, and they should clarify by examples the reciprocal subjective purposiveness about which it was shown above that its form in a given presentation is the beauty of the object of this presentation. Hence the critique of taste is itself only subjective as regards the presentation by which an object is given us: it is the art, or science, of finding rules for the reciprocal relation that understanding and imagination have in the given presentation (without reference to prior sensation or concept), and hence for their accordance or discordance, and of determining them as regards their conditions. The critique of taste is an *art* if it shows this only through examples; it is a *science* if it derives the possibility of such judging from the nature of these powers as cognitive powers as such. It is with the latter alone, with a transcendental critique, that we are here concerned throughout. Its aim is to set forth and justify the subjective principle of taste as an a priori principle of the power of judgment. The critique that is an art merely takes the physiological (in this case psychological) and hence empirical rules by which taste actually proceeds, and (without thinking about [how] they are possible) seeks to apply them to our judging of objects of taste; and it criticizes the products of fine art, just as the *transcendental* critique criticizes our very ability to judge them.

§ 35 The principle of taste is the subjective principle of the power of judgment as such

A judgment of taste differs from a logical one in that a logical judgment subsumes a presentation under concepts of the object, whereas a judgment of taste does not subsume it under any concept at all, since otherwise the necessary universal approval could be [obtained] by compelling [people to give it]. But a judgment of taste does resemble a logical judgment inasmuch as it alleges a universality and necessity, though a universal- 287
ity and necessity that is not governed by concepts of the object and hence is merely subjective. Now since the concepts in a judgment constitute its content (what belongs to the cognition of the object), while a judgment of taste cannot be determined by concepts, its basis is only the subjective formal condition of a judgment as such. The subjective condition of all judgments is our very ability to judge, i.e., the power of judgment. When we use this power of judgment in regard to a presentation by which an object is given, then it requires that there be a harmony between two presentational powers, imagination (for the intuition and the combination of its manifold) and understanding (for the concept that is the presentation of the unity of this combination). Now since a judgment of taste is not based on a concept of the object (in the case of a presentation by which an object is given), it can consist only in the subsumption of the very imagination under the condition [which must be met] for the understanding to proceed in general from intuition to concepts. In other words, since the imagination's freedom consists precisely in its schematizing[5] without a concept, a judgment of taste must rest upon a mere sensation,[6] namely, our sensation of both the imagination in its

freedom and the understanding with its *lawfulness*, as they reciprocally quicken each other; i.e., it must rest on a feeling that allows us to judge the object by the purposiveness that the presentation (by which an object is given) has insofar as it furthers the cognitive powers in their free play. Hence taste, as a subjective power of judgment, contains a principle of subsumption; however, this subsumption is not one of intuitions under *concepts*, but, rather, one of the *power* of intuitions or exhibitions (the imagination) under the *power* of concepts (the understanding), insofar as the imagination *in its freedom* harmonizes with the understanding *in its lawfulness*.

In attempting to discover this legitimating basis by means of a deduction of judgments of taste, we can use as our guide only the formal peculiarities of this kind of judgments, i.e., we must consider merely their logical form.

§ 36 On the problem of a deduction of judgments of taste

With the perception of an object we can directly connect the concept of an object as such, [for] which it contains the empirical predicates, in order to give rise to a cognitive
288 judgment. This is how an empirical judgment is produced.[7] Now this judgment is based on a priori concepts of the systematic unity of the manifold of intuition; hence we can think this manifold as the determination of an object. These concepts (the categories) require a deduction, and this was indeed provided in the *Critique of Pure Reason*,[8] which thus made it possible to solve the problem: How are synthetic cognitive judgments possible a priori? That problem, then, concerned the pure understanding's a priori principles and theoretical judgments.

But we can also directly connect with a perception a feeling of pleasure (or displeasure) and a liking that accompanies the object's presentation and serves it in the place of a predicate. This is how an aesthetic judgment arises, which is not a cognitive judgment. Now if an aesthetic judgment is not a mere judgment of sensation, but a formal judgment of reflection that requires this liking from everyone as necessary, then it must be based on something as its a priori principle. This principle may well be merely subjective (in case an objective one were to be impossible for judgments of this kind), but even then it requires a deduction, in order that we may grasp how an aesthetic judgment can lay claim to necessity. And that is the basis of the problem with which we are now dealing: How are judgments of taste possible? So this problem concerns the a priori principles that the pure power of judgment [uses when it makes] *aesthetic* judgments, i.e., judgments where it does not (as it does in theoretical judgments) merely have to subsume under objective concepts of the understanding, [so that] it is subject to a law,[9] but where it is, subjectively, object to itself as well as law to itself.

We can also think of this problem as follows: How is a judgment possible in which the subject, merely on the basis of his *own* feeling of pleasure in an object, independently of the object's concept, judges this pleasure as one attaching to the presentation of that same object *in all other subjects*, and does so a priori, i.e., without being allowed to wait for other people's assent?

We can readily see that judgments of taste are synthetic; for they go beyond the concept of the object, and even beyond the intuition of the object, and add as a predicate to this intuition something that is not even cognition: namely [a] feeling of
289 pleasure (or displeasure). And yet, that these judgments are, or want to be considered,

a priori judgments as regards the demand that *everyone* assent, a demand they make despite the fact that their predicate (of one's own pleasure [as] connected with the presentation) is empirical, is also already implicit in the expressions used to make that claim. Hence this problem of the critique of judgment is part of the general problem of transcendental philosophy: How are synthetic judgments possible a priori?[10]

§ 37 What is actually asserted a priori about an object in a judgment of taste?

That the presentation of an object is directly connected with a pleasure can only be perceived inwardly, and if we wished to indicate no more than this, the result would be a merely empirical judgment. For I cannot connect a priori a definite feeling (of pleasure or displeasure) with any presentation, except in the case where an underlying a priori principle in reason determines the will; but in that case the pleasure (in moral feeling) is the consequence of that principle, and that is precisely why it is not at all comparable to the pleasure in taste: for it requires a determinate concept of a law, whereas the pleasure in taste is to be connected directly with our mere judging, prior to any concept. That is also why all judgments of taste are singular judgments, because they do not connect their predicate, the liking, with a concept but connect it with a singular empirical presentation that is given.

Hence it is not the pleasure, but *the universal validity of this pleasure*, perceived as connected in the mind with our mere judging of an object, that we present a priori as [a] universal rule for the power of judgment, valid for everyone. That I am perceiving and judging an object with pleasure is an empirical judgment. But that I find the object beautiful, i.e., that I am entitled to require that liking from everyone as necessary, is an a priori judgment.

§ 38 Deduction of judgments of taste[11]

If it is granted that in a pure judgment of taste our liking for the object is connected with our mere judging of the form of the object, then this liking is nothing but [our consciousness of] the form's subjective purposiveness for the power of judgment, which we feel as connected in the mind with the presentation of the object. Now, as far 290
as the formal rules of judging [as such] are concerned, apart from any matter (whether sensation or concept), the power of judgment can be directed only to the subjective conditions for our employment of the power of judgment as such (where it is confined neither to the particular kind of sense involved nor to a[ny] particular concept of the understanding), and hence can be directed only to that subjective [condition] which we may presuppose in all people (as required for possible cognition as such). It follows that we must be entitled to assume a priori that a presentation's harmony with these conditions of the power of judgment is valid for everyone. In other words, it seems that when, in judging an object of sense in general, we feel this pleasure, or subjective purposiveness of the presentation for the relation between our cognitive powers, we must be entitled to require this pleasure from everyone.[12]

Comment

What makes this deduction so easy is that it does not need to justify the objective reality of a concept; for beauty is not a concept of an object, and a judgment of taste is not a cognitive judgment. All it asserts is that we are justified in presupposing universally in all people the same subjective conditions of the power of judgment that we find in ourselves; apart from this it asserts only that we have subsumed the given object correctly under these conditions.[14] It is true that this latter assertion involves unavoidable difficulties that do not attach to the logical power of judgment (since there we subsume under concepts, whereas in the aesthetic power of judgment we subsume
291 under a relation of imagination and understanding, as they harmonize with each other in the presented form of an object, that can only be sensed, so that the subsumption may easily be illusory [*trügen*]). But this does not in any way detract from the legitimacy of the power of judgment's claim in counting on universal assent, a claim that amounts to no more than this: that the principle of judging validly for everyone from subjective bases is correct. For as far as the difficulty and doubt concerning the correctness of the subsumption under that principle is concerned, no more doubt is cast on the legitimacy of the claim that aesthetic judgments as such have this validity, and hence is cast on the principle itself, than the principle of the logical power of judgment, a principle that is objective, is made doubtful by the fact that [sometimes] (though not so often and so easily) this power's subsumption under its principle is faulty as well. But if the question were, How is it possible to assume a priori that nature is a sum [*Inbegriff*] of objects of taste? that problem would have to do with teleology. For if nature offered forms that are purposive for our power of judgment, then this would have to be regarded as a purpose of nature belonging essentially to its concept. But whether this assumption is correct is as yet very doubtful, while the actuality of natural beauties is patent to experience.

* * *

§ 44 On fine art

There is no science of the beautiful [*das Schöne*], but only critique; and there is no fine [*schön*] science,[15] but only fine art. For in a science of the beautiful, whether or not
305 something should be considered beautiful would have to be decided scientifically, i.e., through bases of proof, so that if a judgment about beauty belonged to science then it would not be a judgment of taste. As for a fine science: a science that as a science is to be fine is an absurdity; for if, [treating it] as a science, we asked for reasons and proofs, we would be put off with tasteful phrases (*bons mots*). What has given rise to the familiar expression, *fine science*, is doubtless nothing more than the realization, which is quite correct, that fine art in its full perfection requires much science: e.g., we must know ancient languages, we must have read the authors considered classical, we must know history and be familiar with the antiquities, etc.; and this is why these historical sciences have, through a confusion of words, themselves come to be called fine sciences, because they constitute the foundation and preparation needed for fine art, and in part also because they have come to include even a familiarity with the products of fine art (as in oratory or poetry).

If art merely performs the acts that are required to make a possible object actual, adequately to our *cognition* of that object, then it is *mechanical* art; but if what it intends directly is [to arouse] the feeling of pleasure, then it is called *aesthetic* art. The latter is either *agreeable* or *fine* art. It is agreeable art if its purpose is that the pleasure should accompany presentations that are mere *sensations*; it is fine art if its purpose is that the pleasure should accompany presentations that are *ways of cognizing*.

Agreeable arts are those whose purpose is merely enjoyment. They include [the art of providing] all those charms that can gratify a party at table, such as telling stories entertainingly, animating the group to open and lively conversation, or using jest and laughter to induce a certain cheerful tone among them[16] – a tone such that, as is said, there may be a lot of loose talk over the feast, and no one wants to be held responsible for what he says, because the whole point is the entertainment of the moment, not any material for future meditation or quotation. (Such arts also include the art of furnishing a table so that people will enjoy themselves, or include, at large banquets, presumably even the table-music – a strange thing which is meant to be only an agreeable noise serving to keep the minds in a cheerful mood, and which fosters the free flow of conversation between each person and his neighbor, without anyone's paying the slightest attention to the music's composition.) Also included in these arts are any 306
games that involve no further interest than that of making time go by unnoticed.

Fine art, on the other hand, is a way of presenting that is purposive on its own and that furthers, even though without a purpose, the culture of our mental powers to [facilitate] social communication.

The very concept of the universal communicability of a pleasure carries with it [the requirement] that this pleasure must be a pleasure of reflection rather than one of enjoyment arising from mere sensation. Hence aesthetic art that is also fine art is one whose standard is the reflective power of judgment, rather than sensation proper.[17]

§ 45 Fine art is an art insofar as it seems at the same time to be nature

In [dealing with] a product of fine art we must become conscious that it is art rather than nature, and yet the purposiveness in its form must seem as free from all constraint of chosen rules as if it were a product of mere nature. It is this feeling of freedom in the play of our cognitive powers, a play that yet must also be purposive, which underlies that pleasure which alone is universally communicable although not based on concepts. Nature, we say, is beautiful [*schön*] if it also looks like art; and art can be called fine [*schön*] art only if we are conscious that it is art while yet it looks to us like nature.

For we may say universally, whether it concerns beauty in nature or in art: *beautiful is what we like in merely judging it* (rather than either in sensation proper or through a concept). Now art always has a determinate intention to produce something. But if this something were mere sensation (something merely subjective), to be accompanied by pleasure, then we would [indeed] like this product in judging it, [but] only by means of the feeling of sense. If the intention were directed at producing a determinate object and were achieved by the art, then we would like the object only through concepts. In neither case, then, would we like the art in *merely judging it*, i.e., we would like it not as fine but only as mechanical art.

Therefore, even though the purposiveness in a product of fine art is intentional, it
must still not seem intentional; i.e., fine art must have the *look* of nature even though 307

we are conscious of it as art. And a product of art appears like nature if, though we find it to agree quite *punctiliously* with the rules that have to be followed for the product to become what it is intended to be, it does not do so *painstakingly*. In other words, the academic form must not show; there must be no hint that the rule was hovering before the artist's eyes and putting fetters on his mental powers.

§ 46 Fine art is the art of genius

Genius is the talent (natural endowment) that gives the rule to art. Since talent is an innate productive ability of the artist and as such belongs itself to nature, we could also put it this way: *Genius* is the innate mental predisposition (*ingenium*) *through which* nature gives the rule to art.

Whatever the status of this definition may be, and whether or not it is merely arbitrary, or rather adequate to the concept that we usually connect with the word *genius* . . . still we can prove even now that, in terms of the meaning of the word genius adopted here, fine arts must necessarily be considered arts of *genius*.

For every art presupposes rules, which serve as the foundation on which a product, if it is to be called artistic, is thought of as possible in the first place. On the other hand, the concept of fine art does not permit a judgment about the beauty of its product to be derived from any rule whatsoever that has a *concept* as its determining basis, i.e., the judgment must not be based on a concept of the way in which the product is possible. Hence fine art cannot itself devise the rule by which it is to bring about its product. Since, however, a product can never be called art unless it is preceded by a rule, it must be nature in the subject (and through the attunement of his powers) that gives the rule to art; in other words, fine art is possible only as the product of genius.

What this shows is the following: (1) Genius is a *talent* for producing something for which no determinate rule can be given, not a predisposition consisting of a skill for
308 something that can be learned by following some rule or other; hence the foremost property of genius must be *originality*. (2) Since nonsense too can be original, the products of genius must also be models, i.e., they must be *exemplary*; hence, though they do not themselves arise through imitation, still they must serve others for this, i.e., as a standard or rule by which to judge. (3) Genius itself cannot describe or indicate scientifically how it brings about its products, and it is rather as *nature* that it gives the rule. That is why, if an author owes a product to his genius, he himself does not know how he came by the ideas for it; nor is it in his power [*Gewalt*] to devise such products at his pleasure, or by following a plan, and to communicate [his procedure] to others in precepts that would enable them to bring about like products. (Indeed, that is presumably why the word genius is derived from [Latin] *genius*, [which means] the guardian and guiding spirit that each person is given as his own at birth,[18] and to whose inspiration [*Eingebung*] those original ideas are due.) (4) Nature, through genius, prescribes the rule not to science but to art, and this also only insofar as the art is to be fine art.

* * *

§49 On the powers of the mind which constitute genius

Of certain products that are expected to reveal themselves at least in part to be fine art, we say that they have no *spirit*, even though we find nothing to censure in them as far as taste is concerned. A poem may be quite nice and elegant and yet have no spirit. A story may be precise and orderly and yet have no spirit. An oration may be both thorough and graceful and yet have no spirit. Many conversations are entertaining, but they have no spirit. Even about some woman we will say that she is pretty, communicative, and polite, but that she has no spirit. Well, what do we mean here by spirit?

Spirit [*Geist*] in an aesthetic sense is the animating principle in the mind.[19] But what this principle uses to animate [or quicken] the soul, the material it employs for this, is what imparts to the mental powers a purposive momentum, i.e., imparts to them a play which is such that it sustains itself on its own and even strengthens the powers for such play.

Now I maintain that this principle is nothing but the ability to exhibit *aesthetic ideas*; 314
and by an aesthetic idea I mean a presentation of the imagination which prompts much thought, but to which no determinate thought whatsoever, i.e., no [determinate] *concept*, can be adequate, so that no language can express it completely and allow us to grasp it.[20] It is easy to see that an aesthetic idea is the counterpart (pendant) of a *rational idea*, which is, conversely, a concept to which no *intuition* (presentation of the imagination) can be adequate.

For the imagination ([in its role] as a productive cognitive power) is very mighty when it creates,[21] as it were, another nature out of the material that actual nature gives it. We use it to entertain ourselves when experience strikes us as overly routine. We may even restructure experience; and though in doing so we continue to follow analogical laws, yet we also follow principles which reside higher up, namely, in reason (and which are just as natural to us as those which the understanding follows in apprehending empirical nature). In this process we feel our freedom from the law of association (which attaches to the empirical use of the imagination); for although it is under that law that nature lends us material, yet we can process that material into something quite different, namely, into something that surpasses nature.

Such presentations of the imagination we may call *ideas*. One reason for this is that they do at least strive toward something that lies beyond the bounds of experience, and hence try to approach an exhibition of rational concepts (intellectual ideas), and thus [these concepts] are given a semblance of objective reality. Another reason, indeed the main reason, for calling those presentations ideas is that they are inner intuitions to which no concept can be completely adequate. A poet ventures to give sensible expression to rational ideas of invisible beings, the realm of the blessed, the realm of hell, eternity, creation, and so on. Or, again, he takes [things] that are indeed exemplified in experience, such as death, envy, and all the other vices, as well as love, fame, and so on; but then, by means of an imagination that emulates the example of reason in reaching [for] a maximum, he ventures to give these sensible expression in a way that goes beyond the limits of experience, namely, with a completeness for which no example can be found in nature. And it is actually in the art of poetry that the power [i.e., faculty] of aesthetic ideas can manifest itself to full extent. Considered by itself, however, this power is actually only a talent (of the imagination).

Now if a concept is provided with [*unterlegen*] a presentation of the imagination

315 such that, even though this presentation belongs to the exhibition of the concept, yet it prompts, even by itself, so much thought as can never be comprehended within a determinate concept and thereby the presentation aesthetically expands the concept itself in an unlimited way, then the imagination is creative in [all of] this and sets the power of intellectual ideas (i.e., reason) in motion: it makes reason think more, when prompted by a [certain] presentation, than what can be apprehended and made distinct in the presentation (though the thought does pertain to the concept of the object [presented]).

If forms do not constitute the exhibition of a given concept itself, but are only supplementary [*Neben-*] presentations of the imagination, expressing the concept's implications and its kinship with other concepts, then they are called (aesthetic) *attributes* of an object, of an object whose concept is a rational idea and hence cannot be exhibited adequately. Thus Jupiter's eagle with the lightning in its claws is an attribute of the mighty king of heaven, and the peacock is an attribute of heaven's stately queen. [Through] these attributes, unlike [through] *logical attributes*, [we] do not present the content of our concepts of the sublimity and majesty of creation, but present something different, something that prompts the imagination to spread over a multitude of kindred presentations that arouse more thought than can be expressed in a concept determined by words. These aesthetic attributes yield an *aesthetic idea*, which serves the mentioned rational idea as a substitute for a logical exhibition, but its proper function is to quicken [*beleben*] the mind by opening up for it a view into an immense realm of kindred presentations. Fine art does this not only in painting or sculpture (where we usually speak of attributes); but poetry and oratory also take the spirit that animates [*beleben*] their works solely from the aesthetic attributes of the objects, attributes that accompany the logical ones and that give the imagination a momentum which makes it think more in response to these objects [*dabei*], though in an undeveloped way, than can be comprehended within one concept and hence in one determinate linguistic expression. Here are some examples, though for the sake of brevity I must confine myself to only a few.

The great king, in one of his poems, expresses himself thus:

> Let us part from life without grumbling or regrets,
> Leaving the world behind filled with our good deeds.
> Thus the sun, his daily course completed,
> Spreads one more soft light over the sky;
> And the last rays that he sends through the air
> 316 Are the last sighs he gives the world for its well-being.[22]

The king is here animating his rational idea of a cosmopolitan attitude, even at the end of life, by means of an attribute which the imagination (in remembering all the pleasures of a completed beautiful summer day, which a serene evening calls to mind) conjoins with that presentation, and which arouses a multitude of sensations and supplementary presentations for which no expression can be found. On the other hand, even an intellectual concept may serve, conversely, as an attribute of a presentation of sense and thus animate that presentation by the idea of the supersensible; but [we] may use for this only the aesthetic [element] that attaches subjectively to our consciousness of the supersensible. Thus, for example, a certain poet, in describing a beautiful morning, says: 'The sun flowed forth, as serenity flows from virtue.'[23] The consciousness of virtue, even if we only think of ourselves as in the position of a virtuous person, spreads in the mind a multitude of sublime and calming feelings and a boundless outlook toward a joyful future, such as no expression commensurate with a determinate concept completely attains.[24]

In a word, an aesthetic idea is a presentation of the imagination which is conjoined with a given concept and is connected, when we use imagination in its freedom, with such a multiplicity of partial presentations that no expression that stands for a determinate concept can be found for it. Hence it is a presentation that makes us add to a concept the thoughts of much that is ineffable, but the feeling of which quickens our cognitive powers and connects language, which otherwise would be mere letters, with spirit.

So the mental powers whose combination (in a certain relation) constitutes *genius* are imagination and understanding. One qualification is needed, however. When the imagination is used for cognition, then it is under the constraint of the understanding and is subject to the restriction of adequacy to the understanding's concept. But when the aim is aesthetic, then the imagination is free, so that, over and above that harmony 317
with the concept, it may supply, in an unstudied way, a wealth of undeveloped material for the understanding which the latter disregarded in its concept. But the understanding employs this material not so much objectively, for cognition, as subjectively, namely, to quicken the cognitive powers, though indirectly this does serve cognition too. Hence genius actually consists in the happy relation – one that no science can teach and that cannot be learned by any diligence – allowing us, first, to discover ideas for a given concept, and, second, to hit upon a way of *expressing* these ideas that enables us to communicate to others, as accompanying a concept, the mental attunement that those ideas produce. The second talent is properly the one we call spirit. For in order to express what is ineffable in the mental state accompanying a certain presentation and to make it universally communicable – whether the expression consists in language or painting or plastic art – we need an ability [viz., spirit] to apprehend the imagination's rapidly passing play and to unite it in a concept that can be communicated without the constraint of rules (a concept that on that very account is original, while at the same time it reveals a new rule that could not have been inferred from any earlier principles or examples).

* * *

§56 Presentation of the antinomy of taste 338

There are two commonplaces about taste. The following proposition contains the first of these and is used by everyone who lacks taste but tries to escape censure: *Everyone has his own taste*. That amounts to saying that the basis determining a judgment of taste is merely subjective (gratification or pain), and that such judgments have no right to other people's necessary assent.

The second commonplace about taste, which is used even by those who grant judgments of taste the right to speak validly for everyone, is this: *There is no disputing about taste*. That amounts to saying that, even though the basis determining a judgment of taste may be objective, that basis still cannot be brought to determinate concepts; and hence even proofs do not allow us to *decide* anything about such a judgment, although we can certainly *quarrel* about it, and rightly so. For though *disputing* and *quarreling* are alike in that [we] try to produce agreement between judgments by means of the mutual resistance between them, disputing is different inasmuch as here we hope to produce this agreement according to determinate concepts, by basing a proof on them, so that we assume that the judgment is based on *objective concepts*; and in cases where we think that this cannot be done, we judge that disputing also is impossible.

It is easy to see that between these two commonplaces a proposition is missing. This proposition is not in common use as a proverb, but everyone still has it in mind. It is this: *One can quarrel about taste* (though one cannot dispute about it). This proposition, however, implies the opposite of the first proposition above [Everyone has his own taste]. For if it is granted that we can quarrel about something, then there must be some hope for us to arrive at agreement about it, and so we must be able to count on the judgment's having bases that do not have merely private validity and hence are not merely subjective. But the above principle, *Everyone has his own taste*, says the direct opposite.

Hence the following antinomy emerges concerning the principle of taste:

1 *Thesis*: A judgment of taste is not based on concepts; for otherwise one could dispute about it (decide by means of proofs).
2 *Antithesis*: A judgment of taste is based on concepts; for otherwise, regardless of the variation among [such judgments], one could not even so much as quarrel
339 about them (lay claim to other people's necessary assent to one's judgment).

§ 57 Solution of the antinomy of taste

There is only one way for us to eliminate the conflict between the mentioned principles,[26] on which we base all our judgments of taste (and which are nothing but the two peculiarities of a judgment of taste[27] that were set out in the analytic): We must show that the concept to which we refer the object in such judgments is understood in different senses in those two maxims [or principles] of the aesthetic power of judgment, and show that it is necessary for our transcendental power of judgment to adopt both these senses (or points of view in judging) but that even the illusion arising from our confusion of the two is natural and hence unavoidable.

A judgment of taste must refer to some concept or other, for otherwise it could not possibly lay claim to necessary validity for everyone. And yet it must not be provable *from* a concept, because, while some concepts can be determined, others cannot, but are intrinsically both indeterminate and indeterminable. Concepts of the understanding are of the first kind: for them there can be a corresponding sensible intuition whose predicates determine them. On the other hand, reason has a concept of the second kind: the transcendental concept of the supersensible underlying all that intuition, so that we cannot determine this concept any further theoretically.

Now, on the other hand, a judgment of taste does deal with objects of sense – though not so as to determine a *concept* of these objects for the understanding, since it is not a cognitive judgment. Rather, this judgment is a singular intuitive presentation referred to the feeling of pleasure, and hence is only a private judgment; and to this extent its validity would be restricted to the judging individual: The object is an object of liking *for me*;[28] the same may not apply to others: Everyone has his own taste.

And yet there can be no doubt that in a judgment of taste the presentation of the object (and at the same time of the subject as well) is referred more broadly [i.e., beyond ourselves], and this broader reference is our basis for extending such judgments [and treating them] as necessary for everyone. Hence this extension must be based on some concept or other; but this concept must be one that no intuition can determine, 340
that does not permit us to cognize anything and hence does not permit us *to prove* a judgment of taste; such a mere concept is reason's pure concept of the supersensible[29] underlying the object (as well as underlying the judging subject) as an object of sense and hence as appearance. For unless we assumed that a judgment of taste relies on some concept or other, we could not save its claim to universal validity. Alternatively, if a judgment of taste were based on a concept of the understanding, such as that of perfection, even though merely a confused concept of perfection, to which we could add the sensible intuition of the beautiful as corresponding to it, then it would be possible at least intrinsically to base a judgment of taste on proofs; but that contradicts the thesis.

However, all contradiction disappears if I say this: A judgment of taste is based on a concept (the concept of a general basis of nature's subjective purposiveness for our power of judgment), but this concept does not allow us to cognize and prove anything concerning the object because it is intrinsically indeterminable and inadequate for cognition; and yet this same concept does make the judgment of taste valid for everyone, because (though each person's judgment is singular and directly accompanies his intuition) the basis that determines the judgment lies, perhaps, in the concept of what may be considered the supersensible substrate of humanity.

What is needed to solve an antinomy is only the possibility that two seemingly [*dem Scheine nach*] conflicting propositions are in fact not contradictory but are consistent, even though it would surpass our cognitive power to explain how the concept involved [i.e., how what the concept stands for] is possible. Showing this [consistency] will also allow us to grasp [the fact] that and [the reason] why this illusion [*Schein*] is natural and unavoidable for human reason, and why this illusion remains so even though it ceases to deceive us once we have resolved the seeming contradiction.

For what gives rise to this antinomy is [the fact] that we treat the concept presupposed by the universal validity of a judgment as if that concept had the same meaning in the two conflicting judgments, and yet two opposed predicates are asserted of it. Hence the thesis should instead read: A judgment of taste is not based on *determinate* concepts; but the antithesis should read: A judgment of taste is indeed based on a concept, but on an *indeterminate* one (namely, that of the supersensible substrate of 341
appearances); and then there would be no conflict between the two.

Eliminating this conflict between the claims and counterclaims of taste is the best we can do. It is absolutely impossible to provide a determinate, objective principle of taste that would allow us to guide, to test, and to prove its judgments, because then they would not be judgments of taste.[30] As for the subjective principle – i.e., the indeterminate idea of the supersensible in us – as the sole key for solving the mystery of this ability [i.e., taste] concealed from us even as to its sources, we can do no more than point to it; but there is nothing we can do that would allow us to grasp it any further.

The antinomy I have set forth and settled here is based on the concept of taste in the proper sense, i.e., as an aesthetic power of judgment that merely reflects; and I reconciled the two seemingly conflicting principles [by showing] that *they may both be true*, and that is all we need. If, on the other hand, we assumed, as some do, that the basis determining taste is *agreeableness* (because the presentation underlying a judgment of taste is singular), or, as others would have it, that it is the principle of *perfection* (because the judgment is universally valid), with the definition of taste formulated accordingly, then the result would be an antinomy that we could not possibly settle except by showing that the two opposed (but opposed [as contraries,] not as mere contradictories) *propositions are both false*;[31] and that would prove the concept underlying both of them to be self-contradictory. So we see that the elimination of the antinomy of aesthetic judgment proceeds along lines similar to the solution of the antinomies of pure theoretical reason in the *Critique* [*of Pure Reason*],[32] and we see here too – as well as in the *Critique of Practical Reason*[33] – that the antinomies compel us against our will to look beyond the sensible to the supersensible as the point [where] all our a priori powers are reconciled, since that is the only alternative left to us for bringing reason into harmony with itself.

Comment I

Since we so frequently find occasion in transcendental philosophy to distinguish ideas from concepts of the understanding, it may be useful to introduce technical terms to
342 mark the difference. I think there will be no objection if I propose a few. Ideas, in the broadest sense, are presentations referred to an object according to a certain principle (subjective or objective) but are such that they can still never become cognition of an object. There are two kinds of ideas. One of these is referred to an intuition, according to a merely subjective principle of the mutual harmony of the cognitive powers (imagination and understanding); and these ideas are called *aesthetic*. The other kind is referred to a concept, according to an objective principle, but these ideas still can never yield cognition of the object; they are called *rational* ideas.[34] Rational ideas are *transcendent* concepts; they differ from concepts of the understanding, which are called *immanent* because they can always be supplied with an experience that adequately corresponds to them.

An *aesthetic idea* cannot become cognition because it is an *intuition* (of the imagination) for which an adequate concept can never be found. A *rational idea* can never become cognition because it contains a *concept* (of the supersensible) for which no adequate intuition can ever be given.

I think we may call aesthetic ideas *unexpoundable* presentations of the imagination, and rational ideas *indemonstrable* concepts of reason. [But in saying this] I am presupposing that certainly neither of them lacks a basis, but that (as I said above in explicating ideas generally) they are produced according to certain principles of the cognitive powers to which they belong (aesthetic ideas according to subjective principles, rational ideas according to objective ones).

Concepts of the understanding must, as such, always be demonstrable (if by demonstrating we mean merely *exhibiting*, as we do in anatomy [for example[35]]; i.e., it must always be possible for the object corresponding to such concepts to be given in intuition (pure or empirical), because only in this way can they become cognitions. The concept of *magnitude* can be given in the a priori intuition of space, such as that of a

straight line, and so on; the concept of *cause* can be given in [an intuition of] impenetrability, or [of] the impact of bodies, etc. Hence both these concepts can be supported by an empirical intuition, i.e., the thought of them can be illustrated (demonstrated, displayed) in an example; and this possibility must [always] be there, since otherwise we cannot be certain that the thought is not empty, i.e., devoid of any 343
object.[36]

In logic the terms demonstrable and indemonstrable are usually applied only to *propositions*. But it would be better if there we talked instead about propositions that are only indirectly certain and propositions that are *directly certain*. For pure philosophy also has propositions of both kinds, if we understand by them true propositions that can be proved, or that cannot.[37] For, as philosophy, it can indeed prove [propositions] from a priori grounds, but cannot demonstrate them, unless we totally abandon the meaning of the word demonstrate (*ostendere, exhibere*), which means the same as to exhibit one's concept [not only discursively but] in intuition as well (whether in proving or merely in defining something). If this intuition is a priori, [the exhibition[38]] is called the construction of the concept;[39] but even if the intuition is empirical, [the exhibition] is still a display of the object, which serves to assure us that the concept has objective reality. For example, if an anatomist has set forth the concept of the human eye discursively and goes on to dissect the eye to make the concept intuitable, we say that he demonstrates this organ.

Accordingly, the rational concept of the supersensible substrate of all appearances generally, or the rational concept of the supersensible that must be regarded as underlying our power of choice in relation to moral laws, i.e., the rational concept of transcendental freedom, is an indemonstrable concept and a rational idea, simply because of the type of concept it is; virtue too is such a concept, but [only] in degree. For in the case of the concept of the supersensible, there is not even an intrinsic possibility for anything corresponding to it in quality to be given in experience, whereas in the case of virtue no empirical product of our causality of freedom reaches the degree that the rational idea of virtue prescribes to us as the rule.

Just as in the case of a rational idea the *imagination* with its intuitions does not reach the given concept, so in the case of an aesthetic idea the *understanding* with its concepts never reaches the entire inner intuition that the imagination has and connects with a given presentation. And since bringing a presentation of the imagination to concepts is the same as *expounding* it, aesthetic ideas may be called *unexpoundable* presentations of the imagination (in its free play). Later on I shall have occasion to make some further points about aesthetic ideas.[40] Here I shall merely point out that both kinds of ideas, rational as well as aesthetic, must have their principles, and both must have them in 344
reason: the principles of rational ideas must be objective principles of reason's employment, those of aesthetic ideas subjective ones.

Hence GENIUS can also be explicated as the ability to [exhibit] *aesthetic ideas*.[41] This [explication] indicates at the same time why it is that, in products of genius, art (i.e., production of the beautiful) receives its rule from nature (the nature of the subject) rather than from a deliberate purpose. For we must judge the beautiful not according to concepts, but according to the purposive attunement of the imagination that brings it into harmony with the power of concepts as such. Hence the subjective standard for that aesthetic but unconditioned purposiveness in fine art that is to lay rightful claim to everyone's necessary liking cannot be supplied by any rule or precept, but can be supplied only by that which is merely nature in the subject but which cannot be encompassed by rules or concepts – namely, the supersensible substrate (unattainable by any concept of the understanding) of all his powers; and hence the mentioned standard can be supplied only by [means of] that by reference to which we are to make all our cognitive powers harmonize, [doing] which is the ultimate purpose given us by the intelligible [element] of our nature. It is in this way alone, too, that this purposiveness, for which we cannot prescribe an objective principle, can be based a priori on a principle that is subjective and yet universally valid.

Translated by Werner S. Pluhar

Notes

1 The synthetic method proceeds from principles to their consequences, the analytic method the other way. Cf. the *Logic*, Ak. IX, 149, and the *Prolegomena*, Ak. IV, 263, 275, 276n, 279, and 365. [*Editor:* numbers refer to the pagination of the original Akademie edition, reproduced here in the margins.]

2 Cf. Ak. 232 br. n. 51.

3 Charles Batteux (1713–80), French philosopher and, in particular, aesthetician, and author of several works; Gotthold Ephraim Lessing (1729–81), German dramatist and aesthetician.

4 *Essays, Moral and Political* (1741–42), Essay VIII, 'The Sceptic':

> There is something approaching to principles in mental taste, and critics can reason and dispute more plausibly than cooks or perfumers. We may observe, however, that this uniformity among human kind hinders not, but that there is a considerable diversity in the sentiments of beauty and worth, and that education, custom, prejudice, caprice, and humour frequently vary our taste of this kind. You will never convince a man who is not accustomed to Italian music and has not an ear to follow its intricacies that a Scots tune is not preferable. You have not even any single argument beyond your own taste which you can employ in your behalf; and to your antagonist his particular taste will always appear a more convincing argument to the contrary. If you be wise, each of you will allow that the other may be in the right, and, having many other instances of this diversity of taste, you will both confess that beauty and worth are merely of a relative nature and consist in an agreeable sentiment, produced by an object in a particular mind, according to the peculiar structure and constitution of that mind.

5 I.e., creating a schema; cf. Ak. 253 br. n. 17. Kant is about to say that in a judgment of taste the imagination as such is subsumed under the *understanding* as such. Strictly speaking, however, the imagination is subsumed under the (indeterminate) *schema* of the understanding as such; and this indeterminate schema is the 'condition' which Kant has just mentioned.

6 In the sense of *feeling*, in this case.

7

> As far as *empirical judgments have universal validity* they are JUDGMENTS OF EXPERIENCE; but those *that are valid only subjectively* I call mere JUDGMENTS OF PERCEPTION. The latter require no pure concept of the understanding, but only the logical connection of the perceptions in a thinking subject. Judgments of experience, on the other hand, require, in addition to the presentations of sensible intuition, special *concepts produced originally in the understanding*, and it is these concepts that make the judgment of experience *valid objectively*.
>
> (*Prolegomena*, Ak. IV, 298. Cf. the *Critique of Pure Reason*, A 120, A 374, B 422n.)

8 The *metaphysical* deduction (for this name, see B 159), A 65–83 = B 90–116, is to show what categories there are (in the understanding); the *transcendental* deduction, A 84–130 and B 116–69, is to prove that these categories are objectively valid.

9 Cf. the *Critique of Pure Reason*, A 137–47 = B 176–87, and below, Ak. 351–52.

10 Cf. ibid., B 19. 'A priori' has here been construed adverbially, as modifying 'possible'. It can

also be read as an adjective modifying 'judgments,' so that Kant's question reads, 'How are synthetic a priori judgments possible?' Either reading can be supported by quotes in which the ambiguity does not arise, since Kant switches frequently between these two ways of talking. See, e.g., the passage immediately following the question Kant just quoted, B 20.

11 On the problem as to where the deduction ends (specifically, the problem as to whether the link of beauty to morality is still part of the deduction), see the Translator's Introduction [in the Pluhar translation of the *Critique*], lxi–lxvi.

12 To be justified in laying claim to universal assent to a judgment of the aesthetic power of judgment, which rests merely on subjective bases, one need grant only the following: (1) that in all people the subjective conditions of this power are the same as concerns the relations required for cognition as such between the cognitive powers that are activated in the power of judgment; and this must be true, for otherwise people could not communicate their presentations to one another, indeed they could not even communicate cognition; (2) that the judgment has taken into consideration merely this relation (and hence the *formal condition* of the power of judgment) and is pure, i.e., mingled neither with concepts of the object nor with sensations as the judgment's determining bases. But even if a mistake be made on the latter point,[13] this amounts to nothing but an incorrect application, in a particular case, of an authority given to us by a law, and in no way annuls the authority [itself].

13 Cf. Ak. 216 incl. br. n. 30, as well as the Comment Kant is about to make, but esp. §39, Ak. 293, and §40, Ak. 293–94.

14 Cf. just above, n. 15 and br. n. 16. [*Editor:* here, nn. 12 and 13.]

15 Or 'beautiful' science: Kant is responding, above all, to Alexander Gottlieb Baumgarten and Georg Friedrich Meier.

16 Cf. the *Anthropology*, Ak. VII, 280.

17 *Sinnesempfindung*; see §39, Ak. 291 incl. br. n. 19.

18 Cf. the *Anthropology*, Ak. VII, 225.

19 Cf. ibid., Ak. VII, 225 and 246. Cf. also above, §46, Ak. 308.

20 Cf. §57, Comment I, Ak. 341–44.

21 On the 'productive' imagination, see Ak. 240 br. n. 66; and cf. Ak. 243 br. n. 73, where Kant tells us in what sense the imagination *is not* creative.

22 Kant is giving a German translation (probably his own) of the following lines written in French by Frederick the Great (*Oeuvres de Frédéric le Grand*, 1846ff., x, 203):

Oui, finissons sans trouble, et mourons sans regrets,
En laissant l'Univers comblé de nos bienfaits.
Ainsi l'Astre du jour, au bout de sa carrière,
Répand sur l'horizon une douce lumière,
Et les derniers rayons qu'il darde dans les airs
Sont ses derniers soupirs qu'il donne à l'Univers.

23 From *Akademische Gedichte* (*Academic Poems*) (1782), vol. i, p. 70, by J.Ph.L. Withof (1725–89), professor of morals, oratory, and medicine at Duisburg, Germany. The original poem had 'goodness' instead of 'virtue.'

24 Perhaps nothing more sublime has ever been said, or a thought ever been expressed more sublimely, than in that inscription above the temple of *Isis* (Mother Nature): 'I am all that is, that was, and that will be, and no mortal has lifted my veil.' *Segner*[25] made use of this idea in an ingenious vignette prefixed to his *Naturlehre* [*Natural Science*], so as first to imbue the pupil, whom he was about to lead into this temple, with the sacred thrill that is meant to attune the mind to solemn attentiveness.

25 Johann Andreas von Segner (1704–77), German physicist and mathematician at Jena, Göttingen, and Halle. He is the author of several significant scientific works. He introduced the concept of the surface tension of liquids.

26 The thesis and antithesis.

27 See §31, Ak. 281, and § §32–33, Ak. 281–85.

28 Cf. §7, Ak. 212–13.

29 On Kant's mysterious *switch* from the indeterminate concept of nature's purposiveness (Ak.

180–92 and the third Moment, Ak. 219–36) to the (indeterminate) concept of the *supersensible* (specifically the supersensible as basis of that same purposiveness of nature), see 'Problem I' in the Translator's Introduction [to the Pluhar translation], lxii–lxiii and xciv–xcviii.

30 Cf. §34, Ak. 285–86.
31 Cf. the *Logic*, Ak. IX, 71.
32 For these antinomies and their solution, see A 405–567 = B 432–595.
33 Ak. V, 107–19.
34 Or 'ideas of reason.' Emphasis added.
35 Constructing a (pure) concept is also included. Cf. Ak. 232 br. n. 51.
36 Cf. the *Critique of Pure Reason*, B 291–93.
37 Cf. the *Logic*, Ak. IX, 71 and 110.
38 Correcting '*welche*' to '*welcher*,' as Windelband rightly recommends: Ak. V, 529.
39 Cf. Ak. 232 br. n. 51, and Ak. 351 br. n. 31.
40 See §58, Ak. 350–51, and §60, Ak. 355.
41 Cf. §49, Ak. 313–14.

2

EXTRACTS FROM *AESTHETICS: LECTURES ON FINE ART*

G. W. F. Hegel

[1 Prefatory remarks]

These lectures are devoted to Aesthetics. Their topic is the spacious *realm of the beautiful*; more precisely, their province is *art*, or, rather, *fine art*.

For this topic, it is true, the word Aesthetics, taken literally, is not wholly satisfactory, since 'Aesthetics' means, more precisely, the science of sensation, of feeling. In this sense it had its origin as a new science, or rather as something which for the first time was to become a philosophical discipline,[1] in the school of Wolff at the period in Germany when works of art were treated with regard to the feelings they were supposed to produce, as, for instance, the feeling of pleasure, admiration, fear, pity, and so on. Because of the unsatisfactoriness, or more accurately, the superficiality of this word, attempts were made after all to frame others, e.g. 'Callistics'. But this too appears inadequate because the science which is meant deals not with the beautiful as such but simply with the beauty of art. We will therefore let the word 'Aesthetics' stand; as a mere name it is a matter of indifference to us, and besides it has meanwhile passed over into common speech. As a name then it may be retained, but the proper expression for our science is *Philosophy of Art* and, more definitely, *Philosophy of Fine Art*.

[2] Limitation and defence of aesthetics

By adopting this expression we at once exclude the beauty of nature. Such a limitation of our topic may appear to be laid down arbitrarily, on the principle that every science has authority to demarcate its scope at will. But this is not the sense in which we should take the limitation of aesthetics to the beauty of art. In ordinary life we are of course accustomed to speak of a beautiful colour, a beautiful sky, a beautiful river; likewise of beautiful flowers, beautiful animals, and even more of beautiful people. We will not here enter upon the controversy about how far the attribute of beauty is justifiably ascribed to these and the like, and how far, in general, natural beauty may be put alongside the beauty of art. But we may assert against this view, even at this stage, that the beauty of art is *higher* than nature. The beauty of art is beauty *born of the spirit and born again*,[2] and the higher the spirit and its productions stand above nature and its phenomena, the higher too is the beauty of art above that of nature. Indeed, considered *formally* [i.e. no matter what it says], even a useless notion that enters a man's head is higher than any product of nature, because in such a notion spirituality and freedom are always present. Of course, considered in its *content*, the sun, for example, appears as an absolutely necessary factor [in the universe] while a false notion vanishes as *accidental* and transitory. But, taken by itself, a natural existent like the sun is indifferent, not free and self-conscious in itself; and if we treat it in its necessary connection with other things, then we are not treating it by itself, and therefore not as beautiful.

Now if we said in general that spirit and its artistic beauty stands *higher* than natural beauty, then of course virtually nothing is settled, because 'higher' is a quite vague expression which describes natural and artistic beauty as still standing side by side in the space of imagination and differing only quantitatively and therefore externally. But what is *higher* about the spirit and its artistic beauty is not something merely relative in comparison with nature. On the contrary, spirit is alone the *true*, comprehending everything in itself, so that everything beautiful is truly beautiful only as sharing in this higher sphere and generated by it. In this sense the beauty of nature appears only as a reflection of the beauty that belongs to spirit, as an imperfect incomplete mode [of beauty], a mode which in its *substance* is contained in the spirit itself. – Besides we shall find that a limitation to fine art arises very naturally, since, however much is said about the beauties of nature (less by the ancients than by us), it has not yet entered anyone's head to concentrate on the *beauty* of natural objects and make a science, a systematic exposition, of these beauties. A treatment from the point of view of *utility* has indeed been made and, for example, a scientific account of natural objects useful against diseases has been composed, a *materia medica*, a description of the minerals, chemical products, plants, or animals, which are useful for cures. But the realms of nature have not been classified and examined from the point of view of beauty. In [discussing] natural beauty we feel ourselves too much in a vague sphere, without a *criterion*, and therefore such a classification would provide too little interest for us to undertake it.

These preliminary remarks on beauty in nature and art, on the relation of the two, and the exclusion of the former from the scope of our proper subject, should dispose of the idea that the limitation is due merely to caprice and arbitrariness. The proof of this relation should not come here yet, since its consideration falls within our science itself and is therefore not to be further explained and proved until later [see Part I, ch. II].

But if we now limit ourselves provisionally to the beauty of art, this first step brings us at once up against new difficulties.

* * *

[5] Concept of the beauty of art

After these preliminary remarks, we now come closer to our proper subject, the philosophy of the beauty of art, and, since we are undertaking to treat it scientifically, we have to make a beginning with its Concept. Only when we have established this Concept can we lay down the division, and therefore the plan, of the whole of this science. For a division, if not undertaken in a purely external manner, as it is in a non-philosophical inquiry, must find its principle in the Concept of the subject-matter itself.

Confronted with such a requirement, we are at once met with the question 'whence do we derive this Concept?' If we start with the Concept itself of the beauty of art, it at once becomes a *presupposition* and a mere assumption; mere assumptions, however, philosophical method does not allow; on the contrary, what is to pass muster has to have its truth proved, i.e. has to be shown to be necessary.

About this difficulty, which affects the introduction to every philosophical discipline considered independently and by itself, we will come to an understanding in a short space.

In the case of the object of every science, two things come at once into consideration: (i) that there *is* such an object, and (ii) *what* it is.

On the first point little difficulty usually arises in the ordinary [i.e. physical] sciences. Why, it would at once be ridiculous to require astronomy and physics to prove that there are a sun, stars, magnetic phenomena, etc.! In these sciences which have to do with what is present to sensation, the objects are taken from experience of the external world, and instead of *proving* them, it is thought sufficient to *point* to them. Yet even within the non-philosophical disciplines, doubts may arise about the existence of their objects, as, for example, in psychology, the science of mind, there may be a doubt whether there *is* a soul, a spirit, i.e. an explicitly independent subjective entity distinct from what is material; or in theology, a doubt whether there is a God. If, moreover, the objects are of a subjective sort, i.e. present only in the mind and not as things externally perceptible, we know that in mind there is only what its own activity has produced. Hence there arises at once the chance that men may or may not have produced this inner idea or intuition in themselves, and, even if the former is really the case, that they have not made such an idea vanish again, or at least degraded it to a purely subjective idea whose content has no independent reality of its own. Thus, for example, the beautiful has often been regarded as not being absolutely necessary in our ideas but as a purely subjective pleasure, or a merely accidental sense. Our intuitions, observations, and perceptions of the external world are often deceptive and erroneous, but this is even more true of our inner ideas, even if they have in themselves the greatest vividness and could carry us away into passion irresistibly.

Now the doubt whether an object of our inner ideas and general outlook *is* or is *not*, like the question whether subjective consciousness has generated it in itself and whether the manner and mode in which it has brought it before itself was also in correspondence with the object in its essential nature, is precisely what arouses in men the higher scientific need which demands that, even if we have a notion that an object *is* or that there is such an object, nevertheless the object must be exhibited or proved in accordance with its *necessity*.

With this proof, provided it be developed really scientifically, the other question of *what* an object is, is sufficiently answered at the same time. However, to expound this fully would take us too far afield at this point, and only the following indications can be given.

If the necessity of our subject, the beauty of art, is to be exhibited, we would have to prove that art or the beautiful was a result of an antecedent which, considered according to its true Concept, was such as to lead on with scientific necessity to the Concept of fine art. But since we begin with art and wish to treat of *its* Concept and the realization thereof, not of its antecedent in its essential character (the antecedent pursuant to its own Concept), art has for us, as a particular scientific subject-matter, a presupposition which lies outside our consideration and, handled scientifically as a different subject-matter, belongs to a different philosophical discipline. Thus the only course left to us is to take up the Concept of art *lemmatically*,[3] so to say, and this is the case with all particular philosophical sciences if they are to be treated *seriatim*. For it is only the *whole* of philosophy which is knowledge of the universe as in itself that *one* organic totality which develops itself out of its own Concept and which, in its self-relating necessity, withdrawing into itself to form a whole, closes with itself to form *one* world of truth. In the circlet of this scientific necessity each single part is on the one hand a circle returning into itself, while on the other hand it has at the same time a necessary connection with other parts. It has a backward whence it is itself derived, and a forward to which it ever presses itself on, in so far as it is fertile, engendering an 'other' out of itself once more, and issuing it for scientific knowledge. Thus it is not our present aim, but the task of an encyclopedic development of the whole of philosophy and its particular disciplines, to prove the Idea of the beautiful with which we began, i.e. to derive it necessarily from the presuppositions which antecede it in philosophy and out of the womb of which it is born. For us the Concept of the beautiful and art is a presupposition given by the system of philosophy. But since we cannot here expound this system and the connection of art with it, we have not yet got the Concept of the beautiful before us scientifically. What *is* before us is only elements and aspects of it as they occur already in the different ideas of the beautiful and art held by ordinary people, or have formerly been accepted by them. From this point we intend to pass on to a deeper consideration of these views in order to gain the advantage, in the first place, of acquiring a general idea of our subject, as well as, by a brief critique, a preliminary acquaintance with the higher determinations with which we will have to do in the sequel. In this way our final introductory treatment of the subject will present, as it were, an overture to the lectures on the matter at issue and will tend [to provide] a general collection and direction [of our thoughts] to our proper subject.

* * *

[8] Division of the subject

After the foregoing introductory remarks it is now time to pass on to the study of our subject itself. But the introduction, where we still are, can in this respect do no more than sketch for our apprehension a conspectus of the entire course of our subsequent scientific studies. But since we have spoken of art as itself proceeding from the absolute Idea, and have even pronounced its end to be the sensuous presentation of the Absolute itself, we must proceed, even in this conspectus, by showing, at least in general, how the particular parts of the subject emerge from the conception of artistic beauty as the presentation of the Absolute. Therefore we must attempt, in the most general way, to awaken an idea of this conception.

It has already been said that the content of art is the Idea, while its form is the configuration of sensuous material. Now art has to harmonize these two sides and bring them into a free reconciled totality. The *first* point here is the demand that the content which is to come into artistic representation should be in itself qualified for such representation. For otherwise we obtain only a bad combination, because in that case a content ill-adapted to figurativeness and external presentation is made to adopt this form, or, in other words, material explicitly prosaic is expected to find a really appropriate mode of presentation in the form antagonistic to its nature.

The *second* demand, derived from the first, requires of the content of art that it be not anything abstract in itself, but concrete, though not concrete in the sense in which the sensuous is concrete when it is contrasted with everything spiritual and intellectual and these are taken to be simple and abstract. For everything genuine in spirit and nature alike is inherently concrete and, despite its universality, has nevertheless subjectivity and particularity in itself. If we say, for example, of God that he is simply *one*, the supreme being as such, we have thereby only enunciated a dead abstraction of the sub-rational Understanding. Such a God, not apprehended himself in his concrete truth, will provide no content for art, especially not for visual art. Therefore the Jews and the Turks have not been able by art to represent their God, who does not even amount to such an abstraction of the Understanding, in the positive way that the Christians have. For in Christianity God is set forth in his truth, and therefore as thoroughly concrete in himself, as person, as subject, and, more closely defined, as spirit. What he is as spirit is made explicit for religious apprehension as a Trinity of Persons, which yet at the same time is self-aware as *one*. Here we have essentiality or universality, and particularization, together with their reconciled unity, and only such unity is the concrete. Now since a content, in order to be true at all, must be of this concrete kind, art too demands similar concreteness, because the purely abstract universal has not in itself the determinate character of advancing to particularization and phenomenal manifestation and to unity with itself in these.

Now, *thirdly*, if a sensuous form and shape is to correspond with a genuine and therefore concrete content, it must likewise be something individual, in itself completely concrete and single. The fact that the concrete accrues to both sides of art, i.e. to both content and its presentation, is precisely the point in which both can coincide and correspond with one another; just as, for instance, the natural shape of the human body is such a sensuously concrete thing, capable of displaying spirit, which is concrete in itself, and of showing itself in conformity with it. Therefore, after all, we must put out of our minds the idea that it is purely a matter of chance that to serve as such a genuine shape an actual phenomenon of the external world is selected. For art does not seize upon this form either because it just finds it there or because there is no other; on the contrary, the concrete content itself involves the factor of external, actual, and indeed even sensuous manifestation. But then in return this sensuous concrete thing, which bears the stamp of an essentially spiritual content, is also essentially *for* our inner [apprehension]; the external shape, whereby the content is made visible and imaginable, has the purpose of existing solely for our mind and spirit. For this reason alone are content and artistic form fashioned in conformity with one another. The *purely* sensuously concrete – external nature as such – does not have this purpose for the sole reason of its origin. The variegated richly coloured plumage of birds shines even when unseen, their song dies away unheard; the torch-thistle, which blooms for only one night, withers in the wilds of the southern forests without having been admired, and these forests, jungles themselves of the most beautiful and luxuriant vegetation, with the most sweet-smelling and aromatic perfumes, rot and decay equally unenjoyed. But the work of art is not so naïvely self-centred; it is essentially a question, an address to the responsive breast, a call to the mind and the spirit.

Although illustration by art is not in this respect a matter of chance, it is, on the other hand, not the highest way of apprehending the spiritually concrete. The higher way, in contrast to representation by means of the sensuously concrete, is thinking, which in a relative sense is indeed abstract, but it must be concrete, not one-sided, if it is to be true and rational. How far a specific content has its appropriate form in sensuous artistic representation, or whether, owing to its own nature, it essentially demands a higher, more spiritual, form, is a question of the distinction which appears at once, for example, in a comparison between the Greek gods and God as conceived by Christian ideas. The Greek god is not abstract but individual, closely related to the natural [human] form. The Christian God too is indeed a concrete personality, but is *pure* spirituality and is to be known as *spirit* and in spirit. His medium of existence is therefore essentially inner knowledge and not the external natural form through which he can be represented only imperfectly and not in the whole profundity of his nature.

But since art has the task of presenting the Idea to immediate perception in a sensuous shape and not in the form of thinking and pure spirituality as such, and, since this presenting has its value and dignity in the correspondence and unity of both sides, i.e. the Idea and its outward shape, it follows that the loftiness and excellence of art in attaining a reality adequate to its Concept will depend on the degree of inwardness and unity in which Idea and shape appear fused into one.

In this point of higher truth, as the spirituality which the artistic formation has achieved in conformity with the Concept of spirit, there lies the basis for the division of the philosophy of art. For, before reaching the true Concept of its absolute essence, the spirit has to go through a course of stages, a series grounded in this Concept itself; and to this course of the content which the spirit gives to itself there corresponds a course, immediately connected therewith, of configurations of art, in the form of which the spirit, as artist, gives itself a consciousness of itself.

This course within the spirit of art has itself in turn, in accordance with its own nature, two sides. *First*, this development is itself a spiritual and universal one, since the sequence of definite conceptions of the world, as the definite but comprehensive consciousness of nature, man, and God, gives itself artistic shape.[4] *Secondly*, this inner development of art has to give itself immediate existence and sensuous being, and the specific modes of the sensuous being of art are themselves a totality of necessary differences in art, i.e. the *particular arts*. Artistic configuration and its differences are, on the one hand, as spiritual, of a more universal kind and not bound to *one* material [e.g. stone or paint], and sensuous existence is itself differentiated in numerous ways; but since this existence, like spirit, has the Concept implicitly for its inner soul, a specific sensuous material does thereby, on the other hand, acquire a closer relation and a secret harmony with the spiritual differences and forms of artistic configuration.

However, in its completeness our science is divided into three main sections:

First, we acquire a *universal* part. This has for its content and subject both the universal Idea of artistic beauty as the Ideal, and also the nearer relation of the Ideal to nature on the one hand and to subjective artistic production on the other.

Secondly, there is developed out of the conception of artistic beauty a *particular* part, because the essential differences contained in this conception unfold into a sequence of particular forms of artistic configuration.

Thirdly, there is a *final* part which has to consider the individualization of artistic beauty, since art advances to the sensuous realization of its creations and rounds itself off in a system of single arts and their genera and species.

(i) The Idea of the beauty of art or the Ideal

In the first place, so far as the first and second parts are concerned, we must at once, if what follows is to be made intelligible, recall again that the Idea as the beauty of art is not the Idea as such, in the way that a metaphysical logic has to apprehend it as the Absolute, but the Idea as shaped forward into reality and as having advanced to immediate unity and correspondence with this reality. For the *Idea as such* is indeed the absolute truth itself, but the truth only in its not yet objectified universality, while the Idea as the *beauty of art* is the Idea with the nearer qualification of being both essentially individual reality and also an individual configuration of reality destined essentially to embody and reveal the Idea. Accordingly there is here expressed the demand that the Idea and its configuration as a concrete reality shall be made completely adequate to one another. Taken thus, the Idea as reality, shaped in accordance with the Concept of the Idea, is the *Ideal*.

The problem of such correspondence might in the first instance be understood quite formally in the sense that any Idea at all might serve, if only the actual shape, no matter which, represented precisely this specific Idea. But in that case the demanded *truth* of the Ideal is confused with mere *correctness* which consists in the expression of some meaning or other in an appropriate way and therefore the direct rediscovery of its sense in the shape produced. The Ideal is not to be thus understood. For any content can be represented quite adequately, judged by the standard of its own essence, without being allowed to claim the artistic beauty of the Ideal. Indeed, in comparison with ideal beauty, the representation will even appear defective. In this regard it may be remarked in advance, what can only be proved later, namely that the defectiveness of a work of art is not always to be regarded as due, as may be supposed, to the artist's lack of skill; on the contrary, defectiveness of *form* results from defectiveness of *content*. So, for example, the Chinese, Indians, and Egyptians, in their artistic shapes, images of gods, and idols, never get beyond formlessness or a bad and untrue definiteness of form. They could not master true beauty because their mythological ideas, the content and thought of their works of art, were still indeterminate, or determined badly, and so did not consist of the content which is absolute in itself. Works of art are all the more excellent in expressing true beauty, the deeper is the inner truth of their content and thought. And in this connection we are not merely to think, as others may, of any greater or lesser skill with which natural forms as they exist in the external world are apprehended and imitated. For, in certain stages of art-consciousness and presentation, the abandonment and distortion of natural formations is not unintentional lack of technical skill or practice, but international alteration which proceeds from and is demanded by what is in the artist's mind. Thus, from this point of view, there is imperfect art which in technical and other respects may be quite perfect in its *specific* sphere, and yet it is clearly defective in comparison with the concept of art itself and the Ideal.

Only in the highest art are Idea and presentation truly in conformity with one another, in the sense that the shape given to the Idea is in itself the absolutely true shape, because the content of the Idea which that shape expresses is itself the true and genuine content. Associated with this, as has already been indicated, is the fact that the Idea must be determined in and through itself as a concrete totality, and therefore possess in itself the principle and measure of its particularization and determinacy in external appearance. For example, the Christian imagination will be able to represent God in human form and its expression of *spirit*, only because God himself is here completely known in himself as *spirit*. Determinacy is, as it were, the bridge to appearance. Where this determinacy is not a totality emanating from the Idea itself, where the Idea is not presented as self-determining and self-particularizing, the Idea remains abstract and has its determinacy, and therefore the principle for its particular and solely appropriate mode of appearance, not in itself, but outside itself. On this account, then, the still abstract Idea has its shape also external to itself, not settled by itself. On the other hand, the inherently concrete Idea carries within itself the principle of its mode of appearance and is therefore its own free configurator. Thus the truly concrete Idea alone produces its true configuration, and this correspondence of the two is the Ideal.

(ii) Development of the Ideal into the particular forms of the beauty of art

But because the Idea is in this way a concrete unity, this unity can enter the art-consciousness only through the unfolding and then the reconciliation of the particularizations of the Idea, and, through this development, artistic beauty acquires a *totality of particular stages and forms*. Therefore, after studying artistic beauty in itself and on its own account, we must see how beauty as a whole decomposes into its particular determinations. This gives, as the *second* part of our study, the doctrine of the *forms of art*. These forms find their origin in the different ways of grasping the Idea as content, whereby a difference in the configuration in which the Idea appears is conditioned. Thus the forms of art are nothing but the different relations of meaning and shape, relations which proceed from the Idea itself and therefore provide the true basis for the division of this sphere. For division must always be implicit in the concept, the particularization and division of which is in question.

We have here to consider *three* relations of the Idea to its configuration.

(*a*) *First*, art begins when the Idea, still in its indeterminacy and obscurity, or in bad and untrue determinacy, is made the content of artistic shapes. Being indeterminate, it does not yet possess in itself that individuality which the Ideal demands; its abstraction and one-sidedness leave its shape externally defective and arbitrary. The first form of art is therefore rather a *mere search* for portrayal than a capacity for true presentation; the Idea has not found the form even in itself and therefore remains struggling and striving after it. We may call this form, in general terms, the *symbolic* form of art. In it the abstract Idea has its shape outside itself in the natural sensuous material from which the process of shaping starts[5] and with which, in its appearance, this process is linked. Perceived natural objects are, on the one hand, primarily left as they are, yet at the same time the substantial Idea is imposed on them as their meaning so that they now acquire a vocation to express it and so are to be interpreted as if the Idea itself were present in them. A corollary of this is the fact that natural objects have in them an aspect according to which they are capable of representing a universal meaning. But since a complete correspondence is not yet possible, this relation can concern only an *abstract* characteristic, as when, for example, in a lion strength is meant.

On the other hand, the abstractness of this relation brings home to consciousness even so the foreignness of the Idea to natural phenomena, and the Idea, which has no other reality to express it, launches out in all these shapes, seeks itself in them in their unrest and extravagance, but yet does not find them adequate to itself. So now the Idea exaggerates natural shapes and the phenomena of reality itself into indefiniteness and extravagance; it staggers round in them, it bubbles and ferments in them, does violence to them, distorts and stretches them unnaturally, and tries to elevate their phenomenal appearance to the Idea by the diffuseness, immensity, and splendour of the formations employed. For the Idea is here still more or less indeterminate and unshapable, while the natural objects are thoroughly determinate in their shape.

In the incompatibility of the two sides to one another, the relation of the Idea to the objective world therefore becomes a *negative* one, since the Idea, as something inward, is itself unsatisfied by such externality, and, as the inner universal substance thereof, it persists *sublime* above all this multiplicity of shapes which do not correspond with it. In the light of this sublimity, the natural phenomena and human forms and events are accepted, it is true, and left as they are, but yet they are recognized at the same time as incompatible with their meaning which is raised far above all mundane content.

These aspects constitute in general the character of the early artistic pantheism of the East, which on the one hand ascribes absolute meaning to even the most worthless objects, and, on the other, violently coerces the phenomena to express its view of the world whereby it becomes bizarre, grotesque, and tasteless, or turns the infinite but abstract freedom of the substance [i.e. the one Lord] disdainfully against all phenomena as being null and evanescent. By this means the meaning cannot be completely pictured in the expression and, despite all striving and endeavour the incompatibility of Idea and shape still remains unconquered. – This may be taken to be the first form of art, the symbolic form with its quest, its fermentation, its mysteriousness, and its sublimity.

(*b*) In the *second* form of art which we will call the *classical*, the double defect of the symbolic form is extinguished. The symbolic shape is imperfect because, (i) in it the Idea is presented to consciousness only as indeterminate or determined *abstractly*, and, (ii) for this reason the correspondence of meaning and shape is always defective and must itself remain purely abstract. The classical art-form clears up this double defect; it is the free and adequate embodiment of the Idea in the shape peculiarly appropriate to the Idea itself in its essential nature. With this shape, therefore, the Idea is able to come into free and complete harmony. Thus the classical art-form is the first to afford the production and vision of the completed Ideal and to present it as actualized in fact.

Nevertheless, the conformity of concept and reality in classical art must not be taken in the purely *formal* sense of a correspondence between a content and its external configuration, any more than this could be the case with the Ideal itself. Otherwise every portrayal of nature, every cast of features, every neighbourhood, flower, scene, etc., which constitutes the end and content of the representation, would at once be classical on the strength of such congruity between content and form. On the contrary, in classical art the peculiarity of the content consists in its being itself the concrete Idea, and as such the concretely spiritual, for it is the spiritual alone which is the truly inner [self]. Consequently, to suit such a content we must try to find out what in nature belongs to the spiritual in and for itself. The *original* Concept[6] itself it must be which *invented* the shape for concrete spirit, so that now the *subjective* Concept – here the spirit of art – has merely *found* this shape and made it, as a natural shaped existent, appropriate to free individual spirituality. This shape, which the Idea as spiritual – indeed as individually determinate spirituality – assumes when it is to proceed out into a temporal manifestation, is the human form. Of course personification and anthropomorphism have often been maligned as a degradation of the spiritual, but in so far as art's task is to bring the spiritual before our eyes in a sensuous manner, it must get involved in this anthropomorphism, since spirit appears sensuously in a satisfying way only in its body. The transmigration of souls is in this respect an abstract idea,[7] and physiology should have made it one of its chief propositions that life in its development had necessarily to proceed to the human form as the one and only sensuous appearance appropriate to spirit.

But the human body in its forms counts in classical art no longer as a merely sensuous existent, but only as the existence and natural shape of the spirit, and it must therefore be exempt from all the deficiency of the purely sensuous and from the contingent finitude of the phenomenal world. While in this way the shape is purified in order to express in itself a content adequate to itself, on the other hand, if the correspondence of meaning and shape is to be perfect, the spirituality, which is the content, must be of such a kind that it can express itself completely in the natural human form, without towering beyond and above this expression in sensuous and bodily terms. Therefore here the spirit is at once determined as particular and human, not as purely absolute and eternal, since in this latter sense it can proclaim and express itself only as spirituality.

This last point in its turn is the defect which brings about the dissolution of the classical art-form and demands a transition to a higher form, the *third*, namely the *romantic*.

(*c*) The romantic form of art cancels again the completed unification of the Idea and its reality, and reverts, even if in a higher way, to that difference and opposition of the two sides which in symbolic art remained unconquered. The classical form of art has attained the pinnacle of what illustration by art could achieve, and if there is something defective in it, the defect is just art itself and the restrictedness of the sphere of art. This restrictedness lies in the fact that art in general takes as its subject-matter the spirit (i.e. the *universal*, infinite and concrete in its nature) in a *sensuously* concrete form, and classical art presents the complete unification of spiritual and sensuous existence as the *correspondence* of the two. But in this blending of the two, spirit is not in fact represented in its *true nature*. For spirit is the infinite subjectivity of the Idea, which as absolute inwardness cannot freely and truly shape itself outwardly on condition of remaining moulded into a bodily existence as the one appropriate to it.[8]

Abandoning this [classical] principle, the romantic form of art cancels the undivided unity of classical art because it has won a content which goes beyond and above the classical form of art and its mode of expression. This content – to recall familiar ideas – coincides with what Christianity asserts of God as a spirit, in distinction from the Greek religion which is the essential and most appropriate content for classical art. In classical art the concrete content is *implicitly* the unity of the divine nature with the human, a unity which, just because it is only immediate and implicit, is adequately manifested also in an immediate and sensuous way. The Greek god is the object of naïve intuition and sensuous imagination, and therefore his shape is the bodily shape of man. The range of his power and his being is individual and particular. Contrasted with the individual he is a substance and power with which the individual's inner being is only implicitly at one but without itself possessing this oneness as inward subjective knowledge. Now the higher state is the *knowledge* of that *implicit* unity which is the content of the classical art-form and is capable of perfect presentation in bodily shape. But this elevation of the implicit into self-conscious knowledge introduces a tremendous difference. It is the infinite difference which, for example, separates man from animals. Man is an animal, but even in his animal functions, he is not confined to the implicit, as the animal is; he becomes conscious of them, recognizes them, and lifts them, as, for instance, the process of digestion, into self-conscious science. In this way man breaks the barrier of his implicit and immediate character, so that precisely because he *knows* that he is an animal, he ceases to be an animal and attains knowledge of himself as spirit.

Now if in this way what was implicit at the previous stage, the unity of divine and human nature, is raised from an *immediate* to a *known* unity, the *true* element for the realization of this content is no longer the sensuous immediate existence of the spiritual in the bodily form of man, but instead the *inwardness of self-consciousness*. Now Christianity brings God before our imagination as spirit, not as an individual, particular spirit, but as absolute in spirit and in truth. For this reason it retreats from the sensuousness of imagination into spiritual inwardness and makes this, and not the body, the medium and the existence of truth's content. Thus the unity of divine and human nature is a known unity, one to be realized only by *spiritual* knowing and *in spirit*. The new content, thus won, is on this account not tied to sensuous presentation, as if that corresponded to it, but is freed from this immediate existence which must be set down as negative, overcome, and reflected into the spiritual unity. In this way romantic art is the self-transcendence of art but within its own sphere and in the form of art itself.

We may, therefore, in short, adhere to the view that at this third stage the subject-matter of art is *free concrete spirituality*, which is to be manifested as *spirituality* to the spiritually inward. In conformity with this subject-matter, art cannot work for sensuous intuition. Instead it must, on the one hand, work for the inwardness which coalesces with its object simply as if with itself, for subjective inner depth, for reflective emotion, for feeling which, as spiritual, strives for freedom in itself and seeks and finds its reconciliation only in the inner spirit. This *inner* world constitutes the content of the romantic sphere and must therefore be represented as this inwardness and in the pure appearance of this depth of feeling. Inwardness celebrates its triumph over the external and manifests its victory in and on the external itself, whereby what is apparent to the senses alone sinks into worthlessness.

On the other hand, however, this romantic form too, like all art, needs an external medium for its expression. Now since spirituality has withdrawn into itself out of the external world and immediate unity therewith, the sensuous externality of shape is for this reason accepted and represented, as in symbolic art, as something inessential and transient; and the same is true of the subjective finite spirit and will, right down to the particularity and caprice of individuality, character, action, etc., of incident, plot, etc. The aspect of external existence is consigned to contingency and abandoned to the adventures devised by an imagination whose caprice can mirror what is present to it, *exactly as it is*, just as readily as it can jumble the shapes of the external world and distort them grotesquely. For this external medium has its essence and meaning no longer, as in classical art, in itself and its own sphere, but in the heart which finds its manifestation in itself instead of in the external world and *its* form of reality, and this reconciliation with itself it can preserve or regain in every chance, in every accident that takes independent shape, in all misfortune and grief, and indeed even in crime.

Thereby the separation of Idea and shape, their indifference and inadequacy to each other, come to the fore again, as in symbolic art, but with this essential difference, that, in romantic art, the Idea, the deficiency of which in the symbol brought with it deficiency of shape, now has to appear *perfected* in itself as spirit and heart. Because of this higher perfection, it is not susceptible of an adequate union with the external, since its true reality and manifestation it can seek and achieve only within itself.

This we take to be the general character of the symbolic, classical, and romantic forms of art, as the three relations of the Idea to its shape in the sphere of art. They consist in the striving for, the attainment, and the transcendence of the Ideal as the true Idea of beauty.

(iii) The system of the individual arts

Now the *third* part of our subject, in contradistinction from the two just described, presupposes the concept of the Ideal and also the three general forms of art, since it is only the realization of these in specific sensuous materials. Therefore we now no longer have to do with the inner development of artistic beauty in its general fundamental characteristics. Instead we have to consider how these characteristics pass into existence, are distinguished from one another externally, and actualize every feature in the conception of beauty independently and explicitly as a *work of art* and not merely as a *general form*. But since it is the differences immanent in the Idea of beauty, and proper to it, that art transfers into external existence, it follows that in this Part III the general forms of art must likewise be the fundamental principle for the articulation and determination of the individual arts; in other words, the kinds of art have the same essential distinctions in themselves which we came to recognize in the general forms of art. Now the *external* objectivity into which these forms are introduced through a sensuous and therefore *particular* material, makes these forms *fall apart* from one another independently, to become distinct ways of their realization, i.e. the particular arts. For each form finds its specific character also in a specific external material, and its adequate realization in the mode of portrayal which that material requires. But, on the other hand, these art-forms, universal as they are despite their determinateness, break the bounds of a *particular* realization through a *specific* kind of art and achieve their existence equally through the other arts, even if in a subordinate way. Therefore the particular arts belong, on the one hand, specifically to *one* of the general forms of art and they shape its adequate external artistic actuality, and, on the other hand, in their own individual way of shaping externality, they present the totality of the forms of art.[9]

In general terms, that is to say, in Part III of our subject we have to deal with the beauty of art as it unfolds itself, in the arts and their productions, into a world of actualized beauty. The content of this world is the beautiful, and the true beautiful, as we saw, is spirituality given shape, the Ideal, and, more precisely, absolute spirit, the truth itself. This region of divine truth, artistically represented for contemplation and feeling, forms the centre of the whole world of art. It is the independent, free, and divine shape which has completely mastered the externality of form and material and wears it only as a manifestation of itself. Still, since the beautiful develops itself in this region as *objective* reality and therefore distinguishes within itself its single aspects and factors, granting them independent particularity, it follows that this centre now arrays its extremes, realized in their appropriate actuality, as contrasted with itself. One of these extremes therefore forms a still *spiritless objectivity*, the merely natural environment of God. Here the external as such takes shape as something having its spiritual end and content not in itself but in another.

The other extreme is the Divine as inward, as something known, as the variously particularized *subjective* existence of the Deity: the truth as it is effective and living in the sense, heart, and spirit of individual persons, not remaining poured out into its external shape, but returning into the subjective individual inner life. Thereby the Divine as such is at the same time distinguished from its pure manifestation as *Deity*, and thereby enters itself into the particularity characteristic of all individual subjective knowledge, emotion, perception, and feeling. In the analogous sphere of religion, with which art at its highest stage is immediately connected, we conceive this same difference as follows. *First*, earthly natural life in its finitude confronts us on one side; but then, *secondly*, our consciousness makes *God* its object wherein the difference of objectivity and subjectivity falls away, until, *thirdly*, and lastly, we advance from God as such to worship by the *community*, i.e. to God as living and present in subjective consciousness. These three fundamental differences arise also in the world of art in independent development.

(*a*) The *first* of the particular arts, the one with which we have to begin in accordance with this fundamental characterization of them, is *architecture* as a fine art. Its task consists in so manipulating external inorganic nature that, as an external world conformable to art, it becomes cognate to spirit. Its material is matter itself in its immediate externality as a mechanical heavy mass, and its forms remain the forms of inorganic nature, set in order according to relations of the abstract Understanding, i.e. relations of symmetry. In this material and in these forms the Ideal, as concrete spirituality, cannot be realized. Hence the reality presented in them remains opposed to the Idea, because it is something external not penetrated by the Idea or only in an abstract relation to it. Therefore the fundamental type of the art of building is the *symbolic* form of art. For architecture is the first to open the way for the adequate actuality of the god, and in his service it slaves away with objective nature in order to work it free from the jungle of finitude and the monstrosity of chance. Thereby it levels a place for the god, forms his external environment, and builds for him his temple as the place for the inner composure of the spirit and its direction on its absolute objects. It raises an enclosure for the assembly of the congregation, as protection against the threat of storm, against rain, tempest, and wild animals, and it reveals in an artistic way, even if in an external one, the wish to assemble. This meaning it can build into its material and the forms thereof with greater or lesser effect, in proportion as the determinate character of the content for which it undertakes its work is more significant or insignificant, more concrete or abstract, more profoundly plumbing its own depths, or more obscure and superficial. Indeed in this respect architecture may itself attempt to go so far as to fashion in its forms and material an adequate artistic existence for that content; but in that event it has already stepped beyond its own sphere and is swinging over to sculpture, the stage above it. For its limitation lies precisely in retaining the spiritual, as something inner, over against its own external forms and thus pointing to what has soul only as to something distinct from these.

(*b*) But by architecture, after all, the inorganic external world has been purified, set in order symmetrically, and made akin to spirit, and the god's temple, the house of his community, stands there ready. Then into this temple, *secondly*, the god enters himself as the lightning-flash of individuality striking and permeating the inert mass, and the infinite, and no longer merely symmetrical, form of spirit itself concentrates and gives shape to something corporeal. This is the task of *sculpture*.

In so far as in sculpture the spiritual inner life, at which architecture can only hint, makes itself at home in the sensuous shape and its external material, and in so far as these two sides are so mutually formed that neither preponderates, sculpture acquires the *classical* art-form as its fundamental type. Therefore, no expression is left to the sensuous which is not an expression of spirit itself, just as, conversely, for sculpture no spiritual content can be perfectly represented unless it can be fully and adequately presented to view in bodily form. For through sculpture the spirit should stand before us in blissful tranquillity in its bodily form and in immediate unity therewith, and the form should be brought to life by the content of spiritual individuality. So the external sensuous material is no longer processed either according to its mechanical quality alone, as a mass possessing weight, or in forms of the inorganic world, or as indifferent to colour, etc., but in the ideal forms of the human figure and in all three spatial dimensions too. In this last respect we must claim for sculpture that in it the inward and the spiritual come into appearance for the first time in their eternal peace and essential self-sufficiency. To this peace and unity with itself only that external shape corresponds which itself persists in this unity and peace. This is shape according to its *abstract spatiality*.[10] The spirit which sculpture presents is spirit compact in itself, not variously splintered into the play of accidents and passions. Consequently sculpture does not abandon spirit's external form to this variety of appearance, but picks up therein only this one aspect, abstract spatiality in the totality of its dimensions.

(*c*) Now when architecture has built its temple and the hand of sculpture has set up within it the statues of the god, this sensuously present god is confronted, *thirdly*, in the wide halls of his house, by the *community*. The community is the spiritual reflection into itself of this sensuous existent, and is animating subjectivity and inwardness. With these, therefore, it comes about that the determining principle, alike for the content of art and for the material that represents it outwardly, is particularization and individualization and their requisite subjective apprehension. The compact unity in itself which the god has in sculpture disperses into the plurality of the inner lives of individuals whose unity is not sensuous but purely ideal.[11] And so only here is God himself truly spirit, spirit in his community, God as this to-and-fro, as this exchange of his inherent unity with his actualization in subjective knowing and its individualization as well as in the universality and union of the multitude. In the community God is released alike from the abstraction of undeveloped self-identity and from his sculptural representation as immediately immersed in a bodily medium; and he is raised to spirituality and knowledge, i.e. to spirit's mirror-image which essentially appears as inward and as subjectivity. Consequently the higher content is now the spiritual, the spiritual as absolute. But at the same time, owing to the dispersal mentioned just now, the spiritual appears here as *particular* spirituality, an individual mind. And it is not the self-sufficient peace of the god in himself, but appearance as such, being *for* another, that manifestation of the self, which comes to the fore here as the chief thing; so now what becomes on its own account an object of artistic representation is the most manifold subjectivity in its living movement and activity as human passion, action, and adventure, and, in general, the wide range of human feeling, willing, and neglect.

Now in conformity with this content the sensuous element in art has likewise to show itself particularized in itself and appropriate to subjective inwardness. Material for this is afforded by colour, musical sound, and finally sound as the mere indication of inner intuitions and ideas. And as modes of realizing the content in question by means of these materials we have painting, music, and poetry. Here the sensuous medium appears as particularized in itself and posited throughout as ideal. Thus it best corresponds with the generally spiritual content of art, and the connection of spiritual meaning with sensuous material grows into a deeper intimacy than was possible in architecture and sculpture. Nevertheless this is a more inner unity which lies entirely on the subjective side, and which, in so far as form and content have to particularize themselves and posit themselves as ideal, can only come about at the expense of the objective universality of the content and its fusion with the immediately sensuous element.

Now in these arts form and content raise themselves to ideality, and thus, since they leave behind symbolic architecture and the classical idea of sculpture, they acquire their type from the *romantic* form of art on whose mode of configuration they are adapted to impress themselves in the most appropriate manner. But they are a totality of arts, because the romantic is in itself the most concrete form of art.

The inner articulation of this *third sphere* of the individual arts may be established as follows:

(α) The *first* art, standing next to sculpture, is *painting*. It uses as material for its content, and its content's configuration, visibility as such, in so far as this is at the same time particularized, i.e. developed into colour. True, the material of architecture and sculpture is likewise visible and coloured, but it is not, as in painting, the making visible as such; it is not the simple light which, differentiating itself in its contrast with darkness, and in combination therewith, becomes colour.[12] This quality of visibility inherently subjectivized and posited as ideal, needs neither the abstract mechanical difference of mass operative in heavy matter, as in architecture, not the totality of sensuous spatiality which sculpture retains, even if concentrated and in organic shapes. On the contrary, the visibility and the making visible which belong to painting have their differences in a more ideal way, i.e. in the particular colours, and they free art from the *complete* sensuous spatiality of material things by being restricted to the dimensions of a *plane* surface.

On the other hand, the content too attains the widest particularization. Whatever can find room in the human breast as feeling, idea, and purpose, whatever it is capable of shaping into act, all this multiplex material can constitute the variegated content of painting. The whole realm of particularity from the highest ingredients of spirit right down to the most isolated natural objects finds its place here. For even finite nature in its particular scenes and phenomena can come on the stage in painting, if only some allusion to an element of spirit allies it more closely with thought and feeling.

(β) The *second* art through which the romantic form is actualized is, as contrasted with painting, *music*. Its material, though still sensuous, proceeds to still deeper subjectivity and particularization. I mean that music's positing of the sensuous as ideal is to be sought in the fact that it cancels, and idealizes into the individual singularity of one point, the indifferent self-externality of space, the total appearance of which is accepted by painting and deliberately simulated. But as this negativity, the point is concrete in itself and an active cancellation within the material by being a movement and tremor of the material body in itself in its relation to itself. This incipient ideality of matter, which appears no longer as spatial but as temporal ideality, is sound: the sensuous set down as negated with its abstract visibility changed into audibility, since sound releases the Ideal, as it were, from its entanglement in matter.[13]

Now this earliest inwardness and ensouling of matter affords the material for the still indefinite inwardness and soul of the spirit, and in its tones makes the whole gamut of the heart's feelings and passions resound and die away. In this manner, just as sculpture stands as the centre between architecture and the arts of romantic subjectivity, so music forms the centre of the romantic arts and makes the point of transition between the abstract spatial sensuousness of painting and the abstract spirituality of poetry. Like architecture, music has in itself, as an antithesis to feeling and inwardness, a relation of quantity conformable to the mathematical intellect; it also has as its basis a fixed conformity to law on the part of the notes and their combination and succession.

(γ) Finally, as for the *third*, most spiritual presentation of romantic art, we must look for it in *poetry*. Its characteristic peculiarity lies in the power with which it subjects to spirit and its ideas the sensuous element from which music and painting began to make art free. For sound, the last external material which poetry keeps, is in poetry no longer the feeling of sonority itself, but a *sign*, by itself void of significance, a sign of the idea which has become concrete in itself, and not merely of indefinite feeling and its nuances and gradations. Sound in this way becomes a *word* as a voice inherently articulated, the meaning of which is to indicate ideas and thoughts. The inherently negative point to which music had moved forward now comes forth as the completely concrete point, as the point of the spirit, as the self-conscious individual who out of his own resources unites the infinite *space* of his ideas with the *time* of sound. Yet this sensuous element, which in music was still immediately one with inwardness, is here cut free from the content of consciousness, while spirit determines this content on its own account and in itself and makes it into ideas. To express these it uses sound indeed, but only as a sign in itself without value or content. The sound, therefore, may just as well be a mere letter, since the audible, like the visible, has sunk into being a mere indication of spirit. Therefore the proper element of poetical representation is the poetical *imagination* and the illustration of spirit itself, and since this element is common to all the art-forms, poetry runs through them all and develops itself independently in each of them. Poetry is the universal art of the spirit which has become free in itself and which is not tied down for its realization to external sensuous material; instead, it launches out exclusively in the inner space and the inner time of ideas and feelings. Yet, precisely, at this highest stage, art now transcends itself, in that it forsakes the element of a reconciled embodiment of the spirit in sensuous form and passes over from the poetry of the imagination to the prose of thought.

This we may take to be the articulated totality of the particular arts: the external art of architecture, the objective art of sculpture, and the subjective art of painting, music, and poetry. Of course many other classifications have been attempted, since the work of art presents such a wealth of aspects that, as has often happened, now this one and now that can be made the basis of classification. Consider, for example, the sensuous material. In that case architecture is the crystallization, sculpture the organic configuration, of matter in its sensuous and spatial totality; painting is the coloured surface and line; while, in music, space as such passes over into the inherently filled point of time; until, finally, in poetry the external material is altogether degraded as worthless. Alternatively, these differences have been considered in their totally abstract aspect of space and time. But such abstract characteristics of the work of art may of course, like its material, be consistently pursued in their special features, but they cannot be carried through as the final basis of classification, because any such aspect derives its origin from a higher principle and therefore has to be subordinate thereto.

As this higher principle we have found the art-forms of the symbolical, the classical, and the romantic, which are themselves the universal moments of the Idea of beauty.

The concrete form of their relation to the individual arts is of such a kind that the several arts constitute the real existence of the art-forms. *Symbolic art* attains its most appropriate actuality and greatest application in *architecture*, where it holds sway in accordance with its whole conception and is not yet degraded to be the inorganic nature, as it were, dealt with by another art. For the *classical form*, on the other hand, *sculpture* is its unqualified realization, while it takes architecture only as something surrounding it, and it cannot yet develop painting and music as absolute forms for its content. Finally, the *romantic* art-form masters painting and music, and poetic representation likewise, as modes of expression in a way that is substantive and unqualified. But poetry is adequate to all forms of the beautiful and extends over all of them, because its proper element is beautiful imagination, and imagination is indispensable for every beautiful production, no matter to what form of art it belongs.

Now, therefore, what the particular arts realize in individual works of art is, according to the Concept of art, only the universal forms of the self-unfolding Idea of beauty. It is as the external actualization of this Idea that the wide Pantheon of art is rising. Its architect and builder is the self-comprehending spirit of beauty, but to complete it will need the history of the world in its development through thousands of years.

Translated by T.M. Knox

Notes

1 In Baumgarten's *Aesthetica*, 1750.

2 This is obscure. Bosanquet, in his translation of Hegel's Introduction (London, 1905), p. 39, suggests an allusion to 'born of water and the spirit', but this must be wrong. Hegel means that we have beauty originated by man's mind and also what is reproduced by his mind in his natural world.

3 i.e. assume that it has been demonstrated.

4 i.e. the art expressive of one world-view differs from that which expresses another: Greek art as a whole differs from Christian art as a whole. The sequence of different religions gives rise to a sequence of different art-forms.

5 An unknown block of stone may symbolize the Divine, but it does not represent it. Its natural shape has no connection with the Divine and is therefore external to it and not an embodiment of it. When shaping begins, the shapes produced are symbols, perhaps, but in themselves are fantastic and monstrous.

6 Bosanquet (Introduction, p. 185) seems to be right in suggesting that 'original Concept'

means 'God', and that he *invented* man as an expression of spirit; art *finds* him as appropriate to express the individual spirit. Hegel is fond of the play on words between *erfinden* (invent) and *finden* (find).

7 Bosanquet points out that the idea is abstract because it represents the soul as independent of an appropriate body – the human soul as capable of existing in a beast's body (ibid., p. 186).

8 In other words, thought is 'inwardness' in the sense that thoughts are not outside one another in the way that the parts of a body are. This is why the spirit cannot find an adequate embodiment in things but only in thoughts, or at least only in the inner life.

9 The forms of art are the symbolic, classical, and romantic. The kinds of art are sculpture, painting, etc. There is a sense in which one kind of art (e.g. sculpture) is the adequate mode in which one form of art (e.g. the classical) is actualized. But no form of art is wholly actualized in one kind of art alone; it requires the others, even if they take a subordinate place. Thus while one kind of art may belong *par excellence* to one form of art, it also appears to some extent in the other forms and may be said to present them all. This whole section on the kinds of art is not easily intelligible except in the light of Hegel's full discussion in Part III of these lectures.

10 i.e. shape taken simply as an object occupying space (Bosanquet, Introduction p. 199).

11 The unity of the members of a church is not visible, but exists in their common belief and in the recognition of their community (ibid., p. 200).

12 An obvious reference to Goethe's theory of colour, one of Hegel's favourite topics.

13 For this section on sound and music, see Hegel's *Philosophy of Nature*, i.e. *Part Two of the Encyclopaedia of the Philosophical Sciences*, §§ 300–02. Two English translations are available: A.V. Miller, Oxford, Clarendon Press, 1970, pp. 136–47, and M.J. Petry, London, Allen and Unwin, 1970, vol, 2, pp. 69–82.

3

ON TRUTH AND LIE IN AN EXTRA-MORAL SENSE

Friedrich Nietzsche

1

Once upon a time, in some out of the way corner of that universe which is dispersed into numberless twinkling solar systems, there was a star upon which clever beasts invented knowing. That was the most arrogant and mendacious minute of 'world history,' but nevertheless, it was only a minute. After nature had drawn a few breaths, the star cooled and congealed, and the clever beasts had to die. – One might invent such a fable, and yet he still would not have adequately illustrated how miserable, how shadowy and transient, how aimless and arbitrary the human intellect looks within nature. There were eternities during which it did not exist. And when it is all other with the human intellect, nothing will have happened. For this intellect has no additional mission which would lead it beyond human life. Rather, it is human, and only its possessor and begetter takes it so solemnly – as though the world's axis turned within it. But if we could communicate with the gnat, we would learn that he likewise flies through the air with the same solemnity,[1] that he feels the flying center of the universe within himself. There is nothing so reprehensible and unimportant in nature that it would not immediately swell up like a balloon at the slightest puff of this power of knowing. And just as every porter wants to have an admirer, so even the proudest of men, the philosopher, supposes that he sees on all sides the eyes of the universe telescopically focused upon his action and thought.

It is remarkable that this was brought about by the intellect, which was certainly allotted to these most unfortunate, delicate, and ephemeral beings merely as a device for detaining them a minute within existence. For without this addition they would have every reason to flee this existence as quickly as Lessing's son.[2] The pride connected with knowing and sensing lies like a blinding fog over the eyes and senses of men, thus deceiving them concerning the value of existence. For this pride contains within itself the most flattering estimation of the value of knowing. Deception is the most general effect of such pride, but even its most particular effects contain within themselves something of the same deceitful character.

As a means for the preserving of the individual, the intellect unfolds its principal powers in dissimulation, which is the means by which weaker, less robust individuals preserve themselves – since they have been denied the chance to wage the battle for existence with horns or with the sharp teeth of beasts of prey. This art of dissimulation reaches its peak in man. Deception, flattering, lying, deluding, talking behind the back, putting up a false front, living in borrowed splendor, wearing a mask, hiding behind convention, playing a role for others and for oneself – in short, a continuous fluttering around the *solitary* flame of vanity – is so much the rule and the law among men that there is almost nothing which is less comprehensible than how an honest and pure drive for truth could have arisen among them. They are deeply immersed in illusions and in dream images; their eyes merely glide over the surface of things and see 'forms.' Their senses nowhere lead to truth; on the contrary, they are content to receive stimuli and, as it were, to engage in a groping game on the backs of things. Moreover, man permits himself to be deceived in his dreams every night of his life. His moral sentiment does not even make an attempt to prevent this, whereas there are supposed to be men who have stopped snoring through sheer will power. What does man actually know about himself? Is he, indeed, ever able to perceive himself completely, as if laid out in a lighted display case? Does nature not conceal most things from him – even concerning his own body – in order to confine and lock him within a proud, deceptive consciousness, aloof from the coils of the bowels, the rapid flow of the blood stream, and the intricate quivering of the fibers! She threw away the key. And woe to that fatal curiosity which might one day have the power to peer out and down through a crack in the chamber of consciousness and then suspect that man is sustained in the indifference of his ignorance by that which is pitiless, greedy, insatiable, and murderous – as if hanging in dreams on the back of a tiger. Given this situation, where in the world could the drive for truth have come from?

Insofar as the individual wants to maintain himself against other individuals, he will under natural circumstances employ the intellect mainly for dissimulation. But at the same time, from boredom and necessity, man wishes to exist socially and with the herd; therefore, he needs to make peace and strives accordingly to banish from his world at least the most flagrant *bellum omni contra omnes*.[3] This peace treaty brings in its wake something which appears to be the first step toward acquiring that puzzling truth drive: to wit, *that* which shall count as 'truth' from now on is established. That is to say, a uniformly valid and binding designation is invented for things, and this legislation of language likewise establishes the first laws of truth. For the contrast between truth and lie arises here for the first time. The liar is a person who uses the valid designations, the words, in order to make something which is unreal appear to be real. He says, for example, 'I am rich,' when the proper designation for his condition would be 'poor.' He misuses fixed conventions by means of arbitrary substitutions or even reversals of names. If he does this in a selfish and moreover harmful manner, society will cease to trust him and will thereby exclude him. What men avoid by excluding the liar is not so much being defrauded as it is being harmed by means of fraud. Thus, even at this stage, what they hate is basically not deception itself, but rather the unpleasant, hated consequences of certain sorts of deception. It is in a similarly restricted sense that man now wants nothing but truth: he desires the pleasant, life-preserving consequences of truth. He is indifferent toward pure knowledge which has no consequences; to ward those truths which are possibly harmful and destructive he is even hostilely inclined. And besides, what about these linguistic conventions themselves? Are they perhaps products of knowledge, that is, of the sense of truth? Are designations congruent with things? Is language the adequate expression of all realities?

It is only by means of forgetfulness that man can ever reach the point of fancying himself to possess a 'truth' of the grade just indicated. If he will not be satisfied with truth in the form of tautology, that is to say, if he will not be content with empty husks, then he will always exchange truths for illusions. What is a word? It is the copy in sound of a nerve stimulus. But the further inference from the nerve stimulus to a cause outside of us is already the result of a false and unjustifiable application of the principle of sufficient reason.[4] If truth alone had been the deciding factor in the genesis of language, and if the standpoint of certainty had been decisive for designations, then how could we still dare to say 'the stone is hard,' as if 'hard' were something otherwise familiar to us, and not merely a totally subjective stimulation! We separate things according to gender, designating the tree as masculine and the plant as feminine. What arbitrary assignments![5] How far this oversteps the canons of certainty! We speak of a 'snake': this designation touches only upon its ability to twist itself and could therefore also fit a worm.[6] What arbitrary differentiations! What one-sided preferences, first for this, then for that property of a thing! The various languages placed side by side show that with words it is never a question of truth, never a question of adequate expression; otherwise, there would not be so many languages.[7] The 'thing in itself' (which is precisely what the pure truth, apart from any of its consequences, would be) is likewise something quite incomprehensible to the creator of language and something not in the least worth striving for. This creator only designates the relations of things to men, and for expressing these relations he lays hold of the boldest metaphors. To begin with, a nerve stimulus is transferred into an image:[8] first metaphor. The image, in turn, is imitated in a sound: second metaphor. And each time there is a complete overleaping of one sphere, right into the middle of an entirely new and different one. One can imagine a man who is totally deaf and has never had a sensation of sound and music. Perhaps such a person will gaze with astonishment at Chladni's sound figures; perhaps he will discover their causes in the vibrations of the string and will now swear that he must know what men mean by 'sound.' It is this way with all of us concerning language: we believe that we know something about the things themselves when we speak of trees, colors, snow, and flowers; and yet we possess nothing but metaphors for things – metaphors which correspond in no way to the original entities.[9] In the same way that the sound appears as a sand figure, so the mysterious X of the thing in itself first appears as a nerve stimulus, then as an image, and finally as a sound. Thus the genesis of language does not proceed logically in any case, and all the material within and with which the man of truth, the scientist, and the philosopher later work and build, if not derived from never-never land,[10] is at least not derived from the essence of things.

In particular, let us further consider the formation of concepts. Every word instantly becomes a concept precisely insofar as it is not supposed to serve as a reminder of the unique and entirely individual original experience to which it owes its origin; but rather, a word becomes a concept insofar as it simultaneously has to fit countless more or less similar cases – which means, purely and simply, cases which are never equal and thus altogether unequal. Every concept arises from the equation of unequal things. Just as it is certain that one leaf is never totally the same as another, so it is certain that the concept 'leaf' is formed by arbitrarily discarding these individual differences and by forgetting the distinguishing aspects. This awakens the idea that, in addition to the leaves, there exists in nature the 'leaf': the original model according to which all the leaves were perhaps woven, sketched, measured, colored, curled, and painted – but by incompetent hands, so that no specimen has turned out to be a correct, trustworthy, and faithful likeness of the original model. We call a person 'honest', and then we ask 'why has he behaved so honestly today?' Our usual answer is, 'on account of his honesty.' Honesty! This in turn means that the leaf is the cause of the leaves. We know nothing whatsoever about an essential quality called 'honesty'; but we do know of countless individualized and consequently unequal actions which we equate by omitting the aspects in which they are unequal and which we now designate as 'honest' actions. Finally we formulate from them a *qualitas occulta*[11] which has the name 'honesty.' We obtain the concept, as we do the form, by overlooking what is individual and actual; whereas nature is acquainted with no forms and no concepts, and likewise with no species, but only with an X which remains inaccessible and undefinable for us. For even our contrast between individual and species is something anthropomorphic and does not originate in the essence of things; although we should not presume to claim that this contrast does not correspond to the essence of things: that would of course be a dogmatic assertion and, as such, would be just as indemonstrable as its opposite.

What then is truth? A movable host of metaphors, metonymies, and anthropomorphisms: in short, a sum of human relations which have been poetically and rhetorically intensified, transferred, and embellished, and which, after long usage, seem to a people to be fixed, canonical, and binding. Truths are illusions which we have forgotten are illusions; they are metaphors that have become worn out and have been drained of sensuous force, coins which have lost their embossing and are now considered as metal and no longer as coins.

We still do not yet know where the drive for truth comes from. For so far we have heard only of the duty which society imposes in order to exist: to be truthful means to employ the usual metaphors. Thus, to express it morally, this is the duty to lie according to a fixed convention, to lie with the herd and in a manner binding upon everyone. Now man of course forgets that this is the way things stand for him. Thus he lies in the manner indicated, unconsciously and in accordance with habits which are centuries old; and precisely *by means of this unconsciousness* and forgetfulness he arrives at his sense of truth. From the sense that one is obliged to designate one thing as 'red,' another as 'cold,' and a third as 'mute,' there arises a moral impulse in regard to truth. The venerability, reliability, and utility of truth is something which a person demonstrates for himself from the contrast with the liar, whom no one trusts and everyone excludes. As a '*rational*' being, he now places his behavior under the control of abstractions. He will no longer tolerate being carried away by sudden impressions, by intuitions. First he universalizes all these impressions into less colorful, cooler concepts, so that he can entrust the guidance of his life and conduct to them. Everything which distinguishes man from the animals depends upon this ability to volatilize perceptual metaphors in a schema, and thus to dissolve an image into a concept. For something is possible in the realm of these schemata which could never be achieved with the vivid first impressions: the construction of a pyramidal order according to castes and degrees, the creation of a new world of laws, privileges, subordinations, and clearly marked boundaries – a new world, one which now confronts that other vivid world of first impressions as more solid, more universal, better known, and more human than the immediately perceived world, and thus as the regulative and imperative world. Whereas each perceptual metaphor is individual and without equals and is therefore able to elude all classification, the great edifice of concepts displays the rigid regularity of a Roman columbarium[12] and exhales in logic that strength and coolness which is characteristic of mathematics. Anyone who has felt this cool breath [of logic] will hardly believe that even the concept – which is as bony, foursquare, and transposable as a die – is nevertheless merely the *residue of a metaphor*, and that the illusion which is involved in the artistic transference of a nerve stimulus into images is, if not the mother, then the grandmother of every single concept.[13] But in this conceptual crap game 'truth' means using every die in the designated manner, counting its spots accurately, fashioning the right categories, and never violating the order of caste and class rank. Just as the Romans and Etruscans cut up the heavens with rigid mathematical lines and confined a god within each of the spaces thereby delimited, as within a *templum*,[14] so every people has a similarly mathematically divided conceptual heaven above themselves and henceforth thinks that truth demands that each conceptual god be sought only within *his own* sphere. Here one may certainly admire man as a mighty genius of construction, who succeeds in piling up an infinitely complicated dome of concepts upon an unstable foundation, and, as it were, on running water. Of course, in order to be supported by such a foundation, his construction must be like one constructed of spiders' webs: delicate enough to be carried along by the waves, strong enough not to be blown apart by every wind. As a genius of construction man raises himself far above the bee in the following way: whereas the bee builds with wax that he gathers from nature, man builds with the far more delicate conceptual material which he first has to manufacture from himself. In this he is greatly to be admired, but not on account of his drive for truth or for pure knowledge of things. When someone hides something behind a bush and looks for it again in the same place and finds it there as well, there is not much to praise in such seeking and finding. Yet this is how matters stand regarding seeking and finding 'truth' within the realm of reason. If I make up the definition of a mammal, and then, after inspecting a camel, declare 'look, a mammal,' I have indeed brought a truth to light in this way, but it is a truth of limited value. That is to say, it is a thoroughly anthropomorphic truth which contains not a single point which would be 'true in itself' or really and universally valid apart from man. At bottom, what the investigator of such truths is seeking is only the metamorphosis of the world into man. He strives to understand the world as something analogous to man, and at best he achieves by his struggles the feeling of assimilation. Similar to the way in which astrologers considered the stars to be in man's service and connected with his happiness and sorrow, such an investigator considers the entire universe in connection with man: the entire universe as the infinitely fractured echo of one original sound – man; the entire universe as the infinitely multiplied copy of one original picture – man. His method is to treat man as the measure of all things, but in doing so he again proceeds from the error of believing that he has these things [which he intends to measure] immediately before him as mere objects. He forgets that the original perceptual metaphors are metaphors and takes them to be the things themselves.

Only by forgetting this primitive world of metaphor can one live with any repose, security, and consistency: only by means of the petrification and coagulation of a mass of images which originally streamed from the primal faculty of human imagination like a fiery liquid, only in the invincible faith that *this* sun, *this* window, *this* table is a truth in itself, in short, only by forgetting that he himself is an *artistically creating* subject, does man live with any repose, security, and consistency. If but for an instant he could escape from the prison walls of this faith, his 'self consciousness' would be immediately destroyed. It is even a difficult thing for him to admit to himself that the insect or the bird perceives an entirely different world from the one that man does, and that the question of which of these perceptions of the world is the more correct one is quite meaningless, for this would have to have been decided previously in accordance with the criterion of the *correct perception*, which means, in accordance with a criterion which is *not available*. But in any case it seems to me that 'the correct perception' – which would mean 'the adequate expression of an object in the subject' – is a contradictory impossibility. For between two absolutely different spheres, as between subject and object, there is no causality, no correctness, and no expression; there is, at most, an *aesthetic* relation:[15] I mean, a suggestive transference, a stammering translation into a completely foreign tongue – for which there is required, in any case, a freely inventive intermediate sphere and mediating force. 'Appearance' is a word that contains many temptations, which is why I avoid it as much as possible. For it is not true that the essence of things 'appears' in the empirical world. A painter without hands who wished to express in song the picture before his mind would, by means of this substitution of spheres, still reveal more about the essence of things than does the empirical world. Even the relationship of a nerve stimulus to the generated image is not a necessary one. But when the same image has been generated millions of times and has been handed down for many generations and finally appears on the same occasion every time for all mankind, then it acquires at last the same meaning for men it would have if it were the sole necessary image and if the relationship of the original nerve stimulus to the generated image were a strictly causal one. In the same manner, an eternally repeated dream would certainly be felt and judged to be reality. But the hardening and congealing of a metaphor guarantees absolutely nothing concerning its necessity and exclusive justification.

Every person who is familiar with such considerations has no doubt felt a deep mistrust of all idealism of this sort: just as often as he has quite clearly convinced himself of the eternal consistency, omnipresence, and infallibility of the laws of nature. He has concluded that so far as we can penetrate here – from the telescopic heights to the microscopic depths – everything is secure, complete, infinite, regular, and without any gaps. Science will be able to dig successfully in this shaft forever, and all the things that are discovered will harmonize with and not contradict each other. How little does this resemble a product of the imagination, for if it were such, there should be some place where the illusion and unreality can be divined. Against this, the following must be said: if each of us had a different kind of sense perception – if we could only perceive things now as a bird, now as a worm, now as a plant, or if one of us saw a stimulus as red, another as blue, while a third even heard the same stimulus as a sound – then no one would speak of such a regularity of nature, rather, nature would be grasped only as a creation which is subjective in the highest degree. After all, what is a law of nature as such for us? We are not acquainted with it in itself, but only with its effects, which means in its relation to other laws of nature – which, in turn, are known to us only as sums of relations. Therefore all these relations always refer again to others and are thoroughly incomprehensible to us in their essence. All that we actually know about these laws of nature is what we ourselves bring to them – time and space, and therefore relationships of succession and number. But everything marvelous about the laws of nature, everything that quite astonishes us therein and seems to demand our explanation, everything that might lead us to distrust idealism: all this is completely and solely contained within the mathematical strictness and inviolability of our representations of time and space. But we produce these representations in and from ourselves with the same necessity with which the spider spins. If we are forced to comprehend all things only under these forms, then it ceases to be amazing that in all things we actually comprehend nothing but these forms. For they must all bear within themselves the laws of number, and it is precisely number which is most astonishing in things. All that conformity to law, which impresses us so much in the movement of the stars and in chemical processes, coincides at bottom with those properties which we bring to things. Thus it is we who impress ourselves in this way. In conjunction with this it of course follows that the artistic process of metaphor formation with which every sensation begins in us already presupposes these forms and thus occurs within them. The only way in which the possibility of subsequently constructing a new conceptual edifice from metaphors themselves can be explained is by the firm persistence of these original forms. That is to say, this conceptual edifice is an imitation of temporal, spatial, and numerical relationships in the domain of metaphor.[16]

2

We have seen how it is originally *language* which works on the construction of concepts, a labor taken over in later ages by *science*. Just as the bee simultaneously constructs cells and fills them with honey, so science works unceasingly on this great columbarium of concepts, the graveyard of perceptions. It is always building new, higher stories and shoring up, cleaning, and renovating the old cells; above all, it takes pains to fill up this monstrously towering framework and to arrange therein the entire empirical world, which is to say, the anthropomorphic world. Whereas the man of action binds his life to reason and its concepts so that he will not be swept away and lost, the scientific investigator builds his hut right next to the tower of science so that he will be able to work on it and to find shelter for himself beneath those bulwarks which presently exist. And he requires shelter, for there are frightful powers which continuously break in upon him, powers which oppose scientific 'truth' with completely different kinds of 'truths' which bear on their shields the most varied sorts of emblems.

The drive toward the formation of metaphors is the fundamental human drive, which one cannot for a single instant dispense with in thought, for one would thereby dispense with man himself. This drive is not truly vanquished and scarcely subdued by the fact that a regular and rigid new world is constructed as its prison from its own ephemeral products, the concepts. It seeks a new realm and another channel for its activity, and it finds this in *myth* and in *art* generally. This drive continually confuses the conceptual categories and cells by bringing forward new transferences, metaphors, and metonymies. It continually manifests an ardent desire to refashion the world which presents itself to waking man, so that it will be as colorful, irregular, lacking in results and coherence, charming, and eternally new as the world of dreams. Indeed, it is only by means of the rigid and regular web of concepts that the waking man clearly sees that he is awake; and it is precisely because of this that he sometimes thinks that he must be dreaming when this web of concepts is torn by art. Pascal is right in maintaining that if the same dream came to us every night we would be just as occupied with it as we are with the things that we see every day. 'If a workman were sure to dream for twelve straight hours every night that he was king,' said Pascal, 'I believe that he would be just as happy as a king who dreamt for twelve hours every night that he was a workman.'[17] In fact, because of the way that myth takes it for granted that miracles are always happening, the waking life of a mythically inspired people – the ancient Greeks, for instance – more closely resembles a dream than it does the waking world of a scientifically disenchanted thinker. When every tree can suddenly speak as a nymph, when a god in the shape of a bull can drag away maidens, when even the goddess Athena herself is suddenly seen in the company of Peisistratus driving through the market place of Athens with a beautiful team of horses[18] – and this is what the honest Athenian believed – then, as in a dream, anything is possible at each moment, and all of nature swarms around man as if it were nothing but a masquerade of the gods, who were merely amusing themselves by deceiving men in all these shapes.

But man has an invincible inclination to allow himself to be deceived and is, as it were, enchanted with happiness when the rhapsodist tells him epic fables as if they were true, or when the actor in the theater acts more royally than any real king. So long as it is able to deceive without *injuring*, that master of deception, the intellect, is free; it is released from its former slavery and celebrates its Saturnalia. It is never more luxuriant, richer, prouder, more clever and more daring. With creative pleasure it throws metaphors into confusion and displaces the boundary stones of abstractions, so that, for example, it designates the stream as 'the moving path which carries man where he would otherwise walk.' The intellect has now thrown the token of bondage from itself. At other times it endeavors, with gloomy officiousness, to show the way and to demonstrate the tools to a poor individual who covets existence; it is like a servant who goes in search of booty and prey for his master. But now it has become the master and it dares to wipe from its face the expression of indigence. In comparison with its previous conduct, everything that it now does bears the mark of dissimulation,[19] just as that previous conduct did of distortion.[20] The free intellect copies human life, but it considers this life to be something good and seems to be quite satisfied with it. That immense framework and planking of concepts to which the needy man clings his whole life long in order to preserve himself is nothing but a scaffolding and toy for the most audacious feats of the liberated intellect. And when it smashes this framework to pieces, throws it into confusion, and puts it back together in an ironic fashion, pairing the most alien things and separating the closest, it is demonstrating that it has no need of these makeshifts of indigence and that it will now be guided by intuitions rather than by concepts. There is no regular path which leads from these intuitions into the land of ghostly schemata, the land of abstractions. There exists no word for these intuitions; when man sees them he grows dumb, or else he speaks only in forbidden metaphors and in unheard-of combinations of concepts. He does this so that by shattering and mocking the old conceptual barriers he may at least correspond creatively to the impression of the powerful present intuition.

There are ages in which the rational man and the intuitive man stand side by side, the one in fear of intuition, the other with scorn for abstraction. The latter is just as irrational as the former is inartistic. They both desire to rule over life: the former, by knowing how to meet his principal needs by means of foresight, prudence, and regularity; the latter, by disregarding these needs and, as an 'overjoyed hero,' counting as real only that life which has been disguised as illusion and beauty. Whenever, as was perhaps the case in ancient Greece, the intuitive man handles his weapons more authoritatively and victoriously than his opponent, then, under favorable circumstances, a culture can take shape and art's mastery over life can be established. All the manifestations of such a life will be accompanied by this dissimulation, this disavowal of indigence, this glitter of metaphorical intuitions, and, in general, this immediacy of deception: neither the house, nor the gait, nor the clothes, nor the clay jugs give evidence of having been invented because of a pressing need. It seems as if they were all intended to express an exalted happiness, an Olympian cloudlessness, and, as it were, a playing with seriousness. The man who is guided by concepts and abstractions only succeeds by such means in warding off misfortune, without ever gaining any happiness for himself from these abstractions. And while he aims for the greatest possible freedom from pain, the intuitive man, standing in the midst of a culture, already reaps from his intuition a harvest of continually inflowing illumination, cheer, and redemption – in addition to obtaining a defense against misfortune. To be sure, he suffers more intensely, *when* he suffers; he even suffers more frequently, since he does not understand how to learn from experience and keeps falling over and over again into the same ditch. He is then just as irrational in sorrow as he is in happiness: he cries aloud and will not be consoled. How differently the stoical man who learns from experience and governs himself by concepts is affected by the same misfortunes! This man, who at other times seeks nothing but sincerity, truth, freedom from deception, and protection against ensnaring surprise attacks, now executes a masterpiece of deception: he executes his masterpiece of deception in misfortune, as the other type of man executes his in times of happiness. He wears no quivering and changeable human face, but, as it were, a mask with dignified, symmetrical features. He does not cry; he does not even alter his voice. When a real storm cloud thunders above him, he wraps himself in his cloak, and with slow steps he walks from beneath it.

Translated by Daniel Breazeale

Notes

1 *Pathos.*
2 A reference to the offspring of Lessing and Eva König, who died on the day of his birth.
3 'War of each against all.'
4 Note that Nietzsche is here engaged in an implicit critique of Schopenhauer, who had been guilty of precisely this misapplication of the principle of sufficient reason in his first book, *The Fourfold Root of the Principle of Sufficient Reason*. It is quite wrong to think that Nietzsche was ever wholly uncritical of Schopenhauer's philosophy (see, for example, the little essay, *Kritik der Schopenhauerischen Philosophie* from 1867, in *Nietzsche's Gesammelte Werke (Musarionausgabe)*, Munich, Musarion, 1920–1929, vol. 1, pp. 392–401).
5 *welche willkürlichen Übertragungen*. The specific sense of this passage depends upon the fact that all ordinary nouns in the German language are assigned a gender: the tree is *der Baum*; the plant is *die Pflanze*. This assignment of an original sexual property to all things is the 'transference' in question.
6 This passage depends upon the etymological relation between the German words *Schlange* (snake) and *schlingen* (to wind or twist), both of which are related to the Old High German *slango*.
7 What Nietzsche is rejecting here is the theory that there is a sort of 'naturally appropriate' connection between certain words (or sounds) and things. Such a theory is defended by Socrates in Plato's *Cratylus*.
8 *Ein Nervenreiz, zuerst übertragen in ein Bild*. The 'image' in this case is the visual image, what we 'see.'
9 *Wesenheiten*.
10 *Wolkenkukuksheim*: literally, 'cloud-cuckoo-land.'
11 'Occult quality.'

12 A columbarium is a vault with niches for funeral urns containing the ashes of cremated bodies.

13 i.e. concepts are derived from images, which are, in turn, derived from nerve stimuli.

14 A delimited space restricted to a particular purpose, especially a religiously sanctified area.

15 *ein ästhetisches Verhalten.* A more literal translation of *Verhalten* is 'behavior,' 'attitude,' or perhaps 'disposition.'

16 This is where section 2 of the fair copy made by von Gersdorff ends. But according to Schlechta (in Karl Schlechta and Anni Anders, *Friedrich Nietzche. Von den verborgenen Anfangen seines Philosophierens*, Stuttgart-Bad Cannstadt, Frommann, 1962, pp. 14–15) Nietzsche's preliminary version continued as follows:

> Empty space and empty time are ideas which are possible at any time. Every concept, thus an empty metaphor, is only an imitation of these first ideas: space, time, and causality. Afterwards, the original imaginative act of transference into images: the first provides the matter, the second the qualities which we believe in. Comparison to music. How can one speak of it?

17 *Pensées*, number 386. Actually, Pascal says that the workman would be 'almost as happy' as the king in this case!

18 According to the story told by Herodotus (*Histories* I, 60) the tyrant Peisistratus adopted the following ruse to secure his popular acceptance upon his return from exile: he entered Athens in a chariot accompanied by a woman named Phye who was dressed in the costume of Athena. Thus the people were supposed to have been convinced that it was the goddess herself who was conducting the tyrant back to the Acropolis.

19 *Verstellung.*

20 *Verzerrung.*

Part 2

PHENOMENOLOGY AND HERMENEUTICS

INTRODUCTION

Martin Heidegger	The Origin of the Work of Art
Jean-Paul Sartre	What is Writing?
Emmanuel Levinas	Reality and its Shadow
Mikel Dufrenne	The World of the Aesthetic Object
Gaston Bachelard	The Dialectics of Outside and Inside
Maurice Merleau-Ponty	The Intertwining – The Chiasm
Hans-Georg Gadamer	Aesthetics and Hermeneutics
Gianni Vattimo	The Death or Decline of Art

Phenomenology and hermeneutics are distinct but related theories of experience or, more specifically, theories of how words relate to experience. While the former pays greater attention to the nature of lived experience, and the latter concentrates on problems arising from textual interpretation, both deal in a fundamental way with our status as beings whose existence is enabled and determined by particular physical and cultural conditions. Originally defined, hermeneutics is the art of understanding and interpreting historical texts. In the history of hermeneutics, there are, generally speaking, three phases: theological, romantic, and phenomenological. The first two are characterized by the intention to recover the 'true' meaning a text would have had in the age it was written, free from the mediation and distortion that translation and the passage of time bring. Hermeneutics emerges in the sixteenth century at the time of the Reformation with Martin Luther's concern to retrieve the original meaning of classical and biblical writings. Three centuries later, a comparable desire to know the seminal context and significance of a text is manifest in the romanticism of literary theorists such as Friedrich Ast, Friedrich D.E. Schleiermacher, and Wilhelm Dilthey. What distinguishes twentieth-century hermeneutics (represented below by Heidegger, Gadamer, and Vattimo) from its earlier forms is the recognition that the hermeneut, as an interpreter of texts, is herself rooted in history. As a result, any interpretation she gives of a text, no matter how 'close' she claims to be to identifying the conditions of its production, will always be mediated by the historically constructed assumptions and expectations which constitute her practice as a hermeneut. It is this appreciation of the necessarily perspectival nature of historical, textual interpretation which makes recent hermeneutic theory 'phenomenological'.

The beginnings of phenomenology are most often identified with the work of the late nineteenth-, early twentieth-century German thinkers Franz Brentano (1838–1917) and Edmund Husserl (1859–1938), but the governing principles, I would argue, are first evident in Kant. Phenomenology maintains that the categories with which philosophy has divided up experience in the past are not adequate to experience; they break up continuous experience into things, and let that sense of a lived point-of-contact between mind and reality slip away. Thus, new perspectives on experience are offered which take the intertwined nature of mind and reality as their starting point. Experience, Brentano argues in *Psychology from an Empirical Standpoint* (1874), is necessarily 'intentional', that is to say, it is always object-directed, always experience *of something*. Experience is such that there will always be some content or other of which we are aware, no matter how unprepared we are for describing what is before us, for example, this road, this tree, this red, this buzzing confusion. From the basic, intentional structure of experience, whereby one thing (experience) can open out to become two things (experience *of* something), phenomenology sets out to redescribe appearances. Husserl is the first to conduct a major phenomenological redescription of phenomena. In his later works – principally *Ideas Pertaining to a Pure Phenomenology and to a Phenomenological Philosophy* (1913) and *Cartesian Meditations* (1931)[1] – he performs his phenomenological reduction in order to give verbal expression to mental events as they appear to consciousness, independent of an everyday, uncritical commitment to the existence of other people, places, physical objects, causality, etc.

The premise shared by phenomenology and hermeneutics is that experience has a questioning-character: experience is not the grasping of a pre-formed content but a form of prospection or enquiry; just as a question draws out and determines a range of possible replies, so the manner in which our faculties approach the world shapes how it appears to us. As Brentano shows, experience has as its structure an essential openness which creates a content or an object for itself; this is intentionality. The foundations of this analysis of experience lie with Kant. His Transcendental Deduction, from the *Critique of Pure Reason* (1781, 1787), demonstrates that the conditions of possibility of subjectivity are at one and the same time the conditions of possibility of objectivity. When we perceive or describe or understand something, we don't just receive what's there but, in virtue of the act, bring something new to it and change what's there; it is the active interplay between mind and object which gives experience its textures and meanings. This applies to objects for phenomenology, and to texts for hermeneutics.

Research in these fields is devoted to the perspectives which constitute our outlook on the world and, in particular, to making palpable the way in which these perspectives are active in determining what we take to be real. The aesthetic is particularly significant here since it is a form of experience which tests or exceeds the understanding we have of our cognitive and cultural contact with the world.

Traditionally, the aesthetic has either been defined in opposition to thought or has been denied categorical determination altogether. Thus, not only is it an area of enquiry where the application of concepts is an issue but also, precisely because it has been given this marginal or resistant quality, it is a domain which allows us to see *the conditions that enable conceptual judgement* in operation. Art, for phenomenology and hermeneutics, renders the ground upon which we're standing visible.

Martin Heidegger

Some of the most important connections between phenomenology and hermeneutics occur in the work of Martin Heidegger (1889–1976). A student of Husserl, Heidegger has become one of the most important European philosophers of the twentieth century, influencing thinkers such as Gaston Bachelard, Hans-Georg Gadamer, and Jacques Derrida. However, he was an active member of the National Socialist party during the 1930s and the Second World War, and this has tainted his ideas in many people's eyes.

Heidegger reasserts the Kantian claim that experience is not the reception of sense impressions but a form of prospection or questioning: to have experience is to be in an active state of finding out about the world. In his principal work, *Being and Time* (1927), he asks: what is the meaning of being? What does it mean to have experience, to protrude into the world, to be human? The question of being stimulated the metaphysical schemes of Plato and Aristotle but, since then, according to Heidegger, it has been forgotten. The notion of 'being' has become ordinary and universal, applying to anything and everything in existence. However, what is distinctive about human being, Heidegger avers, is that it is a form of being *for which being itself is an issue*:

> Looking at something, understanding and conceiving it, choosing, access to it – all these ways of behaving are constitutive for our inquiry, and therefore are modes of being for those particular entities which we, the inquirers, are ourselves. Thus to work out the question of being adequately, we must make an entity – the inquirer – transparent in its own being. The very asking of this question is an entity's mode of *being*; and as such it gets its essential character from what is inquired about – namely, being. This entity which each of us is himself and which includes inquiring as one of the possibilities of its being, we shall denote by the term '*Dasein*'.[2]

'Dasein' is an everyday, colloquial German word meaning 'being there' or a human's sense of existence. The fact that being is an issue for us is tremendously important for Heidegger's thesis. Something's 'being an issue', Heidegger writes, 'is a constitutive state of Dasein's being' and this shows that Dasein 'in its being, has a relationship towards that being – a relationship which itself is one of being'. We are not just aware of the world, but *aware of the fact* that we are *aware of the world*. '*Understanding of being*', he asserts, '*is itself a definite characteristic of Dasein's being.* Dasein is ontically distinctive in that it is ontological.'[3] 'Ontic' is Heidegger's term for the objects and events which feature in experience, and 'ontological' refers to the structure of experience, that is, in Heidegger's idiom, the structure of the ontic. What distinguishes Dasein from other kinds of being in the world is that its character, and its character alone, represents the possibility of there being other kinds of being in the world.

Heidegger is pursuing the Kantian project of drawing out the conditions of possibility of experience: the structures which have to be at work in and around experience for there to be any experience at all. Experience takes the form of a question, Heidegger argues, in the sense that there always has to be an opening-up of possibilities in advance of experience in order for experience to take place. Just as the kind of question asked influences the answer, he avows, so the way in which we approach reality affects how it appears. In *Kant and the Problem of Metaphysics* (1929), Heidegger shows that experience is made possible by the imagination projecting the concept of an object in general as a horizon of possibility, and this opens up a 'space' in which objects can appear before consciousness. The 'Kant book' (as Heidegger refers to it) develops some of the connections implicit but never realized in Kant's *Critique of Pure Reason* (1781,

1787) and was written as preparation for the second part of *Being and Time*, but Heidegger never completed the project. The concept of a horizon projected by the imagination prior to experience raises questions concerning the origin and status of the imagination, but these are to be expected and are appropriate to the territory, since both Heidegger and Kant are broaching the dynamic structures which allow things, including consciousness, to come into being in the first place.

If the question of being has been forgotten, if being has become ordinary, then we must draw it out and make it prominent again. Phenomenology, Heidegger asserts, is the method of enquiry whereby something is brought out 'into the open'. He defines it as letting 'that which shows itself be seen from itself in the very way in which it shows itself from itself'.[4] However, this phenomenological disclosure is also hermeneutic, in two senses: (1) because it involves interpretation, and (2) because we are working towards an understanding not just of how things appear to us, but of how things appear *per se*. As Heidegger writes, his enquiry 'becomes a "hermeneutic"' to the extent 'that by uncovering the meaning of being and the basic structures of Dasein in general we may exhibit the horizon for any further ontological study of those entities which do not have the character of Dasein', in other words, we work out 'the conditions on which the possibility of any ontological investigation depends'.[5] This is 'hermeneutic' in the (recent) sense of transcending one's subjective standpoint to approach objectivity. It is reminiscent of Kant's attempt to secure objectivity given his investment of the possibility of experience within the subject. We can make the comparison with conversation again: asking a question elicits a response and, although the response is influenced by the phrasing of the question, it nevertheless represents the willingness to approach a shared understanding which is constitutive of all communication.

Heidegger develops a new understanding of ontology – the way in which experience and the world are shaped and organized – based on processes of disclosing and concealing, opening and closing. Apart from the times when we are amazed by the extent and complexity of the universe, we ordinarily take the existence of objects for granted; we assume they are simply 'there', waiting for us to perceive or interact with them. The tyranny of the ordinary again. Heidegger is interested in how things come to be for us, not so much in the sense of their material origin and constitution, but how they are bound up with our subjective experience and the meanings, values, and dispositions which experience involves. Our everyday ontology of stable, mind-independent objects, he asserts, presupposes a prior, 'fundamental' ontology whereby things are disclosed or concealed. Before things can exist, there have to be the conditions which allow things to come into being or made to appear before consciousness.

The five senses are a good illustration of Heidegger's concept of disclosure.[6] When we see, we are not passively receiving what is 'out there' in the world. Rather, the optical and neural processes that take place within us open up the world for us in a certain way, that is, they allow us to interpret the world in terms of colour and as something which is *continuously there*. Hearing makes the world available to us in alternative ways, allowing us to be aware of things that are not yet visible, e.g., the person singing next door, and to be aware of things *intermittently*, that is, only when they are making a noise. For the blind, rain behaves like light: raindrops bouncing off different surfaces give texture and depth to an otherwise silent, featureless world. Different animals, with differently attuned sensory faculties, have access to realities other than ours. For dogs, a heightened sense of smell makes near-past and near-future events more immediately cognizable, and sonar-like echo-location situates bats in a landscape of reflected sonic pulses.

The text representing Heidegger here is his essay 'The Origin of the Work of Art', first given as a series of lectures in 1935 and 1936. It establishes a theme which links the first four essays in this section. Heidegger, Sartre, and Levinas all consider the ontology of art and the different ways in which art and language create new perspectives on reality, while Dufrenne develops the Heideggerian claim that a work of art brings a world into view. Heidegger discusses art in terms of truth and his ontology of disclosure. The essay follows section 44 of *Being and Time* by referring Heidegger's ontology to the ancient Greek concept of truth as *aletheia. Aletheia* means 'the unconcealedness of beings'. As a concept of truth, it is distinct from and logically prior to our conventional, Roman notion of truth as *veritas* or 'correspondence with the facts'. For there to be any objects to make up states of affairs to which our statements can correspond, there must be the 'truth' which lets these objects first come to be.

Art is true, Heidegger claims, in that it lets us see the tension between concealment and disclosure. He calls this 'the conflict of world and earth': 'world' is used in the sense that any disclosure is the opening of a realm, e.g., the realm of sight, and 'earth' is the concealed domain from which the world emerges. The artwork 'moves the earth itself into the Open of a world and keeps it there'. A Greek temple, Heidegger suggests, opens a world by creating a 'relational context', of 'birth and death, disaster and blessing, victory and disgrace, endurance and decline', and Van Gogh's painting of a peasant's shoes brings out the use-life which the shoes have for their owner, what Heidegger calls 'the equipmentality of equipment'. We experience the *aletheic* truth of art as a form of 'thatness'. We might not be able to say *what* it is about a work that impresses us, but *that* there is something there we are certain of. A sense of 'thatness' stands out, stops us in our tracks. This is consistent with Kant's proposal that it is part of the experience of art for us to be motivated to find new words to describe the experience.

Ultimately, for Heidegger, 'the nature of art is poetry'. It is not his intention to construct a hierarchy of the arts, like Hegel, with poetry at the top. Rather, he is proposing that art is truest, at its most *aletheic*, when it is poetic. Verbal language, Heidegger argues, is the principal form of projection whereby a space is opened, allowing an object to appear. In projection, he writes, 'announcement is made of what it is that beings come into the Open *as*'. When we use words, we are drawing on the associations and significations which constitute everyday discourse. What the poet does is work with these in a way which defamiliarizes the familiar, which makes the usual unusual. An opening appears in the ordinariness of being, allowing new possibilities to come to light. In the 'open place' of projection, Heidegger writes, 'everything is other than usual . . . everything ordinary and hitherto existing becomes an unbeing'. Metaphor is a good example: two familiar but unrelated words are combined to produce a novel description, often leading to a new way of seeing the object in question, e.g., 'time is a river', 'rain is the light of the blind'. Generating 'new' ideas from 'old' concepts reflects the hermeneutic principle of speakers transcending their initial perspectives through conversation. Heidegger does not discuss metaphor here but considers the topic much later in *On the Way to Language*. The nature of language is seldom absent from his thought, but it is in this essay, from 1959, that it receives its most thorough treatment.

Jean-Paul Sartre

The relationship between art and language also concerns Sartre and Levinas. They examine how the form of an artwork – principally, whether it is phenomenal or verbal – affects its capacity to refer beyond itself and stimulate the viewer's sense of her place in a world among others. Through his plays, novels, and philosophical texts, Jean-Paul Sartre (1905–80) displays the central ideas of existentialism. For the existentialist, identity, a sense of who we are and what our place in the world is, is constructed through action and only has meaning when regarded as something dynamic, a propensity to act or to apply oneself. Sartre builds upon nihilism and, following Nietzsche, rejects the belief that human beings derive their identity and motivation from internal, substantive essences, for example, a soul or a continuous self. Epistemologies, such as Platonism and Cartesianism, which seek to explain identity in terms of abiding, essential qualities, Sartre argues, always leave us with the problem of how universal principles apply to particular situations. In response, Sartre radically rethinks the relation between concept and identity to show that it is only through active transformation of or engagement with the world that people and things acquire meanings.

Sartre, like Heidegger, presents subjective experience in the form of a question, but this time the question is 'how should one act?' or 'how should this experience lead to the next?'. In his major work, *Being and Nothingness* (1943), Sartre defines the self as a 'nothingness'. This has two meanings: (1) the self is *not* a *thing*, it is not something which can be captured and defined in the way that a pen or an inkwell can, and, more importantly, (2) the self, he claims, is the absence or gap between one appearance and the next. This gap is essentially a form of questioning through time, created by the structure of experience. An object does not disclose all its possible appearances in one moment. Experience is successive: a continuum in which aspects appear and disappear, in which appearances are revealed and then withdrawn. Impressions move on: this object is not present to me now in exactly the same way it was a moment ago. The next moment always appears as if it were the answer to a question: it might confirm or confound our expectations, or surprise us, or give a negative reply. What is certain is that the next moment won't be the same as before, for even to judge it 'the same' is to give it a different character. It is only in consciousness that the impression of something not being the case can take place, for example, expecting to find thirty pounds in my wallet but finding only twenty, or waiting in a café for a friend who never turns up. It is the possibility of negation, of being surprised by appearances, of having one's expectations confounded, which disengages consciousness from the brute causal order of the world. Because this rupture in the causal order of the world *is* the structure of consciousness for Sartre, there can never be a moment when consciousness is identical with a self which can influence or determine its actions. Consciousness is being-*for-itself* because it can never be identical with a content, cause, or thing. There is nothing – no inner core of being – which can compel me to adopt a particular form of conduct.

As there are no metaphysical essences in Sartre's epistemology to organize and give shape to experience, order has to be made. We define ourselves and our lives by the actions we take. Experience itself, Sartre maintains, is an active process, a series of negotiations between mind and reality. Writing is considered a form of action by Sartre. Not only does it have the same structure as consciousness, but it also changes and gives shape to experience. Putting an event or an object 'into words' gives definition and specificity to what would otherwise just pass us by as the flow of experience. From all that could be said at any one moment, one slice across phenomena is made – 'the root is black' – and the root is carved out as the object of our attention. Consciousness suddenly becomes aware of itself as that which is confronting this object. Producing a description brings the recognition that qualities are present in the root which our words do not cover and, in fact, distances the object further by suggesting connections with other items, e.g., other black things. Sartre's novel *Nausea* (1938) is an account of a writer's coming to terms with the realization that words do not bring us closer to things but rather exacerbate the questioning sense of absence which defines consciousness' relationship with reality.

Sartre has particular views on just how writing gives shape and form to experience. In 'What is Writing?' (1947), he argues that, of all the arts, prose is the only form of representation which returns us to the world. For the prose writer, he claims, words are 'transparent'. This is an unfortunate metaphor, since it is associated historically with the philosophical ideal of passing through concepts to things in themselves. But this is not Sartre's meaning. The prose writer makes her words transparent so that her readers 'may assume full responsibility before the object which has been thus laid bare'. Prose 'utilizes' words as signs: 'The ambiguity of the sign', he suggests, 'implies that one can penetrate it at will like a pane of glass and pursue the thing signified, or turn one's gaze towards its *reality* and consider it as an object.' In contrast, the forms of painting, sculpture, music, and poetry exist as *things* and, as such, have a density of their own which 'withdraws' the audience from the human condition. We are dealing with an ontology of action. Shape has to be given to experience not in a way which isolates objects and distances us from them but in a way which makes them available to us. Prose, for Sartre, organizes experience in a manner which does not draw attention to itself as an external or extra-experiential form of organization.

Emmanuel Levinas

A similar argument is given in 'Reality and its Shadow' (1948): art, Levinas claims, impedes our openness to others. Born in Lithuania, Emmanuel Levinas (b. 1906) spent the greater part of his academic life in France, obtaining French citizenship in 1930. One of the most distinctive features of his work is the importance he assigns to the attitude with which we approach others or the Other. The 'Other' is a technical term from Hegel, denoting that which an individual encounters as distinct from herself, e.g., an object or another person, yet which plays a role in affirming the individual's sense of her own identity. For Levinas, all our dealings with the world, whether they concern art, politics, or science, raise ethical questions of how we ought to behave in the face of someone or something standing before us, and much of his writing is devoted to working out the precise nature of this 'confrontation'.

Art, Levinas suggests, is a 'doubling of reality', like a shadow, and has a 'density of its own' which creates a 'fissure' or an 'interval' (called the 'meanwhile') between art and reality. This makes art 'a dimension of evasion': we become preoccupied with it at the expense of our obligation to deal with others. The idea that art, because of its substantiality, obstructs human activity comes from Plato. But whereas Plato recommends that the artist should be banished from the ideal state, Levinas insists that art can be reintegrated into human affairs through conceptual, philosophical criticism. The critic works not with phenomenal particularities but with conceptual generalities. She lacks 'the force to arouse realities' and so, instead, must 'speak in enigmas, by allusions, by suggestion, in equivocations'. The inherent incompleteness of her medium, Levinas asserts, means she is more attentive to her rootedness in the world among others.

Both 'What is Writing?' and 'Reality and its Shadow' were first published in the journal *Les Temps Modernes*, created by Sartre in 1944. Levinas' article appeared a year after Sartre's, but the editorial board of the journal, of which Sartre was a member, saw fit to add a preface drawing attention to its Sartrean themes. However, Levinas' only knowledge of Sartre's work had come from reading *Being and Nothingness* while he was a prisoner of war, and the book gives little indication of Sartre's later attitude towards the ontology of representation. Nevertheless, Levinas' account differs from Sartre's in that it offers art criticism as a category of writing which reintroduces art back into 'the true homeland of the mind'. Although Sartre had himself already begun to write critical reviews of Giacometti and Alexander Calder, art and language, as they appear in 'What is Writing?', remain divided.

Mikel Dufrenne

Of all the French phenomenologists, Mikel Dufrenne (b. 1910) offers the most systematic account of the relationship between phenomenology and art. He has written three books on aesthetics: *The Phenomenology of Aesthetic Experience* (1953), *La Poétique* (1963), and the three-volume *In the Presence of the Sensuous* (1967, 1976, 1981). Written some years prior to publication as his principal dissertation at the Sorbonne, the *Phenomenology* lays the foundations of Dufrenne's aesthetic theory. His main ambition in the book is to specify what an aesthetic object is and how it can be distinguished from other kinds of objects. The work is vital to any appreciation of Dufrenne's *œuvre* since it contains the first, full articulation of his thesis that 'the a priori is revealed only in the a posteriori'. 'The World of the Aesthetic Object' is from the *Phenomenology* and draws on Kant and Heidegger to show how the a posteriori revealing of the a priori defines an aesthetic object.

What distinguishes an artwork from other forms of representation, Dufrenne claims, is that it *expresses a world.* While an artwork is like a diagram or a sign or a news report in that it *re*-presents for us part of the world, what is unique to the artwork is that it establishes the conditions and interactions which allow the various material elements making up the work to speak to one another, to become significant, to have meaning. In other words, it establishes the conditions which allow representation to occur. How does this count as the expression of a 'world'?

Dufrenne's use of the term furthers Heidegger's proposal that the work of art draws a world from the earth, and refers, with Heidegger, to the Kantian project of demonstrating the conditions of possibility of experience. This is the origin of Dufrenne's interest in the 'a priori'–'a posteriori' relationship: identifying the structures which have to be in place a priori (prior to experience) for there to be any experience and the possibility of knowledge from experience (a posteriori) at all. The world, Dufrenne reminds us, is not a thing; we don't experience the world as an object among others, like a tree or a table or a house. Rather, our sense of 'world', he asserts (acknowledging Kant and Heidegger), is a correlate of the unity which the imagination projects as a horizon for experience. 'World' refers to the sense of objectivity which follows as a result of subjective experience having the same defining conditions as external appearances. Thus, the artwork expresses a world in the sense that it lets us see the structure of experience. Because the artwork is a form of representation which does not take representation for granted but actually deals with how certain marks or impressions can become representation, it stands as the sensuous, a posteriori expression of a priori conditions.

Gaston Bachelard

The career of the French philosopher Gaston Bachelard (1884–1962) embraces physics, psychoanalysis, and phenomenology. As professor of physics at the Collège de Bar-sur-Aube from 1919 to 1930, he became preoccupied with the philosophical issues raised by scientific knowledge. He began to conduct research in the philosophy of science, and in 1940 he was appointed as chair of the history and philosophy of science at the Sorbonne. Running through Bachelard's various specialisms is an interest in the relationship between thought and matter. In *The New Scientific Spirit* (1934), he argues that theory construction and the data generated by experimentation can shape one another; the concepts adopted can affect the way in which objects are studied, and the material data collected can impinge upon or challenge the expectations embodied in the concepts. Development in science occurs, he suggests, not as a process of accumulation, one theory building upon another, but as a series of jumps or discontinuities, in which one theory transcends another. Bachelard's observation anticipates the concept of the 'paradigm shift', articulated by the American philosopher of science Thomas Kuhn in *The Structure of Scientific Revolutions* (1962).[7] The intriguing question here is: how does transcendence happen, how do new ideas emerge? In order to explore how ideas connect with one another and how we behave in and around them – what might be called a 'topography of thought' – Bachelard turns to psychoanalysis and phenomenology.

'The Dialectics of Outside and Inside' is a chapter from *The Poetics of Space* (1957). The book is a wonderful display of the phenomenological principle that thought and experience emerge or unfold themselves from their surrounding, defining conditions. Bachelard's theme is the house or, rather, to acknowledge a sense of 'belonging' to the world, the home: the domain in which we spend most of our time and in which we have the most intimate experiences. 'The Dialectics of Outside and Inside' assesses the 'inner' and 'outer' metaphors which shape philosophy's conception of thought, and considers what the implications for philosophy might be when these terms are taken in a more lived, architectural sense.

In philosophy, and in our general understanding of language, there is the tradition which thinks of a concept as a circle or an enclosure, circumscribing all the entities to which the term refers, e.g., 'red' refers to all possible red things, 'car' refers to all possible cars. But, on this account, *being*, i.e., what something is or is said to be, is reduced to a disjunction: either you are inside or outside the circle. The model is too geometric and too visual, leading the metaphysician to think that outlines exist in nature, and that everything possible is already open to view. To make an authentic study of being, Bachelard proposes, 'it is preferable to follow all the ontological deviations of the various experiences of beings'. Rather than allowing a simplifying geometry to restrict our recognition of what can be, Bachelard argues, we should let our sense of the possibilities of experience be 'ontologically amplified' by the diversities of experience. Thus, he explores our more intimate senses of insides, outsides, doorways, and passageways in order to articulate a more resonant, textured model of thought.

Bachelard focuses on the poet's experience of the house, for the poet gives us 'exaggerated images' and these benefit phenomenology by working against the 'habits of reduction'. Poetry is exaggerated in the sense that it pursues an experience *to the end.* It is like being in a house and not being satisfied with just seeing one room but wanting to explore them all. This gives poetry its own topographic form: the door. The doorway represents the crossing of thresholds, the passage from one world to another, freedom from the confines of reductive metaphysics. The disclosive properties of metaphor are foregrounded by presenting it as the crossing of a threshold, moving from one concept to another. Here is one answer to Bachelard's question of the origin of new ideas, consistent with the large volume of recent research on the role metaphor plays in scientific theory construction. Furthermore, images of opening up a new realm make the doorway a symbol for Heidegger's poetry as *aletheia,* and Bachelard's interlacing structures of thought with the intimate, physical gestures of home is indicative of the relationships being drawn in Merleau-Ponty's phenomenology of the body.

Maurice Merleau-Ponty

French phenomenology, more so than Husserl's and Heidegger's, seeks to 'concretize' the phenomenological method, that is, to show how the structures of experience can be derived from the 'feel' of lived experience. We can see this in the work of the French phenomenologists considered so far: Sartre's 'nothingness' is based on the absence we sense when expectations are not met; for Levinas, philosophical thought should have as its template our interaction with others; Dufrenne's 'artwork' makes visible the projection whereby we create a world for ourselves; and Bachelard constructs ontologies of thought from the experiences of home. Concretization occurs at its fullest, I would argue, in the study of bodily experience conducted by Maurice Merleau-Ponty (1908–61). Those aspects of our being normally regarded as aphysical, abstract, and descriptively elusive, i.e., consciousness, thought, memory, the actual 'having' of experience, Merleau-Ponty declares, can be shown to unfold from our condition as beings physically immersed in the world.

The fundamental premise of phenomenology, as announced above, is that experience is intentional: experience is necessarily experience *of something.* Reality and my perception of it are interwoven in or *as* the texture of experience; the same, single fabric – experience – gives rise to two things – consciousness and reality. This is a response to the problems encountered by traditional rationalist and empiricist theories explaining experience as a binary relation between an isolated mind and an external reality. The body, Merleau-Ponty asserts in his seminal text, *The Phenomenology of Perception* (1945), is not a thing among others in the world but a framework of intentionality. We open onto the world through the body. Not only is it the medium which translates sensation for us but also something active and prospective which moves around and maps out the world for us. The 'counter-pressure' sense of intentionality, of bumping up against the world, for Merleau-Ponty, is the intersecting – but never interlocking – of these two aspects of the body.

'The Intertwining – The Chiasm' (1961) is one of Merleau-Ponty's final essays. It is from *The Visible and the Invisible*, the book he was working on at the time of his death, and explores the sensory and ontological implications of intentionality. Whereas contact between consciousness and reality is traditionally idealized as a perfect fit, Merleau-Ponty assigns the relationship a 'resistance' and 'thickness' which he calls 'flesh' and which, he argues, is the original opening of the subject–object distinction. We normally ascribe a sensory quality, like a colour, either to *the thing* or to *our* perception of the thing, but this assumes that nothing more is taking place in experience other than the meeting of two preformed components. If mind and reality met exactly, he argues, the two would 'blend into' one another and sensation 'would vanish at the moment of formation'. Rather, perception involves a gap, a tension between the way we sense the world to be and how we relate this to past and potential experiences. In order to perceive, one must belong to a world in which one can contextualize the information received:

> Between the exploration [of my hand] and what it will teach me, between my movements and what I touch, there must exist some relationship by principle, some kinship, according to which they are not only, like the pseudopods of the amoeba, vague and ephemeral deformations of the corporeal space, but the initiation to and the opening upon a tactile world. This can happen only if my hand, while it is felt from within, is also accessible from without, itself tangible, for my other hand, for example, if it takes its place among the things it touches, is in a sense one of them, opens finally upon a tangible being of which it is also a part.

The difference between the body as 'sensory' and the body as 'object' occurs because the two cannot coincide; we can touch and be touched, but cannot superpose the two, that is, the hand that is doing the touching cannot simultaneously be the object that is touched, otherwise experience would vanish. The impossibility of superposition is a key premise in Merleau-Ponty's argument, for it is the non-identity – the necessary blindspot, so to speak – which gives perception its thickness and roots intentionality in the body. That which restricts, enables. This is from the 'Working Notes' for *The Visible and the Invisible*:

> *What* it does not see it does not see for reasons of principle, it is because it is consciousness that it does not see. *What* it does not see is what in it prepares the vision of the rest (as the retina is blind at the point where the fibres that will permit the vision spread out into it). *What* it does not see is what makes it see, is its tie to Being, is its corporeity, are the existentials by which the world becomes visible, is the flesh wherein the object is born.[8]

The essay is a wonderful and demanding display of phenomenology working with and against the divisions in everyday language in order to articulate a prior state of being to which these divisions do not apply. The subject–predicate structure of language divides the world into individuals and things, and all our prepositions and attributions of properties are oriented in and around this organized, public world. However, Merleau-Ponty wants to show that the colours, patterns, and textures of sensory experience, *before they are the qualities of objects*, are the thick interactions which manifest the disclosive, intentional structure of experience. What we ordinarily regard as immediate and without substance – the instantaneous reception of a world through sense perception – he is widening into a 'space' or 'texture' which, because it is the original 'opening' of experience, cannot easily be expressed or positioned in ordinary terms. Familiar metaphors appear: cavity, hollow, armature, and horizon. The work that is required in shifting our perspective is appropriate to the argument though. Just as experience, for Merleau-Ponty, is the arching outward enabled by our embodiment, so, working our way through his images and metaphors, we sense how new understanding can arise from rearranging and pressing against the ideas which surround us. The essay is subject to a close-reading by Luce Irigaray in 'The Invisible of the Flesh' and acknowledged by Jacques Lacan in 'Of the Gaze as *Objet Petit a*'. See the 'Psychoanalysis and Feminism' section below.

Hans-Georg Gadamer

The German philosopher Hans-Georg Gadamer (b. 1900) is arguably the most significant figure to emerge in post-Heideggerian hermeneutics. I have shown that the notion of 'gap' or 'opening' represents the structure of consciousness for Heidegger, and the structure of the body for Merleau-Ponty. In a comparable fashion, the true locus of hermeneutics, for Gadamer, is the 'in-between': the gap between the familiarity of a text and its strangeness, as the product of another time, another tradition, or 'simply' another mind.[9] Where familiarity ends and strangeness begins will be governed by the reader's propensities for seeing connections and drawing conclusions and these, in turn, will be supplemented, challenged, or revised as the strange is made familiar or the familiar is made strange. Conversation, with its exchanges of ideas and revisions of opinion, is a good analogy for hermeneutics' 'novelty through transformation'. Gadamer makes the comparison in *Truth and Method* (1960).[10] He is not thinking of those 'conversations' when you are stuck in a corner with a crushing bore who does nothing but spout on about his own interests and achievements, but those occasions when each person wants to understand and pursue what the other has to say.

> To conduct a conversation [Gadamer writes] means to allow oneself to be conducted by the subject matter to which the partners in the dialogue are oriented. It requires that one does not try to argue the other person down but that one really considers the weight of the other's opinion.[11]

In his short but concisely argued essay 'Aesthetics and Hermeneutics', Gadamer relates the experience of art to the hermeneutic question of how one tradition can understand another. He contests the idea that aesthetic experience is the grasping of an original content, whether this refers to the original experience of the artist or something judged to be specific to the time in which the work was produced. Gadamer was a student of Heidegger's, and central to his work is the Heideggerian notion that the way things appear to us or have meaning for us is determined by a horizon of expectation which we project in advance of experience. When we study an artwork, he suggests, the artist's intention to speak meets our own projected desire to understand. The encounter does not reconstruct experience but instead surprises us: it generates new experience through the interrelation of perspectives, and draws attention to our own status as beings who interpret the world. Gadamer appeals to the act of conversation: 'we cannot understand without wanting to understand, that is, without wanting to let something be said . . . Understanding does not occur when we try to intercept what someone wants to say to us by claiming we already know it.'

All human constructions, Gadamer reminds us, are reflections of a culture's orientation towards the world. This applies to hand tools, to language, and to art. Present here is the phenomenological principle that all objects and events are extensions of our involvement with them, that is to say, they are ordered and given meaning by us according to the way we interact or potentially interact with them. They exist as part of a network of possible encounters, with one thing always suggesting or inviting connection with something else. 'Everything points to another thing.' To apprehend an artwork is therefore to bring our faculties into relation with the ideas and judgements which shaped the work. The 'what is said', the 'what could have been said', the 'what they wanted to say', and the 'what was impossible to say' of both the artist's frame of reference and our own interact to generate new chains of interpretation. Thus, the experience of art, Gadamer avers, becomes the experience *of experience*, as the distance between ourselves and the artist – necessary for conversation – makes us aware of the temporal, contingent nature of the terms through which we perceive the world.

Gianni Vattimo

Gianni Vattimo (b. 1936) is Italy's most prominent phenomenological thinker and commentator on the postmodern. A former student of Gadamer's, he translated *Truth and Method* into Italian and, through his critical appraisals of Nietzsche, Heidegger, and Gadamer, he shows how debates within phenomenology and hermeneutics can be applied to questions of postmodernity. Vattimo's essay, 'The Death or Decline of Art', offers a hermeneutics of the concept of 'end'. The end in question, as the title indicates, is Hegel's 'death of art' thesis and, therefore, embraces the end of modernity, where 'modernity' is understood as the ultimate and final dominion of the universal concept over individual phenomena. The essay takes us back to Heidegger's 'Origin of the Work of Art', and shows how Heidegger's ontological treatment of the artwork, in terms of the world-disclosing properties of earth, has implications for the way we classify postmodern art.

Hegel's 'death of art' thesis, Vattimo claims, has to be considered in the light of Heidegger's reworking of metaphysics. Art, in Hegel's dialectical account of consciousness, is essentially the practice of making thought visible but, as consciousness becomes increasingly aware that the material is the mental, so the argument goes, art surrenders its material being and becomes conceptual, becomes philosophy. Although art, as we find it, Vattimo admits, has not turned into thought, it is nevertheless true to say that art is no longer an isolatable event; it is now, instead, one practice among many in the mass media. It has either allowed itself to be taken over by technological means of production – in the process becoming kitsch or, with Marcuse, a boundary-transcending source of emancipation – or, with Adorno, refused to engage with mass culture completely.

However, the death of art, Vattimo claims, 'cannot be understood as a "notion" which could be said to correspond . . . to a certain state of things' but is instead 'an event that constitutes the historical and ontological constellation in which we move'. This is because Heidegger's metaphysics is a departure from the metaphysics underlying Hegel's dialectic and, therefore, a departure from the terms in which the 'death of art' is set. What Heidegger offers is not so much an 'overcoming' (*Überwindung*) as a 'healing' (*Verwindung*) of traditional metaphysics. As Heidegger argues in *Being and Time* and in 'Origin' in relation to art, the absolute, binary ontology of traditional metaphysics, including Hegel's, where something either *is* or *is not*, presupposes a more fundamental ontology in which objects are first allowed to *come into* being, to be disclosed. The way in which ontological conditions of possibility allow experience to open up in front of us, Heidegger argues, is comparable to the way in which a work of art brings a world before us. Things emerge and subside almost with a breathing action, rather than simply switching from 'on' to 'off', on account of the fact that experience is actively determined by propensities within the subject's cognitive and aesthetic faculties.

Heidegger's aesthetics of disclosure, Vattimo declares, changes completely our understanding of the applicability of concepts and the inscription of where one thing or category ends and another begins. Consonant with Bachelard's notion of the concept as 'doorway', Vattimo proposes that the concept does not circumscribe and isolate its referent but, instead, makes it prominent, draws it out, while allowing it to remain a part of a wider fabric of conceptual possibility. The move, he suggests, is away from the 'somewhat grandiose conceptual language' which suited romantic notions of genius and transcendence and towards the acknowledgement of a relational, rising and falling topography of thought. On this account, death or an end is not a moment but a network of transitions in which alternative outcomes are recognized to be potential. Part of the *work* of art, through the world-disclosing properties of earth, is to make us aware that what we initially conceptualize as a negative or antithetical development in fact belongs to a wider complex of association and so any immediate assertion of an end might be premature. We should rather speak of the 'decline' of art, Vattimo suggests, since, in an era of mechanical reproduction and mass culture, 'assumed to signal the death of art', the possibility of new life nevertheless remains.

Notes

1 Edmund Husserl, *Ideas Pertaining to a Pure Phenomenology and to a Phenomenological Philosophy* (1913), trans. F. Kersten, The Hague, Nijhoff, 1982; *Cartesian Meditations* (1931), trans. Dorion Cairns, The Hague, Nijhoff, 1960.

2 Martin Heidegger, *Being and Time*, trans. John Macquarrie and Edward Robinson, Oxford, Blackwell, 1995, H. 7, pp. 26–27. 'H' refers to the pagination of the later German editions, reproduced in the margins of the translation.

3 Ibid., H. 12, p. 32.

4 Ibid., H. 34, p. 58.

5 Ibid., H. 37, p. 62.

6 Ibid., H. 33, p. 57.

7 Thomas Kuhn, *The Structure of Scientific Revolutions*, Chicago, University of Chicago Press, 1962.

8 Maurice Merleau-Ponty, *The Visible and the Invisible*, trans. Alphonso Lingis, Evanston, Illinois, Northwestern University Press, 1968, p. 248.

9 Hans-Georg Gadamer, *Truth and Method*, trans. Joel Weinsheimer and Donald G. Marshall, London, Sheed and Ward, 1993, p. 295.
10 Ibid., pp. 367–69, 383–88, 461–63, 538–39.
11 Ibid., p. 367.

4

THE ORIGIN OF THE WORK OF ART

Martin Heidegger

Origin here means that from and by which something is what it is and as it is. What something is, as it is, we call its essence or nature. The origin of something is the source of its nature. The question concerning the origin of the work of art asks about the source of its nature. On the usual view, the work arises out of and by means of the activity of the artist. But by what and whence is the artist what he is? By the work; for to say that the work does credit to the master means that it is the work that first lets the artist emerge as a master of his art. The artist is the origin of the work. The work is the origin of the artist. Neither is without the other. Nevertheless, neither is the sole support of the other. In themselves and in their interrelations artist and work *are* each of them by virtue of a third thing which is prior to both, namely that which also gives artist and work of art their names – art.

As necessarily as the artist is the origin of the work in a different way than the work is the origin of the artist, so it is equally certain that, in a still different way, art is the origin of both artist and work. But can art be an origin at all? Where and how does art occur? Art – this is nothing more than a word to which nothing real any longer corresponds. It may pass for a collective idea under which we find a place for that which alone is real in art: works and artists. Even if the word art were taken to signify more than a collective notion, what is meant by the word could exist only on the basis of the actuality of works and artists. Or is the converse the case? Do works and artists exist only because art exists as their origin?

Whatever the decision may be, the question of the origin of the work of art becomes a question about the nature of art. Since the question whether and how art in general exists must still remain open, we shall attempt to discover the nature of art in the place where art undoubtedly prevails in a real way. Art is present in the art work. But what and how is a work of art?

What art is should be inferable from the work. What the work of art is we can come to know only from the nature of art. Anyone can easily see that we are moving in a circle. Ordinary understanding demands that this circle be avoided because it violates logic. What art is can be gathered from a comparative examination of actual art works. But how are we to be certain that we are indeed basing such an examination on art works if we do not know beforehand what art is? And the nature of art can no more be arrived at by a derivation from higher concepts than by a collection of characteristics of actual art works. For such a derivation, too, already has in view the characteristics that must suffice to establish that what we take in advance to be an art work is one in fact. But selecting works from among given objects, and deriving concepts from principles, are equally impossible here, and where these procedures are practiced they are a self-deception.

Thus we are compelled to follow the circle. This is neither a makeshift nor a defect. To enter upon this path is the strength of thought, to continue on it is the feast of thought, assuming that thinking is a craft. Not only is the main step from work to art a circle like the step from art to work, but every separate step that we attempt circles in this circle.

In order to discover the nature of the art that really prevails in the work, let us go to the actual work and ask the work what and how it is.

Works of art are familiar to everyone. Architectural and sculptural works can be seen installed in public places, in churches, and in dwellings. Art works of the most diverse periods and peoples are housed in collections and exhibitions. If we consider the works in their untouched actuality and do not deceive ourselves, the result is that the works are as naturally present as are things. The picture hangs on the wall like a rifle or a hat. A painting, e.g., the one by Van Gogh that represents a pair of peasant shoes, travels from one exhibition to another. Works of art are shipped like coal from the Ruhr and logs from the Black Forest. During the First World War Hölderlin's hymns were packed in the soldier's knapsack together with cleaning gear. Beethoven's quartets lie in the storerooms of the publishing house like potatoes in a cellar.

All works have this thingly character. What would they be without it? But perhaps this rather crude and external view of the work is objectionable to us. Shippers or charwomen in museums may operate with such conceptions of the work of art. We, however, have to take works as they are encountered by those who experience and enjoy them. But even the much-vaunted aesthetic experience cannot get around the thingly aspect of the art work. There is something stony in a work of architecture, wooden in a carving, colored in a painting, spoken in a linguistic work, sonorous in a musical composition. The thingly element is so irremovably present in the art work that we are compelled rather to say conversely that the architectural work is in stone, the carving is in wood, the painting in color, the linguistic work in speech, the musical composition in sound. 'Obviously,' it will be replied. No doubt. But what is this self-evident thingly element in the work of art?

Presumably it becomes superfluous and confusing to inquire into this feature, since the art work is something else over and above the thingly element. This something else in the work constitutes its artistic nature. The art work is, to be sure, a thing that is made, but it says something other than the mere thing itself is, *allo agoreuei*. The work makes public something other than itself; it manifests something other; it is an allegory. In the work of art something other is brought together with the thing that is made. To bring together is, in Greek, *sumballein*. The work is a symbol.

Allegory and symbol provide the conceptual frame within whose channel of vision the art work has for a long time been characterized. But this one element in a work that manifests another, this one element that joins with another, is the thingly feature in the art work. It seems almost as though the thingly element in the art work is like the substructure into and upon which the other, authentic element is built. And is it not this thingly feature in the work that the artist really makes by his handicraft?

Our aim is to arrive at the immediate and full reality of the work of art, for only in this way shall we discover real art also within it. Hence we must first bring to view the thingly element of the work. To this end it is necessary that we should know with sufficient clarity what a thing is. Only then can we say whether the art work is a thing, but a thing to which something else adheres; only then can we decide whether the work is at bottom something else and not a thing at all.

Thing and work

What in truth is the thing, so far as it is a thing? When we inquire in this way, our aim is to come to know the thing-being (thingness) of the thing. The point is to discover the thingly character of the thing. To this end we have to be acquainted with the sphere to which all those entities belong which we have long called by the name of thing.

The stone in the road is a thing, as is the clod in the field. A jug is a thing, as is the well beside the road. But what about the milk in the jug and the water in the well? These too are things if the cloud in the sky and the thistle in the field, the leaf in the autumn breeze and the hawk over the wood, are rightly called by the name of thing. All these must indeed be called things, if the name is applied even to that which does not, like those just enumerated, show itself, i.e., that which does not appear. According to Kant, the whole of the world, for example, and even God himself, is a thing of this sort, a thing that does not itself appear, namely, a 'thing-in-itself.' In the language of philosophy both things-in-themselves and things that appear, all beings that in any way are, are called things.

Airplanes and radio sets are nowadays among the things closest to us, but when we have ultimate things in mind we think of something altogether different. Death and judgment – these are ultimate things. On the whole the word 'thing' here designates whatever is not simply nothing. In this sense the work of art is also a thing, so far as it is not simply nothing. Yet this concept is of no use to us, at least immediately, in our attempt to delimit entities that have the mode of being of a thing, as against those having the mode of being of a work. And besides, we hesitate to call God a thing. In the same way we hesitate to consider the peasant in the field, the stoker at the boiler, the teacher in the school as things. A man is not a thing. It is true that we speak of a young girl who is faced with a task too difficult for her as being a young thing, still too young for it, but only because we feel that being human is in a certain way missing here and think that instead we have to do here with the factor that constitutes the thingly character of things. We hesitate even to call the deer in the forest clearing, the beetle in the grass, the blade of grass a thing. We would sooner think of a hammer as a thing, or a shoe, or an ax, or a clock. But even these are not mere things. Only a stone, a clod of earth, a piece of wood are for us such mere things. Lifeless beings of nature and objects of use. Natural things and utensils are the things commonly so called.

We thus see ourselves brought back from the widest domain, within which everything is a thing (thing = *res* = *ens* = an entity), including even the highest and last things, to the narrow precinct of mere things. 'Mere' here means, first, the pure thing, which is simply a thing and nothing more; but then, at the same time, it means that which is only a thing, in an almost pejorative sense. It is mere things, excluding even use-objects, that count as things in the strict sense. What does the thingly character of these things, then, consist in? It is in reference to these that the thingness of things must be determinable. This determination enables us to characterize what it is that is thingly as such. Thus prepared, we are able to characterize the almost palpable reality of works, in which something else inheres.

* * *

That which gives things their constancy and pith but is also at the same time the source of their particular mode of sensuous pressure – colored, resonant, hard, massive – is the matter in things. In this analysis of the thing as matter (*hule*), form (*morphe*) is already coposited. What is constant in a thing, its consistency, lies in the fact that matter stands together with a form. The thing is formed matter. This interpretation appeals to the immediate view with which the thing solicits us by its looks (*eidos*). In this synthesis of matter and form a thing-concept has finally been found which applies equally to things of nature and to use-objects.

This concept puts us in a position to answer the question concerning the thingly element in the work of art. The thingly element is manifestly the matter of which it consists. Matter is the substrate and field for the artist's formative action. But we could have advanced this obvious and well-known definition of the thingly element at the very outset. Why do we make a detour through other current thing-concepts? Because we also mistrust this concept of the thing, which represents it as formed matter.

But is not precisely this pair of concepts, matter–form, usually employed in the domain in which we are supposed to be moving? To be sure. The distinction of matter and form is *the conceptual schema which is used, in the greatest variety of ways, quite generally for all art theory and aesthetics.* This incontestable fact, however, proves neither that the distinction of matter and form is adequately founded, nor that it belongs originally to the domain of art and the art work. Moreover, the range of application of this pair of concepts has long extended far beyond the field of aesthetics. Form and content are the most hackneyed concepts under which anything and everything may be subsumed. And if form is correlated with the rational and matter with the irrational; if the rational is taken to be the logical and the irrational the alogical; if in addition the subject–object relation is coupled with the conceptual pair form–matter; then representation has at its command a conceptual machinery that nothing is capable of withstanding.

If, however, it is thus with the distinction between matter and form, how then shall we make use of it to lay hold of the particular domain of mere things by contrast with all other entities? But perhaps this characterization in terms of matter and form would recover its defining power if only we reversed the process of expanding and emptying these concepts. Certainly, but this presupposes that we know in what sphere of beings they realize their true defining power. That this is the domain of mere things is so far only an assumption. Reference to the copious use made of this conceptual framework in aesthetics might sooner lead to the idea that matter and form are specifications stemming from the nature of the art work and were in the first place transferred from it back to the thing. Where does the matter–form structure have its origin – in the thingly character of the thing or in the workly character of the art work?

The self-contained block of granite is something material in a definite if unshapely form. Form means here the distribution and arrangement of the material parts in spatial locations, resulting in a particular shape, namely that of a block. But a jug, an ax, a shoe are also matter occurring in a form. Form as shape is not the consequence here of a prior distribution of the matter. The form, on the contrary, determines the arrangement of the matter. Even more, it prescribes in each case the kind and selection of the matter – impermeable for a jug, sufficiently hard for an ax, firm yet flexible for shoes. The interfusion of form and matter prevailing here is, moreover, controlled beforehand by the purposes served by jug, ax, shoes. Such usefulness is never assigned or added on afterward to a being of the type of a jug, ax, or pair of shoes. But neither is it something that floats somewhere above it as an end.

Usefulness is the basic feature from which this entity regards us, that is, flashes at us and thereby is present and thus is this entity. Both the formative act and the choice of material – a choice given with the act – and therewith the dominance of the conjunction of matter and form are all grounded in such usefulness. A being that falls under usefulness is always the product of a process of making. It is made as a piece of equipment for something. As determinations of beings, accordingly, matter and form have their proper place in the essential nature of equipment. This name designates what is produced expressly for employment and use. Matter and form are in no case original determinations of the thingness of the mere thing.

A piece of equipment, a pair of shoes for instance, when finished, is also self-contained like the mere thing, but it does not have the character of having taken shape by itself like the granite boulder. On the other hand, equipment displays an affinity with the art work insofar as it is something produced by the human hand. However, by its self-sufficient presence the work of art is similar rather to the mere thing which has taken shape by itself and is self-contained. Nevertheless we do not count such works among mere things. As a rule it is the use-objects around us that are the nearest and authentic things. Thus the piece of equipment is half thing, because characterized by thingliness, and yet it is something more; at the same time it is half art work and yet something less, because lacking the self-sufficiency of the art work. Equipment has a peculiar position intermediate between thing and work, assuming that such a calculated ordering of them is permissible.

The matter–form structure, however, by which the being of a piece of equipment is first determined, readily presents itself as the immediately intelligible constitution of every entity, because here man himself as maker participates in the way in which the piece of equipment comes into being. Because equipment takes an intermediate place between mere thing and work, the suggestion is that nonequipmental beings – things and works and ultimately everything that is – are to be comprehended with the help of the being of equipment (the matter–form structure).

The inclination to treat the matter–form structure as *the* constitution of every entity receives a yet additional impulse from the fact that on the basis of a religious faith, namely, the biblical faith, the totality of all beings is represented in advance as something created, which here means made. The philosophy of this faith can of course assure us that all of God's creative work is to be thought of as different from the action of a craftsman. Nevertheless, if at the same time or even beforehand, in accordance with a presumed predetermination of Thomistic philosophy for interpreting the Bible, the *ens creatum* is conceived as a unity of *materia* and *forma*, then faith is expounded by way of a philosophy whose truth lies in an unconcealedness of beings which differs in kind from the world believed in by faith.

The idea of creation, grounded in faith, can lose its guiding power of knowledge of beings as a whole. But the theological interpretation of all beings, the view of the world in terms of matter and form borrowed from an alien philosophy, having once been instituted, can still remain a force. This happens in the transition from the Middle Ages to modern times. The metaphysics of the modern period rests on the form–matter structure devised in the medieval period, which itself merely recalls in its words the buried natures of *eidos* and *hule*. Thus the interpretation of 'thing' by means of matter and form, whether it remains medieval or becomes Kantian-transcendental, has become current and self-evident. But for that reason, no less than the other interpretations mentioned of the thingness of the thing, it is an encroachment upon the thing-being of the thing.

The situation stands revealed as soon as we speak of things in the strict sense as mere things. The 'mere,' after all, means the removal of the character of usefulness and of being made. The mere thing is a sort of equipment, albeit equipment denuded of its equipmental being. Thing-being consists in what is then left over. But this remnant is not actually defined in its ontological character. It remains doubtful whether the thingly character comes to view at all in the process of stripping off everything equipmental. Thus the third mode of interpretation of the thing, that which follows the lead of the matter–form structure, also turns out to be an assault upon the thing.

These three modes of defining thingness conceive of the thing as a bearer of traits, as the unity of a manifold of sensations, as formed matter. In the course of the history of truth about beings, the interpretations mentioned have also entered into combinations, a matter we may now pass over. In such combination they have further strengthened their innate tendency to expand so as to apply in similar way to thing, to equipment, and to work. Thus they give rise to a mode of thought by which we think not only about thing, equipment, and work but about all beings in general. This long-familiar mode of thought preconceives all immediate experience of beings. The preconception shackles reflection on the being of any given entity. Thus it comes about that prevailing thing-concepts obstruct the way toward the thingly character of the thing as well as toward the equipmental character of equipment, and all the more toward the workly character of the work.

This fact is the reason why it is necessary to know about these thing-concepts, in order thereby to take heed of their derivation and their boundless presumption, but also of their semblance of self-evidence. This knowledge becomes all the more necessary when we risk the attempt to bring to view and express in words the thingly character of the thing, the equipmental character of equipment, and the workly character of the work. To this end, however, only one element is needful: to keep at a distance all the preconceptions and assaults of the above modes of thought, to leave the thing to rest in its own self, for instance, in its thing-being. What seems easier than to let a being be just the being that it is? Or does this turn out to be the most difficult of tasks, particularly if such an intention – to let a being be as it is – represents the opposite of the indifference that simply turns its back upon the being itself in favor of an unexamined concept of being? We ought to turn toward the being, think about it in regard to its being, but by means of this thinking at the same time let it rest upon itself in its very own being.

This exertion of thought seems to meet with its greatest resistance in defining the thingness of the thing; for where else could the cause lie of the failure of the efforts mentioned? The unpretentious thing evades thought most stubbornly. Or can it be that this self-refusal of the mere thing, this self-contained independence, belongs precisely to the nature of the thing? Must not this strange and uncommunicative feature of the nature of the thing become intimately familiar to thought that tries to think the thing? If so, then we should not force our way to its thingly character.

That the thingness of the thing is particularly difficult to express and only seldom expressible is infallibly documented by the history of its interpretation indicated above. This history coincides with the destiny in accordance with which Western thought has hitherto thought the Being of beings. However, not only do we now establish this point; at the same time we discover a clue in this history. Is it an accident that in the interpretation of the thing the view that takes matter and form as guide attains to special dominance? This definition of the thing derives from an interpretation of the equipmental being of equipment. And equipment, having come into being through human making, is particularly familiar to human thinking. At the same time, this familiar being has a peculiar intermediate position between thing and work. We shall follow this clue and search first for the equipmental character of equipment. Perhaps this will suggest something to us about the thingly character of the thing and the workly character of the work. We must only avoid making thing and work prematurely into subspecies of equipment. We are disregarding the possibility, however, that differences relating to the history of Being may yet also be present in the way equipment *is*.

But what path leads to the equipmental quality of equipment? How shall we discover what a piece of equipment truly is? The procedure necessary at present must plainly avoid any attempts that again immediately entail the encroachments of the usual interpretations. We are most easily insured against this if we simply describe some equipment without any philosophical theory.

We choose as example a common sort of equipment – a pair of peasant shoes. We do not even need to exhibit actual pieces of this sort of useful article in order to describe them. Everyone is acquainted with them. But since it is a matter here of direct description, it may be well to facilitate the visual realization of them. For this purpose a pictorial representation suffices. We shall choose a well-known painting by Van Gogh, who painted such shoes several times. But what is there to see here? Everyone knows what shoes consist of. If they are not wooden or bast shoes, there will be leather soles and uppers, joined together by thread and nails. Such gear serves to clothe the feet. Depending on the use to which the shoes are to be put, whether for work in the field or for dancing, matter and form will differ.

Such statements, no doubt correct, only explicate what we already know. The equipmental quality of equipment consists in its usefulness. But what about this usefulness itself? In conceiving it, do we already conceive along with it the equipmental character of equipment? In order to succeed in doing this, must we not look out for useful equipment in its use? The peasant woman wears her shoes in the field. Only here are they what they are. They are all the more genuinely so, the less the peasant woman thinks about the shoes while she is at work, or looks at them at all, or is even aware of them. She stands and walks in them. That is how shoes actually serve. It is in this process of the use of equipment that we must actually encounter the character of equipment.

As long as we only imagine a pair of shoes in general, or simply look at the empty, unused shoes as they merely stand there in the picture, we shall never discover what the equipmental being of the equipment in truth is. From Van Gogh's painting we cannot even tell where these shoes stand. There is nothing surrounding this pair of peasant shoes in or to which they might belong – only an undefined space. There are not even clods of soil from the field or the field-path sticking to them, which would at least hint at their use. A pair of peasant shoes and nothing more. And yet –

From the dark opening of the worn insides of the shoes the toilsome tread of the worker stares forth. In the stiffly rugged heaviness of the shoes there is the accumulated tenacity of her slow trudge through the far-spreading and ever-uniform furrows of the field swept by a raw wind. On the leather lie the dampness and richness of the soil. Under the soles slides the loneliness of the field-path as evening falls. In the shoes vibrates the silent call of the earth, its quiet gift of the ripening grain and its unexplained self-refusal in the fallow desolation of the wintry field. This equipment is pervaded by uncomplaining anxiety as to the certainty of bread, the wordless joy of having once more withstood want, the trembling before the impending childbed and shivering at the surrounding menace of death. This equipment belongs to the *earth*, and it is protected in the *world* of the peasant woman. From out of this protected belonging the equipment itself rises to its resting-within-itself.

But perhaps it is only in the picture that we notice all this about the shoes. The peasant woman, on the other hand, simply wears them. If only this simple wearing were so simple. When she takes off her shoes late in the evening, in deep but healthy fatigue, and reaches out for them again in the still dim dawn, or passes them by on the day of rest, she knows all this without noticing or reflecting. The equipmental quality of the equipment consists indeed in its usefulness. But this usefulness itself rests in the abundance of an essential being of the equipment. We call it reliability. By virtue of this reliability the peasant woman is made privy to the silent call of the earth; by virtue of the reliability of the equipment she is sure of her world. World and earth exist for her, and for those who are with her in her mode of being, only thus – in the equipment. We say 'only' and therewith fall into error; for the reliability of the equipment first gives to the simple world its security and assures to the earth the freedom of its steady thrust.

The equipmental being of equipment, reliability, keeps gathered within itself all things according to their manner and extent. The usefulness of equipment is nevertheless only the essential consequence of reliability. The former vibrates in the latter and would be nothing without it. A single piece of equipment is worn out and used up; but at the same time the use itself also falls into disuse, wears away, and becomes usual. Thus equipmentality wastes away, sinks into mere stuff. In such wasting, reliability vanishes. This dwindling, however, to which use-things owe their boringly obtrusive usualness, is only one more testimony to the original nature of equipmental being. The worn-out usualness of the equipment then obtrudes itself as the sole mode of being, apparently peculiar to it exclusively. Only blank usefulness now remains visible. It awakens the impression that the origin of equipment lies in a mere fabricating that impresses a form upon some matter. Nevertheless, in its genuinely equipmental being, equipment stems from a more distant source. Matter and form and their distinction have a deeper origin.

The repose of equipment resting within itself consists in its reliability. Only in this reliability do we discern what equipment in truth is. But we still know nothing of what we first sought: the thing's thingly character. And we know nothing at all of what we really and solely seek: the workly character of the work in the sense of the work of art.

Or have we already learned something unwittingly, in passing so to speak, about the work-being of the work?

The equipmental quality of equipment was discovered. But how? Not by a description and explanation of a pair of shoes actually present; not by a report about the process of making shoes; and also not by the observation of the actual use of shoes occurring here and there; but only by bringing ourselves before Van Gogh's painting. This painting spoke. In the vicinity of the work we were suddenly somewhere else than we usually tend to be.

The art work let us know what shoes are in truth. It would be the worst self-deception to think that our description, as a subjective action, had first depicted everything thus and then projected it into the painting. If anything is questionable here, it is rather that we experienced too little in the neighborhood of the work and that we expressed the experience too crudely and too literally. But above all, the work did not, as it might seem at first, serve merely for a better visualizing of what a piece of equipment is. Rather, the equipmentality of equipment first genuinely arrives at its appearance through the work and only in the work.

What happens here? What is at work in the work? Van Gogh's painting is the disclosure of what the equipment, the pair of peasant shoes, *is* in truth. This entity emerges into the unconcealedness of its being. The Greeks called the unconcealedness of beings *aletheia*. We say 'truth' and think little enough in using this word. If there occurs in the work a disclosure of a particular being, disclosing what and how it is, then there is here an occurring, a happening of truth at work.

In the work of art the truth of an entity has set itself to work. 'To set' means here: to bring to a stand. Some particular entity, a pair of peasant shoes, comes in the work to stand in the light of its being. The being of the being comes into the steadiness of its shining.

The nature of art would then be this: the truth of beings setting itself to work. But until now art presumably has had to do with the beautiful and beauty, and not with truth. The arts that produce such works are called the beautiful or fine arts, in contrast with the applied or industrial arts that manufacture equipment. In fine art the art itself is not beautiful, but is called so because it produces the beautiful. Truth, in contrast, belongs to logic. Beauty, however, is reserved for aesthetics.

But perhaps the proposition that art is truth setting itself to work intends to revive the fortunately obsolete view that art is an imitation and depiction of reality? The reproduction of what exists requires, to be sure, agreement with the actual being, adaptation to it; the Middle Ages called it *adaequatio*; Aristotle already spoke of *homoiosis*. Agreement with what *is* has long been taken to be the essence of truth. But then, is it our opinion that this painting by Van Gogh depicts a pair of actually existing peasant shoes, and is a work of art because it does so successfully? Is it our opinion that the painting draws a likeness from something actual and transposes it into a product of artistic – production? By no means.

* * *

The work and truth

A building, a Greek temple, portrays nothing. It simply stands there in the middle of the rock-cleft valley. The building encloses the figure of the god, and in this concealment lets it stand out into the holy precinct through the open portico. By means of the temple, the god is present in the temple. This presence of the god is in itself the extension and delimitation of the precinct as a holy precinct. The temple and its precinct, however, do not fade away into the indefinite. It is the temple-work that first fits together and at the same time gathers around itself the unity of those paths and relations in which birth and death, disaster and blessing, victory and disgrace, endurance and decline acquire the shape of destiny for human being. The all-governing expanse of this open relational context is the world of this historical people. Only from and in this expanse does the nation first return to itself for the fulfillment of its vocation.

Standing there, the building rests on the rocky ground. This resting of the work draws up out of the rock the mystery of that rock's clumsy yet spontaneous support. Standing there, the building holds its ground against the storm raging above it and so first makes the storm itself manifest in its violence. The luster and gleam of the stone, though itself apparently glowing only by the grace of the sun, yet first brings to light the light of the day, the breadth of the sky, the darkness of the night. The temple's firm towering makes visible the invisible space of air. The steadfastness of the work contrasts with the surge of the surf, and its own repose brings out the raging of the sea. Tree and grass, eagle and bull, snake and cricket first enter into their distinctive shapes and thus come to appear as what they are. The Greeks early called this emerging and rising in itself and in all things *phusis*. It clears and illuminates, also, that on which and in which man bases his dwelling. We call this ground the *earth*. What this word says is not to be associated with the idea of a mass of matter deposited somewhere, or with the merely astronomical idea of a planet. Earth is that whence the arising brings back and shelters everything that arises without violation. In the things that arise, earth is present as the sheltering agent.

The temple-work, standing there, opens up a world and at the same time sets this world back again on earth, which itself only thus emerges as native ground. But men and animals, plants and things, are never present and familiar as unchangeable objects, only to represent incidentally also a fitting environment for the temple, which one fine day is added to what is already there. We shall get closer to what *is*, rather, if we think of all this in reverse order, assuming of course that we have, to begin with, an eye for how differently everything then faces us. Mere reversing, done for its own sake, reveals nothing.

The temple, in its standing there, first gives to things their look and to men their outlook on themselves. This view remains open as long as the work is a work, as long as the god has not fled from it. It is the same with the sculpture of the god, votive offering of the victor in the athletic games. It is not a portrait whose purpose is to make it easier to realize how the god looks; rather, it is a work that lets the god himself be present and thus *is* the god himself. The same holds for the linguistic work. In the tragedy nothing is staged or displayed theatrically, but the battle of the new gods against the old is being fought. The linguistic work, originating in the speech of the people, does not refer to this battle; it transforms the people's saying so that now every living word fights the battle and puts up for decision what is holy and what unholy, what great and what small, what brave and what cowardly, what lofty and what flighty, what master and what slave (cf. Heraclitus, Fragment 53).

In what, then, does the work-being of the work consist? Keeping steadily in view the points just crudely enough indicated, two essential features of the work may for the moment be brought out more distinctly. We set out here, from the long familiar foreground of the work's being, the thingly character which gives support to our customary attitude toward the work.

When a work is brought into a collection or placed in an exhibition we say also that it is 'set up.' But this setting up differs essentially from setting up in the sense of erecting a building, raising a statue, presenting a tragedy at a holy festival. Such setting up is erecting in the sense of dedication and praise. Here 'setting up' no longer means a bare placing. To dedicate means to consecrate, in the sense that in setting up the work the holy is opened up as holy and the god is invoked into the openness of his presence. Praise belongs to dedication as doing honor to the dignity and splendor of the god. Dignity and splendor are not properties beside and behind which the god, too, stands as something distinct, but it is rather in the dignity, in the splendor that the god is present. In the reflected glory of this splendor there glows, i.e., there lightens itself, what we called the word. To e-rect means: to open the right in the sense of a guiding measure, a form in which what belongs to the nature of being gives guidance. But why is the setting up of a work an erecting that consecrates and praises? Because the work, in its work-being, demands it. How is it that the work comes to demand such a setting up? Because it itself, in its own work-being, is something that sets up. What does the work, as work, set up? Towering up within itself, the work opens up a *world* and keeps it abidingly in force.

To be a work means to set up a world. But what is it to be a world? The answer was hinted at when we referred to the temple. On the path we must follow here, the nature of world can only be indicated. What is more, this indication limits itself to warding off anything that might at first distort our view of the world's nature.

The world is not the mere collection of the countable or uncountable, familiar and unfamiliar things that are just there. But neither is it a merely imagined framework added by our representation to the sum of such given things. The *world worlds*, and is more fully in being than the tangible and perceptible realm in which we believe ourselves to be at home. World is never an object that stands before us and can be seen. World is the ever-nonobjective to which we are subject as long as the paths of birth and death, blessing and curse keep us transported into Being. Wherever those decisions of our history that relate to our very being are made, are taken up and abandoned by us, go unrecognized and are rediscovered by new inquiry, there the world worlds. A stone is worldless. Plant and animal likewise have no world; but they belong to the covert throng of a surrounding into which they are linked. The peasant woman, on the other hand, has a world because she dwells in the overtness of beings, of the things that are. Her equipment, in its reliability, gives to this world a necessity and nearness of its own. By the opening up of a world, all things gain their lingering and hastening, their remoteness and nearness, their scope and limits. In a world's worlding is gathered that spaciousness out of which the protective grace of the gods is granted or withheld. Even this doom of the god remaining absent is a way in which world worlds.

A work, by being a work, makes space for that spaciousness. 'To make space for' means here especially to liberate the Open and to establish it in its structure. This in-stalling occurs through the erecting mentioned earlier. The work as work sets up a world. The work holds open the Open of the world. But the setting up of a world is only the first essential feature in the work-being of a work to be referred to here. Starting again from the foreground of the work, we shall attempt to make clear in the same way the second essential feature that belongs with the first.

When a work is created, brought forth out of this or that work-material – stone, wood, metal, color, language, tone – we say also that it is made, set forth out of it. But just as the work requires a setting up in the sense of a consecrating-praising erection, because the work's work-being consists in the setting up of a world, so a setting forth is needed because the work-being of the work itself has the character of setting forth. The work as work, in its presencing, is a setting forth, a making. But what does the work set forth? We come to know about this only when we explore what comes to the fore and is customarily spoken of as the making or production of works.

To work-being there belongs the setting up of a world. Thinking of it within this perspective, what is the nature of that in the work which is usually called the work material? Because it is determined by usefulness and serviceability, equipment takes into its service that of which it consists: the matter. In fabricating equipment – e.g., an ax – stone is used, and used up. It disappears into usefulness. The material is all the better and more suitable the less it resists perishing in the equipmental being of the equipment. By contrast the temple-work, in setting up a world, does not cause the material to disappear, but rather causes it to come forth for the very first time and to come into the Open of the work's world. The rock comes to bear and rest and so first becomes rock; metals come to glitter and shimmer, colors to glow, tones to sing, the word to speak. All this comes forth as the work sets itself back into the massiveness and heaviness of stone, into the firmness and pliancy of wood, into the hardness and luster of metal, into the lighting and darkening of color, into the clang of tone, and into the naming power of the word.

That into which the work sets itself back and which it causes to come forth in this setting back of itself we called the earth. Earth is that which comes forth and shelters. Earth, self-dependent, is effortless and untiring. Upon the earth and in it, historical man grounds his dwelling in the world. In setting up a world, the work sets forth the earth. This setting forth must be thought here in the strict sense of the word. The work moves the earth itself into the Open of a world and keeps it there. *The work lets the earth be an earth.*

But why must this setting forth of the earth happen in such a way that the work sets itself back into it? What is the earth that it attains to the unconcealed in just such a manner? A stone presses downward and manifests its heaviness. But while this heaviness exerts an opposing pressure upon us it denies us any penetration into it. If we attempt such a penetration by breaking open the rock, it still does not display in its fragments anything inward that has been disclosed. The stone has instantly withdrawn again into the same dull pressure and bulk of its fragments. If we try to lay hold of the stone's heaviness in another way, by placing the stone on a balance, we merely bring the heaviness into the form of a calculated weight. This perhaps very precise determination of the stone remains a number, but the weight's burden has escaped us. Color shines and wants only to shine. When we analyze it in rational terms by measuring its wavelengths, it is gone. It shows itself only when it remains undisclosed and unexplained. Earth thus shatters every attempt to penetrate into it. It causes every merely calculating importunity upon it to turn into a destruction. This destruction may herald itself under the appearance of mastery and of progress in the form of the technical-scientific objectivation of nature, but this mastery nevertheless remains an impotence of will. The earth appears openly cleared as itself only when it is perceived and preserved as that which is by nature undisclosable, that which shrinks from every disclosure and constantly keeps itself closed up. All things of earth, and the earth itself as a whole, flow together into a reciprocal accord. But this confluence is not a blurring of their outlines. Here there flows the stream, restful within itself, of the setting of bounds, which delimits everything present within its presence. Thus in each of the self-secluding things there is the same not-knowing-of-one-another. The earth is essentially self-secluding. To set forth the earth means to bring it into the Open as the self-secluding.

This setting forth of the earth is achieved by the work as it sets itself back into the earth. The self-seclusion of earth, however, is not a uniform, inflexible staying under cover, but unfolds itself in an inexhaustible variety of simple modes and shapes. To be sure, the sculptor uses stone just as the mason uses it, in his own way. But he does not use it up. That happens in a certain way only where the work miscarries. To be sure, the painter also uses pigment, but in such a way that color is not used up but rather only now comes to shine forth. To be sure, the poet also uses the word – not, however, like ordinary speakers and writers who have to use them up, but rather in such a way that the word only now becomes and remains truly a word.

Nowhere in the work is there any trace of a work-material. It even remains doubtful whether, in the essential definition of equipment, what the equipment consists of is properly described in its equipmental nature as matter.

The setting up of a world and the setting forth of earth are two essential features in the work-being of the work. They belong together, however, in the unity of work-being. This is the unity we seek when we ponder the self-subsistence of the work and try to express in words this closed, unitary repose of self-support.

But in the essential features just mentioned, if our account has any validity at all, we have indicated in the work rather a happening and in no sense a repose, for what is rest if not the opposite of motion? It is at any rate not an opposite that excludes motion from itself, but rather includes it. Only what is in motion can rest. The mode of rest varies with the kind of motion. In motion as the mere displacement of a body, rest is, to be sure, only the limiting case of motion. Where rest includes motion, there can exist a repose which is an inner concentration of motion, hence a highest state of agitation, assuming that the mode of motion requires such a rest. Now the repose of the work that rests in itself is of this sort. We shall therefore come nearer to this repose if we can succeed in grasping the state of movement of the happening in work-being in its full unity. We ask: What relation do the setting up of a world and the setting forth of the earth exhibit in the work itself?

The world is the self-disclosing openness of the broad paths of the simple and essential decisions in the destiny of an historical people. The earth is the spontaneous forthcoming of that which is continually self-secluding and to that extent sheltering and concealing. World and earth are essentially different from one another and yet are never separated. The world grounds itself on the earth, and earth juts through world. But the relation between world and earth does not wither away into the empty unity of opposites unconcerned with one another. The world, in resting upon the earth, strives to surmount it. As self-opening it cannot endure anything closed. The earth, however, as sheltering and concealing, tends always to draw the world into itself and keep it there.

The opposition of world and earth is a striving. But we would surely all too easily falsify its nature if we were to confound striving with discord and dispute, and thus see it only as disorder and destruction. In essential striving, rather, the opponents raise each other into the self-assertion of their natures. Self-assertion of nature, however, is never a rigid insistence upon some contingent state, but surrender to the concealed originality of the source of one's own being. In the struggle, each opponent carries the other beyond itself. Thus the striving becomes ever more intense as striving, and more authentically what it is. The more the struggle overdoes itself on its own part, the more inflexibly do the opponents let themselves go into the intimacy of simple belonging to one another. The earth cannot dispense with the Open of the world if it itself is to appear as earth in the liberated surge of its self-seclusion. The world, again, cannot soar out of the earth's sight if, as the governing breadth and path of all essential destiny, it is to ground itself on a resolute foundation.

In setting up a world and setting forth the earth, the work is an instigating of this striving. This does not happen so that the work should at the same time settle and put an end to the conflict in an insipid agreement, but so that the strife may remain a strife. Setting up a world and setting forth the earth, the work accomplishes this striving. The work-being of the work consists in the fighting of the battle between world and earth. It is because the struggle arrives at its high point in the simplicity of intimacy that the unity of the work comes about in the fighting of the battle. The fighting of the battle is the continually self-overreaching gathering of the work's agitation. The repose of the work that rests in itself thus has its presencing in the intimacy of striving.

From this repose of the work we can now first see what is at work in the work. Until now it was a merely provisional assertion that in an art work the truth is set to work. In what way does truth happen in the work-being of the work, i.e., now, how does truth happen in the fighting of the battle between world and earth? What is truth?

How slight and stunted our knowledge of the nature of truth is, is shown by the laxity we permit ourselves in using this basic word. By truth is usually meant this or that particular truth. That means: something true. A cognition articulated in a proposition can be of this sort. However, we call not only a proposition true, but also a thing, true gold in contrast with sham gold. True here means genuine, real gold. What does the expression 'real' mean here? To us it is what is in truth. The true is what corresponds to the real, and the real is what is in truth. The circle has closed again.

What does 'in truth' mean? Truth is the essence of the true. What do we have in mind when speaking of essence? Usually it is thought to be those features held in common by everything that is true. The essence is discovered in the generic and universal concept, which represents the one feature that holds indifferently for many things. This indifferent essence (essentiality in the sense of *essentia*) is, however, only the inessential essence. What does the essential essence of something consist in? Presumably it lies in what the entity *is* in truth. The true essential nature of a thing is determined by way of its true being, by way of the truth of the given being. But we are now seeking not the truth of essential nature but the essential nature of truth. There thus appears a curious tangle. Is it only a curiosity or even merely the empty sophistry of a conceptual game, or is it – an abyss?

Truth means the nature of the true. We think this nature in recollecting the Greek word *aletheia*, the unconcealedness of beings. But is this enough to define the nature of truth? Are we not passing off a mere change of word usage – unconcealedness instead of truth – as a characterization of fact? Certainly we do not get beyond an interchange of names as long as we do not come to know what must have happened in order to be compelled to tell the *nature* of truth in the word 'unconcealedness.'

Does this require a revival of Greek philosophy? Not at all. A revival, even if such an impossibility were possible, would be of no help to us; for the hidden history of Greek philosophy consists from its beginning in this, that it does not remain in conformity with the nature of truth that flashes out in the word *aletheia*, and has to misdirect its knowing and its speaking about the nature of truth more and more into the discussion of a derivative nature of truth. The nature of truth as *aletheia* was not thought out in the thinking of the Greeks nor since then, and least of all in the philosophy that followed after. Unconcealedness is, for thought, the most concealed thing in Greek existence, although from early times it determines the presence of everything present.

Yet why should we not be satisfied with the nature of truth that has by now been familiar to us for centuries? Truth means today and has long meant the agreement or conformity of knowledge with fact. However, the fact must show itself to be fact if knowledge and the proposition that forms and expresses knowledge are to be able to conform to the fact; otherwise the fact cannot become binding on the proposition. How can fact show itself if it cannot itself stand forth out of concealedness, if it does not itself stand in the unconcealed? A proposition is true by conforming to the unconcealed, to what is true. Propositional truth is always, and always exclusively, this correctness. The critical concepts of truth which, since Descartes, start out from truth as certainty, are merely variations of the definition of truth as correctness. This nature of truth which is familiar to us – correctness in representation – stands and falls with truth as unconcealedness of beings.

If here and elsewhere we conceive of truth as unconcealedness, we are not merely taking refuge in a more literal translation of a Greek word. We are reminding ourselves of what, unexperienced and unthought, underlies our familiar and therefore outworn nature of truth in the sense of correctness. We do, of course, occasionally take the trouble to concede that naturally, in order to understand and verify the correctness (truth) of a proposition one really should go back to something that is already evident, and that this presupposition is indeed unavoidable. As long as we talk and believe in this way, we always understand truth merely as correctness, which of course still requires a further presupposition, that we ourselves just happen to make, heaven knows how or why.

But it is not we who presuppose the unconcealedness of beings; rather, the unconcealedness of beings (Being) puts us into such a condition of being that in our representation we always remain installed within and in attendance upon unconcealedness. Not only must that in *conformity* with which a cognition orders itself be already in some way unconcealed. The entire *realm* in which this 'conforming to something' goes on must already occur as a whole in the unconcealed; and this holds equally of that *for* which the conformity of a proposition to fact becomes manifest. With all our correct representations we would get nowhere, we could not even presuppose that there already is manifest something to which we can conform ourselves, unless the unconcealedness of beings had already exposed us to, placed us in that lighted realm in which every being stands for us and from which it withdraws.

But how does this take place? How does truth happen as this unconcealedness? First, however, we must say more clearly what this unconcealedness itself is.

Things are, and human beings, gifts, and sacrifices are, animals and plants are, equipment and works are. That which is, the particular being, stands in Being. Through Being there passes a veiled destiny that is ordained between the godly and the countergodly. There is much in being that man cannot master. There is but little that comes to be known. What is known remains inexact, what is mastered insecure. What is, is never of our making or even merely the product of our minds, as it might all too easily seem. When we contemplate this whole as one, then we apprehend, so it appears, all that is – though we grasp it crudely enough.

And yet – beyond what is, not away from it but before it, there is still something else that happens. In the midst of beings as a whole an open place occurs. There is a clearing, a lighting. Thought of in reference to what is, to beings, this clearing is in a greater degree than are beings. This open center is therefore not surrounded by what is; rather, the lighting center itself encircles all that is, like the Nothing which we scarcely know.

That which is can only be, as a being, if it stands within and stands out within what is lighted in this clearing. Only this clearing grants and guarantees to us humans a passage to those beings that we ourselves are not, and access to the being that we ourselves are. Thanks to this clearing, beings are unconcealed in certain changing degrees. And yet a being can be *concealed*, too, only within the sphere of what is lighted. Each being we encounter and which encounters us keeps to this curious opposition of presence in that it always withholds itself at the same time in a concealedness. The clearing in which beings stand is in itself at the same time concealment. Concealment, however, prevails in the midst of beings in a twofold way.

Beings refuse themselves to us down to that one and seemingly least feature which we touch upon most readily when we can say no more of beings than that they are. Concealment as refusal is not simply and only the limit of knowledge in any given circumstance, but the beginning of the clearing of what is lighted. But concealment, though of another sort, to be sure, at the same time also occurs within what is lighted. One being places itself in front of another being, the one helps to hide the other, the former obscures the latter, a few obstruct many, one denies all. Here concealment is not simple refusal. Rather, a being appears, but it presents itself as other than it is.

This concealment is dissembling. If one being did not simulate another, we could not make mistakes or act mistakenly in regard to beings; we could not go astray and transgress, and especially could never overreach ourselves. That a being should be able to deceive as semblance is the condition for our being able to be deceived, not conversely.

Concealment can be a refusal or merely a dissembling. We are never fully certain whether it is the one or the other. Concealment conceals and dissembles itself. This means: the open place in the midst of beings, the clearing, is never a rigid stage with a permanently raised curtain on which the play of beings runs its course. Rather, the clearing happens only as this double concealment. The unconcealedness of beings – this is never a merely existent state, but a happening. Unconcealedness (truth) is neither an attribute of factual things in the sense of beings, nor one of propositions.

We believe we are at home in the immediate circle of beings. That which is, is familiar, reliable, ordinary. Nevertheless, the clearing is pervaded by a constant concealment in the double form of refusal and dissembling. At bottom, the ordinary is not ordinary; it is extra-ordinary, uncanny. The nature of truth, that is, of unconcealedness, is dominated throughout by a denial. Yet this denial is not a defect or a fault, as though truth were an unalloyed unconcealedness that has rid itself of everything concealed. If truth could accomplish this, it would no longer be itself. *This denial, in the form of a double concealment, belongs to the nature of truth as unconcealedness*. Truth, in its nature, is un-truth. We put the matter this way in order to serve notice, with a possibly surprising trenchancy, that denial in the manner of concealment belongs to unconcealedness as clearing. The proposition, 'the nature of truth is untruth,' is not, however, intended to state that truth is at bottom falsehood. Nor does it mean that truth is never itself but, viewed dialectically, is always also its opposite.

Truth occurs precisely as itself in that the concealing denial, as refusal, provides its constant source to all clearing, and yet, as dissembling, it metes out to all clearing the indefeasible severity of error. Concealing denial is intended to denote that opposition in the nature of truth which subsists between clearing, or lighting, and concealing. It is the opposition of the primal conflict. The nature of truth is, in itself, the primal conflict in which that open center is won within which what is, stands, and from which it sets itself back into itself.

This Open happens in the midst of beings. It exhibits an essential feature which we have already mentioned. To the Open there belong a world and the earth. But the world is not simply the Open that corresponds to clearing, and the earth is not simply the Closed that corresponds to concealment. Rather, the world is the clearing of the paths of the essential guiding directions with which all decision complies. Every decision, however, bases itself on something not mastered, something concealed, confusing; else it would never be a decision. The earth is not simply the Closed but rather that which rises up as self-closing. World and earth are always intrinsically and essentially in conflict, belligerent by nature. Only as such do they enter into the conflict of clearing and concealing.

Earth juts through the world and world grounds itself on the earth only so far as truth happens as the primal conflict between clearing and concealing. But how does truth happen? We answer: it happens in a few essential ways. One of these ways in which truth happens is the work-being of the work. Setting up a world and setting forth the earth, the work is the fighting of the battle in which the unconcealedness of beings as a whole, or truth, is won.

Truth happens in the temple's standing where it is. This does not mean that something is correctly represented and rendered here, but that what is as a whole is brought into unconcealedness and held therein. To hold (*halten*) originally means to tend, keep, take care (*hüten*). Truth happens in Van Gogh's painting. This does not mean that something is correctly portrayed, but rather that in the revelation of the equipmental being of the shoes, that which is as a whole – world and earth in their counterplay – attains to unconcealedness.

Thus in the work it is truth, not only something true, that is at work. The picture that shows the peasant shoes, the poem that says the Roman fountain, do not just make manifest what this isolated being as such is – if indeed they manifest anything at all; rather, they make unconcealedness as such happen in regard to what is as a whole. The more simply and authentically the shoes are engrossed in their nature, the more plainly and purely the fountain is engrossed in its nature – the more directly and engagingly do all beings attain to a greater degree of being along with them. That is how self-concealing being is illuminated. Light of this kind joins its shining to and into the work. This shining, joined in the work, is the beautiful. *Beauty is one way in which truth occurs as unconcealedness.*

We now, indeed, grasp the nature of truth more clearly in certain respects. What is at work in the work may accordingly have become more clear. But the work's now visible work-being still does not tell us anything about the work's closest and most obtrusive reality, about the thingly aspect of the work. Indeed it almost seems as though, in pursuing the exclusive aim of grasping the work's independence as purely as possible, we had completely overlooked the one thing, that a work is always a work, which means that it is something worked out, brought about, effected. If there is anything that distinguishes the work as work, it is that the work has been created. Since the work is created, and creation requires a medium out of which and in which it creates, the thingly element, too, enters into the work. This is incontestable.

* * *

Truth and art

But what looks like the thingly element, in the sense of our usual thing-concepts, in the work taken as object, is, seen from the perspective of the work, its earthy character. The earth juts up within the work because the work exists as something in which truth is at work and because truth occurs only by installing itself within a particular being. In the earth, however, as essentially self-closing, the openness of the Open finds the greatest resistance (to the Open) and thereby the site of the Open's constant stand, where the figure must be fixed in place.

Was it then superfluous, after all, to enter into the question of the thingly character of the thing? By no means. To be sure, the work's work-character cannot be defined in terms of its thingly character, but as against that the question about the thing's thingly character can be brought into the right course by way of a knowledge of the work's work-character. This is no small matter, if we recollect that those ancient, traditional modes of thought attack the thing's thingly character and make it subject to an interpretation of what is as a whole, which remains unfit to apprehend the nature of equipment and of the work, and which makes us equally blind to the original nature of truth.

To determine the thing's thingness neither consideration of the bearer of properties is adequate, nor that of the manifold of sense data in their unity, and least of all that of the matter–form structure regarded by itself, which is derived from equipment. Anticipating a meaningful and weighty interpretation of the thingly character of things, we must aim at the thing's belonging to the earth. The nature of the earth, in its free and unhurried bearing and self-closure, reveals itself, however, only in the earth's jutting into a world, in the opposition of the two. This conflict is fixed in place in the figure of the work and becomes manifest by it. What holds true of equipment – namely that we come to know its equipmental character specifically only through the work itself – also holds of the thingly character of the thing. The fact that we never know thingness directly, and if we know it at all, then only vaguely and thus require the work – this fact proves indirectly that in the work's work-being the happening of truth, the opening up or disclosure of what is, is at work.

* * *

Truth, as the clearing and concealing of what is, happens in being composed, as a poet composes a poem. *All art*, as the letting happen of the advent of the truth of what is, is, as such, *essentially poetry*. The nature of art, on which both the art work and the artist depend, is the setting-itself-into-work of truth. It is due to art's poetic nature that, in the midst of what is, art breaks open an open place, in whose openness everything is other than usual. By virtue of the projected sketch set into the work of the unconcealedness of what is, which casts itself toward us, everything ordinary and hitherto existing becomes an unbeing. This unbeing has lost the capacity to give and keep being as measure. The curious fact here is that the work in no way affects hitherto existing entities by causal connections. The working of the work does not consist in the taking effect of a cause. It lies in a change, happening from out of the work, of the unconcealedness of what is, and this means, of Being.

Poetry, however, is not an aimless imagining of whimsicalities and not a flight of mere notions and fancies into the realm of the unreal. What poetry, as illuminating projection, unfolds of unconcealedness and projects ahead into the design of the figure, is the Open which poetry lets happen, and indeed in such a way that only now, in the midst of beings, the Open brings beings to shine and ring out. If we fix our vision on the nature of the work and its connection with the happening of the truth of what is, it becomes questionable whether the nature of poetry, and this means at the same time the nature of projection, can be adequately thought of in terms of the power of imagination.

The nature of poetry, which has now been ascertained very broadly – but not on that account vaguely, may here be kept firmly in mind as something worthy of questioning, something that still has to be thought through.

If all art is in essence poetry, then the arts of architecture, painting, sculpture, and music must be traced back to poesy. That is pure arbitrariness. It certainly is, as long as we mean that those arts are varieties of the art of language, if it is permissible to characterize poesy by that easily misinterpretable title. But poesy is only one mode of the lighting projection of truth, i.e., of poetic composition in this wider sense. Nevertheless, the linguistic work, the poem in the narrower sense, has a privileged position in the domain of the arts.

To see this, only the right concept of language is needed. In the current view, language is held to be a kind of communication. It serves for verbal exchange and agreement, and in general for communicating. But language is not only and not primarily an audible and written expression of what is to be communicated. It not only puts forth in words and statements what is overtly or covertly intended to be communicated; language alone brings what is, as something that is, into the Open for the first time. Where there is no language, as in the being of stone, plant, and animal, there is also no openness of what is, and consequently no openness either of that which is not and of the empty.

Language, by naming beings for the first time, first brings beings to word and to appearance. Only this naming nominates beings *to* their being *from out of* their being. Such saying is a projecting of the clearing, in which announcement is made of what it is that beings come into the Open *as*. Projecting is the release of a throw by which unconcealedness submits and infuses itself into what is as such. This projective announcement forthwith becomes a renunciation of all the dim confusion in which what is veils and withdraws itself.

Projective saying is poetry: the saying of world and earth, the saying of the arena of their conflict and thus of the place of all nearness and remoteness of the gods. Poetry is the saying of the unconcealedness of what is. Actual language at any given moment is the happening of this saying, in which a people's world historically arises for it and the earth is preserved as that which remains closed. Projective saying is saying which, in preparing the sayable, simultaneously brings the unsayable as such into a world. In such saying, the concepts of an historical people's nature, i.e., of its belonging to world history, are formed for that folk, before it.

Poetry is thought of here in so broad a sense and at the same time in such intimate unity of being with language and word, that we must leave open whether art, in all its modes from architecture to poesy, exhausts the nature of poetry.

Language itself is poetry in the essential sense. But since language is the happening in which for man beings first disclose themselves to him each time as beings, poesy – or poetry in the narrower sense – is the most original form of poetry in the essential sense. Language is not poetry because it is the primal poesy; rather, poesy takes place in language because language preserves the original nature of poetry. Building and plastic creation, on the other hand, always happen already, and happen only, in the Open of saying and naming. It is the Open that pervades and guides them. But for this very reason they remain their own ways and modes in which truth orders itself into work. They are an ever special poetizing within the clearing of what is, which has already happened unnoticed in language.

Art, as the setting-into-work of truth, is poetry. Not only the creation of the work is poetic, but equally poetic, though in its own way, is the preserving of the work; for a work is in actual effect as a work only when we remove ourselves from our commonplace routine and move into what is disclosed by the work, so as to bring our own nature itself to take a stand in the truth of what is.

The nature of art is poetry. The nature of poetry, in turn, is the founding of truth. We understand founding here in a triple sense: founding as bestowing, founding as grounding, and founding as beginning. Founding, however, is actual only in preserving. Thus to each mode of founding there corresponds a mode of preserving. We can do no more now than to present this structure of the nature of art in a few strokes, and even this only to the extent that the earlier characterization of the nature of the work offers an initial hint.

The setting-into-work of truth thrusts up the unfamiliar and extraordinary and at the same time thrusts down the ordinary and what we believe to be such. The truth that discloses itself in the work can never be proved or derived from what went before. What went before is refuted in its exclusive reality by the work. What art founds can therefore never be compensated and made up for by what is already present and available. Founding is an overflow, an endowing, a bestowal.

The poetic projection of truth that sets itself into work as figure is also never carried out in the direction of an indeterminate void. Rather, in the work, truth is thrown toward the coming preservers, that is, toward an historical group of men. What is thus cast forth is, however, never an arbitrary demand. Genuinely poetic projection is the opening up or disclosure of that into which human being as historical is already cast. This is the earth and, for an historical people, its earth, the self-closing ground on which it rests together with everything that it already is, though still hidden from itself. It is, however, its world, which prevails in virtue of the relation of human being to the unconcealedness of Being. For this reason, everything with which man is endowed must, in the projection, be drawn up from the closed ground and expressly set upon this ground. In this way the ground is first grounded as the bearing ground.

All creation, because it is such a drawing-up, is a drawing, as of water from a spring. Modern subjectivism, to be sure, immediately misinterprets creation, taking it as the self-sovereign subject's performance of genius. The founding of truth is a founding not only in the sense of free bestowal, but at the same time foundation in the sense of this ground-laying grounding. Poetic projection comes from Nothing in this respect, that it never takes its gift from the ordinary and traditional. But it never comes from Nothing in that what is projected by it is only the withheld vocation of the historical being of man itself.

Bestowing and grounding have in themselves the unmediated character of what we call a beginning. Yet this unmediated character of a beginning, the peculiarity of a leap out of the unmediable, does not exclude but rather includes the fact that the beginning prepares itself for the longest time and wholly inconspicuously. A genuine beginning, as a leap, is always a head start, in which everything to come is already leaped over, even if as something disguised. The beginning already contains the end latent within itself. A genuine beginning, however, has nothing of the neophyte character of the primitive. The primitive, because it lacks the bestowing, grounding leap and head start, is always futureless. It is not capable of releasing anything more from itself because it contains nothing more than that in which it is caught.

A beginning, on the contrary, always contains the undisclosed abundance of the unfamiliar and extraordinary, which means that it also contains strife with the familiar and ordinary. Art as poetry is founding, in the third sense of instigation of the strife of truth: founding as beginning. Always when that which is as a whole demands, as what is, itself, a grounding in openness, art attains to its historical nature as foundation. This foundation happened in the West for the first time in Greece. What was in the future to be called Being was set into work, setting the standard. The realm of beings thus opened up was then transformed into a being in the sense of God's creation. This happened in the Middle Ages. This kind of being was again transformed at the beginning and in the course of the modern age. Beings became objects that could be controlled and seen through by calculation. At each time a new and essential world arose. At each time the openness of what is had to be established in beings themselves, by the fixing in place of truth in figure. At each time there happened unconcealedness of what is. Unconcealedness sets itself into work, a setting which is accomplished by art.

Whenever art happens – that is, whenever there is a beginning – a thrust enters history, history either begins or starts over again. History means here not a sequence in time of events of whatever sort, however important. History is the transporting of a people into its appointed task as entrance into that people's endowment.

Art is the setting-into-work of truth. In this proposition an essential ambiguity is hidden, in which truth is at once the subject and the object of the setting. But subject and object are unsuitable names here. They keep us from thinking precisely this ambiguous nature, a task that no longer belongs to this consideration. Art is historical, and as historical it is the creative preserving of truth in the work. Art happens as poetry. Poetry is founding in the triple sense of bestowing, grounding, and beginning. Art, as founding, is essentially historical. This means not only that art has a history in the external sense that in the course of time it, too, appears along with many other things, and in the process changes and passes away and offers changing aspects for historiology. Art is history in the essential sense that it grounds history.

Art lets truth originate. Art, founding preserving, is the spring that leaps to the truth of what is, in the work. To originate something by a leap, to bring something into being from out of the source of its nature in a founding leap – this is what the word origin (German *Ursprung*, literally, primal leap) means.

The origin of the work of art – that is, the origin of both the creators and the preservers, which is to say of a people's historical existence, is art. This is so because art is by nature an origin: a distinctive way in which truth comes into being, that is, becomes historical.

We inquire into the nature of art. Why do we inquire in this way? We inquire in this way in order to be able to ask more truly whether art is or is not an origin in our historical existence, whether and under what conditions it can and must be an origin.

Such reflection cannot force art and its coming-to-be. But this reflective knowledge is the preliminary and therefore indispensable preparation for the becoming of art. Only such knowledge prepares its space for art, their way for the creators, their location for the preservers.

In such knowledge, which can only grow slowly, the question is decided whether art can be an origin and then must be a head start, or whether it is to remain a mere appendix and then can only be carried along as a routine cultural phenomenon.

Are we in our existence historically at the origin? Do we know, which means do we give heed to, the nature of the origin? Or, in our relation to art, do we still merely make appeal to a cultivated acquaintance with the past?

For this either–or and its decision there is an infallible sign. Hölderlin, the poet – whose work still confronts the Germans as a test to be stood – named it in saying:

Schwer verlässt
was nahe dem Ursprung wohnet, den Ort.

Reluctantly
that which dwells near its origin departs.
('The Journey,' verses 18–19)

Translated by Albert Hofstadter

5

WHAT IS WRITING?

Jean-Paul Sartre

No, we do not want to 'commit' painting, sculpture, and music 'too', or at least not in the same way.[1] And why would we want to? When a writer of past centuries expressed an opinion about his craft, was he immediately asked to apply it to the other arts? But today it's the thing to 'talk painting' in the jargon of the musician or the literary man and to 'talk literature' in the jargon of the painter, as if at bottom there were only one art which expressed itself indifferently in one or the other of these languages, like the Spinozistic substance which is adequately reflected by each of its attributes.

Doubtless, one could find at the origin of every artistic calling a certain undifferentiated choice which circumstances, education, and contact with the world particularized only later. Besides, there is no doubt that the arts of a period mutually influence each other and are conditioned by the same social factors. But those who want to expose the absurdity of a literary theory by showing that it is inapplicable to music must first prove that the arts are parallel.

Now, there is no such parallelism. Here, as everywhere, it is not only the form which differentiates, but the matter as well. And it is one thing to work with colour and sound, and another to express oneself by means of words. Notes, colours, and forms are not signs. They refer to nothing exterior to themselves. To be sure, it is quite impossible to reduce them strictly to themselves, and the idea of a pure sound, for example, is an abstraction. As Merleau-Ponty has pointed out in *The Phenomenology of Perception*, there is no quality of sensation so bare that it is not penetrated with significance. But the dim little meaning which dwells within it, a light joy, a timid sadness, remains immanent or trembles about it like a heat mist; it *is* colour or sound. Who can distinguish the green apple from its tart gaiety? And aren't we already saying too much in naming 'the tart gaiety of the green apple'? There is green, there is red, and that is all. They are things, they exist by themselves.

It is true that one might, by convention, confer the value of signs upon them. Thus, we talk of the language of flowers. But, if after the agreement, white roses signify 'fidelity' to me, the fact is that I have stopped seeing them as roses. My attention cuts through them to aim beyond them at this abstract virtue. I forget them. I no longer pay attention to their mossy abundance, to their sweet stagnant odour. I have not even perceived them. That means that I have not behaved like an artist. For the artist, the colour, the bouquet, the tinkling of the spoon on the saucer, are *things*, in the highest degree. He stops at the quality of the sound or the form. He returns to it constantly and is enchanted with it. It is this colour-object that he is going to transfer to his canvas, and the only modification he will make it undergo is that he will transform it into an *imaginary* object. He is therefore as far as he can be from considering colours and signs as a *language*.[2]

What is valid for the elements of artistic creation is also valid for their combinations. The painter does not want to draw signs on his canvas, he wants to create a thing.[3] And if he puts together red, yellow, and green, there is no reason why this collection of colours should have a definable significance, that is, should refer particularly to another object. Doubtless the composition is also inhabited by a soul, and since there must have been motives, even hidden ones, for the painter to have chosen yellow rather than violet, it may be asserted that the objects thus created reflect his deepest tendencies. However, they never express his anger, his anguish, or his joy as do words or the expression of the face; they are impregnated with these emotions; and in order for them to have crept into these colours, which by themselves already had something like a meaning, his emotions get mixed up and grow obscure. Nobody can quite recognize them there.

Tintoretto did not choose that yellow rift in the sky above Golgotha to *signify* anguish or to *provoke* it. It is anguish and yellow sky at the same time. Not sky of anguish or anguished sky; it is an anguish become thing, an anguish which has turned into yellow rift of sky, and which thereby is submerged and impasted by the qualities peculiar to things, by their impermeability, their extension, their blind permanence, their externality, and that infinity of relations which they maintain with other things. That is, it is no longer *readable*. It is like an immense and vain effort, forever arrested half-way between sky and earth, to express what their nature keeps them from expressing.

Similarly, the significance of a melody – if one can still speak of significance – is nothing outside the melody itself, unlike ideas, which can be adequately rendered in several ways. Call it joyous or sad. It will always be over and above anything you can say about it. Not because its passions, which are perhaps at the origin of the invented theme, have, by being incorporated into notes, undergone a transubstantiation and a transmutation. A cry of grief is a sign of the grief which provokes it, but a song of grief is both grief itself and something other than grief. Or, if one wishes to adopt the existentialist vocabulary, it is a grief which does not *exist* any more, which *is*. But, you will say, suppose the painter portrays houses? That's just it. He *makes* them, that is, he creates an imaginary house on the canvas and not a sign of a house. And the house which thus appears preserves all the ambiguity of real houses.

The writer can guide you and, if he describes a hovel, make it seem the symbol of social injustice and provoke your indignation. The painter is mute. He presents you with *a* hovel, that's all. You are free to see in it what you like. That attic window will never be the symbol of misery; for that, it would have to be a sign, whereas it is a thing. The bad painter looks for the type. He paints the Arab, the Child, the Woman; the good one knows that neither the Arab nor the proletarian exists either in reality or on his canvas. He offers a workman, a certain workman. And what are we to think about a workman? An infinity of contradictory things. All thoughts and all feelings are there, adhering to the canvas in a state of profound undifferentiation. It is up to you to choose. Sometimes, high-minded artists try to move us. They paint long lines of workmen waiting in the snow to be hired, the emaciated faces of the unemployed, battlefields. They affect us no more than does Greuze with his *Prodigal Son*. And that masterpiece, *The Massacre of Guernica*, does anyone think that it won over a single heart to the Spanish cause? And yet something is said that can never quite be heard and that would take an infinity of words to express. And Picasso's long harlequins, ambiguous and eternal, haunted with inexplicable meaning, inseparable from their stooping leanness and their pale diamond-shaped tights, are emotion become flesh, emotion which the flesh has absorbed as the blotter absorbs ink, and emotion which is unrecognizable, lost, strange to itself, scattered to the four corners of space and yet present to itself.

I have no doubt that charity or anger can produce other objects, but they will likewise be swallowed up; they will lose their name; there will remain only things haunted by a mysterious soul. One does not paint meanings; one does not put them to music. Under these conditions, who would dare require that the painter or musician commit himself?

On the other hand, the writer deals with meanings. Still, a distinction must be made. The empire of signs is prose; poetry is on the side of painting, sculpture, and music. I am accused of detesting it; the proof, so they say, is that *Les Temps Modernes*[4] publishes very few poems. On the contrary, this is proof that we like it. To be convinced, all one need do is take a look at contemporary production. 'At least,' critics say triumphantly, 'you can't even dream of committing it.' Indeed. But why should I want to? Because it uses words as does prose? But it does not use them in the same way, and it does not even *use* them at all. I should rather say that it serves them. Poets are men who refuse to *utilize* language. Now, since the quest for truth takes place in and by language conceived as a certain kind of instrument, it is unnecessary to imagine that they aim to discern or expound the true. Nor do they dream of *naming* the world, and, this being the case, they name nothing at all, for naming implies a perpetual sacrifice of the name to the object named, or, as Hegel would say, the name is revealed as the inessential in the face of the thing which is essential. They do not speak, neither do they keep silent; it is something different. It has been said that they wanted to destroy the 'word' by monstrous couplings, but this is false. For then they would have to be thrown into the midst of utilitarian language and would have had to try to retrieve words from it in odd little groups, as for example 'horse' and 'butter' by writing 'horses of butter'.[5]

Besides the fact that such an enterprise would require infinite time, it is not conceivable that one can keep oneself on the plane of the utilitarian project, consider words as instruments, and at the same time contemplate taking their instrumentality away from them. In fact, the poet has withdrawn from language-instrument in a single movement. Once and for all he has chosen the poetic attitude which considers words as things and not as signs. For the ambiguity of the sign implies that one can penetrate it at will like a pane of glass and pursue the thing signified, or turn one's gaze towards its *reality* and consider it as an object. The man who talks is beyond words and near the object, whereas the poet is on this side of them. For the former, they are domesticated; for the latter they are in the wild state. For the former, they are useful conventions, tools which gradually wear out and which one throws away when they are no longer serviceable; for the latter, they are natural things which sprout naturally upon the earth like grass and trees.

But if he dwells upon words, as does the painter with colours and the musician with sounds, that does not mean that they have lost all meaning in his eyes. Indeed, it is meaning alone which can give words their verbal unity. Without it they are frittered away into sounds and strokes of the pen. Only, it too becomes natural. It is no longer the goal which is always out of reach and which human transcendence is always aiming at, but a property of each term, analogous to the expression of a face, to the little sad or gay meaning of sounds and colours. Having flowed into the word, having been absorbed by its sonority or visual aspect, having been thickened and defaced, it too is a thing, uncreated and eternal.

For the poet, language is a structure of the external world. The speaker is *in a situation* in language; he is invested with words. They are prolongations of his meanings, his pincers, his antennae, his spectacles. He manœuvres them from within; he feels them as if they were his body; he is surrounded by a verbal body which he is hardly aware of and which extends his action upon the world. The poet is outside language. He sees words inside out as if he did not share the human condition, and as if he were first meeting the word as a barrier as he comes towards men. Instead of first knowing things by their name, it seems that first he has a silent contact with them, since, turning towards that other species of thing which for him is the word, touching them, testing them, fingering them, he discovers in them a slight luminosity of their own and particular affinities with the earth, the sky, the water, and all created things.

Not knowing how to use them as a *sign* of an aspect of the world, he sees in the word the *image* of one of these aspects. And the verbal image he chooses for its resemblance to the willow tree or the ash tree is not necessarily the word which we use to designate these objects. As he is already on the outside, he considers words as a trap to catch a fleeing reality rather than as indicators which throw him out of himself into the midst of things. In short, all language is for him the mirror of the world. As a result, important changes take place in the internal economy of the word. Its sonority, its length, its masculine or feminine endings, its visual aspect, compose for him a face of flesh which *represents* rather than expresses meaning. Inversely, as the meaning is *realized*, the physical aspect of the word is reflected within it, and it, in its turn, functions as an image of the verbal body. Like its sign, too, for it has lost its pre-eminence; since words, like things, are given, the poet does not decide whether the former exist for the latter or vice versa.

Thus, between the word and the thing signified, there is established a double reciprocal relation of magical resemblance and meaning. And the poet does not *utilize* the word, he does not choose between different senses given to it; each of them, instead of appearing to him as an autonomous function, is given to him as a material quality which merges before his eyes with the other accepted meanings.

Thus, in each word he realizes, solely by the effect of the poetic *attitude*, the metaphors which Picasso dreamed of when he wanted to do a matchbox which was completely a bat without ceasing to be a matchbox. Florence is city, flower, and woman. It is city-flower, city-woman, and girl-flower all at the same time. And the strange object which thus appears has the liquidity of the *river*, the soft, tawny ardency of *gold*, and finally gives itself up with *propriety* and, by the continuous diminution of the silent *e*, prolongs indefinitely its modest blossoming.[6] To that is added the insidious effect of biography. For me, Florence is also a certain woman, an American actress who played in the silent films of my childhood, and about whom I have forgotten everything except that she was as long as a long evening glove and always a bit weary and always chaste and always married and misunderstood and whom I loved and whose name was Florence.

For the word, which tears the writer of prose away from himself and throws him out into the world, sends back to the poet his own image, like a mirror. This is what justifies the double undertaking of Leiris who, on the one hand, in his *Glossary*, tries to give certain words a *poetic definition*, that is, one which is by itself a synthesis of reciprocal implications between the sonorous body and the verbal soul, and, on the other hand, in a still unpublished work, goes in quest of remembrance of things past, taking as guides a few words which for him are particularly charged with feeling. Thus, the poetic word is a microcosm.

The crisis of language which broke out at the beginning of this century is a poetic crisis. Whatever the social and historical factors, it showed itself in an attack of depersonalization when the writer was confronted by words. He no longer knew how to use them, and, in Bergson's famous formula, he only half recognized them. He approached them with a completely fruitful feeling of strangeness. They were no longer his; they were no longer he; but in those strange mirrors, the sky, the earth, and his own life were reflected. And, finally, they became things themselves, or rather the black heart of things. And when the poet joins several of these microcosms together the case is like that of painters when they assemble their colours on the canvas. One might think that he is composing a sentence, but this is only what it appears to be. He is creating an object. The words-things are grouped by magical associations of fitness and incongruity, like colours and sounds. They attract, repel, and '*burn*' one another, and their association composes the veritable poetic unity which is the *phrase-object*.

More often the poet first has the scheme of the sentence in his mind, and the words follow. But this scheme has nothing in common with what one ordinarily calls a verbal scheme. It does not govern the construction of a meaning. Rather, it is comparable to the creative project by which Picasso, even before touching his brush, prefigures in space the *thing* which will become a buffoon or a harlequin.

> Fuir, là-bas fuir, je sens que des oiseaux sont ivres
> Mais ô mon cœur entends le chant des matelots.

This 'but' which rises like a monolith at the threshold of the sentence does not tie the second line to the preceding one. It colours it with a certain reserved nuance, with 'private associations' which penetrate it completely. In the same way, certain poems begin with 'and'. This conjunction no longer indicates to the mind an operation which is to be carried out; it extends throughout the paragraph to give it the absolute quality of a *sequel*. For the poet, the sentence has a tonality, a taste; by means of it he tastes for their own sake the irritating flavours of objection, of reserve, of disjunction. He carries them to the absolute. He makes them real properties of the sentence, which becomes an utter objection without being an objection *to* anything precise. He finds here those relations of reciprocal implication which we pointed out a short time ago between the poetic word and its meaning; the unit made up of the words chosen functions as an *image* of the interrogative or restrictive nuance, and vice versa, the interrogation is an image of the verbal unit which it delimits.

As in the following admirable lines:

> O saisons! O châteaux!
> Quelle âme est sans défaut?

Nobody is questioned; nobody is questioning; the poet is absent. And the question involves no answer, or rather it is its own answer. Is it therefore a false question? But it would be absurd to believe that Rimbaud 'meant' that everybody has his faults. As Breton said of Saint-Pol Roux, 'If he had meant it, he would have said it.' Nor did he *mean* to say something else. He asked an absolute question. He conferred upon the beautiful word 'âme' an interrogative existence. The interrogation has become a thing as the anguish of Tintoretto became a yellow sky. It is no longer a meaning, but a substance. It is seen from the outside, and Rimbaud invites us to see it from the outside with him. Its strangeness arises from the fact that, in order to consider it, we place ourselves on the other side of the human condition, on the side of God.

If this is the case, one easily understands how foolish it would be to require a poetic commitment. Doubtless, emotion, even passion – and why not anger, social indignation, and political hatred? – are at the origin of the poem. But they are not *expressed* there, as in a pamphlet or in a confession. In so far as the writer of prose exhibits feelings, he illustrates them; whereas, if the poet injects his feelings into his poem, he ceases to recognize them; the words take hold of them, penetrate them, and metamorphose them; they do not signify them, even in his eyes. Emotion has become thing; it now has the opacity of things; it is compounded by the ambiguous properties of the words in which it has been enclosed. And above all, there is always much more in each phrase, in each verse, as there is more than simple anguish in the yellow sky over Golgotha. The word, the phrase-thing, inexhaustible as things, everywhere overflows the feeling which has produced them. How can one hope to provoke the indignation or the political enthusiasm of the reader when the very thing one does is to withdraw him from the human condition and invite him to consider with the eyes of God a language that has been turned inside out? Someone may say, 'You're forgetting the poets of the Resistance. You're forgetting Pierre Emmanuel.' Not a bit! They're the very ones I was going to give as examples.[7]

But even if the poet is forbidden to commit himself, is that a reason for exempting the writer of prose? What do they have in common? It is true that the prose-writer and the poet both write. But there is nothing in common between these two acts of writing except the movement of the hand which traces the letters. Otherwise, their universes are incommunicable, and what is good for one is not good for the other. Prose is, in essence, utilitarian. I would readily define the prose-writer as a man who *makes use* of words. M. Jourdan made prose to ask for his slippers, and Hitler to declare war on Poland. The writer is a *speaker*; he designates, demonstrates, orders, refuses, interpolates, begs, insults, persuades, insinuates. If he does so without any effect, he does not therefore become a poet; he is a writer who is talking and saying nothing. We have seen enough of language inside out; it is now time to look at it right side out.[8]

The art of prose is employed in discourse; its substance is by nature significative; that is, the words are first of all not objects but designations for objects; it is not first of all a matter of knowing whether they please or displease in themselves, but whether they correctly indicate a certain thing or a certain notion. Thus, it often happens that we find ourselves possessing a certain idea that someone has taught us by means of words without being able to recall a single one of the words which have transmitted it to us.

Prose is first of all an attitude of mind. As Valéry would say, there is prose when the word passes across our gaze as the glass across the sun. When one is in danger or in difficulty one grabs any instrument. When the danger is past, one does not even remember whether it was a hammer or a stick; moreover, one never knew; all one needed was a prolongation of one's body, a means of extending one's hand to the highest branch. It was a sixth finger, a third leg, in short, a pure function which one assimilated. Thus, regarding language, it is our shell and our antennae; it protects us against others and informs us about them; it is a prolongation of our senses, a third eye which is going to look into our neighbour's heart. We are within language as within our body. We *feel* it spontaneously while going beyond it towards other ends, as we feel our hands and our feet; we perceive it when it is someone else who is using it, as we perceive the limbs of others. There is the word which is lived and the word which is met. But in both cases it is in the course of an undertaking, either of me acting upon others, or the others upon me. The word is a certain particular moment of action and has no meaning outside it. In certain cases of aphasia the possibilities of acting, of understanding situations, and of having normal relations with the other sex, are lost.

At the heart of this apraxia the destruction of language appears only as the collapse of one of the structures, the finest and the most apparent. And if prose is never anything but the privileged instrument of a certain undertaking, if it is only the poet's business to contemplate words in a disinterested fashion, then one has the right to ask the prose-writer from the very start, 'What is your aim in writing? What undertaking are you engaged in, and why does it require you to have recourse to writing?' In any case this undertaking cannot have pure contemplation as an end. For, intuition is silence, and the end of language is to communicate. One can doubtless *pin down* the results of intuition, but in this case a few words hastily scrawled on paper will suffice; it will always be enough for the author to recognize what he had in mind. If the words are assembled into sentences, with a concern for clarity, a decision foreign to the intuition, to the language itself, must intervene, the decision of confiding to others the results obtained. In each case one must ask the reason for this decision. And the common sense which our pedants too readily forget never stops repeating it. Are we not in the habit of putting this basic question to young people who are thinking of writing: 'Do you have anything to say?' Which means: something which is worth the trouble of being communicated. But what do we mean by something which is 'worth the trouble' if it is not by recourse to a system of transcendent values?

Moreover, to consider only this secondary structure of the undertaking, which is what the *verbal moment* is, the serious error of pure stylists is to think that the word is a gentle breeze which plays lightly over the surface of things, grazing them without altering them, and that the speaker is a pure *witness* who sums up with a word his harmless contemplation. To speak is to act; anything which one names is already no longer quite the same; it has lost its innocence.

If you name the behaviour of an individual, you reveal it to him; he sees himself. And since you are at the same time naming it to all others, he knows that he is *seen* at the moment he *sees* himself. The furtive gesture which he forgot while making it, begins to exist beyond all measure, to exist for everybody; it is integrated into the objective mind; it takes on new dimensions; it is retrieved. After that, how can you expect him to act in the same way? Either he will persist in his behaviour out of obstinacy and with full knowledge of what he is doing, or he will give it up. Thus, by speaking, I reveal the situation by my very intention of changing it; I reveal it to myself and to others *in order* to change it. I strike at its very heart, I transfix it, and I display it in full view; at present

I dispose of it; with every word I utter, I involve myself a little more in the world, and by the same token I emerge from it a little more, since I go beyond it towards the future.

Thus, the prose-writer is a man who has chosen a certain method of secondary action which we may call action by disclosure. It is therefore permissible to ask him this second question: 'What aspect of the world do you want to disclose? What change do you want to bring into the world by this disclosure?' The 'committed' writer knows that words are action. He knows that to reveal is to change and that one can reveal only by planning to change. He has given up the impossible dream of giving an impartial picture of Society and the human condition. Man is the being towards whom no being can be impartial, not even God. For God, if He existed, would be, as certain mystics have seen Him, in a *situation* in relationship to man. And He is also the being Who cannot even see a situation without changing it, for His gaze congeals, destroys, or sculpts, or, as does eternity, changes the object in itself. It is in love, in hate, in anger, in fear, in joy, in indignation, in admiration, in hope, in despair, that man and the world reveal themselves *in their truth*. Doubtless, the committed writer can be mediocre; he can even be conscious of being so; but as one cannot write without the intention of succeeding perfectly, the modesty with which he envisages his work should not divert him from constructing it *as if* it were to have the greatest celebrity. He should never say to himself, 'Bah! I'll be lucky if I have three thousand readers,' but rather, 'What would happen if everybody read what I wrote?' He remembers what Mosca said beside the coach which carried Fabrizio and Sanseverina away, 'If the word Love comes up between them, I'm lost.' He knows that he is the man who names what has not yet been named or what dares not tell its name. He knows that he makes the word 'love' and the word 'hate' *surge up* and with them love and hate between men who had not yet decided upon their feelings. He knows that words, as Brice-Parrain says, are 'loaded pistols'. If he speaks, he fires. He may be silent, but since he has chosen to fire, he must do it like a man, by aiming at targets, and not like a child, at random, by shutting his eyes and firing merely for the pleasure of hearing the shot go off.

Later on we shall try to determine what the goal of literature may be. But from this point on we may conclude that the writer has chosen to reveal the world and particularly to reveal man to other men so that the latter may assume full responsibility before the object which has been thus laid bare. It is assumed that no one is ignorant of the law because there is a code and because the law is written down; thereafter, you are free to violate it, but you know the risks you run. Similarly, the function of the writer is to act in such a way that nobody can be ignorant of the world and that nobody may say that he is innocent of what it's all about. And since he has once committed himself in the universe of language, he can never again pretend that he cannot speak. Once you enter the universe of meanings, there is nothing you can do to get out of it. Let words organize themselves freely and they will make sentences, and each sentence contains language in its entirety and refers back to the whole universe. Silence itself is defined in relationship to words, as the pause in music receives its meaning from the group of notes round it. This silence is a moment of language; being silent is not being dumb; it is to refuse to speak, and therefore to keep on speaking. Thus, if a writer has chosen to remain silent on any aspect whatever of the world, or, according to an expression which says just what it means, to *pass over* it in silence, one has the right to ask him a third question: 'Why have you spoken of this rather than that, and – since you speak in order to bring about change – why do you want to change this rather than that?'

All this does not prevent there being a manner of writing. One is not a writer for having chosen to say certain things, but for having chosen to say them in a certain way. And, to be sure, the style makes the value of the prose. But it should pass unnoticed. Since words are transparent and since the gaze looks through them, it would be absurd to slip in among them some panes of rough glass. Beauty is in this case only a gentle and imperceptible force. In a painting it shines forth at the very first sight; in a book it hides itself; it acts by persuasion like the charm of a voice or a face. It does not coerce; it inclines a person without his suspecting it, and he thinks that he is yielding to arguments when he is really being solicited by a charm that he does not see. The ceremonial of the mass is not faith; it disposes the harmony of words; their beauty, the balance of the phrases, *dispose* the passions of the reader without his being aware and orders them like the mass, like music, like the dance. If he happens to consider them by themselves, he loses the meaning; there remains only a boring seesaw of phrases.

In prose the aesthetic pleasure is pure only if it is thrown in into the bargain. I blush at recalling such simple ideas, but it seems that today they have been forgotten. If that were not the case, would we be told that we are planning the murder of literature, or, more simply, that commitment is harmful to the art of writing? If the contamination of a certain kind of prose by poetry had not confused the ideas of our critics, would they dream of attacking us on the matter of form, when we have never spoken of anything but the content? There is nothing to be said about form in advance, and we have said nothing. Everyone invents his own, and one judges it afterwards. It is true that the subjects suggest the style, but they do not order it. There are no styles ranged a priori outside the literary art. What is more 'committed', what is more boring, than the idea of attacking the Jesuits? Yet, out of this Pascal made his *Provincial Letters*. In short, it is a matter of knowing what one wants to write about, whether butterflies or the condition of the Jews. And when one knows, then it remains to decide how one will write about it.

Often the two choices are only one, but among good writers the second choice never precedes the first. I know that Giraudoux has said that 'the only concern is finding one's style; the idea comes afterwards'; but he was wrong. The idea did not come. On the contrary, if one considers subjects as problems which are always open, as solicitations, as expectations, it will be easily understood that art loses nothing by being committed. On the contrary, just as physics submits to mathematicians new problems which require them to produce a new symbolism, in like manner the always new requirements of the social and the metaphysical involve the artist in finding a new language and new techniques. If we no longer write as they did in the eighteenth century, it is because the language of Racine and Saint-Evremond does not lend itself to talking about locomotives or the proletariat. After that, the purists will perhaps forbid us to write about locomotives. But art has never been on the side of the purists.

If that is the principle of commitment, what objection can one have to it? And above all *what objection has been made to it*? It has seemed to me that my opponents have not had their hearts in their work very much and that their articles contain nothing more than a long scandalized sigh which drags on over two or three columns. I should have liked to know *in the name of what*, with what conception of literature, they condemned commitment. But they have not said; they themselves have not known. The most reasonable thing would have been to support their condemnation on the old theory of art for art's sake. But none of them can accept it. That is also disturbing. We know very well that pure art and empty art are the same thing and that aesthetic purism was a brilliant manœuvre of the bourgeois of the last century who preferred to see themselves denounced as philistines rather than as exploiters. Therefore, they themselves admitted that the writer had to speak about something. But about what? I believe that their embarrassment would have been extreme if Fernandez had not found for them, after the other war, the notion of the *message*. The writer of today, they say, should in no case occupy himself with temporal affairs. Neither should he set up lines without meaning nor seek solely beauty of phrase and of imagery. His function is to deliver messages to his readers. Well, what is a message?

It must be borne in mind that most critics are men who have not had much luck and who, just about the time they were growing desperate, found a quiet little job as cemetery watchmen. God knows whether cemeteries are peaceful; none of them are more cheerful than a library. The dead are there; the only thing they have done is write. They have long since been washed clean of the sin of living, and besides, their lives are known only through other books which other dead men have written about them. Rimbaud is dead. So are Paterne Berrichon and Isabelle Rimbaud. The trouble makers have disappeared; all that remains are the little coffins that are stacked on shelves along the walls like urns in a columbarium. The critic lives badly; his wife does not appreciate him as she ought to; his children are ungrateful; the first of the month is hard on him. But it is always possible for him to enter his library, take down a book from the shelf, and open it. It gives off a slight odour of the cellar, and a strange operation begins which he has decided to call reading. From one point of view it is a possession; he lends his body to the dead in order that they may come back to life. And from another point of view it is a contact with the beyond. Indeed, the book is by no means an object; neither is it an act, nor even a thought. Written by a dead man about dead things, it no longer has any place on this earth; it speaks of nothing which interests us directly. Left to itself, it falls back and collapses; there remain only ink spots on musty paper. And when the critic reanimates these spots, when he makes letters and words of them, they speak to him of passions which he does not feel, of bursts of anger without objects, of dead fears and hopes. It is a whole disembodied world which surrounds him, where human feelings, because they are no longer affecting, have passed on to the status of exemplary feelings and, in short, of *values*. So he persuades himself that he has entered into relations with an intelligible world which is like the truth of his daily sufferings. And their reason for being. He thinks that nature imitates art, as for Plato the world of the senses imitates that of the archetypes. And during the time he is reading, his everyday life becomes an appearance. His nagging wife, his hunchbacked son, they too are appearances. And he will put up with them because Xenophon has drawn the portrait of Xantippe and Shakespeare that of Richard the Third.

It is a holiday for him when contemporary authors do him the favour of dying. Their books, too raw, too living, too urgent, pass on to the other shore; they become less and less affecting and more and more beautiful. After a short stay in Purgatory they go on to people the intelligible heaven with new values. Bergotte, Swann, Siegfried and Bella, and M. Teste are recent acquisitions. He is waiting for Nathanaël and Ménalque. As for the writers who persist in living, he asks them only not to move about too much, and to make an effort to resemble from now on the dead men they will be. Valéry, who for twenty-five years had been publishing posthumous books, managed the matter very nicely. That is why, like some highly exceptional saints, he was canonized during his lifetime. But Malraux is scandalous.

Our critics are Catharists. They don't want to have anything to do with the real world except eat and drink in it, and since it is absolutely necessary to have relations with our fellow-creatures, they have chosen to have them with the defunct. They get excited only about classified matters, closed quarrels, stories whose ends are known. They never bet on uncertain issues, and since history has decided for them, since the objects which terrified or angered the authors they read have disappeared, since bloody disputes seem futile at a distance of two centuries, they can be charmed with balanced periods, and everything happens for them as if all literature were only a vast tautology and as if every new prose-writer had invented a new way of speaking only for the purpose of saying nothing.

To speak of archetypes and 'human nature' – is that speaking in order to say nothing? All the conceptions of our critics oscillate from one idea to the other. And, of course, both of them are false. Our great writers wanted to destroy, to edify, to demonstrate. But we no longer retain the proofs which they have advanced because we have no concern with what they mean to prove. The abuses which they denounced are no longer those of our time. There are others which rouse us which they did not suspect. History has given the lie to some of their predictions, and those which have been fulfilled became true so long ago that we have forgotten that they were at first flashes of their genius. Some of their thoughts are utterly dead, and there are others which the whole human race has taken up to its advantage and which we now regard as commonplace. It follows that the best arguments of these writers have lost their effectiveness. We admire only their order and rigour. Their most compact composition is in our eyes only an ornament, an elegant architecture of exposition, with no more practical application than such architectures as the fugues of Bach and the arabesques of the Alhambra.

We are still moved by the passion of these impassioned geometries when the geometry no longer convinces us. Or rather, by the representation of the passion. In the course of centuries the ideas have turned flat, but they remain the little personal objectives of a man who was once flesh and bone; behind the reasons of reason, which wither, we perceive the reasons of the heart, the virtues, the vices, and that great pain that men have in living. Sade does his best to win us over, but we hardly find him scandalous. He is no longer anything but a soul eaten by a beautiful disease, a pearl-oyster. The *Letter on the Theatre* no longer keeps anyone from going to the theatre, but we find it piquant that Rousseau detested the art of the drama. If we are a bit versed in psycho-analysis, our pleasure is perfect. We shall explain the *Social Contract* by the Oedipus complex and *The Spirit of the Laws* by the inferiority complex. That is, we shall fully enjoy the well-known superiority of live dogs to dead lions. Thus, when a book presents befuddled thoughts which only have the appearance of being reasons before melting under our scrutiny and dwindling into the beatings of a heart, when the teaching that one can draw from it is radically different from what its author intended, the book is called a message. Rousseau, the father of the French Revolution, and Gobineau, the father of racism, both sent us messages. And the critic considers them with equal sympathy. If they were alive, he would have to choose between the two, to love one and hate the other. But what brings them together, above all, is that they are both profoundly and deliciously wrong, and in the same way: they are dead.

Thus, contemporary writers should be advised to deliver messages, that is, voluntarily to limit their writing to the involuntary expression of their souls. I say involuntary because the dead, from Montaigne to Rimbaud, have portrayed themselves completely, but without having meant to – it is something they have simply thrown into the bargain. The surplus which they have given us unintentionally should be the primary and professed goal of living writers. They are not to be forced to give us confessions without any seasoning, nor are they to abandon themselves to the too-naked lyricism of the romantics. But since we find pleasure in foiling the ruses of Chateaubriand or Rousseau, in surprising them in the secret places of their being at the moment they are playing at being the public man, in distinguishing the private motives from their most universal assertions, we shall ask newcomers to procure us this pleasure deliberately. So let them reason, assert, deny, refute, and prove; but the cause they are defending must be only the apparent aim of their discourse; the deeper goal is to yield themselves without seeming to do so. They must first disarm themselves of their arguments as time has done for those of the classic writers; they must bring them to bear upon subjects which interest no one or on truths so general that readers are convinced in advance. As for their ideas, they must give them an air of profundity, but with an effect of emptiness, and they must shape them in such a way that they are obviously explained by an unhappy childhood, a class hatred, or an incestuous love. Let them not presume to think in earnest; thought conceals the man, and it is the man alone who interests us. A bare tear is not lovely. It offends. A good argument also offends, as Stendhal well observed. But an argument that masks a tear – that's what we're after. The argument removes the obscenity from the tears; the tears, by revealing their origin in the passions, remove the aggressiveness from the argument. We shall be neither too deeply touched nor at all convinced, and we shall be able to yield ourselves safely to that moderate pleasure which, as everyone knows, we derive from the contemplation of works of art. Thus, this is 'true', 'pure' literature, a subjective thing which reveals itself under the aspect of the objective, a discourse so curiously contrived that it is equivalent to silence, a thought which debates with itself, a reason which is only the mask of madness, an Eternal which lets it be understood that it is only a moment of History, a historical moment which, by the hidden side which it reveals, suddenly sends back a perpetual lesson to the eternal man, but which is produced against the express wishes of those who do the teaching.

When all is said and done, the message is a soul which is made object. A soul, and what is to be done with a soul? One contemplates it at a respectful distance. It is not customary to show one's soul in society without a powerful motive. But, with certain reservations, convention permits some individuals to put theirs into commerce, and all adults may procure it for themselves. For many people today, works of the mind are thus little wandering souls which one acquires at a modest price; there is good old Montaigne's, dear La Fontaine's, and that of Jean-Jacques and of Jean-Paul and of delicious Gérard. What is called literary art is the sum of the treatments which make them inoffensive. Tanned, refined, chemically treated, they provide their acquirers with the opportunity of devoting some moments of a life completely turned outwards to the cultivation of subjectivity. Custom guarantees it to be without risk. Montaigne's scepticism? Who can take it seriously since the author of the *Essays* got frightened when the plague ravaged Bordeaux? Or Rousseau's humanitarianism, since 'Jean-Jacques' put his children into an orphanage? And the strange revelations of *Sylvie*, since Gérard de Nerval was mad? At the very most, the professional critic will set up infernal dialogues between them and will inform us that French thought is a perpetual colloquy between Pascal and Montaigne. In so doing he has no intention of making Pascal and Montaigne more alive, but of making Malraux and Gide more dead. Finally, when the internal contradictions of the life and the work have made both of them useless, when the message, in its imponderable depth, has taught us these capital truths, 'that man is neither good nor bad', 'that there is a great deal of suffering in human life', 'that genius is only great patience', this dismal bungling will have achieved its ultimate purpose, and the reader, as he lays down the book, will be able to cry out with a tranquil soul, 'All this is only literature.'

But since, for us, writing is an enterprise; since writers are alive before being dead; since we think that we must try to be as right as we can in our books; and since, even if afterwards the centuries show us to be in the wrong, this is no reason why they should prove us wrong in advance; since we think that the writer should commit himself completely in his works, and not in an abjectly passive rôle by putting forward his vices, his misfortunes, and his weaknesses, but as a resolute will and as a choice, as this total enterprise of living that each one of us is, it is then proper that we take up this problem at its beginning and that we, in our turn, ask ourselves: '*Why* does one write?'

Translated by Bernard Frechtman

Notes

1 *Editor's note:* this is how the chapter starts. Sartre's 'No, we do not want to . . .' follows on from the Foreword to *What is Literature?*. Sartre is replying to a 'smart-aleck' who asks 'And poetry? And painting? And music? You want to commit them, too?'. The one-page Foreword, which immediately precedes the chapter, addresses political (and implicitly Communist) commitment in literature, and is a riposte to those critics who think that 'the worst artists are the most committed'. Sartre accuses them of not understanding the nature of writing, and suggests that 'the best answer to give them is to examine the art of writing without prejudice'.

2 At least in general. The greatness and error of Klee lie in his attempt to make a painting both sign and object.

3 I say 'create', not 'imitate', which is enough to squelch the bombast of M. Charles Estienne, who has obviously not understood a word of my argument and who is dead set on tilting at shadows.

4 A periodical edited by M. Sartre. – Translator.

5 This is the example cited by Bataille in *Inner Experience*.

6 This sentence is not fully intelligible in translation as the author is here associating the component sounds of the word Florence with the meaning of the French words they evoke. Thus: FL-OR-ENCE, *fleuve, or*, and *décence*. The latter part of the sentence refers to the practice in French poetry of giving, in certain circumstances, a syllabic value to the otherwise silent terminal *e*. – Translator.

7 If you wish to know the origin of this attitude towards language, the following are a few brief indications.

Originally, poetry creates the *myth*, while the prose-writer draws its *portrait*. In reality, the human act, governed by needs and urged on by the useful is, in a sense, a *means*. It passes unnoticed, and it is the result which counts. When I extend my hand *in order* to take up my pen, I have only a fleeting and obscure consciousness of my gesture; it is the pen which I see. Thus, man is alienated by his ends. Poetry reverses the relationship: the world and things become inessential, become a pretext for the act which becomes its own end. The vase is there so that the girl may perform the graceful act of filling it; the Trojan War, so that Hector and Achilles may engage in that heroic combat. The action, detached from its goals, which become blurred, becomes an act of prowess or a dance. Nevertheless, however indifferent he might have been to the success of the enterprise, the poet, before the nineteenth century, remained in harmony with society as a whole. He did not use language for the end which prose seeks, but he had the same confidence in it as the prose-writer.

With the coming of bourgeois society, the poet puts up a common front with the prose-writer to declare it unliveable. His job is always to create the myth of man, but he passes from white magic to black magic. Man is always presented as the absolute end, but by the success of his enterprise he is sucked into a utilitarian collectivity. The thing that is in the background of his act and that will allow transition to the myth is thus no longer success, but defeat. By stopping the infinite series of his projects like a screen, defeat alone returns him to himself in his purity. The world remains the inessential, but it is now there as a pretext for defeat. The finality of the thing is to send man back to himself by blocking the route. Moreover, it is not a matter of arbitrarily introducing defeat and ruin into the course of the world, but rather of having no eyes for anything but that. Human enterprise has two aspects: it is both success and failure. The dialectical scheme is inadequate for reflecting upon it. We must make our vocabulary and the frames of our reason more supple. Some day I am going to try to describe that strange reality, History, which is neither objective, nor ever quite subjective, in which the dialectic is contested, penetrated, and corroded by a kind of antidialectic, but which is still a dialectic. But that is the philosopher's affair. One does not ordinarily consider the two faces of Janus; the man of action sees one and the poet sees the other. When the instruments are broken and unusable, when plans are blasted and effort is useless, the world appears with a childlike and terrible freshness, without supports, without paths. It has the maximum reality because it is crushing for man, and as action, in any case, generalizes, defeat restores to things their individual reality. But, by an expected reversal, the defeat, considered as a final end, is both a contesting and an appropriation of this universe. A contesting, because man *is worth more* than that which crushes; he no longer contests things in their 'little bit of reality', like the engineer or the captain, but, on the contrary, in their 'too full of reality', by his very existence as a vanquished person; he is the remorse of the world. An appropriation, because the world, by ceasing to be the tool of success, becomes the instrument of failure. So there it is, traversed by an obscure finality; it is its coefficient of adversity which serves, the more human in so far as it is more hostile to man. The defeat itself turns into salvation. Not that it makes us yield to some 'beyond', but by itself it shifts and is metamorphosed. For example, poetic language rises out of the ruins of prose. If it is true that the word is a betrayal and that communication is impossible, then each word by itself recovers its individuality and becomes an instrument of our defeat and a receiver of the incommunicable. It is not that there is *another thing* to communicate; but the communication of prose having miscarried, it is the very meaning of the word which becomes the pure incommunicable. Thus, the failure of communication becomes a suggestion of the incommunicable, and the thwarted project of utilizing words is succeeded by the pure disinterested intuition of the word. Thus, we again meet with the description which we attempted earlier in this study, but in the more general perspective of the absolute valorization of the defeat, which seems to me the original attitude of contemporary poetry. Note also that this choice confers upon the poet a very precise function in the collectivity: in a highly integrated or religious society, the defeat is masked by the State or redeemed by Religion; in a less integrated and secular society, such as our democracies, it is up to poetry to redeem them.

Poetry is a case of the loser winning. And the genuine poet chooses to lose, even if he has to go so far as to die, in order to win. I repeat that I am talking of contemporary poetry. History presents other forms of poetry. It is not my concern to show their connection with ours. Thus, if one absolutely wishes to speak of the commitment of the poet, let us say that he is the man who commits himself to lose. This is the deeper meaning of that tough-luck, of that curse with which he always claims kinship and which he always attributes to an intervention from without; whereas it is his deepest choice, the source, and not the consequence of his poetry. He is certain of the total defeat of the human enterprise and arranges to fail in his own life in order to bear witness, by his individual defeat, to human defeat in general. Thus, he challenges, as we shall see, which is what the prose-writer does too. But the challenge of prose is carried on in the name of a greater success; and that of poetry, in the name of the hidden defeat which every victory conceals.

8 It goes without saying that in all poetry a certain form of prose, that is, of success, is present; and, vice versa, the driest prose always contains a bit of poetry, that is, a certain form of defeat; no prose-writer is *quite* capable of expressing what he wants to say; he says too much or not enough; each phrase is a wager, a risk assumed; the more cautious one is, the more attention the word attracts; as Valéry has shown, no one can understand a word to its very bottom. Thus, each word is used simultaneously for its clear and social meaning and for certain obscure resonances – let me say, almost for its physiognomy. The reader, too, is sensitive to this. At once we are no longer on the level of concerted communication, but on that of grace and chance; the silences of prose are poetic because they mark its limits, and it is for the purpose of greater clarity that I have been considering the extreme cases of pure prose and pure poetry. However, it need not be concluded that we can pass from poetry to prose by a continuous series of intermediate forms. If the prose-writer is too eager to fondle his words, the *eidos* of 'prose' is shattered and we fall into highfalutin nonsense. If the poet relates, explains, or teaches, the poetry complex becomes *prosaic*; he has lost the game. It is a matter of structures, impure, but well-defined.

6

REALITY AND ITS SHADOW

Emmanuel Levinas

Art and criticism

It is generally, dogmatically, admitted that the function of art is expression, and that artistic expression rests on cognition. An artist – even a painter, even a musician – tells. He tells of the ineffable. An artwork prolongs, and goes beyond, common perception. What common perception trivializes and misses, an artwork apprehends in its irreducible essence. It thus coincides with metaphysical intuition. Where common language abdicates, a poem or a painting speaks. Thus an artwork is more real than reality and attests to the dignity of the artistic imagination, which sets itself up as knowledge of the absolute. Though it be disparaged as an aesthetic canon, realism nevertheless retains all its prestige. In fact it is repudiated only in the name of a higher realism. Surrealism is a superlative.

Criticism too professes this dogma. It enters into the artist's game with all the seriousness of science. In artworks it studies psychology, characters, environments, and landscapes – as though in an aesthetic event an object were by the microscope or telescope of artistic vision exposed for the curiosity of an investigator. But, alongside of difficult art, criticism seems to lead a parasitic existence. A depth of reality inaccessible to conceptual intelligence becomes its prey. Or else criticism substitutes itself for art. Is not to interpret Mallarmé to betray him? Is not to interpret his work faithfully to suppress it? To say clearly what he says obscurely is to reveal the vanity of his obscure speech.

Criticism as a distinct function of literary life, expert and professional criticism, appearing as an item in newspapers and journals and in books, can indeed seem suspect and pointless. But it has its source in the mind of the listener, spectator or reader; criticism exists as a public's mode of comportment. Not content with being absorbed in aesthetic enjoyment, the public feels an irresistible need to speak. The fact that there might be something for the public to say, when the artist refuses to say about artwork anything in addition to the work itself, the fact that one cannot contemplate in silence, justifies the critic. He can be defined as the one that still has something to say when everything has been said, that can say about the work something else than that work.

One then has the right to ask if the artist really knows and speaks. He does in a preface or a manifesto, certainly; but then he is himself a part of the public. If art originally were neither language nor knowledge, if it were therefore situated outside of 'being in the world' which is coextensive with truth,[1] criticism would be rehabilitated. It would represent the intervention of the understanding necessary for integrating the inhumanity and inversion of art into human life and into the mind.

Perhaps the tendency to apprehend the aesthetic phenomenon in literature, where speech provides the material for the artist, explains the contemporary dogma of knowledge through art. We are not always attentive to the transformation that speech undergoes in literature. Art as speech, art as knowledge, then brings on the problem of committed art, which is a problem of committed literature.[2] The completion, the indelible seal of artistic production by which the artwork remains essentially disengaged, is underestimated – that supreme moment when the last brush stroke is done, when there is not another word to add to or to strike from the text, by virtue of which every artwork is classical. Such completion is different from the simple interruption which limits language and the works of nature and industry. Yet we might wonder if we should not recognize an element of art in the work of craftsmen, in all human work, commercial and diplomatic, in the measure that, in addition to its perfect adaptation to its ends, it bears witness to an accord with some destiny extrinsic to the course of things, which situates it outside the world, like the forever bygone past of ruins, like the elusive strangeness of the exotic. The artist stops because the work refuses to accept anything more, appears saturated. The work is completed *in spite of* the social or material causes that interrupt it. It does not give itself out as the beginning of a dialogue.

This completion does not necessarily justify the academic aesthetics of art for art's sake. The formula is false inasmuch as it situates art *above* reality and recognizes no master for it, and it is immoral inasmuch as it liberates the artist from his duties as a man and assures him of a pretentious and facile nobility. But a work would not belong to art if it did not have this formal structure of completion, if at least in this way it were not disengaged. We have to understand the value of this disengagement, and first of all its meaning. Is to disengage oneself from the world always to go *beyond*, toward the region of Platonic ideas and toward the eternal which towers above the world? Can one not speak of a disengagement on the hither side – of an interruption of time by a movement going on on the hither side of time, in its 'interstices'?

To go beyond is to communicate with ideas, to understand. Does not the function of art lie in not understanding? Does not obscurity provide it with its very element and a completion sui generis, foreign to dialectics and the life of ideas? Will we then say that the artist knows and expresses the very obscurity of the real? But that leads to a much more general question, to which this whole discussion of art is subordinate: in what does the *non-truth* of being consist? Is it always to be defined by comparison with truth, as what is left over after *understanding*? Does not the commerce with the obscure, as a totally independent ontological event, describe categories irreducible to those of cognition? We should like to show this event in art. Art does not know a particular type of reality; it contrasts with knowledge. It is the very event of obscuring, a descent of the night, an invasion of shadow. To put it in theological terms, which will enable us to delimit however roughly our ideas by comparison with contemporary notions: art does not belong to the order of revelation. Nor does it belong to that of creation, which moves in just the opposite direction.

The imaginary, the sensible, the musical

The most elementary procedure of art consists in substituting for the object its image. Its image, and not its concept. A concept is the object *grasped*, the intelligible object. Already by action we maintain a living relationship with a real object; we grasp it, we conceive it. The image neutralizes this real relationship, this primary conceiving through action. The well-known disinterestedness of artistic vision, which the current aesthetic analysis stops with, signifies above all a blindness to concepts.

But the disinterestedness of the artist scarcely deserves this name. For it excludes freedom, which the notion of disinterestedness implies. Strictly speaking, it also excludes bondage, which presupposes freedom. An image does not engender a *conception*, as do scientific cognition and truth; it does not involve Heidegger's 'letting be', *Sein-lassen*, in which objectivity is transmuted into power.[3] An image marks a hold over us rather than our initiative, a fundamental passivity. Possessed, inspired, an artist, we say, harkens to a muse. An image is musical. Its passivity is directly visible in magic, song, music, and poetry. The exceptional structure of aesthetic existence invokes this singular term magic, which will enable us to make the somewhat worn-out notion of passivity precise and concrete.

The idea of rhythm, which art criticism so frequently invokes but leaves in the state of a vague suggestive notion and catch-all, designates not so much an inner law of the poetic order as the way the poetic order affects us, closed wholes whose elements call for one another like the syllables of a verse, but do so only insofar as they impose themselves on us, disengaging themselves from reality. *But they impose themselves on us without our assuming them.* Or rather, our consenting to them is inverted into a participation. Their entry into us is one with our entry into them. Rhythm represents a unique situation where we cannot speak of consent, assumption, initiative or freedom, because the subject is caught up and carried away by it. The subject is part of its own representation. It is so not even despite itself, for in rhythm there is no longer a oneself, but rather a sort of passage from oneself to anonymity. This is the captivation or incantation of poetry and music. It is a mode of being to which applies neither the form of consciousness, since the I is there stripped of its prerogative to assume, its power, nor the form of unconsciousness, since the whole situation and all its articulations are in a dark light, *present*. Such is a waking dream. Neither habits, reflexes, nor instinct operate in this light. The particular automatic character of a walk or a dance to music is a mode of being where nothing is unconscious, but where consciousness, paralyzed in its freedom, plays, totally absorbed in this playing. To listen to music is in a sense to refrain from dancing or stepping; the movement or gesture is of little import. It would be more appropriate to talk of interest than of disinterestedness with respect to images. An image is interesting, without the slightest sense of utility, interesting in the sense of *involving*, in the etymological sense – to be *among* things which should have had only the status of objects. To be 'among things' is different from Heidegger's 'being-in-the-world'; it constitutes the pathos of the imaginary world of dreams – the subject is among things not only by virtue of its density of being, requiring a 'here', a 'somewhere', and retaining its freedom; it is among things as a thing, as part of the spectacle. It is exterior to itself, but with an exteriority which is not that of a body, since the pain of the I-actor is felt by the I-spectator, and not through compassion. Here we have really an exteriority of the inward. It is surprising that phenomenological analysis never tried to apply this fundamental paradox of rhythm and dreams, which describes a sphere situated outside of the conscious and the unconscious, a sphere whose role in all ecstatic rites has been shown by ethnography; it is surprising that we have stayed with metaphors of 'ideomotor' phenomena and with the study of the prolongation of sensations into actions. Here we shall use the terms rhythm and musical while thinking of this reversal of power into participation.

Then we must detach them from the arts of sound where they are ordinarily envisioned exclusively, and draw them out into a general aesthetic category. Rhythm certainly does have its privileged locus in music, for the musician's element realizes the pure deconceptualization of reality. Sound is the quality most detached from an object. Its relation with the substance from which it emanates is not inscribed in its quality. It resounds impersonally. Even its timbre, a trace of its belonging to an object, is submerged in its quality, and does not retain the structure of a relation. Hence in listening we do not apprehend a 'something', but are without concepts: musicality belongs to sound naturally. And indeed, among all the classes of images distinguished by traditional psychology, the image of sound is most akin to real sound. To insist on the musicality of every image is to see in an image its detachment from an object, that independence from the category of substance which the analyses of our textbooks ascribe to pure sensation not yet converted into perception (sensation as an adjective), which for empirical psychology remains a limit case, a purely hypothetical given.

It is as though sensation free from all conception, that famous sensation that eludes introspection, appeared with images. Sensation is not a residue of perception, but has a function of its own – the hold that an image has over us, a function of rhythm. What is today called being-in-the-world is an existence with concepts. Sensibility takes place as a distinct ontological event, but is realized only by the imagination.

If art consists in substituting an image for being, the aesthetic element, as its etymology indicates, is sensation. The whole of our world, with its elementary and intellectually elaborated givens, can touch us musically, can become an image. That is why classical art which is attached to objects – all those paintings, all those statues representing *something*, all those poems which recognize syntax and punctuation – conforms no less to the true essence of art than the modern works which claim to be pure music, pure painting, pure poetry, because they drive objects out of the world of sounds, colours and words into which those works introduce us – because they break up representation. A represented object, by the simple fact of becoming an image, is converted into a non-object; the image as such enters into categories proper to it which we would like to bring out here. The disincarnation of reality by an image is not equivalent to a simple diminution in degree. It belongs to an ontological dimension that does not extend between us and a reality to be captured, a dimension where commerce with reality is a rhythm.

Image and resemblance

The phenomenology of images insists on their transparency. The intention of one who contemplates an image is said to go directly through the image, as through a window, into the world it represents, and aims at an *object*.[4] Yet nothing is more mysterious than the term 'world it represents' – since representation expresses just that function of an image that still remains to be determined.

The theory of transparency was set up in reaction to the theory of mental images, of an inner tableau which the perception of an object would leave in us. In imagination our gaze then always goes outward, but imagination modifies or neutralizes this gaze: the real world appears in it as it were between parentheses or quote marks. The problem is to make clear what these devices used in writing mean. The imaginary world is said to present itself as unreal – but can one say more about this unreality?

In what does an image differ from a symbol, a sign, or a word? By the very way it refers to its object: resemblance. But that supposes that thought stops on the image itself; it consequently supposes a certain opacity of the image. A sign, for its part, is pure transparency, nowise counting for itself. Must we then come back to taking the image as an independent reality which resembles the original? No, but on condition that we take resemblance not as the result of a comparison between an image and the original, but as the very movement that engenders the image. Reality would not be only what it is, what it is disclosed to be in truth, but would be also its double, its shadow, its image.

Being is not only itself, it escapes itself. Here is a person who is what he is; but he does not make us forget, does not absorb, cover over entirely the objects he holds and the way he holds them, his gestures, limbs, gaze, thought, skin, which escape from under the identity of his substance, which like a torn sack is unable to contain them. Thus a person bears on his face, alongside of its being with which he coincides, its own caricature, its picturesqueness. The picturesque is always to some extent a caricature. Here is a familiar everyday thing, perfectly adapted to the hand which is accustomed to it, but its qualities, colour, form, and position at the same time remain as it were behind its being, like the 'old garments' of a soul which had withdrawn from that thing, like a 'still life'. And yet all this is the person and is the thing. There is then a duality in this person, this thing, a duality in its being. It is what it is and it is a stranger to itself, and there is a relationship between these two moments. We will say the thing is itself and is its image. And that this relationship between the thing and its image is resemblance.

This situation is akin to what a fable brings about. Those animals that portray men give the fable its peculiar colour inasmuch as men are seen *as* these animals and not only *through* these animals; the animals stop and fill up thought. It is in this that all the power and originality of allegory lies. An allegory is not a simple auxiliary to thought, a way of rendering an abstraction concrete and popular for childlike minds, a poor man's symbol. It is an ambiguous commerce with reality in which reality does not refer to itself but to its reflection, its shadow. An allegory thus represents what in the object itself doubles it up. An image, we can say, is an allegory of being.

A being is that which is, that which reveals itself in its truth, and, at the same time, it resembles itself, is its own image. The original gives itself as though it were at a distance from itself, as though it were withdrawing itself, as though something in a being delayed behind being. The consciousness of the absence of the object which characterizes an image is not equivalent to a simple neutralization of the thesis, as Husserl would have it, but is equivalent to an alteration of the very being of the object, where its essential forms appear as a garb that it abandons in withdrawing. To contemplate an image is to contemplate a picture. The image has to be understood by starting with the phenomenology of pictures, and not the converse.

In the vision of the represented object a painting has a density of its own: it is itself an object of the gaze. The consciousness of the representation lies in knowing that the object is not there. The perceived elements are not the object but are like its 'old garments', spots of colour, chunks of marble or bronze. These elements do not serve as symbols, and in the absence of the object they do not force its presence, but by their presence insist on its absence. They occupy its place fully to mark its removal, as though the represented object died, were degraded, were disincarnated in its own reflection. The painting then does not lead us beyond the given reality, but somehow to the hither side of it. It is a symbol in reverse. The poet and painter who have discovered the 'mystery' and 'strangeness' of the world they inhabit every day are free to think that they have gone beyond the real. The mystery of being is not its myth. The artist moves in a universe that precedes (in what sense we will see below) the world of creation, a universe that the artist has already gone beyond by his thought and his everyday actions.

The idea of shadow or reflection to which we have appealed – of an essential doubling of reality by its image, of an ambiguity 'on the hither side' – extends to the light itself, to thought, to the inner life. The whole of reality bears on its face its own allegory, outside of its revelation and its truth. In utilizing images art not only reflects, but brings about this allegory. In art allegory is introduced into the world, as truth is accomplished in cognition. These are two contemporary possibilities of being. Alongside of the simultaneity of the idea and the soul – that is, of being and its disclosure – which the *phaedo* teaches, there is the simultaneity of a being and its reflection. The absolute at the same time reveals itself to reason and lends itself to a sort of erosion, outside of all causality. Non-truth is not an obscure residue of being, but is its sensible character itself, by which there is resemblance and images in the world. Because of resemblance the Platonic world of becoming is a lesser world, of appearances only. As a dialectic of being and non-being, becoming does indeed, since the *Parmenides*, make its appearance in the world of Ideas. It is through imitation that participation engenders shadows, distinct from the participation of the Ideas in one another which is revealed to the understanding. The discussion over the primacy of art or of nature – does art imitate nature or does natural beauty imitate art? – fails to recognize the simultaneity of truth and image.

The notion of shadow thus enables us to situate the economy of resemblance within the general economy of being. Resemblance is not a participation of a being in an idea (the old argument of the third man shows the futility of that); it is the very structure of the sensible as such. The sensible is being insofar as it resembles itself, insofar as, outside of its triumphal work of being, it casts a shadow, emits that obscure and elusive essence, that phantom essence which cannot be identified with the essence revealed in truth. There is not first an image – a neutralized vision of the object – which then differs from a sign or symbol because of its resemblance with the original; the neutralization of position in an image is precisely this resemblance.

The *transdescendence* Jean Wahl speaks of, when separated from the ethical significance it has for him and taken in a strictly ontological sense, can characterize this phenomenon of degradation or erosion of the absolute which we see in images and in resemblance.

The meanwhile

To say that an image is a shadow of being would in turn be only to use a metaphor, if we did not show *where* the hither side we are speaking of is situated. To speak of inertia or death would hardly help us, for first we should have to say what the ontological signification of materiality itself is.

We have envisioned the image as the caricature, allegory or picturesque element which reality bears on its own face. All of Giraudoux's work effects a casting of reality into images, with a consistency which has not been fully appreciated, despite all Giraudoux's glory.[5] But up to now we seemed to be basing our conception on a fissure in being between being and its essence which does not adhere to it but masks and betrays it. But this in fact only enables us to approach the phenomenon we are concerned with. The art called classical – the art of antiquity and of its imitators, the art of ideal forms – corrects the caricature of being – the snub nose, the stiff gesture. Beauty is being dissimulating its caricature, covering over or absorbing its shadow. Does it absorb it completely? It is not a question of wondering whether the perfect forms of Greek art could be still more perfect, nor if they seem perfect in all latitudes of the globe. The insurmountable caricature in the most perfect image manifests itself in its stupidness as an idol. The image *qua* idol leads us to the ontological significance of its unreality. This time the work of being itself, the very *existing* of a being,[6] is doubled up with a semblance of existing.

To say that an image is an idol is to affirm that every image is in the last analysis plastic, and that every artwork is in the end a statue – a stoppage of time, or rather its delay behind itself. But we must show in what sense it stops or delays, and in what sense a statue's existing is a semblance of the existing of being.

A statue realizes the paradox of an instant that endures without a future. Its duration is not really an instant. It does not give itself out here as an infinitesimal element of duration, the instant of a flash; it has in its own way a quasi-eternal duration. We are not thinking just of the duration of an artwork itself as an object, of the permanence of writings in libraries and of statues in museums. Within the life, or rather the death, of a statue, an instant endures infinitely: eternally Laocoon will be caught up in the grip of serpents; the Mona Lisa will smile eternally. Eternally the future announced in the strained muscles of Laocoon will be unable to become present. Eternally, the smile of the Mona Lisa about to broaden will not broaden. An eternally suspended future floats around the congealed position of a statue like a future forever to come. The imminence of the future lasts before an instant stripped of the essential characteristic of the present, its evanescence. It will never have completed its task as a present, as though reality withdrew from its own reality and left it powerless. In this situation the present can assume nothing, can take on nothing, and thus is an impersonal and anonymous instant.

The immobile instant of a statue owes its acuteness to its non-indifference to duration. It does not belong to eternity. But it is not as though the artist had not been able to give it life. It is just that the life of an artwork does not go beyond the limit of an instant. The artwork does not succeed, is bad, when it does not have that aspiration for life which moved Pygmalion. But it is only an aspiration. The artist has given the statue a lifeless life, a derisory life which is not master of itself, a caricature of life. Its presence does not cover over itself and overflows on all sides, does not hold in its own hands the strings of the puppet it is. We can attend to the puppet in the personages of a tragedy and laugh at the Comédie-Française. *Every image is already a caricature*. But this caricature turns into something tragic. The same man is indeed a comic poet and a tragic poet, an ambiguity which constitutes the particular magic of poets like Gogol, Dickens, Tchekov – and Molière, Cervantes, and above all, Shakespeare.

This present, impotent to force the future, is fate itself, that fate refractory to the will of the pagan gods, stronger than the rational necessity of natural laws. Fate does not appear in universal necessity. It is a necessity in a free being, a reverting of freedom into necessity, their simultaneity, a freedom that discovers it is a prisoner. Fate has no place in life. The conflict between freedom and necessity in human action appears in reflection: when action is already sinking into the past, man discovers the motifs that necessitated it. But an antinomy is not a tragedy. In the instant of a statue, in its eternally suspended future, the tragic simultaneity of necessity and liberty, can come to pass: the power of freedom congeals into impotence. And here too we should compare art with dreams: the instant of a statue is a nightmare. Not that the artist represents being crushed by fate – beings enter their fate because they are represented. They are enclosed in their fate but just this is the artwork, an event of darkening of being, parallel with its revelation, its truth. It is not that an artwork reproduces a time that has stopped: in the general economy of being, art is the falling movement on the hither side of time, into fate. A novel is not, as Jean Pouillon thinks, a way of reproducing time; it has its own time, it is a unique way for time to temporalize.

We can then understand that time, apparently introduced into images by the non-plastic arts such as music, literature, theatre and cinema, does not shatter the fixity of images. That the characters in a book are committed to the infinite repetition of the same acts and the same thoughts is not simply due to the contingent fact of the narrative, which is exterior to those characters. They can be narrated because their being *resembles* itself, doubles itself and immobilizes. Such a fixity is wholly different from that of concepts, which initiates life, offers reality to our powers, to truth, opens a dialectic. By its reflection in a narrative, being has a non-dialectical fixity, stops dialectics and time.

The characters of a novel are beings that are shut up, prisoners. Their history is never finished, it still goes on, but makes no headway. A novel shuts beings up in a fate despite their freedom. Life solicits the novelist when it seems to him as if it were already something out of a book. Something somehow completed arises in it, as though a whole set of facts were immobilized and formed a series. They are described between two well-determined moments, in the space of a time existence had traversed as through a tunnel. The events related form a *situation* – akin to a plastic ideal. That is what myth is: the plasticity of a history. What we call the artist's choice is the natural selection of facts and traits which are fixed in a rhythm, and transform time into images.

This plastic issue of the literary work was noted by Proust in a particularly admirable page of *The Prisoner*. In speaking of Dostoyevsky, what holds his attention is neither Dostoyevsky's religious ideas, his metaphysics, nor his psychology, but some profiles of girls, a few images: the house of the crime with its stairway and its *dvornik* in *Crime and Punishment*, Grushenka's silhouette in *Brothers Karamazov*. It is as though we are to think that the plastic element of reality is, in the end, the goal of the psychological novel.

Much is said about atmosphere in novels. Criticism itself likes to adopt this meteorological language. Introspection is taken to be a novelist's fundamental procedure, and one supposes that things and nature can enter into a book only when they are enveloped in an atmosphere composed of human emanations. We think, on the contrary, that an exterior vision – of a total exteriority, like the exteriority in rhythm we have described above, where the subject itself is exterior to itself – is the true vision of the novelist. Atmosphere is the very obscurity of images. The poetry of Dickens, who was surely a rudimentary psychologist, the atmosphere of those dusty boarding schools, the pale light of London offices with their clerks, the antique and second-hand clothing shops, the very characters of Nickleby and Scrooge, only appear in an exterior vision set up as a method. There is no other method. Even the psychological novelist sees his inner life on the outside, not necessarily through the eyes of another, but as one participates in a rhythm or a dream. All the power of the contemporary novel, its art-magic, is perhaps due to this way of seeing inwardness from the outside – which is not all the same as the procedures of behaviorism.

Since Bergson it has become customary to take the continuity of time to be the very essence of duration. The Cartesian teaching of the discontinuity of duration is at most taken as the illusion of a time grasped in its spatial trace, an origin of false problems for minds incapable of conceiving duration. And a metaphor, one that is eminently spatial, of a cross-section made in duration, a photographic metaphor of a snapshot of movement, is accepted as a truism.

We on the contrary have been sensitive to the paradox that an instant can stop. The fact that humanity could have provided itself with art reveals in time the uncertainty of time's continuation and something like a death doubling the impulse of life. The petrification of the instant in the heart of duration – Niobe's punishment – the insecurity of a being which has a presentiment of fate, is the great obsession of the artist's world, the pagan world. Zeno, cruel Zeno – that arrow . . .

Here we leave the limited problem of art. This presentiment of fate in death subsists, as paganism subsists. To be sure, one need only give oneself a constituted duration to remove from death the power to interrupt. Death is then sublated. To situate it in time is precisely to go beyond it, to already find oneself on the other side of the abyss, to have it behind oneself. Death *qua* nothingness is the death of the other, death for the survivor. The time of *dying* itself cannot give itself the other shore. What is unique and poignant in this instant is due to the fact that it cannot pass. In *dying*, the horizon of the future is given, but the future as a promise of a new present is refused; one is in the interval, forever an interval. The characters of certain tales by Edgar Allen Poe must have found themselves in this empty interval. A threat appears to them in the approach of such an empty interval; no move can be made to retreat from its approach, but this approach can never end. This is the anxiety which in other tales is prolonged like a fear of being buried alive. It is as though death were never dead enough, as though parallel with the duration of the living ran the eternal duration of the interval – the *meanwhile*.

Art brings about just this duration in the interval, in that sphere which a being is able to traverse, but in which its shadow is immobilized. The eternal duration of the interval in which a statue is immobilized differs radically from the eternity of a concept; it is the meanwhile, never finished, still enduring – something inhuman and monstrous.

Inertia and matter do not account for the peculiar death of the shadow. Inert matter already refers to a substance to which its qualities cling. In a statue matter knows the death of idols. The proscription of images is truly the supreme command of monotheism, a doctrine that overcomes fate, that creation and revelation in reverse.

For philosophical criticism

Art then lets go of the prey for the shadow.

But in introducing the death of each instant into being, it effects its eternal duration in the meanwhile, has there its uniqueness, its value. Its value then is ambiguous – unique because it is impossible to go beyond it, because, being unable to end, it cannot go toward the *better*. It does not have the quality of the living instant which is open to the salvation of becoming, in which it can end and be surpassed. The value of this instant is thus made of its misfortune. This sad value is indeed the beautiful of modern art, opposed to the happy beauty of classical art.

On the other hand, art, essentially disengaged, constitutes, in a world of initiative and responsibility, a dimension of evasion.

Here we rejoin the most common and ordinary experience of aesthetic enjoyment. It is one of the reasons that bring out the value of art. Art brings into the world the obscurity of fate, but it especially brings the irresponsibility that charms as a lightness and grace. It frees. To make or to appreciate a novel and a picture is to no longer have to conceive, is to renounce the effort of science, philosophy, and action. Do not speak, do not reflect, admire in silence and in peace – such are the counsels of wisdom satisfied before the beautiful. Magic, recognized everywhere as the devil's part, enjoys an incomprehensible tolerance in poetry. Revenge is gotten on wickedness by producing its caricature, which is to take from it its reality without annihilating it; evil powers are conjured by filling the world with idols which have mouths but do not speak. It is as though ridicule killed, as though everything really can end in songs. We find an appeasement when, beyond the invitations to comprehend and act, we throw ourselves into the rhythm of a reality which solicits only its admission into a book or a painting. Myth takes the place of mystery. The world to be built is replaced by the essential completion of its shadow. This is not the disinterestedness of contemplation but of irresponsibility. The poet exiles himself from the city. From this point of view, the value of the beautiful is relative. There is something wicked and egoist and cowardly in artistic enjoyment. There are times when one can be ashamed of it, as of feasting during a plague.

Art then is not committed by virtue of being art. But for this reason art is not the supreme value of civilization, and it is not forbidden to conceive a stage in which it will be reduced to a source of pleasure – which one cannot contest without being ridiculous – having its place, but only a place, in man's happiness. Is it presumptuous to denounce the hypertrophy of art in our times when, for almost everyone, it is identified with spiritual life?

But all this is true for art separated from the criticism that integrates the inhuman work of the artist into the human world. Criticism already detaches it from its irresponsibility by envisaging its technique. It treats the artist as a man at work. Already in inquiring after the influences he undergoes it links this disengaged and proud man to real history. Such criticism is still preliminary. It does not attack the artistic event as such, that obscuring of being in images, that stopping of being in the meanwhile. The value of images for philosophy lies in their position between two times and their ambiguity. Philosophy discovers, beyond the enchanted rock on which it stands, all its possibles swarming about it. It grasps them by interpretation. This is to say that the artwork can and must be treated as a myth: the immobile statue has to be put in movement and made to speak. Such an enterprise is not the same as a simple reconstruction of the original from the copy. Philosophical exegesis will measure the distance that separates myth from real being, and will become conscious of the creative event itself, an event which eludes cognition, which goes from being to being by skipping over the intervals of the meanwhile. Myth is then at the same time untruth and the source of philosophical truth, if indeed philosophical truth involves a dimension of intelligibility proper to it, not content with laws and causes which connect beings to one another, but searching for the work of being itself.

Criticism, in interpreting, will choose and will limit. But if, *qua* choice, it remains on the hither side of the world which is fixed in art, it reintroduces that world into the intelligible world in which it stands, and which is the true homeland of the mind. The most lucid writer finds himself in the world bewitched by its images. He speaks in enigmas, by allusions, by suggestion, in equivocations, as though he moved in a world of shadows, as though he lacked the force to arouse realities, as though he could not go to them without wavering, as though, bloodless and awkward, he always committed himself further than he had decided to do, as though he spills half the water he is bringing us. The most forewarned, the most lucid writer none the less plays the fool. The interpretation of criticism speaks in full self-possession, frankly, through concepts, which are like the muscles of the mind.

Modern literature, disparaged for its intellectualism (which, none the less goes back to Shakespeare, the Molière of *Don Juan*, Goethe, Dostoyevsky), certainly manifests a more and more clear awareness of this fundamental insufficiency of artistic idolatry. In this intellectualism the artist refuses to be only an artist, not because he wants to defend a thesis or cause, but because he needs to interpret his myths himself. Perhaps the doubts that, since the renaissance, the alleged death of God has put in souls have compromised for the artist the reality of the henceforth inconsistent models, have imposed on him the onus of finding his models anew in the heart of his production itself, and made him believe he had a mission to be creator and revealer. The task of criticism remains essential, even if God was not dead, but only exiled. But we cannot here broach the 'logic' of the philosophical exegesis of art; that would demand a broadening of the intentionally limited perspective of this study. For one would have to introduce the perspective of the relation with the other without which being could not be told in its reality, that is, in its time.

Translated by Alphonso Lingis

Notes

All notes are by the translator unless otherwise indicated.

1 Cf. Martin Heidegger, *Being and Time*, trans. John Macquarrie and Edward Robinson, New York and Evanston, Harper and Row, 1962, p. 44.

2 Cf. Jean-Paul Sartre, *Literature and Existentialism*, trans. Bernard Frechtman, New York, Citadel, 1964.

3 Martin Heidegger, *Being and Time*, p. 405. Also 'On the Essence of Truth', trans. John Sallis in *Basic Writings*, ed. David Farrell Krell, New York, Harper and Row, 1993, pp. 127–30.

4 Jean-Paul Sartre, *Imagination, a Psychology of Imagination*, trans. Bernard Frechtman, New York, Washington Square Press, 1966.
5 Editor [Séan Hand]: Jean Giraudoux (1882–1944) wrote modern versions of classical tragedy which emphasized the human qualities inherent in classical myth.
6 Cf. Emmanuel Levinas, *Existence and Existents*, trans. Alphonso Lingis, The Hague, Martinus Nijhoff, 1978, p. 17.

7

THE WORLD OF THE AESTHETIC OBJECT

Mikel Dufrenne

We now proceed to confirm and develop what has already been suggested by the confrontation between the aesthetic object and the ordinary signifying object. The aesthetic object signifies neither in the manner of a history or physics book nor as a signal would. The aesthetic object addresses itself neither to the will so as to inform it nor to the intellect so as to instruct it. It *shows* and sometimes shows only itself, without referring to anything real. In any case, the aesthetic object does not claim to imitate the real (even if some aesthetic theories prescribe such imitation). When the authentic artist draws his inspiration from the real, he does so in order to measure himself against it and to remake it. Even when he celebrates the Creation he competes with it or, like Claudel, at least does not hide the fact that he collaborates with and completes it. In signifying, the aesthetic object does not exist to serve the world. It is, rather, the source of a world which is its own. The justification for speaking of 'world' here will be given below; at present we are content with describing it.

What is this world? Is it only a portion of the real world transposed into the work in such a way that the work represents it? Is the world of Balzac only the world of the Nucingens, the Vautrins, or the Chouans? Is the world of Rouault that of clowns, judges, and Crucifixions? And then what would be the world of Mozart or Chopin? When we name the world of the aesthetic object by its creator, we emphasize the presence of a certain style, a unique way of treating a subject, of making the sensuous serve representation. The Romanesque and the Gothic master builders have the same object; they both wish to erect God's house. But do Saint-Séverin and Sainte-Chapelle produce the same impression? How many painters have treated the Crucifixion? From Rembrandt to Rubens, it is the same Christ, but it is not the same Christianity. On the other hand, when Giraudoux shows us Bardini or Electra, when Bach writes cantatas or a concerto, when Goya paints a festival or a nightmare, it is to the same world that they give us access.[1] Sometimes it is even by means of that world that we identify the work, as surely as we do by the style, since the world is that which the style expresses.

These considerations suffice to inform us that the creator's world cannot be described according to norms valid for the objective world or even for the represented world. The world of the creator is expressed and not represented. It is not without relation to the represented world, but it is not identical with it, since two different subjects can participate equally in the same world, as when Phaedra and Athalie, who live before us on the stage in two different worlds – in two different plays – nevertheless communicate in the same world of Racine. It is not easy to see what this world is, yet we are immediately sensitive to its presence as soon as the aesthetic object introduces it to us. It is not a world of identifiable objects. One can neither explore it nor survey it, because one does not have to take distance into consideration with respect to it. In truth, it is less a world than the atmosphere of a world, in the sense that we say an atmosphere is tense or lively. Thus it is a matter of a certain quality of objects or of beings, but a quality which does not belong to them in their own right, since it is not they that bring it about. The quality in question is like a supervening or impersonal principle in accordance with which we say that there is an electric atmosphere or, as Trénet sang, that there is joy in the air. This principle is embodied in individuals or in things. It is somewhat like the collective consciousness which governs individual consciousness in times of agitation. Whether or not it is a principle of explanation, it is at any rate a reality that we feel keenly when we come into contact with the group from which it emanates. We have much the same experience in a dark forest. It seems to us that individual shadows are not the result of shade, but, on the contrary, that the shadows create the leafy summits and the entanglement of underbrush along with the entire vegetable mass in its damp mystery. The forest prevents us from seeing the tree, and the forest itself is seen only through its atmosphere. But here the atmosphere refers to the real world of men or things. To what does it refer in the aesthetic object? It is not a quality of the real world but of the object itself. The world of the aesthetic object is a world interior to the object. It is as such that we must describe it, leaving until later the examination of its coefficient of reality and its truth with respect to the real world. At the very moment when it proposes the real, the aesthetic object seems to exclude it or to convert it into its own substance. We become engaged in its world only by being diverted from *the* world, even if we do not leave it altogether and if the environment is always *mitgemeint* [cointended]. On the one hand, it is necessary that perception not degenerate into a dream, and there is perception only if we are in the world. On the other hand, the aesthetic object itself must be real in order to thrust itself upon us and to draw us into the world which it opens to us and which is its highest signification.

(a) The represented world

In order to understand the world of the aesthetic object, we must grasp it in its opposition but also in its quite limited relationship to the world as strictly represented. Are we not tempted to identify this latter world immediately with the subject of the work? Let us, therefore, first consider the represented world.[2] At first glance it thrusts itself upon our attention and appears to be the very substance of the work. But does it truly create a world by itself? Does the represented object raise itself to that height? The nature of the world, in fact, is to be open and to refer continually from object to object, extending all limits. The world is the inexhaustible reservoir of being which is attested to quantitatively by the infinite nature of space and time, but which is also symbolized by the myths of an inexhaustible creative power or of an eternal return of forms and kinds. Undoubtedly, the world can be adumbrated by the most humble object as soon as I realize that I cannot coincide with it entirely, that in its very presence it escapes me in some way, and that it is joined to something beyond itself which I am never able to reach or wholly master. In this respect, when the aesthetic object is considered as a thing, it attests to the world. If the world is to take shape in my sight, I must undertake to explore it or let my gaze lose itself at the horizon. I must have some contact with the unlimited. But does the object as aesthetically represented furnish a represented world? Yes and no. Even if the representation does not imitate, it tends to make the object leave its framework, to confer on this object the power of evoking the world in which the object is able to take its place. The real object, in contrast, possesses a plenitude by which it accords with the world as with that which surrounds and extends it.

I read a novel. Some characters evolve before me who have, by virtue of art, a certain density of being and constancy. These characters are present to me as is the hidden side of a cube, which ensures that the cube is more than a superficial spectacle and exists inviscerated in a perceptual field. The characters themselves live in a world which I experience as spatial and temporal density and as a peculiar style.[3] The art of the novelist may, however, take many different paths. It can, for instance, represent the world of things and events, the cosmic and human context, as an independent and primary reality – a sort of Great Being à la Comte, where individuals are sometimes caught in a trap, receiving their fate according to the place they occupy. The classical novel unfolds in this way, even if it depicts the context only in light strokes and reserves the bulk of the work for psychological design. But the novelist can, in contrast, according to a totally different perspective, subordinate the context to the individuals or to one special individual whose consciousness becomes a center of reference which is itself referred to no other. The contemporary novel most often operates in this way. Finally, one can, as it were, merge the two perspectives, obtaining a world which has a cosmic density through an entanglement of diverse aims, as if its substance were made of many adventures, decisions, fears, and hopes. Such appears to be the special unity of Dos Passos and Sartre. At any rate, there are no heroes except those engaged in a world. To conceive a hero of a novel is not only to recognize in him the opacity, the fullness, the secret property of a consciousness, it is also to grasp him in relation to a world which is both a correlative and a destiny, according to the ambiguity of the human condition. The world is suggested in the work by scattered indications whose synthesis we continually effect. This synthesis is realized, not in the manner of a judgment which collects and compares, but because each indication offers more than it is, as when a detail set apart within a whole is corroborated by other details. Yet the whole is never reducible to the sum of the parts, as Balzac sometimes seems to believe. It is in this sense that the indications in a novel are truly expressive, always saying more than their literal meaning. They are the inverse of clear and distinct ideas in which the meaning is rigorously coextensive with the signs. It is possible that the novelist's art – indeed, that of all artists – consists of choosing, of cutting out as much as of adding, for he is not interested in the prodigality of appearances or the indefiniteness of horizons. He retains only that which interests him. What he retains must suffice to allow us to reach a world of which we easily accept the fact that certain aspects are clear and others obscure, but which has the shape of a world all the same. This mixture of the implicit and explicit exists, moreover, in the image of the perceived world.

The represented world also possesses, in its own fashion, the spatiotemporal structure of the perceived world. Space and time here fill a dual function. They serve both to open up a world and to ordain it objectively by creating a world common to the characters and the readers. Even if they are centered in a character who experiences them, they also have meaning for the reader. They possess enough objectivity for the represented world to be identifiable and objective in the manner of the real world of which it is the image, although the represented world can be presented as lived and dominated by a central subjectivity with which the novelist identifies (and does not merely consign to a place in an impersonal world). This world is still subject to the requirements of representation and must appear objective enough for the reader to become oriented there. In the novel, space and time transfer the objectivity of the real to the represented elements. In fact, they appear according to the norms of objectivity, even when there is a flying carpet or seven-league boots to make light of distance. These distances are measurable, and we know it. Paris is at the same distance for heroes of novels and for the real traveler. Undoubtedly that space can be qualified by the restlessness of the hero as well as by his means of locomotion, but, as in the case of the real traveler, it is from an objective given that we understand the restlessness or that we appreciate the airplane he takes. Similarly, the time of the represented world imitates the time of the real world, to the point of reproducing it in the novels which explore the interior monologue, where the time of the reading and the time of the story recounted coincide in a certain fashion.[4] Even the time of legends and myths has the aspect of real time, as when heroes are engaged in adventures. Even more often the time of the novel makes reference to the time of objective history. The story unfolds between dates which exist on a calendar, referring to events which are localized in both history and geography.

There is at the least a sort of osmosis proceeding from the real world to the represented world, even for novelists who have abandoned the naturalistic illusion. Nevertheless, it will be said that the techniques of expressing time vary considerably and that certain novelists make free with objective time. This is certainly so, but it is not because such novelists abandon the time of the real world and claim to invent another time for the world which they represent. Rather, it is because the notion of a real time is itself ambiguous and gives rise to treatments and explanations which are quite diverse. Between objective time and lived time, between time-space and time-duration, the choice is always open. At least time can be described and recounted according to these two perspectives. One perspective orders time according to the causality of things, and the other orders time according to the spontaneity of a consciousness. Thus the novelist is able to choose the most appropriate means to indicate time, depending on whether he writes a story of a consciousness or a story of the world. Wherever he puts the accent, he strives to restore to time, within the world that he represents, the allure which it possesses for him in the real world. And he cannot entirely sacrifice the expression of objective time. Even if the time of the story is nothing but an objectified time and consequently is unable to claim ontological priority, it is nonetheless the means by which we gain access to a subjective time and to a necessary aspect of duration as well. A novelist like Faulkner, who abuses chronology (symbolized by Quentin's watch-smashing in *The Sound and the Fury*) in order to reveal the inanity of a present which is always the replica of a past and has meaning only in reference to the past, cannot prevent the reader from putting time in order so that he can recognize himself in it and give an objective meaning to the lived categories of before and after. Moreover, the novelist himself must provide the means for this act of ordering, e.g., by utilizing grammatical moods. It is due to our ability to reconstitute an objective structure of lived time that what is represented in a novel appears to have the density of a world.

The same holds true for all the representational arts. Each one makes certain privileged objects comply with an over-all scheme and places behind these objects backdrop which gives them, in contrast, more consistency and at the same time the indeterminacy of a world. Undoubtedly this backdrop itself can be minutely represented, as in the novels of Balzac, in early Flemish canvases, and in palaces surrounded by gardens in the French style. Such art neglects only what is intentionally omitted. The same precision attests to an effort to associate the world with the represented object in order to force the world into the structure of the work. One may say that this is a naïve effort. Does not a uniform background, an Elizabethan setting, suffice? Why encumber the aesthetic object and make it compete with the real? The setting [*le décor*], particularly in the theater, serves a double function. One function can be emphasized more than the other, but neither should be wholly neglected. The setting surrounds and delimits the aesthetic object in its sensuous body, and it gives to the represented object the aureole of a world.

In drama, as in the novel, the characters who live before me are also bound up in a world. In Racine's play, Phaedra, the daughter of Minos and Pasiphaé, is caught up in that dark Dionysiac universe in which Theseus, the heroic founder of cities who is freed from the Labyrinth, triumphs, but which condemns her to the infernal gods. Not only do I know of this world: I see it. Phaedra moves in a setting, but the setting signifies much more than it represents. Behind the palace suggested by a porch, a city exists for me from which noises sometimes arise in the wings. Indeed, all of Greece is present, as well as the distant shores – though no more distant for me than for Phaedra – where the survivor Theseus disembarks. But it is not necessary – in fact, it is impossible – that this fabulous geography be offered to the eye. It suffices if it is suggested to the mind by the indications of the text. Thus the signification remains for the most part confined to spoken words. One may here establish a comparison between the setting in the theater and in the film. In the theater, the words are what order the setting and give it its profound truth. It is not at all necessary that the setting create the illusion of reality, since it need only please the eye. Thus it need not compete with the dramatic object, for it is not empowered to constitute in itself an autonomous pictorial or architectural aesthetic object. However lively and pleasant the colors are, they do not possess the dignity of colors in an authentic painting. One covers the set with distempered paint, using the same elementary technique as the house painter. Moreover, the scene designer has no right to use stone, only cardboard and stucco. The setting, in principle, signifies only through the text which it is entrusted to illustrate.[5] In other words, the world of the dramatic work is as much presented to the mind as it is to the senses. It suffices to make only a discreet allusion to the senses, filling them up effortlessly rather than exciting them. For the scenery must not divert the eye from the actor. The scenery acts as a costume for him rather than as a geographical landmark. One of its functions can be seen in the kind of scenery which Christian Bérard composed for *Don Juan* and which involved the division of technical space to regulate the movements of the actors and the unfolding of the action. The setting is to the actor what the stadium is to the athlete or the race track to the horseman. At the same time, the setting encloses the space of the stage, separating it from the wings more strictly than from the audience. The setting is to the play what the frame is to the painting, though it also continues to function as the background. This is particularly evident in the ballet, where the dancers create, through their posture and their grouping, plastic shapes which often serve as a background for a solo or a duet and which themselves need a framework in order to be consolidated and to produce their effect. The setting is the framework of the performance [*représentation*] before becoming the framework of the represented object. It delimits the choreographic space before opening the space of the world where the action unfolds in the ballet. A few curtains suffice for this delimitation, unless the setting is more intimately associated with the aesthetic object.

The setting in the case of film is different. In fact, certain shots can stand out like a tableau – indeed, are sometimes specifically inspired by a pictorial work, so that the setting is first of all the means of framing the composition. Care in composition is required more or less explicitly in all visual art – architecture is the chief example. But the vocation of the cinema that corresponds to its technical possibilities is one that uses all the resources of the image in order to extend the field of representation to the dimensions of the world. Then the represented world, especially in exterior shots, gains the breadth which Van Eyck or Breughel present in their painting without their precise detail. In film, the setting assumes more responsibility than the spoken word for presenting the represented world, since the spoken word cannot have the same importance on the screen that it does on the stage. That which the text says, the screen is always able to show. This does not mean, however, that the value of the film's scenery is measured by its ability to create illusion. In fact, the cinema has taken over all the tricks of perspective that painting has abandoned. *Trompe-l'œil* is king in the cinema. The height of film art is all too often to make the corner of a studio hold a city. It uses miniatures of houses rapidly diminishing in size to obtain a truncated perspective. If necessary, it places extras in the background, among the houses with reduced dimensions – small children ridiculously dressed up in mustaches. Are these artifices still art? In this respect, film, so often eager to imitate the theater, may have something to learn from the latter. Without going to the extent of installing a prompter's box in a corner of the image, film should remember that art must never be ashamed of its medium and of its limits. Film can enlarge our vision without having to deceive us.

In other words, even when it is used to connect a world with the represented action, the setting must be selective and not try to show too much. Moreover, it always acts as some sort of frame. The setting limits the world which it evokes to the dimensions of the aesthetic object, closing it off as much as opening it up. Thus, if the represented world is an image of the real world, it is an image which is inevitably and voluntarily mutilated. That which the work gives us of the real world is only what is necessary to situate the characters or to illuminate the action. Its purpose is not so much to represent a world as to single out some determinate and meaningful object from within it, making this object its property and taking us back to it untiringly. In practical perception the horizon is like a challenge which we must take up, or like a question to which knowledge will provide an answer through an investigation that gradually moves it back. But the world which is the backdrop of the aesthetic object, instead of soliciting our attention, directs it immediately to the foreground, to the essential. Crete, reeking with the blood of the Minotaur, interests us only as a means of understanding Phaedra. The city which spreads out toward an enormous horizon in Van Eyck's *Madonna with Chancellor Rollin* requires only a sidelong look from us. Like the landscape of high rocks behind the *Mona Lisa*, the city is there only to offer the Madonna the same homage that we are supposed to give her. Thus the represented world is not truly a world by itself in the sense that the real world is. It cannot compete with the real world insofar as: (*a*) the represented world claims (and we agree to apply to it) the norm of objectivity; (*b*) one seeks in the represented world the image or the interpretation of the real world; and (*c*) the real world itself is conceived as an objective world which is the measure of all objectivity. If the aesthetic object offers us a world, it is in another manner and according to a mode which should be common to all of the arts, representational or not.

(b) The expressed world

The represented world does not allow us to speak yet of a world of the work which is original and singular. Undoubtedly it is a world distinct from the real world, with all the distance which separates the real from the represented. But it still imitates the real world, even if it is fantastic, since it always forms identifiable objects with the help of elements borrowed from the real, as studies on creative imagination have clearly shown. That is why works which do not raise themselves to the level of expression exhaust their entire ambition in copying the real. In contrast, if the work shuns imitation and constitutes an original creation on the level of representation itself, it is through its desire to be expressive, and, as we shall see, it is the expressed world which animates the represented world.

Moreover, the represented world is not truly a world. It is not self-sufficient; it is indeterminate. This is not only because it is represented and not real but also because it is incomplete. The work by itself affords us only sparse information about itself. However much we may know about this world and however precise our descriptions of it, there is always a beyond, just as there is a third dimension absent from a painting which the imagination tries vainly to fill out by lengthening and enriching the appearance. Undoubtedly this indeterminacy is characteristic of the world. It is that which escapes apprehension and cannot be totalized. It is the possibility of a perpetual progress or a labor of Sisyphus. Space and time, which form its structure, are the source of its indeterminacy. But we must add something else to this negative cosmology. What is the source of our ability to speak of a world if we are doomed to this infinite disorder, continually forced to relate one object to another? We must somehow obtain the idea of a possible totality, a unity for the indefinite. Within the objective world which science seeks to master, we may think that the idea of such unity comes from the very principle of unification. That which assures the unity of the world – that which allows one to think of a world – is the fact that all things are equally subsumed under the conditions of objectivity. What determines the indeterminate is, at the least, the fact that it is indefinitely determinable. Is this fact the source of the idea of world? We shall see. In any event, it cannot be the source for the idea of a world proper to the aesthetic object. We do not perceive the aesthetic object under the sign of determinism, that is, by confining to the understanding the task of pursuing indefinitely the unification of the world. It is deficient works – the ones that offer only an incoherent representation – which hand over to the understanding the chore of ordering the elements which they offer. Genuine works, even when they baffle the understanding, bear in themselves the principle of their unity. Their unity is both the perceived unity of the appearance as rigorously composed and the felt unity of a world represented by the appearance or, rather, emanating from it in such a way that what is represented itself signifies totality and is converted into a world.

What is the source of the unity by which the expressed is able to assume the shape of a world? We already know, from the fact that the consciousness of the artist is expressed through it, since there can be expression only of a subjectivity (and that is why we are able to identify the world of the aesthetic object and the world of the creator; the creator as revealed by the work is the guarantee of what the work reveals). The unity of an atmosphere is thus the unity of a *Weltanschauung*; its coherence is the coherence of a characteristic or quality. This *Weltanschauung* is not a doctrine but rather the vital metaphysical element in all men, the way of being in the world which reveals itself in a personality. We are not surprised that it can turn itself into a world, the world of an aesthetic object, since each man already radiates a world. There is a nimbus of joy around the joyous man. We say of another that he exudes boredom. The effect is such that ordinary objects can change their appearance through the mere presence of someone. But while expression ordinarily remains indistinct, its world blurred, the aesthetic object expresses the world of the artist with greater power and precision and gives it bulk and unity.

Therefore, a higher principle of unity comes to the aesthetic object from the fact that it is capable of expression, that is, from the fact that it signifies not only by representing but, through that which it represents, by producing in the perceiver a certain impression. Thus the aesthetic object manifests a certain quality which words cannot translate but which communicates itself in arousing a feeling. This quality proper to the work – to the works of a single creator or to a single style – is a world atmosphere. How is it produced? Through the ensemble from which it emanates. All the elements of the represented world conspire to produce it, according to their mode of representation. Take the novel, for example. It evokes a world. In its way, the novel establishes a setting in which characters evolve (with the reservation that, except in certain classical novels that are not entirely set free from the theater, the setting is only for us; for the character, it is a context to which he is dialectically bound). But the setting, the characters, and the events which are recounted, with varying degrees of emphasis, are chosen by the novelist, set apart from the undetermined story or outline in order to produce a certain total effect. Moreover, the precise intention which presides over that choice matters little. Whether the novelist wished to demonstrate the motives of a character in showing the hero subject to various tests, wished to sketch a sort of fresco, or simply wished to tell a story, the work, if it is successful, manifests a unity which transcends the detail of the representations. In one instance, the unity will proceed less from the unity of a character than from the unity of a life, a unity resulting from the indefinable resemblance between the actions of one man and thus between the situations in which he is caught and the visages which the world offers to him. In another instance, the unity will arise from a certain allure, from a rhythm common to events, from a style of the world as creating a style of life and not the converse – as in the swarming of bewildered insects in the incoherent universe of Dos Passos, or in the indifferent cruelty of Zola's universe regulated by laws which no Providence promulgates or amends, or in the proliferation of a voluntaristic world in Balzac's works. In still another case, the unity will proceed from the very rhythm of the story, as in the ardent or peaceful breathing of a world which hardens into fatality in the short stories of de Maupassant. In every instance, the choice of the novelist is justified by an identical result, that of producing a certain total effect like that which painters obtain (so obviously that there is no need to stress it) by the rigor with which they harmonize the values and colors of a composition.

What we have said of the setting can now be reconsidered in the light of the idea of the work's unity. The scenery in a play contributes to creating a world, first by enlarging the perspectives of the presentation, by giving a horizon to the represented objects as well as a framework for the actors. But, while assuming this indispensable function, the scenery is also able to combine more directly with the work by participating in its expressive function. Consider a setting like that of Bérard for *Les Bonnes*. Because it is presented as stuffy, sumptuous, and suffocating, an apartment is able to become the principal personage in a play. So, too, is a forest filled with mystery, especially when contrasted with the liberating sea, as Valentine Hugo has demonstrated in the case of *Pelléas et Mélisande*.[6] In such instances, the affective quality of the world matters more than its geography. Things are no longer a mere locus of action, they truly have a meaning by themselves – a meaning which is not their utilitarian meaning. They are aestheticized. The scenery ceases to decorate because it has undertaken the responsibility of expressing the world rather than leaving it to the care of the text. (However, the scenery must remain scenery and avoid deception; itself aestheticized, it belongs to the world of the work and not to the natural world.) The same is true for the architectural setting. If it is the real world which is annexed by the monument, it is more easily converted into an expressed world than into a represented world. For the architectural monument introduces us into a world of its own. Undoubtedly, the elements of this world are less easily distinguished from one another than those of the world of the play. Just as the real mingles with the aesthetic, so that which is represented – for example, the architectural signification, the historical context evoked by the style – mingles with what is expressed: nobility, fervor, majesty, tranquillity. Not to know the interior life of the architectural monument is to refuse it aesthetic quality. Versailles speaks to us through the rigor of its layout, the elegant equilibrium of its proportions, the discreet pomp of its embellishment, the delicate color of the stone. Its pure and measured voice expresses order and clarity and sovereign urbanity in the very countenance of stone. In such a building, man gains stature and solidity by the majesty which resounds in him, rebuking all dissonant emotion like a perfect harmony. And the surroundings – the park, the sky, and even the town – which the palace annexes and aestheticizes speak the same language. The setting is like a bass accompaniment to the clear voice of the monument.

Expression thus establishes a singular world. It is not the unity of a perceivable space, of an addable sum; it is not a unity which can be grasped from the outside, surveyed, and defined. It proceeds from an internal cohesion which is amenable only to the logic of feeling. The unity manifests itself both in what it integrates and in what it excludes. To see what it excludes, let us consider the problems posed by the mingling of genres. When we say that a certain tragic art, like that of Racine, excludes the comic, we mean that the world expressed by the tragedy is a closed world. It is open through the indefinite multiplicity of objects that is able to qualify, but closed – closed inwardly, so to speak, and according to the internal requirements of cohesion – because of what it rejects. And who is the judge of it? How is it possible, except through feeling, to condemn the false notes or to approve the harmony? That is why the problem of the unity of style is unable to receive an objectively and universally valid solution. But, when the work is done, one does know whether there is a unified feeling such as one experiences upon arriving in a coherent world, in a world which is truly a world. And it is notable that, if the internal unity is missing, there is no longer any expressiveness. There are only represented objects, which may be interesting or tedious but which are so diverse that they no longer form a world. This is the case in certain of Hugo's melodramas, or in those novels which 'end well' in order to please the reader. The danger is great, especially for composite works.[7] Moreover, the unity of the expressed world must include as much elasticity as rigor, perhaps because it is not ratified by an explicit logic. That the expression is total does not imply repetition or monotony. The cruel can alternate with the tender, as the tragic sometimes does with the comic, without destroying the unity of expression. Tenderness and buffoonery in Mozart's *Abduction from the Seraglio* form a precious mixture that constitutes a world of smiling liberty where the action delivers love from agony and restores it to innocence. Similarly, the sublime and the vulgar combine to form a world which one can only call Homeric. Just as different modes of behavior of the same man, provided that the behavior is not superficial and mechanical, possess an indefinable resemblance which attests to the reality of the person, so too in the same novel different scenes with different characters can exhibit, beyond their diversity, a subtle resemblance, like objects subject to the same illumination or movements transfigured by the same emotion. Such resemblance is the seal of the creator. It is also perceptible among the movements of a suite or a sonata. It is a long way from a minuet to a jig, from an adagio to a presto, and yet, in the presence of great works, we feel the unity of an atmosphere for which it would be vain to seek the reason in a thematic structure (as we would for cyclical works). The atmosphere changes and yet remains the same, sustaining a kind of organic development which does not change its essence. If the Ninth Symphony possesses such prestige, it is perhaps because of the admirable movement from a muted atmosphere in the beginning to a joyous sense of triumphant and fraternal freedom at the end – while passing through a frantic and then measured scherzo and a meditative adagio, without which the force of the movement would be broken and the spiritual unity destroyed.

Because expression is as much a principle of integration as of exclusion, we must say further that the expressed world clearly has the volume of a world. Like the Einsteinian universe, it is both finite and unlimited. It has an atmosphere that diffuses itself, not because it is ungraspable, but because it has the positive power of extending itself beyond the particular objects of which it is the quality and of drawing other objects to it in order to disclose itself through them. This atmosphere is like the spilled wine of which the poet speaks, which requires an entire sea in order to manifest its inexhaustible power of coloration.[8] The soft, delicate tranquillity which is expressed by the interiors of Vermeer is not contained between the walls which the painting encloses. It radiates upon an infinity of absent objects and constitutes the visage of a world of which it is the potentiality.[9] Thus the world of the aesthetic object certainly has the essential world-property of being open. But it is in intension rather than in extension, or, as we shall say, in depth. The world of the aesthetic object is not indefinite in the way that space and time are – in a mechanical way which becomes evident whenever one wishes to give it an objective representation. Rather, it is indefinite in the sense of a potentiality which no actualization can exhaust. It is an indefinite possibility of objects which are linked and reconciled by a common quality, as a sound is pregnant with innumerable harmonic overtones. In this respect, the aesthetic object has the dimensions of a world, dimensions which defy measurement not because there is always more to measure but because there is nothing yet to measure. This world is not crowded with objects; it precedes them. It is like a faint light in which they are revealed and in which everything that is perceptible in this light is disclosed – or, if one prefers, like an atmosphere in which all those things that can display themselves are revealed.

Thus the world of the aesthetic object is not yet structured in accordance with space and time but is rather the potentiality of space and time – as it is of objects as well. It cannot possess an objective space and time, since there is objectivity only in relation to objects which serve to order such space and time. Here we are not yet on the level of objects which the work can represent. Nor does the world of the aesthetic object possess a lived space and time. For space and time are lived only by appealing to objective space and time and through individual consciousnesses, and in the expressed world we fall short of represented personages. This is why we must try to catch space and time at their roots, where they are different from what they are in the represented world – a world for which they may lay the foundation. For representation as such flattens out space and above all stops time. Time as represented is time comprehended, and one can comprehend time only by invoking chronology. That is why the novelist often chooses the lazy solution of merely following chronology. At any rate, if the novel is incapable of *expressing* time, tricks designed to make living time appear, such as those which appear in Pouillon's analysis, are in vain. We return in the end to chronology.[10] For objective time to become animated, we must feel it spread through the aesthetic object, the aesthetic object must itself become temporal, and we must take charge of this temporality. We shall explore later in more detail the idea that the aesthetic object is able to be the source of its own time and space. This idea is posed to us now under another aspect, namely, that in expressing a world the aesthetic object already expresses a preobjective space and time *as* this world. And it is certainly the same idea, since the aesthetic object is capable of expression only in terms of its being. If it expresses space and time, this is because it is capable of spatializing and temporalizing in some way and not simply because it represents space and time objectively defined. Nor is it the case that the aesthetic object locates itself through its matter in the space and time of the ordinary world. Rather, the aesthetic object is the covert source of a space and time of its own.

In fact, the aesthetic object clearly manifests such space and time in its expression. The architectural monument has a grandeur or a loftiness incommensurable with its surface or its height. The symphony or the novel has a rhythm, a force, or a restraint of which an objective measure like the metronome gives only an impoverished image. We should realize that, in seeking to grasp expression, we disclose an unpopulated world, one which is only the promise of a world. The space and time which we find there are not structures of an organized world but qualities of an expressed world which is a prelude to knowledge. We already have this experience in the real world, where the first determinations of space and time – the far and the near, the absent and the present, the repeatable and the irrevocable – appear to us in impatience, dreaming, nostalgia, astonishment, and repulsion. In this way space is animated and hollowed out, and we respond to it through movement or through a plan, the rough draft of a movement. And it is thus that the aesthetic object possesses a spatiality of its own. In the presence of the Winged Victory, we are at first aware of an animated atmosphere of wind and of upward movement, creating a space which is that of taking flight and which has the dimensions of an ethereal world. The space of the garret where the dancer Babilée struggles like an animal caught in a trap (in the ballet staged by Roland Petit, *Le Jeune Homme et la mort*) is a closed and asphyxiating space which only death is able to open up and join to the horizons of the city, to the everyday life illuminated by the Eiffel Tower. Similarly, in Mallarmé's work, the feeling of emptiness which is communicated to us by the mysterious and chilling aspect of the verse hollows out space as the locus of a perpetual absence, and this emptiness precedes the being through which it speaks.

But it is above all time, in its preobjective form, which the aesthetic object manifests in its expression. There is (and we shall return to this point) a duration peculiar to the musical object. This duration is always movement, a movement which includes the movement of a soul fascinated by sound and immersed in a certain atmosphere. Objective time is still only an external means for the object to manifest this internal temporality of a world without objects or referents, and yet a world which is recognizable and imperiously offered. The titles of the movements or the indications of the tempo exhibit both the quality of the duration for the listener and the cadence of the rhythm for the performer – in short, the means of using the objective time which is like the prime matter of the work. In the literary work, there is likewise a temporality of the atmosphere that emanates from the peculiar style of the narrative and is independent of historical time. The rhythm of *Macbeth* is precipitate, whereas the action is spread out over years – twenty years, according to the chronicles on which the play is based. The rhythm of Joyce's *Ulysses* is extremely slow, whereas the action unfolds in twenty-four hours. Thus the atmosphere, depending on whether it is tragic or liberated, light or heavy, cheerful or suffocating, suggests a duration which shrinks or slackens, drags or quickens. Undoubtedly, if the expressed belongs inevitably to the represented, one could say that the duration is a function of the way in which the represented characters live time. Because Macbeth is fascinated, then corrupted, by crime, his will hurls him toward his own destruction; the fall of a soul into the snare of fatality is thus a movement uniformly accelerated. It is Macbeth's time – that of the evil project which he forms and of which he is captive, caught in its trap like the consciousness of a dreamer – which guides the theatrical time. Similarly, it is Bloom's time which guides the rhythm of the novel, a way of living without the future in an inconsistent universe whose only truth lies in a past which is more legendary than historical and which one recounts instead of repeating. But, conversely, one can say that there is a temporality of the tragic or of the aesthetic, that is, a temporality of the atmosphere which governs represented space and time and prepares us to grasp the space and time lived by the characters and even a sense of objective space and time. In truth, if there is a time peculiar to the work, it is not easily distinguishable from the time represented in the work. And yet the distinction is necessary, since represented time is a time which is said or shown but is not lived. At the limit, represented time is a time without temporalization, an arrested time such as we find in a painting representing dawn or twilight, or in Leconte de Lisle's poem, 'Midi, roi des étés.' It is time as an object, a time which is no longer time. Expressed time, in contrast, is a genuine time, since it is truly lived and grasped by the spectator capable of associating himself with the aesthetic object. It is in the spectator that the atmosphere temporalizes itself, that the quality of the world awakens the promise of time. In fact, the spectator experiences this temporality only because he also participates in the historical time which the characters live. Conversely, the spectator participates in historical time only because he is taken up in the atmosphere and is sensitive to its own duration.

(c) The represented world and the expressed world

The fact that it is difficult to distinguish between these two types of time, the nascent temporality in the expressed world and the time of the represented object, alerts us to the close relationship established between the expressed and the represented. We have said both that the expressed is like the effect of the represented and that the expressed precedes and heralds the represented. Both propositions are true. The relation of the expressed and the represented can be compared with that of the a priori and the a posteriori. The expressed is, as it were, the possibility of the represented, and the represented is the reality of the expressed. Together with the style which gives them body, they compose the world of the aesthetic object. We shall confirm this when we examine the structure of the aesthetic object since in it the signification is immanent in the sign. Meanwhile, we shall concentrate on the element of signification in order to specify the relationship between the represented and the expressed.

The verb 'to express' requires a subject, and in the present case the subject is the work. It is the *work* which expresses. Yet the work is first of all that which it represents. For this reason, the unity of the expression also depends on the represented objects – which tells us as well that the reflection attached to those objects will be an indispensable moment of aesthetic experience. In arts that are wholly representational in character, represented objects have a primary place, and it appears that they bear the expression in themselves and in such a way that we can read it directly. There is a world of *Hamlet* on the condition that the drama recount a story in which the characters meet, and events link up, in a certain setting. All the features furnished by the creator are here the witnesses and guardians of the expressed world, for example, the cock and donkey of Chagall, the dishonest soubrettes of Molière, the elongated bodies of El Greco. In the case of the writer, it is a matter of his key words, the system of images peculiar to him, and the arsenal of his adjectives (though he is not always so poverty-stricken in this regard as claims the professor in Giraudoux's *Juliette au pays des hommes*). With his treasure of words, the writer strives not so much to describe or mimic a pre-existing world as to evoke a world re-created by him.[11] All that is represented or suggested in this fashion signifies beyond the explicit meaning, as a word does in terms of its intonation. But it signifies still more radically, because the affective coefficient with which the magic of style endows the representation not only tends to emphasize the meaning but also to free it. The represented object becomes a symbol, but a symbol that is not swallowed up in an external signification (as happens in allegory), since this object does not pretend to translate a concept whose comprehension would render it useless. The represented object is not a springboard which one abandons at the moment of leaping from the sensuous to the intelligible. The expressed world is not another world but the expansion of represented objects to the dimensions of a world. When Valéry sings of the palm, a world opens to us where everything is palmlike – softly curved and fecund, patient, and rich with the grace of gesture and fulfillment.[12] But in the nonrepresentational arts, the work is expressive through the form of the sensuous, and the reading of expression cannot traverse the level of representation. This conclusion brings us to the second, and essential, form of the relationship between the expressed and the represented.

For the represented world has, conversely, need of the expressed world. More specifically, represented objects constitute a world only on the condition that the expression present a unity in multiplicity, somewhat like Claude Bernard's notion of a controlling idea which presides over the constitution of an organism. This primacy of the expressed is explicable in two propositions. First, it gives rise to represented objects. We have said that the atmosphere was produced by the objects, and we must now add that the objects are produced by the atmosphere. The paradox of this dialectical relationship tends to be blunted if one restricts oneself to the example of a nonrepresentational art like music, for then only one of the terms is entirely true. Musical expression does not result from represented objects. On the contrary, musical expression tends to arouse representations in the form of images which are often undesirable and which are a way for the atmosphere to crystallize into a world. This happens needlessly, because the work does not require it and the expressed world should suffice by itself. We even risk losing sight of the multitude of imaginary objects. But we must add that imagination is not responsible for this temptation – to which, however, it easily succumbs. Expression naturally solicits representation as a complement, yet expression is able to do without representation. This solicitation is authorized, on the contrary, in representational arts, where, paradoxically, the atmosphere seems to give rise to the represented world. Is this not what Malraux wishes to say in terms of the psychology of creation when he writes, in reference to Faulkner's *Sanctuary*, 'I would be not at all surprised if . . . the work were for him, not a story of which the unfolding determines tragic situations, but, on the contrary, a story born of tragedy, of the opposition and the crushing of unknown persons, and if the imagination serves only to lead logically from the characters to this original situation'?[13] Aesthetic experience confirms this observation. It is often through a certain atmosphere into which we are initially thrown that we apprehend the represented object. In the theater, for example, the first scenes directly instill in us a certain emotion which orients our entire comprehension. It is not sufficient that a problem be posed or an intrigue outlined, for it is also necessary that there be communicated to us a certain world-quality within which the problem or intrigue takes on meaning.

In other words, the expressed has primacy in a second sense. It transfigures the represented and confers on it a meaning through which it becomes inexhaustible – an inexhaustibility differing from that which it enjoys within reality. One may believe that this transformation occurs through the object's becoming unreal by being transported into the work, as if one were transplanting it, like a living species. To be sure, this conversion from the real to the unreal is important. We have already ascertained its effects in speaking of the innocuous character of the represented object. We may add here that the techniques peculiar to each art, the material conditions of the representation, are able to alter the shape of the object and even its affective character. One knows, for example, how in film a quite insignificant object is able to move us – a tear becomes unbearable, simply because its presence on the screen is unexpected and insistent. But in the present case, it is a matter of a metamorphosis which does not derive from material conditions but from the fact that the represented object is integrated into a new world. Heidegger says that 'Being is unable to manifest itself in any fashion if it is unable to find some way of entering into a world.'[14] It is through the transcendence of Dasein that this *Urgeschichte* is realized. One can say that the same unexpected event happens to the represented object, imparting to the aesthetic object something like the transcendence of Dasein. To express is to transcend toward a meaning, and the luminescence of the meaning – the quality of the atmosphere – gives rise to a new countenance for the object. What strange fragrance the fleurs-de-lis of medieval Annunciations take on in illuminating an immediately present world of purity and faith! And when it is Rimbaud who evokes illuminated manuscripts in the secret and amazing world which is peculiar to them, with what color they adorn themselves! Even the cinema in this way can convert the objects which it represents, and not only by exiling them on the screen. One thinks of the furnishings of a room in Rune Hagberg's astonishing film, *Après le crépuscule vient la nuit*. And we must go even farther. Not only does expression confer on what is represented that 'aura,' in Focillon's term, by which it becomes expressive (it is understood that the relation is dialectical, and that at the same time it is because what is represented is expressive that there is an expression). Furthermore, expression consecrates that which is objective in what is represented, that in it which imitates the real. It is because we are sensitive to that which the palm in Valéry's poem expresses, to that surplus of meaning with which it is charged, that we go straight to its vegetable existence, perceive its fullness, glimpse its solemn and peaceful curve, and make it truly a palm for us. When Rimbaud writes, 'O seasons, O castles!' in order to express the world of the helpless and miserable soul in a universe too full and too beautiful – to which the soul can become equal only in an act of denial – then seasons and castles are there in all their glory.[15] It is in like manner that the space and time of the novel or of theater can become veridical. They are objective at the level of the represented, but we have observed that the novelist can experiment with this objectivity without obscuring or annulling it (and thereby depriving space and time of their most pregnant meaning). For space and time form the matrix of the world insofar as the world is external to us and resists us. The novelist experiments in order to animate space and time, allowing us to seize again, on the level of expression, the movement through which they originally reveal the subject. The temporality or spatiality which the aesthetic object expresses, both by its structure and through the contrivances of representation, and with which the spectator is invited to associate himself, establish rather than destroy the objectivity of represented space and time and thus bring about the intelligibility of the narrative. Similarly, an adjective can found a substantive, creating an object by means of the expression which the adjective confers on the substantive – unless the substantive, poetically employed, contains its own adjective in the way that a sound vibrates with its harmonic overtones. The expressed thus confirms the represented in its objective being. The expressed founds the represented while at the same time being founded on it.

In short, the expressed world is like the soul of the represented world, which is, as it were, its body. The relationship which unites them renders them inseparable, and it is together that they constitute the world of the aesthetic object – a world through which this object gains depth. And it is due to their conjugal status that we are able to define the world of a work or of a creator in terms of what it contains. We can say that the world of Balzac is defined by a given social group in which a certain character circulates, or that the world of Cézanne is Provence, an osseous and ardent land, a land of persons who have the motionless opacity of that land. But then we must not forget that there is still another factor – that these landscapes, natural or human, express a certain vision of the world, composing an atmosphere to which a nonrepresentational art like music gives us direct access. In short, the world of the work is a finite but unlimited totality, a totality which the work shows through both its form and its content, while soliciting reflection as well as feeling. This world is the work itself, considered not in its immediate and meaningless reality as a mute thing without a soul but as a thing which surpasses itself toward its meaning – that is, as a quasi subject.

(d) The objective world and the world of the aesthetic object

One question still remains in abeyance, whether it is legitimate to use the term 'world' in order to designate that which the aesthetic object signifies, in particular the surplus of meaning by which the expressed overflows the represented. We have not inquired into the extent to which the world of the aesthetic object testifies to the objective world. We shall have to confront the problem later, when we inquire about the truth of the aesthetic object. But now we must justify the use we have already made of the notion of world. One objection is likely to be raised immediately – is this notion not applicable exclusively to the real? Is there not in the end a single world, the one in which representations and significations are given? Is not a world which is a function of signs a myth? For the understanding, the only world is the objective world. And reason, even if it is responsible for the *idea* of the world – the 'cosmological idea' – only carries understanding to its limit. Furthermore, an existential conception of the world which subjectifies it in linking it to the work of art, and through the latter to a concrete subject, would be nonsense. Must we accept this objection? That the world of the work is not a real world, in the sense that the objects among which I live are real, is evident. But for all that, does it deserve the title of world?

First of all, we may observe with Jaspers that the notion of an objective and total world is unspecifiable. As soon as I analyze it, I discover that it returns me to my own world, the world where I am and that I am – a world which is for me at one and the same time a correlate and a destiny. The earth is both the planet that revolves around the sun according to astronomy and the earth which sustains me ('precious firmness, o feeling of the earth!') and which, as Husserl says, 'does not, qua *Urarché*, move.' Thus 'if I speak of "the world," I immediately allude to two worlds which remain in spite of all distinctions.'[16] It is notable that science itself meets with this ambiguity (and has on occasion pointed it out to philosophers) when it finds itself obliged to renounce the idea of an objective world which is unique and universal. Indeed, biologists, and even sociologists who follow suit, orient their investigations towards the world as environment, as that which constitutes living beings, but also as that which is constituted by them through an irreducible reciprocal causality. It is here that we encounter the notion of a world which we can call 'subjective' in order to oppose it to an impersonal objective world which could be known only by a disembodied reason and which natural science strives to elaborate. But it is necessary to recall that, for the individual who lives it, his world is by no means subjective. It is real, pressing, and irreducible. For this reason, when reflection discovers such a world, it can no longer accord a monopoly to the objective world, the world that physics, or rather the metaphysics of nature in Kant's sense, knows. This 'subjective' world is neither the true world with respect to which other worlds would be only illusory nor the total world of which the others would be mere parts. On the contrary, it derives its value from the fact that it is deeply rooted in the human experience of the world which is the common world of coexistence. The world of the subject is not a subjectified world but a world in which and on which the subject harmonizes with other subjects. Such a subject is not an inalienable subjectivity but an existence 'given to itself.'[17] Thus this world appeals to an objective treatment which makes it appear as common to all subjects and thereby rejects the claims of the solipsistic *cogito* – in short, it appeals to science. But not even science challenges the initial experience of the subjective world. On the one hand, to the degree that science gets rid of its prejudice of scientism, it takes the subjective world seriously. Ought not the biologist who studies the spider's world in relation to its behavior have a feeling for its world through a kind of sympathy with the spider? In any case, such sympathy is quite evident when the question is, for the psychiatrist, that of grasping the perceptual field of a patient, as in Gelb's analysis of Schneider, or, for the sociologist, that of grasping the cultural field of the primitive.[18] On the other hand, it is possible that the reflection which is associated with a properly objective world is experienced only on the condition of first feeling it. Of course, reflection is conscious of feeling only to reject it, and the objections of Valéry and Pascal to this strategy of reflection pertain. But perhaps it was first necessary to contemplate the sky and be frightened by the silence of infinite spaces in order to conceive subsequently the astronomical world.[19] Similarly, it may be necessary first to feel chemical bodies, even at the price of the deviations with which imagination exploits this feeling, in order later to constitute a positive chemistry.[20] And when the theory of relativity teaches us that, by virtue of the mechanical equivalence of rest and uniform rectilinear transformation as stated by the principle of identity, all observation is dependent on the observer, such a theory appears to give a scientific transposition of the idea that all apprehension of a world is linked to a feeling of the world.

The objective world thus has no other prerogative than that of being the limit toward which each subjective world tends when the latter ceases being lived in order to be thought. It is an unspecifiable limit, because thought is always the thought of someone and is brought forth from an initial experience.[21] It is in the subjective world, then, that we must seek the root of the notion of the world and the fundamental relation of the world to a subjectivity – a subjectivity which is not a pure transcendental subjectivity, but precisely a subjectivity that defines itself by its relation to a world through the style of its being in the world. And it is thus that the idea of a world peculiar to the aesthetic object is justified as the expression of a creative subjectivity.

In fact, if we now stop short of the distinction between the subjective and the objective, what does the idea of the world signify? Kant tells us that it is an idea of reason which presupposes the establishment by understanding of an order among phenomena. For reason 'applies itself to understanding . . . being the faculty which secures the unity of the rules of understanding under principles.'[22] So close is the relation with understanding that Kant, after having said that 'the pure concepts of reason . . . which are *transcendental ideas* . . . are imposed by the very nature of reason itself,'[23] adds that 'pure and transcendental concepts can issue only from the understanding; reason does not really generate any concept; the most it can do is to *free* a concept of *understanding* from the unavoidable limitations of possible experience,'[24] so that the transcendental ideas are 'simply categories extended to the unconditioned.'[25] Thus the idea of the world is strictly unconditioned: 'What reason is really seeking . . . is solely the unconditioned.'[26] The idea of the totality of phenomena is only an application and an illustration of the idea of a primordial unity. It is because 'this *unconditioned* is always contained in the *absolute totality of the series* as represented in imagination' that 'reason here adopts the method of starting from the idea of totality, though what it really has in view is the *unconditioned*.'[27] Thus the unconditioned is not the last member of a series, the final and inaccessible object of representation. Rather, it is the soul of the series, that by which the series is a series. The principle 'to which all experience is subordinate, but which is never itself an object of experience,'[28] cannot be determined by a logical derivation analogous to that which allows the categories of understanding to be derived from judgments. Can we not say, then, that although the unconditioned is inaccessible to understanding, it nevertheless reveals itself to feeling – that the idea of the world is in the first place a feeling of the world (just as the moral law, a practical expression of reason, is grasped first through respect)? Furthermore, can we not say that the unconditioned proceeds from the very being of subjectivity? If the world is not the indefinite totality of phenomena but rather their unity (a unity which is like the quality that generates the series), and if the unconditioned is above all a mode of openness, is this not because subjectivity is itself an openness and, as Heidegger would say, transcendental?

As a matter of fact, on this precise point, which alone concerns us here, Heidegger carries on from Kant. He distinguishes, with Kant, two meanings of the term 'world,' one properly cosmological and attached to traditional metaphysics, and the other existential and found not only in the *Anthropology* but also in the *Critique of Pure Reason*. For the world, as the totality of phenomena, is an unconditioned that is still relative to a finite consciousness, and Kant distinguishes it from the transcendental ideal, which is the totality of all things as the object of the *intuitus originarius*.[29] He alludes at the same time to the finitude of consciousness and to the being of man, whose fundamental structure is finitude. Heidegger's interpretation consists in adding to this allusion the analysis of the *Anthropology*, where, as Kant says, 'the concept of the world designates the concept that involves what necessarily interests each man.'[30] In the last analysis, 'the world designates Dasein in the ground of its being.'[31] But we cannot call the world, even when it is defined as correlative to the transcendence of the subject, 'subjective.' Heidegger takes care to stress this: the subject is not subjective. Nor is that which corresponds to it, since it is defined precisely by the movement of transcendence: 'The world does not become a being within the sphere of the subjective.'[32] By producing the world 'before itself,' the subject discovers himself as belonging to a world. Thus the possibility arises of an objective treatment of the world as a world where I am (and not as a world that I am) – a treatment which will denounce the world as subjective from the outset and will consider the subject as merely one being among others, thereby neglecting the subject's power to transcend. The tension between the subjective world and the objective world has its source in the original experience of the world, which still falls short of the distinction between the objective and the subjective. In any case, the fact that the subject finds himself bound to the world, although suggesting an objective conception of the world as the locus or the totality of phenomena independent of subjectivity, does not disqualify the subjective world for the benefit of the objective world which rational thought strives to elaborate. It is thus that the aesthetic object can appear both as being in the world and as opening up a world.

But with what right do we invoke the aesthetic object here? Is it a subjectivity, a Dasein? Undoubtedly, the interpretation of the subjectivity of the subject which Heidegger proposes seeks above all to 'make possible the problem of Being.' Viewing the being of subjectivity as transcendence, Heidegger is led to propose that transcendence is itself an adventure of being.[33] But it remains that phenomenology is also able to lead to an existential psychoanalysis, on the condition that one accept the transition from the transcendental to the empirical, from the ontological to the anthropological.[34] The fundamental project which constitutes the subject as transcendence and discloses the world can be made determinate in singular projects, each of which discloses a peculiar world. In this case, the world is the singular world of a subject who loses nothing of his quality as subject when his project is the concrete project of a singular being in the world. We can thus speak of the world of a subject. But what of a world of the aesthetic object? We may speak of this too – if the aesthetic object is a quasi subject, that is, if it is capable of expression. In order to express, the aesthetic object must transcend itself toward a signification which is not the explicit signification attached to representations but a more fundamental signification that projects a world. In aesthetic experience, the unconditioned is the atmosphere of a world which is revealed by the expression through which the transcendence of the subject manifests itself. Moreover, we are justified in treating the aesthetic object as a quasi subject, because it is the work of a creator. A subject always appears in the aesthetic object, and that is why one is able to speak indifferently of a world of the creator or of a world of the work. The aesthetic object contains the subjectivity of the subject who has created it and expresses himself in it, and whom in turn it manifests.

Furthermore, the immanence of the creator in the aesthetic object guarantees the reality of the world of this object. For we are now facing a final problem whose answer we can only begin to sketch: is this world real? The question is in fact ambiguous but nevertheless cannot be evaded. For the question poses itself with persistence, whether it be when one opposes the singular world to an objective and total world, or whether it be when one considers that what the aesthetic object says or suggests is unreal or make-believe (because that which is represented only imitates the real, with more or less success, but is not itself real). Thus two implicit affirmations come together to disqualify the truth of the aesthetic object, that of the primacy of the objective world and that of the vanity of art, all of whose resources and ambition should go into imitating the world. The first affirmation leads to the view that the world of the aesthetic object is unreal, since it constitutes a personal interpretation of a world which is in itself impersonal. Reality is measured in terms of objectivity, so that night, for example, is real as an astronomical phenomenon but not real as gloom, as horror, or as that great peace of which Péguy speaks. To this view, we have replied that, even if the world does indeed authorize that quest for objectivity which entails that subjectivity deny itself – or at least make itself, as Jaspers says, exact – the notion of the world nonetheless has its root in the singular disclosure which is effected by subjectivity. The real then becomes what this subjectivity makes real, and the horror or the serenity of the night is as real as the astronomical fact of night. And the objective world cannot be invoked as embracing or explaining the subjective worlds – any more than optics explains vision when it substitutes a mechanical schema for vision, or than the world of the doctor comprehends the world of the sick, or than the world of the economist reconciles the worlds of management and proletariat. Nor can the world of the aesthetician reduce or replace the world of each creator. Moreover, the world of the aesthetic object is not unreal just because it is make-believe. Certainly, the represented object is unreal. Even for those who believe in hell, the demons of Bosch are unreal. The most exact portrait is unreal, since it does not proffer the subject himself. But the represented is not the essential element. The represented is only a means of saying something. And that which is said is real as soon as the objective world is no longer regarded as the absolute norm of the real. Even if demons are unreal, the world of Bosch is real – as the world of Mozart is real, even though nothing is represented in it. And if one is persistent, one can find a basis for the reality of these worlds in the objective world, since the aesthetic object is after all installed there. The creator has lived in the objective world. Yet it is the subjective worlds which finally *speak* and express a world that is as real as any other. The problem which remains is that of knowing to what extent this world is true and whether, in order to be true, it must be compared with the objective world. We shall approach this problem later.

It suffices for us to have shown that the aesthetic object is, like subjectivity itself, the source of a peculiar world that cannot be reduced to the objective world. We suspect that this world cannot reveal itself except to a subject who would be not only the witness of its epiphany but also capable of associating himself with the movement of the subjectivity which produced it – in brief, a subject who, instead of making himself a consciousness in general so as to think the objective world, responds to the subjectivity of the work through his own subjectivity. We have pointed to the form which aesthetic perception takes in this case – feeling, the specific mode of apprehending the expressed world. The study of aesthetic perception will attempt to establish this thesis in greater detail. But meanwhile, we must return to the being of the aesthetic object, which is in the world and contains its own world.

Translated by Edward S. Casey et al.

Notes

1 Is this still true when one compares Van Gogh's *The Potato Eaters* or his first landscapes, inspired by Corot, with the Arlesian canvases? Does it hold when one considers Rimbaud's first poems (which imitate Banville) alongside *Illuminations*? Certain creators are like Proteus. There are two remarks which must be made in this connection. First, when it is a question of the phenomenal creator, the one of whom the work speaks to us, and not of the actual creator, it is not, strictly speaking, the world of the creator to which one refers but the world of the aesthetic object. It is not the world of Racine but the world of the author of *Phèdre*. And if we do speak of a world of Racine, it is after the fact, when we have discovered an essential kinship between the world of the author of *Phèdre* and that of *Athalie*. Besides, it is noteworthy that modern culture strives to establish that relationship, in offering the complete works of an author or in collecting the chief works of a musician on recordings or of a painter in a museum. Then the style of the creator appears. The effect of the aggregate thus produced is incomparable. Each work is understood alongside the others, without losing its uniqueness. All of them fade away as if each were a voice in a single choir, a province of the same world. This is why we are able to speak of a world of the creator, but always on condition that we do not forget that the creator is revealed only through his works, and that his world is the one expressed in his works.

2 We shall limit ourselves to the representational arts. Whether there are truly nonrepresentational arts can be determined only by studying the nature and function of the subject in the structure of the aesthetic object.

3 How that is possible we are not able to discuss here. The imagination plays a role in it, perhaps not only in Sartre's sense but also in Kant's. The world as an idea of reason would have its root in the imagination as the unlimited power of disclosure. But the imagination opens up, whereas reason demands the possibility of closure, of achieving synthesis. Imagination poses an entirely valid standard, although one which is always on the horizon of knowing or acting.

4 Jean Pouillon points this out in *Temps et roman*, Paris, Gallimard, 1946, p. 186.

5 We shall see, however, that it is able to signify by itself and thus to be more directly associated with the aesthetic object.

6 This is the way that Gordon Craig conceives of the scenery:

> It is idle to talk about the distraction of scenery, because the question here is not how to create some distracting scenery, but rather how to create a place which harmonizes with the thoughts of the poet . . . Take *Macbeth* . . . I see two things. I see a lofty and steep rock, and I see the moist cloud which envelops the head of this rock. That is to say, a place for fierce and warlike men to inhabit, a place for phantoms to nest in. Ultimately this moisture will destroy the rock; ultimately these spirits will destroy the men.
>
> (Edward Gordon Craig, *On the Art of the Theatre*, New York, Theatre Arts Books, 1956, p. 22)

7 See Benedetto Croce, *The Essence of Aesthetic*, trans. Douglas Ainslie, London, Heinemann, 1921, pp. 36–37.
8 Dufrenne is thinking of the poem. 'Le Vin perdu,' by Paul Valéry. – Translator.
9 And that is why we are able to recognize it elsewhere, when we come back to the real, in the peacefulness of a landscape, in the serenity of a countenance, or wherever else. If it is possible that in a sense the aesthetic is the truth of the real, we shall see that it is because of this potentiality.
10 This is perhaps what distinguishes a novel like Aldous Huxley's *Eyeless in Gaza* from a novel like Virginia Woolf's *The Waves*. In the latter, we feel a certain quality of time whereby we are taken into an atmosphere of the unchanging, to the extent that the story communicates the lightness of childhood, the heaviness of memories, and the sclerosis of aging. [See Pouillon, *Temps et roman*. – Translator.]
11 For 'there are no adjectives in nature,' as Claude Roy remarks in his *Descriptions critiques* (Paris, Gallimard, 1949), a book which he dedicates to Colette.
12 Dufrenne refers to Paul Valéry's poem, 'Palme.' – Translator.
13 See André Malraux, *La Psychologie de l'art*, Geneva, Skira, 1947. – Translator.
14 See Martin Heidegger, 'What is Metaphysics?,' trans. R.F.C. Hull and Alan Crick in *Existence and Being*, ed. W. Brock, Chicago, Regnery, 1950. – Translator.
15 Arthur Rimbaud, 'A Season in Hell,' *Rimbaud: Complete Works, Selected Letters*, trans. Wallace Fowlie, Chicago, University of Chicago Press, 1966, p. 201.
16 Karl Jaspers, *Philosophy*, trans. E.B. Ashton, Chicago, University of Chicago Press, 1969, I, pp. 58f. Jaspers returns here to Heidegger's *Being and Time*, 'which has said the essential on the question'; and we shall ourselves call upon Heidegger in a moment.
17 One finds this expression in the work of both Jaspers and Merleau-Ponty.
18 See E. Gelb and K. Goldstein, *Psychologische Analysen hirnpathologischer Fälle*, Leipzig, Barth, 1920. – Translator.
19 'The eternal silence of these infinite spaces frightens me' (Blaise Pascal, *Pensées*, New York, E.P. Dutton, 1958, no. 206). – Translator.
20 Bachelard has demonstrated this clearly in *La Formation de l'esprit scientifique*, 4th ed., Paris, Vrin, 1938.
21 Conversely, the fact that the subjective world (at least in terms of human intersubjectivity) tends toward that limit prevents us from thinking that there is a numberable multiplicity of such worlds, and, for example, as many worlds as there are particular consciousness. For to suppose a countable plurality would be to suppose a totality, and, consequently, to come back to the idea that the subjective worlds are set apart from an objective world given or conceived previously.
22 Immanuel Kant, *Critique of Pure Reason*, trans. Norman Kemp Smith, New York, St. Martin's Press, 1929, B 359, p. 303.
23 Ibid., A 327, B 384, pp. 318–19.
24 Ibid., A 409, B 435, p. 386.
25 Ibid.
26 Ibid., A 416, B 444, p. 391.
27 Ibid., A 417, B 445, p. 391.
28 Ibid., A 311, B 367, pp. 308–09.
29 Dufrenne here refers to Kant's distinction between a derivative (*intuitus derivativus*) and an

original intuition, which, as Kant says, 'seems to belong solely to the primordial being.' See *Critique of Pure Reason*, B 72, p. 90. – Translator.

30 Cited by Martin Heidegger, *Kant and the Problem of Metaphysics*, trans. James S. Churchill, Bloomington, Indiana University Press, 1962.

31 By slipping from the cosmological to the existential, Heidegger rejoins the general interpretation which he gives of Kant in returning the transcendental to transcendence, and he illuminates the world by the notion of being-in-the-world. A world appears, a being 'enters a world,' because Dasein transcends toward it in a movement which constitutes it. It is clearly toward the world and not toward such and such a being that it transcends, for it is from the totality that Dasein is able to enter into relation with such and such a being. (Provided that one understands the world not as an ontic series but as ontological totality. Heidegger warns us on that matter in *The Essence of Reasons*, trans. Terrence Malick, Evanston, Illinois, Northwestern University Press, 1969. The analysis of *Umwelt* in *Being and Time* gives an initial characterization of the phenomenon of the world which only facilitates the transcendental analysis.) Thus Dasein 'finds itself in the midst of being and enters into relation with it' – whereas we shall say that Dasein has the feeling of a world, especially in view of the fact that Heidegger himself refers to the *Befindlichkeit* where that relation is expressed. In other words, 'that human reality transcends amounts to saying: in the essence of its being human reality is the *shaping of a world*' (*Essence of Reasons*, pp. 109 f.).

32 Ibid.

33 See Martin Heidegger, 'Letter on Humanism,' trans. E. Lohner, in *Philosophy in the Twentieth Century*, ed. W. Barrett and H. B. Aiken, New York, Random House, 1962, III, pp. 270ff.

34 In our own view, this transition is, for ontology, a decisive and inevitable trial. It is necessary to return to the cave.

8

THE DIALECTICS OF OUTSIDE AND INSIDE

Gaston Bachelard

Les géographies solennelles des limites humaines . . .
(Paul Eluard,
Les Yeux fertiles, p. 42)

(The solemn geographies of human limits)

Car nous sommes où nous ne sommes pas.
(Pierre-Jean Jouve,
Lyrique, p. 59)

(For we are where we are not.)

Une des maximes d'éducation pratique qui ont régi mon enfance: 'Ne mange pas la bouche ouverte.'
(Colette,
Prisons et paradis, p. 79)

(One of the maxims of practical education that governed my childhood: 'Don't eat with your mouth open.')

I

Outside and inside form a dialectic of division, the obvious geometry of which blinds us as soon as we bring it into play in metaphorical domains. It has the sharpness of the dialectics of *yes* and *no*, which decides everything. Unless one is careful, it is made into a basis of images that govern all thoughts of positive and negative. Logicians draw circles that overlap or exclude each other, and all their rules immediately become clear. Philosophers, when confronted with outside and inside, think in terms of being and non-being. Thus profound metaphysics is rooted in an implicit geometry which – whether we will or no – confers spatiality upon thought; if a metaphysician could not draw, what would he think? Open and closed, for him, are thoughts. They are metaphors that he attaches to everything, even to his systems.

In a lecture given by Jean Hyppolite on the subtle structure of denegation (which is quite different from the simple structure of negation) Hyppolite spoke[1] of 'a first myth of outside and inside.' And he added: 'you feel the full significance of this myth of outside and inside in alienation, which is founded on these two terms. Beyond what is expressed in their formal opposition lie alienation and hostility between the two.' And so, simple geometrical opposition becomes tinged with a[g]gressivity. Formal opposition is incapable of remaining calm. It is obsessed by the myth. But this action of the myth throughout the immense domain of imagination and expression should not be studied by attributing to it the false light of geometrical intuitions.[2]

'This side' and 'beyond' are faint repetitions of the dialectics of inside and outside: everything takes form, even infinity. We seek to determine being and, in so doing, transcend all situations, to give a situation of all situations. Man's being is confronted with the world's being, as though primitivity could be easily arrived at. The dialectics of *here* and *there* has been promoted to the rank of an absolutism according to which these unfortunate adverbs of place are endowed with unsupervised powers of ontological determination. Many metaphysical systems would need mapping. But in philosophy, all short-cuts are costly, and philosophical knowledge cannot advance from schematized experiments.

II

I should like to examine a little more closely, this geometrical cancerization of the linguistic tissue of contemporary philosophy.

For it does indeed seem as though an artificial syntax welded adverbs and verbs together in such a way as to form excrescences. By multiplying hyphens, this syntax obtains words that are sentences in themselves, in which the outside features blend with the inside. Philosophical language is becoming a language of agglutination.

Sometimes, on the contrary, instead of becoming welded together, words loosen their intimate ties. Prefixes and suffixes – especially prefixes – become unwelded: they want to think for themselves. Because of this, words are occasionally thrown out of balance. Where is the main stress, for instance, in *being-there* (être-là): on *being*, or on *there*? In *there* – which it would be better to call *here* – shall I first look for my being? Or am I going to find, in my being, above all, certainty of my fixation in a *there*? In any case, one of these terms always weakens the other. Often the *there* is spoken so forcefully that the ontological aspects of the problems under consideration are sharply summarized in a geometrical fixation. The result is dogmatization of philosophemes as soon as they are expressed. In the tonal quality of the French language, the *là* (there) is so forceful, that to designate being (*l'être*) by *être-là* is to point an energetic forefinger that might easily relegate intimate being to an exteriorized place.

But why be in such a hurry to make these first designations? One has the impression that metaphysicians have stopped taking time to think. To make a study of being, in my opinion, it is preferable to follow all the ontological deviations of the various experiences of being. For, in reality, the experiences of being that might justify 'geometrical' expression are among the most indigent . . . In French, one should think twice before speaking of *l'être-là*. Entrapped in being, we shall always have to come out of it. And when we are hardly outside of being, we always have to go back into it.

Thus, in being, everything is circuitous, roundabout, recurrent, so much talk; a chaplet of sojournings, a refrain with endless verses.

But what a spiral man's being represents![3] And what a number of invertible dynamisms there are in this spiral! One no longer knows *right away* whether one is running toward the center or escaping. Poets are well acquainted with the existence of this hesitation of being, as exemplified in this poem by Jean Tardieu:

> *Pour avancer je tourne sur moi-même*
> *Cyclone par l'immobile habité.*
> (Jean Tardieu,
> *Les Témoins invisibles*, p. 36)

> (In order to advance, I walk the treadmill of myself
> Cyclone inhabited by immobility.)

> *Mais au-dedans, plus de frontières!*

> (But within, no more boundaries!)

Thus, the spiraled being who, from outside, appears to be a well-invested center, will never reach his center. The being of man is an unsettled being which all expression unsettles. In the reign of the imagination, an expression is hardly *proposed*, before being needs another expression, before it must be the being of another expression.

In my opinion, verbal conglomerates should be avoided. There is no advantage to metaphysics for its thinking to be cast in the molds of linguistic fossils. On the contrary, it should benefit by the extreme mobility of modern languages and, at the same time, remain in the homogeneity of a mother tongue; which is what real poets have always done.

To benefit by all the lessons of modern psychology and all that has been learned about man's being through psychoanalysis, metaphysics should therefore be resolutely discursive. It should beware of the privileges of evidence that are the property of geometrical intuition. Sight says too many things at one time. Being does not see itself. Perhaps it listens to itself. It does not stand out, it is not *bordered* by nothingness: one is never sure of finding it, or of finding it solid, when one approaches a center of being. And if we want to determine man's being, we are never sure of being closer to ourselves if we 'withdraw' into ourselves, if we move toward the center of the spiral; for often it is in the heart of being that being is errancy. Sometimes, it is in being outside itself that being tests consistencies. Sometimes, too, it is closed in, as it were, on the outside. Later, I shall give a poetic text in which the prison is on the outside.

If we multiplied images, taking them in the domains of lights and sounds, of heat and cold, we should prepare a slower ontology, but doubtless one that is more certain than the ontology that reposes upon geometrical images.

I have wanted to make these general remarks because, from the point of view of geometrical expressions, the dialectics of outside and inside is supported by a reinforced geometrism, in which limits are barriers. We must be free as regards all *definitive* intuitions – and geometrism records definitive intuitions – if we are to follow the daring of poets (as we shall do later) who invite us to the finesses of experience of intimacy, to 'escapades' of imagination.

First of all, it must be noted that the two terms 'outside' and 'inside' pose problems of metaphysical anthropology that are not symmetrical. To make inside concrete and outside vast is the first task, the first problem, it would seem, of an anthropology of the imagination. But between concrete and vast, the opposition is not a true one. At the slightest touch, asymmetry appears. And it is always like that: inside and outside do not receive in the same way the qualifying epithets that are the measure of our adherence. Nor can one *live* the qualifying epithets attached to inside and outside in the same way. Everything, even size, is a human value, and we have already shown, in a preceding chapter, that miniature can accumulate size. It is *vast* in its way.

In any case, inside and outside, as experienced by the imagination, can no longer be taken in their simple reciprocity; consequently, by omitting geometrical references when we speak of the first expressions of being, by choosing more concrete, more phenomenologically exact inceptions, we shall come to realize that the dialectics of inside and outside multiply with countless diversified nuances.

Pursuing my usual method, I should like to discuss my thesis on the basis of an example of concrete poetics, for which I shall ask a poet to provide an image that is sufficiently new in its *nuance of being* to furnish a lesson in ontological amplification. Through the newness of the image and through its amplification, we shall be sure to reverberate above, or on the margin of reasonable certainties.

III

In a prose-poem entitled: *L'espace aux ombres* Henri Michaux writes:[4]

L'espace, mais vous ne pouvez concevoir, cet horrible en dedans–en dehors qu'est le vrai espace.

Certaines (ombres) surtout se bandant une dernière fois, font un effort désespéré pour 'être dans leur seule unité.' Mal leur en prend. J'en rencontrai une.

Détruite par châtiment, elle n'était plus qu'un bruit, mais énorme.

Un monde immense l'entendait encore, mais elle n'était plus, devenue seulement et uniquement un bruit, qui allait rouler encore des siècles mais destiné à s'éteindre complètement, comme si elle n'avait jamais été.

Shade-Haunted Space

(Space, but you cannot even conceive the horrible inside–outside that real space is.

Certain (shades) especially, girding their loins one last time, make a desperate effort to 'exist as a single unity.' But they rue the day. I met one of them.

Destroyed by punishment, it was reduced to a noise, a thunderous noise.

An immense world still heard it, but it no longer existed, having become simply and solely a noise, which was to rumble on for centuries longer, but was fated to die out *completely*, as though it had never existed.)

If we examine closely the lesson in philosophy the poet gives us, we shall find in this passage a spirit that has lost its 'being-there' (être-là), one that has so declined as to fall from *the being of its shade* and mingle with the rumors of being, in the form of meaningless noise, of a confused hum that *cannot be located.* It once was. But wasn't it merely the noise that it has become? Isn't its punishment the fact of having become the mere echo of the meaningless, useless noise it once was? Wasn't it formerly what it is now: a sonorous echo from the vaults of hell? It is condemned to repeat the word of its evil intention, a word which, being imprinted in being, has overthrown being.[5] And we are in hell, and a part of us is always in hell, walled-up, as we are, in the world of evil intentions. Through what naïve intuition do we locate evil, which is boundless, in a hell? This spirit, this shade, this noise of a shade which, the poet tells us, desires its unity, may be heard on the outside without it being possible to be sure that it is inside. In this 'horrible inside–outside' of unuttered words and unfulfilled intentions, within itself, being is slowly digesting its nothingness. The process of its reduction to nothing will last 'for centuries.' The hum of the being of rumors continues both in time and in space. In vain the spirit gathers its remaining strength. It has become the backwash of expiring being. Being is alternately condensation that disperses with a burst, and dispersion that flows back to a center. Outside and inside are both intimate – they are always ready to be reversed, to exchange their hostility. If there exists a border-line surface between such an inside and outside, this surface is painful on both sides. When we experience this passage by Henri Michaux, we absorb a mixture of being and nothingness. The center of 'being-there' wavers and trembles. Intimate space loses its clarity, while exterior space loses its void, void being the raw material of possibility of being. We are banished from the realm of possibility.

In this drama of intimate geometry, where should one live? The philosopher's advice to withdraw into oneself in order to take one's place in existence, loses its value, and even its significance, when the supplest image of 'being-there' has just been experienced through the ontological nightmare of this poet. Let us observe, however, that this nightmare is not visually frightening. The fear does not come from the outside. Nor is it composed of old memories. It has no past, no physiology. Nothing in common, either, with having one's breath taken away. Here fear is being itself. Where can one flee, where find refuge? In what shelter can one take refuge? Space is nothing but a 'horrible outside–inside.'

And the nightmare is simple, because it is radical. It would be intellectualizing the experience if we were to say that the nightmare is the result of a sudden doubt as to the certainty of inside and the distinctness of outside. What Michaux gives us as an a priori of being is the entire space-time of ambiguous being. In this ambiguous space, the mind has lost its geometrical homeland and the spirit is drifting.

Undoubtedly, we do not have to pass through the narrow gate of such a poem. The philosophies of anguish want principles that are less simplified. They do not turn their attention to the activity of an ephemeral imagination, for the reason that they inscribed anguish in the heart of being long before images had given it reality. Philosophers treat themselves to anguish, and all they see in the images are manifestations of its causality. They are not at all concerned with living the being of the image. Phenomenology of the imagination must assume the task of seizing this ephemeral being. In fact, phenomenology can learn from the very brevity of the image. What strikes us here is that the metaphysical aspect originates on the very level of the image, on the level of an image which disturbs the notions of a spatiality commonly considered to be able to reduce these disturbances and restore the mind to a statute of indifference to space that does not have to localize dramatic events.

Personally, I welcome this poet's image as a little piece of experimental folly, like a virtual grain of hashish without which it is impossible to enter into the reign of the imagination. And how should one receive an exaggerated image, if not by exaggerating it a little more, by personalizing the exaggeration? The phenomenological gain appears right away: in prolonging *exaggeration*, we may have the good fortune to avoid the habits of *reduction*. With space images, we are in a region where reduction is easy, commonplace. There will always be someone who will do away with all complications and oblige us to leave as soon as there is mention of space – whether figurative or not – or of the opposition of outside and inside. But if reduction is easy, exaggeration is all the more interesting, from the standpoint of phenomenology. This problem is very favorable, it seems to me, for marking the opposition between reflexive reduction and pure imagination. However, the direction of psychoanalytical interpretation – which is more liberal than classical literary criticism – follows the diagram of reduction. Only phenomenology makes it a principle to examine and test the psychological being of an image, before any reduction is undertaken. The dialectics of the dynamisms of reduction and exaggeration can throw light on the dialectics of psychoanalysis and phenomenology. It is, of course, phenomenology which gives us the psychic positivity of the image. Let us therefore transform our amazement into admiration. We can even begin by admiring. Then, later, we shall see whether or not it will be necessary to organize our disappointment through criticism and reduction. To benefit from this active, immediate admiration, one has only to follow the positive impulse of exaggeration. Here I read Michaux's poem over and over, and I accept it as a phobia of inner space, as though hostile remoteness had already become oppressive in the tiny cell represented by inner space. With this poem, Henri Michaux has juxtaposed in us claustrophobia and agoraphobia; he has aggravated the line of demarcation between outside and inside. But in doing so, from the psychological standpoint, he has demolished the lazy certainties of the geometrical intuitions by means of which psychologists sought to govern the space of intimacy. Even figuratively, nothing that concerns intimacy can be shut in, nor is it possible to fit into one another, for purposes of designating depth, impressions that continue to *surge up*. A fine example of phenomenological notation may be seen in the following simple line by a symbolist poet: 'The pansy took on new life when it became a corolla . . . '[6]

A philosopher of the imagination, therefore, should follow the poet to the ultimate extremity of his images, without ever reducing this extremism, which is the specific phenomenon of the poetic impulse. In a letter to Clara Rilke, Rilke wrote:

> Works of art always spring from those who have faced the danger, gone to the very end of an experience, to the point beyond which no human being can go. The further one dares to go, the more decent, the more personal, the more unique a life becomes.[7]

But is it necessary to go and look for 'danger' other than the danger of writing, of expressing oneself? Doesn't the poet put language in danger? Doesn't he utter words that are dangerous? Hasn't the fact that, for so long, poetry has been the echo of heartache, given it a pure dramatic tonality? When we really live a poetic image, we learn to know, in one of its tiny fibres, a becoming of being that is an awareness of the *being's inner disturbance*. Here being is so sensitive that it is upset by a word. In the same letter, Rilke adds: 'This sort of derangement, which is peculiar to us, must go into our work.'

Exaggeration of images is in fact so *natural* that however original a poet may be, one often finds the same impulse in another poet. Certain images used by Jules Supervielle, for instance, may be compared with the Michaux image we have just been studying. Supervielle also juxtaposes claustrophobia and agoraphobia when he writes: '*Trop d'espace nous étouffe beaucoup plus que s'il n'y en avait pas assez*.' (Too much space smothers us much more than if there were not enough.)[8]

Supervielle is also familiar with 'exterior dizziness' (p. 21). And elsewhere he speaks of 'interior immensity.' Thus the two spaces of inside and outside exchange their dizziness.

In another text by Supervielle, which Christian Sénéchal points out in his book on Supervielle, *the prison is outside*. After endless rides on the South American pampas, Supervielle wrote: 'Precisely because of too much riding and too much freedom, and of the unchanging horizon, in spite of our desperate gallopings, the pampa assumed the aspect of a prison for me, a prison that was bigger than the others.'

IV

If, through poetry, we restore to the activity of language its free field of expression, we are obliged to supervise the use of fossilized metaphors. For instance, when open and closed are to play a metaphorical rôle, shall we harden or soften the metaphor? Shall we repeat with the logicians that a door must be open or closed? And shall we find in this maxim an instrument that is really effective for analyzing human passions? In any case, such tools for analysis should be sharpened each time they are used. Each metaphor must be restored to its surface nature; it must be brought up out of habit of expression to actuality of expression. For it is dangerous, in expressing oneself, to be 'all roots.'

The phenomenology of the poetic imagination allows us to explore the being of man considered as the being of a *surface*, of the surface that separates the region of the same from the region of the other. It should not be forgotten that in this zone of sensitized surface, before being, one must speak, if not to others, at least to oneself. And advance always. In this orientation, the universe of speech governs all the phenomena of being, that is, the new phenomena. By means of poetic language, waves of newness flow over the surface of being. And language bears within itself the dialectics of open and closed. Through *meaning* it encloses, while through poetic expression, it opens up.

It would be contrary to the nature of my inquiries to summarize them by means of radical formulas, by defining the being of man, for instance, as the being of an ambiguity. I only know how to work with a philosophy of detail. Then, on the surface of being, in that region where being *wants* to be both visible and hidden, the movements of opening and closing are so numerous, so frequently inverted, and so charged with hesitation, that we could conclude on the following formula: man is half-open being.

V

But how many daydreams we should have to analyze under the simple heading of Doors! For the door is an entire cosmos of the Half-open. In fact, it is one of its primal images, the very origin of a daydream that accumulates desires and temptations: the temptation to open up the ultimate depths of being, and the desire to conquer all reticent beings. The door schematizes two strong possibilities, which sharply classify two types of daydream. At times, it is closed, bolted, padlocked. At others, it is open, that is to say, wide open.

But then come the hours of greater imagining sensibility. On May nights, when so many doors are closed, there is one that is just barely ajar. We have only to give it a very slight push! The hinges have been well oiled. And our fate becomes visible.

And how many doors were doors of hesitation! In *La Romance du retour*, by Jean Pellerin, this tender, delicate poet wrote:[9]

La porte me flaire, elle hésite.

(The door scents me, it hesitates.)

In this verse, so much psychism is transferred to the object that a reader who attaches importance to objectivity will see in it mere brain-play. If such a document had its source in some remote mythology, we should find it more readily acceptable. But why not take the poet's verse as a small element of spontaneous mythology? Why not sense that, incarnated in the door, there is a little threshold god? And there is no need to return to a distant past, a past that is no longer our own, to find sacred properties attributed to the threshold. In the third century, Porphyrus wrote: 'A threshold is a sacred thing.'[10] But even if erudition did not permit us to refer to such a sacralization, why should we not react to sacralization through poetry, through a poem of our own time, tinged with fantasy, perhaps, but which is in harmony with primal values?

Another poet, with no thought of Zeus, discovered the majesty of the threshold within himself and wrote the following:

Je me surprends à définir le seuil
Comme étant le lieu géométrique
Des arrivées et des départs
Dans la Maison du Père.[11]

(I find myself defining threshold
As being the geometrical place
Of the comings and goings
In my Father's House.)

And what of all the doors of mere curiosity, that have tempted being for nothing, for emptiness, for an unknown that is not even imagined?

Is there one of us who hasn't in his memories a Bluebeard chamber that should not have been opened, even half-way? Or – which is the same thing for a philosophy that believes in the primacy of the imagination – that should not even have been imagined open, or capable of opening half-way?

How concrete everything becomes in the world of the spirit when an object, a mere door, can give images of hesitation, temptation, desire, security, welcome and respect. If one were to give an account of all the doors one has closed and opened, of all the doors one would like to re-open, one would have to tell the story of one's entire life.

But is he who opens a door and he who closes it the same being? The gestures that make us conscious of security or freedom are rooted in a profound depth of being. Indeed, it is because of this 'depth' that they become so normally symbolical. Thus René Char takes as the theme of one of his poems this sentence by Albert the Great: 'In Germany there once lived twins, one of whom opened doors by touching them with his right arm, and the other who closed them by touching them with his left arm.' A legend like this, treated by a poet, is naturally not a mere reference. It helps the poet sensitize the world at hand, and refine the symbols of everyday life. The old legend becomes quite new when the poet makes it his own. He knows that there are two 'beings' in a door, that a door awakens in us a two-way dream, that it is doubly symbolical.

And then, onto what, toward what, do doors open? Do they open for the world of men, or for the world of solitude? Ramon Gomez de la Serna wrote: 'Doors that open on the countryside seem to confer freedom behind the world's back.'[12]

VI

As soon as the word *in* appears in an expression, people are inclined not to take literally the *reality of the expression*, and they translate what they believe to be figurative language into reasonable language. It is not easy for me, indeed it seems futile, to follow, for instance, the poet – I shall furnish documentation on the subject – who says that the house of the past is alive in his own head. I immediately interpret: the poet simply wants to say that an old memory has been preserved *in* his mind. The exaggerated nature of the image that seeks to upset the relationship of contained to container makes us shrink in the presence of what can appear to be mental derangement of images. We should be more indulgent if we were reading a fever chart. By following the labyrinth of fever that runs through the body, by exploring the 'seats of fever,' or the pains that inhabit a hollow tooth, we should learn that the imagination localizes suffering and creates and recreates imaginary anatomies. But I shall not use in this work the numerous documents that psychiatry provides. I prefer to underline my break with causalism by rejecting all organic causality. For my problem is to discuss the images of a pure, free imagination, a liberating imagination that has no connection with organic incitements.

These documents of absolute poetics exist. The poet does not shrink before reversals of dovetailings. Without even thinking that he is scandalizing reasonable men, contrary to the most ordinary common sense, he actually experiences reversal of dimensions or inversion of the perspective of inside and outside.

The abnormal nature of the image does not mean that it is artificially produced, for the imagination is the most natural of faculties. No doubt the images I plan to examine could not figure in a psychology of projects, even of *imaginary projects*. For every project is a contexture of images and thoughts that supposes a grasp of reality. We need not consider it, consequently, in a doctrine of pure imagination. It is even useless to *continue* an image, or to *maintain* it. All we want is for it to exist.

Let us study then, in all phenomenological simplicity, the documents furnished by poets.

In his book: *Où boivent les loups*, Tristan Tzara writes (p. 24):

Une lente humilité pénètre dans la chambre
Qui habite en moi dans la paume du repos.

(A slow humility penetrates the room
That dwells in me in the palm of repose.)

In order to derive benefit from the oneirism of such an image, one must no doubt first place oneself 'in the palm of repose,' that is, withdraw into oneself, and condense oneself in the being of a repose, which is the asset one has most easily 'at hand.' Then the great stream of simple humility that is in the silent room flows into ourselves. The intimacy of the room becomes our intimacy. And correlatively, intimate space has become so quiet, so simple, that all the quietude of the room is localized and centralized in it. The room is very deeply our room, it is in us. We no longer *see* it. It no longer *limits* us, because we are in the very ultimate depth of its repose, in the repose that it has conferred upon us. And all our former rooms come and fit into this one. How simple everything is!

In another passage, which is even more enigmatic for the reasonable mind, but quite as clear for anyone who senses the topoanalytical inversions of images, Tzara writes:

Le marché du soleil est entré dans la chambre
Et la chambre dans la tête bourdonnante.

(The market of the sun has come into my room
And the room into my buzzing head.)

In order to accept and hear this image, one must experience the strange whir of the sun as it comes into a room in which one is alone, for it is a fact that the first ray *strikes* the wall. These sounds will be heard also – over and beyond the fact – by those who know that every one of the sun's rays carries with it bees. Then everything starts buzzing and one's head is a hive, the hive of the sounds of the sun.

To begin with, Tzara's image was overcharged with surrealism. But if we overcharge it still more, if we increase the charge of image, if we go beyond the barriers set up by criticism, then we really enter into the surrealistic action of a pure image. And the exaggerated nature of the image is thus proved to be active and communicable, this means that it started well: the sunny room is buzzing *in* the head of the dreamer.

A psychologist will say that all my analysis does is to relate daring, too daring, 'associations.' And a psychoanalyst will agree perhaps to 'analyze' this daring; he is accustomed to doing this. Both of them, if they take the image as symptomatic, will try to find reasons and causes for it. A phenomenologist has a different approach. He takes the image just as it is, just as the poet created it, and tries to make it his own, to feed on this rare fruit. He brings the image to the very limit of what he is able to imagine. However far from being a poet he himself may be, he tries to repeat its creation for himself and, if possible, continue its exaggeration. Here association ceases to be fortuitous, but is sought after, willed. It is a poetic, specifically poetic, constitution. It is sublimation that is entirely rid of the organic or psychic weights from which one wanted to be free. In other words, it corresponds to pure sublimation.

Of course, such an image is not received in the same way every day. Psychically speaking, it is never objective. Other commentaries could renew it. Also, to receive it properly, one should be in the felicitous mood of super-imagination.

Once we have been touched by the grace of super-imagination, we feel it in the presence of the simpler images through which the exterior world deposits virtual elements of highly-colored space in the heart of our being. The image with which Pierre-Jean Jouve *constitutes* his secret being is one of these. He places it in his most intimate cell:

> *La cellule de moi-même emplit d'étonnement*
> *La muraille peinte à la chaux de mon secret.*
> (*Les Noces*, p. 50)

> (The cell of myself fills with wonder
> The white-washed wall of my secret.)

The room in which the poet pursues such a dream as this is probably not 'white-washed.' But this room in which he is writing is so quiet, that it really deserves its name, which is, the 'solitary' room! It is inhabited thanks to the image, just as one inhabits an image which is 'in the imagination.' Here the poet inhabits the cellular image. This image does not transpose a reality. It would be ridiculous, in fact, to ask the dreamer its dimensions. It does not lend itself to geometrical intuition, but is a solid framework for secret being. And secret being feels that it is guarded more by the whiteness of the lime-wash than by the strong walls. The cell of the secret is white. A single value suffices to coordinate any number of dreams. And it is always like that, the poetic image is under the domination of a heightened quality. The whiteness of the walls, alone, protects the dreamer's *cell*. It is stronger than all geometry. It is a part of the cell of intimacy.

Such images lack stability. As soon as we depart from expression as it is, as the author gives it, in all spontaneity, we risk relapsing into literal meaning. We also risk being bored by writing that is incapable of condensing the intimacy of the image. And we have to withdraw deep into ourselves, for instance, to read this fragment by Maurice Blanchot in the tonality of being in which it was written:

> About this room, which was plunged in utter darkness, I knew everything, I had entered into it, I bore it within me, I made it live, with a life that is not life, but which is stronger than life, and which no force in the world can vanquish.[13]

One feels in these repetitions, or to be more exact, in this constant strengthening of an image into which one has entered (and not of a room into which one has entered, a room which the author bears within himself, and which he has made live with a life that does not exist in life), one feels, as I said, that it is not the writer's intention merely to describe his *familiar* abode. Memory would *encumber* this image by stocking it with *composite memories* from several periods of time. Here everything is simpler, more radically simple. Blanchot's room is an abode of intimate space, it is his inner room.

We share the writer's image, thanks to what we are obliged to call a *general image*, that is, an image which participation keeps us from confusing with a *generality*. We individualize this general image right away. We live in it, we enter into it the way Blanchot enters into his. Neither word nor idea suffices, the writer must help us to reverse space; and shun description, in order to have a more valid experience of the hierarchy of repose.

Often it is from the very fact of concentration in the most restricted intimate space that the dialectics of inside and outside draws its strength. One feels this elasticity in the following passage by Rilke:[14] 'And there is almost no space here; and you feel almost calm at the thought that it is impossible for anything very large to hold in this narrowness.' There is consolation in knowing that one is in an atmosphere of calm, in a narrow space. Rilke achieved this narrowness intimately, in inner space where everything is commensurate with inner being. Then, in the next sentence, the text continues dialectically:

> But outside, everything is immeasurable. And when the level rises outside, it also rises in you, not in the vessels that are partially controlled by you, or in the phlegm of your most unimpressionable organs: but it grows in the capillary veins, drawn upward into the furthermost branches of your infinitely ramified existence. This is where it rises, where it overflows from you, higher than your respiration, and, as a final resort, you take refuge, as though on the tip of your breath. Ah! where, where next? Your heart banishes you from yourself, your heart pursues you, and you are already almost beside yourself, and you can't stand it any longer. Like a beetle that has been stepped on, you flow from yourself, and your lack of hardness or elasticity means nothing any more.
>
> Oh night without objects. Oh window muffled on the outside, oh, doors carefully closed; customs that have come down from times long past, transmitted, verified, never entirely understood. Oh silence in the stair-well, silence in the adjoining rooms, silence up there, on the ceiling. Oh mother, oh one and only you, who faced all this silence, when I was a child.

I have given this long passage without cuts for the reason that it has dynamic continuity. Inside and outside are not abandoned to their geometrical opposition. From what overflow of a ramified interior does the substance of being run, does the outside call? Isn't the exterior an old intimacy lost in the shadow of memory? In what silence does the stairwell resound? In this silence there are soft foot-steps: the mother comes back to watch over her child, as she once did. She restores to all these confused, unreal sounds their concrete, familiar meaning. Limitless night ceases to be empty space. This passage by Rilke, which is assailed by such frights, finds its peace. But by what a long, circuitous route! In order to experience it in the reality of the images, one would have to remain the contemporary of an osmosis between intimate and undetermined space.

I have presented texts that were as varied as possible, in order to show that there exists a play of values, which makes everything in the category of simple determinations fall into second place. The opposition of outside and inside ceases to have as coefficient its geometrical evidence.

To conclude this chapter, I shall consider a fragment in which Balzac defines determined opposition in the face of affronted space. This text is all the more interesting in that Balzac felt obliged to correct it.

In an early version of *Louis Lambert*, we read:

> When he used his entire strength, he grew unaware, as it were, of his physical life, and only existed through the all-powerful play of his interior organs, the range of which he constantly maintained and, according to his own admirable expression, he made *space withdraw before his advance*.[15]

In the final version, we read simply: 'He left space, as he said, behind him.'

What a difference between these two movements of expression! What decline of power of being faced with space, between the first and second forms! In fact, one is puzzled that Balzac should have made such a correction. He returned, in other words, to 'indifferent space.' In a meditation on the subject of being, one usually puts space between parentheses, in other words, one leaves space 'behind one.' As a sign of the lost 'tonalization' of being, it should be noted that 'admiration' subsided. The second mode of expression is no longer, according to the author's own admission, *admirable*. Because it really was admirable, this power to make *space withdraw*, to put space, all space, outside, in order that meditating being might be free to think.

Translated by Maria Jolas

Notes

1 Jean Hyppolite, Spoken commentary on the *Verneinung* (negation) of Freud. See *La Psychanalyse*, No. 1, 1956, p. 35.
2 Hyppolite brings out the deep psychological inversion of negation in denegation. Later, I plan to give examples of this inversion, on the simple level of images.
3 Spiral? If we banish geometry from philosophical intuitions, it reappears almost immediately.
4 Henri Michaux, *Nouvelles de l'étranger*, Paris, Mercure de France, 1952.
5 Another poet writes: 'To think that a mere word, a name, suffices to make the dividing walls of your strength come tumbling down.' Pierre Reverdy, *Risques et périls*, p. 23.
6 André Fontainas, *L'Ornement de la solitude*, Paris, Mercure de France, 1899, p. 22.
7 *Lettres*, Paris, Stock, p. 167.
8 Jules Supervielle, *Gravitations*, p. 19.
9 Jean Pellerin, *La Romance du retour*, N.R.F. 1921, p. 18.
10 Porphyrus, *The Nymph's Cave*, § 27.
11 Michel Barrault, *Dominicale*, I, p. 11.
12 Ramon Gomez de la Serna, *Echantillons*, Paris, Grasset, p. 167.
13 Maurice Blanchot, *L'Arrêt de mort*, p. 124.
14 Rilke, French translation, p. 106, of *Les Cahiers*.
15 Ed. Jean Pommier, *Corti*, p. 19.

9

THE INTERTWINING – THE CHIASM

Maurice Merleau-Ponty

If it is true that as soon as philosophy declares itself to be reflection or coincidence it prejudges what it will find, then once again it must recommence everything, reject the instruments reflection and intuition had provided themselves, and install itself in a locus where they have not yet been distinguished, in experiences that have not yet been 'worked over,' that offer us all at once, pell-mell, both 'subject' and 'object,' both existence and essence, and hence give philosophy resources to redefine them. Seeing, speaking, even thinking (with certain reservations, for as soon as we distinguish thought from speaking absolutely we are already in the order of reflection), are experiences of this kind, both irrecusable and enigmatic. They have a name in all languages, but a name which in all of them also conveys significations in tufts, thickets of proper meanings and figurative meanings, so that, unlike those of science, not one of these names clarifies by attributing to what is named a circumscribed signification. Rather, they are the repeated index, the insistent reminder of a mystery as familiar as it is unexplained, of a light which, illuminating the rest, remains at its source in obscurity. If we could rediscover within the exercise of seeing and speaking some of the living references that assign them such a destiny in a language, perhaps they would teach us how to form our new instruments, and first of all to understand our research, our interrogation, themselves.

The visible about us seems to rest in itself. It is as though our vision were formed in the heart of the visible, or as though there were between it and us an intimacy as close as between the sea and the strand. And yet it is not possible that we blend into it, nor that it passes into us, for then the vision would vanish at the moment of formation, by disappearance of the seer or of the visible. What there is then are not things first identical with themselves, which would then offer themselves to the seer, nor is there a seer who is first empty and who, afterward, would open himself to them – but something to which we could not be closer than by palpating it with our look, things we could not dream of seeing 'all naked' because the gaze itself envelops them, clothes them with its own flesh. Whence does it happen that in so doing it leaves them in their place, that the vision we acquire of them seems to us to come from them, and that to be seen is for them but a degradation of their eminent being? What is this talisman of color, this singular virtue of the visible that makes it, held at the end of the gaze, nonetheless much more than a correlative of my vision, such that it imposes my vision upon me as a continuation of its own sovereign existence? How does it happen that my look, enveloping them, does not hide them, and, finally, that, veiling them, it unveils them?[1]

We must first understand that this red under my eyes is not, as is always said, a *quale*, a pellicle of being without thickness, a message at the same time indecipherable and evident, which one has or has not received, but of which, if one has received it, one knows all there is to know, and of which in the end there is nothing to say. It requires a focusing, however brief; it emerges from a less precise, more general redness, in which my gaze was caught, into which it sank, before – as we put it so aptly – *fixing* it. And, now that I have fixed it, if my eyes penetrate into it, into its fixed structure, or if they start to wander round about again, the *quale* resumes its atmospheric existence. Its precise form is bound up with a certain wooly, metallic, or porous [?] configuration or texture, and the *quale* itself counts for very little compared with these participations. Claudel has a phrase saying that a certain blue of the sea is so blue that only blood would be more red. The color is yet a variant in another dimension of variation, that of its relations with the surroundings: this red is what it is only by connecting up from its place with other reds about it, with which it forms a constellation, or with other colors it dominates or that dominate it, that it attracts or that attract it, that it repels or that repel it. In short, it is a certain node in the woof of the simultaneous and the successive. It is a concretion of visibility, it is not an atom. The red dress a fortiori holds with all its fibers onto the fabric of the visible, and thereby onto a fabric of invisible being. A punctuation in the field of red things, which includes the tiles of roof tops, the flags of gatekeepers and of the Revolution, certain terrains near Aix or in Madagascar, it is also a punctuation in the field of red garments, which includes, along with the dresses of women, robes of professors, bishops, and advocate generals, and also in the field of adornments and that of uniforms. And its red literally is not the same as it appears in one constellation or in the other, as the pure essence of the Revolution of 1917 precipitates in it, or that of the eternal feminine, or that of the public prosecutor, or that of the gypsies dressed like hussars who reigned twenty-five years ago over an inn on the Champs-Elysées. A certain red is also a fossil drawn up from the depths of imaginary worlds. If we took all these participations into account, we would recognize that a naked color, and in general a visible, is not a chunk of absolutely hard, indivisible being, offered all naked to a vision which could be only total or null, but is rather a sort of straits between exterior horizons and interior horizons ever gaping open, something that comes to touch lightly and makes diverse regions of the colored or visible world resound at the distances, a certain differentiation, an ephemeral modulation of this world – less a color or a thing, therefore, than a difference between things and colors, a momentary crystallization of colored being or of visibility. Between the alleged colors and visibles, we would find anew the tissue that lines them, sustains them, nourishes them, and which for its part is not a thing, but a possibility, a latency, and a *flesh* of things.

If we turn now to the seer, we will find that this is no analogy or vague comparison and must be taken literally. The look, we said, envelops, palpates, espouses the visible things. As though it were in a relation of pre-established harmony with them, as though it knew them before knowing them, it moves in its own way with its abrupt and imperious style, and yet the views taken are not desultory – I do not look at a chaos, but at things – so that finally one cannot say if it is the look or if it is the things that command. What is this prepossession of the visible, this art of interrogating it according to its own wishes, this inspired exegesis? We would perhaps find the answer in the tactile palpation where the questioner and the questioned are closer, and of which, after all, the palpation of the eye is a remarkable variant. How does it happen that I give to my hands, in particular, that degree, that rate, and that direction of movement that are capable of making me feel the textures of the sleek and the rough? Between the exploration and what it will teach me, between my movements and what I touch, there must exist some relationship by principle, some kinship, according to which they are not only, like the pseudopods of the amoeba, vague and ephemeral deformations of the corporeal space, but the initiation to and the opening upon a tactile world. This can happen only if my hand, while it is felt from within, is also accessible from without, itself tangible, for my other hand, for example, if it takes its place among the things it touches, is in a sense one of them, opens finally upon a tangible being of which it is also a part. Through this crisscrossing within it of the touching and the tangible, its own movements incorporate themselves into the universe they interrogate, are recorded on the same map as it; the two systems are applied upon one another, as the two halves of an orange. It is no different for the vision – except, it is said, that here the exploration and the information it gathers do not belong 'to the same sense.' But this delimitation of the senses is crude. Already in the 'touch' we have just found three distinct experiences which subtend one another, three dimensions which overlap but are distinct: a touching of the sleek and of the rough, a touching of the things – a passive sentiment of the body and of its space – and finally a veritable touching of the touch, when my right hand touches my left hand while it is palpating the things, where the 'touching subject' passes over to the rank of the touched, descends into the things, such that the touch is formed in the midst of the world and as it were in the things. Between the massive sentiment I have of the sack in which I am enclosed, and the control from without that my hand exercises over my hand, there is as much difference as between the movements of my eyes and the changes they produce in the visible. And as, conversely, every experience of the visible has always been given to me within the context of the movements of the look, the visible spectacle belongs to the touch neither more nor less than do the 'tactile qualities.' We must habituate ourselves to think that every visible is cut out in the tangible, every tactile being in some manner promised to visibility, and that there is encroachment, infringement, not only between the touched and the touching, but also between the tangible and the visible, which is encrusted in it, as, conversely, the tangible itself is not a nothingness of visibility, is not without visual existence. Since the same body sees and touches, visible and tangible belong to the same world. It is a marvel too little noticed that every movement of my eyes – even more, every displacement of my body – has its place in the same visible universe that I itemize and explore with them, as, conversely, every vision takes place somewhere in the tactile space. There is double and crossed situating of the visible in the tangible and of the tangible in the visible; the two maps are complete, and yet they do not merge into one. The two parts are total parts and yet are not superposable.

Hence, without even entering into the implications proper to the seer and the visible, we know that, since vision is a palpation with the look, it must also be inscribed in the order of being that it discloses to us; he who looks must not himself be foreign to the world that he looks at. As soon as I see, it is necessary that the vision (as is so well indicated by the double meaning of the word) be doubled with a complementary vision or with another vision: myself seen from without, such as another would see me, installed in the midst of the visible, occupied in considering it from a certain spot. For the moment we shall not examine how far this identity of the seer and the visible goes, if we have a complete experience of it, or if there is something missing, and what it is. It suffices for us for the moment to note that he who sees cannot possess the visible unless he is possessed by it, unless he *is of it*,[2] unless, by principle, according to what is required by the articulation of the look with the things, he is one of the visibles, capable, by a singular reversal, of seeing them – he who is one of them.[3]

We understand then why we see the things themselves, in their places, where they are, according to their being which is indeed more than their being-perceived – and why at the same time we are separated from them by all the thickness of the look and of the body; it is that this distance is not the contrary of this proximity, it is deeply consonant with it, it is synonymous with it. It is that the thickness of flesh between the seer and the thing is constitutive for the thing of its visibility as for the seer of his corporeity; it is not an obstacle between them, it is their means of communication. It is for the same reason that I am at the heart of the visible and that I am far from it: because it has thickness and is thereby naturally destined to be seen by a body. What is indefinable in the *quale*, in the color, is nothing else than a brief, peremptory manner of giving in one sole something, in one sole tone of being, visions past, visions to come, by whole clusters. I who see have my own depth also, being backed up by this same visible which I see and which, I know very well, closes in behind me. The thickness of the body, far from rivaling that of the world, is on the contrary the sole means I have to go unto the heart of the things, by making myself a world and by making them flesh.

The body interposed is not itself a thing, an interstitial matter, a connective tissue, but a *sensible for itself*, which means, not that absurdity: color that sees itself, surface that touches itself – but this paradox [?]: a set of colors and surfaces inhabited by a touch, a vision, hence an *exemplar sensible*, which offers to him who inhabits it and senses it the wherewithal to sense everything that resembles himself on the outside, such that, caught up in the tissue of the things, it draws it entirely to itself, incorporates it, and, with the same movement, communicates to the things upon which it closes over that identity without superposition, that difference without contradiction, that divergence between the within and the without that constitutes its natal secret.[4] The body unites us directly with the things through its own ontogenesis, by welding to one another the two outlines of which it is made, its two laps: the sensible mass it is and the mass of the sensible wherein it is born by segregation and upon which, as seer, it remains open. It is the body and it alone, because it is a two-dimensional being, that can bring us to the things themselves, which are themselves not flat beings but beings in depth, inaccessible to a subject that would survey them from above, open to him alone that, if it be possible, would coexist with them in the same world. When we speak of the flesh of the visible, we do not mean to do anthropology, to describe a world covered over with all our own projections, leaving aside what it can be under the human mask. Rather, we mean that carnal being, as a being of depths, of several leaves or several faces, a being in latency, and a presentation of a certain absence, is a prototype of Being, of which our body, the sensible sentient, is a very remarkable variant, but whose constitutive paradox already lies in every visible. For already the cube assembles within itself incompossible *visibilia*, as my body is at once phenomenal body and objective body, and if finally it is, it, like my body, is by a *tour de force*. What we call a visible is, we said, a quality pregnant with a texture, the surface of a depth, a cross section upon a massive being, a grain or corpuscle borne by a wave of Being. Since the total visible is always behind, or after, or between the aspects we see of it, there is access to it only through an experience which, like it, is wholly outside of itself. It is thus, and not as the bearer of a knowing subject, that our body commands the visible for us, but it does not explain it, does not clarify it, it only concentrates the mystery of its scattered visibility; and it is indeed a paradox of Being, not a paradox of man, that we are dealing with here. To be sure, one can reply that, between the two 'sides' of our body, the body as sensible and the body as sentient (what in the past we called objective body and phenomenal body), rather than a spread, there is the abyss that separates the In Itself from the For Itself. It is a problem – and we will not avoid it – to determine how the sensible sentient can also be thought. But here, seeking to form our first concepts in such a way as to avoid the classical impasses, we do not have to honor the difficulties that they may present when confronted with a *cogito*, which itself has to be re-examined. Yes or no: do we have a body – that is, not a permanent object of thought, but a flesh that suffers when it is wounded, hands that touch? We know: hands do not suffice for touch – but to decide for this reason alone that our hands do not touch, and to relegate them to the world of objects or of instruments, would be, in acquiescing to the bifurcation of subject and object, to forego in advance the understanding of the sensible and to deprive ourselves of its lights. We propose on the contrary to take it literally to begin with. We say therefore that our body is a being of two leaves, from one side a thing among things and otherwise what sees them and touches them; we say, because it is evident, that it unites these two properties within itself, and its double belongingness to the order of the 'object' and to the order of the 'subject' reveals to us quite unexpected relations between the two orders. It cannot be by incomprehensible accident that the body has this double reference; it teaches us that each calls for the other. For if the body is a thing among things, it is so in a stronger and deeper sense than they: in the sense that, we said, it *is of them*, and this means that it detaches itself upon them, and, accordingly, detaches itself from them. It is not simply a thing *seen* in fact (I do not see my back), it is visible by right, it falls under a vision that is both ineluctable and deferred. Conversely, if it touches and sees, this is not because it would have the visibles before itself as objects: they are about it, they even enter into its enclosure, they are within it, they line its looks and its hands inside and outside. If it touches them and sees them, this is only because, being of their family, itself visible and tangible, it uses its own being as a means to participate in theirs, because each of the two beings is an archetype for the other, because the body belongs to the order of the things as the world is universal flesh. One should not even say, as we did a moment ago, that the body is made up of two leaves, of which the one, that of the 'sensible,' is bound up with the rest of the world. There are not in it two leaves or two layers; fundamentally it is neither thing seen only nor seer only, it is Visibility sometimes wandering and sometimes reassembled. And as such it is not in the world, it does not detain its view of the world as within a private garden: it sees the world itself, the world of everybody, and without having to leave 'itself,' because it is wholly – because its hands, its eyes, are nothing else than – this reference of a visible, a tangible-standard to all those whose resemblance it bears and whose evidence it gathers, by a magic that is the vision, the touch themselves. To speak of leaves or of layers is still to flatten and to juxtapose, under the reflective gaze, what coexists in the living and upright body. If one wants metaphors, it would be better to say that the body sensed and the body sentient are as the obverse and the reverse, or again, as two segments of one sole circular course which goes above from left to right and below from right to left, but which is but one sole movement in its two phases. And everything said about the sensed body pertains to the whole of the sensible of which it is a part, and to the world. If the body is one sole body in its two phases, it incorporates into itself the whole of the sensible and with the same movement incorporates itself into a 'Sensible in itself.' We have to reject the age-old assumptions that put the body in the world and the seer in the body, or, conversely, the world and the body in the seer as in a box. Where are we to put the limit between the body and the world, since the world is flesh? Where in the body are we to put the seer, since evidently there is in the body only 'shadows stuffed with organs,' that is, more of the visible? The world seen is not 'in' my body, and my body is not 'in' the visible world ultimately: as flesh applied to a flesh, the world neither surrounds it nor is surrounded by it. A participation in and kinship with the visible, the vision neither envelops it nor is enveloped by it definitively. The superficial pellicle of the visible is only for my vision and for my body. But the depth beneath this surface contains my body and hence contains my vision. My body as a visible thing is contained within the full spectacle. But my seeing body subtends this visible body, and all the visibles with it. There is reciprocal insertion and intertwining of one in the other. Or rather, if, as once again we must, we eschew the thinking by planes and perspectives, there are two circles, or two vortexes, or two spheres, concentric when I live naïvely, and as soon as I question myself, the one slightly decentered with respect to the other . . .

We have to ask ourselves what exactly we have found with this strange adhesion of the seer and the visible. There is vision, touch, when a certain visible, a certain tangible, turns back upon the whole of the visible, the whole of the tangible, of which it is a part, or when suddenly it finds itself *surrounded* by them, or when between it and them, and through their commerce, is formed a Visibility, a Tangible in itself, which belong properly neither to the body *qua* fact nor to the world *qua* fact – as upon two mirrors facing one another where two indefinite series of images set in one another arise which belong really to neither of the two surfaces, since each is only the rejoinder of the other, and which therefore form a couple, a couple more real than either of them. Thus since the seer is caught up in what he sees, it is still himself he sees: there is a fundamental narcissism of all vision. And thus, for the same reason, the vision he exercises, he also undergoes from the things, such that, as many painters have said, I feel myself looked at by the things, my activity is equally passivity – which is the second and more profound sense of the narcissim: not to see in the outside, as the others see it, the contour of a body one inhabits, but especially to be seen by the outside, to exist within it, to emigrate into it, to be seduced, captivated, alienated by the phantom, so that the seer and the visible reciprocate one another and we no longer know which sees and which is seen. It is this Visibility, this generality of the Sensible in itself, this anonymity innate to Myself that we have previously called flesh, and one knows there is no name in traditional philosophy to designate it. The flesh is not matter, in the sense of corpuscles of being which would add up or continue on one another to form beings. Nor is the visible (the things as well as my own body) some 'psychic' material that would be – God knows how – brought into being by the things factually existing and acting on my factual body. In general, it is not a fact or a sum of facts 'material' or 'spiritual.' Nor is it a representation for a mind: a mind could not be captured by its own representations; it would rebel against this insertion into the visible which is essential to the seer. The flesh is not matter, is not mind, is not substance. To designate it, we should need the old term 'element,' in the sense it was used to speak of water, air, earth, and fire, that is, in the sense of a *general thing*, midway between the spatio-temporal individual and the idea, a sort of incarnate principle that brings a style of being wherever there is a fragment of being. The flesh is in this sense an 'element' of Being. Not a fact or a sum of facts, and yet adherent to *location* and to the *now*. Much more: the inauguration of the *where* and the *when*, the possibility and exigency for the fact; in a word: facticity, what makes the fact be a fact. And, at the same time, what makes the facts have meaning, makes the fragmentary facts dispose themselves about 'something.' For if there is flesh, that is, if the hidden face of the cube radiates forth somewhere as well as does the face I have under my eyes, and coexists with it, and if I who see the cube also belong to the visible, I am visible from elsewhere, and if I and the cube are together caught up in one same 'element' (should we say of the seer, or of the visible?), this cohesion, this visibility by principle, prevails over every momentary discordance. In advance every vision or very partial visible that would here definitively come to naught is not nullified (which would leave a gap in its place), but, what is better, it is replaced by a more exact vision and a more exact visible, according to the principle of visibility, which, as though through a sort of abhorrence of a vacuum, already invokes the true vision and the true visible, not only as substitutes for their errors, but also as their explanation, their relative justification, so that they are, as Husserl says so aptly, not erased, but 'crossed out' . . . Such are the extravagant consequences to which we are led when we take seriously, when we question, vision. And it is, to be sure, possible to refrain from doing so and to move on, but we would simply find again, confused, indistinct, non-clarified, scraps of this ontology of the visible mixed up with all our theories of knowledge, and in particular with those that serve, desultorily, as vehicles of science. We are, to be sure, not finished ruminating over them. Our concern in this preliminary outline was only to catch sight of this strange domain to which interrogation, properly so-called, gives access . . .

But this domain, one rapidly realizes, is unlimited. If we can show that the flesh is an ultimate notion, that it is not the union or compound of two substances, but thinkable by itself, if there is a relation of the visible with itself that traverses me and constitutes me as a seer, this circle which I do not form, which forms me, this coiling over of the visible upon the visible, can traverse, animate other bodies as well as my own. And if I was able to understand how this wave arises within me, how the visible which is yonder is simultaneously my landscape, I can understand a fortiori that elsewhere it also closes over upon itself and that there are other landscapes besides my own. If it lets itself be captivated by one of its fragments, the principle of captation is established, the field open for another Narcissus, for an 'intercorporeity.' If my left hand can touch my right hand while it palpates the tangibles, can touch it touching, can turn its palpation back upon it, why, when touching the hand of another, would I not touch in it the same power to espouse the things that I have touched in my own? It is true that 'the things' in question are my own, that the whole operation takes place (as we say) 'in me,' within my landscape, whereas the problem is to institute another landscape. When one of my hands touches the other, the world of each opens upon that of the other because the operation is reversible at will, because they both belong (as we say) to one sole space of consciousness, because one sole man touches one sole thing through both hands. But for my two hands to open upon one sole world, it does not suffice that they be given to one sole *consciousness* – or if that were the case the difficulty before us would disappear: since other bodies would be known by me in the same way as would be my own, they and I would still be dealing with the same world. No, my two hands touch the same things because they are the hands of one same body. And yet each of them has its own tactile experience. If nonetheless they have to do with one sole tangible, it is because there exists a very peculiar relation from one to the other, across the corporeal space – like that holding between my two eyes – making of my hands one sole organ of experience, as it makes of my two eyes the channels of one sole Cyclopean vision. A difficult relation to conceive – since one eye, one hand, are capable of vision, of touch, and since what has to be comprehended is that these visions, these touches, these little subjectivities, these 'consciousnesses of . . . ,' could be assembled like flowers into a bouquet, when each being 'consciousness of,' being For Itself, reduces the others into objects. We will get out of the difficulty only by renouncing the bifurcation of the 'consciousness of' and the object, by admitting that my synergic body is not an object, that it assembles into a cluster the 'consciousnesses' adherent to its hands, to its eyes, by an operation that is in relation to them lateral, transversal; that 'my consciousness' is not the synthetic, uncreated, centrifugal unity of a multitude of 'consciousnesses of . . . ' which would be centrifugal like it is, that it is sustained, subtended, by the prereflective and preobjective unity of my body. This means that while each monocular vision, each touching with one sole hand has its own visible, its tactile, each is bound to every other vision, to every other touch; it is bound in such a way as to make up with them the experience of one sole body before one sole world, through a possibility for reversion, reconversion of its language into theirs, transfer, and reversal, according to which the little private world of each is not juxtaposed to the world of all the others, but surrounded by it, levied off from it, and all together are a Sentient in general before a Sensible in general. Now why would this generality, which constitutes the unity of my body, not open it to other bodies? The handshake too is reversible; I can feel myself touched as well and at the same time as touching, and surely there does not exist some huge animal whose organs our bodies would be, as, for each of our bodies, our hands, our eyes are the organs. Why would not the synergy exist among different organisms, if it is possible within each? Their landscapes interweave, their actions and their passions fit together exactly: this is possible as soon as we no longer make belongingness to one same 'consciousness' the primordial definition of sensibility, and as soon as we rather understand it as the return of the visible upon itself, a carnal adherence of the sentient to the sensed and of the sensed to the sentient. For, as overlapping and fission, identity and difference, it brings to birth a ray of natural light that illuminates all flesh and not only my own. It is said that the colors, the tactile reliefs given to the other, are for me an absolute mystery, forever inaccessible. This is not completely true; for me to have not an idea, an image, nor a representation, but as it were the imminent experience of them, it suffices that I look at a landscape, that I speak of it with someone. Then, through the concordant operation of his body and my own, what I see passes into him, this individual green of the meadow under my eyes invades his vision without quitting my own, I recognize in my green his green, as the customs officer recognizes suddenly in a traveler the man whose description he had been given. There is here no problem of the *alter ego* because it is not *I* who sees, not *he* who sees, because an anonymous visibility inhabits both of us, a vision in general, in virtue of that primordial property that belongs to the flesh, being here and now, of radiating everywhere and forever, being an individual, of being also a dimension and a universal.

What is open to us, therefore, with the reversibility of the visible and the tangible, is – if not yet the incorporeal – at least an intercorporeal being, a presumptive domain of the visible and the tangible, which extends further than the things I touch and see at present.

There is a circle of the touched and the touching, the touched takes hold of the touching; there is a circle of the visible and the seeing, the seeing is not without visible existence;[5] there is even an inscription of the touching in the visible, of the seeing in the tangible – and the converse; there is finally a propagation of these exchanges to all the bodies of the same type and of the same style which I see and touch – and this by virtue of the fundamental fission or segregation of the sentient and the sensible which, laterally, makes the organs of my body communicate and founds transitivity from one body to another.

As soon as we see other seers, we no longer have before us only the look without a pupil, the plate glass of the things with that feeble reflection, that phantom of ourselves they evoke by designating a place among themselves whence we see them: henceforth, through other eyes we are for ourselves fully visible; that lacuna where our eyes, our back, lie is filled, filled still by the visible, of which we are not the titulars. To believe that, to bring a vision that is not our own into account, it is to be sure inevitably, it is always from the unique treasury of our own vision that we draw, and experience therefore can teach us nothing that would not be outlined in our own vision. But what is proper to the visible is, we said, to be the surface of an inexhaustible depth: this is what makes it able to be open to visions other than our own. In being realized, they therefore bring out the limits of our factual vision, they betray the solipsist illusion that consists in thinking that every going beyond is a surpassing accomplished by oneself. For the first time, the seeing that I am is for me really visible; for the first time I appear to myself completely turned inside out under my own eyes. For the first time also, my movements no longer proceed unto the things to be seen, to be touched, or unto my own body occupied in seeing and touching them, but they address themselves to the body in general and for itself (whether it be my own or that of another), because for the first time, through the other body, I see that, in its coupling with the flesh of the world, the body contributes more than it receives, adding to the world that I see the treasure necessary for what the other body sees. For the first time, the body no longer couples itself up with the world, it clasps another body, applying [itself to it][6] carefully with its whole extension, forming tirelessly with its hands the strange statue which in its turn gives everything it receives; the body is lost outside of the world and its goals, fascinated by the unique occupation of floating in Being with another life, of making itself the outside of its inside and the inside of its outside. And henceforth movement, touch, vision, applying themselves to the other and to themselves, return toward their source and, in the patient and silent labor of desire, begin the paradox of expression.

Yet this flesh that one sees and touches is not all there is to flesh, nor this massive corporeity all there is to the body. The reversibility that defines the flesh exists in other fields; it is even incomparably more agile there and capable of weaving relations between bodies that this time will not only enlarge, but will pass definitively beyond the circle of the visible. Among my movements, there are some that go nowhere – that do not even go find in the other body their resemblance or their archetype; these are the facial movements, many gestures, and especially those strange movements of the throat and mouth that form the cry and the voice. Those movements end in sounds and I hear them. Like crystal, like metal and many other substances, I am a sonorous being, but I hear my own vibration from within; as Malraux said, I hear myself with my throat. In this, as he also has said, I am incomparable; my voice is bound to the mass of my own life as is the voice of no one else. But if I am close enough to the other who speaks to hear his breath and feel his effervescence and his fatigue, I almost witness, in him as in myself, the awesome birth of vociferation. As there is a reflexivity of the touch, of sight, and of the touch–vision system, there is a reflexivity of the movements of phonation and of hearing; they have their sonorous inscription, the vociferations have in me their motor echo. This new reversibility and the emergence of the flesh as expression are the point of insertion of speaking and thinking in the world of silence.[7]

At the frontier of the mute or solipsist world where, in the presence of other seers, my visible is confirmed as an exemplar of a universal visibility, we reach a second or figurative meaning of vision, which will be the *intuitus mentis* or idea, a sublimation of the flesh, which will be mind or thought. But the factual presence of other bodies could not produce thought or the idea if its seed were not in my own body. Thought is a relationship with oneself and with the world as well as a relationship with the other; hence it is established in the three dimensions at the same time. And it must be brought to appear directly in the infrastructure of vision. Brought to appear, we say, and not brought to birth: for we are leaving in suspense for the moment the question whether it would not be already implicated there. Manifest as it is that feeling is dispersed in my body, that for example my hand touches, and that consequently we may not in advance ascribe feeling to a thought of which it would be but a mode – it yet would be absurd to conceive the touch as a colony of assembled tactile experiences. We are not here proposing any empiricist genesis of thought: we are asking precisely what is that central vision that joins the scattered visions, that unique touch that governs the whole tactile life of my body as a unit, that *I think* that must be able to accompany all our experiences. We are proceeding toward the center, we are seeking to comprehend how there is a center, what the unity consists of, we are not saying that it is a sum or a result; and if we make the thought appear upon an infrastructure of vision, this is only in virtue of the uncontested evidence that one must see or feel in some way in order to think, that every thought known to us occurs to a flesh.

Once again, the flesh we are speaking of is not matter. It is the coiling over of the visible upon the seeing body, of the tangible upon the touching body, which is attested in particular when the body sees itself, touches itself seeing and touching the things, such that, simultaneously, *as* tangible it descends among them, *as* touching it dominates them all and draws this relationship and even this double relationship from itself, by dehiscence or fission of its own mass. This concentration of the visibles about one of them, or this bursting forth of the mass of the body toward the things, which makes a vibration of my skin become the sleek and the rough, makes me *follow with my eyes* the movements and the contours of the things themselves, this magical relation, this pact between them and me according to which I lend them my body in order that they inscribe upon it and give me their resemblance, this fold, this central cavity of the visible which is my vision, these two mirror arrangements of the seeing and the visible, the touching and the touched, form a close-bound system that I count on, define a vision in general and a constant style of visibility from which I cannot detach myself, even when a particular vision turns out to be illusory, for I remain certain in that case that in looking closer I would have had the true vision, and that in any case, whether it be this one or another, *there is a true vision*. The flesh (of the world or my own) is not contingency, chaos, but a texture that returns to itself and conforms to itself. I will never see my own retinas, but if one thing is certain for me it is that *one* would find at the bottom of my eyeballs those dull and secret membranes. And finally, I believe it – I believe that I have a man's senses, a human body – because the spectacle of the world that is my own, and which, to judge by our confrontations, does not notably differ from that of the others, with me as with them refers with evidence to typical dimensions of visibility, and finally to a virtual focus of vision, to a detector also typical, so that at the joints of the opaque body and the opaque world there is a ray of generality and of light. Conversely, when, starting from the body, I ask how it makes itself a seer, when I examine the critical region of the aesthesiological body, everything comes to pass (as we have shown in an earlier work)[8] as though the visible body remained incomplete, gaping open; as though the physiology of vision did not succeed in closing the nervous functioning in upon itself, since the movements of fixation, of convergence, are suspended upon the advent to the body of a visible world for which they were supposed to furnish the explanation; as though, therefore, the vision came suddenly to give to the material means and instruments left here and there in the working area a convergence which they were waiting for; as though, through all these channels, all these prepared but unemployed circuits, the current that will traverse them was rendered probable, in the long run inevitable: the current making of an embryo a newborn infant, of a visible a seer, and of a body a mind, or at least a flesh. In spite of all our substantialist ideas, the seer is being premeditated in counterpoint in the embryonic development; through a labor upon itself the visible body provides for the hollow whence a vision will come, inaugurates the long maturation at whose term suddenly it will see, that is, will be visible for itself, will institute the interminable gravitation, the indefatigable metamorphosis of the seeing and the visible whose principle is posed and which gets underway with the first vision. What we are calling flesh, this interiorly worked-over mass, has no name in any philosophy. As the formative medium of the object and the subject, it is not the atom of being, the hard in itself that resides in a unique place and moment: one can indeed say of my body that it is not *elsewhere*, but one cannot say that it is *here* or *now* in the sense that objects are; and yet my vision does not soar over them, it is not the being that is wholly knowing, for it has its own inertia, its ties. We must not think the flesh starting from substances, from body and spirit – for then it would be the union of contradictories – but we must think it, as we said, as an element, as the concrete emblem of a general manner of being. To begin with, we spoke summarily of a reversibility of the seeing and the visible, of the touching and the touched. It is time to emphasize that it is a reversibility always imminent and never realized in fact. My left hand is always on the verge of touching my right hand touching the things, but I never reach coincidence; the coincidence eclipses at the moment of realization, and one of two things always occurs: either my right hand really passes over to the rank of touched, but then its hold on the world is interrupted; or it retains its hold on the world, but then I do not really touch *it* – my right hand touching, I palpate with my left hand only its outer covering. Likewise, I do not hear myself as I hear the others, the sonorous existence of my voice is for me as it were poorly exhibited; I have rather an echo of its articulated existence, it vibrates through my head rather than outside. I am always on the same side of my body; it presents itself to me in one invariable perspective. But this incessant escaping, this impotency to superpose exactly upon one another the touching of the things by my right hand and the touching of this same right hand by my left hand, or to superpose, in the exploratory movements of the hand, the tactile experience of a point and that of the 'same' point a moment later, or the auditory experience of my own voice and that of other voices – this is not a failure. For if these experiences never exactly overlap, if they slip away at the very moment they are about to rejoin, if there is always a 'shift,' a 'spread,' between them, this is precisely because my two hands are part of the same body, because it moves itself in the world, because I hear myself both from within and from without. I experience – and as often as I wish – the transition and the metamorphosis of the one experience into the other, and it is only as though the hinge between them, solid, unshakeable, remained irremediably hidden from me. But this hiatus between my right hand touched and my right hand touching, between my voice heard and my voice uttered, between one moment of my tactile life and the following one, is not an ontological void, a non-being: it is spanned by the total being of my body, and by that of the world; it is the zero of pressure between two solids that makes them adhere to one another. My flesh and that of the world therefore involve clear zones, clearings, about which pivot their opaque zones, and the primary visibility, that of the *quale* and of the things, does not come without a second visibility, that of the lines of force and dimensions, the massive flesh without a rarefied flesh, the momentary body without a glorified body. When Husserl spoke of the horizon of the things – of their exterior horizon, which everybody knows, and of their 'interior horizon,' that darkness stuffed with visibility of which their surface is but the limit – it is necessary to take the term seriously. No more than are the sky or the earth is the horizon a collection of things held together, or a class name, or a logical possibility of conception, or a system of 'potentiality of consciousness': it is a new type of being, a being by porosity, pregnancy, or generality, and he before whom the horizon opens is caught up, included within it. His body and the distances participate in one same corporeity or visibility in general, which reigns between them and it, and even beyond the horizon, beneath his skin, unto the depths of being.

We touch here the most difficult point, that is, the bond between the flesh and the idea, between the visible and the interior armature which it manifests and which it conceals. No one has gone further than Proust in fixing the relations between the visible and the invisible, in describing an idea that is not the contrary of the sensible, that is its lining and its depth. For what he says of musical ideas he says of all cultural beings, such as *The Princess of Clèves* and *René*, and also of the essence of love which 'the little phrase' not only makes present to Swann, but communicable to all who hear it, even though it is unbeknown to themselves, and even though later they do not know how to recognize it in the loves they only witness. He says it in general of many other notions which are, like music itself 'without equivalents,' 'the notions of light, of sound, of relief, of physical voluptuousness, which are the rich possessions with which our inward domain is diversified and adorned.'[9] Literature, music, the passions, but also the experience of the visible world are – no less than is the science of Lavoisier and Ampère – the exploration of an invisible and the disclosure of a universe of ideas.[10] The difference is simply that this invisible, these ideas, unlike those of that science, cannot be detached from the sensible appearances and be erected into a second positivity. The musical idea, the literary idea, the dialectic of love, and also the articulations of the light, the modes of exhibition of sound and of touch speak to us, have their logic, their coherence, their points of intersection, their concordances, and here also the appearances are the disguise of unknown 'forces' and 'laws.' But it is as though the secrecy wherein they lie and whence the literary expression draws them were their proper mode of existence. For these truths are not only hidden like a physical reality which we have not been able to discover, invisible in fact but which we will one day be able to see facing us, which others, better situated, could already see, provided that the screen that masks it is lifted. Here, on the contrary, there is no vision without the screen: the ideas we are speaking of would not be better known to us if we had no body and no sensibility; it is then that they would be inaccessible to us. The 'little phrase,' the notion of the light, are not exhausted by their manifestations, any more than is an 'idea of the intelligence'; they could not be given to us *as ideas* except in a carnal experience. It is not only that we would find in that carnal experience the *occasion* to think them; it is that they owe their authority, their fascinating, indestructible power, precisely to the fact that they are in transparency behind the sensible, or in its heart. Each time we want to get at it[11] immediately, or lay hands on it, or circumscribe it, or see it unveiled, we do in fact feel that the attempt is misconceived, that it retreats in the measure that we approach. The explicitation does not give us the idea itself; it is but a second version of it, a more manageable derivative. Swann can of course close in the 'little phrase' between the marks of musical notation, ascribe the 'withdrawn and chilly tenderness' that makes up its essence or its sense to the narrow range of the five notes that compose it and to the constant recurrence of two of them: while he is thinking of these signs and this sense, he no longer has the 'little phrase' itself, he has only 'bare values substituted for the mysterious entity he had perceived, for the convenience of his understanding.'[12] Thus it is essential to this sort of ideas that they be 'veiled with shadows,' appear 'under a disguise.' They give us the assurance that the 'great unpenetrated and discouraging night of our soul' is not empty, is not 'nothingness'; but these entities, these domains, these worlds that line it, people it, and whose presence it feels like the presence of someone in the dark, have been acquired only through its commerce with the visible, to which they remain attached. As the secret blackness of milk, of which Valéry spoke, is accessible only through its whiteness, the idea of light or the musical idea doubles up the lights and sounds from beneath, is their other side or their depth. Their carnal texture presents to us what is absent from all flesh; it is a furrow that traces itself out magically under our eyes without a tracer, a certain hollow, a certain interior, a certain absence, a negativity that is not nothing, being limited very precisely to *these* five notes between which it is instituted, to that family of sensibles we call lights. We do not see, do not hear the ideas, and not even with the mind's eye or with the third ear: and yet they are there, behind the sounds or between them, behind the lights or between them, recognizable through their always special, always unique manner of entrenching themselves behind them, 'perfectly distinct from one another, unequal among themselves in value and in significance.'[13]

With the first vision, the first contact, the first pleasure, there is initiation, that is, not the positing of a content, but the opening of a dimension that can never again be closed, the establishment of a level in terms of which every other experience will henceforth be situated. The idea is this level, this dimension. It is therefore not a *de facto* invisible, like an object hidden behind another, and not an absolute invisible, which would have nothing to do with the visible. Rather it is the invisible *of* this world, that which inhabits this world, sustains it, and renders it visible, its own and interior possibility, the Being of this being. At the moment one says 'light,' at the moment that the musicians reach the 'little phrase,' there is no lacuna in me; what I live is as 'substantial,' as 'explicit,' as a positive thought could be – even more so: a positive thought is what it is, but, precisely, is only what it is and accordingly cannot hold us. Already the mind's volubility takes it elsewhere. We do not possess the musical or sensible ideas, precisely because they are negativity or absence circumscribed; they possess us. The performer is no longer producing or reproducing the sonata: he feels himself, and the others feel him to be at the service of the sonata; the sonata sings through him or cries out so suddenly that he must 'dash on his bow' to follow it. And these open vortexes in the sonorous world finally form one sole vortex in which the ideas fit in with one another. 'Never was the spoken language so inflexibly necessitated, never did it know to such an extent the pertinence of the questions, the evidence of the responses.'[14] The invisible and, as it were, weak being is alone capable of having this close texture. There is a strict ideality in experiences that are experiences of the flesh: the moments of the sonata, the fragments of the luminous field, adhere to one another with a cohesion without concept, which is of the same type as the cohesion of the parts of my body, or the cohesion of my body with the world. Is my body a thing, is it an idea? It is neither, being the measurant of the things. We will therefore have to recognize an ideality that is not alien to the flesh, that gives it its axes, its depth, its dimensions.

But once we have entered into this strange domain, one does not see how there could be any question of *leaving* it. If there is an animation *of* the body; if the vision and the body are tangled up in one another; if, correlatively, the thin pellicle of the *quale*, the surface of the visible, is doubled up over its whole extension with an invisible reserve; and if finally, in our flesh as in the flesh of things, the actual, empirical, ontic visible, by a sort of folding back, invagination, or padding, exhibits a visibility, a possibility that is not the shadow of the actual but is its principle, that is not the proper contribution of a 'thought' but is its condition, a style, allusive and elliptical like every style, but like every style inimitable, inalienable, an interior horizon and an exterior horizon between which the actual visible is a provisional partitioning and which, nonetheless, open indefinitely only upon other visibles – then (the immediate and dualist distinction between the visible and the invisible, between extension and thought, being impugned, not that extension be thought or thought extension, but because they are the obverse and the reverse of one another, and the one forever behind the other) there is to be sure a question as to how the 'ideas of the intelligence' are initiated over and beyond, how from the ideality of the horizon one passes to the 'pure' ideality, and in particular by what miracle a created generality, a culture, a knowledge come to add to and recapture and rectify the natural generality of my body and of the world. But, however we finally have to understand it, the 'pure' ideality already streams forth along the articulations of the aesthesiological body, along the contours of the sensible things, and, however new it is, it slips through ways it has not traced, transfigures horizons it did not open, it derives from the fundamental mystery of those notions 'without equivalent,' as Proust calls them, that lead their shadowy life in the night of the mind only because they have been divined at the junctures of the visible world. It is too soon now to clarify this type of surpassing that does not leave its field of origin. Let us only say that the pure ideality is itself not without flesh nor freed from horizon structures: it lives off them, though they be another flesh and other horizons. It is as though the visibility that animates the sensible world were to emigrate, not outside of every body, but into another less heavy, more transparent body, as though it were to change flesh, abandoning the flesh of the body for that of language, and thereby would be emancipated but not freed from every condition. Why not admit – what Proust knew very well and said in another place – that language as well as music can sustain a sense by virtue of its own arrangement, catch a meaning in its own mesh, that it does so without exception each time it is conquering, active, creative language, each time something is, in the strong sense, said? Why not admit that, just as the musical notation is a *facsimile* made after the event, an abstract portrait of the musical entity, language as a system of explicit relations between signs and signified, sounds and meaning, is a result and a product of the operative language in which sense and sound are in the same relationship as the 'little phrase' and the five notes found in it afterwards? This does not mean that musical notation and grammar and linguistics and the 'ideas of the intelligence' – which are acquired, available, honorary ideas – are useless, or that, as Leibniz said, the donkey that goes straight to the fodder knows as much about the properties of the straight line as we do; it means that the system of objective relations, the acquired ideas, are themselves caught up in something like a second life and perception, which make the mathematician go straight to entities no one has yet seen, make the *operative* language and algorithm make use of a second visibility, and make ideas be the other side of language and calculus. When I think they animate my interior speech, they haunt it as the 'little phrase' possesses the violinist, and they remain beyond the words as it remains beyond the notes – not in the sense that under the light of another sun hidden from us they would shine forth but because they are that certain divergence, that never-finished differentiation, that openness ever to be reopened between the sign and the sign, as the flesh is, we said, the dehiscence of the seeing into the visible and of the visible into the seeing. And just as my body sees only because it is a part of the visible in which it opens forth, the sense upon which the arrangement of the sounds opens reflects back upon that arrangement. For the linguist language is an ideal system, a fragment of the intelligible world. But, just as for me to see it is not enough that my look be visible for *X*, it is necessary that it be visible for itself, through a sort of torsion, reversal, or specular phenomenon, which is given from the sole fact that I am born; so also, if my words have a meaning, it is not *because* they present the systematic organization the linguist will disclose, it is because that organization, like the look, refers back to itself: the operative Word is the obscure region whence comes the instituted light, as the muted reflection of the body upon itself is what we call natural light. As there is a reversibility of the seeing and the visible, and as at the point where the two metamorphoses cross what we call perception is born, so also there is a reversibility of the speech and what it signifies; the signification is what comes to seal, to close, to gather up the multiplicity of the physical, physiological, linguistic means of elocution, to contract them into one sole act, as the vision comes to complete the aesthesiological body. And, as the visible takes hold of the look which has unveiled it and which forms a part of it, the signification rebounds upon its own means, it annexes to itself the speech that becomes an object of science, it antedates itself by a retrograde movement which is never completely belied – because already, in opening the horizon of the nameable and of the sayable, the speech acknowledged that it has its place in that horizon; because no locutor speaks without making himself in advance allocutary, *be it only for himself*; because with one sole gesture he closes the circuit of his relation to himself and that of his relation to the others and, with the same stroke, also sets himself up as *delocutary*, speech of which one speaks: he offers himself and offers every word to a universal Word. We shall have to follow more closely this transition from the mute world to the speaking world. For the moment we want only to suggest that one can speak neither of a destruction nor of a conservation of silence (and still less of a destruction that conserves or of a realization that destroys – which is not to solve but to pose the problem). When the silent vision falls into speech, and when the speech in turn, opening up a field of the nameable and the sayable, inscribes itself in that field, in its place, according to its truth – in short, when it metamorphoses the structures of the visible world and makes itself a gaze of the mind, *intuitus mentis* – this is always in virtue of the same fundamental phenomenon of reversibility which sustains both the mute perception and the speech and which manifests itself by an almost carnal existence of the idea, as well as by a sublimation of the flesh. In a sense, if we were to make completely explicit the architectonics of the human body, its ontological framework, and how it sees itself and hears itself, we would see that the structure of its mute world is such that all the possibilities of language are already given in it. Already our existence as seers (that is, we said, as beings who turn the world back upon itself and who pass over to the other side, and who catch sight of one another, who see one another with eyes) and especially our existence as sonorous beings for others and for ourselves contain everything required for there to be speech from the one to the other, speech about the world. And, in a sense, to understand a phrase is nothing else than to fully welcome it in its sonorous being, or, as we put it so well, to *hear what it says* (*l'entendre*). The meaning is not on the phrase like the butter on the bread, like a second layer of 'psychic reality' spread over the sound: it is the totality of what is said, the integral of all the differentiations of the verbal chain; it is given with the words for those who have ears to hear. And conversely the whole landscape is overrun with words as with an invasion, it is henceforth but a variant of speech before our eyes, and to speak of its 'style' is in our view to form a metaphor. In a sense the whole of philosophy, as Husserl says, consists in restoring a power to signify, a birth of meaning, or a wild meaning, an expression of experience by experience, which in particular clarifies the special domain of language. And in a sense, as Valéry said, language is everything, since it is the voice of no one, since it is the very voice of the things, the waves, and the forests. And what we have to understand is that there is no dialectical reversal from one of these views to the other; we do not have to reassemble them into a synthesis: they are two aspects of the reversibility which is the ultimate truth.

Translated by Alphonso Lingis

Notes

1 Editor [Claude Lefort]: Here in the course of the text itself, these lines are inserted:

> it is that the look is itself incorporation of the seer into the visible, quest for itself, which *is of it*, within the visible – it is that the visible of the world is not an envelope of *quale*, but what is between the qualia, a connective tissue of exterior and interior horizons – it is as flesh offered to flesh that the visible has its aseity, and that it is mine – The flesh as *Sichtigkeit* and generality. → whence vision is question and response . . . The openness through flesh: the two leaves of my body and the leaves of the visible world . . . It is

between these intercalated leaves that there is visibility . . . My body model of the things and the things model of my body: the body bound to the world through all its parts, up against it → all this means: the world, the flesh not as fact or sum of facts, but as the locus of an inscription of truth: the false crossed out, not nullified.

2 The *Uerpräsentierbarkeit* is the flesh.
3 The visible is not a tangible zero, the tangible is not a zero of visibility (relation of encroachment).
4 Editor: Here, in the course of the text itself, between brackets, these lines are inserted:

One can say that we perceive the things themselves, that we are the world that thinks itself – or that the world is at the heart of our flesh. In any case, once a body–world relationship is recognized, there is a ramification of my body and a ramification of the world and a correspondence between its inside and my outside, between my inside and its outside.

5 Editor: Here is inserted between brackets, in the course of the text itself, the note: 'what are these adhesions compared with those of the voice and the hearing?'
6 Editor: These words, which we reintroduce into the text, had been erased apparently by error.
7 Editor: Inserted here between brackets:

in what sense we have not yet introduced thinking: to be sure, we are not in the in itself. From the moment we said *seeing*, *visible*, and described the dehiscence of the sensible, we were, if one likes, in the order of thought. We were not in it in the sense that the thinking we have introduced was *there is*, and not *it appears to me that* . . . (appearing that would make up the whole of being, self-appearing). Our thesis is that this *there is* by inherence is necessary, and our problem to show that thought, in the restrictive sense (pure signification, thought of seeing and of feeling), is comprehensible only as the accomplishment by other means of the will of the *there is*, by sublimation of the *there is* and realization of an invisible that is exactly the reverse of the visible, the power of the visible. Thus between sound and meaning, speech and what it means to say, there is still the relation of reversibility, and no question of priority, since the exchange of words is exactly the differentiation of which the thought is the integral.

8 *The Structure of Behavior*, trans. Alden L. Fisher, Boston, 1963.
9 *Du côté de chez Swann*, II, Paris, 1926, p. 190. [English translation by C.K. Scott Moncrieff, *Swann's Way*, New York, 1928, p. 503.]
10 Ibid., p. 192. [Eng. trans., p. 505.]
11 Editor: It: that is, the idea.
12 *Du côté de chez Swann*, II, p. 189. [Eng. trans., p. 503.]
13 Ibid.
14 Ibid., p. 192. [Eng. trans., p. 505.]

10

AESTHETICS AND HERMENEUTICS

Hans-Georg Gadamer

If we define the task of hermeneutics as the bridging of personal or historical distance between minds, then the experience of art would seem to fall entirely outside its province. For of all the things that confront us in nature and history, it is the work of art that speaks to us most directly. It possesses a mysterious intimacy that grips our entire being, as if there were no distance at all and every encounter with it were an encounter with ourselves. We can refer to Hegel in this connection. He considered art to be one of the forms of Absolute Spirit, that is, he saw in art a form of Spirit's self-knowledge in which nothing alien and unredeemable appeared, a form in which there was no contingency of the actual, no unintelligibility of what is merely given. In fact, an absolute contemporaneousness exists between the work and its present beholder that persists unhampered despite every intensification of the historical consciousness. The reality of the work of art and its expressive power cannot be restricted to its original historical horizon, in which the beholder was actually the contemporary of the creator. It seems instead to belong to the experience of art that the work of art always has its own present. Only in a limited way does it retain its historical origin within itself. The work of art is the expression of a truth that cannot be reduced to what its creator actually thought in it. Whether we call it the unconscious creation of the genius or consider the conceptual inexhaustibility of every artistic expression from the point of view of the beholder, the aesthetic consciousness can appeal to the fact that the work of art communicates itself.

The hermeneutical perspective is so comprehensive, however, that it must even include the experience of beauty in nature and art. If it is the fundamental constitution of the historicity of human Dasein to mediate itself to itself understandingly – which necessarily means to the whole of its own experience of the world – then *all* tradition belongs to it. Tradition encompasses institutions and life-forms as well as texts. Above all, however, the encounter with art belongs within the process of integration that is involved in all human life that stands within traditions. Indeed, it is even a question as to whether the peculiar contemporaneousness of the work of art does not consist precisely in its being open in a limitless way to ever new integrations. The creator of a work of art may intend the public of his own time, but the real being of his work is what it is able to say, and this being reaches fundamentally beyond any historical confinement. In this sense, the work of art occupies a timeless present. But this statement does not mean that it involves no task of understanding, or that we do not find its historical heritage within it. The claim of historical hermeneutics is legitimated precisely by the fact that while the work of art does not intend to be understood historically and offers itself instead in an absolute presence, it nevertheless does not permit just any forms of comprehension. In all the openness and all the richness of its possibilities for comprehension, it permits – indeed even requires – the application of a standard of appropriateness. It may remain undecided whether the claim to appropriateness of comprehension raised at any particular time is correct. Kant was right in asserting that universal validity is required of the judgment of taste, though its recognition cannot be compelled by reasons. This holds true for every interpretation of works of art as well. It holds true for the active interpretation of the reproductive artist or the reader, as well as for that of the scientific interpreter.

One can ask skeptically if a concept of the work of art that regards it as being open to ever newer comprehension does not already belong to a secondary world of aesthetic cultivation. In its origins, is not a work of art the bearer of a meaningful life-function within a cultic or social context? And is it not within this context alone that it receives its full determination of meaning? Still it seems to me that this question can also be reversed: Is it really the case that a work of art, which comes out of a past or alien life-world and is transferred into our historically educated world, becomes a mere object of aesthetic-historical enjoyment and says nothing more of what it originally had to say? 'To say something,' 'to have something to say' – are these simply metaphors grounded in an undetermined aesthetic formative value that is the real truth? Or is the reverse the case? Is the aesthetic quality of formation only the condition for the fact that the work bears its meaning within itself and has something to say to us? This question gives us access to the real problematic dimension of the theme 'aesthetics and hermeneutics.'

The inquiry developed here deliberately transforms the systematic problem of *aesthetics* into the question of the experience of *art*. In its actual genesis and also in the foundation Kant provided for it in his *Critique of Aesthetic Judgment*, it is certainly true that philosophical aesthetics covered a much broader area, since it included the beautiful in nature and art, indeed, even the sublime. It is also incontestable that in Kant's philosophy natural beauty had a methodical priority for the basic determinations of the judgment of aesthetic taste, and especially for his concept of 'disinterested pleasure.' However, we must admit that natural beauty does not 'say' anything in the sense that works of art, created by and for men, say something to us. One can rightly assert that a work of art does not satisfy in a 'purely aesthetic' way, in the same sense as a flower or perhaps an ornament does. With respect to art, Kant speaks of an 'intellectualized' pleasure. But this formulation does not help. The 'impure,' intellectualized pleasure that the work of art evokes is still what really interests us as aestheticians. Indeed, the sharper reflection that Hegel brought to the question of the relation of natural and artistic beauty led him to the valid conclusion that natural beauty is a reflection of the beauty of art. When something natural is regarded and enjoyed as beautiful, it is not a timeless and wordless givenness of the 'purely aesthetic' object that has its exhibitive ground in the harmony of forms and colors and symmetry of design, as it might seem to a Pythagorizing, mathematical mind. How nature pleases us belongs instead to the context that is stamped and determined by the artistic creativity of a particular time. The aesthetic history of a landscape – for instance, the Alpine landscape – or the transitional phenomenon of garden art are irrefutable evidence of this. We are justified, therefore, in proceeding from the work of art rather than from natural beauty if we want to define the relation between aesthetics and hermeneutics. In any case, when we say that the work of art *says* something to us and that it thus belongs to the matrix of things we have to understand, our assertion is not a metaphor, but has a valid and demonstrable meaning. Thus the work of art is an object of hermeneutics.

According to its original definition, hermeneutics is the art of clarifying and mediating by our own effort of interpretation what is said by persons we encounter in tradition. Hermeneutics operates wherever what is said is not immediately intelligible. Yet this philological art and pedantic technique has long since assumed an altered and broadened form. Since the time of this original definition, the growing historical consciousness has made us aware of the misunderstanding and the possible unintelligibility of all tradition. Also, the decay of Christian society in the West – in continuation of a process of individualization that began with the Reformation – has allowed the individual to become an ultimately indissoluble mystery to others. Since the time of the German romantics, therefore, the task of hermeneutics has been defined as avoiding misunderstanding. With this definition, hermeneutics acquires a domain that in principle reaches as far as the expression of meaning as such. Expressions of meaning are first of all linguistic manifestations. As the art of conveying what is said in a foreign language to the understanding of another person, hermeneutics is not without reason named after Hermes, the interpreter of the divine message to mankind. If we recall the origin of the name hermeneutics, it becomes clear that we are dealing here with a language event, with a translation from one language to another, and therefore with the relation of two languages. But insofar as we can only translate from one language to another if we have understood the meaning of what is said and construct it anew in the medium of the other language, such a language event presupposes understanding.

Now these obvious conclusions become decisive for the question that concerns us here – the question of the language of art and the legitimacy of the hermeneutical point of view with respect to the experience of art. Every interpretation of the intelligible that helps others to understanding has the character of language. To that extent, the entire experience of the world is linguistically mediated, and the broadest concept of tradition is thus defined – one that includes what is not itself linguistic, but is capable of linguistic interpretation. It extends from the 'use' of tools, techniques, and so on through traditions of craftsmanship in the making of such things as various types of implements and ornamental forms through the cultivation of practices and customs to the establishing of patterns and so on. Does the work of art belong in this category, or does it occupy a special position? Insofar as it is not directly a question of *linguistic* works of art, the work of art does in fact seem to belong to such nonlinguistic tradition. And yet the experience and understanding of a work of art is different from the understanding of the tool or the practices handed on to us from the past.

If we follow an old definition from Droysen's hermeneutics, we can distinguish between sources [*Quellen*] and vestiges [*Überresten*]. Vestiges are fragments of a past world that have survived and assist us in the intellectual reconstruction of the world of which they are a remnant. Sources, on the other hand, constitute a linguistic tradition, and they thus serve our understanding of a linguistically interpreted world. Now where does an archaic image of a god belong, for instance? Is it a vestige, like any tool? Or is it a piece of world-interpretation, like everything that is handed on linguistically?

Sources, says Droysen, are records handed down for the purpose of recollection. Monuments are a hybrid form of sources and vestiges, and to this category he assigns 'works of art of every kind,' along with documents, coins, and so on. It may seem this way to the historian, but the work of art as such is a historical document neither in its intention nor in the meaning it acquires in the experience of the work of art. To be sure, we talk of artistic monuments, as if the production of a work of art had a documentary intention. There is a certain truth in the assertion that permanence is essential to every work of art – in the transitory arts, of course, only in the form of their repeatability. The successful work 'stands.' (Even the music hall artist can say this of his act.) But the explicit aim at recollection through the presentation of something, as it is found in the genuine document, is not present in the work of art. We do not want to refer to anything that once was by means of presentation. Just as little could it be a guarantee of its permanence, since it depends for its preservation on the approving taste or sense of quality of later generations. Precisely this dependence on a preserving will means that the work of art is handed on in the same sense as our literary sources are. At any rate, 'it speaks' not only as remnants of the past speak to the historical investigator or as do historical documents that render something permanent. What we are calling the language of the work of art, for the sake of which the work is preserved and handed on, is the language the work of art itself speaks, whether it is linguistic in nature or not. The work of art says something to the historian: it says something to each person as if it were said especially to him, as something present and contemporaneous. Thus our task is to understand the meaning of what it says and to make it clear to ourselves and others. Even the nonlinguistic work of art, therefore, falls within the province of the proper task of hermeneutics. It must be integrated into the self-understanding of each person.[1]

In this comprehensive sense, hermeneutics includes aesthetics. Hermeneutics bridges the distance between minds and reveals the foreignness of the other mind. But revealing what is unfamiliar does not mean merely reconstructing historically the 'world' in which the work had its original meaning and function. It also means apprehending what is said to us, which is always more than the declared and comprehended meaning. Whatever says something to us is like a person who says something. It is alien in the sense that it transcends us. To this extent, there is a double foreignness in the task of understanding, which in reality is one and the same foreignness. It is this way with all speech. Not only does it say something, but *someone* says something to someone else. Understanding speech is not understanding the wording of what is said in the step-by-step execution of word meanings. Rather, it occurs in the unitary meaning of what is said – and this always transcends what is expressed by what is said. It may be difficult to understand what is said in a foreign or ancient language, but it is still more difficult to let something be said to us even if we understand what is said right away. Both of these things are the task of hermeneutics. We cannot understand without wanting to understand, that is, without wanting to let something be said. It would be an inadmissible abstraction to contend that we must first have achieved a contemporaneousness with the author or the original reader by means of a reconstruction of his historical horizon before we could begin to grasp the meaning of what is said. A kind of anticipation of meaning guides the effort to understand from the very beginning.

But what holds in this fashion for all speaking is valid in an eminent way for the experience of art. It is more than an anticipation of meaning. It is what I would like to call surprise at the meaning of what is said. The experience of art does not only understand a recognizable meaning, as historical hermeneutics does in its handling of texts. The work of art that says something confronts us itself. That is, it expresses something in such a way that what is said is like a discovery, a disclosure of something previously concealed. The element of surprise is based on this. 'So true, so filled with being' [*So wahr, so seiend*] is not something one knows in any other way. Everything familiar is eclipsed. To understand what the work of art says to us is therefore a self-encounter. But as an encounter with the authentic, as a familiarity that includes surprise, the experience of art is *experience* in a real sense and must master ever anew the task that experience involves: the task of integrating it into the whole of one's own orientation to a world and one's own self-understanding. The language of art is constituted precisely by the fact that it speaks to the self-understanding of *every* person, and it does this as ever present and by means of its own contemporaneousness. Indeed, precisely the contemporaneousness of the work allows it to come to expression in language. Everything depends on how something is said. But this does not mean we should reflect on the means of saying it. Quite the contrary, the more convincingly something is said, the more self-evident and natural the uniqueness and singularity of its declaration seems to be, that is, it concentrates the attention of the person being addressed entirely upon what is said and prevents him from moving to a distanced aesthetic differentiation. Over against the real intention, which aims at what is said, reflection upon the means of the declaration is indeed always secondary and in general is excluded where men speak to each other face to face. For what is said is not something that presents itself as a kind of content of judgment, in the logical form of a judgment. Rather, it is what we want to say and what we will allow to be said to us. Understanding does not occur when we try to intercept what someone wants to say to us by claiming we already know it.

All these observations hold especially for the language of art. Naturally it is not the artist who is speaking here. The artist's own comments about what is said in one or another of his works may certainly be of possible interest too. But the language of art means the excess of meaning that is present in the work itself. The inexhaustibility that distinguishes the language of art from all translation into concepts rests on this excess of meaning. It follows that in understanding a work of art we cannot be satisfied with the cherished hermeneutical rule that the *mens auctoris* limits the task of understanding posed in a text. Rather, just this expansion of the hermeneutical perspective to include the language of art makes it obvious how little the subjectivity of the act of meaning suffices to denote the object of understanding. But this fact has a general significance, and to that extent aesthetics is an important element of general hermeneutics. That should be conclusively indicated. Everything that in the broadest sense speaks to us as tradition poses the task of understanding, without understanding in general being taken to mean the new actualization in oneself of another person's thoughts. We learn this fact with convincing clarity not only from the experience of art (as explained above), but also from the understanding of history. For the real task of historical study is not to understand the subjective intentions, plans, and experiences of the men who are involved in history. Rather, it is the great matrix of the meaning of history that must be understood and that requires the interpretive effort of the historian. The subjective intentions of men standing within the historical process are seldom or never such that a later historical evaluation of events confirms their assessment by contemporaries. The significance of the events, their connection and their involvements as they are represented in historical retrospect, leave the *mens auctoris* behind them, just as the experience of the work of art leaves the *mens auctoris* behind it.

The universality of the hermeneutical perspective is all-encompassing. I once formulated this idea by saying that being that can be understood is language.[2] This is certainly not a metaphysical assertion. Instead, it describes, from the medium of understanding, the unrestricted scope possessed by the hermeneutical perspective. It would be easy to show that all historical experience satisfies this proposition, as does the experience of nature. In the last analysis, Goethe's statement 'Everything is a symbol' is the most comprehensive formulation of the hermeneutical idea. It means that everything points to another thing. This 'everything' is not an assertion about each being, indicating what it is, but an assertion as to how it encounters man's understanding. There is nothing that cannot mean something to it. But the statement implies something else as well: nothing comes forth in the one meaning that is simply offered to us. The impossibility of surveying all relations is just as much present in Goethe's concept of the symbolic as is the vicarious function of the particular for the representation of the whole. For only because the universal relatedness of being is concealed from human eyes does it need to be discovered. As universal as the hermeneutical idea is that corresponds to Goethe's words, in an eminent sense it is fulfilled only by the experience of art. For the distinctive mark of the language of art is that the individual art work gathers into itself and expresses the symbolic character that, hermeneutically regarded, belongs to all beings. In comparison with all other linguistic and nonlinguistic tradition, the work of art is the absolute present for each particular present, and at the same time holds its word in readiness for every future. The intimacy with which the work of art touches us is at the same time, in enigmatic fashion, a shattering and a demolition of the familiar. It is not only the 'This art thou!' disclosed in a joyous and frightening shock; it also says to us; 'Thou must alter thy life!'

Translated by David E. Linge

Notes

1 It is in this sense that I criticized Kierkegaard's concept of the aesthetic (as he himself does). Cf. Hans-Georg Gadamer, *Wahrheit und Methode*: *Grundzüge einer philosophischen Hermeneutik*, Tübingen, Mohr, 1960, pp. 91ff.

2 Cf. ibid., p. 450.

11

THE DEATH OR DECLINE OF ART

Gianni Vattimo

As is the case with many of Hegel's ideas, the notion of the death of art has turned out to be prophetic with regard to the development of advanced industrial society. This is so even though the death of art in the contemporary world does not have quite the same meaning that it does for Hegel, but rather – as Adorno repeatedly shows – a strangely perverted one. Is it not perhaps true that the universalization of the domain of information could be interpreted as a perverted realization of the triumph of absolute spirit? The utopia of the return of the spirit to itself – that is, the coincidence between Being and a completely transparent self-consciousness – occurs in some way in our everyday life as a generalization of the realm of means of communication and of the universe of representation diffused by these same means, which can no longer be distinguished from 'reality'. Naturally, the realm of the mass media is not the Hegelian absolute spirit; it is instead perhaps a caricature of it. In any event, though, the mass media are not simply a perversion of it in the sense of a degeneration, but rather something which contains, as is often the case with perversions, cognitive and practical possibilities which need to be explored, and which probably delineate the shape of things to come.

It should be noted right away, even if our argument will not proceed any further in these very general terms, that when we discuss the death of art we are speaking within the framework of this effective perverted realization of the Hegelian absolute spirit. Or rather, in what amounts to the same thing, we are speaking within the framework of an accomplished metaphysics that has arrived at its end, in the sense in which Heidegger – who sees Nietzsche's work as a philosophical announcement of this – speaks of such an occurrence. To bring into play another Heideggerian term, the fact that we speak from within this framework indicates that what is at stake is not so much an *Überwindung* as a *Verwindung* of metaphysics.[1] It is not an overcoming of the perverted realization of the absolute spirit, or, in the case at hand, of the death of art, but rather a healing of it and a resignation to it. The death of art is a phrase that describes or, better still, constitutes the epoch of the end of metaphysics as prophesied by Hegel, as lived by Nietzsche and as registered by Heidegger. In this epoch thought stands in a position of *Verwindung* in regard to metaphysics. Metaphysics is not abandoned like an old, worn-out garment, for it still constitutes our 'humanity' in *geschicklich* terms; we yield to it, we heal ourselves from it, we are resigned to it as something that is destined to us.

Like the whole of the heritage of metaphysics, the death of art cannot be understood as a 'notion' which could be said to correspond (or fail to correspond) to a certain state of things, or which is more or less logically contradictory and could therefore be replaced by some other 'notion', or whose origin, ideological significance, and so on could be explained. It is instead an event that constitutes the historical and ontological constellation in which we move. This constellation is a network of historical and cultural events and of the words which belong to them, at once describing and co-determining them. The death of art concerns us in this *geschicklich* sense of what is 'destined' for us, and is something which we simply cannot ignore. First of all, it concerns us as the prophecy or utopia of a society in which art no longer exists as a specific phenomenon, but has been suppressed and ablated – in a Hegelian way – through a general aestheticization of existence. The last prominent figure to proclaim loudly the death of art was Herbert Marcuse, or at least the Marcuse who was a guru of the 1968 student revolt. From his point of view, the death of art appears as a readily available possibility for a technologically advanced society – that is to say, in our own terms, in a society with a fully realized metaphysics. Now, such a possibility does not exist only as a theoretical utopia. Starting with the early twentieth-century avant-garde movements, the practice of the arts forms part of a wider phenomenon of the 'explosion' of aesthetics beyond the institutional limits which are traditionally assigned to it. The poetics of the avant-garde reject the limitations which philosophy, especially of the neo-Kantian and neo-idealist sort, had previously imposed upon art. Avant-garde art refuses to be considered as a place of non-theoretical and non-practical experience, and instead claims to be the model for a privileged mode of knowledge of the real, a moment of subversion of the hierarchized structure of the individual and society, and thus an instrument of true social and political action. The heritage of the early avant-garde is maintained by the later avant-garde movements, although at a less totalizing and less metaphysical level, which continue to argue in favour of exploding the traditional confines of aesthetics. This explosion becomes, for instance, a negation of the places which had traditionally been assigned to aesthetic experience, such as the concert hall, the theatre, the gallery, the museum, and the book. A series of developments occur – earth-works, body art, street theatre, and so on – which appear somewhat more limited in regard to the revolutionary metaphysical ambitions of the earlier avant-garde movements, but also more concretely within reach for contemporary artistic experience. No longer is art to be rendered out-of-date and suppressed by a future revolutionary society; rather, the experience of art as an integral aesthetic fact is immediately to be sought out. As a consequence, the status of the work becomes constitutively ambiguous: the work no longer seeks a success which would permit it to position itself within a determinate set of values (the imaginary museum of objects possessed of aesthetic quality), but rather defines its success fundamentally in terms of rendering problematic such a set of values, and in overcoming – at least momentarily – the limits of the latter. In this perspective, one of the criteria for evaluation of the work of art seems to be, first and foremost, the ability of the work to call into question its own status. It may do this either directly (and thus often quite crudely) or indirectly, for instance as an ironization of literary genres, as rewriting, as a poetics of citation, or as a use of photography not for creating certain formal effects but for its most elementary function of duplication. In all these phenomena, which are present in different ways in contemporary artistic experience, it is not merely a matter of the sort of self-reference which, in many aesthetic theories, seems constitutive of all art; rather, it is a question of facts which are specifically linked to the death of art in the sense of an explosion of aesthetics which also occurs in these forms of self-ironization of the artistic operation.

The impact of technology is a decisive fact for the passage from the explosion of aesthetics as it appears in the early avant-garde movements – which conceive of the death of art as the suppression of the limits of aesthetics in order to move toward a metaphysical, or historical and political, meaning of the work – to the explosion which appears in the newer avant-garde movements. Technology is taken here to mean what it does for Walter Benjamin in his 1936 essay on 'The Work of Art in the Age of Mechanical Reproduction'. Art's escape from institutional confines no longer either exclusively or principally appears to be linked, in this perspective, to the utopia of metaphysical or revolutionary reintegration of existence; rather, it seems connected to the advent of new technologies which in fact at once permit and determine a form of generalization of aestheticity. With the advent of the ability to reproduce art by mechanical means, the works of the past lose their aura, that is, the halo that surrounds them and isolates them (and together with them the aesthetic realm of experience as well) from the rest of existence. Forms of art are born for which reproducibility is constitutive, such as film and photography: such works not only have no original, but tend to collapse the difference between producer and user because they rely upon the technological use of machines, thus eliminating any argument about the genius of the artist (which is, in essence, the aura as seen from the artist's point of view).

The idea that aesthetic experience is decisively transformed in the era of mass reproduction, as Benjamin contends, represents the moment of passage from a utopian and revolutionary meaning for the death of art to a technological one instead, which ultimately takes the form of a theory of mass culture. This is so even if, as is well known, Benjamin himself would have never made such a claim: he rather distinguishes between a 'good' (socialist) and a 'bad' (fascist) aestheticization of experience. The death of art is not only what will result from the revolutionary reintegration of existence; it is what we are already living in a mass culture, for such a culture produces a generalized aestheticization of life. This can be said to occur because the mass media – who, to be sure, distribute information, culture, and entertainment, but always according to the general criteria of the 'beautiful', that is, the formal attractiveness of products – have assumed in the life of each individual an infinitely more important role than in any other era of the past. An identification between the domain of the mass media and the aesthetic itself is certainly open to objection. However, such an identification becomes relatively simple to sustain if it is kept in mind that, over and beyond the function of distributing information, the mass media serve to produce a consensus through the establishment and intensification of a common language of social life. The mass media do not provide a means for the masses which is at the service of the masses; it is the means *of* the masses, in the sense in which the masses as such are constituted by the mass media as a public realm of common consensus, taste, and feeling. This function, which is usually called (in a pejorative sense) the organization of consensus, is an exquisitely aesthetic one. This becomes clear if we recall one of the fundamental meanings that has been attributed to the term 'aesthetic' since the *Critique of Judgement*: aesthetic pleasure is not defined as that which the subject experiences in relation to the object, but is rather that pleasure which derives from the recognition of belonging to a group – which, for Kant, is humanity itself as an ideal – that shares the same capacity for appreciating the beautiful.

This point of view may be found to exist in different ways: in the theoretical return to Hegelian concepts by revolutionary ideology, in early and 'neo-'avant-garde poetics, and in the experience of the mass media as the distributor of aesthetic products which are also the sites upon which a consensus is organized. In this perspective the death of art signifies two things: in a strong – and utopian – sense, it indicates the end of art as a specific fact, separate from the rest of experience, thanks to the renewal and re-integration of existence; in a weak – or real – sense, it points to aestheticization as an extension of the domain of the mass media.

The way in which artists often respond to the death of art at the hands of the mass media also belongs to the category of death, for it appears as a suicidal gesture of protest. To protest against *Kitsch*, a manipulative mass culture, and the aestheticization of existence at a low and weak level, authentic art has often taken refuge in programmatically aporetic positions which deny any possibility of immediate enjoyment of the work (its 'gastronomic' aspect, as it were), refuse to communicate anything at all, and opt for silence instead. Adorno finds this to be the crucial lesson of Beckett's work, as is well known, and in various ways sees the same as holding true for many artistic avant-garde movements; in a world where consensus is produced by manipulation, authentic art speaks only by lapsing into silence, and aesthetic experience arises only as the negation of all its traditional and canonical characteristics, starting with the pleasure of the beautiful itself. Even in Adorno's negative aesthetics, as in the case of the utopia of a general aestheticization of experience, the chief criterion for evaluating the work of art is its greater or lesser capacity for self-negation. If the meaning of art resides in its production of a reintegration of existence, the work of art will appear valid precisely to the degree that it leads back to such a reintegration and necessarily dissolves into it. If, instead, the meaning of the work is found in its resistance to the omnipotence of *Kitsch*, then once again its validity coincides with its own self-negation. In a sense that needs to be more closely examined, the work of art, in present conditions, displays characteristics analogous to Heidegger's notion of Being: it arises only as that which at the same time withdraws from us.

(Naturally, it should not be forgotten that for Adorno the criterion of evaluation of the work of art is not only and explicitly the self-negation of its own status. There is instead also the technical tradition of each art to consider, as that which assures the possibility of a relation between the history of art and the history of spirit. Through artistic technique, above all, the work of art is realized as a fact of the spirit, that is, as containing a truth or a spiritual significance. Since Adorno is not an optimistic Hegelian and does not believe in progress, he sees the technical aspect of art as in the last analysis only a means for guaranteeing a more perfect impenetrability of the work of art and as a means for reinforcing its screen of silence.)

In this sort of philosophical phenomenology of the contemporary *Wesen* of art (in the Heideggerian sense of the term), more is involved than merely the different forms of the death of art as a utopia of reintegration, as an aestheticization of mass culture, and as authentic art's suicide and silence. Other facts need to be considered here as well, facts which constitute the rather surprising survival of art in the traditional and institutional sense. For there are still, after all, theatres, concert halls, and galleries, and there are artists who produce works which unproblematically fit into these frameworks. At the theoretical level, this means that the evaluation of these works cannot be based especially and exclusively on their capacity for self-negation. In the face of the different manifestations of the death of art, the fact that there are still 'works of art' in the institutional sense of the term appears as an alternative to the former and as something irreducible to it. In other words, such works appear as an ensemble of *objects differentiated from each other not only on the basis* of their greater or lesser degree of negativity in respect to the status of art. The world of effective artistic production cannot be described in an adequate way solely on the basis of this criterion. We are continually faced with differentiations of value that elude such a simplistic classification, and that cannot be said to belong to it even in a mediated way. Theory has to reflect most carefully upon this problem, since the notion of the death of art – which appears so simplificatory and comforting in its metaphysical compactness – could serve theory as a convenient means to avoid confronting it at all.

The survival of a world of artistic products with its own internal order, however, has a constitutive relation to the three different manifestations of the death of art defined above. It would be easy to show that the history of painting – or, better still, of the visual arts – and the history of poetry over the past few decades have meaning only if placed in relation to the world of images of the mass media or the language of this same world. This is a matter, once again, of relations which in general can be said to belong to the Heideggerian category of *Verwindung*, for they are ironical–iconical relations that at once duplicate and break down the images and words produced by mass culture, but not only in order to negate such a culture. The fact that in spite of everything else, vital works of 'art' still are produced today probably depends upon this. For these products are the place in which – in a complex system of relations – the three different aspects of the death of art (as utopia, as *Kitsch*, and as silence) are brought into play and come into contact with each other. The philosophical description of this situation could finally become complete through the recognition that the key element in the persistent life of art and in its products – which nevertheless continue to define themselves from inside the institutional frame of art – is precisely this interplay of the various aspects of its own death.

This is the situation with which aesthetic philosophy must deal. Because it persists in always announcing and always once again deferring the death of art, such a situation could be called the *decline* of art.

Traditional aesthetic philosophy has a difficult time taking the measure of this particular group of phenomena, for traditional concepts appear devoid of any basis in concrete experience. It is always somewhat uncomfortable, for anyone concerned with aesthetics who tries to describe the contemporary experience of art and of the beautiful with the somewhat grandiose conceptual language inherited from earlier philosophy, when the former and the latter come into contact with each other. Do we still really find the work of art to be an exemplary work of genius, a concrete manifestation of an idea, or a 'setting-into-work of truth'? Certainly, such an inflated description of the work of art could be undermined at the level of utopia and social critique: we no longer encounter works of art which can be described in these terms because the world of an integrated and authentic human experience is no longer or not yet real. Alternatively, we could entirely reject the conceptual terminology of traditional aesthetics by having recourse instead to the 'positive' notions of this or that 'human science', whether it be semiotics, psychology, anthropology, sociology, or whatever. Both of these approaches remain deeply – or, as Nietzsche would say, reactively – linked to tradition. They both suppose that the world of aesthetic concepts handed down by tradition is still the only possible one for the construction of a philosophical discourse on art. They thus either maintain it by preserving it in a negative perspective (whether utopian or critical), or by declaring that aesthetic philosophy no longer has any meaning. In both cases (although on different levels) we see that the death of aesthetic philosophy mirrors the death of art in the various senses discussed above. The aesthetics inherited from tradition, however, could be neither the only possible conceptual system nor simply an ensemble of notions which are false because they have no connection to experience itself. Like metaphysics (in Heidegger's sense of the term), traditional aesthetics is a destiny for us: it is something to which we must yield, from which we must heal ourselves, and to which we must resign ourselves. The grandiose nature of the concepts which have come down to us from the aesthetics developed within the metaphysical tradition is linked to the essence of this same metaphysics. Heidegger has described it primarily as objectivizing thought, and in general as that epoch of the history of Being in which Being arises and occurs as presence. We may add that this epoch is also especially characterized by the fact that Being arises in it as *force*, namely as grandeur, evidence, definiteness, and permanence – and also, probably, as domination. With the positioning of the problem of Being and time the *Verwindung* of metaphysics begins, and this positioning cannot be interpreted solely as the strategic manœuvre of any single philosopher. Being now arises, as is already announced in Nietzsche's nihilism, as that which disappears and perishes: from the discourse of *Sein und Zeit* on, Being is not that which remains, but rather that which is born and dies.

The situation of the death – or, better, of the decline – of art in which we are living today is philosophically interpretable as one aspect of the more general event, concerning Being itself, which is the *Verwindung* of metaphysics. How is this the case? To answer this question, we need to look at it in a way that has only infrequently been considered by previous readers of Heidegger: what we experience in the moment of the decline of art is describable in terms of the Heideggerian notion of the work of art as the 'setting-into-work of truth'.

In the era of mechanical reproduction aesthetic experience grows ever closer to what Benjamin calls 'distracted perception'. This perception no longer encounters the 'work of art', of which the aura was once an integral part. It may therefore be said that the experience of art no longer arises, or has yet to arise, but this admission is still always set in the framework of an acceptance of the concepts of metaphysical aesthetics. It is instead possible, though, that it is precisely in the distracted experience of art that seems to be the only one available to us in our present condition that the *Wesen* of art summons us in a sense that requires us to step beyond metaphysics. The experience of a distracted perception no longer comes into contact with works themselves, but rather operates in an atmosphere of twilight, decline, and disseminated meanings as well. This occurs in the same way in which, for instance, moral experience is no longer forced to choose between the absolute values of good and evil, but only between micrological facts in regard to which traditional notions appear grandiose and empty, as is the case with art. In *Human All Too Human* (vol. I, aphorism 34), Nietzsche describes this situation in terms of an opposition between the resentful individual who lives the loss of the pathos and the metaphysical dimensions of existence as a tragedy and the individual who is instead 'free of emphasis'.

The Heideggerian notion of the 'setting-into-work of truth' can be, from a philosophical point of view, productively applied to this same situation. For Heidegger, the work is an 'exhibition' (*Aufstellung*) of a world and a 'production' (*Herstellung*) of the earth.[2] Heidegger emphasizes the notion of 'exhibition' in the same terms we use for 'putting on' an exhibition in a museum or gallery, for instance; for it implies that the work of art has the function of founding and constituting the outlines which define an historical world. A society or social group – in short, an historical world – recognizes the constitutive traits of its own experience of the world (for instance, the implicit criteria for distinguishing between good and evil, truth and error, etc.) in a work of art. This idea affirms the inaugural nature of the work, which depends upon Kant's thesis of the absolute originality of artistic genius. However, *Aufstellung* also refers us to the notion, developed out of the philosophy of Dilthey, that in the work of art, more than in any other product of the spirit, the truth of any historical epoch is revealed. The essential element here is not so much the inaugurality of the work, or a 'truth' which could be opposed to error, as the constitution of the fundamental outlines of a given historical existence, that is, what is called (in depreciatory terms) the aesthetic function as an organization of consensus. In the work each individual's sense of membership in a historical world may be recognized and intensified. In this way the distinction on the basis of which Adorno rejects the world of mass-media-oriented culture as pure ideology can be eliminated: for this distinction is one of a presumed use-value of the work which could be opposed to its exchange-value, namely to its functioning only as a distinguishing sign of recognition for groups and societies. The work as a 'setting-into-work of truth' – in its exhibition of a world – is the place where a sense of membership in a group is made recognizable and is intensified. This function, which is crucial for Heidegger's notion of the exhibition of a world, may belong not only to the work as a great individual achievement. For it is in fact a function which persists and is even more fully suitable in the situation in which individual works, along with their aura, disappear in a setting of relatively functional products that have, however, an analogous value.

The full implications of the Heideggerian notion of the work of art as a 'setting-into-work of truth' can be understood, however, only by examining its other aspect as a 'production' of the earth. In his 1936 essay, the idea of the work as a *Herstellung* of the earth is associated with both the materiality of the work and, especially, the fact that by virtue of this materiality (which is never to be understood as 'physical') the work occurs as something which is always kept in reserve. In the work, the earth is not, strictly speaking, matter; it is the presence of the work as such, namely its concrete appearance as something which always calls attention to itself. Even here, as in the case of the notion of 'world', we need to disentangle the meaning of Heidegger's argument (more than forty years later) from the metaphysical misunderstandings that threaten to compromise it. For the earth is the *hic et nunc* of the work, to which each new interpretation always returns and which always leads to new readings and therefore new possible 'worlds'. If we look carefully at Heidegger's text – for example where he speaks of the earth in the Greek temple as being in relation to the seasons, to the natural decay of matter, etc., or where he speaks of the conflict between world and earth as that in which truth opens up as *aletheia* – we discover that the earth is the dimension which in the work connects the world as a system of discrete and unfolded meanings to its 'other', the *physis*, which sets in motion the tendentially immobile structures of historical/social worlds through its rhythms. In short, the work of art is the 'setting-into-work of truth' because in it the opening up of a world as a context of referrals – like a language – is permanently connected to the earth as the 'other' of the world; and the earth has for Heidegger the features of *physis* (not in his 1936 essay, but in his writings on Hölderlin), which is defined by the fact of birth and growth and death. Earth and *physis* are that which *zeitigt* – or, literally, that which develops as a living being; they are also, however, that which is 'temporalized', in the etymological sense of the verb that Heidegger explores in *Sein und Zeit*. As the 'other' of the world, the earth is that which does not endure. On the contrary, it is that which appears always to withdraw into a 'naturality' that entails *Zeitigen*, namely birth and growth, and bears on its face the traces of the passage of time. The work of art is the one kind of artifact which registers ageing as a positive event that actively contributes to determine new possibilities of meaning.

This second aspect of Heidegger's notion of the work as a 'setting-into-work of truth' seems significant precisely because it points us in the direction of the temporality of the work of art, in a sense that has always eluded traditional metaphysical aesthetics. All the difficulties that aesthetic philosophy encounters in accounting for the experience of the decline of art, distracted perception, and mass culture, derive from the fact that it continues to think in terms of the work as a necessarily eternal form, and, at a deeper level, in terms of Being as permanence, grandeur, and force. The decline of art is instead an aspect of the more general situation of the end of metaphysics, in which thought is called upon to perform a *Verwindung* of metaphysics, in all the various senses of the term that have been discussed above. Aesthetics can fulfil its task as a philosophical aesthetics, from this point of view, if it is able to recognize in the various elements which are assumed to signal the death of art the announcement of an epoch of Being in which – in the perspective of an 'ontology of decline' – thought may open itself up to the only partially negative and 'fallen' meaning (in the sense of *Verfallenheit*) which the experience of aestheticity has acquired in the era of mechanical reproduction and mass culture.

Translated by Jon R. Snyder

Notes

1 Martin Heidegger, *Vorträge und Aufsätze*, Pfullingen, Neske, 1954; repr. 1978, pp. 71ff.

2 Cf. Heidegger, 'The Origin of the Work of Art' (1936), in *Poetry, Language, Thought*, trans. Albert Hofstadter (1971; repr. New York, Harper and Row, 1975), pp. 15–87. [*Editor:* an abridged version of the essay appears above, pp. 80–101.]

Part 3

MARXISM AND CRITICAL THEORY

INTRODUCTION

Karl Marx

Marxism represents a broad, extremely influential, and sometimes ambiguous, body of thought. Breadth and ambiguity here are indices of the extent to which the ideas of Karl Marx (1818–83) have been embellished and transformed through interpretation and application. Interestingly enough, this is not out of keeping with Marx's thesis: ideas are aspects of our practical involvement with the world and, therefore, will undergo change through being 'lived'. His is a philosophy which invites application, due to the emphasis it places on the subject–object or individual–world relationship being an evolutionary, open-ended dynamic. The concept of revolution immanent in his dialectic proved to be very attractive to the socialist movement emerging in the second half of the nineteenth century. The economic divisions created by industrialization were becoming increasingly apparent, and Marx was offering a quasi-scientific integration of historical perspective and social change which concluded by sounding the 'knell' of capitalist inequality.

A lot of what has come to be understood as Marxism derives from the writings of Friedrich Engels (1829–95). Marx and Engels were close friends and collaborators – they co-wrote *The Communist Manifesto* (1848)[1] – and, after Marx's death, Engels edited his unfinished manuscripts and became the leading disseminator and popularizer of Marx's ideas. Inevitably, there were subtle shifts in emphasis with Engels' interpretation of Marx. Engels' interest in Darwinism prompted him, in his book *Anti-Dühring* (1877–78),[2] to attribute dialectical transition to nature itself, whereas Marx insisted that transition was a property of *the interaction between* subject and nature. Furthermore, because *Anti-Dühring* contained such an accessible exposition of the unwieldy *Capital*, it was the *Capital as summarized by Engels* upon which the first generation of Marxist thinkers based their position. *Capital* provides detailed analysis of one particular socio-economic structure but gives little insight into the philosophical arguments behind Marx's thesis. Inevitably, with dissemination, claims were simplified and conclusions were allowed to ossify away from their original context of argumentation, thus reducing an elegant thesis to dogmatic ideology. The reformulations of Marx imposed by Lenin and Stalin follow more from Engels' popularized account and are actually antithetical to much of his original writing.

Marx's principal influence is Hegel. To overcome the incongruities he perceives in Kant's philosophy between thought and reality, Hegel proposes that the two are in fact one, that reality *is* thought. Description, for Hegel, is a positive act because it puts us in a position where we can compare our statement with reality, become aware of its partiality and inadequacy – *a moment in thought* – and then offer a revised, more adequate judgement. Through this dialectic, we eventually arrive at the final stage of Absolute Consciousness when we realize that thought and that which we think about are of the same order. Two aspects of this process are particularly important for Marx. The first is precisely that *it is a process.* A statement never stands in isolation but has implicit within it the act of comparison that propagates the next. Thus, each statement contains its predecessor and anticipates its successor, an action Hegel refers to as 'supersession' (*Aufhebung*, also translated as 'sublation'; literally, 'carrying over'). The second point Marx draws from Hegel's dialectic is that we mistake the world to be something opposite and distinct from ourselves when, as becomes clear with Absolute Consciousness, it is part of us, an aspect of thought. The world, in this sense, Hegel claims, is 'alienated' from us or 'placed outside' ourselves (*Entäusserung*).

Although impressed by the concept of the dialectic, Marx's early contact with the anti-idealism of Ludwig Feuerbach (1804–72) and the Young Hegelians in Berlin convinced him that the basis of human existence was not thought but social, practical activity. The human being, Marx asserts, is first and foremost related to the world through his or her *labour.* 'Labour' is a technical term for Marx, and it is important to distinguish his sense of the term from the meaning it has acquired within capitalist economies. The concept plays an ontological role in his thesis. 'Labour', for Marx, does not simply denote the work you do or have to do but refers to the physical transformations the individual makes as a being rooted in the world. Labour, he announces in *Capital*, is 'the universal condition for the metabolic interaction (*Stoffwechsel*) between man and Nature, the everlasting Nature-imposed condition of human experience'.[3]

What is distinctive about this labour-ontology is that it is fundamentally social: the interventions we make in the world bind us to others. This is one of Marx's most important claims, argued for in 'Estranged Labour', part of the *Economic and Philosophical Manuscripts.* 'What is true of man's relationship to his labour, to the product of his labour and to himself', he asserts, 'is also true of his relationship to other men, and to the labour and the object of the labour of other men'.[4] This sociability Marx calls our 'species-being'. Man is a species-being 'because he looks upon himself as a universal'.[5] Both man and animals are a part of nature and fashion it to suit their needs. However, whereas animals produce 'only when immediate physical need compels them to do so', man 'produces even when he is free from physical need and truly produces only in freedom from such need'.[6] Man produces not just for himself but for his kind, for his universal. The human world is a created world, a world in which we see *the labour of others* and where human intervention is a 'speaking to others'.

This might all seem very rosy, but Marx is not painting a picture of the ideal communist state.

Rather, he is performing conceptual analysis: showing how key concepts can be related in order to develop a line of thought against capitalism. The concept of 'labour' cannot be separated from the concept of 'species-being'; as a concept, practical activity cannot be divorced from interaction with other people. This, he claims, is precisely what capitalism does. Under capitalism, the labour of the individual is alienated (in Hegel's sense of the term) from her species-being. The basis of capitalism is private property. Those who *supply labour* are divided from those who *own capital*, 'the power to command labour and its products'.[7] The product of a person's labour is owned by the capitalist and sold by him to yield a profit, instead of remaining in a condition of species-interrelationship; what would otherwise exist as a *universal* relationship is objectified into the property of particular individuals. Because one stage of the dialectic is necessarily superseded by another, the transition from alienated perception to Absolute Consciousness for Hegel is an inevitability, and Marx claims this for the relationship between capitalism and communism. Just as alienated perception and the world undergo mutual transformation until their identity is realized, so man, through his fundamentally active engagement with nature and nature *as it is compartmentalized by man*, works towards the abolition of private property and class division and, therefore, to reintegration with his species-being.

The extract representing Marx is 'Private Property and Communism', a fragment from the *Economic and Philosophical Manuscripts*, written in 1844 when Marx was in Paris and only twenty-five. The *Manuscripts* were first published in 1932 by the Marx–Engels Institute but were coolly received. They were marginalized as the 'early writings', in contrast to his later 'mature system', on the grounds that their argumentation was inconsistent with what Marxism had become, and the rigidification which had set in under Stalin did not encourage speculative interpretation. However, these early, philosophical texts are, without a doubt, among Marx's most important writings, since they represent the transition in his thought from the critique of Hegel to the conceptual and ontological foundations of his own political philosophy.

Although Marx provides no specific, sustained discussion of art or aesthetics, the theory of being he proposes holds immense significance for our understanding of sensory and aesthetic experience. It is no doubt already apparent from the definition of species-being given above that art, as something which is *not* produced in response to an immediate animalistic need, is, for Marx, an expression of species-being. 'Private Property and Communism' is, in many ways, an account of how we can think of the aesthetic in these terms. The notion of objectivity is central to the discussion, since it is conceptualized in two antithetical ways: objectivity as an externalized object, and as an expressive relation. These correspond to capitalism and communism respectively. On the one hand, capitalism transforms our fundamental species relationship with the world into the ownership of particular things by certain individuals. On the other, communism, in Marx's sense of the term, is 'the supersession of private property': the realization that what is alien and external is in fact social and relational.

Just what 'relational objectivity' amounts to Marx considers with reference to sense experience. A world occupied by private property encourages us to think of sensation as something we *have*: the consumption or possession of something that is other than ourselves. However, in relational terms, sensation is *of itself* objective. The way in which the world appears to us is determined by the way in which we, that is, our senses, approach it. Just as vision exists for the eye and sound for the ear, etc., so the objectivity of human sensation is confirmed by the fact that the world, through our labour, our involvement with it, is a human world. 'A musical ear, an eye for the beauty of form', Marx argues, only come into being 'through the existence of *their* objects, through *humanized* nature'. This is not to anthropomorphize nature, for anthropomorphization can only occur if the 'human' is situated over and above the 'natural', whereas Marx already includes the former within the latter. With the supersession of private property, sensation ceases to be the having of an item (inward and passive) and becomes an expression (outward and active) of participation in species-being. The labour of the artist becomes the manipulation of human media, e.g., paint, or the humanization of matter, e.g., stone, with the intention of making the finished object 'speak' to its audience. This is aesthetics as sociability. The immersion of the human in the natural sees Marx extend the entwinement of concept and object inaugurated by Kant and Hegel and, in so doing, finds him anticipating phenomenology's presentation of the aesthetic in terms of disclosure and conversation.

Georg Lukács

The writings of the Hungarian philosopher Georg Lukács (1885–1971) span political theory and literary theory. He is the first thinker to develop a systematic Marxist aesthetics and thereby to make aesthetics an organic part of Marxist philosophy. He was also active politically: a member of the Hungarian Communist Party, a participant in the revolution against Rakosi's Stalinist regime, and a member of Nagy's short-lived revolutionary government (1956). He began preparing his Marxist theory of art in the early 1950s. This was a period when his ideas were attracting censure from other intellectuals within the Communist Party. His support for the Hungarian revolution of 1956 led to his deportation to Romania and to his expulsion from the party a year later when he returned to Hungary. The essay 'Specific Particularity as the Central Category of Aesthetics' originally appeared in *The German Journal for Philosophy* in 1956,[8] and was reprinted in the book *On Particularity as a Category of Aesthetics* in 1957. This was the last of Lukács' writings to be published in Hungary until his readmission to the Communist Party ten years later. He nevertheless continued to concentrate on aesthetics during this time and published a much larger work, *The Specific Nature of the Aesthetic* (*Die Eigenart des Aesthetischen*) – a study of the differences between artistic, scientific, and everyday representations of reality – in Germany in 1963. It is interesting to note that writing this book made the ideas contained in *On Particularity* even more important for Lukács. As he admits in the 'Afterword' to the 1967 German edition of *On Particularity*, 'particularity' is not just 'a central category' of aesthetics but '*the* central category'. Neither book has been translated into English, and 'Specific Particularity' is a specially commissioned translation (from the German by Nicholas Walker) for this volume.

Lukács adopts the term 'particularity' (*Besonderheit*) to denote the form an artist is able to give to reality, a form which avoids both the abstract generality of the universal concept and the uncontextualizable detail of the individual thing. The particular, for Lukács, exists midway between the individual and the universal. The 'individual' is what we are immediately confronted with in experience, e.g., 'this stone', 'this chair', 'this colour', whereas the 'universal' denotes the abstract, general term, e.g., the concept 'stone', the concept 'colour', which allows us to think of individuals as having certain characteristics. Knowledge consists of judgements made up of universals, that is, judgements which indicate that we have met this *kind of object* before, know how to categorize it, and have some idea of how to deal with it. Just how universals and individuals stand in relation to one another, though, has always been a problem for philosophy, since the two are of seemingly distinct and incompatible orders. The individual is something unique and of the moment, whereas the universal is something general which applies to an indefinite number of cases. However, following Hegel and Marx, the two emerge as interrelated poles in a dialectical, material relationship. Hegel's dialectic shows that it is in contrast to the generality of the concept that the object's individual detail is brought to light, and this relationship can occur, Marx argues, because consciousness is immersed in the world through its practical engagement with it.

The individual–universal relationship has two guises in Lukács' essay. The first is epistemological in that it represents the distinction between art and science. Both forms of knowledge work in the middle ground between the two poles, but in different ways. The scientist merely 'passes through' particularity, either in abstracting universals from individuals or in using universals to focus on new individuals. In contrast, the artist wants to retain and give expression to the particular tension which exists between sensuous individuality and universal recognition. Particularity though, Lukács asserts, is not a fixed point but a *Spielraum*; literally, a 'space for play'. Walker's translation of the term as 'leeway' captures this sense of dynamic. It is not a balance which is sought, but a sensitivity to the different emphases which are possible and which might be appropriate. Titian and Breughel incline towards the universal, Lukács suggests, whereas the impressionists emphasize the individual.

Another aspect of an artwork's particularity is the tension it creates between its individual form and the genre or category to which it belongs. The genre of a work provides the context necessary for the viewer to appreciate the construction of meaning within the work, and represents the conventions and options available to the artist within a way of working. The individual–universal distinction is playing a historical role here. A way of working is historical, Lukács observes, since it is an index of the means of production and, therefore, the economic and social conditions of the time. Bourgeois aesthetics values the artwork as something timeless and ineffable, and takes the emphasis on genre determination to be a detraction from the work's ineffability. This treats 'artwork' and 'genre' as antithetical poles. However, on a dialectical materialist account, as offered by Lukács here, the two terms are mutually defining components. The artistic expression of particularity, as noted above, is a tensional enquiry, with the consequence that the polar extremes of individual and universal are not left unaffected. Much aesthetic merit consists in testing the boundaries of a medium or importing conventions from another genre. Genuine fulfilment of an aesthetic rule or law, Lukács notes, 'can only be accomplished if the law in question is reborn, extended and rendered more concrete in the act of fulfilment itself'. By making 'particularity' the central category of aesthetics, Lukács allows both the production and the classification of art to become the process through which we see the historical interaction between thought and our practical engagement with the world. While art and science are related in their mediation of the universal and the particular, it is the historical development of art which makes their epistemologies visible.

Theodor W. Adorno

The single, most prominent body of Marxist enquiry in twentieth-century western Europe was the 'Frankfurt School' of critical theory: originally a core group of German-born Jewish intellectuals (Theodor W. Adorno, Leo Lowenthal, Herbert Marcuse, Max Horkheimer, Friedrich Pollock) at the Institute of Social Research, established in Frankfurt in 1923, followed by a 'second generation' of theorists (Jürgen Habermas, Alfred Schmidt, Albrecht Wellmer) who joined Horkheimer and Adorno when the Institute returned to Frankfurt in 1950 after wartime exile. Their research challenged the alienating effect of rationality which, it was argued, mediated between capitalism, fascism and Enlightenment thought and, latterly, they articulated a social epistemology to counter the positivistic and scientific model of truth as verification. Adorno and Marcuse do the most to develop a critical aesthetic theory, while Habermas relates aesthetic experience to his broader thesis on the overcoming of categorial divisions within modernity.

Through the content and style of his writing, the German philosopher and musicologist Theodor W. Adorno (1903–69) works against the limitations of binary thinking – thinking in terms of concepts 'consuming' objects – in order to bring new conceptual possibilities to light. The Marxist, materialist conception of history asserts that thought and culture are inextricably linked. The objects and structures which populate our lives cannot be dissociated from the concepts and structures we use to think. Western, Enlightenment thought, Adorno claims, is governed by the binary, epistemological model of the knowing subject and the object he perceives. Knowledge, on this account, is idealized as the subject consuming, mastering, or identifying himself with the object; in other words, the subject arranging his categories so that they 'capture' the object. This is manifest in the commodity fetishism of capitalism whereby we equate ourselves with the items we buy; objects acquire an allure and an independence of their own, removed from the labour behind them, which has to be possessed.

Art, however, for Adorno, offers social and conceptual emancipation. It is, he claims, 'autonomous'. Although rooted in a particular cultural context, art nevertheless generates its own novel structures of meaning, independent of any worldly content. He cites music as the purest art because it does not refer directly to the world; all other art forms, e.g., literature, painting, film, are burdened by their representational value (see 'In nuce' below, pp. 250–51). Through creating meaning and value which exceed its material origins, art challenges dominant structures of understanding. Art's capacity to generate new meaning is a version of the old philosophical problem, first considered by Plato in the *Meno*, of how new ideas can arise from old. (Plato argues that new ideas are recollections of direct experience of the Forms from a previous existence. Marcuse alludes to the theory in 'Nature and Revolution' below.) It appears here in the form set by Hegel and Marx, whereby human involvement in reality, either through perception or labour, allows the world to throw back a new conceptual or humanized appearance.

Adorno's writing is performative. His philosophical position is articulated not just through *what he says* but also through *how he says it*. If philosophy is to generate new, emancipatory concepts and avoid the contradictions of binary thinking, Adorno reasons, then it must become more like art. He draws his inspiration from music. Adorno studied composition under Alban Berg in Vienna between 1925 and 1927 and was especially sympathetic to the atonality of Arnold Schönberg's 'new music'. Whereas traditional, diatonic music is consonant with abstraction, summary, and ease of recognition, 'new' atonality draws attention to the structure of a composition as a series of decisions whose outcomes cannot be universalized. It is the same irreducibility to a concept which motivates Adorno's philosophy. His dense, tortuous prose and the lack of unity or orientation which results, are intended to resist the transparency and ease of consumption of linear, continuous, recapitulative argument. His style might be described as 'constellational', following the 'constellation' metaphor he uses to explicate his epistemology in *Negative Dialectics*. Understanding occurs not through a unified hierarchy of concepts, he argues, but through the constellational proximities and distances which exist between terms and which will always, ultimately, frustrate classification.[9] Parataxis is his preferred form of composition: clauses placed one after the other with little or no indication of the thesis or argument which might bind them together. Some key works, such as *Minima Moralia* (1951), *Negative Dialectics* (1966), and *Aesthetic Theory* (1970), are made up entirely of aphorisms: individual excursions, each a couple or so pages long, which, on the one hand, give the impression of being self-contained and independent but, on the other, knit together to form an irreducible network of conceptual counterpoint and cross-referral. The texture of the interaction which takes place between ideas, the conceptual friction that is generated, and the possibility of new insights being thrown back, are the objects of Adorno's philosophical aesthetics. His writing is philosophy made into art or a philosophy *of* art, where the 'of' is not placing the philosopher at a distance but making his thought itself 'of art'.

Contradiction in any discussion is a significant outcome, Adorno avers, because it shows how the attempt to step outside a way of thinking only reinvokes the very concepts one is hoping to exceed. The fact that contradiction arises and not, as with Hegel, the dominion of the concept over the object, is taken by Adorno as evidence of the historical and material rootedness of thought, an affirmation of its contingency and necessary undetachability from the particular. Several examples of this kind of analysis appear below in the extracts from *Minima Moralia: Reflections from Damaged Life*. The book interweaves meditations on the experience of exile with some of the most concise, lucid, though nonetheless demanding, formulations of arguments that are central to Adorno's entire *œuvre*. Taste, he writes in 'Damper and drum', 'is the most accurate seismograph of historical experience' because, throughout history, it is always 'reacting against itself'. The sharp edges of the will to shock have been machined by antecedent aesthetic conventions. It is 'the fine filigree of his late bourgeois organization' that allows the individual to rebel against 'the fine filigree of late bourgeois organization'. However, without this supersessive retention of an order, he warns us, the possibility of subjective expression in art would be cancelled out by the 'matter of factness' of cinematic representation. Every artwork contains the contradiction which is at the heart of Kant's *Critique of Judgment*: the concept of purposiveness without a purpose. As Adorno writes in 'Art Object': 'the very glorification of the artefact is itself inseparable from the rational purposefulness from which art seeks to break away'. The purpose of art, he suggests, is to 'push this contradiction to the extreme' and to realize itself in its 'resultant downfall'. But by Adorno's own lights, this will not be an eternal descent.

Herbert Marcuse

Whereas Adorno rejects the *telos* of conceptual unity in Hegel, Herbert Marcuse (1898–1978) emphasizes the anticipatory, revolutionary aspect of *Aufhebung* in the dialectic, so that it becomes a theory of experience which allows a *telos* of utopian possibility always to be visible in the material conditions of society. Born in Berlin, Marcuse joined the Frankfurt Institute of Social Research in 1932. One year later, with the Nazi rise to power, he followed Horkheimer and other colleagues to New York, and remained in the United States for the rest of his teaching career. His wide-ranging research combines Hegelian Marxism with insights drawn from phenomenology, existentialism, psychoanalysis, and aesthetics.

Characteristic of Marcuse's Hegelianism is the claim that negation entails affirmation. While his pessimistic *One-Dimensional Man: Studies in the Ideology of Advanced Industrial Society* (1964) shares Horkheimer and Adorno's opinion that there is no longer any effective potential for dissent, *Counterrevolution and Revolt* (1972), written shortly after the student rebellions of 1968, displays a renewed commitment to the possibility of social change. Although 'the highest stage of capitalist development corresponds, in the advanced capitalist countries, to a low of revolutionary potential', he observes, the 'inner dynamic of capitalism' nevertheless changes the pattern of revolution, with the consequence that the dynamic of capitalism in fact 'extends the potential mass base for revolution, and it necessitates the revival of the radical rather than minimum goals of socialism'.[10] The argument is, in effect, a retrieval of the most important yet subtle and easily overlooked adjustment Hegel is asking us to make. Concept and object are placed in a dialectical relationship not to sustain philosophy's privileging of the universal over the particular (the reading of Hegel to which Adorno inclines) but to show that any incongruity or inadequacy which exists between them can be turned around to become a force for the dissolution of their binary opposition.

'Nature and Revolution', from *Counterrevolution and Revolt*, shows how changes in the structure of society are linked to changes in our sensory experience of reality. The essay builds upon the dynamic species relationship Marx constructs between nature and the senses in 'Private Property and Communism'. Human perception, Marcuse avers, constitutes a 'radical sensibility'. Far from being merely receptive and passive, sensation is the process which binds us materially and socially to the world; it shapes 'the categories under which the world is ordered, experienced, changed'. The emancipation of the senses, he argues, would transform nature from being an object of capitalist exploitation to being 'an environment for the human being as "species-being"'. Sensory emancipation, for Marcuse, is achieved through art. If the premise, from Marx, is accepted that human aesthetic sensibility is an expression of species-being, i.e., man's interrelationship with nature, then human sensory gratification, e.g., the experience of beauty, is also the release of 'nature's *own* gratifying forces'. On this account, and wholly consistent with the Hegelian thesis that a negative can become a positive, art and the experience of beauty, both largely reconstructed in the eighteenth century as an affirmation of bourgeois, capitalist identity, are transformed into experiences which can motivate social change away from capitalism.

The article gives us an insight into one of the major disputes in Marxist aesthetics: does art best serve the Marxist cause by being a mimetic representation of the world – showing reality as it is or how it ought to be – or by carving out a region of its own (art for art's sake) which, in virtue of its relative autonomy, becomes a source of social critique? Some Marxist philosophers (notably Lukács in his criticism of expressionism) attack the latter view on the grounds that aesthetic autonomy, as they see it, reinforces the bourgeois notion of an independent self, utterly removed from wider, social concerns. Marcuse, though, defends the autonomy of art against such opposition in his most well-known work on aesthetics, *The Aesthetic Dimension: Toward a Critique of Marxist Aesthetics* (1977). Aesthetic experience, conceived as an independent phenomenon, he declares, enables the individual to 'withdraw from the reality of bourgeois society' and 'become a powerful force in *invalidating* the actually prevailing bourgeois values'.[11] His account of aesthetic transformation in 'Nature and Revolution' anticipates this position.

Marcuse cites feminism as an example of aesthetic transformation. By denying women full participation in the workplace, and by determining them as tender, receptive, and sensuous, he suggests, capitalism has allowed women to remain relatively free from the 'brutalities' of capitalist economy so that, collectively, they constitute a fund of sensibility which holds out the promise of emancipation. Just how 'woman' is to be conceptualized here is an ontological question, not an empirical one. 'Woman' is being considered not just as one category among others but as a category which underlines a whole new theory of being and, therefore, which affects how we understand the applicability of concepts in general. The contrast between 'woman' as an ontological essence and as an existentialist dynamic is one of the main arenas for discussion in the feminist aesthetics of Julia Kristeva and Luce Irigaray.

Jürgen Habermas

The 'inner logic' of concepts which allows negation to transform itself into affirmation also occupies the work of Jürgen Habermas (b. 1929), a leading figure within the Frankfurt School's 'second generation'. Our use of concepts, according to Habermas, is intertwined with modernity's compartmentalization of society into different interest or power groups, e.g., scientific, economic, administrative, cultural, and his writing remains committed to the possibility of consensus or reconciliation between these divisions. Whereas Adorno's and Marcuse's assessments of the dynamics of contradiction take their lead from Hegel, Habermas draws on Kant's transcendental philosophy and attributes the possibility of emancipation to the interrelationship of the different domains, in a fashion comparable to the aesthetic's mediation between morality and cognition in the *Critique of Judgment.* This thesis is based on the work of his colleague Albrecht Wellmer and discussed below in 'Modernity versus Postmodernity' (1980) and 'Questions and Counterquestions' (1984).

Another source of Habermas' Kantianism is the transcendental semantics of Karl-Otto Apel, prominent in (what is arguably) Habermas' principal work, the two-volume *Theory of Communicative Action* (1981). Here he introduces the concept of 'life-world': a concept of social interaction, comparable in its ontological ambition to Marx's 'species-being', but slanted more to the conditions which allow communication between groups to take place. Just as any experience, with Kant, presupposes an a priori determinative structure, so any act of communication, Habermas argues, presupposes certain shared conditions which enable both parties to recognize one another as interlocutors, and it is in the universality of these conditions, he declares, that the possibility of consensus lies.

His argument has attracted a lot of criticism, based mainly on the poststructuralist premise that the fundamentally differential nature of meaning precludes the possibility of there being a common, locatable ground for verbal exchange. However, in response, one might draw on the Gadamerian, hermeneutic tradition which, also in line with Kant, insists that there doesn't have to be a ground of correspondence, for the simple reason that experience is inherently differential anyway. On this account, difference is a necessary and enabling condition (as in, say, the difference between concept and intuition), rather than an incompatibility preventing contact.

Whereas poststructuralism and postmodernism assert that the categories of the Enlightenment are politically suspect for leaving certain forms of experience unacknowledged, Habermas stands by the emancipatory potential of the Enlightenment project. In 'Modernity versus Postmodernity', he considers the possibility that aesthetic modernity might reintegrate us with the life-world. The paper is the address he gave upon receiving the Theodor W. Adorno prize from the city of Frankfurt in 1980. Habermas' argument turns upon the 'inner logic' of the aesthetic resisting the divisive specialization exercised by modernity as a whole and promoting social integration through the cross-referral of categories. Aesthetic modernity, in its most recent guise, Habermas suggests, is a condition of perceptual revolution: the modern 'is "the new" which will be overcome and made obsolete through the necessity of the next style'. The drive to find new, unexplored regions within a territory has its origins in the eighteenth century. Enlightenment thought consolidates the independence of human perception from the teachings of the Church first instituted in the Renaissance. Whereas the Renaissance is defined by renewed interest in pre-Christian and ancient Greek texts, the Enlightenment introduces a compartmentalization of knowledge – into science, morality, and art – on the understanding that truth consists in the careful scrutiny and rationalization of what is appropriate to each domain – an 'inner logic', as Habermas refers to it – and that the depth of knowledge generated by specialization would promote justice, moral progress, and the development of the self. However, this has not happened. Specialization has instead come to mean 'separation from the hermeneutics of everyday communication'. In art, since the middle of the nineteenth century, there has been the 'distinct consciousness of art for art's sake', and twentieth-century attempts to bring art and life together, for example, Dada, the ready-made, conceptualism, have only served to deepen the Enlightenment's divisions.

'Postmodernity' in the essay title refers to the various neo-conservative intellectual positions which, in recent decades, have either given up on modernity as a force for positive social change or have claimed it to be responsible for the alienating tendencies within society. However, Habermas urges us to learn from the mistakes of modernity and see it as a project not yet complete; the divisions imposed by specialization can be retrieved from their schema of alienation. Rather than contributing to the divisions which carve society into alienated sectors, the category of aesthetic modernity, Habermas declares, following Wellmer, can work towards social reintegration by being combined with other categories, for example, creating situations which allow art to relate to the layman and not just to the expert who works exclusively within art criticism. This turns the logic of the aesthetic against itself, transforming an act of division into an act of cross-referral, in keeping with Kant's situation of the aesthetic as that which stimulates moral reasoning and the construction of knowledge. The aesthetic experience 'not only renews the interpretation of our needs in whose light we perceive the world' but also affects 'our cognitive significations and our normative expectations and changes the manner in which all these moments refer to one another'.

The analysis of the 'inner logic' of concepts takes an interesting turn with Habermas. It is clear from 'Questions and Counterquestions' that he sees Kant as a representative of the Enlightenment's strict demarcation of cognition, morality, and taste and not as an agent of reconciliation. In other words, Habermas doesn't recognize that Kant underpins Wellmer's thesis of conceptual integration. While it is true that Kant's critical philosophy involves systematic division, e.g., sensibility and understanding, theoretical cognition and practical cognition, determinative judgement and reflective judgement, it takes a wilfully selective reading of the three *Critiques* not to appreciate that these divisions are in place as the foundations for a theory of interrelationship. It is an unavoidable feature of grammar that one can only assert the interaction between things by first referring to them individually as separate things. By not recognizing that the origins of Wellmer's thesis are Kantian, Habermas' own writing becomes a display of just how difficult it is to determine the point when the 'inner logic' of a concept transforms it from being the imposition of a boundary to being a principle of boundary-transcendence.

The extract from 'Questions and Counterquestions' which follows 'Modernity versus Postmodernity' is Habermas' response to the various theorists who have commented upon his account of aesthetic modernity. It features some impressive descriptions of how aesthetic experience can break down entrenched categorial divisions. Works of art, Habermas avers, give us 'the inner logical differentiation of special sorts of experience' and generate 'increased sensitivity to what remains unassimilated in the interpretative achievements of pragmatic, epistemic, and moral mastery of the demands and challenges of everyday situations'. This structure of mutual illumination is essentially metaphorical – two normally unrelated concepts combined to create a proposition which generates novel perspectives on both – and invites us to compare Habermas' hermeneutics of conceptual cross-fertilization with the phenomenological accounts of, say, Heidegger and Bachelard, and the ethical issues raised by poststructuralism's reliance on metaphor.

Fredric Jameson

As can be seen from the previous papers in this section, the epistemological questions of how a concept cuts up the world and how matter pushes back and resists the concept are central themes in Marxist aesthetics: the 'particularity' of an artwork, Lukács claims, repositions the individual and the universal with respect to one another; Adorno uses contradiction and performative prose to transcend the limits of simple concept–object distinctions; the dialectical relationship between affirmation and negation, Marcuse asserts, means that what is initially alienated and marginalized, in virtue of its alienation, can muster the critical force necessary to reassert itself; and the category of aesthetic modernity, for Habermas, has the capacity to transform its categoriality into an act of interconceptual communication. That these questions are so prominent, I suggest, is the result of Kant's and Hegel's influence, with some expansion from Marx. Kant tells us that our concepts determine the shape of reality, and Hegel modifies this with the observation that the process of perception involves becoming aware of the inadequacy of our concepts and having them negated by the world. Furthermore, the epistemology underlying Marx's concepts of labour and species-being makes the question of conceptual order and determination a consequence of our practical engagement in the world.

The American literary and cultural theorist Fredric Jameson (b. 1934) is equally sensitive to the dynamics of the concept. He is one of the leading theorists of postmodernism, and concentrates on articulating the postmodern as the cultural expression of late capitalism which, through the tensions and inflexions of aesthetic experience, allows us to study the determinants of social change in the particular. What distinguishes Jameson from his predecessors is a reluctance to make his cultural analyses part of a moralizing, totalizing account of history, a position which has worried many thinkers on the Left. The postmodern, he claims, is a radical new cultural order and distinctive of this order is a complexity of conceptual borrowing and intermingling which prevents any simple or straightforward assimilation of it in the name of a given or predicted end. As he writes in 'Marxism and Postmodernism', his interest lies in 'the conditions of possibility' which entitle the theorist to draw her concepts rather than in the 'speculation and hypothetical analysis' which, to his mind, smacks of 'analysis of moments in the past when such conceptuality seemed possible'.[12]

Thus 'Postmodernism and Consumer Society', the essay representing Jameson below, concludes with the question of the critical or emancipatory status of postmodern art left unanswered. The essay shows how two postmodern aesthetic practices – pastiche and schizophrenia – 'reproduce' and 'reinforce' the 'logic of consumer capitalism', but refrains from suggesting how they might resist its logic. Pastiche is the form of parodic or mimical expression which results when the concept of an authentic or appropriate style is no longer available, while schizophrenia refers to the complete and utter disorientation an interpreter experiences when, in the absence of a familiar, shared narrative, she is confronted by a network of competing styles. These are discussed in relation to architecture, literature, and film. The essay is, for many, the foundation for all Jameson's subsequent writing on the postmodern, since it is his seminal articulation of the notion of a reproductive logic. The text presented below is the original address he gave to the Whitney Museum of Contemporary Arts in 1982, containing his core arguments for the relation between postmodernism and late capitalism. A longer version, with expanded sections on visual art, literature, technology, and the city, appeared in *New Left Review* in 1984 under the title 'Postmodernism, or the Cultural Logic of Late Capitalism'.

Adorno, Habermas, and Lyotard all share a commitment to the longevity of modernism's potential to generate new, destabilizing forms of representation, and both Habermas and Lyotard are keen to emphasize the revisionary dynamic of the modern against what they perceive to be the less fervent, more recapitulative aspects of the postmodern. However, for Jameson, the postmodern is an entirely separate category from the modern. Modernity's potential for generating new aesthetic forms, he argues, has been exhausted; there are simply no more new styles left to be discovered. The reason for this, he suggests, is that the intimate tie of aesthetic modernity between a 'unique private world' of experience and the particular stylistic practice dedicated to it has been severed. Changes in the social order of capitalism after the Second World War have brought a level of linguistic fragmentation which makes any single, one-to-one correspondence between experience and expression impossible. The consumer society, multinational capitalism, the media explosion, and electronic information introduce their own internal contradictions and provoke external resistance, and 'postmodernism' is the 'periodizing concept' Jameson uses 'to correlate the emergence of new formal features in culture' with the conflicting forces of late capitalism.

Notes

1 Karl Marx, *The Communist Manifesto,* with Friedrich Engels, ed. David McLellan, Oxford, Oxford University Press, 1998.
2 Friedrich Engels, *Anti-Dühring: Herr Eugen Dühring's Revolution in Science* (1878), Moscow, Foreign Language Publishing House, 1954; London, Lawrence and Wishart, 1955.
3 Karl Marx, *Capital,* vol. 1, Moscow, 1965, pp. 183–84, and quoted by Lucio Colletti in Marx, *Early Writings,* trans. Rodney Livingstone and Gregor Benton, London, Penguin, 1992, p. 28.
4 Marx, 'Estranged Labour', *Early Writings,* p. 330.
5 Ibid., p. 327.
6 Ibid., p. 329.
7 Marx, 'Profit of Capital', *Early Writings,* p. 295.
8 Lukács founded *The German Journal for Philosophy* with his friend Ernst Bloch in 1953.
9 Theodor W. Adorno, *Negative Dialectics,* trans. E.B. Ashton, London, Routledge, 1973, p. 162.
10 Herbert Marcuse, *Counterrevolution and Revolt,* Boston, Beacon Press, 1972, p. 5.
11 Herbert Marcuse, *The Aesthetic Dimension: Toward a Critique of Marxist Aesthetics,* trans. Herbert Marcuse and Erica Sherover, Boston, Beacon Press, 1977, p. 4.
12 Fredric Jameson, *The Cultural Turn: Selected Writings on the Postmodern, 1983–1998,* London, Verso, 1998, pp. 40–41.

12

PRIVATE PROPERTY AND COMMUNISM

Karl Marx

ad page xxxix.[1] But the antithesis between *propertylessness* and *property* is still an indifferent antithesis, not grasped in its *active connection*, its *inner* relation, not yet grasped as *contradiction*, as long as it is not understood as the antithesis between *labour* and *capital*. In its initial form this antithesis can manifest itself even without the advanced development of private property, as for example in ancient Rome, in Turkey, etc. In such cases it does not yet *appear* as established by private property itself. But labour, the subjective essence of private property as exclusion of property, and capital, objective labour as exclusion of labour, constitute *private property* in its developed relation of contradiction: a vigorous relation, therefore, driving towards resolution.

ad ibidem. The supersession [*Aufhebung*] of self-estrangement follows the same course as self-estrangement. *Private property* is first considered only in its objective aspect, but still with labour as its essence. Its form of existence is therefore *capital*, which is to be abolished 'as such' (Proudhon). Or the *particular form* of labour – levelled down, parcelled and therefore unfree – is taken as the source of the *harmfulness* of private property and its humanly estranged existence. For example, Fourier, like the Physiocrats, regarded agriculture as at least the *best* form of labour, while Saint-Simon on the other hand declared *industrial labour* as such to be the essence and consequently wants *exclusive* rule by the industrialists and the improvement of the condition of the workers. Finally, *communism*[2] is the *positive* expression of the abolition of private property and at first appears as *universal* private property. In grasping this relation in its *universality*, communism is

(1) in its initial form only a *generalization* and *completion* of that relation (of private property). As such it appears in a dual form: on the one hand the domination of *material* property bulks so large that it threatens to destroy *everything* which is not capable of being possessed by everyone as private property; it wants to abstract from talent, etc., by *force*. Physical, immediate *possession* is the only purpose of life and existence as far as this communism is concerned; the category of *worker* is not abolished but extended to all men; the relation of private property remains the relation of the community to the world of things; ultimately this movement to oppose universal private property to private property is expressed in bestial form – *marriage* (which is admittedly a *form* of *exclusive private property*) is counterposed to the *community of women*, where women become *communal* and *common* property. One might say that this idea of a *community of women* is the *revealed secret* of this as yet wholly crude and

unthinking communism. Just as women are to go from marriage into general prostitution, so the whole world of wealth – i.e. the objective essence of man – is to make the transition from the relation of exclusive marriage with the private owner to the relation of universal prostitution with the community. This communism, inasmuch as it negates the *personality* of man in every sphere, is simply the logical expression of the private property which is this negation. Universal *envy* constituting itself as a power is the hidden form in which *greed* reasserts itself and satisfies itself, but in *another* way. The thoughts of every piece of private property as such are *at least* turned against *richer* private property in the form of envy and the desire to level everything down; hence these feelings in fact constitute the essence of competition. The crude communist is merely the culmination of this envy and desire to level down on the basis of a *preconceived* minimum. It has a *definite, limited* measure. How little this abolition of private property is a true appropriation is shown by the abstract negation of the entire world of culture and civilization, and the return to the *unnatural* simplicity of the *poor*, unrefined man who has no needs and who has not even reached the stage of private property, let alone gone beyond it.

(For crude communism) the community is simply a community of *labour* and equality of *wages*, which are paid out by the communal capital, the *community* as universal capitalist. Both sides of the relation are raised to an *imaginary* universality – *labour* as the condition in which everyone is placed and *capital* as the acknowledged universality and power of the community.

In the relationship with *woman*, as the *prey* and handmaid of communal lust, is expressed the infinite degradation in which man exists for himself, for the secret of this relationship has its *unambiguous*, decisive, *open* and revealed expression in the relationship of *man* to *woman* and in the manner in which the *direct*, *natural* species-relationship is conceived. The immediate, natural, necessary relation of human being to human being is the *relationship* of *man* to *woman*. In this *natural* species-relationship the relation of man to nature is immediately his relation to man, just as his relation to man is immediately his relation to nature, his own *natural* condition. Therefore this relationship *reveals* in a *sensuous* form, reduced to an observable *fact*, the extent to which the human essence has become nature for man or nature has become the human essence for man. It is possible to judge from this relationship the entire level of development of mankind. It follows from the character of this relationship how far *man* as a *species-being*, as *man*, has become himself and grasped himself; the relation of man to woman is the most *natural* relation of human being to human being. It therefore demonstrates the extent to which man's *natural* behaviour has become *human* or the extent to which his *human* essence has become a *natural* essence for him, the extent to which his *human nature* has become *nature* for him. This relationship also demonstrates the extent to which man's *needs* have become *human* needs, hence the extent to which the *other*, as a human being, has become a need for him, the extent to which in his most individual existence he is at the same time a communal being.

The first positive abolition of private property – *crude* communism – is therefore only a *manifestation* of the vileness of private property trying to establish itself as the *positive community*.

(2) Communism (a) still of a political nature, democratic or despotic; (b) with the abolition of the state, but still essentially incomplete and influenced by private property, i.e. by the estrangement of man. In both forms communism already knows

itself as the reintegration or return of man into himself, the supersession of man's self-estrangement; but since it has not yet comprehended the positive essence of private property or understood the *human* nature of need, it is still held captive and contaminated by private property. True, it has understood its concept, but not yet its essence.

(3) *Communism*[3] is the *positive* supersession of *private property* as *human self-estrangement*, and hence the true *appropriation* of the *human* essence through and for man; it is the complete restoration of man to himself as a *social*, i.e. human, being, a restoration which has become conscious and which takes place within the entire wealth of previous periods of development. This communism, as fully developed naturalism, equals humanism, and as fully developed humanism equals naturalism; it is the *genuine* resolution of the conflict between man and nature, and between man and man, the true resolution of the conflict between existence and being, between objectification and self-affirmation, between freedom and necessity, between individual and species. It is the solution of the riddle of history and knows itself to be the solution.

The entire movement of history is therefore both the *actual* act of creation of communism – the birth of its empirical existence – and, for its thinking consciousness, the *comprehended* and *known* movement of its *becoming*; whereas the other communism, which is not yet fully developed, seeks in isolated historical forms opposed to private property a historical proof for itself, a proof drawn from what already exists, by wrenching isolated moments from their proper places in the process of development (a hobby horse Cabet, Villegardelle, etc., particularly like to ride) and advancing them as proofs of its historical pedigree. But all it succeeds in showing is that by far the greater part of this development contradicts its assertions and that if it did once exist, then the very fact that it existed in the *past* refutes its claim to *essential being* [*Wesen*].

It is easy to see how necessary it is for the whole revolutionary movement to find both its empirical and its theoretical basis in the movement of *private property* or, to be more exact, of the economy.

This *material*, immediately *sensuous* private property is the material, sensuous expression of *estranged human* life. Its movement – production and consumption – is the sensuous revelation of the movement of all previous production, i.e. the realization or reality of man. Religion, the family, the state, law, morality, science, art, etc., are only *particular* modes of production and therefore come under its general law. The positive supersession of *private property*, as the appropriation of *human* life, is therefore the positive supersession of all estrangement, and the return of man from religion, the family, the state, etc., to his *human*, i.e. *social* existence. Religious estrangement as such takes place only in the sphere *of consciousness*, of man's inner life, but economic estrangement is that of *real life* – its supersession therefore embraces both aspects. Clearly the nature of the movement in different countries initially depends on whether the actual and *acknowledged* life of the people has its being more in consciousness or in the external world, in ideal or in real life. Communism begins with atheism (Owen), but atheism is initially far from being *communism*, and is for the most part an abstraction. The philanthropy of atheism is therefore at first nothing more than an abstract *philosophical* philanthropy, while that of communism is at once *real* and directly bent towards *action*.

We have seen how, assuming the positive supersession of private property, man produces man, himself and other men; how the object, which is the direct activity of his individuality, is at the same time his existence for other men, their existence and their existence for him. Similarly, however, both the material of labour and man as subject are the starting-point as well as the outcome of the movement (and the historical *necessity* of private property lies precisely in the fact that they must be this starting-point). So the *social* character is the general character of the whole movement; *just as* society itself produces *man* as *man*, so it is *produced* by him. Activity and consumption, both in their content and in their *mode of existence*, are *social* activity and *social* consumption. The *human* essence of nature exists only for *social* man; for only here does nature exist for him as a *bond* with other *men*, as his existence for others and their existence for him, as the vital element of human reality; only here does it exist as the *basis* of his own *human* existence. Only here has his *natural* existence become his *human* existence and nature become man for him. *Society* is therefore the perfected unity in essence of man with nature, the true resurrection of nature, the realized naturalism of man and the realized humanism of nature.[4]

Social activity and social consumption by no means exist *solely* in the form of a *directly* communal activity and a directly *communal* consumption, even though *communal* activity and *communal* consumption, i.e. activity and consumption that express and confirm themselves directly in *real association* with other men, occur wherever that *direct* expression of sociality [*Gesellschaftlichkeit*] springs from the essential nature of the content of the activity and is appropriate to the nature of the consumption.

But even if I am active in the field of science, etc. – an activity which I am seldom able to perform in direct association with other men – I am still *socially* active because I am active as a *man*. It is not only the material of my activity – including even the language in which the thinker is active – which I receive as a social product. My *own* existence *is* social activity. Therefore what I create from myself I create for society, conscious of myself as a social being.

My *universal* consciousness is only the *theoretical* form of that whose *living* form is the *real* community, society, whereas at present *universal* consciousness is an abstraction from real life and as such in hostile opposition to it. Hence the *activity* of my universal consciousness – as activity – is my *theoretical* existence as a social being.

It is above all necessary to avoid once more establishing 'society' as an abstraction over against the individual. The individual *is* the *social being*. His vital expression – even when it does not appear in the direct form of a *communal* expression, conceived in association with other men – is therefore an expression and confirmation of *social life*. Man's individual and species-life are not two *distinct things*, however much – and this is necessarily so – the mode of existence of individual life is a more *particular* or a more *general* mode of the species-life, or species-life a more *particular* or more *general* individual life.

As *species-consciousness* man confirms his real *social life* and merely repeats in thought his actual existence; conversely, species-being confirms itself in species-consciousness and exists for itself in its universality, as a thinking being.

Man, however much he may therefore be a *particular* individual – and it is just this particularity which makes him an individual and a real *individual* communal being – is just as much the *totality*, the ideal totality, the subjective existence of thought and experienced society for itself; he also exists in reality as the contemplation and true enjoyment of social existence and as a totality of vital human expression.

It is true that thought and being are *distinct*, but at the same time they are in *unity* with one another.

Death appears as the harsh victory of the species over the particular individual, and seemingly contradicts their unity; but the particular individual is only a *particular species-being*, and as such mortal.

(4) Just as *private property* is only the sensuous expression of the fact that man becomes *objective* for himself and at the same time becomes an alien and inhuman object for himself, that his expression of life [*Lebensäusserung*] is his alienation of life [*Lebensentäusserung*], and that his realization is a loss of reality, an *alien* reality, so the positive supersession of private property, i.e. the *sensuous* appropriation of the human essence and human life, of objective man and of human *works* by and for man, should not be understood only in the sense of *direct*, one-sided *consumption*, of *possession*, of *having*. Man appropriates his integral essence in an integral way, as a total man. All his *human* relations to the world – seeing, hearing, smelling, tasting, feeling, thinking, contemplating, sensing, wanting, acting, loving – in short, all the organs of his individuality, like the organs which are directly communal in form, are in their *objective* approach or in their *approach to the object* the appropriation of that object. This appropriation of *human* reality, their approach to the object, is the *confirmation of human reality*.[5] It is human *effectiveness* and human *suffering*, for suffering, humanly conceived, is an enjoyment of the self for man.

Private property has made us so stupid and one-sided that an object is only *ours* when we have it, when it exists for us as capital or when we directly possess, eat, drink, wear, inhabit it, etc., in short, when we *use* it. Although private property conceives all these immediate realizations of possession only as *means of life*; and the life they serve is the *life* of *private property*, labour and capitalization.

Therefore *all* the physical and intellectual senses have been replaced by the simple estrangement of *all* these senses – the sense of *having*. So that it might give birth to its inner wealth, human nature had to be reduced to this absolute poverty. (On the category of *having* see Hess in *Einundzwanzig Bogen*.)[6]

The supersession of private property is therefore the complete *emancipation* of all human senses and attributes; but it is this emancipation precisely because these senses and attributes have become *human*, subjectively as well as objectively. The eye has become a *human* eye, just as its *object* has become a social, *human* object, made by man for man. The *senses* have therefore become *theoreticians* in their immediate praxis. They relate to the *thing* for its own sake, but the thing itself is an *objective human* relation to itself and to man,[7] and vice versa. Need or enjoyment have therefore lost their *egoistic* nature, and nature has lost its mere *utility* in the sense that its use has become *human* use.

Similarly, the senses and enjoyment of other men have become my *own* appropriation. Apart from these direct organs, *social* organs are therefore created in the *form* of society; for example, activity in direct association with others, etc. has become an organ of my *life expression* and a mode of appropriation of *human* life.

Obviously the *human* eye takes in things in a different way from the crude non-human eye, the human *ear* in a different way from the crude ear, etc.

To sum up: it is only when man's object becomes a *human* object or objective man that man does not lose himself in that object. This is only possible when it becomes a *social* object for him and when he himself becomes a social being for himself, just as society becomes a being for him in this object.

On the one hand, therefore, it is only when objective reality universally becomes for man in society the reality of man's essential powers, becomes human reality, and thus the reality of his *own* essential powers, that all *objects* become for him the *objectification of himself*, objects that confirm and realize his individuality, *his* objects, i.e. *he himself* becomes the object. The *manner* in which they become his depends on the *nature* of the *object* and the nature of the *essential power* that corresponds to *it*; for it is just the *determinateness* of this relation that constitutes the particular, *real* mode of affirmation. An object is different for the *eye* from what it is for the *ear*, and the eye's object *is* different from the *ear's*. The peculiarity of each essential power is precisely its *peculiar essence*, and thus also the peculiar mode of its objectification, of its *objectively real*, living *being*. Man is therefore affirmed in the objective world not only in thought but with *all* the senses.

On the other hand, let us look at the question in its subjective aspect: only music can awaken the musical sense in man and the most beautiful music has *no* sense for the unmusical ear, because my object can only be the confirmation of one of my essential powers, i.e. can only be for me in so far as my essential power exists for me as a subjective attribute (this is because the sense of an object for me extends only as far as *my* sense extends, only has sense for a sense that corresponds to that object). In the same way, and for the same reasons, the *senses* of social man are *different* from those of non-social man. Only through the objectively unfolded wealth of human nature can the wealth of subjective *human* sensitivity – a musical ear, an eye for the beauty of form, in short, *senses* capable of human gratification – be either cultivated or created. For not only the five senses, but also the so-called spiritual senses, the practical senses (will, love, etc.), in a word, the *human* sense, the humanity of the senses – all these come into being only through the existence of *their* objects, through *humanized* nature. The *cultivation* of the five senses is the work of all previous history. *Sense* which is a prisoner of crude practical need has only a *restricted* sense. For a man who is starving the human form of food does not exist, only its abstract form exists; it could just as well be present in its crudest form, and it would be hard to say how this way of eating differs from that of *animals*. The man who is burdened with worries and needs has no *sense* for the finest of plays; the dealer in minerals sees only the commercial value, and not the beauty and peculiar nature of the minerals; he lacks a mineralogical sense; thus the objectification of the human essence, in a theoretical as well as a practical respect, is necessary both in order to make man's *senses human* and to create an appropriate *human sense* for the whole of the wealth of humanity and of nature.

Just as in its initial stages society is presented with all the material for this *cultural development* through the movement of *private property* and of its wealth and poverty – both material and intellectual wealth and poverty – so the society that is *fully developed* produces man in all the richness of his being, the *rich* man who is *profoundly and abundantly endowed with all the senses*, as its constant reality. It can be seen how subjectivism and objectivism, spiritualism and materialism, activity and passivity [*Leiden*], lose their antithetical character, and hence their existence as such antitheses, only in the social condition; it can be seen how the resolution of the *theoretical* antitheses themselves is possible *only* in a *practical* way, only through the practical energy of man, and how their resolution is for that reason by no means only a problem of knowledge, but a *real* problem of life, a problem which *philosophy* was unable to solve precisely because it treated it as a *purely* theoretical problem.

It can be seen how the history of *industry* and the *objective* existence of industry as it has developed is the *open* book of the essential powers of man, man's psychology present in tangible form; up to now this history has not been grasped in its connection with the *nature* of man, but only in an external utilitarian aspect, for man, moving in the realm of estrangement, was only capable of conceiving the general existence of man – religion, or history in its abstract and universal form of politics, art, literature, etc. – as the reality of man's essential powers and as *man's species-activity*. In *everyday, material industry* (which can just as easily be considered as a part of that general development as that general development itself can be considered as a *particular* part of industry, since all human activity up to now has been labour, i.e. industry, self-estranged activity) we find ourselves confronted with the *objectified powers of the human essence*, in the form of *sensuous, alien, useful objects*, in the form of estrangement. A *psychology* for which this book, the most tangible and accessible part of history, is closed, can never become a *real* science with a genuine content. What indeed should we think of a science which *primly* abstracts from this large area of human labour, and fails to sense its own inadequacy, even though such an extended wealth of human activity says nothing more to it perhaps than what can be said in one word – 'need', 'common need'?

The *natural sciences* have been prolifically active and have gathered together an ever growing mass of material. But philosophy has remained just as alien to them as they have remained alien to philosophy. Their momentary union was only a *fantastic illusion*. The will was there, but not the means. Even historiography only incidentally takes account of natural science, which it sees as contributing to enlightenment, utility and a few great discoveries. But natural science has intervened in and transformed human life all the more *practically* through industry and has prepared the conditions for human emancipation, however much its immediate effect was to complete the process of dehumanization. *Industry* is the *real* historical relationship of nature, and hence of natural science, to man. If it is then conceived as the *exoteric* revelation of man's *essential powers*, the *human* essence of nature or the *natural* essence of man can also be understood. Hence natural science will lose its abstractly material, or rather idealist, orientation and become the basis of *human* science, just as it has already become – though in an *estranged* from – the basis of actual human life. The idea of *one* basis for life and another for *science* is from the very outset a lie. Nature as it comes into being in human history – in the act of creation of human society – is the *true* nature of man; hence nature as it comes into being through industry, though in an *estranged* form, is true *anthropological* nature.

Sense perception (see Feuerbach) must be the basis of all science. Only when science starts out from sense perception in the dual form of *sensuous* consciousness and *sensuous* need – i.e. only when science starts out from nature – is it *real* science. The whole of history is a preparation, a development, for '*man*' to become the object of *sensuous* consciousness and for the needs of 'man as man' to become [sensuous] needs. History itself is a *real* part of *natural history* and of nature's becoming man. Natural science will in time subsume the science of man just as the science of man will subsume natural science: there will be *one* science.

Man is the immediate object of natural science; for immediate *sensuous nature* for man is, immediately, human sense perception (an identical expression) in the form of the *other* man who is present in his sensuous immediacy for him. His own sense perception only exists as human sense perception for himself through the *other* man. But *nature* is the immediate object of the *science of man.* Man's first object – man – is nature, sense perception; and the particular sensuous human powers, since they can find objective realization only in *natural* objects, can find self-knowledge only in the science of nature in general. The element of thought itself, the element of the vital expression of thought – *language* – is sensuous nature. The *social* reality of nature and *human* natural science or the *natural science of man* are identical expressions.

It can be seen how the *rich man* and the wealth of *human* need take the place of the *wealth* and *poverty* of political economy. The *rich* man is simultaneously the man *in need of* a totality of vital human expression; he is the man in whom his own realization exists as inner necessity, as *need.* Given socialism, not only man's *wealth* but also his *poverty* acquire a *human* and hence a social significance. Poverty is the passive bond which makes man experience his greatest wealth – the *other* man – as need. The domination of the objective essence within me, the sensuous outburst of my essential activity, is *passion*, which here becomes the *activity* of my being.

(5) A *being* sees himself as independent only when he stands on his own feet, and he only stands on his own feet when he owes his *existence* to himself. A man who lives by the grace of another regards himself as a dependent being. But I live completely by the grace of another if I owe him not only the maintenance of my life but also its *creation*, if he is the *source* of my life. My life is necessarily grounded outside itself if it is not my own creation. The *creation* is therefore an idea which is very hard to exorcize from the popular consciousness. This consciousness is *incapable of comprehending* the self-mediated being [*Durchsichselbstsein*] of nature and of man, since such a being contradicts all the *palpable evidence* of practical life.

The creation of the *earth* received a heavy blow from the science of *geogeny*, i.e. the science which depicts the formation of the earth, its coming to be, as a process of self-generation. *Generatio aequivoca*[8] is the only practical refutation of the theory of creation.

Now it is easy to say to a particular individual what Aristotle said: You were begotten by your father and your mother, which means that in you the mating of two human beings, a human species-act, produced another human being. Clearly, then, man also owes his existence to man in a physical sense. Therefore you should not only keep sight of the *one* aspect, the *infinite* progression which leads you on to the question: 'Who begot my father, his grandfather, etc.?' You should also keep in mind the *circular movement* sensuously perceptible in that progression whereby man reproduces himself in the act of begetting and thus always remains the subject. But you will reply: I grant you this circular movement, but you must also grant me the right to progress back to the question: Who begot the first man, and nature in general? I can only answer: Your question is itself a product of abstraction. Ask yourself how you arrived at that question. Ask yourself whether your question does not arise from a standpoint to which I cannot reply because it is a perverse one. Ask yourself whether that progression exists as such for rational thought. If you ask about the creation of nature and of man, then you are abstracting from nature and from man. You assume them as *non-existent* and want me to prove to you that they *exist.* My answer is: Give up your abstraction and you will then give up your question. But if you want to hold on to your abstraction, then do so consistently, and if you assume the non-existence of man and nature, then assume also your own non-existence, for you are also nature and man. Do not think and do not ask me questions, for as soon as you think and ask questions, your *abstraction* from the existence of nature and man has no meaning. Or are you such an egoist that you assume everything as non-existent and still want to exist yourself?

You can reply: I do not want to assume the nothingness of nature, etc. I am only asking how it *arose*, just as I might ask the anatomist about the formation of bones, etc.

But since for socialist man the *whole of what is called world history* is nothing more than the creation of man through human labour, and the development of nature for man, he therefore has palpable and incontrovertible proof of his self-mediated *birth*, of his *process of emergence*. Since the *essentiality* [*Wesenhaftigkeit*] of man and of nature, man as the existence of nature for man and nature as the existence of man for man, has become practically and sensuously perceptible, the question of an *alien* being, a being above nature and man – a question which implies an admission of the unreality of nature and of man – has become impossible in practice. *Atheism*, which is a denial of this unreality, no longer has any meaning, for atheism is a *negation of God*, through which negation it asserts the *existence of man*. But socialism as such no longer needs such mediation. Its starting-point is the *theoretically and practically sensuous consciousness* of man and of nature as *essential beings*. It is the *positive self-consciousness* of man, no longer mediated through the abolition of religion, just as *real life* is positive reality no longer mediated through the abolition of private property, through *communism*. Communism is the act of positing as the negation of the negation, and is therefore a *real* phase, necessary for the next period of historical development, in the emancipation and recovery of mankind. *Communism* is the necessary form and the dynamic principle of the immediate future but communism is not as such the goal of human development – the form of human society.[9]

Translated by Rodney Livingstone and Gregor Benton

Notes

1 *Editor's note:* 'Private Property and Communism' is a fragment from the third of Marx's *Economic and Philosophical Manuscripts* and was written as an appendix to a page in the second manuscript, 'The Relationship of Private Property', much of which is missing. The fragment begins with these words.

2 'Communism' in this sense is, of course, the 'crude communism' of utopian thinkers such as Fourier, Proudhon and Babeuf, and is later contrasted with Marx's own conception of communism.

3 Having discussed the nature of 'crude communism', Marx now goes on to describe his own conception of communism.

4 Prostitution is only a *particular* expression of the *universal* prostitution of the *worker*, and since prostitution is a relationship which includes not only the prostituted but also the prostitutor – whose infamy is even greater – the capitalist is also included in this category. [*This note was inserted by Marx at the bottom of his manuscript page without any further indication of reference.*]

5 It is therefore just as varied as the *determinations* of the *human essence* and *activities*. [*Marx's note*]

6 Cf. Moses Hess, 'Philosophie der Tat', printed in *Einundzwanzig Bogen aus der Schweiz*, Zurich, Erster Teil, 1843, p. 329.

7 In practice I can only relate myself to a thing in a human way if the thing is related in a human way to man. [*Marx's note*]

8 Spontaneous generation.
9 The meaning of this sentence is unclear. 'Communism . . . as such' is sometimes taken as referring to the 'crude communism' discussed earlier. On the other hand, the sentence can be interpreted as meaning that communism is not the final stage in the development of humanity, but will in its turn be transcended by a richer and higher stage.

13

SPECIFIC PARTICULARITY AS THE CENTRAL CATEGORY OF AESTHETICS

Georg Lukács

Goethe's discovery in elucidating the aesthetic category of specific particularity [*das Besondere*] would seem at first sight to be quite minor. It refers to the way in which the artist reflects [*wiederspiegelt*] objective reality by bringing its movement to stand, by fixing and bestowing shape upon it in a quite specific and particular manner, rather than by concentrating upon the universal or individual dimension of reality as scientific knowledge attempts to do in accordance with its concrete purposes in each case. Knowledge which is bound up with the sphere of everyday praxis can only ever be defined in each case in relation to its concrete practical task. Both scientific knowledge and artistic creation (including the aesthetic reception of reality with respect to specific ways of experiencing natural beauty, for example) differentiate themselves out during the course of the long historical development of humanity. The explicit specialization of these different domains and the superiority they enjoy with respect to the immediate practical sphere of everyday life, from which indeed they first and only gradually emerged, would never have been accomplished without some such process.

Attempting to define the peculiar character of the different forms of human activity will inevitably result in misleading conclusions if we fail to grasp that it is the same objective reality which finds itself reflected in all three cases, and indeed the same not merely in respect to its substantive content but also to its forms and categories. Of course it is true that this long-established and successfully accomplished process of specialization leads to the formation of specifically differentiated modes of perception, both natural and artificial in character, which respond to things, forms and relationships that would never have become accessible to the immediate praxis of everyday life. And here we must consider not merely the innumerable instruments of knowledge which have emerged along with developments in economic life, technology and the natural sciences, but also the further development of man's natural modes of perception through the increasingly specialized needs of the labouring process, and through the fruitful and beneficial interaction between the products of science and art, the results of labour and everyday praxis in general. The differentiation which is produced by social-historical development does not therefore serve to isolate the particular modes of human behaviour from one another. On the contrary: the greater the specialization, the more fruitful the interaction and mutually beneficial effect of these modes of behaviour can prove to be, unless the social structure itself exerts a destructive influence, as it does with the capitalist division of labour.

The materialist break with idealist philosophy finds exemplary expression with this insistence upon the priority of a single shared objective reality. Subjective idealism on the other hand conjures up quite specific and mutually incomparable 'worlds' by appeal to the so-called a priori forms of specific modes of relating to reality, something which is particularly marked in the case of Simmel's thought. The dialectical conception proper to materialism thus consists, on the one hand, in affirming the substantive and formal unity of the world that is reflected, but also emphasizes, on the other hand, the non-mechanical, non-photographic character of this reflection [*Wiederspiegelung*], the active dimension which characterizes the subject's concrete engagement with the reflected world in the form of socially conditioned questions and problems produced in the development of productive forces and modified by the changes in the relations of production.

It is only in this context that the peculiar character of aesthetic reflection can properly be grasped. The question concerning the community of form and content also involves the categories of individuality [*Einzelheit*], particularity [*Besonderheit*] and universality [*Allgemeinheit*]. And it is not merely the intrinsic totality or the serial order of these categories which is at issue. For it is also necessary – in a quite general sense – to recognise that these categories stand objectively in a constant dialectical interrelationship, that they constantly pass over into one another, and further, subjectively, that the unbroken movement involved in the process of reflecting reality leads from one extreme to the other. It is this latter movement which properly reveals the peculiar character of aesthetic reflection. In the case of theoretical knowledge this movement really proceeds in both directions, from one extreme to the other, with the middle term, the category of particularity, playing a mediating role in both cases. In artistic reflection, on the other hand, the middle term literally becomes the middle, where the movement in question is gathered and centred in a single point. In this connection, therefore, we are presented with a movement from particularity to universality (and back again) as well as a movement from particularity to individuality (and likewise back again), and in both cases the movement to particularity is conclusive. Aesthetic reflection, like the cognitive reflection of science, aims to grasp and reveal the totality of reality in all of its unfolded substantive and formal richness, to reproduce the latter with the specific means at its disposal. Insofar as aesthetic reflection decisively modifies the subjective process, in the manner outlined above, it also produces qualitative modifications in its mirroring image of the world. The moment of particularity here becomes an ineliminable fixed point upon which the entire world of artistic forms is built. The reciprocal reversion and transition of the categories finds itself modified here: for both individuality and universality always appear as sublated [*aufgehoben*], gathered up and preserved, in the moment of specific particularity.

Here indeed it is necessary in turn to introduce an emphatic qualification concerning the overall unity which characterizes all the ways of reflecting reality. In analysing the process of theoretical knowledge we have already stressed the tendency constantly to expand the limits of universality, and individuality as well, and this is also something which affects the process of aesthetic reflection. There would be no history of art if, along with the transformations of life itself, a further expansion in the limits of the known world, a further development of the instruments which allow us to comprehend the world, did not make itself felt within the domain of art as well. But whereas the domain of theoretical reflection involves a continuous development which can be pursued indefinitely, the sublation of universality and individuality into particularity (a non-reciprocal process in the last analysis, although a certain reciprocity may of course be necessary and possible in the preparatory stages of artistic production) fixes a certain stage of human development for consciousness. An even higher stage of development is naturally intrinsically possible and necessary. But an authentic artistic creation, fashioned in such a way as to give optimal shape to the specific particularity of a given stage of development, still preserves its validity – its artistic validity – even if all the constructive elements involved in it have long since been superseded by the evolving forms and techniques of art. The process in which art approaches truth here assumes a specific and emphatic character of its own: the higher stage does not always have to represent an immediate continuation of an earlier one, as is generally the case with the advance of science. Rather the next stage, even while exploiting all the experience that has been accumulated through previous works and creative processes associated with them, always begins in a certain sense again from scratch. Reactionary philosophical positions appeal to this peculiar character which belongs to the aesthetic reflection of reality in order to mystify the nature of art in an irrationalist manner. But our own reflections have shown that every specific character which attaches to the production and the existence of art can be explained in an entirely rational manner – in a dialectically rational manner – from the process of reflection in general.

As far as the sublation [*Aufhebung*] of the two extremes of universality and individuality into particularity is concerned, the properly elaborated theory of reflection shows just how fundamentally false all such irrational theories of art are. Above all, this process of sublation never involves a loss or disappearance, but always a certain preservation. This is something that must be particularly emphasized, above all, with respect to the role of universality within aesthetic reflection. Every significant form of art engages intensively with all the major problems of its age; it is only in periods of decadence that we find an avoidance of such questions, something which finds expression partly in the lack of genuine universality in the works themselves, partly in the naked articulation of universalities which, distorted and substantively false, have not been artistically sublated in the works in question.

But we must also add something that takes us beyond the parameters of the present discussion: this sublation of universality into artistic particularity can assume the most varied of forms, depending upon period, genre, and the specific nature of the individual artist. It can take on the essentially lyrical form of individual subjective experience and pathos, or, as in the case of drama, find itself entirely absorbed and objectified in external figures and situations, and so forth. But it is quite certain that the deepest source of all such artistic universalization ultimately lies in the objective universalization of life itself and its concrete manifestations. Of course, it is also true with many important artists that the assistance provided by science and philosophy plays a significant role here. But this only proves to be really fruitful if such assistance does not take the form of a ready-made and instantly applicable theory, but rather as a means of grasping the phenomena of life in a deeper, richer and more comprehensive fashion. Dobroljubow, whom no one could possibly accuse of overemphasizing the autonomy of art, expresses the point this way:

> The really gifted writers were always capable of grasping those truths which the philosophers had only surmised in theory, of presenting them and their effects in the context of life itself. As the perfect representatives of the most highly developed stage of human consciousness in a particular epoch they were able to survey and depict the life of man and nature from this elevated perspective . . . But this is not generally accomplished by the writer merely borrowing ideas from the philosopher and then realising them in the resulting works. No, rather both the writer and the philosopher function independently, both draw upon the same original source, real life itself, but they engage the matter in hand in a different way in each case.[1]

This implies that great art can certainly attain the most progressive level with respect to the ideas it harbours, namely the level which points most decisively to the future, but without thereby forfeiting anything of its own particular artistic character and independence.

The relationship between specific particularity and individuality represents a never-ending process of sublation, with an even stronger emphasis, in a certain sense, upon the moment of preservation. Engels touches upon this problem in his letter of criticism to Minna Kautsky: 'Everyone is a type, but also a specific and individual human being at the same time, a "This" as old Hegel used to say, and this is how it must be.'[2] Our reflections above have already shown the necessity of the demand that individuality should be sublated and thus preserved: without the preservation of individuality it is quite impossible for any phenomenon, whatever it may be, to express its own underlying essence as this phenomenon in an immediate manner. Nonetheless, it seems indispensable here to clarify the sublated character of such individuality rather more precisely. For there is no question, on the one hand, that both the constantly changing and the more permanent features of individuality are equally important considered in terms of their immediacy. On the other hand, these features also relate in extraordinarily diverse ways to the underlying mediations by virtue of which every individuality stands in relation to particularity and universality. If the individual moment therefore is to find its true expression, these often ramifying and complex mediations must also receive due emphasis and recognition in accordance with their own intrinsic significance. But this structural displacement within the sphere of individuality also signifies the sublation, its elevation into the sphere of specific particularity (the determinate and the typical). The greater the artist's understanding of human beings and the world they inhabit, and the more he or she is capable of uncovering such mediations, and where necessary pursuing them in terms of their utmost universality, the more vigorous and effective the sublation involved proves itself to be. The greater the artist's creative powers, the more vividly he or she is capable of returning these uncovered mediations to a new immediacy and centring them organically in the latter: in other words, in fashioning something specific and particular out of the individual phenomenon.

Here too the development of art reveals how the genuine dialectic that is required in this connection finds historical expression and recognition in the most varied of ways. Aristotle had already noted the development which leads from the iambic poets to the comic dramatists, manifest in the fact that typical human characteristics rather than individual human beings had eventually become the objects of satire. This conception of individuality – or in specifically Aristotelian terms of the individual figures of myth, legend and history, etc. – still plays a major role in Lessing's *Hamburg Dramaturgy*. Naturally the precise terminology is not aesthetically important here. For it is quite possible to imagine a satirical treatment of some definite individual, including all the attendant features of his individual nature, which successfully accomplished the sublation of individuality into specific particularity (the typical). On the other hand, characterization in terms of the typical does not of itself guarantee any genuine sublation into specific particularity. Here too the decisive thing is the movement that unfolds with respect to the content of the individual phenomenon, that is: whether the characteristic features which connect the latter with society and the world through objective interaction are preserved precisely as mediating factors and returned to a new form of specific particularity (i.e. are dialectically sublated in it). Once again it is the periods of decadence in which this richer determination of individuality is lost. Of course, the theory and practice of decadence always emphasize the moment of individuality which then gets fetishized as the absolutely unique, the unrepeatable, the ineliminable, etc. In reality what has happened here is merely that the perceptual means of reflecting reality have lost contact with the 'social amalgam', as Gorky puts it, have taken to overemphasizing the moment of purely immediate individuality precisely because the artists in question have lost the capacity to transcend the latter and attain to true concreteness.

Guy de Maupassant interestingly relates the way in which Flaubert helped him to become a writer. Amongst other things, his master once told him:

> The real task is to consider long and carefully what it is one wishes to express, and to discover an aspect which no one has ever seen or articulated before . . . In order to describe a flame, or a tree in the plain, we must observe this flame, this tree, for a long time until it is no longer the same as any other flame, any other tree, that we have ever seen . . . We must, in other words, reveal just why this cab horse is not the same as the fifty other ones that come before or after it.[3]

These remarks are interesting in two respects. In the first place, they reveal how theory often lags far behind actual practice, even in the case of very thoughtful and significant artists. If Flaubert had really written in this way, and if Maupassant had only learned this from him, then both of them would be naturalist writers long since forgotten. But apart from that, the remarks are also interesting for a second reason in so far as they indicate the dead-end that awaits every aesthetic which overemphasizes the moment of individuality. For it is clear that Flaubert expects the truly original artist to focus precisely upon the individual phenomenon in its immediacy. Any connection and interaction of the individual phenomenon with the surrounding world (with society and nature) is supposed to vanish in order that the specific characteristics of the isolated individual phenomenon may be captured. On the one hand, this really represents a Sisyphean labour because the attainment of the end would actually involve the destruction of all artistic interest. A tree or a cab horse (or a human being for that matter) are only worthy of interest through their interactions with the surrounding world. On the other hand, artistic achievement in the field of literature spontaneously accomplishes the work of sublation. Hegel was quite right in claiming that the simplest word already harbours within it a moment of universalization with respect to the individual object which it names: at the very least it subsumes the latter under a general representation, or reveals a network of relationships, etc. Flaubert's vigorous defence of the moment of individuality thus reveals – contrary to his own intentions – that while art can certainly never dispense with such individuality, and must constantly struggle to grasp it, art can only properly call the latter its own once it has been sublated in the form of specific particularity.

As far as the category of particularity itself is concerned, we must always bear in mind that the two extremes (individuality and universality) represent certain ever-extendable end-points, although they are indeed at any given moment specific points, whereas particularity as the middle term presents us rather with a field, a certain leeway, an intermediate domain. In the case of aesthetic reflection, where the middle is fixed as the focus of the entire movement, this structure is inevitably subjected to radical transformation. But this seems to raise an insoluble problem for the theory of aesthetic reflection: that of precisely determining the middle-point at all. When we consider the structure of theoretical reflection, this appears from the beginning as an insoluble task, for every decision must appear – from the standpoint of aesthetic reflection in general – to be arbitrary; there is no conceivable universally valid criterion which would allow a decision here.

It was necessary to insist upon this difficulty precisely in order fully to clarify the distinction between theoretical and aesthetic reflection. In fact there is no theoretical criterion here, and the artistic criterion involved embraces (abstractly considered) the open domain of particularity itself; the focus of the middle-point can, generally speaking and in principle, transpire anywhere within the leeway of this domain [*Spielraum*]. It might seem as though we had thereby merely avoided the difficulty in question, perhaps even displaced it into the sphere of the irrational and the arbitrary rather than satisfactorily resolving it. And we must indeed concede: within the parameters of the present discussion, which claims merely to provide a somewhat epistemological analysis of aesthetic reflection, there is no possibility of discovering a concrete criterion. But of itself this implies neither irrationality nor arbitrariness in our approach. The necessity for this purely abstract determination of the issue, provisionally coupled as it is with a complete abstention of judgement on concrete cases, has yet to reveal its express justification and fertility for aesthetics in general.

We have already pointed out that only a dialectical theory of reflection is capable of grounding the objectivity of the aesthetic picturing of reality without establishing its hierarchical subordination with respect to the theoretical domain, that is, without transforming art into a species of imperfect knowledge or a preparatory stage of theoretical understanding. The apparent difficulty already mentioned, the need to assume an organizing middle-point in the sphere of particularity with regard to the dynamic reflection of reality while not being able to identify it, actually provides the epistemological justification for the intrinsic variety of the aesthetically configurable world, for the variety of artforms, of genres and styles, etc. The epistemological dimension of aesthetics must be content to recognize its own incapacity to find a concrete criterion for every case here. Of course, it also recognizes at the same time, given the generally accepted relativity in the sphere of particularity, in relation to both the universal and the individual moments, that this relativity can in principle find expression from any particular point. And this means that the field of particularity either below or above the selected middle-point can, from this perspective, suddenly pass over without contradiction into the universal or the individual, or better put, can traverse the path to universality or to individuality as the case may be.

It would be worse than merely superficial to regard this fact as a purely formal possibility of arbitrary combination. Although we are necessarily treating the question from an abstractly epistemological standpoint in the present context, it should be obvious that the proper content of the question concerns the position of the work of art in its relation to reality, the precise manner, the depth and breadth with which the work of art presents *sui generis* some reality or other for our actual perception. And it is precisely those who regard the work of art from the standpoint of life, rather than formalistically, who are forced to concede the following: it is exactly here, in the choice of the middle and focal point in the field of particularity, that the most important questions concerning the ideal content and the actual configuration of the work are properly decided. The fact that we cannot deduce any aesthetic principles from the absolutely universal and abstract principle of mimetic reflection itself only represents a disadvantage from a dogmatic standpoint which would attempt to prescribe strict and formally derivable rules for art in general. The historical fact that there is a multiplicity of artforms, or of different styles within a single artform, thereby – and indeed above all thereby – now receives an epistemological grounding.

Any attempt even to outline a systematic account of this acknowledged multiplicity naturally lies quite beyond the bounds of the present discussion. That is a task which belongs to the more concrete aspects of aesthetics which deal with the system of the arts in general, with the aesthetic analysis of particular styles, etc. Here it is only possible to offer some – purely illustrative – suggestions in order to clarify the theoretical structure of the argument. One should think, for example, of the difference between drama on the one side and epic narrative on the other (particularly in its modern form in the novel). It is immediately obvious that the drama treats its figures and situations in a much more universal manner than does the epic; that the individual features of the phenomena are presented much more sparingly and in much less concrete detail; in drama every individual detail receives a certain symbolic and symptomatic emphasis which it cannot and should not acquire to nearly the same extent in the field of epic. And it is equally obvious that this in no way represents a 'defect' on the part of either of these literary genres. Of course there have always been dogmatic theorists who have defended such positions. On closer examination, however, it soon becomes clear that this involved making naturalistic claims upon drama or formalistic claims upon narrative art, that it was impossible to ground or extend the aesthetic essence of drama or epic in this way, that such approaches merely encouraged the ossification or dissolution of the specific forms of drama and epic. And all of this signifies, in short, that drama generally reveals a tendency to determine the crystallizing and focal point of particularity as closer to the universal, whereas the epic seems rather to propel its focal point more in the direction of individuality. One can also identify a similar distinction between the classical short story or novella and the novel in the broader sense in so far as the former tends to concentrate its picture of reality, with a certain similarity to the drama, more in the direction of greater universality.

Of course the differentiation suggested here is still extremely abstract in character. At best it merely indicates a general tendency and direction within the open domain of particularity and is unable to provide any criterion to determine the position of the middle or focal point, and in fact, if we were to compare the drama of Shakespeare with that of Racine, or Greek tragedy with modern bourgeois drama, we would also find – within the general difference of direction as identified by the theory of genre – certain divergent tendencies: Racine locates his focal point much closer to the universal than does Shakespeare, whereas modern bourgeois drama vigorously returns it to the domain of individuality. But even with this observation we find ourselves indulging in an over-generalization that is far removed from the actual concrete reality of the work of art. For these claims really only point us towards *tendencies* which are socially and historically conditioned. The same writer in the same genre can determine the focal point quite differently within the course of several individual works. It can fall not merely within the leeway intrinsically provided by the sphere of particularity, but also within the context of the universal historical tendencies of the age or within the context of the writer's individual way of handling a particular genre; in this respect one only has to compare Goethe's *Iphigenia* with *The Natural Daughter*, not to mention the even more glaring contrasts provided by *Goetz von Berlichingen*.

We are thus presented here with a series of perspectives: the general principles of aesthetics as a whole, the concretely particular principles of genre, the historical differentiation in the development of genre, and the individual configuration of the work of art. It is only upon the last of these levels that the focal point of the work can be determined in a concrete manner. But this recognition does not imply a purely individualistic relativism. For the series we have presented here, incomplete as it is and simply indicative of the principal stages involved, really is a series. For it presents the ever more precise and concrete effective determinations which can only find their real and final realization in the individual work of art itself, something which must be recognized if aesthetics is not to degenerate into a pseudo-system of abstract prescriptions and mechanical rules. But it also represents a real series in the sense that the same dominant factors are at work within it and find their concrete fulfilment in the individual work of art.

This brings up an ancient and very puzzling question of aesthetics: the apparent difficulty involved in reconciling the fact that while every real work of art represents something incomparable, unique and individual, it can only be regarded as a genuine work of art if it also fulfils its own intrinsic principle, and this is something which involves general aesthetic principles as well. Although this is a very ancient question, it is only with Kant that it received the formulation which was to become so significant for the later development of bourgeois art theory. Kant tells us:

> For every art presupposes rules through the foundation of which a product, if it supposed to be an artistic product, can first be represented as possible. But the concept of fine art does not permit us to derive any judgement concerning the beauty of its product from any rule which has a *concept* as its determining ground, i.e., the judgement cannot be based on the kind of concept which shows how the product is possible. Fine art therefore cannot of itself think out the rules whereby it is supposed to bring forth its product. For although no product can be called art without a preceding rule, nature must provide the rule in the subject of art (and through the determination of its faculties), that is, fine art is only possible as the product of genius.[4]

It is necessary here to distinguish the justified aspect of Kant's approach from the irrationalist tendency which also arises from the fact that Kant continues to hover uncertainly between a metaphysical and a dialectical position. The irrationalist tendency finds expression in his already familiar doctrine that judgements of beauty lie beyond the world of concepts. When Kant therefore allows nature to 'provide the rule to art', something which is merely the consequence of his conception of art as the work of genius, he dissolves the metaphysically insoluble question through a spurious answer with irrationalist overtones. And modern bourgeois aesthetics has not succeeded in advancing beyond this point either – one only has to consider Croce or Simmel in this respect.

In spite of this, Kant's approach to the question does contain a genuine problem concerning the relationship of aesthetic principles and the individual work of art. Of course it is true that Kant also obstructs the path towards a rational solution by determining aesthetic principles in terms of 'rules', something which not merely expresses his own metaphysical preconceptions but also a certain entanglement of his art theory in the courtly-feudal doctrines of the seventeenth and eighteenth centuries. But the problem of how works of art succeed in fulfilling aesthetic laws still remains a real problem, because every such fulfilment, if it really is genuine, can only be accomplished if the law in question is reborn, extended and rendered more concrete in the act of fulfilment itself. Any simple 'application' of aesthetic laws to art would entail the destruction of the aesthetic essence of the works involved. We can only properly discuss this question in another context, and at a more concrete stage of our aesthetic theory. But the path we have suggested still provides the appropriate methodological access to a solution. Here too – in opposition to any irrationalism that always insists upon an unmediated methodological contrast between abstract law on the one hand and individual 'uniqueness' on the other – it is necessary to recall Marx's observation, made precisely with regard to the question of the historical development of art: 'The difficulty consists solely in the quite general manner in which these contradictions are grasped. As soon as they are specified, they are already solved.'[5] The expression about 'specifying' here is extremely important precisely by virtue of its opposition to universal generalization. It indicates that the concretization we have been discussing cannot proceed from the abstract universal (the rule) to the purely individual and hence indeterminable moment (the genius), that we must rather take the constant concretization of particularity, with as many concrete mediations as possible, as our aim. Historical materialism provides just such a method for the theoretical-aesthetic perspective in general, and it is on this basis, and in the application of this method, that these problems can and must be addressed.

Complicated as these problems may initially appear to be, there is in fact a simplifying abstraction which underlies them all, and one which must also be translated into concrete form if we are properly to understand the significance of specific particularity as the central category, as it were the 'domain-defining' category of aesthetics as such. In order to understand the decisive distinction between scientific and aesthetic reflection, it was necessary to emphasize that the moment of particularity which figured in the scientific domain as a mediating 'field' necessarily appears in the aesthetic domain as the organizing middle and focal point. This opposition serves in fact to illuminate the fundamental distinction, even when it is formulated in this initial and baldly abstract fashion. But as far as aesthetics itself is concerned this is a purely provisional abstraction which merely prepares us for a true understanding of the issue, and helps us to grasp particularity properly as the organizing focal point of the aesthetic. But considered more carefully, it is not really a question of a point in the strict sense, but rather of the focal middle within a dynamic interplay of moments. This does not entail any fundamental modification of our earlier observations, since we are continuing as before to emphasize that the actual manner in which a work is configured depends upon where this focal point is chosen with regard to the poles of universality and individuality. The concretizing modification introduced here merely consists in stressing that the choice of such a central point, which determines the specific artistic character of the work in each case, also involves a process of movement around this centre, a movement in the sphere of particularity. Now this observation expresses a universally known and recognized aesthetic fact, namely that the style, tone and mood of a work can remain entirely unified in an artistic sense even when a powerful ebb and flow prevails within this unity, when specific aspects of the work approach more closely to the pole of universality, while others approach more closely to the pole of individuality, at least under the condition that such movements are accomplished within the same sphere of particularity, that they are all ideally and formally rigorously related to one another.

In order to dispel likely misunderstanding here, it should be stressed that this approach makes no attempt to characterize in any exhaustive fashion the systems of movement which transpire within a work of art. On the contrary. We are speaking here exclusively of the movements *within* particularity, and indeed both in the direction of universality and in the direction of individuality. The crucial movement of feelings and passions in a poetic work of art, for example, their frequently tumultuous ebb and flow, no more belongs in the immediate circle of our present reflections than the closely connected dynamic tensions in the works of Michelangelo. Such phenomena can certainly manifest themselves on the same level of particularity, but of course they do not have to do so.

One does not really have to look very far to find these abstract observations confirmed in the actual practice of art. But it would be quite superficial simply to identify this specific and more or less extended dynamic leeway with the idea that the focal point's closer proximity to universality must produce a narrower dynamic leeway, while its closer proximity to individuality necessarily produces a greater one. Of course there are cases where this happens. One only has to consider the comparison between Racine and Shakespeare we mentioned above. But Dante, whose proximity to the pole of universality will surely be challenged by nobody, successfully gave shape to one of the most comprehensive examples of dynamic interaction in the history of literature, whereas a very large proportion of modern realist novels, which generally seek their focal point in the direction of individuality rather than universality, work relatively speaking with a much more reduced domain of action and reaction. (Of course there are also exceptions here, like Dickens and Balzac.) We encounter the same thing when we think of Titian or Breughel on the one hand, and the impressionists on the other. Here too any schematizing approach would prove as dangerous and inadequate as it did in our earlier analyses, where the focal point, which has now been defined concretely, was still interpreted – with a provisional abstraction – as the organizing middle term, as if it were a point. The essential and concrete intellectual approach to the essence of art now consists in grasping the artistic organization of a 'world' dynamically as a system of movements, as a system of tensions and contrasts. The way in which the reciprocal relationships of these dynamic moments and elements unfolds is here too naturally conditioned by socio-historical factors, by aspects of genre, and by personal-artistic considerations. In order to avoid falling prey to dogmatism, the theory of reflection can and should erect only the most general of structures in this connection.

It must also be noted, of course, that every such domain which permits the free play of spontaneity, every such dynamic field of the creative leeway, must be grounded in the artistic ideality of the work of art in question. However pronounced the emphasis in one direction or the other may be, whether upwards towards the universal or downwards towards the individual, this has nothing to do, where a genuine work of art is concerned, with an explicit and deliberate universalizing rhetoric on the one hand or with any naturalistic immersion in singular features on the other. It is quite true that Dickens in some of his novels, for example, describes the 'overlying' social sphere by recourse to satirical generalization, and the 'underlying' sphere with loving attention to the little details of everyday life, and equally that some of Titian's great works reveal specific features which, considered entirely on their own, would produce the typical impression of genre painting, etc. But in all such cases we are nonetheless presented with a great range of human experience, artistically configured and grounded in a certain view of the world as it is, with an image of internal differences and contradictions which are rigorously related to one another in the medium of artistic ideality, which mutually reinforce each other precisely through such contrast effects, and which thus enrich the content of the work in its unity without ever threatening to dissolve the specific particularity of the latter into the purely universal or individual.

The leeway which is involved here can be greater or smaller as the case may be. But even in works which strictly maintain a single quality or tone throughout, a certain internal tension can also be identified. That is why we described our earlier attempt to define the focal point as a provisional and introductory abstraction. For here too the different forms of reflection represent the highest universalizations of the reflected content. Even if particularity plays a different role in the categorial system of aesthetic reflection than it does in the case of science, it still retains that specific character already identified in our discussion of the scientific reflection of reality, namely that of representing a 'field' of mediations between the extremes of the universal and the individual. The significance and function of particularity has certainly changed, in accordance with the peculiar character of aesthetic reflection, but its essential place and structure has remained the same. This once again reveals, from a new perspective, the fundamental principle of the theory of reflection: namely, that the scientific and the aesthetic reproduction of reality are reproductions of a single objective reality, and that therefore – despite all the necessary modifications – the fundamental structures involved must somehow broadly correspond with one another.

This problematic also implies the firm recognition of two things. On the one hand, objective reality, independent as it is of human consciousness, objectively and immanently contains all three categories (individuality, particularity, universality), and the fact that reflection transcends immediate and individual givenness implies no abandonment of objectivity, no special 'mental structure' or 'sovereign creativity' on the part of the knowing or artistic subject. On the other hand, the categories of universalization (including therefore particularity) possess no independent existence as such within reality itself, but represent necessarily recurrent determinations immanent within all reality. Any attempt to isolate these determinations, to inflate them into individual forms with a supposedly autonomous existence of their own, involves a typically idealist falsification of the essence and structure of objective reality. Aristotle had already clearly recognized this in his polemic against the Platonic doctrine of Forms.

The question may therefore well arise: does our conception of the central significance of particularity in the system of aesthetic categories not itself run the risk of falling victim to a vulgar species of Platonic idealism? We believe that precisely the opposite is in fact the case. A brief explanation of this potential misunderstanding may also help to clarify the specific character of aesthetic reflection even further. It must be stressed, above all, that the independent shape in which particularity manifests itself in art is not some concept which claims to be thought (idea) and reality in one, as in Platonic idealism, in medieval conceptual realism, or in Hegel's notion of the 'world spirit'. On the contrary, the 'independent shape' which particularity assumes as the work of art is, in the first place, something expressly created by human beings, something which never claims to possess reality in the same sense in which objective reality exists. In the second place, it is nonetheless true that the work of art presents itself to us as a 'reality' in its own right, in the sense that our thoughts, wishes or whatever cannot change its being or specific character; we must respond to it as it is, and can only – subjectively – commend or repudiate it as the case may be. In the third place, however, the 'reality' of the work of art is present to the senses. The sublation of immediate individuality in artistic reflection also always involves, in contrast to scientific reflection, a preservation, and that in the most literal sense. Particularity no more acquires an independent shape with regard to individuality than does universality with regard to objective reality itself. Particularity is manifestly present in all the appearing forms of immediate individuality but can never be separated out from those forms. This means, in the fourth place, that the elevation of every individual detail to the level of particularity can only be accomplished by the intensification and concentration of its immediate sensible and perceptible character. It is only in this way that the manifest indwelling presence of particularity can realize itself in every individual phenomenon, as well as the totality and the system of such phenomena, in the work of art itself; and it is only in this way that the work as a whole can embody precisely the particularity of a creatively articulated 'world' and allow us to experience that world. The independent form of the work is therefore a reflection of essential connections, contexts and manifestations of reality itself. The work is capable of standing before us as an independent form because, and only because, in this respect it faithfully reflects the structure of objective reality. This perspective is diametrically opposed to that of Plato's doctrine of Ideas, and Plato himself was much more consistent therefore in repudiating the products of art than those later thinkers, like Plotinus or Schelling, who attempted to derive the truth-content and the range of types of artwork from a consideration of the ideal world itself. The truth of artistic form finds its most natural and emphatic expression precisely here in this its essentially anti-Platonic tendency.

If dialectical materialism has successfully identified the most universal structural character of the theory of reflection in the field of aesthetics, the task must then be to explicate and explain the historical process and the social specificity of art in a concrete fashion with all the means at the disposal of historical materialism. This method, constantly articulating itself in terms of concrete cases, must above all elucidate the necessity of the genres, the various forms of which express and define quite universal and, therefore, in their principal features, constantly recurring relationships between man and society, between man and nature, mediated as the latter always is through society. These relationships are subject to major transformations during the course of history, and it is the task of historical materialism to identify the social causes and the aesthetic manifestations of such changes. If the question is posed in this way, it is clear that the specific investigation of particular works of art merely represents a concrete extension of the same method, that the path of general research here (evolutionary in perspective and oriented towards genre) is by no means inimical to the analysis of particular works, something which is indeed often the case in bourgeois aesthetics. Naturally the process of aesthetic analysis is not completed once we have identified the focal point involved in the particular work of art, or better expressed, the dynamic interplay of mutually related elements within the sphere of particularity which emerges around that focal point. On the contrary, it is only here that the analysis properly begins. In the present context it is naturally impossible to present the various tasks and principles which result from such an approach. We merely note here in brief that the task of aesthetics is, in every concrete case, to investigate in a concrete fashion whether the artist's choice of focal point in particular properly corresponds to the intellectual content, the material, the theme, etc., of the work, whether from the standpoint of appropriate expression the focal point has been situated too high or too low. The whole question of form, the relation to the principles of the relevant genre, is intimately connected with this question of substantive content. Even the most cursory enumeration of the principal tasks here cannot fail to emphasize that we are not concerned with making any simple comparison of 'timeless' principles and then applying them to individual works of art (as with all dogmatic aesthetics), but rather with determining whether, for example, the particular work in question has contributed to a legitimate extension of these principles, etc. And finally it would be necessary to examine the individual work of art itself in order to see how the choice of focal point in the broader sense we have discussed above determines and influences the aesthetic vitality of the composition, of the individual forms, of the particular details, etc., how the consistency of the aesthetic execution and realization (or possibly any apparent deviation from such consistency) enhances or inhibits the aesthetic unity and living spontaneity of the work.

These considerations have rather led us away from our original question which essentially concerned the dialectical materialist interpretation of the specific features of aesthetic reflection. But it was necessary at least to outline the problems arising from this approach in order to show that the apparently indeterminate focal point of a work and the creative leeway it vouchsafes in the sphere of particularity in no way represents a lacuna in the dialectical materialist theory of reflection. On the contrary, it provides the point of departure for a concrete and quite undogmatic analysis of all the ramifications of artistic practice throughout its historical development, and one which will lead us to an entirely concrete evaluation of the success or failure of an individual work of art. The extremely complex questions of aesthetics will prove quite insoluble without this kind of interaction between the dialectical materialist and the historical materialist method. That is why we found it necessary at least to suggest a rough schema of the issues involved here. We should also note that we have only illuminated the dialectical materialist approach to aesthetic reflection in the first place from one, albeit extremely important, general perspective. We have not attempted to exhaust the possibilities implicit in this approach, which will be the task of an aesthetic system also elaborated on the basis of historical materialism. And in the second place, we have as yet only indicated the problem involved in the question of particularity as a category of aesthetic reflection. For the concrete realization of this problem in the field of dialectical materialism would take us far beyond what we have already elucidated, would have to reveal not merely the categories of aesthetic reflection but, taking this as the point of departure, would also have to clarify the general structure of works of art and the principal types of concrete aesthetic comportment involved. That is the task for continued investigation.

Translated by Nicholas Walker

Notes

1 Nikolai A. Dobroljubow, *Ausgewählte philosophische Schriften*, Moscow, 1949, pp. 617–18.
2 Friedrich Engels to Minna Kautsky on 26 November 1885; cf. Mikhail Lifschitz, *Marx und Engels über Literatur und Kunst*, Berlin, 1948, p. 102.
3 Guy de Maupassant, *Etudes sur le roman*, *Œuvres complètes*, Paris, 1935, X, pp. 281–83.
4 Immanuel Kant, *The Critique of Judgement*, § 46.
5 Karl Marx, *Grundrisse der politischen Ökonomie* (1859), p. 30.

Translator's note

The generic terms *Allgemeinheit, Besonderheit* and *Einzelheit* have generally been translated as *universality, particularity* and *individuality*, and the nominalized forms *das Allgemeine, das Besondere*, and *das Einzelne* as *the universal, the particular* and *the individual* respectively. As will readily be seen from the details of Lukács' discussion, these expressions carry a more precise sense in the German philosophical tradition than they generally do in everyday or theoretical contexts in English. English usage often simply identifies the 'singular', the 'particular' or the 'individual' in order to designate the individual subject of a proposition in contrast to a 'universal' term or class concept, whereas in German logical usage the terms are used to designate quantitative judgements (All S are P, Some S are P, This S is P). In Lukács the expression 'particularity' or 'the particular' is primarily employed to characterize something individual of universal significance but which is qualified in a quite specific or particular fashion. The singular object, pre-eminently the work of art, is thus apprehended neither as a sheerly unique individual 'this', nor as a mere example of an abstract universal 'such'.

14

EXTRACTS FROM *MINIMA MORALIA*

Reflections from Damaged Life

Theodor W. Adorno

91 Vandals

The haste, nervousness, restlessness observed since the rise of the big cities is now spreading in the manner of an epidemic, as did once the plague and cholera. In the process forces are being unleashed that were undreamed of by the scurrying passer-by of the nineteenth century. Everybody must have projects all the time. The maximum must be extracted from leisure. This is planned, used for undertakings, crammed with visits to every conceivable site or spectacle, or just with the fastest possible locomotion. The shadow of all this falls on intellectual work. It is done with a bad conscience, as if it had been poached from some urgent, even if only imaginary occupation. To justify itself in its own eyes it puts on a show of hectic activity performed under great pressure and shortage of time, which excludes all reflection, and therefore itself. It often seems as if intellectuals reserved for their actual production only those hours left over from obligations, excursions, appointments and unavoidable amusements. There is something repulsive, yet to a certain degree rational, about the prestige gained by those who can present themselves as such important people that they have to be on the spot everywhere. They stylize their lives with intentionally ham-acted discontent as a single *acte de présence*. The pleasure with which they turn down an invitation by reference to another previously accepted, signals a triumph between competitors. As here, so generally, the forms of the production process are repeated in private life, or in those areas of work exempted from these forms themselves. The whole of life must look like a job, and by this resemblance conceal what is not yet directly devoted to pecuniary gain. But the fear thus expressed only reflects a much deeper one. The unconscious innervations which, beyond thought processes, attune individual existence to historical rhythms, sense the approaching collectivization of the world. Yet since integral society does not so much take up individuals positively within itself as crush them to an amorphous and malleable mass, each individual dreads the process of absorption, which is felt as inevitable. Doing things and going places is an attempt by the sensorium to set up a kind of counter-irritant against a threatening collectivization, to get in training for it by using the hours apparently left to freedom to coach oneself as a member of the mass. The technique is to try to outdo the danger. One lives in a sense even worse, that is, with even less self, than one expects to have to live. At the same time one learns through this playful excess of self-loss that to live in earnest without a self could be easier, not more difficult. All this is done in great haste, for no warning bells will announce the earthquake. If one does not take part, and that means, if one does not swim bodily in the human stream, one fears, as when delaying too long to join a totalitarian party, missing the bus and bringing on oneself the vengeance of the collective. Pseudo-activity is an insurance, the expression of a readiness for self-surrender, in which one senses the only guarantee of self-preservation. Security is glimpsed in adaptation to the utmost insecurity. It is seen as a licence for flight that will take one somewhere else with the utmost speed. In the fanatical love of cars the feeling of physical homelessness plays a part. It is at the bottom of what the bourgeois were wont to call, mistakenly, the flight from oneself, from the inner void. Anyone who wants to move with the times is not allowed to be different. Psychological emptiness is itself only the result of the wrong kind of social absorption. The boredom that people are running away from merely mirrors the process of running away, that started long before. For this reason alone the monstrous machinery of amusement keeps alive and constantly grows bigger without a single person being amused by it. It channels the urge to be in on the act, which otherwise, indiscriminately, anarchically, as promiscuity or wild aggression, would throw itself on the collective, itself consisting of none other than those on the move. Most closely related to them are addicts. Their impulse reacts exactly to the dislocation of mankind that has led from the murky blurring of the difference between town and country, the abolition of the house, via the processions of millions of unemployed, to the deportations and uprooting of peoples on the devastated European continent. The nullity and lack of content of all collective rituals since the Youth Movement emerges retrospectively as a groping anticipation of stunning historical blows. The countless people who suddenly succumb to their own quantity and mobility, to the swarming getaway as to a drug, are recruits to the migration of nations, in whose desolated territories bourgeois history is preparing to meet its end.

92 Picture-book without pictures[1]

The objective tendency of the Enlightenment, to wipe out the power of images over man, is not matched by any subjective progress on the part of enlightened thinking towards freedom from images. While the assault on images irresistibly demolishes, after metaphysical Ideas, those concepts once understood as rational and genuinely attained by thought, the thinking unleashed by the Enlightenment and immunized against thinking is now becoming a second figurativeness, thought without images or spontaneity. Amid the network of now wholly abstract relations of people to each other and to things, the power of abstraction is vanishing. The estrangement of schemata and classifications from the data subsumed beneath them, indeed the sheer quantity of the material processed, which has become quite incommensurable with the horizons of individual experience, ceaselessly enforces an archaic retranslation into sensuous signs. The little silhouettes of men or houses that pervade statistics like hieroglyphics may appear in each particular case accidental, mere auxiliary means. But it is not by chance that they have such a resemblance to countless advertisements, newspaper stereotypes, toys. In them representation triumphs over what is represented. Their outsize, simplistic and therefore false comprehensibility corroborates the incomprehensibility of the intellectual processes themselves, from which their falseness – their blind, unthinking subsumption – is inseparable. The omnipresent images are none, because they present the wholly general, the average, the standard model, as something unique or special, and so deride it. The abolition of the particular is turned insidiously into something particular. The desire for particularity has silted up while still at the stage of a need, and is reproduced on all sides by mass-culture, on the pattern of the comic strip. What was once called intellect is superseded by illustrations. It is not only that people are no longer able to imagine what is not shown and drilled into them in abbreviated form. Even the joke, in which once the freedom of the mind collided with the facts and exploded them, has gone over to illustration. The pictorial jokes filling magazines are for the most part pointless, devoid of meaning. They consist of nothing beyond a challenge to the eye to compete with the situation. One is supposed, schooled by countless precedents, to see what is 'going on' more quickly than the moments of significance in the situation can unfold. What is acted out by such pictures and then re-enacted by the well-versed onlooker, in the instantaneous sizing-up of the situation, the unresisting submission to the empty predominance of things, is the jettisoning of all meaning like ballast. The joke of our time is the suicide of intention. He who 'cracks' it is rewarded by admission to the collective of laughers, who have cruel things on their side. If one strove to understand such jokes by thinking, one would fall helplessly behind the runaway tempo of things, which tear along even in the simplest caricature as in the mad race at the end of a film cartoon. Cleverness turns straight into stupidity in face of regressive progress. The only comprehension left to thought is horror at the incomprehensible. Just as the reflective onlooker, meeting the laughing placard of a toothpaste beauty, discerns in her flashlight grin the grimace of torture, so from every joke, even from every pictorial representation, he is assailed by the death sentence on the subject, which is implicit in the universal triumph of subjective reason.

93 Intention and reproduction

The pseudo-realism of the culture industry, its style, is in no need of fraudulent fabrication by film-magnates and their lackeys, but is dictated, under the prevailing conditions of production, by the stylistic principles of naturalism itself. If the film were to give itself up to the blind representation of everyday life, following the precepts of, say, Zola, as would indeed be practicable with moving photography and sound-recording, the result would be a construction alien to the visual habits of the audience, diffuse, unarticulated outwards. Radical naturalism, to which the technique of film lends itself, would dissolve all surface coherence of meaning and finish up as the antithesis of familiar realism. The film would turn into an associative stream of images, deriving its form from their pure, immanent construction. Yet if, for commercial reasons, or even with some disinterested intention, it strives to choose words and gestures in a way that relates them to an idea conferring meaning, this perhaps inevitable attempt finds itself in equally inevitable contradiction with the presupposition of naturalism. The less dense reproduction of reality in naturalist literature left room for intentions: in the unbroken duplication achieved by the technical apparatus of film every intention, even that of truth, becomes a lie. The word that is intended to impress on the audience the character of the speaker or even the meaning of the whole, sounds, compared to the literal fidelity of its reproduction, 'unnatural'. It justifies the world as having been itself similarly meaningful, before the first deliberate fraud, the first real distortion was committed. No-one talks, no-one moves like this, whereas the film unceasingly urges that everyone does. One is trapped: conformism is produced a priori by meaning in itself, no matter what the concrete meaning may be, while it is only by meaning something that conformism, the respectful reiteration of the factual, could be shaken. True intentions would only be possible by renouncing intention. That this and realism are incompatible, that synthesis becomes a lie, stems from the concept of significance. It is ambiguous. It refers without distinction to the organization of the subject matter as such and to its communication to the audience. This ambiguity is, however, no accident. Significance designates the point of equilibrium between reason and communication. It is both right, in that the objective figure, the realized expression, turns outward from itself and speaks, and wrong, in that the figure is corrupted by counting in the interlocutor. Every artistic and even theoretical work must show itself able to meet the danger of such ambiguity. Significant form, however esoteric, makes concessions to consumption; lack of significance is dilettantism by its immanent criteria. Quality is decided by the depth at which the work incorporates the alternatives within itself, and so masters them.

94 All the world's not a stage

The coming extinction of art is prefigured in the increasing impossibility of representing historical events. That there is no adequate drama about Fascism is not due to lack of talent; talent is withering through the insolubility of the writer's most urgent task. He has to choose between two principles, both equally inappropriate to the subject: psychology and infantilism. The former, now aesthetically obsolete, has been used by significant artists only as a trick and with a bad conscience, since modern drama came to see its object in politics. In his preface to *Fiesco* Schiller argues:

> If it is true that only emotion arouses emotion, the political hero must, it seems to me, be an unsuitable subject for the stage to the same extent that he is obliged to neglect the man in order to be the political hero. It was not my intention to give my plot the living glow which is the pure product of enthusiasm, but to spin the cold, sterile drama of state from the human heart, and so to connect it again to the human heart – to involve the man through his statesman's intelligence – and to draw human situations from an ingenious intrigue – that was my intention. Also, my relation to the ordinary world made me more familiar with the heart than with the council-chamber, and perhaps this very political weakness has become a poetic strength.

Perhaps not. The connection of alienated history to the human heart was already in Schiller's case a pretext for justifying the inhumanity of history as humanly comprehensible, and was given the lie whenever his technique equated the 'man' and the 'statesman's intelligence', as in the burlesque and fortuitous murder of Leonore by the betrayer of his own conspiracy. The tendency towards aesthetic re-privatization pulls the ground from under art in its attempt to conserve humanism. The cabals of Schiller's too-well constructed plays are impotent auxiliary constructions straddling the passions of the characters and a social and political reality already incommensurable with them, no longer comprehensible in terms of human motivations. Recently this has taken the form of a trashy biographical literature eager to bring the famous humanly closer to the humble reader. The same urge towards false humanization underlies the calculated re-introduction of plot, of action as a coherent meaning harmoniously performed. On the presuppositions of photographic realism this would not be tenable in film. In arbitrarily reinstating it, the cinema has disregarded the experience of the great novels on which it parasitically lives; they derived their meaning precisely from the dissolution of coherent meaning.

To clear all this aside, however, and to seek to portray the political scene as abstract and extra-human, excluding the deceptive mediations of the psychological, is to do no better. For it is just the essential abstractness of what really happens which rebuts the aesthetic image. To make this abstractness expressible at all, the writer is forced to translate it into a kind of children's language, into archetypes, and so a second time to 'bring it home', no longer to the emotions but to those check-points in comprehension which precede even the constitution of language, and cannot be sidestepped even by epic theatre. The appeal to these authorities is in itself a formal sanction of the subject's dissolution in collective society. The object, however, is scarcely less falsified by such translation than would be a religious war by its deduction from the erotic needs of a queen. For as infantile as today's simplistic drama are the very people whose portrayal it abjures. Yet the political economy that it takes upon itself to portray instead, if it remains in principle unchanged, in each of its moments is so differentiated and advanced, as to exclude schematic parables. To present processes within large-scale industry as transactions between crooked vegetable dealers suffices for a momentary shock-effect, but not for dialectical theatre. The illustration of late capitalism by images from the agrarian or criminal registers does not permit the monstrosity of modern society to emerge in full clarity from the complex phenomena masking it. Rather, the unconcern for the phenomena, which ought themselves to be derived visibly from their essence, distorts the essence. It harmlessly interprets the seizure of power on the highest level as the machination of rackets outside society, not as the coming-to-itself of society as such.[2] The impossibility of portraying Fascism springs from the fact that in it, as in its contemplation, subjective freedom no longer exists. Total unfreedom can be recognized, but not represented. Where freedom occurs as a motif in political narratives today, as in the praise of heroic resistance, it has the embarrassing quality of impotent reassurance. The outcome always appears decided in advance by high politics, and freedom is manifested only ideologically, as talk about freedom, in stereotyped declamations, not in humanly commensurable actions. Art is least to be saved by stuffing the extinct subject like a museum piece, and the object, the purely inhuman, which alone is worthy of art today, escapes its reach at once by excess and inhumanity.

95 Damper and drum

Taste is the most accurate seismograph of historical experience. Unlike almost all other faculties, it is even able to register its own behaviour. Reacting against itself, it recognizes its own lack of taste. Artists who repel or shock, spokesmen of unbridled cruelty, are governed, in their idiosyncrasy, by taste; the cultivation of a fine sensibility, the domain of nervous neo-romantics, is as patently coarse and unfeeling, even to its protagonists, as is Rilke's line: 'For poverty's a great glow from within . . . ' The delicate shudder, the pathos of being different, are now no more than stock masks in the cult of oppression. It is precisely the nerves most highly-developed aesthetically that now find self-righteous aestheticism intolerable. The individual is so thoroughly historical that he is able, with the fine filigree of his late bourgeois organization, to rebel against the fine filigree of late bourgeois organization. In repugnance for all artistic subjectivism, for expression and exaltation, the flesh creeps at the lack of historical tact, just as subjectivity itself earlier flinched from bourgeois conventions. Even the rejection of mimesis, the deepest concern of the new matter-of-factness in art, is mimetic. Judgement on subjective expression is not passed from outside, in political and social reflection, but within immediate impulses, every one of which, shamed in face of the culture industry, averts its eyes from its mirror image. Heading the list is the proscription of erotic pathos, evinced no less by the shift of lyrical accents than by the collective ban on sexuality in Kafka's works. In art since Expressionism the prostitute has become a key figure, though in reality she is dying out, since it is only by portrayal of figures devoid of shame that sex can now be handled without aesthetic embarrassment. Such displacements in the deepest levels of our reaction have brought about the decay of art in its individualistic form, without a collective form being possible. It is beyond the faith and independence of the individual artist to hold unwaveringly to the expressive sphere and to oppose the brutal compulsion of collectivization; rather he must feel this compulsion, even against his will, in the most secret cells of his isolation, if he is not, through anachronistic humanity, to fall untruthfully and helplessly behind the inhuman. Even intransigent literary Expressionism, Stramm's poetry, Kokoschka's dramas,[3] show as the reverse-side of their genuine radicalism a naive aspect of liberal trustfulness. Progress beyond them, however, is no less questionable. Works of art which attempt consciously to eliminate innocuous absolute subjectivity, raise in so doing the demand for a positive community, not present in themselves, but which they arbitrarily quote. This merely makes them mouthpieces of doom and victims of an ultimate naivety which cancels them out: that of still being art at all. The aporia of responsible work benefits the irresponsible. Should it once prove possible to do away with nerves entirely, then no herbicide will avail against the renascent springtime of song, and the national front extending all the way from barbaric Futurism to the ideology of the cinema, will go entirely unopposed.

96 Palace of Janus

If one gave way to a need to place the system of the culture industry in a wide, world-historical perspective, it would have to be defined as the systematic exploitation of the ancient fissure between men and their culture. The dual nature of progress, which always developed the potential of freedom simultaneously with the reality of oppression, gave rise to a situation where peoples were more and more inducted into the control of nature and social organization, but grew at the same time, owing to the compulsion under which culture placed them, incapable of understanding in what way culture went beyond such integration. What has become alien to men is the human component of culture, its closest part, which upholds them against the world. They make common cause with the world against themselves, and the most alienated condition of all, the omnipresence of commodities, their own conversion into appendages of machinery, is for them a mirage of closeness. The great works of art and philosophical constructions have remained uncomprehended not through their too great distance from the heart of human experience, but the opposite; and this incomprehension could itself be accounted for easily enough by too great comprehension: shame at involvement in universal injustice that would become overwhelming as soon as one allowed oneself to understand. Instead, people cling to what mocks them in confirming the mutilation of their essence by the smoothness of its own appearance. On such inevitable delusions lackeys of the existing order have in all phases of urban civilization parasitically dwelt: later Attic comedy, Hellenistic arts and crafts, are already kitsch, even though they have not yet at their disposal the technique of mechanical reproduction and that industrial apparatus whose archetype the ruins of Pompeii readily conjure up. Reading popular novels a hundred years old like those of Cooper, one finds in rudimentary form the whole pattern of Hollywood. The stagnation of the culture industry is probably not the result of monopolization, but was a property of so-called entertainment from the first. Kitsch is composed of that structure of invariables which the philosophical lie ascribes to its solemn designs. On principle, nothing in them must change, since the whole mischief is intended to hammer into men that nothing must change. But as long as civilization followed its course randomly and anonymously, the objective spirit was not aware of this barbaric element as a necessary part of itself. Under the illusion of directly helping freedom, when it was mediating domination, it at least disdained to assist in directly reproducing the latter. It proscribed kitsch, that followed it like a shadow, with a fervour certainly itself expressive of the bad conscience of high culture, half aware that under domination it ceases to be culture, and reminded by kitsch of its own degradation. Today, when the consciousness of rulers is beginning to coincide with the overall tendency of society, the tension between culture and kitsch is breaking down. Culture no longer impotently drags its despised opponent behind it, but is taking it under its direction. In administering the whole of mankind, it administers also the breach between man and culture. Even the coarseness, insensitivity and narrowness objectively imposed on the oppressed, are manipulated with subjective mastery in humour. Nothing more exactly characterizes the condition of being at once integral and antagonistic than this incorporation of barbarity. Here, however, the will of the controllers can invoke that of the world. Their mass society did not first produce the trash for the customers, but the customers themselves. It is they who hungered for films, radio and magazines; whatever remained unsatisfied in them through the order which takes from them without giving in exchange what it promises, only burned with impatience for their gaoler to remember them, and at last offer them stones in his left hand for the hunger from which he withholds bread in his right. Unresistingly, for a quarter of a century, elderly citizens, who should have known of something different, have been falling into the arms of the culture industry which so accurately calculates their famished hearts. They have no cause to take umbrage at a youth corrupted to the marrow by Fascism. This subjectless, culturally disinherited generation are the true heirs of culture.

97 Monad

The individual owes his crystallization to the forms of political economy, particularly to those of the urban market. Even as the opponent of the pressure of socialization he remains the latter's most particular product and its likeness. What enables him to resist, that streak of independence in him, springs from monadological individual interest and its precipitate, character. The individual mirrors in his individuation the preordained social laws of exploitation, however mediated. This means too, however, that his decay in the present phase must itself not be deduced individualistically, but from the social tendency which asserts itself by means of individuation and not merely as its enemy. On this point reactionary cultural criticism diverges from the other kind. Reactionary criticism often enough attains insight into the decay of individuality and the crisis of society, but places the ontological responsibility for this on the individual as such, as something discrete and internal: for this reason the accusation of shallowness, lack of faith and substance, is the last word it has to say, and return to the past its solace. Individualists like Huxley and Jaspers damn the individual for his mechanical emptiness and neurotic weakness, but the trend of their condemnation is rather to sacrifice the individual himself than to criticize the social *principium individuationis*. As half-truths their polemics are already the whole untruth. Society is seen by them as an unmediated community of men, from whose attitudes the whole follows, instead of as a system not only encompassing and deforming them, but even reaching down into that humanity which once conditioned them as individuals. By this exclusively human interpretation of the situation as it is, the crude material reality that binds human beings to inhumanity is accepted even while being accused. In its better days, when it reflected historically, the bourgeoisie was well aware of such interconnections, and it is only since its doctrine has degenerated to obtuse apologetics against socialism that it has forgotten them. It is not the least merit of Jakob Burckhardt's history of Greek civilization to have connected the drying-up of Hellenistic individuality not only with the objective decline of the *polis*, but precisely with the cult of the individual:

> But following the deaths of Demosthenes and Phocion, the city is surprisingly depleted of political personalities, and not only of them: Epicurus, born as early as 342 of an Attic cleruch family on Samos, is the last Athenian of any kind to have world-historical importance.

The situation in which the individual was vanishing was at the same time one of unbridled individualism, where 'all was possible': 'Above all, individuals are now worshipped instead of gods.'[4] That the setting-free of the individual by the undermining of the *polis* did not strengthen his resistance, but eliminated him and individuality itself, in the consummation of dictatorial states, provides a model of one of the central contradictions which drove society from the nineteenth century to Fascism. Beethoven's music, which works within the forms transmitted by society and is ascetic towards the expression of private feelings, resounds with the guided echo of social conflict, drawing precisely from this asceticism the whole fullness and power of individuality. That of Richard Strauss, wholly at the service of individual claims and dedicated to the glorification of the self-sufficient individual, thereby reduces the latter to a mere receptive organ of the market, an imitator of arbitrarily chosen ideas and styles. Within repressive society the individual's emancipation not only benefits but damages him. Freedom from society robs him of the strength for freedom. For however real he may be in his relations to others, he is, considered absolutely, a mere abstraction. He has no content that is not socially constituted, no impulse transcending society that is not directed at assisting the social situation to transcend itself. Even the Christian doctrine of death and immortality, in which the notion of absolute individuality is rooted, would be wholly void if it did not embrace humanity. The single man who hoped for immortality absolutely and for himself alone, would in such limitation only inflate to preposterous dimensions the principle of self-preservation which the injunction that 'He that loses his life, shall save it' holds in check. Socially, the absolute status granted to the individual marks the transition from the universal mediation of social relation – a mediation which, as exchange, always also requires curtailment of the particular interests realized through it – to direct domination, where power is seized by the strongest. Through this dissolution of all the mediating elements within the individual himself, by virtue of which he was, in spite of everything, also a part of a social subject, he regresses, impoverished and coarsened, to the state of a mere social object. As something abstractly realized, in Hegel's sense, the individual cancels himself out: the countless people who know nothing but their naked, prowling interest are those who capitulate the moment organization and terror overtake them. If today the trace of humanity seems to persist only in the individual in his decline, it admonishes us to make an end of the fatality which individualizes men, only to break them completely in their isolation. The saving principle is now preserved in its antithesis alone.

98 Bequest

Dialectical thought is an attempt to break through the coercion of logic by its own means. But since it must use these means, it is at every moment in danger of itself acquiring a coercive character: the ruse of reason would like to hold sway over the dialectic too. The existing cannot be overstepped except by means of a universal derived from the existing order itself. The universal triumphs over the existing through the latter's own concept, and therefore, in its triumph, the power of mere existence constantly threatens to reassert itself by the same violence that broke it. Through the absolute rule of negation, the movement of thought as of history becomes, in accordance with the pattern of immanent antithesis, unambiguously, exclusively, implacably positive. Everything is subsumed under the principal economic phases and their development, which each in turn historically shape the whole of society; thought in its entirety has something of what Parisian artists call le *genre chef d'œuvre*. That calamity is brought about precisely by the stringency of such development; that this stringency is itself linked to domination, is, at the least, not made explicit in critical theory, which, like traditional theory, awaits salvation from stage-by-stage progression. Stringency and totality, the bourgeois intellectual ideals of necessity and generality, do indeed circumscribe the formula of history, but for just this reason the constitution of society finds its precipitate in those great, immovable, lordly concepts against which dialectical criticism and practice are directed. If Benjamin said that history had hitherto been written from the standpoint of the victor, and needed to be written from that of the vanquished,[5] we might add that knowledge must indeed present the fatally rectilinear succession of victory and defeat, but should also address itself to those things which were not embraced by this dynamic, which fell by the wayside – what might be called the waste products and blind spots that have escaped the dialectic. It is in the nature of the defeated to appear, in their impotence, irrelevant, eccentric, derisory. What transcends the ruling society is not only the potentiality it develops but also all that which did not fit properly into the laws of historical movement. Theory must needs deal with cross-grained, opaque, unassimilated material, which as such admittedly has from the start an anachronistic quality, but is not wholly obsolete since it has outwitted the historical dynamic. This can most readily be seen in art. Children's books like *Alice in Wonderland* or *Struwwelpeter*, of which it would be absurd to ask whether they are progressive or reactionary, contain incomparably more eloquent ciphers even of history than the high drama of Hebbel, concerned though it is with the official themes of tragic guilt, turning points of history, the course of the world and the individual, and in Satie's pert and puerile piano pieces there are flashes of experience undreamed of by the school of Schönberg, with all its rigour and all the pathos of musical development behind it. The very grandeur of logical deductions may inadvertently take on a provincial quality. Benjamin's writings are an attempt in ever new ways to make philosophically fruitful what has not yet been foreclosed by great intentions. The task he bequeathed was not to abandon such an attempt to the estranging enigmas of thought alone, but to bring the intentionless within the realm of concepts: the obligation to think at the same time dialectically and undialectically.

* * *

135 Sacrificial lamb

Dictating is not only more comfortable, more conducive to concentration, it has an additional substantive benefit. Dictation makes it possible for the writer, in the earliest phases of production, to manœuvre himself into the position of critic. What he sets down is tentative, provisional, mere material for revision, yet appears to him, once transcribed, as something estranged and in some measure objective. He need have no fear of committing something inadequate to paper, for he is not the one who has to write it: he outwits responsibility in its interests. The risk of formulation takes the innocuous form first of the casually delivered memorandum and then of work on something already existing, so that he no longer properly perceives his own audacity. In face of the difficulty, now grown to desperate proportions, of every theoretical utterance, such tricks become a blessing. They are technical aids to the dialectical procedure which makes statements in order to withdraw them and yet to hold them fast. But thanks are due to the person taking down the dictation, if at the right moment he pulls up the writer by contradiction, irony, nervosity, impatience and disrespect. He incurs wrath, so diverting it from the store of bad conscience with which otherwise the writer would mistrust his own work and therefore dig in his heels all the more defiantly over his supposedly sacred text. The emotion that turns ungratefully on his troublesome helper, benignly purifies his relation to his subject.

136 Exhibitionist

Artists do not sublimate. That they neither satisfy nor repress their desires, but transform them into socially desirable achievements, their works, is a psycho-analytical illusion; incidentally, legitimate works of art are today without exception socially undesired. Rather, artists display violent instincts, free-floating and yet colliding with reality, marked by neurosis. Even the philistine's dream of the actor or violinist as the synthesis of a bundle of nerves and a tugger of heart-strings, has more truth than the no less philistine economic theory of instincts according to which the favourite children of renunciation get rid of the stuff in symphonies and novels. Their lot is rather a hysterically excessive lack of inhibition over every conceivable fear; narcissism taken to its paranoiac limit. To anything sublimated they oppose idiosyncrasies. They are implacable towards aesthetes, indifferent to a carefully-tended environment, and in tastefully-conducted lives they recognize diminished reactions against pressures to diminution as surely as do the psychologists, by whom they are themselves misunderstood. From Mozart's letters to his little Augsburg cousin to the jibes of the embittered private tutor, they have been attracted by the coarse, the inane, the indecent. They do not fit into Freudian theory because it lacks an adequate concept of expression, despite all its insight into the workings of symbolism in dream and neuroses. That an instinctual impulse expressed uncensored cannot be called repressed even though it no longer wishes to reach the goal it cannot find, is no doubt obvious. On the other hand, the analytic distinction between motor – 'real' – and hallucinatory satisfaction is an extension of that between satisfaction and undisguised expression. But expression is not hallucination. It is appearance, measured by the reality principle that it wishes to circumvent. Never, however, does subjective material attempt through appearance, as it does through the symptom, to substitute itself delusively for reality. Expression negates reality by holding up to it what is unlike it, but it never denies reality; it looks straight in the eye the conflict that results blindly in the symptom. What expression has in common with repression is that its movement is blocked by reality. That movement, and the whole complex of experience of which it is a part, is denied direct communication with its object. As expression it achieves unfalsified manifestation of itself and so of the resistance to it, in sensuous imitation. It is so strong that it suffers modification to a mere image, the price of survival, without mutilation on its outward path. In place of the goal, and of subjective, censorial 'elaboration', it sets an objective, polemical self-revelation. This distinguishes it from sublimation: each successful expression of the subject, one might say, is a small victory over the play of forces in its own psychology. The pathos of art is bound up with the fact that precisely by withdrawing into imagination it renders the superior power of reality its due, and yet does not resign itself to adaptation, does not prolong external violence in internal deformation. Those who accomplish this, have without exception to pay dearly for it as individuals, left helplessly behind by their expression, which has outstripped their psychology. Thereby, however, they no less than their products instil doubts as to the ranking of art-works as cultural achievements by definition. No work of art, within the organization of society, can escape its involvement in culture, but there is none, if it is more than mere handicraft, which does not make culture a dismissive gesture: that of having become a work of art. Art is as inimical to 'art' as are artists. In renouncing the goal of instinct they remain faithful to it, and unmask the socially desirable activity naively glorified by Freud as sublimation – which probably does not exist.

137 Small sorrows, great songs[6]

Contemporary mass-culture is historically necessary not merely as a result of the encompassment of life in its totality by monster enterprises, but as a consequence of what seems most utterly opposed to the standardization of consciousness predominant today, aesthetic subjectivism. True, the more artists have journeyed into the interior, the more they have learned to forgo the infantile fun of imitating external reality. But at the same time, by dint of reflecting on the psyche, they have found out more and more how to control themselves. The progress in technique that brought them ever greater freedom and independence of anything heterogeneous, has resulted in a kind of reification, technification of the inward as such. The more masterfully the artist expresses himself, the less he has to 'be' what he expresses, and the more what he expresses, indeed the content of subjectivity itself, becomes a mere function of the production process. Nietzsche had an inkling of this when he taxed Wagner, that tamer of expression, with hypocrisy, without perceiving that this was not a matter of psychology but of a historical tendency. The transformation of expressive content from an undirected impulse into material for manipulation makes it palpable, exhibitable, saleable. The lyrical subjectivism of Heine, for example, does not stand in simple contradiction to his commercial traits; the saleable is itself subjectivity administrated by subjectivity. The virtuoso use of the 'scale' characteristic of nineteenth-century performers is transformed by an internal impulsion, without any need for betrayal, into journalism, spectacle, calculation. The law of motion of art, which amounts to the control and therefore the objectification of the subject by itself, means its downfall: the hostility to art of film, which passes in administrative review all materials and emotions in order to sell them most effectively to the public, the second stage of externality, has its source in art, in the growing domination over inner nature. The much-lauded play-acting of modern artists, their exhibitionism, is the gesture whereby they put themselves as goods on the market.

138 Who is who

The artist's or scholar's flattering conviction of his own naivety and purity is prolonged in his propensity to explain difficulties by the devious interests, the practical, calculating mentality of those who contract his services. But just as every construction that acquits oneself and convicts the world, all insistence on one's own qualifications, tends precisely to acquit the world in oneself, so the same holds good for the antithesis of pure intentions and cunning. Premeditating, guided by a thousand political and tactical considerations, cautious and suspicious – just such is the attitude adopted today by the intellectual outsider who knows what to expect. The insiders, however, whose realm has long since coalesced across party frontiers into 'living-space', no longer need the calculation ascribed to them. They are so dependably committed to the rules of reason's game, their interests have so unquestionably sedimented in their thinking, that they have again become ingenuous. In seeking out their dark designs, one's judgement is indeed metaphysically true, in that they are akin to the sombre course of the world, but psychologically false: one succumbs to the objective increase of persecution-mania. They who, through their function, commit base and treacherous acts, who sell themselves and their friends to power, need no cunning or *arrière-pensée*, no plans elaborated by the ego, rather they need only give way to their own reactions, unthinkingly satisfy the demands of the moment, to perform effortlessly what others could achieve only by unfathomable scheming. They inspire trust just by proclaiming it. They see their own advantage, live from hand to mouth and commend themselves as both unegoistic and subscribers to a state of things which can be relied on to let them go short of nothing. Because all pursue without conflict solely their own particular interests, these appear in turn as universal and, in this way, disinterested. Their gestures are candid, spontaneous, disarming. They are nice and their opponents unpleasant. Since they no longer have the independence to perform an act in opposition to their interests, they rely on the goodwill of others, and themselves radiate it. Abstract interest, being wholly mediated, creates a second immediacy, while the man not yet wholly encompassed compromises himself as unnatural. If he is not to come to grief he must ceremoniously outdo the world in worldliness and is easily convicted of his maladroit excess. Suspicion, power-greed, lack of comradeship, deceit, vanity and inconsistency are a compelling reproach to him. Social witchcraft inescapably turns him who does not play the game into a self-seeker, and he who, lacking a self, lives by the principle of reality, is called selfless.

139 Addressee unknown

Cultivated philistines are in the habit of requiring that a work of art 'give' them something. They no longer take umbrage at works that are radical, but fall back on the shamelessly modest assertion that they do not understand. This eliminates even opposition, their last negative relationship to truth, and the offending object is smilingly catalogued among its kind, consumer commodities that can be chosen or refused without even having to take responsibility for doing so. One is just too stupid, too old-fashioned, one simply can't keep up, and the more one belittles oneself the more one can be sure of swelling the mighty unison of the *vox inhumana populi*, the judging power of the petrified *Zeitgeist*. Incomprehensibility, that benefits no-one, from being an inflammatory crime becomes pitiable folly. Together with the barb one deflects the temptation. That one must be given something, apparently the postulate of substantiality and fullness, cuts both off and impoverishes giving. In this, however, human relationships are like aesthetic. The reproach that someone gives one nothing is pitiful. If the relation has grown sterile, it should be broken off. But he who holds it fast and yet complains, is always devoid of the organ of receiving: fantasy. Both must give something, happiness, as precisely what is not exchangeable, not open to complaint, but such giving is inseparable from taking. All is over if what one finds for the other no longer reaches him. There is no love that is not an echo. In myths the warrant of grace was the acceptance of sacrifice; it is this acceptance that love, the re-enactment of sacrifice, beseeches if it is not to feel under a curse. The decay of giving is today matched by a hardness towards receiving. But this comes to the same thing as the denial of real happiness, that alone permits men to cling to their kind of happiness. The rampart would only be breached if they were to accept from others what, with a wry face, they refuse themselves. But this they find difficult because of the effort demanded by taking. Besotted with technique, they transfer their hatred for the superfluous exertion of their existence, to the expense of energy that pleasure, as a moment of their being, needs even in all its sublimations. Though facilitated in countless ways, their practice remains absurd toil; yet to squander strength on their lives' secret, happiness, is something they cannot endure. Here the watchword is 'relax and take it easy', a formula borrowed from the language of the nursing-home, not of exuberance. Happiness is obsolete: uneconomic. For its idea, sexual union, is the opposite of slackness, a blessed straining, just as that of all subjected labour is cursed.

140 Consecutio temporum[7]

When my first composition teacher, trying to knock the atonal nonsense out of me, found his tales of erotic scandals about the new composers proving ineffective, he switched his attack to what he suspected as my weak spot, by showing himself up-to-date. The ultra-modern, his argument ran, was no longer modern, the stimulations I sought were already numb, the expressive figures that excited me belonged to an outdated sentimentality, and the new youth had, as he liked to put it, more red blood-corpuscles. His own pieces, in which oriental themes were regularly extended by the chromatic scale, betrayed the same ultra-subtle deliberations as the manœuvres of a conservatory director with a bad conscience. But I was soon to discover that the fashion he opposed to my modernity did actually resemble, in the primeval habitat of the great *salons*, what he had hatched up in the provinces. Neo-classicism, that form of reaction which not only fails to acknowledge itself as such but even passes off its reactionary moment as ahead of its time, was the advance-guard of a massive tendency which under Fascism and mass-culture quickly learned to be rid of tender concern for the endlessly tiresome sensibilities of artists, and to combine the spirit of Courths-Mahler[8] with that of technical progress. The modern has really become unmodern. Modernity is a qualitative, not a chronological, category. Just as it cannot be reduced to abstract form, with equal necessity it must turn its back on conventional surface coherence, the appearance of harmony, the order corroborated merely by replication. The stalwarts of the Fascist fighting leagues, thundering fulsomely against Futurism, saw more clearly in their rage than did the Moscow censors who placed Cubism on the Index because, in its private impropriety, it failed to measure up to the spirit of the collective age, or the brazen theatre critics who find a play by Strindberg or Wedekind *passé* but a piece of underground reportage up-to-date. All the same, their blasé philistinism utters an appalling truth: that the procession of total society which would like to force its organization on all expression, is in fact leaving behind the power which opposes what Lindbergh's wife called the wave of the future, that is, the critical construction of being. This is not merely outlawed by a corrupt public opinion, but the prevailing absurdity affects its very substance. The might of what is, constraining the mind to follow its example, is so overwhelming that even the unassimilated expression of protest assumes in face of it a home-spun, aimless, inexperienced quality reminiscent of the provincialism that once so prophetically suspected modernity of backwardness. Matching the psychological regression of individuals who exist without a self, is a regression of the objective spirit, in which obtuseness, primitivism and the bargain-sale set up what historically has long since decayed as the newest historical power, and consign to the day before yesterday everything that does not zealously join the march of regression. This *quid pro quo* of progress and reaction makes orientation in contemporary art almost as difficult as in politics, and furthermore paralyses production itself, where anyone who clings to extreme intentions is made to feel like a backwoodsman, while the conformist no longer lingers bashfully in arbours, literary or horticultural,[9] but hurtles forward, rocket-powered, into the pluperfect.

141 La nuance/encor'[10]

The demand that thinking and information dispense with nuances cannot be summarily dismissed as bowing to the prevalent obtuseness. Were linguistic nuance no longer perceptible, it would be itself implicated, not merely reception. Language is by its own objective substance social expression, even where it has abruptly severed itself from society as individual. Changes that it undergoes in communication involve the writer's uncommunicative material. Words and phrases spoilt by use do not reach the secluded workshop intact. And the historical damage cannot be repaired there. History does not merely touch on language, but takes place in it. What continues to be used in spite of usage smacks of simple-minded provincialism or cosy restoration. So thoroughly have all nuances been perverted and sold off as 'flavour' that even advanced literary subtleties recall debased words like 'gloaming', 'pensive', 'verdant', 'fragrant'. The measures against banality are becoming banal, arty-crafty, with an undertone of moping consolation from that womanly world whose soulfulness complete with lutes and traditional costume, was politically co-ordinated in Germany. In the cultivated superior trash with which the intellectuals who survive there happily compete for the vacant posts of culture, what yesterday had a linguistically conscious air hostile to convention, reads today as olde-worlde prettifying. German culture seems faced with the alternative between a loathsome second *Biedermeier* or paper administrative philistinism. Yet this simplification, suggested not only by market interests but by cogent political motives and finally by the historical state of the language itself, does not so much overcome nuances as it tyrannically furthers their decay. It offers sacrifices to omnipotent society. But the latter, by virtue of its very omnipotence, is as incommensurable and alien to the subject of knowledge and expression as it ever was in the milder days when it spurned the language of common speech. The fact that human beings are absorbed by the totality without being humanly equal to it, makes institutionalized linguistic forms as vacuous as naively individualistic tone-values, and equally fruitless is the attempt to turn the tables on the former by admitting them to the literary medium: people incapable of reading a diagram posing as engineers. The collective language attractive to the writer who suspects his isolation of romanticism, is no less romantic: he usurps the voice of those for whom he cannot speak directly, as one of them, because his language, through reification, is as divorced from them as all are from each other; because the present form of the collective is in itself speechless. No collective entrusted today with expressing the subject, thereby becomes a subject. He who does not chime in with the official hymnic tone of festivals to liberation supervised by totalitarians, but seriously espouses the *aridité* recommended ambiguously enough by Roger Caillois, merely submits to an objective discipline as privation, without receiving anything concrete and general in exchange. The contradiction between the abstractness of the language that wants to do away with bourgeois subjectivism, and its emphatically concrete objects, does not reside in the incapacity of writers but in a historical antinomy. The subject wants to cede himself to the collective without being cancelled by it. Therefore his very forfeiture of the private becomes private, chimerical. His language, imitating single-handed the taut construction of society, fondly believes it has wakened cement to speech. As punishment, this unauthorized communal language commits incessant *faux pas*, matter-of-factness at the expense of matter and fact, not so very different from a bourgeois waxing eloquent. The conclusion to be drawn from the decay of nuance is not to cling obstinately to forms that have decayed, nor yet to extirpate them altogether, but rather to try to out-nuance them, to push them to the point where from subjective shading they switch to being a pure, specific definition of the object. The writer must combine the tightest control in ensuring that the word refers, without sidelong glances, to the matter alone, with the shedding of all phrases, the patient effort to detect what linguistically, in itself, carries meaning and what does not[.] But those in fear of falling in spite of everything behind the *Zeitgeist*, of being cast on the refuse-heap of discarded subjectivity, should be reminded that *arriviste* timeliness and progressive content are no longer the same. In an order which liquidates the modern as backward, this backwardness, once condemned, can be invested with the truth over which the historical process obliviously rolls. Because no other truth can be expressed than that which is able to fill the subject, anachronism becomes the refuge of modernity.

142 By this does German song abide[11]

Free verse was rejected by artists like George as a miscarried form, a hybrid between metre and prose. They are refuted by Goethe and by Hölderlin's late hymns. Their technical eye takes free verse at face value. They stop their ears to history by which free verse is stamped. Only in the period of their decay are free rhythms no more than prose periods printed one below the other, in elevated tone. Where free verse proves a form in its own right, it has emerged from the metrical strophe, transcending subjectivity. It turns the pathos of metre against its own claims, a strict negation of ultimate strictness, just as musical prose, emancipated from the symmetry of the eight-beat rhythm, owes its existence to the implacable principles of construction which matured in the articulation of tonal regularity. In free rhythms the ruins of the artistically rhymeless classical strophe grow eloquent. Jutting their alien contours into the newer languages, they are suited by their strangeness to express what is not exhausted by communication. But they yield, unrescuable, to the flood of the languages in which they once stood erect. Only brokenly, marooned in the realm of communication and distinguishable from it by no capricious convolutions, do they signify distance and stylization, as if incognito, and without privilege, until in poetry like Trakl's the waves of dream close over the helpless verses. Not without reason was the epoch of free rhythms that of the French Revolution, the solemn entrance of human dignity and equality. But does not the conscious practice of such verses resemble the law followed by language as a whole in its unconscious history? Is not all carefully-fashioned prose really a system of free rhythms, an attempt to make the magic charm of the absolute coincide with the negation of its appearance, an effort of the mind to save the metaphysical power of expression by means of its own secularization? Were this so, a ray of light would fall on the sisyphean burden that every prose-writer has shouldered, now that demythologization has led to the destruction of language itself. Linguistic quixotry has become obligatory, since the putting-together of each sentence contributes to the decision whether language as such, ambiguous since primeval times, will succumb to commercialism and the consecrated lie that is a part of it, or whether it will make itself a sacred text by diffidence towards the sacral element on which it lives. Prose isolates itself so ascetically from poetry for the sake of invoking song.

143 In nuce

The task of art today is to bring chaos into order.

Artistic productivity is the capacity for being voluntarily involuntary.

Art is magic delivered from the lie of being truth.

Since works of art are sprung, for better or worse, from fetishes – are artists to be blamed if their attitude to their products is slightly fetishistic?

The art-form which has from earliest times laid the highest claims to spirituality, as representation of Ideas, drama, depends equally, by its innermost presuppositions, on an audience.

Just as, according to Benjamin, painting and sculpture translate the mute language of things into a higher but similar one, so it might be supposed that music rescues name as pure sound – but at the cost of severing it from things.

Perhaps the strict and pure concept of art is applicable only to music, while great poetry or great painting – precisely the greatest – necessarily brings with it an element of subject-matter transcending aesthetic confines, undissolved in the autonomy of form. The more profound and consequential an aesthetic theory, the more inappropriate it becomes to such works as the major novels of the nineteenth century. Hegel seized this advantage in his polemic against Kant.

The belief put about by aesthetic theorists that a work of art is to be understood as an object of immediate contemplation, purely on its own terms, is unsound. It is limited not merely by the cultural presuppositions of each work, its 'language', which only the initiate can follow. Even where there are no such difficulties, the work of art demands more than that one should merely abandon oneself to it. Anyone wishing to find the *Fledermaus* beautiful must know that it is the *Fledermaus*: his mother must have told him that it is not about the winged animal but a fancy-dress costume; he must remember having been told: tomorrow you can go to see the *Fledermaus*. To be within tradition used to mean: to experience the work of art as something sanctioned, valid: to participate through it in all the reactions of those who had seen it previously. Once this falls away, the work is exposed in its nakedness and fallibility. The plot, from a ritual, becomes idiocy, the music, from a canon of significant figures, flat and stale. It is really no longer so beautiful. From this mass-culture draws its right of adaptation. The weakness of all traditional culture outside its tradition provides the pretext for improving, and so barbarically mutilating it.

The comfort that flows from great works of art lies less in what they express than in the fact that they have man[a]ged to struggle out of existence. Hope is soonest found among the comfortless.

Kafka: the solipsist without ipseity.

Kafka, though an avid reader of Kierkegaard, is connected with existentialist philosophy only to the extent that one speaks of down-and-outs as 'annihilated existences'.

Surrealism breaks the *promesse du bonheur*. It sacrifices, to the appearance of happiness transmitted by any integral form, concern for its truth.

144 Magic Flute

The ideology of cultural conservatism which sees enlightenment and art as simple antitheses is false, among other reasons, in overlooking the moment of enlightenment in the genesis of beauty. Enlightenment does not merely dissolve all the qualities that beauty adheres to, but posits the quality of beauty in the first place. The disinterested pleasure that according to Kant is aroused by works of art, can only be understood by virtue of historical antitheses still at work in each aesthetic object. The thing disinterestedly contemplated pleases because it once claimed the utmost interest and thus precluded contemplation. The latter is a triumph of enlightened self-discipline. Gold and precious stones, in the perception of which beauty and luxury still coexist undistinguished, were honoured as magical. The radiance they reflect was thought their own essence. Under their power falls whatever is touched by their light. This was early used in the mastering of nature. Jewels were seen as instruments for subjugating the course of the world by its own cunningly usurped power. The magic adhered to the illusion of omnipotence. This illusion was dispelled by mind's self-enlightenment, but the magic has survived as the power of radiant things over men, in whom they once instilled a dread that continues to hold their eyes spellbound, even after they have seen through its claim to domination. Contemplation, as a residue of fetishist worship, is at the same time a stage in overcoming it. As radiant things give up their magic claims, renounce the power with which the subject invested them and hoped with their help himself to wield, they become transformed into images of gentleness, promises of a happiness cured of domination over nature. This is the primeval history of luxury, that has migrated into the meaning of all art. In the magic of what reveals itself in absolute powerlessness, of beauty, at once perfection and nothingness, the illusion of omnipotence is mirrored negatively as hope. It has escaped every trial of strength. Total purposelessness gives the lie to the totality of purposefulness in the world of domination, and only by virtue of this negation, which consummates the established order by drawing the conclusion from its own principle of reason, has existing society up to now become aware of another that is possible. The bliss of contemplation consists in disenchanted charm. Radiance is the appeasement of myth.

145 Art-object

Accumulated domestic monstrosities can shock the unwary by their relation to works of art. Even the hemispherical paper-weight with a fir-tree landscape submerged under glass and below it a greeting from Bad Wildungen has some resemblance to Stifter's green Fichtau,[12] even the polychrome garden dwarf to a little wight from Balzac or Dickens. This is the fault neither simply of the subjects nor of the abstract similarity of all aesthetic appearance. Rather the existence of trash expresses inanely and undisguisedly the fact that men have succeeded in reproducing from within themselves a piece of what otherwise imprisons them in toil, and in symbolically breaking the compulsion of adaptation by themselves creating what they feared; and an echo of the same triumph resounds in the mightiest works, though they seek to forgo it, imagining themselves pure self unrelated to any model. In both cases freedom from nature is celebrated, yet remains mythically entrapped. What men trembled before, they have placed at their own disposal. Great paintings and picture-postcards have in common that they have put primeval images at our fingertips. The illustration of *L'automne* in the schoolbook is a *déjà-vu*, the Eroica, like great philosophy, represents the idea as a total process, yet as if it were directly, sensuously present. In the end indignation over kitsch is anger at its shameless revelling in the joy of imitation, now placed under taboo, while the power of works of art still continues to be secretly nourished by imitation. What escapes the jurisdiction of existence and its purposes is not only a protesting better world but also a more stupid one incapable of self-assertion. This stupidity grows, the more autonomous art idolizes its isolated, allegedly innocent self-assertion instead of its real one, guilty and imperious. The subjective act, by presenting itself as the successful rescue of objective meaning, becomes untrue. Of this it is convicted by kitsch; the latter's lie does not even feign truth. It incurs hostility because it blurts out the secret of art and the affinity of culture to savagery. Every work of art has its irresoluble contradiction in the 'purposefulness without purpose' by which Kant defined the aesthetic; in the fact that it is an apotheosis of making, of the nature-ruling capacity that, as a second creation, postulates itself as absolute, purpose-free, existing in itself, whereas after all the act of making, indeed the very glorification of the artefact, is itself inseparable from the rational purposefulness from which art seeks to break away. The contradiction between what is and what is made, is the vital element of art and circumscribes its law of development, but it is also art's shame: by following, however indirectly, the existing pattern of material production and 'making' its objects, art as akin to production cannot escape the question 'what for?' which it aims to negate. The closer the mode of production of artefacts comes to material mass-production, the more naively it provokes that fatal question. Works of art, however, try to silence it. 'Perfection', as Nietzsche put it, 'must not have become',[13] that is, it should not appear made. Yet the more consequentially it distances itself, through perfection, from making, the more fragile its own made existence necessarily becomes: the endless pains to eradicate the traces of making, injure works of art and condemn them to be fragmentary. Art, following the decay of magic, has taken upon itself the transmission of images to posterity. But in this task it employs the same principle that destroyed images: the stem of its Greek name is the same as that of technique. Its paradoxical entanglement in the process of civilization brings it into conflict with its own idea. The archetypes of our time, synthetically concocted by film and hit-song for the bleak contemplation of the late industrial era, do not merely liquidate art but, by their blatant feeblemindedness, blast into daylight the delusion that was always immured in the oldest works of art and which still gives the maturest their power. Luridly the horror of the ending lights up the deception of the origin. – It is the fortune and limitation of French art never to have entirely eradicated the pride in making little pictures, just as it differs most obviously from German art in not acknowledging the concept of kitsch. In countless significant manifestations it casts a conciliatory glance at what pleases because it was skilfully made: sublime artistry keeps a hold on sensuous life by a moment of harmless pleasure in the *bien fait*. While the absolute claim of perfection without becoming, the dialectic of truth and appearance, is thus renounced, the untruth of those dubbed by Haydn the Grand Moguls is also avoided; they, determined to have no truck with the winsome vignette or figurine, succumb to fetishism by driving out all fetishes. Taste is the ability to keep in balance the contradiction in art between the made and the apparent not-having-become; true works of art, however, never at one with taste, are those which push this contradiction to the extreme, and realize themselves in their resultant downfall.

146 Toy shop

Hebbel, in a surprising entry in his diary, asks what takes away 'life's magic in later years'.

> It is because in all the brightly-coloured contorted marionettes, we see the revolving cylinder that sets them in motion, and because for this very reason the captivating variety of life is reduced to wooden monotony. A child seeing the tightrope-walkers singing, the pipers playing, the girls fetching water, the coachmen driving, thinks all this is happening for the joy of doing so; he can't imagine that these people also have to eat and drink, go to bed and get up again. We however, know what is at stake.

Namely, earning a living, which commandeers all those activities as mere means, reduces them to interchangeable, abstract labour-time. The quality of things ceases to be their essence and becomes the accidental appearance of their value. The 'equivalent form'[14] mars all perceptions: what is no longer irradiated by the light of its own self-determination as 'joy in doing', pales to the eye. Our organs grasp nothing sensuous in isolation, but notice whether a colour, a sound, a movement is there for its own sake or for something else; wearied by a false variety, they steep all in grey, disappointed by the deceptive claim of qualities still to be there at all, while they conform to the purposes of appropriation, indeed largely owe their existence to it alone. Disenchantment with the contemplated world is the sensorium's reaction to its objective role as a 'commodity world'. Only when purified of appropriation would things be colourful and useful at once: under universal compulsion the two cannot be reconciled. Children, however, are not so much, as Hebbel thought, subject to illusions of 'captivating variety', as still aware, in their spontaneous perception, of the contradiction between phenomenon and fungibility that the resigned adult no longer sees, and they shun it. Play is their defence. The unerring child is struck by the 'peculiarity of the equivalent form': 'use-value becomes the form of manifestation, the phenomenal form of its opposite, value.'[15]

In his purposeless activity the child, by a subterfuge, sides with use-value against exchange value. Just because he deprives the things with which he plays of their mediated usefulness, he seeks to rescue in them what is benign towards men and not what subserves the exchange relation that equally deforms men and things. The little trucks travel nowhere and the tiny barrels on them are empty; yet they remain true to their destiny by not performing, not participating in the process of abstraction that levels down that destiny, but instead abide as allegories of what they are specifically for.

Scattered, it is true, but not ensnared, they wait to see whether society will finally remove the social stigma on them; whether the vital process between men and things, praxis, will cease to be practical. The unreality of games gives notice that reality is not yet real. Unconsciously they rehearse the right life. The relation of children to animals depends entirely on the fact that Utopia goes disguised in the creatures whom Marx even begrudged the surplus value they contribute as workers. In existing without any purpose recognizable to men, animals hold out, as if for expression, their own names, utterly impossible to exchange. This make them so beloved of children, their contemplation so blissful. I am a rhinoceros, signifies the shape of the rhinoceros. Fairy-tales and operettas know such images, and the ridiculous question of the woman: how do we know that Orion is really called Orion, rises to the stars.

147 Novissimum organum[16]

It has long been demonstrated that wage-labour formed the masses of the modern epoch, indeed created the worker himself. As a general principle the individual is not merely the biological basis, but the reflection of the social process; his consciousness of himself as something in-itself is the illusion needed to raise his level of performance, whereas in fact the individuated function in the modern economy as mere agents of the law of value. The inner constitution of the individual, not merely his social role, could be deduced from this. Decisive here, in the present phase, is the category of the organic composition of capital. By this the theory of accumulation meant the 'growth in the mass of the means of production, as compared with the mass of the labour-power that vivifies them'.[17] If the integration of society, particularly in totalitarian states, designates subjects more and more exclusively as partial moments in the network of material production, then the 'alteration of the technical composition of capital' is prolonged within those encompassed, and indeed constituted, by the technological demands of the production process. The organic composition of man is growing. That which determines subjects as means of production and not as living purposes, increases with the proportion of machines to variable capital. The pat phrase about the 'mechanization' of man is deceptive because it thinks of him as something static which, through an 'influence' from outside, an adaptation to conditions of production external to him, suffers certain deformations. But there is no substratum beneath such 'deformations', no ontic interior on which social mechanisms merely act externally: the deformation is not a sickness in men but in the society which begets its children with the 'hereditary taint' that biologism projects on to nature. Only when the process that begins with the metamorphosis of labour-power into a commodity has permeated men through and through and objectified each of their impulses as formally commensurable variations of the exchange relationship, is it possible for life to reproduce itself under the prevailing relations of production. Its consummate organization demands the coordination of people that are dead. The will to live finds itself dependent on the denial of the will to live: self-preservation annuls all life in subjectivity. Compared to this, all the achievements of adaptation, all the acts of conformity described by social psychology and cultural anthropology, are mere epiphenomena. The organic composition of man refers by no means only to his specialized technical faculties, but – and this the usual cultural criticism will not at any price admit – equally to their opposite, the moments of naturalness which once themselves sprung from the social dialectic and are now succumbing to it. Even what differs from technology in man is now being incorporated into it as a kind of lubrication. Psychological differentiation, originally the outcome both of the division of labour that dissects man according to sectors of the production process and of freedom, is finally itself entering the service of production. 'The specialized "virtuoso" ', one dialectician wrote thirty years ago,

> the vendor of his objectified and reified faculties . . . lapses into a contemplative attitude towards the workings of his own objectified and reified faculties. This phenomenon can be seen at its most grotesque in journalism. Here it is subjectivity itself, knowledge, temperament and powers of expression that are reduced to an abstract mechanism, functioning autonomously and divorced both from the personality of their 'owner' and from the material and concrete nature of the subject-matter in hand. The journalist's 'lack of convictions', the prostitution of his experiences and beliefs is comprehensible only as the apogee of capitalist reification.[18]

What was here noted among the 'degenerate manifestations' of the bourgeoisie, which it still itself denounced, has since emerged as the social norm, as the character of irreproachable existence under late industrialism. It has long ceased to be a matter of the mere sale of the living. Under a priori saleability the living has made itself, as something living, a thing, equipment. The ego consciously takes the whole man into its service as a piece of apparatus. In this re-organization the ego as business-manager delegates so much of itself to the ego as business-mechanism, that it becomes quite abstract, a mere reference-point: self-preservation forfeits its self. Character traits, from genuine kindness to the hysterical fit of rage, become capable of manipulation, until they coincide exactly with the demands of a given situation. With their mobilization they change. All that is left are the light, rigid, empty husks of emotions, matter transportable at will, devoid of anything personal. They are no longer the subject; rather, the subject responds to them as to his internal object. In their unbounded docility towards the ego they are at the same time estranged from it: being wholly passive they nourish it no longer. This is the social pathogenesis of schizophrenia. The severance of character traits both from their instinctual basis and from the self, which commands them where it formerly merely held them together, causes man to pay for his increasing inner organization with increasing disintegration. The consummation of the division of labour within the individual, his radical objectification, leads to his morbid scission. Hence the 'psychotic character', the anthropological pre-condition of all totalitarian mass-movements. Precisely this transition from firm characteristics to push-button behaviour-patterns – though apparently enlivening – is an expression of the rising organic composition of man. Quick reactions, unballasted by a mediating constitution, do not restore spontaneity, but establish the person as a measuring instrument deployed and calibrated by a central authority. The more immediate its response, the more deeply in reality mediation has advanced: in the prompt, unresistant reflexes the subject is entirely extinguished. So too, biological reflexes, the models of the present social ones, are – when measured against subjectivity – objectified, alien: not without reason are they often called 'mechanical'. The closer organisms are to death, the more they regress to such twitching. Accordingly the destructive tendencies of the masses that explode in both varieties of totalitarian state are not so much death-wishes as manifestations of what they have already become. They murder so that whatever to them seems living, shall resemble themselves.

Translated by E.F.N. Jephcott

Notes

1 Title of a work by Hans Christian Andersen.
2 This passage is a criticism of Brecht's play *The Resistible Rise of Arturo Ui*. Adorno later developed this critique of Brecht's theatre in his essay entitled 'Engagement' in *Noten zur Literatur III*, Frankfurt, 1965, pp. 109–35.
3 August Stramm (1874–1915) was a laconic expressionist poet before the First World War; Oskar Kokoschka (born 1886), before acquiring prominence as a painter, wrote a series of imagistic dramas in the period 1907–1919.
4 Jakob Burckhardt, *Griechische Kulturgeschichte*, Berlin, 1902, vol. IV, pp. 515–16.
5 Walter Benjamin, *Illuminations*, London, 1973, pp. 258–59.
6 Inversion of the lines by Heine: *Aus meinem grossen Schmerzen / mach' ich die kleinen Lieder* ('From my great sorrows, I make small songs'), in his *Lyrisches Intermezzo*, XXXVI.
7 'Sequence of tenses.'
8 Hedwig Courths-Maler [*editor:* the 'Mahler' here is incorrect] (1867–1950): best-seller novelist of popular sentimental romances.
9 Allusion to *Die Gartenlaube*, an illustrated family magazine of patriotic-conservative tendency in the late nineteenth century.
10 *Car nous voulons la nuance encor', / Pas la couleur, rien que la nuance!* – lines from Verlaine's poem *Art Poétique*, a symbolist manifesto.
11 *Dem folgt deutscher Gesang*: last line of Hölderlin's poem *Patmos*.
12 Fichtau is the idyllic valley that appears in Adalbert Stifter's tales *Die Narrenburg* and *Prokopus*.
13 *Nietzsche, Werke*, Munich, 1954, vol. I, p. 545 (*Human All-Too-Human*, Edinburgh–London, 1910, p. 153).
14 See Marx, *Capital*, vol. I, Moscow, 1961, pp. 55ff.
15 Ibid., p. 56.
16 Superlatization of the title of Bacon's treatise *Novum Organum*.
17 Marx, *Capital*, vol. 1, p. 622.
18 Georg Lukács, *History and Class-Consciousness*, London, 1971, p. 100.

15

NATURE AND REVOLUTION

Herbert Marcuse

I

The novel historical pattern of the coming revolution is perhaps best reflected in the role played by a new sensibility in radically changing the 'style' of the opposition. I have sketched out this new dimension in *An Essay on Liberation*; here I shall attempt to indicate what is at stake, namely, a new relation between man and nature – his own, and external nature. The radical transformation of nature becomes an integral part of the radical transformation of society. Far from being a mere 'psychological' phenomenon in groups or individuals, the new sensibility is the medium in which social change becomes an individual need, the mediation between the political practice of 'changing the world' and the drive for personal liberation.

What is happening is the discovery (or rather, rediscovery) of nature as an ally in the struggle against the exploitative societies in which the violation of nature aggravates the violation of man. The discovery of the liberating forces of nature and their vital role in the construction of a free society becomes a new force in social change.

What is involved in the liberation of nature as a vehicle of the liberation of man?

This notion refers to (1) *human* nature: man's primary impulses and senses as foundation of his rationality and experience and (2) *external* nature: man's existential environment, the 'struggle with nature' in which he forms his society. It must be stressed from the beginning that, in both of these manifestations, nature is a historical entity: man encounters nature as transformed by society, subjected to a specific rationality which became, to an ever-increasing extent, technological, instrumentalist rationality, bent to the requirements of capitalism. And this rationality was also brought to bear on man's own nature, on his primary drives. To recall only two characteristic contemporary forms of the adaptation of primary drives to the needs of the established system: the social steering of *aggressiveness* through transferring the aggressive act to technical instruments, thus reducing the sense of guilt; and the social steering of *sexuality* through controlled desublimation, the plastic beauty industry, which leads to a reduction of the sense of guilt and thus promotes 'legitimate' satisfaction.

Nature is a part of history, an object of history; therefore, 'liberation of nature' cannot mean returning to a pre-technological stage, but advancing to the use of the achievements of technological civilization for freeing man and nature from the destructive abuse of science and technology in the service of exploitation. Then, certain lost qualities of artisan work may well reappear on the new technological base.

In the established society, nature itself, ever more effectively controlled, has in turn become another dimension for the control of man: the extended arm of society and its power. Commercialized nature, polluted nature, militarized nature cut down the life environment of man, not only in an ecological but also in a very existential sense. It blocks the erotic cathexis (and transformation) of his environment: it deprives man from finding himself in nature, beyond and this side of alienation; it also prevents him from recognizing nature as a *subject* in its own right – a subject with which to live in a common human universe. This deprivation is not undone by the opening of nature to massive fun and togetherness, spontaneous as well as organized – a release of frustration which only adds to the violation of nature.

Liberation of nature is the recovery of the life-enhancing forces in nature, the sensuous aesthetic qualities which are foreign to a life wasted in unending competitive performances: they suggest the new qualities of *freedom*. No wonder then that the 'spirit of capitalism' rejects or ridicules the idea of liberated nature, that it relegates this idea to the poetic imagination. Nature, if not left alone and protected as 'reservation,' is treated in an aggressively scientific way: it is there for the sake of domination; it is value-free matter, material. This notion of nature is a *historical* a priori, pertaining to a specific form of society. A free society may well have a very different a priori and a very different object; the development of the scientific concepts may be grounded in an experience of nature as a totality of life to be protected and 'cultivated,' and technology would apply this science to the reconstruction of the environment of life.

Domination of man through the domination of nature: the concrete link between the liberation of man and that of nature has become manifest today in the role which the ecology drive plays in the radical movement. The pollution of air and water, the noise, the encroachment of industry and commerce on open natural space have the physical weight of enslavement, imprisonment. The struggle against them is a political struggle; it is obvious to what extent the violation of nature is inseparable from the economy of capitalism. At the same time, however, the political function of ecology is easily 'neutralized' and serves the beautification of the Establishment. Still, the physical pollution practiced by the system must be combated here and now – just as its mental pollution. To drive ecology to the point where it is no longer containable within the capitalist framework means first extending the drive *within* the capitalist framework.[1]

The relation between nature and freedom is rarely made explicit in social theory. In Marxism too, nature is predominantly an object, the adversary in man's 'struggle with nature,' the field for the ever more rational development of the productive forces.[2] But in this form, nature appears as that which capitalism has *made* of nature: matter, raw material for the expanding and exploiting administration of men and things. Does this image of nature conform to that of a free society? Is nature only a productive force – or does it also exist '*for its own sake*' and, in *this* mode of existence, for *man*?

In the treatment of *human* nature, Marxism shows a similar tendency to minimize the role of the natural basis in social change – a tendency which contrasts sharply with the earlier writings of Marx. To be sure, 'human nature' would be different under socialism to the degree to which men and women would, for the first time in history, develop and fulfill their own needs and faculties in association with each other. But this change is to come about almost as a by-product of the new socialist institutions. Marxist emphasis on the development of political consciousness shows little concern with the roots of liberation in individuals, i.e., with the roots of social relationships there where individuals most directly and profoundly experience their world and themselves: in their *sensibility*, in their instinctual needs.

In *An Essay on Liberation*, I suggested that without a change in this dimension, the old Adam would be reproduced in the new society, and that the construction of a free society *presupposes* a break with the familiar experience of the world: with the mutilated sensibility. Conditioned and 'contained' by the rationality of the established system, sense experience tends to 'immunize' man against the very unfamiliar experience of the possibilities of human freedom. The development of a radical, nonconformist sensibility assumes vital political importance in view of the unprecedented extent of social control perfected by advanced capitalism: a control which reaches down into the instinctual and physiological level of existence. Conversely, resistance and rebellion, too, tend to activate and operate on this level.

'Radical sensibility': the concept stresses the active, constitutive role of the senses in shaping reason, that is to say, in shaping the categories under which the world is ordered, experienced, changed. The senses are not merely passive, receptive: they have their own 'syntheses' to which they subject the primary data of experience. And these syntheses are not only the pure 'forms of intuition' (space and time) which Kant recognized as an inexorable a priori *ordering* of sense data. There are perhaps also other syntheses, far more concrete, far more 'material,' which may constitute an empirical (i.e., historical) a priori of experience. Our world emerges not only in the pure forms of time and space, but also, and *simultaneously*, as a totality of sensuous qualities – object not only of the eye (synopsis) but of *all* human senses (hearing, smelling, touching, tasting). It is this qualitative, elementary, unconscious, or rather preconscious, constitution of the world of experience, it is this primary experience itself which must change radically if social change is to be radical, qualitative change.

II

The subversive potential of the sensibility, and nature as a field of liberation are central themes in Marx's *Economic and Philosophic Manuscripts*. They have been reread and reinterpreted again and again, but these themes have been largely neglected. Recently, the Manuscripts served to justify the concept of 'humanistic socialism' in opposition to the bureaucratic-authoritarian Soviet model; they provided a powerful impetus in the struggle against Stalinism and post-Stalinism. I believe that in spite of their 'prescientific' character, and in spite of the prevalence of Feuerbach's philosophic naturalism, these writings espouse the most radical and integral idea of socialism, and that precisely here, 'nature' finds its place in the theory of revolution.

I recall briefly the principal conception of the Manuscripts. Marx speaks of the 'complete emancipation of all human senses and qualities'[3] as the feature of socialism: only this emancipation is the 'transcendence of private property.' This means the emergence of a new type of man, different from the human subject of class society in his very nature, in his physiology: 'the *senses* of the social man are *other* than those of the non-social man.'[4]

'*Emancipation of the senses*' implies that the senses become 'practical' in the reconstruction of society, that they generate new (socialist) relationships between man and man, man and things, man and nature. But the senses become also 'sources' of a new (socialist) *rationality*: freed from that of exploitation. The emancipated senses would repel the instrumentalist rationality of capitalism while preserving and developing its achievements. They would attain this goal in two ways: *negatively* – inasmuch as the Ego, the other, and the object world would no longer be experienced in the context of aggressive acquisition, competition, and defensive possession; *positively* – through the 'human appropriation of nature,' i.e., through the transformation of nature into an environment (medium) for the human being as 'species being'; free to develop the specifically human faculties: the creative, aesthetic faculties.

'Only through the objectively unfolded richness of man's essential being is the richness of subjective human sensibility (a musical ear, an eye for beauty of form – in short, *senses* capable of human gratification, senses affirming themselves as essential powers of man) either cultivated or brought into being.'[5] The emancipated senses, in conjunction with a natural science proceeding on their basis, would guide the 'human appropriation' of nature. Then, nature would have 'lost its mere utility,'[6] it would appear not merely as stuff – organic or inorganic matter – but as life force in its own right, as subject–object;[7] the striving for life is the substance common to man and nature. Man would then form a living object. The senses would 'relate themselves to the thing for the sake of the thing.'[8] And they can do so only inasmuch as the thing itself is objectified human *Verhalten*: objectification of human relationships and is thus itself humanly related to man.[9]

This outrageously unscientific, metaphysical notion foreshadows the mature materialistic theory: it grasps the world of things as objectified human labor, shaped by human labor. Now if this forming human activity produces the technical and natural environment of an acquisitive and repressive society, it will also produce a dehumanized nature; and radical social change will involve a radical transformation of nature.

Also of the *science* of nature? Nature as manifestation of subjectivity; the idea seems inseparable from teleology – long since taboo in Western science. Nature as object per se fitted all too well into the universe of the capitalist treatment of matter to allow discarding the taboo. It seemed entirely justified by the increasingly effective and profitable mastery of nature which was achieved under this taboo.

Is it true that the recognition of nature as a subject is metaphysical teleology incompatible with scientific objectivity? Let us take Jacques Monod's statement of the meaning of objectivity in science:

> What I have tried to show . . . is that the scientific attitude implies what I call the postulate of objectivity – that is to say, the fundamental postulate that there is no plan, that there is no intention in the universe.[10]

The idea of the liberation of nature stipulates no such plan or intention in the universe: liberation is the possible plan and intention of human beings, brought to bear upon nature. However, it does stipulate that nature is susceptible to such an undertaking, and that there are forces in nature which have been distorted and suppressed – forces which could support and enhance the liberation of man. This capacity of nature may be called 'chance,' or 'blind freedom,' and it may give good meaning to the human effort to redeem this blindness – in Adorno's words: to help nature 'to open its eyes,' to help it 'on the poor earth to become what perhaps it would like to be.'[11]

Nature as subject without teleology, without 'plan' and 'intention': this notion goes well with Kant's 'purposiveness without purpose.' The most advanced concepts of the Third Critique have not yet been explored in their truly revolutionary significance. The aesthetic form in art has the aesthetic form in nature (*das Naturschöne*) as its correlate, or rather desideratum. If the idea of beauty pertains to nature as well as to art, this is not merely an analogy, or a human idea imposed on nature – it is the insight that the aesthetic form, as a token of freedom, is a mode (or moment?) of existence of the human as well as the natural universe, an objective quality. Thus Kant attributes the beautiful in nature to nature's 'capacity to form itself, in its freedom, also in an aesthetically purposive way, according to chemical laws.'[12]

The Marxian conception understands nature as a universe which becomes the congenial medium for human gratification to the degree to which nature's *own* gratifying forces and qualities are recovered and released. In sharp contrast to the capitalist exploitation of nature, its 'human appropriation' would be nonviolent, nondestructive: oriented on the life-enhancing, sensuous, aesthetic qualities inherent in nature. Thus transformed, 'humanized,' nature would respond to man's striving for fulfillment, nay, the latter would not be possible without the former. Things have their 'inherent measure' (*inhärentes Mass*):[13] this measure is *in* them, is the potential enclosed in them; only man can free it and, in doing so, free his own human potential. Man is the only being who can 'form things in accordance with the laws of beauty.'[14]

Aesthetics of liberation, beauty as a 'form' of freedom: it looks as if Marx has shied away from this anthropomorphist, idealistic conception. Or is this apparently idealistic notion rather the *enlargement of the materialistic base*? For 'man is directly a *natural being*; he is a corporeal, living, real, sensuous, objective being' who has 'real, sensuous objects' as the objects of his life.[15] And his senses ('like those organs which are directly social in their form')[16] are active, practical in the 'appropriation' of the object world; they express the social existence of man, his 'objectification.' This is no longer Feuerbach's 'naturalism' but, on the contrary, the extension of Historical Materialism to a dimension which is to play a vital role in the liberation of man.

There is, however, a definite internal limit to the idea of the liberation of nature through 'human appropriation.' True, the aesthetic dimension is a vital dimension of freedom; true, it repels violence, cruelty, brutality, and by this token will become an essential quality of a free society, not as a separate realm of 'higher culture,' but as a driving force and *motive* in the *construction* of such a society. And yet, certain brute facts, unconquered and perhaps unconquerable facts, call for skepticism. Can the human appropriation of nature ever achieve the elimination of violence, cruelty, and brutality in the daily sacrifice of animal life for the physical reproduction of the human race? To treat nature 'for its own sake' sounds good, but it is certainly not for the sake of the animal to be eaten, nor probably for the sake of the plant. The end of this war, the perfect peace in the animal world – this idea belongs to the Orphic myth, not to any conceivable historical reality. In the face of the suffering inflicted by man on man, it seems terribly 'premature' to campaign for universal vegetarianism or synthetic foodstuffs; as the world is, priority must be on *human* solidarity among human beings. And yet, no free society is imaginable which does not, under its 'regulative idea of reason,' make the concerted effort to reduce consistently the suffering which man imposes on the animal world.

Marx's notion of a human appropriation of nature retains something of the *hubris* of domination. 'Appropriation,' no matter how human, remains appropriation of a (living) object by a subject. It offends that which is essentially other than the appropriating subject, and which exists precisely as object in its own right – that is, as subject! The latter may well be hostile to man, in which case the relation would be one of struggle; but the struggle may also subside and make room for peace, tranquillity, fulfillment. In this case, not appropriation but rather its negation would be the non-exploitative relation: surrender, 'letting-be,' acceptance . . . But such surrender meets with the impenetrable resistance of matter; nature is not a manifestation of 'spirit,' but rather its essential *limit*.

III

Although the historical concept of nature as a dimension of social change does not imply teleology and does not attribute a 'plan' to nature, it does conceive of nature as subject–object: as a *cosmos* with its own potentialities, necessities, and chances. And these potentialities can *be*, not only in the sense of their value-free function in theory and practice, but also as bearers of *objective values*. These are envisaged in such phrases as 'violation of nature,' 'suppression of nature.' Violation and suppression then mean that human action against nature, man's interrelation with nature, offends against certain objective *qualities* of nature – qualities which are essential to the enhancement and fulfillment of life. And it is on such objective grounds that the liberation for man to his own humane faculties is linked to the liberation of nature – that 'truth' is attributable to nature not only in a mathematical but also in an existential sense. The emancipation of man involves the recognition of such truth in things, in nature. The Marxian vision recaptures the ancient theory of knowledge as *recollection*: 'science' as the *re*discovery of the true *Forms* of things, distorted and denied in the established reality, the perpetual *materialistic core of idealism*. The 'idea,' as the term for these Forms, is not a 'mere' idea, but an image illuminating what is false, distorted in the way in which things are 'given,' what is missing in their familiar perception, in the mutilated experience which is the work of society.

Recollection thus is not remembrance of a Golden Past (which never existed), of childhood innocence, primitive man, et cetera. Recollection as epistemological faculty rather is synthesis, reassembling the bits and fragments which can be found in the distorted humanity and distorted nature. This recollected material has become the domain of the imagination, it has been sanctioned by the repressive societies in art, and as 'poetic truth' – poetic truth only, and therefore not much good in the actual transformation of society. These images may well be called 'innate ideas' inasmuch as they cannot possibly be given in the immediate experience which prevails in the repressive societies. They are given rather as the *horizon* of experience under which the immediately given forms of things appear as 'negative,' as denial of their inherent possibilities, their truth. But in this sense, they are 'innate' in man as *historical* being; they are themselves historical because the possibilities of liberation are always and everywhere historical possibilities. Imagination, *as knowledge*, retains the insoluble tension between idea and reality, the potential and the actual. This is the *idealistic core* of dialectical materialism: the transcendence of freedom beyond the given forms. In this sense too, Marxian theory is the historical heir of German Idealism.

Freedom thus becomes a 'regulative concept of reason' guiding the practice of changing reality in accordance with its 'idea,' i.e., its own potentialities – to make reality free for its truth. Dialectical materialism understands freedom as historical, empirical transcendence, as a force of social change, transcending its immediate form also in a socialist society – not toward ever more production, not toward Heaven or Paradise, but toward an ever more peaceful, joyful struggle with the inexorable resistance of society and nature. This is the philosophical core of the theory of the permanent revolution.

As such force, freedom is rooted in the primary drives of men and women, it is the vital need to enhance their life instincts. Prerequisite is the capacity of the senses to experience not only the 'given' but also the 'hidden' qualities of things which would make for the betterment of life. The radical redefinition of sensibility as 'practical' desublimates the idea of freedom without abandoning its transcendent content: the senses are not only the basis for the *epistemological* constitution of reality, but also for its *transformation*, its *subversion* in the interest of liberation.

Human freedom is thus rooted in the human *sensibility*: the senses do not only 'receive' what is given to them, in the form in which it appears, they do not 'delegate' the transformation of the given to another faculty (the understanding); rather, they discover or *can* discover by themselves, in their 'practice,' new (more gratifying) possibilities and capabilities, forms and qualities of things, and can urge and guide their realization. The emancipation of the senses would make freedom what it is not yet: a sensuous need, an objective of the Life Instincts (*Eros*).

In a society based on alienated labor, human sensibility is *blunted*: men perceive things only in the forms and functions in which they are given, made, used by the existing society; and they perceive only the possibilities of transformation as defined by, and confined to, the existing society.[17] Thus, the existing society is *reproduced* not only in the mind, the consciousness of men, but *also in their senses*; and no persuasion, no theory, no reasoning can break this prison, unless the fixed, petrified *sensibility* of the individuals is '*dissolved*,' *opened* to *a new dimension of history*, until the oppressive familiarity with the given object world is broken – broken in a *second alienation*: that from the alienated society.

Today, in the revolt against the 'consumer society,' sensibility strives to become 'practical,' the vehicle for radical reconstruction, for new ways of life. It has become a force in the *political* struggle for liberation.[18] And that means: the individual emancipation of the senses is supposed to be the beginning, even the foundation, of *universal* liberation, the free society is to take roots in new instinctual needs. How is this possible? How can 'humanity,' human solidarity as '*concrete universal*' (and not as abstract value), as real force, as 'praxis,' originate in the individual sensibility; how can objective freedom originate in the most subjective faculties of man?

We are faced with the *dialectic* of the universal and the particular: how can the human sensibility, which is *principium individuationis*, also generate a *universalizing* principle?

I refer again to the philosophical treatment of this problem in German idealism: here is the intellectual origin of the Marxian concept. For *Kant*: a universal sensorium (the pure forms of intuition) constitutes the one unified framework of sense experience, thus validating the universal categories of the understanding. For *Hegel*: reflection on the content and mode of *my* immediate sense certainty reveals the 'We' in the 'I' of intuition and perception. When the still unreflected consciousness has reached the point where it becomes conscious of itself and its relation to its objects, where it has experienced a 'trans-sensible' world 'behind' the sensuous appearance of things, it discovers that *we* ourselves are behind the curtain of appearance. And this 'we' unfolds as social reality in the struggle between Master and Servant for 'mutual recognition.'

This is the turning point on the road that leads from Kant's effort to reconcile man and nature, freedom and necessity, universal and particular, to Marx's materialistic solution: Hegel's *Phenomenology* breaks with Kant's transcendental conception: history and society enter into the theory of knowledge (and into the very structure of knowledge) and do away with the 'purity' of the a priori: the materialization of the idea of freedom begins. But a closer look shows that the same tendency was already present in Kant's philosophy: in the development from the First to the Third Critique.

1 In the *First Critique*, the freedom of the subject is present only in the epistemological syntheses of the sense data; freedom is relegated to the transcendental Ego's pure syntheses: it is the power of the a priori by virtue of which the transcendental subject constitutes the objective world of experience; theoretical knowledge.
2 In the *Second Critique*, the realm of *praxis* is reached with the stipulation of the autonomy of the moral person: his power to *originate* causation without breaking the universal causation which governs nature: necessity. The price: subjection of the sensibility to the categorical imperative of reason. The relation between human freedom and natural necessity remains obscure.
3 In the *Third Critique*, man and nature are joined in the aesthetic dimension, the rigid 'otherness' of nature is reduced, and Beauty appears as 'symbol of morality.' The union of the realm of freedom and that of necessity is here conceived not as the mastery of nature, not as bending nature to the purposes of man, but as attributing to nature an ideal purposiveness 'of its own: a purposiveness without purpose.'

But it is only the *Marxian* conception which, while preserving the critical, transcendent element of idealism, uncovers the material, historical ground for the reconciliation of human freedom and natural necessity; subjective and objective freedom. This union presupposes liberation: the revolutionary *praxis* which is to abolish the institutions of capitalism and to replace them by socialist institutions and relationships. But in this transition, the emancipation of the senses must accompany the emancipation of consciousness, thus involving the *totality* of human existence. The individuals themselves must change in their very instincts and sensibilities if they are to build, in association, a *qualitatively* different society. But why the emphasis on *aesthetic* needs in this reconstruction?

IV

It is not just in passing and out of exuberance that Marx speaks of the formation of the object world 'in accordance with the laws of beauty' as a feature of free human practice. Aesthetic qualities are essentially nonviolent, nondomineering . . . – qualities which, in the domain of the arts, and in the repressive use of the term 'aesthetic' as pertaining to the sublimated 'higher culture' only, are divorced from the social reality and from 'practice' as such. The revolution would undo this repression and recapture aesthetic needs as a subversive force, capable of counteracting the dominating aggressiveness which has shaped the social and natural universe. The faculty of being 'receptive,' 'passive,' is a precondition of freedom: it is the ability to see things in their own right, to experience the joy enclosed in them, the erotic energy of nature – an energy which is there to be liberated; nature, too, awaits the revolution! This receptivity is itself the soil of creation: it is opposed, not to productivity, but to *destructive* productivity.

The latter has been the ever more conspicuous feature of male domination; inasmuch as the 'male principle' has been the ruling mental and physical force, a free society would be the 'definite negation' of this principle – it would be a *female* society. In this sense, it has nothing to do with matriarchy of any sort; the image of the woman as mother is itself repressive; it transforms a biological fact into an ethical and cultural value and thus it supports and justifies her social repression. At stake is rather the ascent of Eros over aggression, in men *and* women; and this means, in a male-dominated civilization, the 'femalization' of the male. It would express the decisive change in the instinctual structure: the weakening of primary aggressiveness which, by a combination of biological and social factors, has governed the patriarchal culture.

In this transformation, the Women's Liberation Movement becomes a radical force to the degree to which it transcends the entire sphere of aggressive needs and performances, the entire social organization and division of functions. In other words, the movement becomes radical to the degree to which it aims, not only at equality *within* the job and value structure of the *established* society (which would be the equality of dehumanization) but rather at a change in the structure itself (the basic demands of equal opportunity, equal pay, and release from full-time household and child care are a prerequisite). Within the established structure, neither men nor women are free – and the dehumanization of men may well be greater than that of women since the former suffer not only the conveyor belt and assembly line but also the standards and 'ethics' of the 'business community.'

And yet, the liberation of women would be more sweeping than that of men because the repression of women has been constantly fortified by the social use of their biological constitution. The bearing of children, being a mother, is supposed to be not only their natural function but also the fulfillment of their 'nature' – and so is being a wife, since the reproduction of the species occurs within the framework of the monogamous patriarchal family. Outside this framework, the woman is still predominantly a plaything or a temporary outlet for sexual energy not consummated in marriage.

Marxian theory considers sexual exploitation as the primary, original exploitation, and the Women's Liberation Movement fights the degradation of the woman to a 'sexual object.' But it is difficult to overcome the feeling that here, repressive qualities characteristic of the bourgeois-capitalist organization of society enter into the fight against this organization. Historically, the image of the woman as sexual object, and her exchange value on the market, devalue the earlier repressive images of the woman as mother and wife. These earlier images were essential to the bourgeois ideology during a period of capitalist development now left behind: the period where some 'inner-worldly asceticism' was still operative in the dynamic of the economy. In comparison, the present image of the woman as sexual object is a *desublimation* of bourgeois morality – characteristic of a 'higher stage' of capitalist development. Here, too, the commodity form is universalized: it now invades formerly sanctified and protected realms. The (female) body, as seen and plastically idealized by *Playboy*, becomes desirable merchandise with a high exchange value. Disintegration of bourgeois morality, perhaps – but *cui bono*? To be sure, this new body image promotes sales, and the plastic beauty may not be the real thing, but they stimulate aesthetic-sensuous needs which, in their development, must become incompatible with the body as instrument of alienated labor. The male body, too, is made the object of sexual image creation – also plasticized and deodorized . . . clean exchange value. After the secularization of religion, after the transformation of ethics into Orwellian hypocrisy – is the 'socialization' of the body as sexual object perhaps one of the last decisive steps toward the completion of the exchange society: the completion which is the beginning of the end?

Still, the publicity with the body (at present, the female body) as object is dehumanizing, the more so since it plays up to the dominant male as the aggressive subject for whom the female is there, to be taken, to be laid. It is in the nature of sexual relationships that both, male and female, are object *and* subject at the same time; erotic and aggressive energy are fused in both. The surplus-aggression of the male is socially conditioned – as is the surplus-passivity of the female. But beneath the social factors which determine male aggressiveness and female receptivity, a *natural* contrast exists: it is the woman who 'embodies,' in a literal sense, the promise of peace, of joy, of the end of violence. Tenderness, receptivity, sensuousness have become features (or mutilated features) of her body – features of her (repressed) humanity. These female qualities may well be socially determined by the development of capitalism. The process is truly dialectical.[19] Although the reduction of the concrete individual faculties to abstract labor power established an abstract equality between men and women (equality before the machine), this abstraction was less complete in the case of women. They were employed in the material process of production to a lesser extent than men. Women were fully employed in the household, the family, which was supposed to be the sphere of realization for the bourgeois individual. However, this sphere was isolated from the productive process and thus contributed to the women's mutilation. And yet, this isolation (separation) from the alienated work world of capitalism enabled the woman to remain less brutalized by the Performance Principle, to remain closer to her sensibility: more human than men. That this image (and reality) of the woman has been determined by an aggressive, male-dominated society does not mean that this determination must be rejected, that the liberation of women must overcome the female 'nature.' This equalization of male and female would be regressive: it would be a new form of female acceptance of a male principle. Here too the historical process is dialectical: the patriarchal society has created a female image, a female counter-force, which may still become one of the gravediggers of patriarchal society. In this sense too, the woman holds the promise of liberation. It is the woman who, in Delacroix' painting, holding the flag of the revolution, leads the people on the barricades. She wears no uniform; her breasts are bare, and her beautiful face shows no trace of violence. But she has a rifle in her hand – for the end of violence is still to be fought for . . .

Notes

1 See Murray Bookchin, 'Ecology and Revolutionary Thought' and 'Towards a Liberatory Technology,' in *Post-Scarcity Anarchism*, Berkeley, Ramparts Press, 1971.

2 See Alfred Schmidt, *Der Begriff der Natur in der Lehre von Marx*, Frankfurt, Europäische Verlagsanstalt, 1962.

3 Karl Marx, *The Economic and Philosophic Manuscripts of 1844*, ed. Dirk J. Struik, New York, International Publishers, 1964, p. 139 [p. 214 in this volume].
4 Ibid., p. 141 [p. 215].
5 Ibid., p. 141 [p. 215].
6 Ibid., p. 139 [p. 214].
7 'The sun is the object of the plant . . . just as the plant is an object for the sun' (ibid., p. 181).
8 Ibid., p. 139 [p. 214].
9 'For the sake of the thing' – an illustration:

> In Yugoslavia, they sell wooden cutting boards which, on one side, are painted with very colorful, pretty flower patterns; the other side is unpainted. The boards bear the imprint: 'don't hurt my pretty face, use other side.' Childish anthropomorphism? Certainly. But can we perhaps imagine that the people who had this idea, and those users who pay attention to it, have a quite natural, instinctual aversion against violence and destruction, that they have indeed a 'human relation' to matter, that matter to them is part of the *life* environment and thus assumes traits of a living object?

10 Interview with the *New York Times*, March 15, 1971.
11 Theodor W. Adorno, *Aesthetische Theorie*, Frankfurt/Main, Suhrkamp, 1970, pp. 100, 107.
12 *Critique of Judgement*, S 58.
13 Marx, *Manuscripts*, p. 114.
14 Ibid.
15 Ibid., p. 181.
16 Ibid., p. 139 [p. 214].
17 For the following see my *An Essay on Liberation*, Boston, Beacon Press, 1969, pp. 36ff.
18 The fight for the People's Park in Berkeley, which was met with brute force by the armed guardians of law and order, shows the explosion of sensibility in political action.
19 This dialectic is the center of Angela Davis's paper 'Marxism and Women's Liberation' (not yet published). Written in jail, this paper is the work of a great woman, militant, intellectual.

16

MODERNITY VERSUS POSTMODERNITY[1]

Jürgen Habermas

In 1980, architects were admitted to the Biennial in Venice, following painters and filmmakers. The note sounded at this first Architecture Biennial was one of disappointment. I would describe it by saying that those who exhibited in Venice formed an avant-garde of reversed fronts. I mean that they sacrificed the tradition of modernity in order to make room for a new historicism. Upon this occasion, a critic of the German newspaper, *Frankfurter Allgemeine Zeitung*, advanced a thesis whose significance reaches beyond this particular event; it is a diagnosis of our times: 'Postmodernity definitely presents itself as Antimodernity.' This statement describes an emotional current of our times which has penetrated all spheres of intellectual life. It has placed on the agenda theories of post-enlightenment, postmodernity, even of posthistory.

From history we know the phrase:

'The Ancients and the Moderns'

Let me begin by defining these concepts. The term 'modern' has a long history, one which has been investigated by Hans Robert Jauss. The word 'modern' in its Latin form 'modernus' was used for the first time in the late fifth century in order to distinguish the present, which had become officially Christian, from the Roman and pagan past. With varying content, the term 'modern' again and again expresses the consciousness of an epoch that relates itself to the past of antiquity, in order to view itself as the result of a transition from the old to the new.

Some writers restrict this concept of 'modernity' to the Renaissance, but this is historically too narrow. People considered themselves modern during the period of Charles the Great, in the twelfth century, as well as in France of the late seventeenth century, at the time of the famous 'Querelle des Anciens et des Modernes.' This is to say, the term 'modern' appeared and reappeared exactly during those periods in Europe when the consciousness of a new epoch formed itself through a renewed relationship to the ancients – whenever, moreover, antiquity was considered a model to be recovered through some kind of imitation.

The spell which the classics of the ancient world cast upon the spirit of later times was first dissolved with the ideals of the French Enlightenment. Specifically, the idea of being 'modern' by looking back to the ancients changed with the belief, inspired by modern science, in the infinite progress of knowledge and in the infinite advance towards social and moral betterment. Another form of modernist consciousness was formed in the wake of this change. The romantic modernist sought to oppose the antique ideals of the classicists; he looked for a new historical epoch, and found it in the idealized Middle Ages. However, this new ideal age, established early in the nineteenth century, did not remain a fixed ideal. In the course of the nineteenth century, there emerged out of this romantic spirit that radicalized consciousness of modernity which freed itself from all specific historical ties. This most recent modernism simply makes an abstract opposition between tradition and the present; and we are, in a way, still the contemporaries of that kind of aesthetic modernity which first appeared in the midst of the nineteenth century. Since then, the distinguishing mark of works, which count as modern, is the 'new.' The characteristic of such works is 'the new' which will be overcome and made obsolete through the novelty of the next style. But, while that which is merely 'stylish' will soon become out-moded, that which is modern preserves a secret tie to the classical. Of course, whatever can survive time has always been considered to be a classic. But the emphatically modern document no longer borrows this power of being a classic from the authority of a past epoch; instead, a modern work becomes a classic because it has once been authentically modern. Our sense of modernity creates its own self-enclosed canons of being classic. In this sense we speak, e.g., in view of the history of modern art, of classical modernity. The relation between 'modern' and 'classical' has definitely lost a fixed historical reference.

The discipline of aesthetic modernity

The spirit and discipline of aesthetic modernity assumed clear contours in the work of Baudelaire. Modernity then unfolded in various avant-garde movements, and finally reached its climax in the Café Voltaire of the Dadaists, and in Surrealism. Aesthetic modernity is characterized by attitudes which find a common focus in a changed consciousness of time. This time consciousness expresses itself through metaphors of the vanguard and the avant-garde. The avant-garde understands itself as invading unknown territory, exposing itself to the dangers of sudden, of shocking encounters, conquering an as yet unoccupied future. The avant-grade must find a direction in a landscape into which no one seems to have yet ventured.

But these forward gropings, this anticipation of an undefined future and the cult of the new, mean in fact the exaltation of the present. The new time consciousness, which enters philosophy in the writings of Bergson, does more than express the experience of mobility in society, acceleration in history, of discontinuity in everyday life. The new value placed on the transitory, the elusive, and the ephemeral, the very celebration of dynamism, discloses the longing for an undefiled, an immaculate and stable present.

This explains the rather abstract language in which the modernist temper has spoken of the 'past.' Individual epochs lose their distinct forces. Historical memory is replaced by the heroic affinity of the present with the extremes of history: a sense of time wherein decadence immediately recognizes itself in the barbaric, the wild and the primitive. We observe the anarchistic intention of blowing up the continuum of history, and we can account for it in terms of the subversive force of this new aesthetic consciousness. Modernity revolts against the normalizing functions of tradition; modernity lives on the experience of rebelling against all that is normative. This revolt is one way to neutralize the standards of both, morality and utility. This aesthetic consciousness continuously stages a dialectical play between secrecy and public scandal; it is addicted to the fascination of that horror which accompanies the act of profaning, and is yet always in flight from the trivial results of profanation.

On the other hand, the time consciousness articulated in avant-garde art is not simply ahistorical; it is directed against what might be called a false normativity in history. The modern, avant-garde spirit has sought, instead, to use the past in a different way; it disposes over those pasts which have been made available by the objectifying scholarship of historicism, but it opposes at the same time a neutralized history, which is locked up in the museum of historicism.

Drawing upon the spirit of surrealism, Walter Benjamin constructs the relationship of modernity to history, in what I would call a post-historicist attitude. He reminds us of the self-understanding of the French Revolution: 'The Revolution cited ancient Rome, just as fashion cites an antiquated dress. Fashion has a scent for what is current, whenever this moves within the thicket of what was once.' This is Benjamin's concept of the *Jetztzeit*, of the present as a moment of revelation; a time, in which splinters of a messianic presence are enmeshed. In this sense, for Robespierre, the antique Rome was a past laden with momentary revelations.

Now, this spirit of aesthetic modernity has recently begun to age. It has been recited once more in the 1960s; after the 1970s, however, we must admit to ourselves that this modernism arouses a much fainter response today than it did fifteen years ago. Octavio Paz, a fellow traveller of modernity, noted already in the middle of the 1960s that 'the avant-garde of 1967 repeats the deeds and gestures of those of 1917. We are experiencing the end of the idea of modern art.' The work of Peter Bürger has since taught us to speak of 'post-avant-garde' art; this term is chosen to indicate the failure of the surrealist rebellion. But, what is the meaning of this failure? Does it signal a farewell to modernity? Thinking more generally, does the existence of a post-avant-garde mean there is a transition to that broader phenomenon called postmodernity?

This is in fact how Daniel Bell, the most brilliant of the American neoconservatives, interprets matters. In his book, *The Cultural Contradictions of Capitalism*, Bell argues that the crises of the developed societies of the West are to be traced back to a split between culture and society. Modernist culture has come to penetrate the values of everyday life; the life-world is infected by modernism. Because of the forces of modernism, the principle of unlimited self-realization, the demand for authentic self-experience and the subjectivism of a hyperstimulated sensitivity have come to be dominant. This temperament unleashes hedonistic motives irreconcilable with the discipline of professional life in society, Bell says. Moreover, modernist culture is altogether incompatible with the moral basis of a purposive rational conduct of life. In this manner, Bell places the burden of responsibility for the dissolution of the Protestant ethic (a phenomenon which has already disturbed Max Weber), on the 'adversary culture.' Culture, in its modern form, stirs up hatred against the conventions and virtues of an everyday life, which has become rationalized under the pressures of economic and administrative imperatives.

I would call your attention to a complex wrinkle in this view. The impulse of modernity, we are told on the other hand, is exhausted; anyone who considers himself avant-garde can read his own death warrant. Although the avant-garde is still considered to be expanding, it is supposedly no longer creative. Modernism is dominant but dead. For the neoconservative, the question then arises: how can norms arise in society which will limit libertinism, reestablish the ethic of discipline and work? What new norms will put a brake on the leveling caused by the social welfare state, so that the virtues of individual competition for achievement can again dominate? Bell sees a religious revival to be the only solution. Religious faith tied to a faith in tradition will provide individuals with clearly defined identities, and with existential security.

Cultural modernity and societal modernization

One can certainly not conjure up by magic the compelling beliefs which command authority. Analyses like Bell's, therefore, only result in an attitude which is spreading in Germany no less than here in the States: an intellectual and political confrontation with the carriers of cultural modernity. I cite Peter Steinfells, an observer of the new style which the neoconservatives have imposed upon the intellectual scene in the 1970s.

> The struggles takes the form of exposing every manifestation of what could be considered an oppositionist mentality and tracing its 'logic' so as to link it to various forms of extremism: drawing the connection between modernism and nihilism . . . between government regulation and totalitarianism, between criticism of arms expenditures and subservience to communism, between Women's liberation or homosexual rights and the destruction of the family . . . between the Left generally and terrorism, anti-semitism, and fascism . . .[2]

The *ad hominem* approach and the bitterness of these intellectual accusations have also been trumpeted loudly in Germany. They should not be explained so much in terms of the psychology of neoconservative writers; rather, they are rooted in the analytical weaknesses of neoconservative doctrine itself.

Neoconservatism shifts onto cultural modernism the uncomfortable burdens of a more or less successful capitalist modernization of the economy and society. The neoconservative doctrine blurs the relationship between the welcomed process of societal modernization on the one hand, and the lamented cultural development on the other. The neoconservative does not uncover the economic and social causes for the altered attitudes towards work, consumption, achievement, and leisure. Consequently, he attributes all of the following – hedonism, the lack of social identification, the lack of obedience, narcissism, the withdrawal from status and achievement competition – to the domain of 'culture.' In fact, however, culture is intervening in the creation of all these problems in only a very indirect and mediated fashion.

In the neoconservative view, those intellectuals who still feel themselves committed to the project of modernity are then presented as taking the place of those unanalyzed causes. The mood which feeds neoconservatism today in no way originates from the discontents about the antinomian consequences of a culture breaking from the museums into the stream of ordinary life. These discontents have not been called into life by modernist intellectuals. They are rooted in deep seated reactions against the process of *societal* modernization. Under the pressures of the dynamics of economic growth and the organizational accomplishments of the state, this social modernization penetrates deeper and deeper into previous forms of human existence. I would describe this subordination of the life-worlds under the system's imperatives as a matter of disturbing the communicative infrastructure of everyday life.

Thus, for example, neo-populist protests only bring to expression in pointed fashion a widespread fear regarding the destruction of the urban and natural environment, and of forms of human sociability. There is a certain irony about these protests in terms of neoconservatism. The tasks of passing on a cultural tradition, of social integration, and of socialization require the adherence to a criterion of communicative rationality. The occasions for protest and discontent originate exactly when spheres of communicative action, centered on the reproduction and transmission of values and norms, are penetrated by a form of modernization guided by standards of economic and administrative rationality; however, those very spheres are dependent on quite different standards of rationalization – on the standards of what I would call communicative rationality. But, neoconservative doctrines turn our attention precisely away from such societal processes: they project the causes, which they do not bring to light, onto the plane of a subversive culture and its advocates.

To be sure, cultural modernity generates its own aporias as well. Independently from the consequences of *societal* modernization, and from *within the perspective* of *cultural* development itself, there originate motives for doubting the project of modernity. Having dealt with a feeble kind of criticism of modernity – that of neoconservatism – let me now move our discussion of modernity and its discontents into a different domain that touches on these aporias of cultural modernity, issues which often serve only as a pretense for those positions (which either call for a postmodernity, or recommend a return to some form of premodernity or which throw modernity radically overboard).

The project of Enlightenment

The idea of modernity is intimately tied to the development of European art; but what I call 'the project of modernity' comes only into focus when we dispense with the usual concentration upon art. Let me start a different analysis by recalling an idea from Max Weber. He characterized cultural modernity as the separation of the substantive reason expressed in religion and metaphysics into three autonomous spheres. They are: science, morality and art. These came to be differentiated because the unified world conceptions of religion and metaphysics fell apart. Since the eighteenth century, the problems inherited from these older world-views could be rearranged so as to fall under specific aspects of validity: truth, normative rightness, authenticity and beauty. They could then be handled as questions of knowledge, or of justice and morality, or of taste. Scientific discourse, theories of morality, jurisprudence, the production and criticism of art, could in turn be institutionalized. Each domain of culture could be made to correspond to cultural professions, in which problems could be dealt with as the concern of special experts. This professionalized treatment of the cultural tradition brings to the fore the intrinsic structures of each of the three dimensions of culture. There appear the structures of cognitive–instrumental, moral–practical, and of aesthetic–expressive rationality, each of these under the control of specialists who seem more adept at being logical in these particular ways than other people are. As a result, the distance has grown between the culture of the experts and that of the larger public. What accrues to culture through specialized treatment and reflexion does not immediately and necessarily become the property of everyday praxis. With cultural rationalization of this sort, the threat increases that the life-world, whose traditional substance has already been devalued, will become more and more impoverished.

The project of modernity formulated in the eighteenth century by the philosophers of the Enlightenment consisted in their efforts to develop objective science, universal morality and law, and autonomous art, according to their inner logic. At the same time, this project intended to release the cognitive potentials of each of these domains to set them free from their esoteric forms. The Enlightenment philosophers wanted to utilize this accumulation of specialized culture for the enrichment of everyday life, that is to say, for the rational organization of everyday social life.

Enlightenment thinkers of the cast of mind of Condorcet still had the extravagant expectation that the arts and the sciences would promote not only the control of natural forces, but would also further understanding of the world and of the self, would promote moral progress, the justice of institutions, and even the happiness of human beings. The twentieth century has shattered this optimism. The differentiation of science, morality, and art has come to mean the autonomy of the segments treated by the specialist and at the same time letting them split off from the hermeneutics of everyday communication. This splitting off is the problem that has given rise to those efforts to 'negate' the culture of expertise. But the problem won't go away: should we try to hold on to the *intentions* of the Enlightenment, feeble as they may be, or should we declare the entire project of modernity a lost cause? I now want to return to the problem of artistic culture, having explained why, historically, that aesthetic modernity is a part only of cultural modernity in general.

The false programs of the negation of culture

Greatly oversimplifying, I would say in the history of modern art one can detect a trend toward ever greater autonomy in the definition and practice of art. The category of 'beauty' and the domain of beautiful objects were first constituted in the Renaissance. In the course of the eighteenth century, literature, the fine arts and music were institutionalized as activities independent from sacred and courtly life. Finally, around the middle of the nineteenth century an aestheticist conception of art emerged, which encouraged the artist to produce his work according to the distinct consciousness of art for art's sake. The autonomy of the aesthetic sphere could then become a deliberate project: the talented artist could lend authentic expression to those experiences he had in encountering his own de-centered subjectivity, detached from the constraints of routinized cognition and everyday action.

In the mid-nineteenth century, in painting and literature, a movement began which Octavio Paz finds epitomized already in the art criticism of Baudelaire. Color, lines, sounds and movement ceased to serve primarily the cause of representation; the media of expression and the techniques of production themselves became the aesthetic object. Theodor W. Adorno could therefore begin his *Aesthetic Theory* with the following sentence: 'It is now taken for granted that nothing which concerns art can be taken for granted any more: neither art itself, nor art in its relationship to the whole, nor even the right of art to exist.' And this is what surrealism then denied: *das Existenzrecht der Kunst als Kunst*. To be sure, surrealism would not have challenged the right of art to exist, if modern art no longer had advanced a promise of happiness concerning its own relationship 'to the whole' of life. For Schiller, such a promise was delivered by aesthetic intuition, but not fulfilled by it. Schiller's *Letters on the Aesthetic Education of Man* speak to us of a utopia reaching beyond art itself. But by the time of

Baudelaire, who repeated this *promesse de bonheur*, via art, the utopia of reconciliation with society had gone sour. A relation of opposites had come into being; art had become a critical mirror, showing the irreconcilable nature of the aesthetic and the social world. This modernist transformation was all the more painfully realized, the more art alienated itself from life and withdrew into the untouchableness of complete autonomy. Out of such emotional currents finally gathered those explosive energies which unloaded themselves in the surrealist attempt to blow up the autarkical sphere of art and to force a reconciliation of art and life.

But all those attempts to level art and life, fiction and praxis, appearance and reality to one plane; the attempts to remove the distinction between artifact and object of use, between conscious staging and spontaneous excitement; the attempts to declare everything to be art and everyone to be artist, to retract all criteria and to equate aesthetic judgment with the expression of subjective experiences – all these undertakings have proved themselves to be sort of nonsense experiments. These experiments have served to bring back to life, and to illuminate all the more glaringly, exactly those structures of art which they were meant to dissolve. They gave a new legitimacy, as an end in itself, to appearance as the medium of fiction, to the transcendence of the art work over society, to the concentrated and planned character of artistic production as well as to the special cognitive status of judgments of taste. The radical attempt to negate art has ended up ironically by giving due exactly to these categories through which Enlightenment aesthetics had circumscribed its object domain. The surrealists waged the most extreme warfare, but two mistakes in particular destroyed their revolt. First, when the containers of an autonomously developed cultural sphere are shattered, the contents get dispersed. Nothing remains from a desublimated meaning or a destructured form; an emancipatory effect does not follow.

Their second mistake has more important consequences. In everyday communication, cognitive meanings, moral expectations, subjective expressions and evaluations must relate to one another. Communication processes need a cultural tradition covering all spheres – cognitive, moral–practical and expressive. A rationalized everyday life, therefore, could hardly be saved from cultural impoverishment through breaking open a single cultural sphere – art – and so providing access to just one of the specialized knowledge complexes. The surrealist revolt would have replaced only one abstraction.

In the sphere of theoretical knowledge and morality as well, there are parallels to this failed attempt of what we might call the false negation of culture. Only they are less pronounced. Since the days of the Young Hegelians, there has been talk about the negation of philosophy. Since Marx, the question of the relationship of theory and practice has been posed. However, Marxist intellectuals joined a social movement; and only at its peripheries were there sectarian attempts to carry out a program of the negation of philosophy similar to the surrealist program to negate art. A parallel to the surrealist mistakes becomes visible in these programs when one observes the consequences of dogmatism and of moral rigorism.

A reified everyday praxis can be cured only by creating unconstrained interaction of the cognitive with the moral–practical and the aesthetic–expressive elements. Reification cannot be overcome by forcing just one of those highly stylized cultural spheres to open up and become more accessible. Instead, we see under certain circumstances a relationship emerge between terroristic activities and the over-extension of any one of these spheres into other domains: examples would be tendencies to aestheticize politics, or to replace politics by moral rigorism or to submit it to the dogmatism of a doctrine. These phenomena should not lead us, however, into denouncing the intentions of the surviving Enlightenment tradition as intentions rooted in a 'terroristic reason.' Those who lump together the very project of modernity with the state of consciousness and the spectacular action of the individual terrorist are no less short-sighted than those who would claim that the incomparably more persistent and extensive bureaucratic terror practiced in the dark, in the cellars of the military and secret police, and in camps and institutions, is the *raison d'être* of the modern state, only because this kind of administrative terror makes use of the coercive means of modern bureaucracies.

Alternatives

I think that instead of giving up modernity and its project as a lost cause, we should learn from the mistakes of those extravagant programs which have tried to negate modernity. Perhaps the types of reception of art may offer an example which at least indicates the direction of a way out.

Bourgeois art had two expectations at once from its audiences. On the one hand, the layman who enjoyed art should educate himself to become an expert. On the other hand, he should also behave as a competent consumer who uses art and relates aesthetic experiences to his own life problems. This second, and seemingly harmless, manner of experiencing art has lost its radical implications, exactly because it had a confused relation to the attitude of being expert and professional.

To be sure, artistic production would dry up, if it were not carried out in the form of a specialized treatment of autonomous problems, and if it were to cease to be the concern of experts who do not pay so much attention to exoteric questions. Both artists and critics accept thereby the fact that such problems fall under the spell of what I earlier called the 'inner logic' of a cultural domain. But this sharp delineation, this exclusive concentration on one aspect of validity alone, and the exclusion of aspects of truth and justice, breaks down as soon as aesthetic experience is drawn into an individual life history and is absorbed into ordinary life. The reception of art by the layman, or by the 'everyday expert,' goes in a rather different direction than the reception of art by the professional critic.

Albrecht Wellmer has drawn my attention to one way that an aesthetic experience which is not framed around the experts' critical judgments of taste can have its significance altered: as soon as such an experience is used to illuminate a life-historical situation and is related to life problems, it enters into a language game which is no longer that of the aesthetic critic. The aesthetic experience then not only renews the interpretation of our needs in whose light we perceive the world. It permeates as well our cognitive significations and our normative expections and changes the manner in which all these moments refer to one another. Let me give an example of this process.

This manner of receiving and relating to art is suggested in the first volume of the work *The Aesthetics of Resistance* by the German-Swedish writer Peter Weiss. Weiss describes the process of reappropriating art by presenting a group of politically motivated, knowledge-hungry workers in 1937 in Berlin. These were young people, who, through an evening high school education, acquired the intellectual means to fathom the general and the social history of European art. Out of the resilient edifice of the objective mind, embodied in works of art which they saw again and again in the museums in Berlin, they started removing their own chips of stone, which they gathered together and reassembled in the context of their own milieu. This milieu was far removed from that of traditional education as well as from the then existing regime. These young workers went back and forth between the edifice of European art and their own milieu until they were able to illuminate both.

In examples like this which illustrate the reappropriation of the expert's culture from the standpoint of the life-world, we can discern an element which does justice to the intentions of the hopeless surrealist revolts, and to Brecht's and Benjamin's interests in how artworks (which have lost their aura) can still be received in illuminating ways. In sum, the project of modernity has not yet been fulfilled. And the reception of art is only one of at least three of its aspects. The project aims at a differentiated relinking of modern culture with an everyday praxis that still depends on vital heritages, but would be impoverished through mere traditionalism. This new connection, however, can only be established under the condition that societal modernization will also be steered in a different direction. The life-world has to become able to develop institutions out of itself which sets limits to the internal dynamics and to the imperatives of an almost autonomous economic system and its administrative complements.

If I am not mistaken, the chances for this today are not very good. More or less in the entire Western world, a climate has developed that furthers capitalist modernization processes as well as trends critical of cultural modernism. The disillusionment with the very failures of those programs that called for the negation of art and philosophy has come to serve as a pretense for conservative positions. Let me briefly distinguish the antimodernism of the young conservatives from the premodernism of the old conservatives and from the postmodernism of the neoconservatives.

The *Young Conservatives* recapitulate the basic experience of aesthetic modernity. They claim as their own the revelations of a decentered subjectivity, emancipated from the imperatives of work and usefulness, and with this experience they step outside the modern world. On the basis of modernistic attitudes, they justify an irreconcilable anti-modernism. They remove into the sphere of the far away and the archaic the spontaneous powers of imagination, of self-experience and of emotionality. To instrumental reason, they juxtapose in manichean fashion a principle only accessible through evocation, be it the will to power or sovereignty, Being or the dionysiac force of the poetical. In France this line leads from Bataille via Foucault to Derrida.

The *Old Conservatives* do not allow themselves to be contaminated by cultural modernism. They observe the decline of substantive reason, the differentiation of science, morality and art, the modern world view and its merely procedural rationality, with sadness and recommend a withdrawal to a position *anterior* to modernity.

Neo-Aristotelianism, in particular, enjoys a certain success today. In view of the problematic of ecology, it allows itself to call for a cosmological ethic. As belonging to this school, which originates with Leo Strauss, one can count for example the interesting works of Hans Jonas and Robert Spaemann.

Finally, the *Neoconservatives* welcome the development of modern science, as long as this only goes beyond its sphere to carry forward technical progress, capitalist growth and rational administration. Moreover, they recommend a politics of defusing the explosive content of cultural modernity. According to one thesis, science, when properly understood, has become irrevocably meaningless for the orientation of the life-world. A further thesis is that politics must be kept as far aloof as possible from the demands of moral–practical justification. And a third thesis asserts the pure immanence of art, disputes that it has a utopian content, and points to its illusory character in order to limit the aesthetic experience to privacy. One could name here the early Wittgenstein, Carl Schmitt of the middle period, and Gottfried Benn of the late period. But with the decisive confinement of science, morality and art to autonomous spheres separated from the life-world and administered by experts, what remains from the project of cultural modernity is only what we would have if we were to give up the project of modernity altogether. As a replacement one points to traditions, which, however, are held to be immune to demands of (normative) justification and validation.

This typology is like any other, of course, a simplification; but it may not prove totally useless for the analysis of contemporary intellectual and political confrontations. I fear that the ideas of anti-modernity, together with an additional touch of premodernity, are becoming popular in the circles of alternative culture. When one observes the transformations of consciousness within political parties in Germany, a new ideological shift (*Tendenzwende*) becomes visible. And this is the alliance of postmodernists with premodernists. It seems to me that there is no party in particular that monopolizes the abuse of intellectuals and the position of neoconservatism. I therefore have good reason to be thankful for the liberal spirit in which the city of Frankfurt offers me a prize bearing the name of Theodor Adorno. Adorno, a most significant son of this city, who as philosopher and writer has stamped the image of the intellectual in our country in incomparable fashion; even more, who has become the very image of emulation for the intellectual.

Translated by Seyla Ben-Habib

Notes

1 This essay was delivered as a James Lecture of the New York Institute for the Humanities at New York University on March 5, 1981. It had been delivered first in German in September 1980 when Habermas was awarded the Theodor W. Adorno prize by the city of Frankfurt.

2 *Editor's note:* Peter Steinfells, *The Neoconservatives*, New York, 1979, p. 65.

17

EXTRACT FROM 'QUESTIONS AND COUNTERQUESTIONS'[1]

Jürgen Habermas

III

With a great deal of hermeneutic sensitivity, Martin Jay has collected and interpreted my scattered remarks on the question of aesthetic modernity. In every case these remarks had a secondary character to the extent that they arose only in the context of other themes and always in relation to the discussions among Adorno, Benjamin, and Marcuse. In *The Theory of Communicative Action*, my discussion of Max Weber's theory of culture and his diagnosis of the times required understanding the autonomous art that emerged in modern Europe (together with art criticism institutionalized since the eighteenth century) as the product of a disintegration and the result of a process of rationalization. Weber describes the rationalization of worldviews as a process of decomposition and differentiation. On the one hand, the basic substantial concepts with which the world-orders of salvation history and cosmology were constructed have been dissolved; with this dissolution, ontic, moral, and expressive aspects are no longer fused into one and the same concept. Without the possibility of recourse to God and the cosmic order as origins, theological and metaphysical forms of grounding lose their credibility. On the other hand, alongside a subjectivized 'faith,' there arose profane forms of 'knowledge' which are relatively independent of one another; philosophy, forced into the position of mediator, becomes dependent on them. As documented in the division of Kant's three *Critiques*, questions of truth are differentiated from questions of justice, and these in turn from questions of taste.

Originating in the eighteenth century, idealistic aesthetics strictly distinguished aesthetic pleasure from other 'empirical' forms of satisfaction: that is, it separated the beautiful and the sublime, on the one hand, from the useful and the desirable, on the other. Art emerges with its own proper claim, *along with* science and technology, law, and morality. Max Weber speaks of the inner logic or intrinsic meaning (*Eigensinn*) of these three cultural value spheres, which are also separated from each other institutionally in the form of functionally specified systems of action. Since the investigations of Arnold Hauser into the social history of modern art, this *institutional* differentiation of art has often been analyzed.[2]

There is no need here to go into the external aspects of the transformation of the forms of the production of art, the purposes to which it was put, or the modes of its reception in the transition from sacrally bound art, through the art of the court and patron, to bourgeois commercialized art.[3] What is in dispute are the internal aspects of the 'inner logic' of autonomous art since the eighteenth century. One of the two questions raised by Martin Jay is the extent to which one can speak of an aesthetic–practical rationality, or even of a learning process, in this sphere.

There is an unmistakable indicator for the fact that a certain type of 'knowing' is objectified in art works, albeit in a different way than in theoretical discourse or in legal or moral representations: these objectivations of mind are also fallible and hence criticizable. Art criticism arose at the same time as the autonomous work of art; and, since then, the insight has established itself that the work of art calls for interpretation, evaluation, and even the 'linguistification' (*Versprachlichung*) of its semantic content. Art criticism has developed forms of argumentation that specifically differentiate it from the forms of theoretical and moral–practical discourse.[4] As distinct from merely subjective preference, the fact that we link judgments of taste to a criticizable claim presupposes non-arbitrary standards for the judgment of art. As the philosophical discussion of 'artistic truth' reveals, works of art raise claims with regard to their unity (harmony: *Stimmigkeit*), their authenticity, and the success of their expressions by which they can be measured and in terms of which they may fail. For that reason I believe that a pragmatic logic of argumentation is the most appropriate guiding thread through which the 'aesthetic–practical' type of rationality can be differentiated over and against other types of rationality.

If we speak about 'learning processes,' it is the works of art themselves, and not the discourses about them, that are the locus of directed and cumulative transformations. As McCarthy correctly notes, what accumulates are not epistemic contents, but rather the effects of the inner logical differentiation of special sorts of experience: precisely those aesthetic experiences of which only a decentered, unbound subjectivity is capable. Authentic experiences of this type are possible only to the extent that the categories of the patterned expectations of organized daily experience collapse, that the routines of daily action and conventions of ordinary life are destroyed, and the normality of foreseeable and accountable certainties are suspended. The ever more radical uncoupling of this potential for experience, the purification of the aesthetic from admixtures of the cognitive, the useful, and the moral, is mirrored in the reflections of the early Romantic period (especially in Friedrich Schlegel), in the aestheticism of Baudelaire and the Symbolists, in the program of *l'art pour l'art*, in the surrealistic celebration of illumination through shock effects with its ambivalence of attraction and repulsion, of broken continuity, of the shudder of profanization, of agitated disgust: in short, in the reflection on those moments in which the bewildered subject 'transgresses his boundaries,' as Bataille puts it. What is reflected in these interpretations and declarations is a transformation of the form of aesthetic experience, induced by avant-garde art itself, in the direction of the decentering and unbounding of subjectivity. At the same time, this decentering indicates an increased sensitivity to what remains unassimilated in the interpretative achievements of pragmatic, epistemic, and moral mastery of the demands and challenges of everyday situations; it effects an openness to the expurgated elements of the unconscious, the fantastic, and the mad, the material and the bodily, thus to everything in our speechless contact with reality which is fleeting, so contingent, so immediate, so individualized, simultaneously so far and so near that it escapes our usual categorial grasp.

Benjamin called this style of experience 'concentrated distraction' and set it off from the contemplative style of experience. It is in this direction that the characteristics and tendencies of the development of avant-garde art, analyzed repeatedly since Benjamin and Adorno, point. The loss of aura and the importance of allegory are continuous with the destruction of the organically unified work of art and its pretended totality of meaning; one can think here of the incorporation of the ugly, of the negative as such. By treating materials, methods, and techniques reflectively, the artist opens up a space for experiment and play and transfers the activity of the genius to 'free construction' (*Freie Arbeit*).[5] Forced novelty, dependence on the latest trends, and the accelerated pace of fads perpetuate the creative break with tradition and serve to make all stylistic means equally accessible. Art becomes a laboratory, the critic an expert, the development of art the medium of a learning process – here, naturally, not in the sense of an accumulation of epistemic *contents*, of an aesthetic 'progress' – which is possible only in individual dimensions – but nonetheless in the sense of a concentrically expanding, advancing exploration of a realm of possibilities structurally opened up with the autonomization of art. (I do not know whether or not the results of Piaget's genetic psychology are as appropriate for the analysis of this 'level of learning' as they are for the analysis of the stages of postconventional conception of law and morality. I tend to be rather sceptical.)

Martin Jay's other question concerns the relation between the independence of art in a culture of experts and the cultural impoverishment of the life-world. Jay asks why I don't decide unambiguously between Adorno and Benjamin, between the esotericism of the exclusive, often hermetically sealed, avant-garde work of art, and the hope for profane illumination in exoteric mass art. He notes that I seem to find some truth in both positions.

Peter Bürger takes an unambiguous position. In his view, the impulse of several avant-garde movements to rebel against the institutionalization of art, against its being split off from the life-world, was correct despite the failure of the surrealistic revolt.[6] I do not differ with this judgment *per se*. The intention of redeeming a promise of happiness, whose superabundance radiates beyond art, is part of art itself. But this intention cannot be realized in the way in which the surrealists wanted: through the liquidation of appearance as the medium of artistic representation. This false *Aufhebung* of art into life certainly does preclude the possibility of a correct mediation of art with the life-world. An aesthetic experience that is not simply to be transposed into judgments of taste by the professional arbiters, that is not merely to circulate in the realm of art alone, would entail a change in the status of an as it were experimentally unbound subjectivity.

If aesthetic experience is incorporated into the context of individual life-histories, if it is utilized to illuminate a situation and to throw light on individual life-problems – if it communicates at all its impulses to a collective form of life – then art enters into a language game which is no longer that of aesthetic criticism, but belongs, rather, to everyday communicative practice. Then it no longer only affects our evaluative language or only renews the interpretation of needs that color our perceptions; rather, it reaches into our cognitive interpretations and normative expectations and transforms the totality in which these moments are related to each other. In this respect, modern art harbors a utopia that becomes a reality to the degree that the mimetic powers sublimated in the work of art find resonance in the mimetic relations of a balanced and undistorted intersubjectivity of everyday life. However, this does not require the *liquidation* of an art set off from life in the medium of *appearance*, but rather a *changed constellation* of art and the life-world.

I developed these ideas earlier at the suggestion of Albrecht Wellmer.[7] In the meantime, Wellmer has elaborated them in such an ingenious way that I can here be content simply to refer to his treatment.[8] I do not wish to retrace Wellmer's subtle line of argument but only to repeat his main thesis in order to offer it as an answer to Martin Jay's question. The fact that we can dispute the reasons for evaluating a work of art in aesthetic discourse is, as we said, an unmistakable indication for a validity claim inherent in works of art. The aesthetic 'validity' or 'unity' that we attribute to a work refers to its singularly illuminating power to open our eyes to what is seemingly familiar, to disclose anew an apparently familiar reality. This validity claim admittedly stands for a *potential* for 'truth' that can be released only in the whole complexity of life-experience; therefore this 'truth-potential' may not be connected to (or even identified with) one of the three validity claims constitutive for communicative action, as I have been previously inclined to maintain. The one-to-one relationship which exists between the prescriptive validity of a norm and the normative validity claims raised in regulative speech acts is not a proper model for the relation between the potential for truth of works of art and the transformed relations between self and world aesthetic experience. [As Wellmer writes:]

> Neither truth nor truthfulness may be attributed unmetaphorically to works of art, if one understands 'truth' and 'truthfulness' in the sense of a pragmatically differentiated, everyday concept of truth. We can explain the way in which truth and truthfulness – and even normative correctness – are metaphorically interlaced in works of art only by appealing to the fact that the work of art, as a symbolic formation with an aesthetic validity claim, is at the same time an object of the life-world experience, in which the three validity domains are unmetaphorically intermeshed.[9]

Translated by James Bohman

Notes

1 This [part of the] essay is a response to Martin Jay, 'Habermas and Modernism' . . . published in *Praxis International* vol. 4, no. 1 (April 1984) and Thomas McCarthy, 'Reflections on Rationalism in *The Theory of Communicative Action*', *Praxis International* vol. 4, no. 2 (July 1984). When writing this response, I had not yet read the careful chapter on my work by Martin Jay in his *Marxism and Totality* (Berkeley, 1984), pp. 423–60.

2 P. Bürger, *Theory of the Avant Garde*, Minneapolis, 1983; also his 'Institution Kunst,' *Vermittlung, Rezeption, Funktion*, Frankfurt, 1979 and his *Kritik der idealistischen Asthetik*, Frankfurt, 1983.

3 J. Habermas, *Theory of Communicative Action*, Boston, Beacon Press, 1984, vol. 1, pp. 157ff.

4 Ibid., pp. 40ff., and the references given there.

5 P. Bürger, *Kritik*, pp. 104ff.

6 See also P. Bürger, 'Das Altern der Moderne,' *Adorno Konferenz 1983*, ed. Habermas and Freideburg, Frankfurt, 1983, pp. 177ff.

7 Habermas, 'Modernity versus Postmodernity' [see pp. 275–77, this volume].

8 On the following, see A. Wellmer, 'Wahrheit, Schein, Versöhnung,' *Adorno-Konferenz*, pp. 138ff.

9 Ibid., p. 165.

18

POSTMODERNISM AND CONSUMER SOCIETY

Fredric Jameson

The concept of postmodernism is not widely accepted or even understood today. Some of the resistance to it may come from the unfamiliarity of the works it covers, which can be found in all the arts: the poetry of John Ashbery, for instance, as well as the much simpler talk poetry that came out of the reaction against complex, ironic, academic modernist poetry in the 1960s; the reaction against modern architecture and in particular against the monumental buildings of the International Style; the pop buildings and decorated sheds celebrated by Robert Venturi in his manifesto *Learning from Las Vegas*; Andy Warhol, pop art and the more recent Photorealism; in music, the moment of John Cage but also the later synthesis of classical and 'popular' styles found in composers like Philip Glass and Terry Riley, and also punk and new wave rock with such groups as the Clash, Talking Heads and the Gang of Four; in film, everything that comes out of Godard – contemporary vanguard film and video – as well as a whole new style of commercial or fiction films, which has its equivalent in contemporary novels, where the works of William Burroughs, Thomas Pynchon and Ishmael Reed on the one hand, and the French new novel on the other, are also to be numbered among the varieties of what can be called postmodernism.

This list would seem to make two things clear at once. First, most of the postmodernisms mentioned above emerge as specific reactions against the established forms of high modernism, against this or that dominant high modernism which conquered the university, the museum, the art gallery network and the foundations. Those formerly subversive and embattled styles – Abstract Expressionism; the great modernist poetry of Pound, Eliot or Wallace Stevens; the International Style (Le Corbusier, Gropius, Mies van der Rohe); Stravinsky; Joyce, Proust and Mann – felt to be scandalous or shocking by our grandparents are, for the generation which arrives at the gate in the 1960s, felt to be the establishment and the enemy – dead, stifling, canonical, the reified monuments one has to destroy to do anything new. This means that there will be as many different forms of postmodernism as there were high modernisms in place, since the former are at least initially specific and local reactions against those models. That obviously does not make the job of describing postmodernism as a coherent thing any easier, since the unity of this new impulse – if it has one – is given not in itself but in the very modernism it seeks to displace.

The second feature of this list of postmodernisms is the effacement of some key boundaries or separations, most notably the erosion of the older distinction between high culture and so-called mass or popular culture. This is perhaps the most distressing development of all from an academic standpoint, which has traditionally had a vested interest in preserving a realm of high or elite culture against the surrounding environment of philistinism, of schlock and kitsch, of TV series and *Reader's Digest* culture, and in transmitting difficult and complex skills of reading, listening and seeing to its initiates. But many of the newer postmodernisms have been fascinated precisely by that whole landscape of advertising and motels, of the Las Vegas strip, of the Late Show and B-grade Hollywood film, of so-called paraliterature with its airport paperback categories of the gothic and the romance, the popular biography, the murder mystery and the science fiction or fantasy novel. They no longer 'quote' such 'texts' as a Joyce might have done, or a Mahler; they incorporate them, to the point where the line between high art and commercial forms seems increasingly difficult to draw.

A rather different indication of this effacement of the older categories of genre and discourse can be found in what is sometimes called contemporary theory. A generation ago there was still a technical discourse of professional philosophy – the great systems of Sartre or the phenomenologists, the work of Wittgenstein or analytical or common language philosophy – alongside which one could still distinguish that quite different discourse of the other academic disciplines – of political science, for example, or sociology or literary criticism. Today, increasingly, we have a kind of writing simply called 'theory' which is all or none of those things at once. This new kind of discourse, generally associated with France and so-called French theory, is becoming widespread and marks the end of philosophy as such. Is the work of Michel Foucault, for example, to be called philosophy, history, social theory or political science? It's undecidable, as they say nowadays, and I will suggest that such 'theoretical discourse' is also to be numbered among the manifestations of postmodernism.

Now I must say a word about the proper use of this concept: it is not just another word for the description of a particular style. It is also, at least in my use, a periodizing concept whose function is to correlate the emergence of new formal features in culture with the emergence of a new type of social life and a new economic order – what is often euphemistically called modernization, post-industrial or consumer society, the society of the media or the spectacle, or multinational capitalism. This new moment of capitalism can be dated from the post-war boom in the United States in the late 1940s and early 1950s or, in France, from the establishment of the Fifth Republic in 1958. The 1960s are in many ways the key transitional period, a period in which the new international order (neo-colonialism, the Green Revolution, computerization and electronic information) is at one and the same time set in place and is swept and shaken by its own internal contradictions and by external resistance. I want here to sketch a few of the ways in which the new postmodernism expresses the inner truth of that newly emergent social order of late capitalism, but will have to limit the description to only two of its significant features, which I will call pastiche and schizophrenia; they will give us a chance to sense the specificity of the postmodernist experience of space and time respectively.

Pastiche eclipses parody

One of the most significant features or practices in postmodernism today is pastiche. I must first explain this term (from the language of the visual arts), which people generally tend to confuse with or assimilate to that related verbal phenomenon called parody. Both pastiche and parody involve the imitation or, better still, the mimicry of other styles and particularly of the mannerisms and stylistic twitches of other styles. It is obvious that modern literature in general offers a very rich field for parody, since the great modern writers have all been defined by the invention or production of rather unique styles: think of the Faulknerian long sentence or of D.H. Lawrence's characteristic nature imagery; think of Wallace Steven's peculiar way of using abstractions; think also of mannerisms of the philosophers, of Heidegger for example, or Sartre; think of the musical styles of Mahler or Prokofiev. All of these styles, however different from one another, are comparable in this: each is quite unmistakable; once one of them is learned, it is not likely to be confused with something else.

Now parody capitalizes on the uniqueness of these styles and seizes on their idiosyncrasies and eccentricities to produce an imitation which mocks the original. I won't say that the satiric impulse is conscious in all forms of parody: in any case, a good or great parodist has to have some secret sympathy for the original, just as a great mimic has to have the capacity to put himself/herself in the place of the person imitated. Still, the general effect of parody is – whether in sympathy or with malice – to cast ridicule on the private nature of these stylistic mannerisms and their excessiveness and eccentricity with respect to the way people normally speak or write. So there remains somewhere behind all parody the feeling that there is a linguistic norm in contrast to which the styles of the great modernists can be mocked.

But what would happen if one no longer believed in the existence of normal language, of ordinary speech, of the linguistic norm (the kind of clarity and communicative power celebrated by Orwell in his famous essay 'Politics and the English Language', say)? One could think of it in this way: perhaps the immense fragmentation and privatization of modern literature – its explosion into a host of distinct private styles and mannerisms – foreshadows deeper and more general tendencies in social life as a whole. Supposing that modern art and modernism – far from being a kind of specialized aesthetic curiosity – actually anticipated social developments along these lines; supposing that in the decades since the emergence of the great modern styles society had itself begun to fragment in this way, each group coming to speak a curious private language of its own, each profession developing its private code or idiolect, and finally each individual coming to be a kind of linguistic island, separated from everyone else? But then in that case, the very possibility of any linguistic norm in terms of which one could ridicule private languages and idiosyncratic styles would vanish, and we would have nothing but stylistic diversity and heterogeneity.

That is the moment at which pastiche appears and parody has become impossible. Pastiche is, like parody, the imitation of a peculiar or unique style, the wearing of a stylistic mask, speech in a dead language: but it is a neutral practice of such mimicry, without parody's ulterior motive, without the satirical impulse, without laughter, without that still latent feeling that there exists something *normal* compared with which what is being imitated is rather comic. Pastiche is blank parody, parody that has lost its sense of humour: pastiche is to parody what that curious thing, the modern practice of a kind of blank irony, is to what Wayne Booth calls the stable and comic ironies of the eighteenth century.[1]

The death of the subject

But now we need to introduce a new piece into this puzzle, which may help to explain why classical modernism is a thing of the past and why postmodernism should have taken its place. This new component is what is generally called the 'death of the subject' or, to say it in more conventional language, the end of individualism as such. The great modernisms were, as we have said, predicated on the invention of a personal, private style, as unmistakable as your fingerprint, as incomparable as your own body. But this means that the modernist aesthetic is in some way organically linked to the conception of a unique self and private identity, a unique personality and individuality, which can be expected to generate its own unique vision of the world and to forge its own unique, unmistakable style.

Yet today, from any number of distinct perspectives, the social theorists, the psychoanalysts, even the linguists, not to speak of those of us who work in the area of culture and cultural and formal change, are all exploring the notion that this kind of individualism and personal identity is a thing of the past; that the old individual or individualist subject is 'dead'; and that one might even describe the concept of the unique individual and the theoretical basis of individualism as ideological. There are in fact two positions on all this, one of which is more radical than the other. The first one is content to say: yes, once upon a time, in the classic age of competitive capitalism, in the heyday of the nuclear family and the emergence of the bourgeoisie as the hegemonic social class, there was such a thing as individualism, as individual subjects. But today, in the age of corporate capitalism, of the so-called organization man, of bureaucracies in business as well as in the state, of demographic explosion – today, that older bourgeois individual subject no longer exists.

Then there is a second position, the more radical of the two – what one might call the poststructuralist position. It adds: not only is the bourgeois individual subject a thing of the past, it is also a myth; it never really existed in the first place; there have never been autonomous subjects of that type. Rather, this construct is merely a philosophical and cultural mystification which sought to persuade people that they 'had' individual subjects and possessed some unique personal identity.

For our purposes, it is not particularly important to decide which of these positions is correct (or rather, which is more interesting and productive). What we have to retain from all this is rather an aesthetic dilemma: because if the experience and the ideology of the unique self, an experience and ideology which informed the stylistic practice of classical modernism, is over and done with, then it is no longer clear what the artists and writers of the present period are supposed to be doing. What is clear is merely that the older models – Picasso, Proust, T.S. Eliot – do not work any more (or are positively harmful), since nobody has that kind of unique private world and style to express any longer. And this is perhaps not merely a 'psychological' matter: we also have to take into account the immense weight of seventy or eighty years of classical modernism itself. This is yet another sense in which the writers and artists of the present day will no longer be able to invent new styles and worlds – they've already been invented; only a limited number of combinations are possible; the unique ones have been thought of already. So the weight of the whole modernist aesthetic tradition – now dead – also 'weighs like a nightmare on the brain of the living', as Marx said in another context.

Hence, once again, pastiche: in a world in which stylistic innovation is no longer possible, all that is left is to imitate dead styles, to speak through the masks and with the voices of the styles in the imaginary museum. But this means that contemporary or postmodernist art is going to be about art itself in a new kind of way; even more, it means that one of its essential messages will involve the necessary failure of art and the aesthetic, the failure of the new, the imprisonment in the past.

The nostalgia mode

As this may seem very abstract, I want to give a few examples, one of which is so omnipresent that we rarely link it with the kinds of developments in high art discussed here. This particular practice of pastiche is not high-cultural but very much within mass culture, and it is generally known as the 'nostalgia film' (what the French neatly call *la mode rétro* – retrospective styling). We must conceive of this category in the broadest way. Narrowly, no doubt, it consists merely of films about the past and about specific generational moments of that past. Thus, one of the inaugural films in this new 'genre' (if that's what it is) was Lucas's *American Graffiti*, which in 1973 set out to recapture all the atmosphere and stylistic peculiarities of the 1950s United States: the United States of the Eisenhower era. Polanski's great film *Chinatown* (1974) does something similar for the 1930s, as does Bertolucci's *The Conformist* (1969) for the Italian and European context of the same period, the fascist era in Italy; and so forth. We could go on listing these films for some time. But why call them pastiche? Are they not, rather, work in the more traditional genre known as the historical film – work which can more simply be theorized by extrapolating that other well-known form, the historical novel?

I have my reasons for thinking that we need new categories for such films. But let me first add some anomalies: supposing I suggested that *Star Wars* (George Lucas, 1977) is also a nostalgia film. What could that mean? I presume that we can agree that this is not a historical film about our own intergalactic past. Let me put it somewhat differently: one of the most important cultural experiences of the generations that grew up from the 1930s to the 1950s was the Saturday afternoon serial of the Buck Rogers type – alien villains, true American heroes, heroines in distress, the death ray or the doomsday box, and the cliff-hanger at the end whose miraculous solution was to be witnessed next Saturday afternoon. *Star Wars* reinvents this experience in the form of a pastiche; there is no point to a parody of such serials, since they are long extinct. Far from being a pointless satire of such dead forms, *Star Wars* satisfies a deep (might I even say repressed?) longing to experience them again: it is a complex object in which on some first level children and adolescents can take the adventures straight, while the adult public is able to gratify a deeper and more properly nostalgic desire to return to that older period and to live its strange old aesthetic artefacts through once again. This film is thus *metonymically* a historical or nostalgia film. Unlike *American Graffiti*, it does not reinvent a picture of the past in its lived totality; rather, by reinventing the feel and shape of characteristic art objects of an older period (the serials), it seeks to reawaken a sense of the past associated with those objects. *Raiders of the Lost Ark* (1981), meanwhile, occupies an intermediary position here: on some level it is about the 1930s and 1940s, but in reality it too conveys that period metonymically through its own characteristic adventure stories (which are no longer ours).

Now let me discuss another anomaly which may take us further towards understanding nostalgia film in particular and pastiche generally. This one involves a recent film called *Body Heat* (Lawrence Kasdan, 1981), which, as has abundantly been pointed out by the critics, is a kind of distant remake of *Double Indemnity* (1944). (The allusive and elusive plagiarism of older plots is, of course, also a feature of pastiche.) Now *Body Heat* is technically not a nostalgia film, since it takes place in a contemporary setting, in a little Florida village near Miami. On the other hand, this technical contemporaneity is most ambiguous indeed: the credits – always our first cue – are all lettered in a 1930s Art-Deco style which cannot but trigger nostalgic reactions (first to *Chinatown*, no doubt, and then beyond it to some more historical referent). Then the very style of the hero himself is ambiguous: William Hurt is a new star but has nothing of the distinctive style of the preceding generation of male superstars like Steve McQueen or Jack Nicholson, or rather, his persona here is a kind of mix of their characteristics with an older role of the type generally associated with Clark Gable. So here too there is a faintly archaic feel to all this. This spectator begins to wonder why this story, which could have been situated anywhere, is set in a small Florida town, in spite of its contemporary reference. One begins to realize after a while that the small town setting has a crucial strategic function: it allows the film to do without most of the signals and references which we might associate with the contemporary world, with consumer society – the appliances and artefacts, the high rises, the object world of late capitalism. Technically, then, its objects (its cars, for instance) are 1980s products, but everything in the film conspires to blur that immediate contemporary reference and to make it possible to receive this too as nostalgia work – as a narrative set in some indefinable nostalgic past, an eternal 1930s, say, beyond history. It seems to me exceedingly symptomatic to find the very style of nostalgia films invading and colonizing even those movies today which have contemporary settings, as though, for some reason, we were unable today to focus our own present, as though we had become incapable of achieving aesthetic representations of our own current experience. But if that is so, then it is a terrible indictment of consumer capitalism itself – or, at the very least, an alarming and pathological symptom of a society that has become incapable of dealing with time and history.

So now we come back to the question of why nostalgia film or pastiche is to be considered different from the older historical novel or film. I should also include in this discussion the major literary example of all this, to my mind: the novels of E.L. Doctorow – *Ragtime*, with its turn-of-the-century atmosphere, and *Loon Lake*, for the most part about our 1930s. But these are, in my opinion, historical novels in appearance only. Doctorow is a serious artist and one of the few genuinely left or radical novelists at work today. It is no disservice to him, however, to suggest that his narratives do not represent our historical past so much as they represent our ideas or cultural stereotypes about that past. Cultural production has been driven back inside the mind, within the monadic subject: it can no longer look directly out of its eyes at the real world for the referent but must, as in Plato's cave, trace its mental images of the world on its confining walls. If there is any realism left here, it is a 'realism' which springs from the shock of grasping that confinement and of realizing that, for whatever peculiar reasons, we seem condemned to seek the historical past through our own pop images and stereotypes about the past, which itself remains forever out of reach.

Postmodernism and the city

Now, before I try to offer a somewhat more positive conclusion, I want to sketch the analysis of a full-blown postmodern building – a work which is in many ways uncharacteristic of that postmodern architecture whose principal names are Robert Venturi, Charles Moore, Michael Graves and more recently Frank Gehry, but which to my mind offers some very striking lessons about the originality of postmodernist space. Let me amplify the figure which has run through the preceding remarks, and make it even more explicit: I am proposing the notion that we are here in the presence of something like a mutation in built space itself. My implication is that we ourselves, the human subjects who happen into this new space, have not kept pace with that evolution; there has been a mutation in the object, unaccompanied as yet by any equivalent mutation in the subject; we do not yet possess the perceptual equipment to match this new hyperspace, as I will call it, in part because our perceptual habits were formed in that older kind of space I have called the space of high modernism. The newer architecture – like many of the other cultural products I have evoked in the preceding remarks – therefore stands as something like an imperative to grow new organs to expand our sensoria and our bodies to some new, as yet unimaginable, perhaps ultimately impossible, dimensions.

The Bonaventure Hotel

The building whose features I will enumerate here is the Westin Bonaventure Hotel, built in the new Los Angeles downtown by the architect and developer John Portman, whose other works include the various Hyatt Regencies, the Peachtree Center in Atlanta, and the Renaissance Center in Detroit. I must mention the populist aspect of the rhetorical defence of postmodernism against the elite (and utopian) austerities of the great architectural modernisms: it is generally affirmed that these newer buildings are popular works on the one hand; and that they respect the vernacular of the American city fabric on the other. That is to say that they no longer attempt, as did the masterworks and monuments of high modernism, to insert a different, distinct, an elevated, a new utopian language into the tawdry and commercial sign-system of the surrounding city, but on the contrary, seek to speak that very language, using its lexicon and syntax, that has been emblematically 'learned from Las Vegas'.

On the first of these counts, Portman's Bonaventure fully confirms the claim: it is a popular building, visited with enthusiasm by locals and tourists alike (although Portman's other buildings are even more successful in this respect). The populist insertion into the city fabric is, however, another matter, and it is with this that we will begin. There are three entrances to the Bonaventure: one from Figueroa, and the other two by way of elevated gardens on the other side of the hotel, which is built into the remaining slope of the former Beacon Hill. None of these is anything like the old hotel marquee, or the monumental *porte-cochère* with which the sumptuous buildings of yesteryear were wont to stage your passage from city street to the older interior. The entryways of the Bonaventure are, as it were, lateral and rather backdoor affairs: the gardens in the back admit you to the sixth floor of the towers, and even there you must walk down one flight to find the elevator by which you gain access to the lobby. Meanwhile, what one is still tempted to think of as the front entry, on Figueroa, admits you, baggage and all, onto the second-storey balcony, from which you must take an escalator down to the main registration desk. More about these elevators and escalators in a moment. What I first want to suggest about these curiously unmarked ways-in is that they seem to have been imposed by some new category of closure governing the inner space of the hotel itself (and this over and above the material constraints under which Portman had to work). I believe that, with a certain number of other characteristic postmodern buildings, such as the Beaubourg in Paris, or the Eaton Center in Toronto, the Bonaventure aspires to being a total space, a complete world, a kind of miniature city (and I would want to add that to this new total space corresponds a new collective practice, a new mode in which individuals move and congregate, something like the practice of a new and historically original kind of hyper-crowd). In this sense, then, the mini-city of Portman's Bonaventure ideally ought not to have entrances at all (since the entryway is always the seam that links the building to the rest of the city that surrounds it), for it does not wish to be a part of the city, but rather its equivalent and its replacement or substitute. That is, however, obviously not possible or practical, hence the deliberate downplaying and reduction of the entrance function to its bare minimum. But this disjunction from the surrounding city is very different from that of the great monuments of the International Style: there, the act of disjunction was violent, visible and had a very real symbolic significance – as in Le Corbusier's great *pilotis*, whose gesture radically separates the new utopian space of the modern from the degraded and fallen city fabric, which it thereby explicitly repudiates (although the gamble of the modern was that this new utopian space, in the virulence of its Novum, would fan out and transform that eventually by the power of its new spatial language). The Bonaventure, however, is content to 'let the fallen city fabric continue to be in its being' (to parody Heidegger); no further effects – no larger protopolitical utopian transformation – are either expected or desired.

This diagnosis is, to my mind, confirmed by the great reflective glass skin of the Bonaventure, whose function might first be interpreted as developing a thematics of reproductive technology. Now, on a second reading, one would want to stress the way in which the glass skin repels the city outside; a repulsion for which we have analogies in those reflective sunglasses which make it impossible for your interlocutor to see your own eyes and thereby achieve a certain aggressivity towards and power over the Other. In a similar way, the glass skin achieves a peculiar and placeless dissociation of the Bonaventure from its neighbourhood: it is not even an exterior, inasmuch as when you seek to look at the hotel's outer walls you cannot see the hotel itself, but only the distorted images of everything that surrounds it.

Now I want to say a few words about escalators and elevators. Given their very real pleasures in Portman's architecture – particularly these last, which the artist has termed 'gigantic kinetic sculptures' and which certainly account for much of the spectacle and the excitement of the hotel interior, especially in the Hyatts, where like great Japanese lanterns or gondolas they ceaselessly rise and fall – and given such a deliberate marking and foregrounding in their own right, I believe one has to see such 'people movers' (Portman's own term, adapted from Disney) as something a little more meaningful than mere functions and engineering components. We know in any case that recent architectural theory has begun to borrow from narrative analysis in other fields, and to attempt to see our physical trajectories through such buildings as virtual narratives or stories, as dynamic paths and narrative paradigms which we as visitors are asked to fulfil and to complete with our own bodies and movements. In the Bonaventure, however, we find a dialectical heightening of this process. It seems to me that not only do the escalators and elevators here henceforth replace movement, but also and above all designate themselves as new reflexive signs and emblems of movement proper (something which will become evident when we come to the whole question of what remains of older forms of movement in this building, most notably walking itself). Here the narrative stroll has been underscored, symbolized, reified and replaced by a transportation machine which becomes the allegorical signifier of that older promenade we are no longer allowed to conduct on our own. This is a dialectical intensification of the autoreferentiality of all modern culture, which tends to turn upon itself and designate its own cultural production as its content.

I am more at a loss when it comes to conveying the thing itself, the experience of space you undergo when you step off such allegorical devices into the lobby or atrium, with its great central column, surrounded by a miniature lake, the whole positioned between the four symmetrical residential towers with their elevators, and surrounded by rising balconies capped by a kind of greenhouse roof at the sixth level. I am tempted to say that such space makes it impossible for us to use the language of volume or volumes any longer, since these last are impossible to seize. Hanging streamers indeed suffuse this empty space in such a way as to distract systematically and deliberately from whatever form it might be supposed to have; while a constant busyness gives the feeling that emptiness is here absolutely packed, that it is an element within which you yourself are immersed, without any of that distance that formerly enabled the perception of perspective or volume. You are in this hyperspace up to your eyes and your body; and if it seemed to you before that the suppression of depth observable in postmodern painting or literature would necessarily be difficult to achieve in architecture itself, perhaps you may now be willing to see this bewildering immersion as its formal equivalent in the new medium.

Yet escalator and elevator are also, in this context, dialectical opposites; and we may suggest that the glorious movement of the elevator gondolas is also a dialectical compensation for this filled space of the atrium – it gives us the chance of a radically different, but complementary, spatial experience: that of rapidly shooting up through the ceiling and outside, along one of the four symmetrical towers, with the referent, Los Angeles itself, spread out breathtakingly and even alarmingly before us. But even this vertical movement is contained: the elevator lifts you to one of those revolving cocktail lounges, in which you, seated, are again passively rotated about and offered a contemplative spectacle of the city itself, now transformed into its own images by the glass windows through which you view it.

Let me quickly conclude all this by returning to the central space of the lobby itself (with the passing observation that the hotel rooms are visibly marginalized: the corridors in the residential sections are low-ceilinged and dark, most depressingly functional indeed, while one understands that the rooms – frequently redecorated – are in the worst taste). The descent is dramatic enough, plummeting back down through the roof to splash down in the lake; what happens when you get there is something else, which I can only try to characterize as milling confusion, something like the vengeance this space takes on those who still seek to walk through it. Given the absolute symmetry of the four towers, it is quite impossible to get your bearings in this lobby; recently, colour coding and directional signals have been added in a pitiful, rather desperate and revealing attempt to restore the co-ordinates of an older space. I will take as the most dramatic practical result of this spatial mutation the notorious dilemma of the shopkeepers on the various balconies: it has been obvious, since the very opening of the hotel in 1977, that nobody could ever find any of these stores, and even if you located the appropriate boutique, you would be most unlikely to be as fortunate a second time; as a consequence, the commercial tenants are in despair and all the merchandise is marked down to bargain prices. When you recall that Portman is a businessman as well as an architect, and a millionaire developer, an artist who is at one and the same time a capitalist in his own right, you cannot but feel that here too something of a 'return of the repressed' is involved.

So I come finally to my principal point here, that this latest mutation in space – postmodern hyperspace – has finally succeeded in transcending the capacities of the individual human body to locate itself, to organize its immediate surroundings perceptually, and to map cognitively its position in a mappable external world. And I have already suggested that this alarming disjunction between the body and its built environment – which is to the initial bewilderment of the older modernism as the velocities of spacecraft are to those of the automobile – can itself stand as the symbol and analogue of that even sharper dilemma, which is the incapacity of our minds, at least at present, to map the great global, multinational and decentred communicational network in which we find ourselves caught as individual subjects.

The new machine

But as I am anxious that Portman's space not be perceived as something either exceptional or seemingly marginalized and leisure-specialized on the order of Disneyland, I would like in passing to juxtapose this complacent and entertaining (although bewildering) leisure-time space with its analogue in a very different area, namely the space of postmodern warfare, in particular as Michael Herr evokes it in his great book on the experience of Vietnam, *Dispatches*. The extraordinary linguistic innovations of this work may be considered postmodern in the eclectic way in which its language impersonally fuses a whole range of contemporary collective idiolects, most notably rock language and black language, but the fusion is dictated by problems of content. This first terrible postmodernist war cannot be recounted in any of the traditional paradigms of the war novel or movie – indeed, that breakdown of all previous narrative paradigms is, along with the breakdown of any shared language through which a veteran might convey such experience, among the principal subjects of the book and may be said to open up the place of a whole new reflexivity. Benjamin's account of Baudelaire, and of the emergence of modernism from a new experience of city technology which transcends all the older habits of bodily perception, is both singularly relevant here and singularly antiquated, in the light of this new and virtually unimaginable quantum leap in technological alienation:

> He was a moving-target-survivor subscriber, a true child of the war, because except for the rare times when you were pinned or stranded the system was geared to keep you mobile, if that was what you thought you wanted. As a technique for staying alive it seemed to make as much sense as anything, given naturally that you were there to begin with and wanted to see it close; it started

> out sound and straight but it formed a cone as it progressed, because the more you moved the more you saw, the more you saw the more besides death and mutilation you risked, and the more you risked of that the more you would have to let go of one day as a 'survivor'. Some of us moved around the war like crazy people until we couldn't see which way the run was taking us anymore, only the war all over its surface with occasional, unexpected penetration. As long as we could have choppers like taxis it took real exhaustion or depression near shock or a dozen pipes of opium to keep us even apparently quiet, we'd still be running around inside our skins like something was after us, ha, ha, La Vida Loca. In the months after I got back the hundreds of helicopters I'd flown in began to draw together until they'd formed a collective meta-chopper, and in my mind it was the sexiest thing going; saver–destroyer, provider–waster, right hand–left hand, nimble, fluent, canny and human; hot steel, grease, jungle-saturated canvas webbing, sweat cooling and warming up again, cassette rock and roll in one ear and door-gun fire in the other, fuel, heat, vitality and death, death itself, hardly an intruder.[2]

In this new machine, which does not, like the older modernist machinery of the locomotive or the airplane, represent motion, but which can only be represented *in motion*, something of the mystery of the new postmodernist space is concentrated.

The aesthetic of consumer society

Now I must try, in conclusion, to characterize the relationship of cultural production of this kind to social life in this country today. This will also be the moment to address the principal objection to concepts of postmodernism of the type I have sketched here: namely that all the features we have enumerated are not new at all but abundantly characterized modernism proper or what I call high modernism. Was not Thomas Mann, after all, interested in the idea of pastiche, and is not 'The Oxen of the Sun' chapter of *Ulysses* its most obvious realization? Can Flaubert, Mallarmé and Gertrude Stein not be included in an account of postmodernist temporality? What is so new about all of this? Do we really need the concept of postmodernism?

One kind of answer to this question would raise the whole issue of periodization and of how a historian (literary or other) posits a radical break between two henceforth distinct periods. I must limit myself to the suggestion that radical breaks between periods do not generally involve complete changes of content but rather the restructuring of a certain number of elements already given: features that in an earlier period or system were subordinate now become dominant, and features that had been dominant again become secondary. In this sense, everything we have described here can be found in earlier periods and most notably within modernism proper. My point is that until the present day those things have been secondary or minor features of modernist art, marginal rather than central, and that we have something new when they become the central features of cultural production.

But I can argue this more concretely by turning to the relationship between cultural production and social life generally. The older or classical modernism was an oppositional art; it emerged within the business society of the gilded age as scandalous and offensive to the middle-class public – ugly, dissonant, bohemian, sexually shocking. It was something to make fun of (when the police were not called in to seize the books or close the exhibitions): an offense to good taste and to common sense, or, as Freud and Marcuse would have put it, a provocative challenge to the reigning reality- and performance-principles of early twentieth-century middle-class society. Modernism in general did not go well with overstuffed Victorian furniture, with Victorian moral taboos, or with the conventions of polite society. This is to say that whatever the explicit political content of the great high modernisms, the latter were always in some mostly implicit ways dangerous and explosive, subversive within the established order.

If then we suddenly return to the present day, we can measure the immensity of the cultural changes that have taken place. Not only are Joyce and Picasso no longer weird and repulsive, they have become classics and now look rather realistic to us. Meanwhile, there is very little in either the form or the content of contemporary art that contemporary society finds intolerable and scandalous. The most offensive forms of this art – punk rock, say, or what is called sexually explicit material – are all taken in its stride by society, and they are commercially successful, unlike the productions of the older high modernism. But this means that even if contemporary art has all the same formal features as the older modernism, it has still shifted its position fundamentally within our culture. For one thing, commodity production and in particular our clothing, furniture, buildings and other artefacts are now intimately tied in with styling changes which derive from artistic experimentation; our advertising, for example, is fed by modernism in all the arts and inconceivable without. For another, the classics of high modernism are now part of the so-called canon and are taught in schools and universities – which at once empties them of any of their older subversive power. Indeed, one way of marking the break between the periods and of dating the emergence of postmodernism is precisely to be found there: at the moment (the early 1960s, one would think) in which the position of high modernism and its dominant aesthetics become established in the academy and are henceforth felt to be academic by a whole new generation of poets, painters and musicians.

But one can also come at the break from the other side, and describe it in terms of periods of recent social life. As I have suggested, Marxists and non-Marxists alike have come around to the general feeling that at some point following World War Two a new kind of society began to emerge (variously described as post-industrial society, multinational capitalism, consumer society, media society and so forth). New types of consumption; planned obsolescence; an ever more rapid rhythm of fashion and styling changes; the penetration of advertising, television and the media generally to a hitherto unparalleled degree throughout society; the replacement of the old tension between city and country, centre and province, by the suburb and by universal standardization; the growth of the great networks of superhighways and the arrival of automobile culture – these are some of the features which would seem to mark a radical break with that older pre-war society in which high modernism was still an underground force.

I believe that the emergence of postmodernism is closely related to the emergence of this new moment of late consumer or multinational capitalism. I believe also that its formal features in many ways express the deeper logic of this particular social system. I will only be able, however, to show this for one major theme: namely the disappearance of a sense of history, the way in which our entire contemporary social system has little by little begun to lose its capacity to retain its own past, has begun to live in a perpetual present and in a perpetual change that obliterates traditions of the kind which all earlier social information have had, in one way or another, to preserve. Think only of the media exhaustion of news: of how Nixon and, even more so, Kennedy, are figures from a now distant past. One is tempted to say that the very function of the news media is to relegate such recent historical experiences as rapidly as possible into the past. The informational function of the media would thus be to help us forget, to serve as the very agents and mechanisms for our historical amnesia.

But in that case the two features of postmodernism on which I have dwelt here – the transformation of reality into images, the fragmentation of time into a series of perpetual presents – are both extraordinarily consonant with this process. My own conclusion here must take the form of a question about the critical value of the newer art. There is some agreement that the older modernism functioned against its society in ways which are variously described as critical, negative, contestatory, subversive, oppositional and the like. Can anything of the sort be affirmed about postmodernism and its social moment? We have seen that there is a way in which postmodernism replicates or reproduces – reinforces – the logic of consumer capitalism; the more significant question is whether there is also a way in which it resists that logic. But that is a question we must leave open.

Notes

1 Wayne C. Booth, *The Rhetoric of Irony*, Chicago, 1975.
2 Michael Herr, *Dispatches*, New York, 1977, pp. 8–9.

Part 4

MODERNISM

INTRODUCTION

Georg Simmel	Value and Money
Walter Benjamin	The Work of Art in the Age of Mechanical Reproduction
Maurice Blanchot	The Original Experience
Ernst Bloch	Artistic Illusion as Visible Anticipatory Illumination

There are a number of different aspects to the 'modern'. Principally, the term denotes the period in the history of ideas characterized by the development of man's self-image as an autonomous rational being, distinct from God who, through reason and sensory knowledge, is able to know and manipulate the world. The work of the French rationalist philosopher René Descartes (1596–1650) is often cited as the threshold of modern thought. His *cogito* argument – 'I think, therefore, I am' – identifies the essence of the human being with reason and makes the material aspects of human life, that is, the body, sensory experience, and the natural world, subordinate to rational enquiry. 'Modernity' is the name given to the 'modern' as it applies to cultural experience and society and, as a period, is generally held to begin with the Industrial Revolution in the second half of the eighteenth century. Advances in engineering, the manipulation of materials, and mass construction allowed Western man to exert his influence on the world in an unprecedented way, and meant that human sensibilities began to confront an ever-increasing number of man-made objects and opportunities. Concrete form was thus given to the Cartesian model of the human being as an entity which surveys and acts upon the physical world.

Art and aesthetic experience are, of course, not exempt from these social and ontological changes, and the term 'modernism' is used to cover the period in the arts when composers, writers, artists, and performers react to and accommodate the dynamics of modernity. In this time, from the mid-nineteenth century onwards, an interesting dialectic of reaction, appropriation, and subversion emerges between art and technology. On the one hand, artists begin to define their output in terms of what mechanical reproduction *is not*. To give some examples: modern visual art, starting with impressionism, produces images which photography cannot and, with modern literature, James Joyce introduces contingency and human, unconscious chance into the form of his writing as a response to the typewriter's mechanization of prose. However, on the other hand, it is the availability of these inventions and new possibilities that inspire and give context to the very reactions against them. The 'painted light' of impressionism cannot be divorced from the interest in light created by photography and contemporaneous studies in physics, and the typewriter becomes the machine which promotes unconscious, non-sentential 'automatic' writing.

A similar contradiction affects the modernist's attention to the materiality of her medium. One property of modernist artworks is that their significance resides not so much in *what* they represent as in *the way they represent it*. Emphasis is placed on the transformation or distortion which occurs as a result of the properties inherent in the medium. Art is *intrinsically* valuable, it is claimed, because something is mediated or realized through the process of creation which cannot be achieved by mechanical or mass production. Yet, in trying to define art in opposition to the changes brought about by modernity, certain modern lines of thought are relied upon. First, art is made Cartesian, since the refractive possibilities of art mean it can be presented as 'intellectualized' perception and, therefore, at a remove from ordinary sensation. Second, if art becomes this revolutionary quest for new forms of notation and representation, then it inadvertently allies itself with the economic drive to manipulate material in the name of the 'new'. Critical theory has already shown us some of the complications involved in positioning aesthetic experience within modernity. In this section, Georg Simmel, Walter Benjamin, Maurice Blanchot, and Ernst Bloch extend the debate, paying special attention to notions of distance and defamiliarization as the means by which we measure the aesthetic and ontological dimensions of modern experience.

Georg Simmel

The German philosopher Georg Simmel (1858–1918) is a seminal figure in the sociology of culture. A contemporary of Ferdinand de Saussure and Sigmund Freud, he is one of the first thinkers to stress the interrelationship between consciousness and socio-economic conditions. Although most of his work remains untranslated into English (there are twenty-four volumes in the German collected works), the book he held to be his most important – *The Philosophy of Money* (1900, revised 1907) – is available in translation. In it, Simmel shows how the textures and particularities of consciousness and self-hood are woven into modern urban, economic existence. Money is theoretically significant for him in that it represents the widest form of social and worldly interaction. Whereas barter systems require a coincidence of need, a monetary system is abstract and universal, making an unlimited number of exchanges possible. Against the Marxist criticism that money is man's otherwise continuous and communal interaction with the world alienated and objectified as a quantity, Simmel maintains that, while money might sever traditional, local ties, it nevertheless allows the individual to come into contact with a wider circle of people and objects.

Simmel makes it clear in the 'Preface' to *The Philosophy of Money* that his work is not an economic science of money. His main concern is to show how 'the surface level of economic affairs' is a facet of 'the ultimate values and things of importance in all that is human'. The unity of his investigations, he suggests, lies in 'the possibility – which must be demonstrated – of finding in each of life's details the totality of its meaning'.[1] In this respect, Simmel likens his way of working more to art than to philosophy, for the former concentrates on a particular subject – 'a person, a landscape, a mood' – and relates it to the world, whereas the latter, in confronting its problems, reduces the world to what happens to be manageable.[2]

Kant is one of Simmel's main influences. Just as Kant demonstrates the links between the internal, analytic structure of conceptual judgement and the shape of external, synthetic experience, so *The Philosophy of Money* has a two-part analytic–dialectic structure: the 'analytical part' studies concepts in general, making 'the essence of money intelligible from the conditions and connections of life in general', while the 'synthetic part' looks at how concepts apply to experience, making 'the essence and organization of the [conditions and connections of life] intelligible from the effectiveness of money'.[3]

Furthermore, Simmel's theory of value in *The Philosophy of Money* is founded upon Kantian epistemology, as is evident in the opening section of the first chapter, reproduced below. 'Value and Money' explores the relationship between value, cognition, and economic activity. Our sense of value, of worth, of significance, Simmel declares, has the same structure as cognition. In order for us to find something valuable or meaningful, there must be a distance or divide between consciousness and its object, otherwise there would be no difference between the way objects are arranged in nature and the way we arrange them according to our priorities. Occasions when the loss of an object makes us realize just how important it was to us are reminiscent of the 'distance' in value. Similarly, a gap must open up between subject and object for there to be any experience at all: there has to be some sense that what I perceive is other than me for there to be an awareness of both self and world. On this account, subjectivity and objectivity are abstractions from experience, based on the Kantian premise that the two are in fact interwoven as a condition of possibility of experience. Following Kant's dictum that the possibility of experience is the possibility of the objects of experience, Simmel argues that 'the possibility of desire is the possibility of the objects of desire. The object thus formed, which is characterized by its separation from the subject, who at the same time establishes it and seeks to overcome it by his desire, is for us a value'.

The origin of aesthetic experience provides Simmel with an analogy for the process whereby value emerges as something distant from the brute causal order of things. The appreciation of art or beauty, he affirms, is an objective and 'distant' phenomenon in the sense that 'when I call an object beautiful, its quality and significance become much more independent of the arrangements and the needs of the subject than if it is merely useful'. Thus, disinterested reflection, where we are not interested in the thing itself but in the way it stimulates our faculties, exemplifies the process of objectification whereby value emerges as a zone of appreciation distinct from a mere utilitarian handling of objects. What is especially significant about Simmel's analogy with aesthetic value is that it allows him to show that distance is not a principle of alienation but one of motivation and integration: 'the longing, effort and sacrifice that separate us from objects are also supposed to lead us towards them'; we are temporarily stopped in our tracks by an artwork only for our practical engagement with things to be reaffirmed. The aesthetic, reciprocal relationship between 'withdrawal and approach' he also finds in economic activity's creation and overcoming of distance. In the same way that the aesthetic detaches itself from practical value but nonetheless directs us back to the world, so money comes into being as an independent system of exchange that *nevertheless* extends our potential for activity in the world. It can always be asked whether the status of art and the status of money are such that they return us to our engagement with others or that they become ends in themselves. This is a principal concern of critical theory. The question is not addressed in 'Value and Money' although, later in *The Philosophy of Money*, Simmel does claim of the miser (and therefore, by analogy, the capitalist), who hoards money as an end in itself, that his is a perverted use of money.[4] Beyond this, the political and ethical implications of the ontologies of art and economic exchange remain ongoing debates in contemporary theory.

Walter Benjamin

The German theorist and critic Walter Benjamin (1892–1940) is one of the leading thinkers on modernity. The scope and diversity of his work are uncannily appropriate to his position on modern culture. With stylistic forms including prose, dialogue, and aphorism, and subjects ranging from colour in Kant, German tragic drama, translation, and history, to surrealism, Baudelaire, city life, and the arcades of Paris, his *œuvre* represents the fragmentary, ever-changing flow of stimuli he held to be definitive of modern urban experience. The observations he made on suicide in his study of Baudelaire, however, have assumed a terrible poignancy. Benjamin took his own life on the night of 25 September 1940 while fleeing from the Nazis. Refused a pass at the French–Spanish border, he could not face the thought of being captured by the Gestapo. Suicide, Benjamin wrote in *Charles Baudelaire*, 'is not a resignation but a heroic passion. It is *the* achievement of modernism in the realm of the passions'.[5] The concept of suicide as a heroic act is based upon Baudelaire's concept of the modern artist as hero, defiant in the face of hostility. Suicide is 'an act which seals a heroic will that makes no concessions to a mentality inimical towards this will'.[6] The Cartesian structure of modernism and modernity means the individual is always ultimately conceived as an entity who stands before or against the world. Even the Second World War can be seen to rest upon the oppositions of modernity when one considers the technological mastery which enabled it, and the commitment to a universal, overriding truth which motivated it. On these terms, suicide becomes the expression of a will that makes no concessions to modernity.

'The Work of Art in the Age of Mechanical Reproduction' (1936) considers the changes undergone by art and representation in modernity. With connections being drawn between art, politics, and signification, and with implications that prepare the ground for postmodernity, it is understandable why this has become the essay for which Benjamin is most well known. A pre-modern work of art, Benjamin suggests, invites critical contemplation because it is 'authentic': it is rooted in a tradition and, therefore, requires knowledge of the tradition in order to be appreciated. However, mechanical reproduction threatens authenticity, since works can be reproduced out of context and *ad infinitum*, reduced to one unit among many in a homogeneous flow of moving images. The work of art, in this respect, to introduce Benjamin's famous concept, is losing its 'aura'.

Benjamin defines 'aura' in terms of distance. Scanning a mountain range on the horizon or watching the play of shadows cast by a branch, as experiences, are outside us and cannot be brought any nearer without changing the nature of the experience. Both the mountain range and the branch, Benjamin avers, have to be in their particular setting otherwise we would not be able to appreciate the way *their position in relation to us* affects our sensibilities. Against this, he claims, mechanical reproduction seeks to give us everything here and now. It nullifies the aura of natural and historical objects by bringing them closer, by effacing the relationships which locate an object and which make it the particular thing it is. Earlier techniques of reproduction, worked by hand, took time to complete and their end products required time for contemplation, whereas film and photography reproduce their objects and deliver their images with an immediacy that leaves no time for the formation of critical judgement after the initial impact. Art is now something that happens to us rather than an object which we frame and consider from a distance.

The epilogue to 'The Work of Art' relates perception in modernity to the prospect of war. The final paragraph offers sombre reflection: 'mankind's self-alienation has reached such a degree', Benjamin writes, 'that it can experience its own self-destruction as an aesthetic pleasure of the first-order'. War, he suggests, is a fascist response to the unemployment and the inequalities which result when 'the tremendous means of production' are not properly integrated in society. It is an analogous lack of integration that Benjamin finds in the experience of film; in this case, a lack of integration with the faculties of contemplation and judgement which allow the viewer to consider the implications of what she is seeing. Just as war is regarded as the provider of solutions, so it becomes a source of artistic gratification for a medium in which any objective, referential value is suspended.

Experience has certainly borne out Benjamin's claim that perception changes with technology, and the interwoven logics of representation and war have been developed by Baudrillard. However, what has also emerged is that perception evolves in such a way as to generate the possibility of critical distance and scope for new forms of reproduction. Thus, for example, we are now sufficiently familiar with film in order to be able to locate any example within a genre and, therefore, to experience a gap between image and object rather than just a homogeneous flow with no room for comment. This possibility was either something Benjamin failed to anticipate or something he judged to be too optimistic for the time in which he was writing. The question nevertheless raises an interesting contrast between Benjamin and Simmel. Whereas the aesthetic in Benjamin's account loses its auratic, critical dimension to technology, Simmel sees the economic framework of modernity keeping perception and its object in a healthy dialectic of withdrawal and approach, and he holds onto the aesthetic as a realm which exemplifies this dialectical tension.

Maurice Blanchot

The *œuvre* of the French author Maurice Blanchot (b. 1907) might be summed up as a philosophy of uniqueness. To want to sum up Blanchot's output, though, is to be horribly insensitive to the ideas contained in his novels and critical essays. Blanchot is one of the many twentieth-century Continentals who use the style of their writing to display or perform their thesis; others include Adorno, Bataille, Derrida, Deleuze, and Irigaray. Often described by commentators as 'limpid', Blanchot's prose is transparent yet winding and liquid, touching upon a subject but always leaving you with the feeling that the question is the answer. He is positioned here as a modernist for his avowal of the singularity of the artwork. The question 'what is art?' is a particularly modernist question in the sense that it seeks a realm to call art's own in the face of ever-growing mechanical reproduction. Blanchot's approach is to insist that, if the uniqueness of art is to be ensured, then the question must always remain, to some extent, open. He draws attention to the materiality of writing – the structures and textures inherent in the organization of prose – but, rather than aspiring to a Joycean or Adornian unreadability, he combines lucidity with oxymoron and paradox to thwart the reader's expectations, for example, the artwork is 'a relation with what admits of no relations' and the duplicity of art is 'forgetfulness profoundly forgotten'.

'The Original Experience' is from *The Space of Literature* (1955), a collection of essays exploring the question 'what is literature?'. 'Space', as Smock tells us in her 'Translator's

Introduction', is a rendering of '*espace*' but should not be taken in the sense of a straightforward 'realm' or 'domain'. Instead, to honour Blanchot's intent, we should think of it as the space of 'interval' or 'withdrawal', a space which prevents the full meaning and significance of a work ever being available to the reader. The artwork, Blanchot avers, is never something that can be present with itself. Art is caught up in processes and forms of approach which remove or conceal anything that might resemble an essence as soon as one begins to work towards it; it is 'the intertwining of the Yes and of the No, the ebb and flow of the essential ambiguity'. Space is considered in 'The Original Experience' through the motifs of risk, exile, and death. Both 'risk' (from Rilke) and 'exile' (from Saint-John Perse) have the binary characteristics of inclusion and exclusion, and hold their opposites in a tensile relationship. Just as exile thrusts the individual into the realm that a community negates in order to maintain itself, so risk involves placing one's being and possessions outside oneself in order to reaffirm or consolidate them.

However, it is the indeterminacies surrounding the concept of death which Blanchot uses to keep the question and the space of art open. Death poses a 'radical reversal', a state of undecidability which, he muses, is 'the *original experience* [that] the work [of art] must touch'. With giddying verbal agility, Blanchot takes us from 'the end' as that which no longer 'gives man the power to end – to limit, to separate, and thus to grasp' to death as 'that which never happens to me, so that never do I die'. Rather, others die. Death is something I can never experience. I might witness the passing of others and experience pain and suffering as my own life draws to a close, but death is never present to me as an event or an appointment. It is simply the absence of my relationships with others. Comparisons can be drawn with Heidegger and Levinas. In *Being and Time*, death is conceptualized by Heidegger not as a realizable, empirical event but as a primordial, impending possibility which we are forever thrown towards; it is, he avows, the opening of the horizon in front of which experience takes place.[7] And for Levinas, in 'Time and the Other', the approach of death becomes a relationship with 'something that is absolutely other' in which the individual is made fully aware of the respect for possibility and contingency there must be if the totalizing, homogenizing tendencies of thought are to be resisted.[8] An inevitability which cannot be experienced but which nevertheless opens up the experience of otherness for us stands, on Blanchot's terms, as the paradox which forever leaves the question of art unanswerable.

Ernst Bloch

The concept of hope is central to the work of the German philosopher Ernst Bloch (1885–1977), and is also responsible for much of the controversy surrounding his life. He assigns hope an ontological role, and sets it against the political and economic inequalities created by modern technology. Wishful thinking is theorized as a fundamental capacity to look beyond our present circumstances and visualize what is needed to transform things for the better. The relevance of any idea or artefact, Bloch claims, never belongs entirely to the time of its construction but always points towards 'future maturity'. The Parthenon, he comments in a 1968 interview, 'cannot be written off just because it was built by a slaveholding society'.[9] With any object or idea, there is always an excess of potential meaning which allows it to be appropriated for another cause. Since Hegel is one of Bloch's main influences, it is not surprising that his account should have a lot in common with the critical theorist view that an ostensibly 'negative' system of values nevertheless carries within it the seeds of its own sublation. However, although Bloch was committed to Marxism as the only credible form of social critique, his insistence that ideas always existed as part of an ongoing, utopian dynamic meant that he often adopted political stances which orthodox Marxists found disturbing. His assertion of a dialectical relationship between the 'hopeful' individual and social freedom led him into a long dispute with his old friend Georg Lukács over the emancipatory value of expressionism (Bloch was for, Lukács against), and his defence of Stalinist Russia (which he saw in a positive light when compared with the threat of fascism) prompted members of the Frankfurt School to ostracize him when he followed them to America in 1938.

Throughout his life, Bloch remained committed to the view that art and literature were the primary sources of hope in a society. Ontological hope is made tangible in art as visible 'anticipatory illumination'. The phrase is Zipes and Mecklenburg's translation of the original '*Vor-Schein*'; other translators have used 'preappearance' (Plaice *et al.* in *The Principle of Hope*) and 'ontological anticipation' (Jameson in *Marxism and Form*).[10] 'Anticipatory illumination' refers to the capacity of the individual to look beyond life in its present form with the conviction that new, alternative futures are realizable. It is an extension of Bloch's thesis that 'truth is not the reflection of facts but of processes' and, in 'Literature and Socialist Objects' (1938), where he first coins the term, he describes it as 'the indication of the tendency and latency of that which has not yet become and needs its activator'.[11] Distance appears again as the central metaphor. One understanding of art, Bloch observes, is that its images and narratives, as departures from reality, are just opiates for the people, illusions that merely gratify our sensibilities in a disinterested fashion. However, against this, Bloch argues that the 'illusions' of art can stimulate anticipation of what is to come by distancing the viewer from her current standpoint. He is drawing here on the avant-garde project of defamiliarization: the search for new forms of representation which break with convention and deliver reality (or an unrecognized aspect of it) to us in a way which reinvigorates our perception of the world. Expressionist art achieves this the most, Bloch avers, through its use of montage: the metaphor-like technique of taking a term or image from one context and reapplying it in another. Shocked and unsettled by this intervention in the routine order of representation, the viewer is thrown back from the regular patterns of her everyday life and encouraged to reflect upon what might lie beyond the categories and classifications of her present existence.

Metaphor is also a distinctive feature of Bloch's prose. His description of a single subject can often involve the combination of radically different images and tropes, requiring the reader to make several leaps in thought. The metaphors of 'rounding', 'fragment', and 'horizon' are at the root of the late essay 'Artistic Illusion as Visible Anticipatory Illumination' (1959), possibly Bloch's richest exposition of the mechanisms by which art opens up new possibilities. An artwork is 'rounded' in the sense that the elements within it are arranged not for an explosive effect but in order to achieve a tension, a tension which lets the universal be seen in the particular. As Bloch admits, Aristotle's thoughts on entelechy – the realization by a particular of the potential contained in its universal – are not far away. Suddenly, the 'fragmentary' becomes a very important ontological category, for the illuminatory capacity of an artwork is seen to follow from the recognition that both art and world exist in a state of incompleteness, in a state of needing-to-be-realized. A world conceived in pieces, where some of those pieces are art, however, is a utopian image, for it signifies a world under construction, a world with 'real possibilities within it'. The relationship between art and world is the relationship between fragment and horizon. A fragment's jagged edge is what is immediately present to us yet, as a fragment, it implies the possibility of completion, where the intervening distance is pictured not as a finished jigsaw but as 'matter that is pending in the process', a movement that is visible but whose outcomes remain to be decided.

Notes

1 Georg Simmel, *The Philosophy of Money*, trans. Tom Bottomore and David Frisby, London, Routledge, 1990, p. 55.
2 Ibid., p. 55.
3 Ibid., p. 54.
4 Ibid., pp. 228–57.
5 Walter Benjamin, *Charles Baudelaire*, trans. Harry Zohn and Quinton Hoare, London, Verso, 1983, p. 75.
6 Ibid., p. 75.
7 Martin Heidegger, *Being and Time*, trans. John Macquarrie and Edward Robinson, Oxford, Blackwell, 1995, §§46–53.
8 Emmanuel Levinas, 'Time and the Other', *The Levinas Reader*, ed. Séan Hand, Oxford, Blackwell, 1996, p. 43.
9 Interview with Michael Landmann, quoted by Jack Zipes in his 'Introduction' to Ernst Bloch, *The Utopian Function of Art and Literature*, trans. Jack Zipes and Frank Mecklenburg, Cambridge, Massachusetts, MIT Press, 1996, p. xii. Original source: Michael Landmann, 'Talking with Ernst Bloch: Korcula, 1968', *Telos*, 1975, vol. 25, pp. 183–84.
10 See Ernst Bloch, *The Principle of Hope*, vol. 1, trans. Neville Plaice, Stephen Plaice, and Paul Knight, Cambridge, Massachusetts, MIT Press, 1986, and Fredric Jameson, *Marxism and Form*, Princeton, Princeton University Press, 1971.
11 Quoted by Jack Zipes in his 'Introduction' to Ernst Bloch, *The Utopian Function of Art and Literature*, p. xx. Original source: Ernst Bloch, 'Dichtung und sozialistische Gegenstände', *Literarische Aufsätze*, in *Gesamtausgabe*, vol. 9, Frankfurt am Main, Suhrkamp, 1977, p. 141.

19

VALUE AND MONEY

Georg Simmel

Reality and value as mutually independent categories through which our conceptions become images of the world

The order in which things are placed as natural entities is based on the proposition that the whole variety of their qualities rests upon a uniform law of existence. Their equality before the law of nature, the constant sum of matter and energy, the convertibility of the most diverse phenomena into one another, transform the differences that are apparent at first sight into a general affinity, a universal equality. Yet on a closer view this means only that the products of the natural order are beyond any question of a law. Their absolute determinateness does not allow any emphasis that might provide confirmation or doubt of their particular quality of being. But we are not satisfied with this indifferent necessity that natural science assigns to objects. Instead, disregarding their place in that series we arrange them in another order – an order of value – in which equality is completely eliminated, in which the highest level of one point is adjacent to the lowest level of another; in this series the fundamental quality is not uniformity but difference. The value of objects, thoughts and events can never be inferred from their mere natural existence and content, and their ranking according to value diverges widely from their natural ordering. Nature, on many occasions, destroys objects that, in terms of their value, might claim to be preserved, and keeps in existence worthless objects which occupy the place of the more valuable ones. This is not to say that there is a fundamental opposition between the two series, or that they are mutually exclusive. Such a view would imply a relation between the two series; it would establish, indeed, a diabolical world, determined by values, but with the signs reversed. The case is, rather, that the relation between these series is completely accidental. With the same indifference, nature at one time offers us objects that we value highly, at another time withholds them. The occasional harmony between the series, the realization through the reality series of demands derived from the value series, shows the absence of any logical relationship between them just as strikingly as does the opposite case. We may be aware of the same life experience as both real and valuable, but the experience has quite a different meaning in the two cases. The series of natural phenomena could be described in their entirety without mentioning the value of things; and our scale of valuation remains meaningful, whether or not any of its objects appear frequently or at all in reality. Value is an addition to the completely determined objective being, like light and shade, which are not inherent in it but come from a different source. However, we should avoid one misinterpretation; namely, that the formation of value concepts, as a psychological fact, is quite distinct from the natural process. A superhuman mind, which could understand by means of natural laws everything that happens in the world, would also comprehend the fact that people have concepts of values. But these would have no meaning or validity for a being that conceived them purely theoretically, beyond their psychological existence. The meaning of value concepts is denied to nature as a mechanical causal system, while at the same time the psychic experiences that make values a part of our consciousness themselves belong to the natural world. Valuation as a real psychological occurrence is part of the natural world; but what we mean by valuation, its conceptual meaning, is something independent of this world; is not part of it, but is rather the whole world viewed from a particular vantage point. We are rarely aware of the fact that our whole life, from the point of view of consciousness, consists in experiencing and judging values, and that it acquires meaning and significance only from the fact that the mechanically unfolding elements of reality possess an infinite variety of values beyond their objective substance. At any moment when our mind is not simply a passive mirror or reality – which perhaps never happens, since even objective perception can arise only from valuation – we live in a world of values which arranges the contents of reality in an autonomous order.

Thus, value is in a sense the counterpart to being, and is comparable to being as a comprehensive form and category of the world view. As Kant pointed out, being is not a quality of objects; for if I state that an object, which so far existed only in my thoughts, exists, it does not acquire a new quality, because otherwise it would not be the same object that I thought of, but another one. In the same way, an object does not gain a new quality if I call it valuable; it is valued because of the qualities that it has. It is precisely its whole already determined being that is raised to the sphere of value. This is supported by a thorough analysis of our thinking. We are able to conceive the contents of our world view without regard for their real existence or non-existence. We can conceive the aggregates of qualities that we call objects, including all the laws of their interrelation and development, in their objective and logical significance, and we can ask – quite independently of this – whether, where and how often all these concepts or inner notions are realized. The conceptual meaning and determinateness of the objects is not affected by the question as to whether they do exist, nor by the question whether and where they are placed in the scale of values. However, if we want to establish either a theory or a practical rule, we cannot escape the necessity to answer these two questions. We must be able to say of each object that it exists or does not exist and each object must have a definite place for us in the scale of values, from the highest through indifference to negative values. Indifference is a rejection of positive value; the *possibility* of interest remains inactive but is always in the background. The significance of this requirement, which determines the constitution of our world view, is not altered by the fact that our powers of comprehension are often insufficient to decide upon the reality of concepts, or by the fact that the range and certainty of our feelings are often inadequate to rank things according to their value, especially in any permanently and universal fashion. Over against the world of mere concepts, of objective qualities and determinations, stand the great categories of being and value, inclusive forms that take their material from the world of pure contents. Both categories have the quality of being fundamental, that is irreducible to each other or to other simpler elements. Consequently, the being of objects can never be inferred logically; being is rather a primary form of our perception, which can be sensed, experienced and believed, but cannot be deduced for somebody who does not yet know it. When this form of perception has once grasped a specific content – by a non-logical act – it can then be interpreted in its logical context and developed as far as this logical context reaches. As a rule, we are able to state why we assume the reality of a particular phenomenon; namely, because we have already assumed another phenomenon with which this one is connected by its specific characteristics. The reality of the first one, however, can be shown only by tracing it in similar fashion to a more fundamental one. This regression requires a final member whose existence depends only upon a sense of conviction, affirmation and acceptance, a sense that is directly given. Valuation has exactly the same relation to objects. All proofs of the value of an object are nothing more than the necessity of recognizing for that object the same value as has been assumed, and for the time being accepted, as indubitable for another object. We will later analyse the motives of this action. Here it will suffice to say that what we consider a proof of value is only the transference of an existing value to a new object. It does not reveal the essence of value, or the reason why value was originally attached to the object from which it is transferred to others.

If we accept the existence of a value, then the process of its realization, its evolution, can be comprehended rationally, because in general it follows the structure of the contents of reality. That there is a value at all, however, is a primary phenomenon. Value inferences only make known the conditions under which values are realized, yet without being produced by these conditions, just as theoretical proofs only prepare the conditions that favour the sense of affirmation or of existence. The question as to what value really is, like the question as to what being is, is unanswerable. And precisely because they have the same formal relation to objects, they are as alien to each other as are thought and extension for Spinoza. Since both express the same absolute substance, each in its own way and perfect in itself, the one can never encroach upon the other. They never impinge upon each other because they question the concepts of objects from completely different points of view. But this disjunctive parallelism of reality and value does not divide the world into a sterile duality, which the mind with its need for unity could never accept – even though its destiny and the method of its quest may be to move incessantly from diversity to unity and from unity to diversity. What is common to value and reality stands above them: namely the contents, which Plato called 'ideas', the qualitative, that which can be signified and expressed in our concepts of reality and value, and which can enter into either one or the other series. Below these two categories lies what is common to both: the soul, which absorbs the one or produces the other in its mysterious unity. Reality and value are, as it were, two different languages by which the logically related contents of the world, valid in their ideal unity, are made comprehensible to the unitary soul, or the languages in which the soul can express the pure image of these contents which lies beyond their differentiation and opposition. These two compilations made by the soul, through perceiving and through valuing, may perhaps once more be brought together in a metaphysical unity, for which there is no linguistic term unless it be in religious symbols. There is perhaps a cosmic ground where the heterogeneity and divergencies that we experience between reality and value no longer exist, where both series are revealed as one; this unity either being unaffected by the two categories, and standing beyond them in majestic indifference, or signifying a harmonious interweaving of both, which is shattered and distorted into fragments and contrasts only by our way of regarding it, as if we had an imperfect visual faculty.

The psychological fact of objective value

The characteristic feature of value, as it appears in contrast to reality, is usually called its subjectivity. Since one and the same object can have the highest degree of value for one soul and the lowest for another, and vice versa, and since on the other hand the most extensive and extreme differences between objects are compatible with equality of value, there appears to remain only the subject with his customary or exceptional, permanent or changing, moods and responses as the ground for valuation. This subjectivity, needless to say, has nothing to do with the subjectivity that refers to 'my perception' of the totality of the world. For the subjectivity of value contrasts value with the given objects, regardless of the way they are conceived. In other words, the subject who comprehends all objects is different from the subject who is confronted with the objects; the subjectivity that value shares with all other objects does not play any role here. Nor is his subjectivity merely caprice; independence from reality does not mean that value can be bestowed here and there with unrestrained and capricious freedom. Value exists in our consciousness as a fact that can no more be altered than can reality itself. The subjectivity of value, therefore, is first of all only negative, in the sense that value is not attached to objects in the same way as is colour or temperature. The latter, although determined by our senses, are accompanied by a feeling of their direct dependence upon the object; but in the case of value we soon learn to disregard this feeling because the two series constituted by reality and by value are quite independent of each other. The only cases more interesting than this general characterization are those in which psychological facts appear to lead to an opposite view.

In whatever empirical or transcendental sense the difference between objects and subjects is conceived, value is never a 'quality' of the objects, but a judgement upon them which remains inherent in the subject. And yet, neither the deeper meaning and content of the concept of value, nor its significance for the mental life of the individual, nor the practical social events and arrangements based upon it, can be sufficiently understood by referring value to the 'subject'. The way to a comprehension of value lies in a region in which that subjectivity is only provisional and actually not very essential.

The distinction between subject and object is not as radical as the accepted separation of these categories in practical life and in the scientific world would have us believe. Mental life begins with an undifferentiated state in which the Ego and its objects are not yet distinguished; consciousness is filled with impressions and perceptions while the bearer of these contents has still not detached himself from them. It is as a result of a second-stage awareness, a later analysis, that a subject in particular real conditions comes to be distinguished from the content of his consciousness in those conditions. This development obviously leads to a situation where a man speaks of himself as 'I' and recognizes the existence of other objects external to this 'I'. Metaphysics sometimes claims that the transcendent essence of being is completely unified, beyond the opposition of subject–object, and this has a psychological counterpart in the simple, primitive condition of being possessed by the content of a perception, like a child who does not yet speak of himself as 'I', or as may perhaps be observed in a rudimentary form at all stages of life. This unity from which the categories of subject and object develop in relation to each other – in a process to be examined later – appears to us as a subjective unity because we approach it with the concept of objectivity developed later; and because we do not have a proper term for such unities, but name them usually after one of the partial elements that appear in the subsequent analysis. Thus, it has been asserted that all actions are essentially egoistic, whereas egoism has a meaning only within a system of action and by contrast with its correlate, altruism. Similarly, pantheism has described the universality of being as God, although a positive concept of God depends on its contrast with everything empirical. This evolutionary relation between subject and object is repeated finally on a large scale: the intellectual world of classical antiquity differs from that of modern times chiefly in the fact that only the latter has, on the one hand, developed a comprehensive and clear concept of the Ego, as shown by the significance of the problem of liberty which was unknown in ancient times; and on the other, expressed the independence and force of the concept of the object through the idea of unalterable laws of nature. Antiquity was much closer than were later periods to the stage of indifference in which the contents of the world were conceived as such, without being apportioned between subject and object.

Objectivity in practice as standardization or as a guarantee for the totality of subjective values

This development which separates subject and object appears to be sustained on both sides by the same theme, but operating at different levels. Thus, the awareness of being a subject is already an objectification. This is a basic feature of the mind in its form as personality. The fundamental activity of our mind, which determines its form as a whole, is that we can observe, know and judge ourselves just like any other 'object'; that we dissect the Ego, experienced as a unity, into a perceiving subject and a perceived object, without its losing its unity, but on the contrary with its becoming aware of its unity through this inner antagonism. The mutual dependence of subject and object is here drawn together in a single point; it has affected the subject itself, which otherwise stands confronting the world as object. Thus man has realized the basic form of his relation to the world, of his acceptance of the world, as soon as he becomes aware of himself and calls himself 'I'. But before that happens there exists – in respect of meaning as well as of mental growth – a simple perception of content which does not distinguish between subject and object and is not yet divided between them. Regarded from the other side, this content itself, as a logical and conceptual entity, likewise lies beyond the distinction between subjective and objective reality. We can think of any object simply in terms of its qualities and their interconnection without asking whether or not this ideal complex of qualities has an objective existence. To be sure, so far as such a pure objective content is thought, it becomes a conception and to that extent a subjective structure. But the subjective is here only the dynamic act of conception, the function that apprehends the content; in itself this content is thought of as being independent of the act of conceiving. Our mind has a remarkable ability to think of contents as being independent of the act of thinking; this is one of its primary qualities, which cannot be reduced any further. The contents have their conceptual or objective qualities and relationships which can be apprehended but which are not thereby completely absorbed; they exist whether or not they are part of my representation and whether or not they are part of objective reality. The content of a representation does not coincide with the representation of contents. The simple undifferentiated conception that consists only in becoming aware of a content cannot be characterized as subjective, because it does not yet know the contrast between subject and object. Similarly, the pure content of objects or conceptions is not objective, but escapes equally this differential form and its opposite, while being ready to present itself in one or the other. Subject and object are born in the same act: logically, by presenting the conceptual ideal content first as a content of representation, and then as a content of objective reality; psychologically, when the still ego-less representation, in which person and object are undifferentiated, becomes divided and gives rise to a distance between the self and its object, through which each of them becomes a separate entity.

Economic value as the objectification of subjective values

This process, which finally produces our intellectual world view, also occurs in the sphere of our volitional practical activity. Here also the distinction between the desiring, consuming, valuing subject and the valued object does not comprehend all aspects of mental life, nor all the objective circumstances of practical activity. Human enjoyment of an object is a completely undivided act. At such moments we have an experience that does not include an awareness of an object confronting us or an awareness of the self as distinct from its present condition. Phenomena of the basest and the highest kind meet here. The crude impulse, particularly an impulse of an impersonal, general nature, wants to release itself towards an object and to be satisfied, no matter how; consciousness is exclusively concerned with satisfaction and pays no attention to its bearer on one side or its object on the other. On the other hand, intense aesthetic enjoyment displays the same form. Here too 'we forget ourselves', but at the same time we no longer experience the work of art as something with which we are confronted, because our mind is completely submerged in it, has absorbed it by surrendering to it. In this case, as in the other, our psychological condition is not yet, or is no longer, affected by the contrast between subject and object. Only a new process of awareness releases those categories from their undisturbed unity; and only then is the pure enjoyment of the content seen as being on the one hand a state of the subject confronting an object, and on the other the effect produced by an object that is independent of the subject. This tension, which disrupts the naive–practical unity of subject and object and makes us conscious of each in relation to the other, is brought about originally through the mere fact of desire. In desiring what we do not yet own or enjoy, we place the content of our desire outside ourselves. In empirical life, I admit, the finished object stands before us and is only then desired – if only because, in addition to our will, many other theoretical and emotional events contribute to the objectification of mental contents. Within the practical world, however, in relation to its inner order and intelligibility, the origin of the object itself, and its being desired by the subject, are correlative terms – the two aspects of this process of differentiation which splits the immediate unity of the process of enjoyment. It has been asserted that our conception of objective reality originates in the resistance that objects present to us, especially through our sense of touch. We can apply this at once to the practical problem. We desire objects only if they are not immediately given to us for our use and enjoyment; that is, to the extent that they resist our desire. The content of our desire becomes an object as soon as it is opposed to us, not only in the sense of being impervious to us, but also in terms of its distance as something not-yet-enjoyed, the subjective aspect of this condition being desire. As Kant has said: the possibility of experience is the possibility of the objects of experience – because to have experiences means that our consciousness creates objects from sense impressions. In the same way, the possibility of desire is the possibility of the objects of desire. The object thus formed, which is characterized by its separation from the subject, who at the same time establishes it and seeks to overcome it by his desire, is for us a value. The moment of enjoyment itself, when the opposition between subject and object is effaced, consumes the value. Value is only reinstated as contrast, as an object separated from the subject. Such trivial experiences as that we appreciate the value of our possessions only after we have lost them, that the mere withholding of a desired object often endows it with a value quite disproportionate to any possible enjoyment that it could yield, that the remoteness, either literal or figurative, of the objects of our enjoyment shows them in a transfigured light and with heightened attractions – all these are derivatives, modifications and hybrids of the basic fact that value does not originate from the unbroken unity of the moment of enjoyment, but from the separation between the subject and the content of enjoyment as an object that stands opposed to the subject as something desired and only to be attained by the conquest of distance, obstacles and difficulties. To reiterate the earlier analogy: in the final analysis perhaps, reality does not press upon our consciousness through the resistance that phenomena exert, but we register those representations which have feelings of resistance and inhibition associated with them, as being objectively real, independent and external to us. Objects are not difficult to acquire because they are valuable, but we call those objects valuable that resist our desire to possess them. Since the desire encounters resistance and frustration, the objects gain a significance that would never have been attributed to them by an unchecked will.

Value, which appears at the same time and in the same process of differentiation as the desiring Ego and as its correlate, is subordinate to yet another category. It is the same category as applies to the object that is conceived in theoretical representations. We concluded, in that case, that the contents that are realized in the objective world and also exist in us as subjective representations have, in addition, a peculiar ideal dignity. The concepts of the triangle or of the organism, causality or the law of gravitation have a logical sense, an inner structural validity which indeed determines their realization in space and in consciousness; but even if they were never realized, they would still belong to the ultimate unanalysable category of the valid and significant, and would differ entirely from fantastic and contradictory conceptual notions to which they might be akin in their reference to physical and mental non-reality. The value that is attributed to the objects of subjective desire is analogous to this, with the qualifications required by its different sphere. Just as we represent certain statements as true while recognizing that their truth is independent of our representation, so we sense that objects, people and events are not only appreciated as valuable by us, but would still be valuable if no one appreciated them. The most striking example is the value that we assign to people's dispositions or characters, as being moral, dignified, strong or beautiful. Whether or not such inner qualities ever show themselves in deeds that make possible or demand recognition, and whether their bearer himself reflects upon them with a sense of his own value, appears to us irrelevant to their real value; still more, this unconcern for recognition endows these values with their characteristic colouring. Furthermore, intellectual energy and the fact that it brings the most secret forces and arrangements of nature into the light of consciousness; the power and the rhythm of emotions that, in the limited sphere of the individual soul, are yet much more significant than the external world, even if the pessimistic view of the predominance of suffering in the world is true; the fact that, regardless of man, nature moves according to reliable fixed norms, that the manifold natural forms are not incompatible with a more profound unity of the whole, that nature's mechanism can be interpreted through ideas and also produces beauty and grace – all this leads us to conceive that the world is valuable no matter whether these values are experienced consciously or not. This extends all the way down to the economic value that we assign to any object of exchange, even though nobody is willing to pay the price, and even though the object is not in demand at all and remains unsaleable. Here too a basic capacity of the mind becomes apparent: that of separating itself from the ideas that it conceives and representing these ideas as if they were independent of its own representation. It is true that every value that we experience is a sentiment; but what we mean by this sentiment is a significant content which is realized psychologically through the sentiment yet is neither identical with it nor exhausted by it. Obviously this category lies beyond the controversy about the subjectivity or objectivity of value, because it denies the relation to a subject that is indispensable for the existence of an 'object'. It is rather a third term, an ideal concept which enters into the duality but is not exhausted by it. In conformity with the practical sphere to which it belongs, it has a particular form of relationship to the subject which does not exist for the merely abstract content of our theoretical concepts. This form may be described as a claim or demand. The value that attaches to any object, person, relationship or happening demands recognition. This demand exists, as an event, only within ourselves as subjects; but in accepting it we sense that we are not merely satisfying a claim imposed by ourselves upon ourselves, or merely acknowledging a quality of the object. The ability of a tangible symbol to awaken in us religious feelings; the moral challenge to revolutionize particular conditions of life or to leave them alone, to develop or retard them; the feeling of obligation not to remain indifferent to great events, but to respond to them; the right of what is perceived to be interpreted in an aesthetic context – all of these are claims that are experienced or realized exclusively within the Ego and have no counterpart or objective point of departure in the objects themselves, but which, as claims, cannot be traced either to the Ego or to the objects to which they refer. Regarded from a naturalistic point of view such a claim may appear subjective, while from the subject's point of view it appears to be objective; in fact, it is a third category, which cannot be derived from either subject or object, but which stands, so to speak, between us and the objects. I have observed that the value of things belongs among those mental contents that, while we conceive them, we experience at the same time as something independent within our representation, and as detached from the function by which it exists in us. This representation, when its content is a value, appears upon closer scrutiny as a sense that a claim is being made. The 'function' is a demand which does not exist as such outside ourselves, but which originates in an ideal realm which does not lie within us. It is not a particular quality of the objects of valuation, but consists rather in the significance that the objects have for us as subjects through their position in the order of that ideal realm. This value, which we conceive as being independent of its recognition, is a metaphysical category, and as such it stands as far beyond the dualism of subject and object as immediate enjoyment stands below it. The latter is a concrete unity to which the differentiating categories have not yet been applied; the former is an abstract or ideal unity, in whose self-subsistent meaning the dualism has again disappeared, just as the contrast between the empirical Ego and the empirical Non-Ego disappears in the all-comprehending system of consciousness that Fichte calls the Ego. At the moment of complete fusion of the function and its content, enjoyment cannot be called subjective, because there is no counterposed object that would justify the concept of a subject. Likewise, this independent, self-justifying value is not objective simply because it is conceived as independent by the subject who conceives it; although it becomes manifest within the subject as a claim for recognition, it will not forfeit anything of its reality if this claim is not fulfilled.

This metaphysical sublimation of value does not play any role in the valuations of daily life, which are concerned only with values in the consciousness of the subject and with the objectivity that emerges as a counterposed object in this psychological process of valuation. I showed earlier that this process of the formation of values develops with the increase in distance between the consumer and the cause of his enjoyment. The differences in valuation which have to be distinguished as subjective and objective, originate from such variations in distance, measured not in terms of enjoyment, in which the distance disappears, but in terms of desire, which is engendered by the distance and seeks to overcome it. At least in the case of those objects whose valuation forms the basis of the economy, value is the correlate of demand. Just as the world of being is my representation, so the world of value is my demand. However, in spite of the logical–physical necessity that every demand expects to be satisfied by an object, the psychological structure of demand is such that in most cases it is focused upon the satisfaction itself, and the object becomes a matter of indifference so long as it satisfies the need. When a man is satisfied with any woman whatsoever, without exercising an individual choice, when he eats anything at all that he can chew and digest, when he sleeps at any resting place, when his cultural needs can be satisfied by the simplest materials offered by nature, then his practical consciousness is completely subjective, he is inspired exclusively by the agitations and satisfactions of his own subjective condition and his interest in objects is limited to their being the causes of these effects. This fact is observed in the naive need for projection by primitive man, who directs his life towards the outside world and takes his inner life for granted. But the conscious wish cannot always be taken as a sufficient index of the really effective valuation. Often enough it is some expediency in the direction of our practical activities that leads us to regard an object as valuable, and it is not in fact the significance of the object but the possible subjective satisfaction that excites us. From this condition – which is not always temporally prior but is, so to speak, the simplest and most fundamental and thus in a systematic sense prior – consciousness is led to the object along two roads which finally merge. When an identical need rejects a number of possible satisfactions, perhaps all but one, and when, therefore, it is not satisfaction as such but satisfaction by a specific object that is desired, there begins a fundamental reorientation from the subject to the object. It may be said that this is still only a question of the subjective satisfaction of need, but that in this second case the need is differentiated to such an extent that only a specific object can satisfy it. In this case also the object is only the cause of sensation and is not valued in itself. Such an objection would indeed nullify the difference, if it were the case that the differentiation of the impulse directed it exclusively upon a single satisfying object and ruled out the possibility of satisfaction through any other object. However, this is a very rare and exceptional case. The broader basis from which even the most highly differentiated impulses evolve, and the original diffuseness of need which includes only a drive but not yet a definite single goal, remain as a substratum upon which a consciousness of the individual character of more specific desires for satisfaction develops. The circle of objects that can satisfy the subject's needs is diminished as he becomes more refined, and the objects desired are set in a sharper contrast with all the others that might satisfy the need but are no longer acceptable. It is well known from psychological investigations that this difference between objects is largely responsible for directing consciousness towards them and endowing them with particular significance. At this stage the need seems to be determined by the object; feeling is guided increasingly by its *terminus ad quem* instead of its *terminus a quo*, in the measure that impulse no longer rushes upon every possible satisfaction. Consequently, the place that the object occupies in our consciousness becomes larger. There is also another reason for this. So long as man is dominated by his impulses the world appears to him as an undifferentiated substance. Since it represents for him only an irrelevant means for the satisfaction of his drives – and this effect may arise from all kinds of causes – he has no interest in the nature of the objects themselves. It is the fact that we need a particular single object that makes us acutely aware that we need an object at all. But such awareness is, so to speak, more theoretical – and it diminishes the blind energy of the impulse which is directed only to its own extinction.

Since the differentiation of need goes hand in hand with the reduction of its elemental power, consciousness becomes more able to accommodate the object. Or regarded from the other aspect: because consciousness is constrained by the refinement and specialization of need to take a greater interest in the object, a certain amount of force is removed from the solipsistic need. Everywhere the weakening of the emotions, that is to say of the absolute surrender of the Ego to his momentary feelings, is correlated with the objectification of representations, with their appearance in a form of existence that stands over against us. Thus, for instance, talking things over is one of the most powerful means for subduing emotions. The inner process is, as it were, projected by the word into the external world; it now stands over against the individual like a tangible structure, and the intensity of the emotions is diverted. The tranquillization of the passions, and the representation of the objective world as existing and significant, are two sides of one and the same basic process. The diversion of inner interest from mere need and its satisfaction to the object itself, as a result of diminishing the possibility of satisfying the need, can obviously be brought about and strengthened just as well from the side of the object, if the latter makes satisfaction difficult, rare, and to be attained only indirectly or by exceptional effort. Even if we assume a highly differentiated desire concentrated upon selected objects, satisfaction might still be regarded as more or less a matter of course so long as there is no difficulty or resistance. What really matters, in order to conceive the independent significance of objects, is the distance between them and our impression of them. It is one of the numerous cases in which one has to stand back from the objects, to establish a distance between them and oneself, in order to get an objective picture of them. This is certainly no less subjective a view than the unclear or distorted picture that is obtained when the distance is too great or too small; but inner expediential reasons of our cognition lay a special emphasis upon subjectivity in the case of these extremes. At first, the object exists only in our relationship to it and is completely absorbed in this relationship; it becomes something external and opposed to us only in the degree that it escapes from this connection. Even the desire for objects, which recognizes their autonomy while seeking to overcome it, develops only when want and satisfaction do not coincide. The possibility of enjoyment must be separated, as an image of the future, from our present condition in order for us to desire things that now stand at a distance from us. Just as in the intellectual sphere the original oneness of perception, which we can observe in children, is only gradually divided into awareness of the self and of the object, so the naive enjoyment of objects only gives way to an awareness of the significance of things, and respect for them, when the objects are somewhat withdrawn. Here, too, the relationship between the weakening of desire and the beginning of an objectification of values is apparent, since the decline of the elemental strength of volition and feeling favours the growing awareness of the self. So long as a person surrenders unreservedly to a momentary feeling and is completely possessed by it, the Ego cannot develop. The awareness of a self that exists beyond its various emotions can emerge only when it appears as an enduring entity amid all these changes, and when the emotions do not absorb the whole self. The emotions must leave a part of the self untouched, as a neutral point for their contrasts, so that a certain reduction and limitation of the emotions allows the self to develop as the unchanging bearer of diverse contents. In all areas of our life Ego and object are related concepts, which are not yet separated in the initial forms of representation and only become differentiated through each other; and in just the same way, the independent value of objects develops only by contrast with an Ego that has become independent. Only the repulsions that we experience, the difficulties of attaining an object, the waiting and the labour that stand between a wish and its fulfilment, drive the Ego and the object apart; otherwise they remain undeveloped and undifferentiated in the propinquity of need and satisfaction. Whether the effective definition of the object arises from its scarcity, in relation to demand, or from the positive effort to acquire it, there is no doubt that only in this way is distance established between the object and ourselves which enables us to accord it a value beyond that of being merely enjoyed.

It may be said, therefore, that the value of an object does indeed depend upon the demand for it, but upon a demand that is no longer purely instinctive. On the other hand, if the object is to remain an economic value, its value must not be raised so greatly that it becomes an absolute. The distance between the self and the object of demand could become so large – through the difficulties of procuring it, through its exorbitant price, through moral or other misgivings that counter the striving after it – that the act of volition does not develop, and the desire is extinguished or becomes only a vague wish. The distance between subject and object that establishes value, at least in the economic sense, has a lower and an upper limit; the formula that the amount of value equals the degree of resistance to the acquisition of objects, in relation to natural, productive and social opportunities, is not correct. Certainly, iron would not be an economic value if its acquisition encountered no greater difficulty than the acquisition of air for breathing; but these difficulties had to remain within certain limits if the tools were to be manufactured which made iron valuable. To take another example: it has been suggested that the pictures of a very productive painter would be less valuable than those of one who was less productive, assuming equal artistic talent. But this is true only above a certain quantitative level. A painter, in order to acquire the fame that raises the price of his pictures, is obliged to produce a certain number of works. Again, the scarcity of gold in some countries with a paper currency has created a situation in which ordinary people will not accept gold even when it is offered to them. In the particular case of precious metals, whose suitability as the material of money is usually attributed to their scarcity, it should be noted that scarcity can only become significant above a considerable volume, without which these metals could not serve the practical demand for money and consequently could not acquire the value they possess as money. It is, perhaps, only the avaricious desire for an unlimited quantity of goods, in terms of which all values are scarce, that leads us to overlook that a certain proportion between scarcity and non-scarcity, and not scarcity itself, is the condition of value. The factor of scarcity has to be related to the significance of the sense for differences; the factor of abundance to the significance of habituation. Life in general is determined by the proportion of these two facts: that we need variety and change of content just as we need familiarity; and this general need appears here in the specific form that the value of objects requires, on the one hand, scarcity – that is to say, differentiation and particularity – while on the other hand it needs a certain comprehensiveness, frequency and permanence in order that objects may enter the realm of values.

An analogy with aesthetic value

I would like to show the universal significance of distance for supposedly objective valuation by an example that has nothing to do with economic values and which therefore illustrates the general principle, namely aesthetic valuation. What we call the enjoyment of the beauty of things developed relatively late. For no matter how much immediate sensual enjoyment may exist even today in the individual case, the specific quality of aesthetic enjoyment is the ability to appreciate and enjoy the object, not simply an experience of sensual or supra-sensual stimulation. Every cultivated person is able to make a clear distinction in principle between the aesthetic and the sensual enjoyment of female beauty, even though he may not be able to draw the line between these components of his impression on a particular occasion. In the one case we surrender to the object, while in the other case the object surrenders to us. Even though aesthetic value, like any other value, is not an integral part of the object but is rather a projection of our feelings, it has the peculiarity that the projection is complete. In other words, the content of the feeling is, as it were, absorbed by the object and confronts the subject as something which has autonomous significance, which is inherent in the object. What was the historical psychological process in which this objective aesthetic pleasure in things emerged, given that primitive enjoyment which was the basis for any more refined appreciation must have been tied to direct subjective satisfaction and utility? Perhaps we can find a clue in a very simple observation. If an object of any kind provides us with great pleasure or advantage we experience a feeling of joy at every later viewing of this object, even if any use or enjoyment is now out of the question. This joy, which resembles an echo, has a unique psychological character determined by the fact that we no longer want anything from the object. In place of the former concrete relationship with the object, it is now mere contemplation that is the source of enjoyable sensation; we leave the being of the object untouched, and our sentiment is attached only to its appearance, not to that which in any sense may be consumed. In short, whereas formerly the object was valuable as a means for our practical and eudaemonistic ends, it has now become an object of contemplation from which we derive pleasure by confronting it with reserve and remoteness, without touching it. It seems to me that the essential features of aesthetic enjoyment are foreshadowed here, but they can be shown more plainly if we follow the changes in sensation from the sphere of individual psychology to that of the species as a whole. The attempt has often been made to derive beauty from utility, but as a rule this has led only to a philistine coarsening of beauty. This might be avoided if the practical expediency and sensual eudaemonistic immediacy were placed far enough back in the history of the species, as a result of which an instinctive, reflex-like sense of enjoyment in our organism were attached to the appearance of objects; the physico-psychic connection would then be genetic and would become effective in the individual without any consciousness on his part of the utility of the object. There is no need to enter into the controversy about the inheritance of such acquired associations; it suffices here that the events occur as if such qualities were inheritable. Consequently, the beautiful would be for us what once proved useful for the species, and its contemplation would give us pleasure without our having any practical interest in the object as individuals. This would not of course imply uniformity or the reduction of individual taste to an average or collective level. These echoes of an earlier general utility are absorbed into the diversity of individual minds and transformed into new unique qualities, so that one might say that the detachment of the pleasurable sensation from the reality of its original cause has finally become a form of our consciousness, quite independent of the contents that first gave rise to it, and ready to absorb any other content that the psychic constellation permits. In those cases that offer realistic pleasure, our appreciation of the object is not specifically aesthetic, but practical; it becomes aesthetic only as a result of increasing distance, abstraction and sublimation. What happens here is the common phenomenon that, once a certain connection has been established, the connecting link itself disappears because it is no longer required. The connection between certain useful objects and the sense of pleasure has become so well established for the species through inheritance or some other mechanism, that the mere sight of these objects becomes pleasurable even in the absence of any utility. This explains what Kant calls 'aesthetic indifference', the lack of concern about the real existence of an object so long as its 'form', i.e. its visibility, is given. Hence also the radiance and transcendence of the beautiful, which arises from the temporal remoteness of the real motives in which we now discover the aesthetic. Hence the idea that the beautiful is something typical, supra-individual, and universally valid; for the evolution of the species has long ago eliminated from these inner states of mind anything specific and individual in the motives and experiences. In consequence it is often impossible to justify on rational grounds aesthetic judgments or the opposition that they sometimes present to what is useful and agreeable to the individual. The whole development of objects from utility value to aesthetic value is a process of objectification. When I call an object beautiful, its quality and significance become much more independent of the arrangements and the needs of the subject than if it is merely useful. So long as objects are merely useful they are interchangeable and everything can be replaced by anything else that performs the same service. But when they are beautiful they have a unique individual existence and the value of one cannot be replaced by another even though it may be just as beautiful in its own way. We need not pursue these brief remarks on the origin of aesthetic value into a discussion of all the ramifications of the subject in order to recognize that the objectification of value originates in the relative distance that emerges between the direct subjective origin of the valuation of the object and our momentary feeling concerning the object. The more remote for the species is the utility of the object that first created an interest and a value and is now forgotten, the purer is the aesthetic satisfaction derived from the mere form and appearance of the object. The more it stands before us in its own dignity, the more we attribute to it a significance that is not exhausted by haphazard subjective enjoyment, and the more the relationship of valuing the objects merely as means is replaced by a feeling of their independent value.

Economic activity establishes distances and overcomes them

I have chosen the above example because the objectifying effect of what I have called 'distance' is particularly clear when it is a question of distance in time. The process is, of course, intensive and qualitative, so that any quantitative designation in terms of distance is more or less symbolic. The same effect can be brought about by a number of other factors, as I have already mentioned: for example, by the scarcity of an object, by the difficulties of acquisition, by the necessity of renunciation. Even though in these economically important instances the significance of the objects remains a significance *for us* and so dependent upon our appreciation, the decisive change is that the objects confront us after these developments as independent powers, as a world of substances and forces that determine by their own qualities whether and to what extent they will satisfy our needs, and which demand effort and hardship before they will surrender to us. Only if the question of renunciation arises – renunciation of a feeling that really matters – is it necessary to direct attention upon the object itself. The situation, which is represented in stylized form by the concept of Paradise, in which subject and object, desire and satisfaction are not yet divided from each other – a situation that is not restricted to a specific historical epoch, but which appears everywhere in varying degrees – is destined to disintegrate, but also to attain a new reconciliation. The purpose of establishing a distance is that it should be overcome. The longing, effort and sacrifice that separate us from objects are also supposed to lead us towards them. Withdrawal and approach are in practice complementary notions, each of which presupposes the other; they are two sides of our relationship to objects, which we call subjectively our desire and objectively their value. We have to make the object enjoyed more remote from us in order to desire it again, and in relation to the distant object this desire is the first stage of approaching it, the first ideal relation to it. This dual significance of desire – that it can arise only at a distance from objects, a distance that it attempts to overcome, and yet that it presupposes a closeness between the objects and ourselves in order that the distance should be experienced at all – has been beautifully expressed by Plato in the statement that love is an intermediate state between possession and deprivation. The necessity of sacrifice, the experience that the satisfaction of desire has a price, is only the accentuation or intensification of this relationship. It makes us more distinctly aware of the distance between our present self and the enjoyment of things, but only by leading along the road towards overcoming it. This inner development towards the simultaneous growth of distance and approach also appears as a historical process of differentiation. Culture produces a widening circle of interests; that is, the periphery within which the objects of interest are located becomes farther and farther removed from the centre, the Ego. This increase in distance, however, depends upon a simultaneous drawing closer. If objects, persons and events hundreds or thousands of miles away acquire a vital importance for modern man, they must have been brought much closer to him than to primitive man, for whom they simply do not exist because the positive distinction between close and far has not yet been made. These two notions develop in a reciprocal relation from the original undifferentiated state. Modern man has to work in a different way, to apply a much greater effort than primitive man; the distance between him and the objects of his endeavours is much greater and much more difficult obstacles stand in his way, but on the other hand he acquires a greater quantity of objects, ideally through his desire and in practice through his work. The cultural process – which transposes the subjective condition of impulse and enjoyment into the valuation of objects – separates more distinctly the elements of our dual relationship of closeness and distance.

The subjective events of impulse and enjoyment become objectified in value; that is to say, there develop from the objective conditions obstacles, deprivations, demands for some kind of 'price' through which the cause or content of impulse and enjoyment is first separated from us and becomes, by this very act, an object and a value. The fundamental conceptual question as to the subjectivity or objectivity of value is misconceived. The subjectivity of value is quite erroneously based upon the fact that no object can ever acquire universal value, but that value changes from place to place, from person to person, and even from one hour to the next. This is a case of confusing subjectivity with the individuality of value. The fact that I want to enjoy, or do enjoy, something is indeed subjective in so far as there is no awareness of or interest in the object as such. But then an altogether new process begins: the process of valuation. The content of volition and feeling assumes the form of the object. This object now confronts the subject with a certain degree of independence, surrendering or refusing itself, presenting conditions for its acquisition, placed by his original capricious choice in a law-governed realm of necessary occurrences and restrictions. It is completely irrelevant here that the contents of these forms of objectivity are not the same for all subjects. If we assumed that all human beings evaluated objects in exactly the same way, this would not increase the degree of objectivity beyond that which exists in an individual case; for if any object is valued rather than simply satisfying desire it stands at an objective distance from us that is established by real obstacles and necessary struggles, by gain and loss, by considerations of advantage and by prices. The reason why the misleading question about the objectivity or subjectivity of value is raised again and again is that we find empirically an infinite number of objects that are entirely the products of representations. But if an object in its finished form arises first in our consciousness, its value seems to reside entirely in the subject; the aspect from which I began – the classification of objects in the two series of being and value – seems to be identical with the division between objectivity and subjectivity. But this fails to take into account that the object of volition is different from the object of representation. Even though both may occupy the same place in the series of space, time and quality, the desired object confronts us in a different way and has quite a different significance from the represented object. Consider the analogy of love. The person we love is not the same being as our reason represents. I am not referring here to the distortions or falsifications that emotions may produce in the object of cognition; for these remain within the sphere of representation and of intellectual categories, even though the content is modified. It is in a completely different way from that of intellectual representations that the beloved person is an object to us. Despite the logical identity it has a different meaning for us, just as the marble of the Venus de Milo means different things for a crystallographer and an art critic. A single element of being, although recognized as one and the same, can become an object for us in quite different ways: as an object of representation, and as an object of desire. Within each of these categories the confrontation between subject and object has other causes and other effects, so that it leads only to confusion if the practical relation between man and his object is equated with the alternative between subjectivity and objectivity which is valid only in the realm of intellectual representation. For even though the value of an object is not objective in the same manner as colour or weight, it is also not at all subjective in the sense of corresponding with this kind of objectivity; such subjectivity would apply rather to a perception of colour resulting from a deception of the senses, or of any other quality of the object based on a mistaken conclusion, or of a quality suggested by superstition. The practical relation to objects, however, produces a completely different kind of objectivity, because the conditions of reality withdraw the object of desire and enjoyment from the subjective realm and thus produce the specific category that we call value.

Within the economic sphere, this process develops in such a way that the content of the sacrifice or renunciation that is interposed between man and the object of his demand is, at the same time, the object of someone else's demand. The one has to give up the possession or enjoyment that the other wants in order to persuade the latter to give up what he owns and what the former wants. I shall show that the subsistence economy of an isolated producer can be reduced to the same formula. Two value formations are interwoven; a value has to be offered in order to acquire a value. Thus it appears that there is a *reciprocal* determination of value by the objects. By being exchanged, each object acquires a practical realization and measure of its value through the other object. This is the most important consequence and expression of the distance established between the objects and the subject. So long as objects are close to the subjects, so long as the differentiation of demand, scarcity, difficulties and resistance to acquisition have not yet removed the objects to a distance from the subject, they are, so to speak, desire and enjoyment, but not yet objects of desire and enjoyment. The process that I have outlined through which they become objects is brought to completion when the object, which is at the same time remote and yet overcomes the distance, is produced specifically for this purpose. Thus, pure economic objectivity, the detachment of the object from any subjective relationship to the subject, is established; and since production is carried out for the purpose of exchange with another object, which has a corresponding role, the two objects enter into a reciprocal objective relationship. The form taken by value in exchange places value in a category beyond the strict meaning of subjectivity and objectivity. In exchange, value becomes supra-subjective, supra-individual, yet without becoming an objective quality and reality of the things themselves. Value appears as the demand of the object, transcending its immanent reality, to be exchanged and acquired only for another corresponding value. The Ego, even though it is the universal source of values, becomes so far removed from the objects that they can measure their significance by each other without referring in each case to the Ego. But this real relationship between values, which is executed and supported by exchange, evidently has its purpose in eventual subjective enjoyment, that is, in the fact that we receive a greater quantity and intensity of values than would be possible without exchange transactions. It has been said that the divine principle, after having created the elements of the world, withdrew and left them to the free play of their own powers, so that we can now speak of an objective cosmos, subject to its own relations and laws; and further, that the divine power chose this independence of the cosmic process as the most expedient means of accomplishing its own purposes for the world. In the same way, we invest economic objects with a quantity of value as if it were an inherent quality, and then hand them over to the process of exchange, to a mechanism determined by those quantities, to an impersonal confrontation between values, from which they return multiplied and more enjoyable to the final purpose, which was also their point of origin: subjective experience. This is the basis and source of that valuation which finds its expression in economic life and whose consequences represent the meaning of money.

Translated by Tom Bottomore and David Frisby

20

THE WORK OF ART IN THE AGE OF MECHANICAL REPRODUCTION

Walter Benjamin

Our fine arts were developed, their types and uses were established, in times very different from the present, by men whose power of action upon things was insignificant in comparison with ours. But the amazing growth of our techniques, the adaptability and precision they have attained, the ideas and habits they are creating, make it a certainty that profound changes are impending in the ancient craft of the Beautiful. In all the arts there is a physical component which can no longer be considered or treated as it used to be, which cannot remain unaffected by our modern knowledge and power. For the last twenty years neither matter nor space nor time has been what it was from time immemorial. We must expect great innovations to transform the entire technique of the arts, thereby affecting artistic invention itself and perhaps even bringing about an amazing change in our very notion of art.[1]

(Paul Valéry, *Pièces sur l'art*, 'La Conquète de l'ubiquité.' Paris)

Preface

When Marx undertook his critique of the capitalistic mode of production, this mode was in its infancy. Marx directed his efforts in such a way as to give them prognostic value. He went back to the basic conditions underlying capitalistic production and through his presentation showed what could be expected of capitalism in the future. The result was that one could expect it not only to exploit the proletariat with increasing intensity, but ultimately to create conditions which would make it possible to abolish capitalism itself.

The transformation of the superstructure, which takes place far more slowly than that of the substructure, has taken more than half a century to manifest in all areas of culture the change in the conditions of production. Only today can it be indicated what form this has taken. Certain prognostic requirements should be met by these statements. However, theses about the art of the proletariat after its assumption of power or about the art of a classless society would have less bearing on these demands than theses about the developmental tendencies of art under present conditions of production. Their dialectic is no less noticeable in the superstructure than in the economy. It would therefore be wrong to underestimate the value of such theses as a weapon. They brush aside a number of outmoded concepts, such as creativity and genius, eternal value and mystery – concepts whose uncontrolled (and at present almost uncontrollable) application would lead to a processing of data in the Fascist sense. The concepts which are introduced into the theory of art in what follows differ from the more familiar terms in that they are completely useless for the purposes of fascism. They are, on the other hand, useful for the formulation of revolutionary demands in the politics of art.

I

In principle a work of art has always been reproducible. Man-made artifacts could always be imitated by men. Replicas were made by pupils in practice of their craft, by masters for diffusing their works, and, finally, by third parties in the pursuit of gain. Mechanical reproduction of a work of art, however, represents something new. Historically, it advanced intermittently and in leaps at long intervals, but with accelerated intensity. The Greeks knew only two procedures of technically reproducing works of art: founding and stamping. Bronzes, terracottas, and coins were the only art works which they could produce in quantity. All others were unique and could not be mechanically reproduced. With the woodcut graphic art became mechanically reproducible for the first time, long before script became reproducible by print. The enormous changes which printing, the mechanical reproduction of writing, has brought about in literature are a familiar story. However, within the phenomenon which we are here examining from the perspective of world history, print is merely a special, though particularly important, case. During the Middle Ages engraving and etching were added to the woodcut; at the beginning of the nineteenth century lithography made its appearance.

With lithography the technique of reproduction reached an essentially new stage. This much more direct process was distinguished by the tracing of the design on a stone rather than its incision on a block of wood or its etching on a copperplate and permitted graphic art for the first time to put its products on the market, not only in large numbers as hitherto, but also in daily changing forms. Lithography enabled graphic art to illustrate everyday life, and it began to keep pace with printing. But only a few decades after its invention, lithography was surpassed by photography. For the first time in the process of pictorial reproduction, photography freed the hand of the most important artistic functions which henceforth devolved only upon the eye looking into a lens. Since the eye perceives more swiftly than the hand can draw, the process of pictorial reproduction was accelerated so enormously that it could keep pace with speech. A film operator shooting a scene in the studio captures the images at the speed of an actor's speech. Just as lithography virtually implied the illustrated newspaper, so did photography foreshadow the sound film. The technical reproduction of sound was tackled at the end of the last century. These convergent endeavors made predictable a situation which Paul Valéry pointed up in this sentence:

> Just as water, gas, and electricity are brought into our houses from far off to satisfy our needs in response to a minimal effort, so we shall be supplied with visual or auditory images, which will appear and disappear at a simple movement of the hand, hardly more than a sign.
>
> (Ibid., p. 226)

Around 1900 technical reproduction had reached a standard that not only permitted it to reproduce all transmitted works of art and thus to cause the most profound change in their impact upon the public; it also had captured a place of its own among the artistic processes. For the study of this standard nothing is more revealing than the nature of the repercussions that these two different manifestations – the reproduction of works of art and the art of the film – have had on art in its traditional form.

II

Even the most perfect reproduction of a work of art is lacking in one element: its presence in time and space, its unique existence at the place where it happens to be. This unique existence of the work of art determined the history to which it was subject throughout the time of its existence. This includes the changes which it may have suffered in physical condition over the years as well as the various changes in its ownership.[2] The traces of the first can be revealed only by chemical or physical analyses which it is impossible to perform on a reproduction; changes of ownership are subject to a tradition which must be traced from the situation of the original.

The presence of the original is the prerequisite to the concept of authenticity. Chemical analyses of the patina of a bronze can help to establish this, as does the proof that a given manuscript of the Middle Ages stems from an archive of the fifteenth century. The whole sphere of authenticity is outside technical – and, of course, not only technical – reproducibility.[3] Confronted with its manual reproduction, which was usually branded as a forgery, the original preserved all its authority; not so *vis-à-vis* technical reproduction. The reason is twofold. First, process reproduction is more independent of the original than manual reproduction. For example, in photography, process reproduction can bring out those aspects of the original that are unattainable to the naked eye yet accessible to the lens, which is adjustable and chooses its angle at will. And photographic reproduction, with the aid of certain processes, such as enlargement or slow motion, can capture images which escape natural vision. Secondly, technical reproduction can put the copy of the original into situations which would be out of reach for the original itself. Above all, it enables the original to meet the beholder halfway, be it in the form of a photograph or a phonograph record. The cathedral leaves its locale to be received in the studio of a lover of art; the choral production, performed in an auditorium or in the open air, resounds in the drawing room.

The situations into which the product of mechanical reproduction can be brought may not touch the actual work of art, yet the quality of its presence is always depreciated. This holds not only for the art work but also, for instance, for a landscape which passes in review before the spectator in a movie. In the case of the art object, a most sensitive nucleus – namely, its authenticity – is interfered with whereas no natural object is vulnerable on that score. The authenticity of a thing is the essence of all that is transmissible from its beginning, ranging from its substantive duration to its testimony to the history which it has experienced. Since the historical testimony rests on the authenticity, the former, too, is jeopardized by reproduction when substantive duration ceases to matter. And what is really jeopardized when the historical testimony is affected is the authority of the object.[4]

One might subsume the eliminated element in the term 'aura' and go on to say: that which withers in the age of mechanical reproduction is the aura of the work of art.

This is a symptomatic process whose significance points beyond the realm of art. One might generalize by saying: the technique of reproduction detaches the reproduced object from the domain of tradition. By making many reproductions it substitutes a plurality of copies for a unique existence. And in permitting the reproduction to meet the beholder or listener in his own particular situation, it reactivates the object reproduced. These two processes lead to a tremendous shattering of tradition which is the obverse of the contemporary crisis and renewal of mankind. Both processes are intimately connected with the contemporary mass movements. Their most powerful agent is the film. Its social significance, particularly in its most positive form, is inconceivable without its destructive, cathartic aspect, that is, the liquidation of the traditional value of the cultural heritage. This phenomenon is most palpable in the great historical films. It extends to ever new positions. In 1927 Abel Gance exclaimed enthusiastically: 'Shakespeare, Rembrandt, Beethoven will make films . . . all legends, all mythologies and all myths, all founders of religion, and the very religions . . . await their exposed resurrection, and the heroes crowd each other at the gate.'[5] Presumably without intending it, he issued an invitation to a far-reaching liquidation.

III

During long periods of history, the mode of human sense perception changes with humanity's entire mode of existence. The manner in which human sense perception is organized, the medium in which it is accomplished, is determined not only by nature but by historical circumstances as well. The fifth century, with its great shifts of population, saw the birth of the late Roman art industry and the Vienna Genesis, and there developed not only an art different from that of antiquity but also a new kind of perception. The scholars of the Viennese school, Riegl and Wickhoff, who resisted the weight of classical tradition under which these later art forms had been buried, were the first to draw conclusions from them concerning the organization of perception at the time. However far-reaching their insight, these scholars limited themselves to showing the significant, formal hallmark which characterized perception in late Roman times. They did not attempt – and, perhaps, saw no way – to show the social transformations expressed by these changes of perception. The conditions for an analogous insight are more favorable in the present. And if changes in the medium of contemporary perception can be comprehended as decay of the aura, it is possible to show its social causes.

The concept of aura which was proposed above with reference to historical objects may usefully be illustrated with reference to the aura of natural ones. We define the aura of the latter as the unique phenomenon of a distance, however close it may be. If, while resting on a summer afternoon, you follow with your eyes a mountain range on the horizon or a branch which casts its shadow over you, you experience the aura of those mountains, of that branch. This image makes it easy to comprehend the social bases of the contemporary decay of the aura. It rests on two circumstances, both of which are related to the increasing significance of the masses in contemporary life. Namely, the desire of contemporary masses to bring things 'closer' spatially and humanly, which is just as ardent as their bent toward overcoming the uniqueness of every reality by accepting its reproduction.[6] Every day the urge grows stronger to get hold of an object at very close range by way of its likeness, its reproduction.

Unmistakably, reproduction as offered by picture magazines and newsreels differs from the image seen by the unarmed eye. Uniqueness and permanence are as closely linked in the latter as are transitoriness and reproducibility in the former. To pry an object from its shell, to destroy its aura, is the mark of a perception whose 'sense of the universal equality of things' has increased to such a degree that it extracts it even from a unique object by means of reproduction. Thus is manifested in the field of perception what in the theoretical sphere is noticeable in the increasing importance of statistics. The adjustment of reality to the masses and of the masses to reality is a process of unlimited scope, as much for thinking as for perception.

IV

The uniqueness of a work of art is inseparable from its being imbedded in the fabric of tradition. This tradition itself is thoroughly alive and extremely changeable. An ancient statue of Venus, for example, stood in a different traditional context with the Greeks, who made it an object of veneration, than with the clerics of the Middle Ages, who viewed it as an ominous idol. Both of them, however, were equally confronted with its uniqueness, that is, its aura. Originally the contextual integration of art in tradition found its expression in the cult. We know that the earliest art works originated in the service of a ritual – first the magical, then the religious kind. It is significant that the existence of the work of art with reference to its aura is never entirely separated from its ritual function.[7] In other words, the unique value of the 'authentic' work of art has its basis in ritual, the location of its original use value. This ritualistic basis, however remote, is still recognizable as secularized ritual even in the most profane forms of the cult of beauty.[8] The secular cult of beauty, developed during the Renaissance and prevailing for three centuries, clearly showed that ritualistic basis in its decline and the first deep crisis which befell it. With the advent of the first truly revolutionary means of reproduction, photography, simultaneously with the rise of socialism, art sensed the approaching crisis which has become evident a century later. At the time, art reacted with the doctrine of *l'art pour l'art*, that is, with a theology of art. This gave rise to what might be called a negative theology in the form of the idea of 'pure' art, which not only denied any social function of art but also any categorizing by subject matter. (In poetry, Mallarmé was the first to take this position.)

An analysis of art in the age of mechanical reproduction must do justice to these relationships, for they lead us to an all-important insight: for the first time in world history, mechanical reproduction emancipates the work of art from its parasitical dependence on ritual. To an ever greater degree the work of art reproduced becomes the work of art designed for reproducibility.[9] From a photographic negative, for example, one can make any number of prints; to ask for the 'authentic' print makes no sense. But the instant the criterion of authenticity ceases to be applicable to artistic production, the total function of art is reversed. Instead of being based on ritual, it begins to be based on another practice – politics.

V

Works of art are received and valued on different planes. Two polar types stand out: with one, the accent is on the cult value; with the other, on the exhibition value of the work.[10] Artistic production begins with ceremonial objects destined to serve in a cult. One may assume that what mattered was their existence, not their being on view. The elk portrayed by the man of the Stone Age on the walls of his cave was an instrument of magic. He did expose it to his fellow men, but in the main it was meant for the spirits. Today the cult value would seem to demand that the work of art remain hidden. Certain statues of gods are accessible only to the priest in the cella; certain Madonnas remain covered nearly all year round; certain sculptures on medieval cathedrals are invisible to the spectator on ground level. With the emancipation of the various art practices from ritual go increasing opportunities for the exhibition of their products. It is easier to exhibit a portrait bust that can be sent here and there than to exhibit the statue of a divinity that has its fixed place in the interior of a temple. The same holds for the painting as against the mosaic or fresco that preceded it. And even though the public presentability of a mass originally may have been just as great as that of a symphony, the latter originated at the moment when its public presentability promised to surpass that of the mass.

With the different methods of technical reproduction of a work of art, its fitness for exhibition increased to such an extent that the quantitative shift between its two poles turned into a qualitative transformation of its nature. This is comparable to the situation of the work of art in prehistoric times when, by the absolute emphasis on its cult value, it was, first and foremost, an instrument of magic. Only later did it come to be recognized as a work of art. In the same way today, by the absolute emphasis on its exhibition value the work of art becomes a creation with entirely new functions, among which the one we are conscious of, the artistic function, later may be recognized as incidental.[11] This much is certain: today photography and the film are the most serviceable exemplifications of this new function.

VI

In photography, exhibition value begins to displace cult value all along the line. But cult value does not give way without resistance. It retires into an ultimate retrenchment: the human countenance. It is no accident that the portrait was the focal point of early photography. The cult of remembrance of loved ones, absent or dead, offers a last refuge for the cult value of the picture. For the last time the aura emanates from the early photographs in the fleeting expression of a human face. This is what constitutes their melancholy, incomparable beauty. But as man withdraws from the photographic image, the exhibition value for the first time shows its superiority to the ritual value. To have pinpointed this new stage constitutes the incomparable significance of Atget, who, around 1900, took photographs of deserted Paris streets. It has quite justly been said of him that he photographed them like scenes of crime. The scene of a crime, too, is deserted; it is photographed for the purpose of establishing evidence. With Atget, photographs become standard evidence for historical occurrences, and acquire a hidden political significance. They demand a specific kind of approach; free-floating contemplation is not appropriate to them. They stir the viewer; he feels challenged by them in a new way. At the same time picture magazines begin to put up signposts for him, right ones or wrong ones, no matter. For the first time, captions have become obligatory. And it is clear that they have an altogether different character than the title of a painting. The directives which the captions give to those looking at pictures in illustrated magazines soon become even more explicit and more imperative in the film where the meaning of each single picture appears to be prescribed by the sequence of all preceding ones.

VII

The nineteenth-century dispute as to the artistic value of painting versus photography today seems devious and confused. This does not diminish its importance, however; if anything, it underlines it. The dispute was in fact the symptom of a historical transformation the universal impact of which was not realized by either of the rivals. When the age of mechanical reproduction separated art from its basis in cult, the semblance of its autonomy disappeared forever. The resulting change in the function of art transcended the perspective of the century; for a long time it even escaped that of the twentieth century, which experienced the development of the film.

Earlier much futile thought had been devoted to the question of whether photography is an art. The primary question – whether the very invention of photography had not transformed the entire nature of art – was not raised. Soon the film theoreticians asked the same ill-considered question with regard to the film. But the difficulties which photography caused traditional aesthetics were mere child's play as compared to those raised by the film. Whence the insensitive and forced character of early theories of the film. Abel Gance, for instance, compares the film with hieroglyphs:

> Here, by a remarkable regression, we have come back to the level of expression of the Egyptians . . . Pictorial language has not yet matured because our eyes have not yet adjusted to it. There is as yet insufficient respect for, insufficient cult of, what it expresses.[12]

Or, in the words of Séverin-Mars:

> What art has been granted a dream more poetical and more real at the same time! Approached in this fashion the film might represent an incomparable means of expression. Only the most high-minded persons, in the most perfect and mysterious moments of their lives, should be allowed to enter its ambience.[13]

Alexandre Arnoux concludes his fantasy about the silent film with the question: 'Do not all the bold descriptions we have given amount to the definition of prayer?'[14] It is instructive to note how their desire to class the film among the 'arts' forces these theoreticians to read ritual elements into it – with a striking lack of discretion. Yet when these speculations were published, films like *L'Opinion publique* and *The Gold Rush* had already appeared. This, however, did not keep Abel Gance from adducing hieroglyphs for purposes of comparison, nor Séverin-Mars from speaking of the film as one might speak of paintings by Fra Angelico. Characteristically, even today ultra-reactionary authors give the film a similar contextual significance – if not an outright sacred one, then at least a supernatural one. Commenting on Max Reinhardt's film version of *A Midsummer Night's Dream*, Werfel states that undoubtedly it was the sterile copying of the exterior world with its streets, interiors, railroad stations, restaurants, motorcars, and beaches which until now had obstructed the elevation of the film to the realm of art. 'The film has not yet realized its true meaning, its real possibilities . . . these consist in its unique faculty to express by natural means and with incomparable persuasiveness all that is fairylike, marvelous, supernatural.'[15]

VIII

The artistic performance of a stage actor is definitely presented to the public by the actor in person; that of the screen actor, however, is presented by a camera, with a twofold consequence. The camera that presents the performance of the film actor to the public need not respect the performance as an integral whole. Guided by the cameraman, the camera continually changes its position with respect to the performance. The sequence of positional views which the editor composes from the material supplied him constitutes the completed film. It comprises certain factors of movement which are in reality those of the camera, not to mention special camera angles, close-ups, etc. Hence, the performance of the actor is subjected to a series of optical tests. This is the first consequence of the fact that the actor's performance is presented by means of a camera. Also, the film actor lacks the opportunity of the stage actor to adjust to the audience during his performance, since he does not present his performance to the audience in person. This permits the audience to take the position of a critic, without experiencing any personal contact with the actor. The audience's identification with the actor is really an identification with the camera. Consequently the audience takes the position of the camera; its approach is that of testing.[16] This is not the approach to which cult values may be exposed.

IX

For the film, what matters primarily is that the actor represents himself to the public before the camera, rather than representing someone else. One of the first to sense the actor's metamorphosis by this form of testing was Pirandello. Though his remarks on the subject in his novel *Si Gira* were limited to the negative aspects of the question and to the silent film only, this hardly impairs their validity. For in this respect, the sound film did not change anything essential. What matters is that the part is acted not for an audience but for a mechanical contrivance – in the case of the sound film, for two of them. 'The film actor,' wrote Pirandello,

> feels as if in exile – exiled not only from the stage but also from himself. With a vague sense of discomfort he feels inexplicable emptiness: his body loses its corporeality, it evaporates, it is deprived of reality, life, voice, and the noises caused by his moving about, in order to be changed into a mute image, flickering an instant on the screen, then vanishing into silence . . . The projector will play with his shadow before the public, and he himself must be content to play before the camera.[17]

This situation might also be characterized as follows: for the first time – and this is the effect of the film – man has to operate with his whole living person, yet forgoing its aura. For aura is tied to his presence; there can be no replica of it. The aura which, on the stage, emanates from Macbeth, cannot be separated for the spectators from that of the actor. However, the singularity of the shot in the studio is that the camera is substituted for the public. Consequently, the aura that envelops the actor vanishes, and with it the aura of the figure he portrays.

It is not surprising that it should be a dramatist such as Pirandello who, in characterizing the film, inadvertently touches on the very crisis in which we see the theater. Any thorough study proves that there is indeed no greater contrast than that of the stage play to a work of art that is completely subject to or, like the film, founded in, mechanical reproduction. Experts have long recognized that in the film 'the greatest effects are almost always obtained by "acting" as little as possible.' In 1932 Rudolf Arnheim saw 'the latest trend . . . in treating the actor as a stage prop chosen for its characteristics and . . . inserted at the proper place.'[18] With this idea something else is closely connected. The stage actor identifies himself with the character of his role. The film actor very often is denied this opportunity. His creation is by no means all of a piece; it is composed of many separate performances. Besides certain fortuitous considerations, such as cost of studio, availability of fellow players, décor, etc., there are elementary necessities of equipment that split the actor's work into a series of mountable episodes. In particular, lighting and its installation require the presentation of an event that, on the screen, unfolds as a rapid and unified scene, in a sequence of separate shootings which may take hours at the studio; not to mention more obvious montage. Thus a jump from the window can be shot in the studio as a jump from a scaffold, and the ensuing flight, if need be, can be shot weeks later when outdoor scenes are taken. Far more paradoxical cases can easily be construed. Let us assume that an actor is supposed to be startled by a knock at the door. If his reaction is not satisfactory, the director can resort to an expedient: when the actor happens to be at the studio again he has a shot fired behind him without his being forewarned of it. The frightened reaction can be shot now and be cut into the screen version. Nothing more strikingly shows that art has left the realm of the 'beautiful semblance' which, so far, had been taken to be the only sphere where art could thrive.

X

The feeling of strangeness that overcomes the actor before the camera, as Pirandello describes it, is basically of the same kind as the estrangement felt before one's own image in the mirror. But now the reflected image has become separable, transportable. And where is it transported? Before the public.[19] Never for a moment does the screen actor cease to be conscious of this fact. While facing the camera he knows that ultimately he will face the public, the consumers who constitute the market. This market, where he offers not only his labour but also his whole self, his heart and soul, is beyond his reach. During the shooting he has as little contact with it as any article made in a factory. This may contribute to that oppression, that new anxiety which, according to Pirandello, grips the actor before the camera. The film responds to the shriveling of the aura with an artificial build-up of the 'personality' outside the studio. The cult of the movie star, fostered by the money of the film industry, preserves not the unique aura of the person but the 'spell of the personality,' the phony spell of a commodity. So long as the movie-makers' capital sets the fashion, as a rule no other revolutionary merit can be accredited to today's film than the promotion of a revolutionary criticism of traditional concepts of art. We do not deny that in some cases today's films can also promote revolutionary criticism of social conditions, even of the distribution of property. However, our present study is no more specifically concerned with this than is the film production of Western Europe.

It is inherent in the technique of the film as well as that of sports that everybody who witnesses its accomplishments is somewhat of an expert. This is obvious to anyone listening to a group of newspaper boys leaning on their bicycles and discussing the outcome of a bicycle race. It is not for nothing that newspaper publishers arrange races for their delivery boys. These arouse great interest among the participants, for the victor has an opportunity to rise from delivery boy to professional racer. Similarly, the newsreel offers everyone the opportunity to rise from passer-by to movie extra. In this way any man might even find himself part of a work of art, as witness Vertoff's *Three Songs about Lenin* or Ivens' *Borinage*. Any man today can lay claim to being filmed. This claim can best be elucidated by a comparative look at the historical situation of contemporary literature.

For centuries a small number of writers were confronted by many thousands of readers. This changed toward the end of the last century. With the increasing extension of the press, which kept placing new political, religious, scientific, professional, and local organs before the readers, an increasing number of readers became writers – at first, occasional ones. It began with the daily press opening to its readers space for 'letters to the editor.' And today there is hardly a gainfully employed European who could not, in principle, find an opportunity to publish somewhere or other comments on his work, grievances, documentary reports, or that sort of thing. Thus, the distinction between author and public is about to lose its basic character. The difference becomes merely functional; it may vary from case to case. At any moment the reader is ready to turn into a writer. As expert, which he had to become willy-nilly in an extremely specialized work process, even if only in some minor respect, the reader gains access to authorship. In the Soviet Union work itself is given a voice. To present it verbally is part of a man's ability to perform the work. Literary license is now founded on polytechnic rather than specialized training and thus becomes common property.[20]

All this can easily be applied to the film, where transitions that in literature took centuries have come about in a decade. In cinematic practice, particularly in Russia, this change-over has partially become established reality. Some of the players whom we meet in Russian films are not actors in our sense but people who portray *themselves* – and primarily in their own work process. In Western Europe the capitalistic exploitation of the film denies consideration to modern man's legitimate claim to being reproduced. Under these circumstances the film industry is trying hard to spur the interest of the masses through illusion-promoting spectacles and dubious speculations.

XI

The shooting of a film, especially of a sound film, affords a spectacle unimaginable anywhere at any time before this. It presents a process in which it is impossible to assign to a spectator a viewpoint which would exclude from the actual scene such extraneous accessories as camera equipment, lighting machinery, staff assistants, etc. – unless his eye were on a line parallel with the lens. This circumstance, more than any other, renders superficial and insignificant any possible similarity between a scene in the studio and one on the stage. In the theater one is well aware of the place from which the play cannot immediately be detected as illusionary. There is no such place for the movie scene that is being shot. Its illusionary nature is that of the second degree, the result of cutting. That is to say, in the studio the mechanical equipment has penetrated so deeply into reality that its pure aspect freed from the foreign substance of equipment is the result of a special procedure, namely, the shooting by the specially adjusted camera and the mounting of the shot together with other similar ones. The equipment-free aspect of reality here has become the height of artifice; the sight of immediate reality has become an orchid in the land of technology.

Even more revealing is the comparison of these circumstances, which differ so much from those of the theater, with the situation in painting. Here the question is: How does the cameraman compare with the painter? To answer this we take recourse to an analogy with a surgical operation. The surgeon represents the polar opposite of the magician. The magician heals a sick person by the laying on of hands; the surgeon cuts into the patient's body. The magician maintains the natural distance between the patient and himself; though he reduces it very slightly by the laying on of hands, he greatly increases it by virtue of his authority. The surgeon does exactly the reverse; he greatly diminishes the distance between himself and the patient by penetrating into the patient's body, and increases it but little by the caution with which his hand moves among the organs. In short, in contrast to the magician – who is still hidden in the medical practitioner – the surgeon at the decisive moment abstains from facing the patient man to man; rather, it is through the operation that he penetrates into him.

Magician and surgeon compare to painter and cameraman. The painter maintains in his work a natural distance from reality, the cameraman penetrates deeply into its web.[21] There is a tremendous difference between the pictures they obtain. That of the painter is a total one, that of the cameraman consists of multiple fragments which are assembled under a new law. Thus, for contemporary man the representation of reality by the film is incomparably more significant than that of the painter, since it offers, precisely because of the thoroughgoing permeation of reality with mechanical equipment, an aspect of reality which is free of all equipment. And that is what one is entitled to ask from a work of art.

XII

Mechanical reproduction of art changes the reaction of the masses toward art. The reactionary attitude toward a Picasso painting changes into the progressive reaction toward a Chaplin movie. The progressive reaction is characterized by the direct, intimate fusion of visual and emotional enjoyment with the orientation of the expert. Such fusion is of great social significance. The greater the decrease in the social significance of an art form, the sharper the distinction between criticism and enjoyment by the public. The conventional is uncritically enjoyed, and the truly new is criticized with aversion. With regard to the screen, the critical and the receptive attitudes of the public coincide. The decisive reason for this is that individual reactions are predetermined by the mass audience response they are about to produce, and this is nowhere more pronounced than in the film. The moment these responses become manifest they control each other. Again, the comparison with painting is fruitful. A painting has always had an excellent chance to be viewed by one person or by a few. The simultaneous contemplation of paintings by a large public, such as developed in the nineteenth century, is an early symptom of the crisis of painting, a crisis which was by no means occasioned exclusively by photography but rather in a relatively independent manner by the appeal of art works to the masses.

Painting simply is in no position to present an object for simultaneous collective experience, as it was possible for architecture at all times, for the epic poem in the past, and for the movie today. Although this circumstance in itself should not lead one to conclusions about the social role of painting, it does constitute a serious threat as soon as painting, under special conditions and, as it were, against its nature, is confronted directly by the masses. In the churches and monasteries of the Middle Ages and at the princely courts up to the end of the eighteenth century, a collective reception of paintings did not occur simultaneously, but by graduated and hierarchized mediation. The change that has come about is an expression of the particular conflict in which painting was implicated by the mechanical reproducibility of paintings. Although paintings began to be publicly exhibited in galleries and salons, there was no way for the masses to organize and control themselves in their reception.[22] Thus the same public which responds in a progressive manner toward a grotesque film is bound to respond in a reactionary manner to surrealism.

XIII

The characteristics of the film lie not only in the manner in which man presents himself to mechanical equipment but also in the manner in which, by means of this apparatus, man can represent his environment. A glance at occupational psychology illustrates the testing capacity of the equipment. Psychoanalysis illustrates it in a different perspective. The film has enriched our field of perception with methods which can be illustrated by those of Freudian theory. Fifty years ago, a slip of the tongue passed more or less unnoticed. Only exceptionally may such a slip have revealed dimensions of depth in a conversation which had seemed to be taking its course on the surface. Since the *Psychopathology of Everyday Life* things have changed. This book isolated and made analyzable things which had heretofore floated along unnoticed in the broad stream of perception. For the entire spectrum of optical, and now also acoustical, perception the film has brought about a similar deepening of apperception. It is only an obverse of this fact that behavior items shown in a movie can be analyzed much more precisely and from more points of view than those presented on paintings or on the stage. As compared with painting, filmed behavior lends itself more readily to analysis because of its incomparably more precise statements of the situation. In comparison with the stage scene, the filmed behavior item lends itself more readily to analysis because it can be isolated more easily. This circumstance derives its chief importance from its tendency to promote the mutual penetration of art and science. Actually, of a screened behavior item which is neatly brought out in a certain situation, like a muscle of a body, it is difficult to say which is more fascinating, its artistic value or its value for science. To demonstrate the identity of the artistic and scientific uses of photography which heretofore usually were separated will be one of the revolutionary functions of the film.[23]

By close-ups of the things around us, by focusing on hidden details of familiar objects, by exploring commonplace milieus under the ingenious guidance of the camera, the film, on the one hand, extends our comprehension of the necessities which rule our lives; on the other hand, it manages to assure us of an immense and unexpected field of action. Our taverns and our metropolitan streets, our offices and furnished rooms, our railroad stations and our factories appeared to have us locked up hopelessly. Then came the film and burst this prison-world asunder by the dynamite of the tenth of a second, so that now, in the midst of its far-flung ruins and debris, we calmly and adventurously go traveling. With the close-up, space expands; with slow motion, movement is extended. The enlargement of a snapshot does not simply render more precise what in any case was visible, though unclear: it reveals entirely new structural formations of the subject. So, too, slow motion not only presents familiar qualities of movement but reveals in them entirely unknown ones 'which, far from looking like retarded rapid movements, give the effect of singularly gliding, floating, supernatural motions.'[24] Evidently a different nature opens itself to the camera than opens to the naked eye – if only because an unconsciously penetrated space is substituted for a space consciously explored by man. Even if one has a general knowledge of the way people walk, one knows nothing of a person's posture during the fractional second of a stride. The act of reaching for a lighter or a spoon is familiar routine, yet we hardly know what really goes on between hand and metal, not to mention how this fluctuates with our moods. Here the camera intervenes with the resources of its lowerings and liftings, its interruptions and isolations, its extensions and accelerations, its enlargements and reductions. The camera introduces us to unconscious optics as does psychoanalysis to unconscious impulses.

XIV

One of the foremost tasks of art has always been the creation of a demand which could be fully satisfied only later.[25] The history of every art form shows critical epochs in which a certain art form aspires to effects which could be fully obtained only with a changed technical standard, that is to say, in a new art form. The extravagances and crudities of art which thus appear, particularly in the so-called decadent epochs, actually arise from the nucleus of its richest historical energies. In recent years, such barbarisms were abundant in Dadaism. It is only now that its impulse becomes discernible: Dadaism attempted to create by pictorial – and literary – means the effects which the public today seeks in the film.

Every fundamentally new, pioneering creation of demands will carry beyond its goal. Dadaism did so to the extent that it sacrificed the market values which are so characteristic of the film in favor of higher ambitions – though of course it was not conscious of such intentions, as here described. The Dadaists attached much less importance to the sales value of their work than to its uselessness for contemplative immersion. The studied degradation of their material was not the least of their means to achieve this uselessness. Their poems are 'word salad' containing obscenities and every imaginable waste product of language. The same is true of their paintings, on which they mounted buttons and tickets. What they intended and achieved was a relentless destruction of the aura of their creations, which they branded as reproductions with the very means of production. Before a painting of Arp's or a poem by August Stramm it is impossible to take time for contemplation and evaluation as one would before a canvas of Derain's or a poem by Rilke. In the decline of middle-class society, contemplation became a school for asocial behavior; it was countered by distraction as a variant of social conduct.[26] Dadaistic activities actually assured a rather vehement distraction by making works of art the center of scandal. One requirement was foremost: to outrage the public.

From an alluring appearance or persuasive structure of sound the work of art of the Dadaists became an instrument of ballistics. It hit the spectator like a bullet, it happened to him, thus acquiring a tactile quality. It promoted a demand for the film, the distracting element of which is also primarily tactile, being based on changes of place and focus which periodically assail the spectator. Let us compare the screen on which a film unfolds with the canvas of a painting. The painting invites the spectator to contemplation; before it the spectator can abandon himself to his associations. Before the movie frame he cannot do so. No sooner has his eye grasped a scene than it is already changed. It cannot be arrested. Duhamel, who detests the film and knows nothing of its significance, though something of its structure, notes this circumstance as follows: 'I can no longer think what I want to think. My thoughts have been replaced by moving images.'[27] The spectator's process of association in view of these images is indeed interrupted by their constant, sudden change. This constitutes the shock effect of the film, which, like all shocks, should be cushioned by heightened presence of mind.[28] By means of its technical structure, the film has taken the physical shock effect out of the wrappers in which Dadaism had, as it were, kept it inside the moral shock effect.[29]

XV

The mass is a matrix from which all traditional behavior toward works of art issues today in a new form. Quantity has been transmuted into quality. The greatly increased mass of participants has produced a change in the mode of participation. The fact that the new mode of participation first appeared in a disreputable form must not confuse the spectator. Yet some people have launched spirited attacks against precisely this superficial aspect. Among these, Duhamel has expressed himself in the most radical manner. What he objects to most is the kind of participation which the movie elicits from the masses. Duhamel calls the movie

> a pastime for helots, a diversion for uneducated, wretched, worn-out creatures who are consumed by their worries . . . a spectacle which requires no concentration and presupposes no intelligence . . . which kindles no light in the heart and awakens no hope other than the ridiculous one of someday becoming a 'star' in Los Angeles.[30]

Clearly, this is at bottom the same ancient lament that the masses seek distraction whereas art demands concentration from the spectator. That is a commonplace. The question remains whether it provides a platform for the analysis of the film. A closer look is needed here. Distraction and concentration form polar opposites which may be stated as follows: A man who concentrates before a work of art is absorbed by it. He enters into this work of art the way legend tells of the Chinese painter when he viewed his finished painting. In contrast, the distracted mass absorbs the work of art. This is most obvious with regard to buildings. Architecture has always represented the prototype of a work of art the reception of which is consummated by a collectivity in a state of distraction. The laws of its reception are most instructive.

Buildings have been man's companions since primeval times. Many art forms have developed and perished. Tragedy begins with the Greeks, is extinguished with them, and after centuries its 'rules' only are revived. The epic poem, which had its origin in the youth of nations, expires in Europe at the end of the Renaissance. Panel painting is a creation of the Middle Ages, and nothing guarantees its uninterrupted existence. But the human need for shelter is lasting. Architecture has never been idle. Its history is more ancient than that of any other art, and its claim to being a living force has significance in every attempt to comprehend the relationship of the masses to art. Buildings are appropriated in a twofold manner: by use and by perception – or rather, by touch and sight. Such appropriation cannot be understood in terms of the attentive concentration of a tourist before a famous building. On the tactile side there is no counterpart to contemplation on the optical side. Tactile appropriation is accomplished not so much by attention as by habit. As regards architecture, habit determines to a large extent even optical reception. The latter, too, occurs much less through rapt attention than by noticing the object in incidental fashion. This mode of appropriation, developed with reference to architecture, in certain circumstances acquires canonical value. For the tasks which face the human apparatus of perception at the turning points of history cannot be solved by optical means, that is, by contemplation, alone. They are mastered gradually by habit, under the guidance of tactile appropriation.

The distracted person, too, can form habits. More, the ability to master certain tasks in a state of distraction proves that their solution has become a matter of habit. Distraction as provided by art presents a covert control of the extent to which new tasks have become soluble by apperception. Since, moreover, individuals are tempted to avoid such tasks, art will tackle the most difficult and most important ones where it is able to mobilize the masses. Today it does so in the film. Reception in a state of distraction, which is increasing noticeably in all fields of art and is symptomatic of profound changes in apperception, finds in the film its true means of exercise. The film with its shock effect meets this mode of reception halfway. The film makes the cult value recede into the background not only by putting the public in the position of the critic, but also by the fact that at the movies this position requires no attention. The public is an examiner, but an absent-minded one.

Epilogue

The growing proletarianization of modern man and the increasing formation of masses are two aspects of the same process. Fascism attempts to organize the newly created proletarian masses without affecting the property structure which the masses strive to eliminate. Fascism sees its salvation in giving these masses not their right, but instead a chance to express themselves.[31] The masses have a right to change property relations; Fascism seeks to give them an expression while preserving property. The logical result of Fascism is the introduction of aesthetics into political life. The violation of the masses, whom Fascism, with its *Führer* cult, forces to their knees, has its counterpart in the violation of an apparatus which is pressed into the production of ritual values.

All efforts to render politics aesthetic culminate in one thing: war. War and war only can set a goal for mass movements on the largest scale while respecting the traditional property system. This is the political formula for the situation. The technological formula may be stated as follows: Only war makes it possible to mobilize all of today's technical resources while maintaining the property system. It goes without saying that the Fascist apotheosis of war does not employ such arguments. Still, Marinetti says in his manifesto on the Ethiopian colonial war:

> For twenty-seven years we Futurists have rebelled against the branding of war as antiaesthetic . . . Accordingly we state: . . . War is beautiful because it establishes man's dominion over the subjugated machinery by means of gas masks, terrifying megaphones, flame throwers, and small tanks. War is beautiful because it initiates the dreamt-of metalization of the human body. War is beautiful because it enriches a flowering meadow with the fiery orchids of machine guns. War is beautiful because it combines the gunfire, the cannonades, the cease-fire, the scents, and the stench of putrefaction into a symphony. War is beautiful because it creates new architecture, like that of the big tanks, the geometrical formation flights, the smoke spirals from burning villages, and many others . . . Poets and artists of Futurism! . . . remember these principles of an aesthetics of war so that your struggle for a new literature and a new graphic art . . . may be illumined by them!

This manifesto has the virtue of clarity. Its formulations deserve to be accepted by dialecticians. To the latter, the aesthetics of today's war appears as follows: If the natural utilization of productive forces is impeded by the property system, the increase in technical devices, in speed, and in the sources of energy will press for an unnatural utilization, and this is found in war. The destructiveness of war furnishes proof that society has not been mature enough to incorporate technology as its organ, that technology has not been sufficiently developed to cope with the elemental forces of society. The horrible features of imperialistic warfare are attributable to the discrepancy between the tremendous means of production and their inadequate utilization in the process of production – in other words, to unemployment and the lack of markets. Imperialistic war is a rebellion of technology which collects, in the form of 'human material,' the claims to which society has denied its natural material. Instead of draining rivers, society directs a human stream into a bed of trenches; instead of dropping seeds from airplanes, it drops incendiary bombs over cities; and through gas warfare the aura is abolished in a new way.

'*Fiat ars – pereat mundus*,' says Fascism, and, as Marinetti admits, expects war to supply the artistic gratification of a sense perception that has been changed by technology. This is evidently the consummation of '*l'art pour l'art*.' Mankind, which in Homer's time was an object of contemplation for the Olympian gods, now is one for itself. Its self-alienation has reached such a degree that it can experience its own destruction as an aesthetic pleasure of the first order. This is the situation of politics which Fascism is rendering aesthetic. Communism responds by politicizing art.

Translated by Harry Zohn

Notes

1 Quoted from Paul Valéry, *Aesthetics*, 'The Conquest of Ubiquity,' translated by Ralph Manheim, New York, Pantheon Books, Bollingen Series, 1964, p. 225.

2 Of course, the history of a work of art encompasses more than this. The history of the *Mona Lisa*, for instance, encompasses the kind and number of its copies made in the seventeenth, eighteenth, and nineteenth centuries.

3 Precisely because authenticity is not reproducible, the intensive penetration of certain (mechanical) processes of reproduction was instrumental in differentiating and grading authenticity. To develop such differentiations was an important function of the trade in works of art. The invention of the woodcut may be said to have struck at the root of the quality of authenticity even before its late flowering. To be sure, at the time of its origin a medieval picture of the Madonna could not yet be said to be 'authentic.' It became 'authentic' only during the succeeding centuries and perhaps most strikingly so during the last one.

4 The poorest provincial staging of *Faust* is superior to a Faust film in that, ideally, it competes with the first performance at Weimar. Before the screen it is unprofitable to remember traditional contents which might come to mind before the stage – for instance, that Goethe's friend Johann Heinrich Merck is hidden in Mephisto, and the like.

5 Abel Gance, 'Le Temps de l'image est venu,' *L'Art cinématographique*, vol. 2, Paris, 1927, pp. 94f.

6 To satisfy the human interest of the masses may mean to have one's social function removed from the field of vision. Nothing guarantees that a portraitist of today, when painting a famous surgeon at the breakfast table in the midst of his family, depicts his social function more precisely than a painter of the seventeenth century who portrayed his medical doctors as representing this profession, like Rembrandt in his *Anatomy Lesson*.

7 The definition of the aura as a 'unique phenomenon of a distance however close it may be' represents nothing but the formulation of the cult value of the work of art in categories of space and time perception. Distance is the opposite of closeness. The essentially distant object is the unapproachable one. Unapproachability is indeed a major quality of the cult image. True to its nature, it remains 'distant, however close it may be.' The closeness which one may gain from its subject matter does not impair the distance which it retains in its appearance.

8 To the extent to which the cult value of the painting is secularized the ideas of its fundamental uniqueness lose distinctness. In the imagination of the beholder the uniqueness of the phenomena which hold sway in the cult image is more and more displaced by the empirical uniqueness of the creator or of his creative achievement. To be sure, never completely so; the concept of authenticity always transcends mere genuineness. (This is particularly apparent in the collector who always retains some traces of the fetishist and who, by owning the work of art, shares in its ritual power.) Nevertheless, the function of the concept of authenticity remains determinate in the evaluation of art; with the secularization of art, authenticity displaces the cult value of the work.

9 In the case of films, mechanical reproduction is not, as with literature and painting, an external condition for mass distribution. Mechanical reproduction is inherent in the very technique of film production. This technique not only permits in the most direct way but virtually causes mass distribution. It enforces distribution because the production of a film is so expensive that an individual who, for instance, might afford to buy a painting no longer can afford to buy a film. In 1927 it was calculated that a major film, in order to pay its way, had to reach an audience of nine million. With the sound film, to be sure, a setback in its international distribution occurred at first: audiences became limited by language barriers. This coincided with the Fascist emphasis on national interests. It is more important to focus on this connection with Fascism than on this setback, which was soon minimized by synchronization. The simultaneity of both phenomena is attributable to the depression. The same disturbances which, on a larger scale, led to an attempt to maintain the existing property structure by sheer force led the endangered film capital to speed up the development of the sound film. The introduction of the sound film brought about a temporary relief, not only because it again brought the masses into the theaters but also because it merged new capital

from the electrical industry with that of the film industry. Thus, viewed from the outside, the sound film promoted national interests, but seen from the inside it helped to internationalize film production even more than previously.

10 This polarity cannot come into its own in the aesthetics of Idealism. Its idea of beauty comprises these polar opposites without differentiating between them and consequently excludes their polarity. Yet in Hegel this polarity announces itself as clearly as possible within the limits of Idealism. We quote from his *Philosophy of History*:

> Images were known of old. Piety at an early time required them for worship, but it could do without *beautiful* images. These might even be disturbing. In every beautiful painting there is also something nonspiritual, merely external, but its spirit speaks to man through its beauty. Worshipping, conversely, is concerned with the work as an object, for it is but a spiritless stupor of the soul ... Fine art has arisen ... in the church ... although it has already gone beyond its principle as art.

Likewise, the following passage from *The Philosophy of Fine Art* indicates that Hegel sensed a problem here.

> We are beyond the stage of reverence for works of art as divine and objects deserving our worship. The impression they produce is one of a more reflective kind, and the emotions they arouse require a higher test.
>
> G.W.F. Hegel, *The Philosophy of Fine Art*, trans., with notes, by F.P.B. Osmaston, London, 1920, vol. 1, p. 12.

The transition from the first kind of artistic reception to the second characterizes the history of artistic reception in general. Apart from that, a certain oscillation between these two polar modes of reception can be demonstrated for each work of art. Take the Sistine Madonna. Since Hubert Grimme's research it has been known that the Madonna originally was painted for the purpose of exhibition. Grimme's research was inspired by the question: What is the purpose of the molding in the foreground of the painting which the two cupids lean upon? How, Grimme asked further, did Raphael come to furnish the sky with two draperies? Research proved that the Madonna had been commissioned for the public lying-in-state of Pope Sixtus. The Popes lay in state in a certain side chapel of St. Peter's. On that occasion Raphael's picture had been fastened in a nichelike background of the chapel, supported by the coffin. In this picture Raphael portrays the Madonna approaching the papal coffin in clouds from the background of the niche, which was demarcated by green drapes. At the obsequies of Sixtus a pre-eminent exhibition value of Raphael's picture was taken advantage of. Some time later it was placed on the high altar in the church of the Black Friars at Piacenza. The reason for this exile is to be found in the Roman rites which forbid the use of paintings exhibited at obsequies as cult objects on the high altar. This regulation devalued Raphael's picture to some degree. In order to obtain an adequate price nevertheless, the Papal See resolved to add to the bargain the tacit toleration of the picture above the high altar. To avoid attention the picture was given to the monks of the far-off provincial town.

11 Bertolt Brecht, on a different level, engaged in analogous reflections:

> If the concept of 'work of art' can no longer be applied to the thing that emerges once the work is transformed into a commodity, we have to eliminate this concept with cautious care but without fear, lest we liquidate the function of the very thing as well. For it has to go through this phase without mental reservation, and not as noncommittal deviation from the straight path; rather, what happens here with the work of art will change it fundamentally and erase its past to such an extent that should the old concept be taken up again – and it will, why not? – it will no longer stir any memory of the thing it once designated.

12 Abel Gance, 'Le Temps de l'image', pp. 100–01.

13 Séverin-Mars, quoted by Abel Gance, ibid., p. 100.

14 Alexandre Arnoux, *Cinéma pris*, 1929, p. 28.

15 Franz Werfel, 'Ein Sommernachtstraum, ein Film von Shakespeare und Reinhardt,' *Neues Wiener Journal*, cited in *Lu* 15, November 1935.

16 'The film . . . provides – or could provide – useful insight into the details of human actions . . . Character is never used as a source of motivation; the inner life of the persons never supplies the principal cause of the plot and seldom is its main result' (Bertolt Brecht, *Versuche*, 'Der Dreigroschenprozess,' p. 268). The expansion of the field of the testable which mechanical equipment brings about for the actor corresponds to the extraordinary expansion of the field of the testable brought about for the individual through economic conditions. Thus, vocational aptitude tests become constantly more important. What matters in these tests are segmental performances of the individual. The film shot and the vocational aptitude test are taken before a committee of experts. The camera director in the studio occupies a place identical with that of the examiner during aptitude tests.

17 Luigi Pirandello, *Si Gira*, quoted by Léon Pierre-Quint, 'Signification du cinéma,' *L'Art cinématographique*, pp. 14–15.

18 Rudolf Arnheim, *Film als Kunst*, Berlin, 1932, pp. 176f. In this context certain seemingly unimportant details in which the film director deviates from stage practices gain in interest. Such is the attempt to let the actor play without make-up, as made among others by Dreyer in his *Jeanne d'Arc*. Dreyer spent months seeking the forty actors who constitute the Inquisitors' tribunal. The search for these actors resembled that for stage properties that are hard to come by. Dreyer made every effort to avoid resemblances of age, build, and physiognomy. If the actor thus becomes a stage property, this latter, on the other hand, frequently functions as actor. At least it is not unusual for the film to assign a role to the stage property. Instead of choosing at random from a great wealth of examples, let us concentrate on a particularly convincing one. A clock that is working will always be a disturbance on the stage. There it cannot be permitted its function of measuring time. Even in a naturalistic play, astronomical time would clash with theatrical time. Under these circumstances it is highly revealing that the film can, whenever appropriate, use time as measured by a clock. From this more than from many other touches it may clearly be recognized that under certain circumstances each and every prop in a film may assume important functions. From here it is but one step to Pudovkin's statement that 'the playing of an actor which is connected with an object and is built around it . . . is always one of the strongest methods of cinematic construction' (W. Pudovkin, *Filmregie und Filmmanuskript*, Berlin, 1928, p. 126). The film is the first art form capable of demonstrating how matter plays tricks on man. Hence, films can be an excellent means of materialistic representation.

19 The change noted here in the method of exhibition caused by mechanical reproduction applies to politics as well. The present crisis of the bourgeois democracies comprises a crisis of the conditions which determine the public presentation of the rulers. Democracies exhibit a member of government directly and personally before the nation's representatives. Parliament is his public. Since the innovations of camera and recording equipment make it possible for the orator to become audible and visible to an unlimited number of persons, the presentation of the man of politics before camera and recording equipment becomes paramount. Parliaments, as much as theaters, are deserted. Radio and film not only affect the function of the professional actor but likewise the function of those who also exhibit themselves before this mechanical equipment, those who govern. Though their tasks may be different, the change affects equally the actor and the ruler. The trend is toward establishing controllable and transferable skills under certain social conditions. This results in a new selection, a selection before the equipment from which the star and the dictator emerge victorious.

20 The privileged character of the respective techniques is lost. Aldous Huxley writes:

> Advances in technology have led . . . to vulgarity . . . Process reproduction and the rotary press have made possible the indefinite multiplication of writing and pictures. Universal education and relatively high wages have created an enormous public who know how to read and can afford to buy reading and pictorial matter. A great industry has been called into existence in order to supply these commodities. Now, artistic talent is a very rare

> phenomenon; whence it follows . . . that, at every epoch and in all countries, most art has been bad. But the proportion of trash in the total artistic output is greater now than at any other period. That it must be so is a matter of simple arithmetic. The population of Western Europe has a little more than doubled during the last century. But the amount of reading – and seeing – matter has increased, I should imagine, at least twenty and possibly fifty or even a hundred times. If there were n men of talent in a population of x millions, there will presumably be 2n men of talent among 2x millions. The situation may be summed up thus. For every page of print and pictures published a century ago, twenty or perhaps even a hundred pages are published today. But for every man of talent then living, there are now only two men of talent. It may be of course that, thanks to universal education, many potential talents which in the past would have been stillborn are now enabled to realize themselves. Let us assume, then, that there are now three or even four men of talent to every one of earlier times. It still remains true to say that the consumption of reading – and seeing – matter has far outstripped the natural production of gifted writers and draughtsmen. It is the same with hearing-matter. Prosperity, the gramophone and the radio have created an audience of hearers who consume an amount of hearing-matter that has increased out of all proportion to the increase of population and the consequent natural increase of talented musicians. It follows from all this that in all the arts the output of trash is both absolutely and relatively greater than it was in the past; and that it must remain greater for just so long as the world continues to consume the present inordinate quantities of reading-matter, seeing-matter, and hearing-matter.
>
> (Aldous Huxley, *Beyond the Mexique Bay. A Traveller's Journal*, London, 1949, pp. 274ff. First published in 1934)

This mode of observation is obviously not progressive.

21 The boldness of the cameraman is indeed comparable to that of the surgeon. Luc Durtain lists among specific technical sleights of hand those

> which are required in surgery in the case of certain difficult operations. I choose as an example a case from oto-rhinolaryngology; . . . the so-called endonasal perspective procedure; or I refer to the acrobatic tricks of larynx surgery which have to be performed following the reversed picture in the laryngoscope. I might also speak of ear surgery which suggests the precision work of watchmakers. What range of the most subtle muscular acrobatics is required from the man who wants to repair or save the human body! We have only to think of the couching of a cataract where there is virtually a debate of steel with nearly fluid tissue, or of the major abdominal operations (laparotomy).
>
> (Luc Durtain, *op. cit.*)

[*Editor:* although this note refers to a previous citation, there is in fact no reference giving the bibliographical details either in Zohn's translation or in the collection, edited by Hannah Arendt, where the translation appears.]

22 This mode of observation may seem crude, but as the great theoretician Leonardo has shown, crude modes of observation may at times be usefully adduced. Leonardo compares painting and music as follows:

> Painting is superior to music because, unlike unfortunate music, it does not have to die as soon as it is born . . . Music which is consumed in the very act of its birth is inferior to painting which the use of varnish has rendered eternal.
>
> (Trattato I, 29)

23 Renaissance painting offers a revealing analogy to this situation. The incomparable development of this art and its significance rested not least on the integration of a number of new sciences, or at least of new scientific data. Renaissance painting made use of anatomy and perspective, of mathematics, meteorology, and chromatology. Valéry writes:

> What could be further from us than the strange claim of a Leonardo to whom painting was a supreme goal and the ultimate demonstration of knowledge? Leonardo was convinced that painting demanded universal knowledge, and he did not even shrink from a theoretical analysis which to us is stunning because of its very depth and precision.
>
> (Paul Valéry, *Pièces sur l'art*, 'Autour de Corot,' Paris, p. 191)

24 Rudolf Arnheim, *Film als Kunst*, p. 138.

25 'The work of art,' says André Breton, 'is valuable only in so far as it is vibrated by the reflexes of the future.' Indeed, every developed art form intersects three lines of development. Technology works toward a certain form of art. Before the advent of the film there were photo booklets with pictures which flitted by the onlooker upon pressure of the thumb, thus portraying a boxing bout or a tennis match. Then there were the slot machines in bazaars; their picture sequences were produced by the turning of a crank.

Secondly, the traditional art forms in certain phases of their development strenuously work toward effects which later are effortlessly attained by the new ones. Before the rise of the movie the Dadaists' performances tried to create an audience reaction which Chaplin later evoked in a more natural way.

Thirdly, unspectacular social changes often promote a change in receptivity which will benefit the new art form. Before the movie had begun to create its public, pictures that were no longer immobile captivated an assembled audience in the so-called *Kaiserpanorama*. Here the public assembled before a screen into which stereoscopes were mounted, one to each beholder. By a mechanical process individual pictures appeared briefly before the stereoscopes, then made way for others. Edison still had to use similar devices in presenting the first movie strip before the film screen and projection were known. This strip was presented to a small public which stared into the apparatus in which the succession of pictures was reeling off. Incidentally, the institution of the *Kaiserpanorama* shows very clearly a dialectic of the development. Shortly before the movie turned the reception of pictures into a collective one, the individual viewing of pictures in these swiftly outmoded establishments came into play once more with an intensity comparable to that of the ancient priest beholding the statue of a divinity in the cella.

26 The theological archetype of this contemplation is the awareness of being alone with one's God. Such awareness, in the heyday of the bourgeoisie, went to strengthen the freedom to shake off clerical tutelage. During the decline of the bourgeoisie this awareness had to take into account the hidden tendency to withdraw from public affairs those forces which the individual draws upon in his communion with God.

27 Georges Duhamel, *Scènes de la vie future*, Paris, 1930, p. 52.

28 The film is the art form that is in keeping with the increased threat to his life which modern man has to face. Man's need to expose himself to shock effects is his adjustment to the dangers threatening him. The film corresponds to profound changes in the apperceptive apparatus – changes that are experienced on an individual scale by the man in the street in big-city traffic, on a historical scale by every present-day citizen.

29 As for Dadaism, insights important for Cubism and Futurism are to be gained from the movie. Both appear as deficient attempts of art to accommodate the pervasion of reality by the apparatus. In contrast to the film, these schools did not try to use the apparatus as such for the artistic presentation of reality, but aimed at some sort of alloy in the joint presentation of reality and apparatus. In Cubism, the premonition that this apparatus will be structurally based on optics plays a dominant part; in Futurism, it is the premonition of the effects of this apparatus which are brought out by the rapid sequence of the film strip.

30 Duhamel, *Scènes de la vie future*, p. 58.

31 One technical feature is significant here, especially with regard to newsreels, the propagandist importance of which can hardly be overestimated. Mass reproduction is aided especially by the reproduction of masses. In big parades and monster rallies, in sports events, and in war, all of which nowadays are captured by camera and sound recording, the masses are brought face to face with themselves. This process, whose significance need not be stressed, is intimately connected with the development of the techniques of reproduction and photography.

Mass movements are usually discerned more clearly by a camera than by the naked eye. A bird's-eye view best captures gatherings of hundreds of thousands. And even though such a view may be as accessible to the human eye as it is to the camera, the image received by the eye cannot be enlarged the way a negative is enlarged. This means that mass movements, including war, constitute a form of human behavior which particularly favors mechanical equipment.

21

THE ORIGINAL EXPERIENCE

Maurice Blanchot

Investigations on the subject of art such as those the esthetician pursues bear no relation to the concern for the work of which we speak. Esthetics talks about art, makes of it an object of reflection and of knowledge. Esthetics explains art by reducing it or then again exalts by elucidating it, but in all events art for the esthetician is a present reality around which he constructs plausible thoughts at no risk.

The work is deeply concerned for art. This is to say that for the work, art is never a given, and that the work can find art only by continuing toward its own completion in radical uncertainty, for it cannot know in advance whether art is what it is. As long as the work can serve art by serving other values, these permit the work to find art without having to seek it, and indeed allow that the finding not even be an issue. A work inspired by faith need not (and should not) trouble about itself. It bears witness to this faith, and if it does so poorly, if it fails, faith is not affected. Today the work has no faith other than itself. And this faith is absolute passion for that which depends upon the work alone to give it life. Yet the work by itself can discover only the absence of art. Perhaps the work has the power to present art, but only if it hides from itself that it is seeking by seeking art where the impossible preserves it. And because of this, when the work takes itself to be the task of grasping art in its essence, the impossible is its task, and the work is only realized as an infinite searching. For the characteristic most proper to the origin is to be always veiled by that of which it is the origin.

In advance of a particular work, does art not exist in other works which have already provided illustrious examples? Did Cézanne not think he encountered it in the Venetian paintings at the Louvre? If Rilke honors Hölderlin, does he not count on him for the certainty that the poem, that poetry exists? Perhaps Cézanne knows that art dwells in Venice, but the work of Cézanne does not know this. Cézanne spoke of *realization*, the supreme quality, and believed that thus he represented to himself the essence of Venetian art. But his work cannot hold this 'realization' to be essential except by achieving it.

Doubtless one can conceive of such seeking, and describe it and trace the successive steps in what seems to us to be artistic creation. Malraux, for example, has shown that the artist becomes aware of his future work by living in that embodied consciousness of art, so to speak, which the Museum is for him, and which is art, not immobilized in its particular manifestations, but perceived in the changes which make of given works moments in an actual duration, and of art the always incomplete sense of such a movement. This is a significant idea, but mainly it helps us to understand or to imagine how the work is always lacking with respect to itself. For the implication is that, without the collection of all the works which incarnate it in time, art does not exist, yet that art is 'true' only in the work always still to come.

The habits of thought which we owe to the commonplaces of subjective art lead us to believe that the artist or writer seeks to express himself and that for him what is missing from the Museum and from literature is he. What torments him, what he strives to fashion into a work, is said to be this expression of himself which he forms by means of an artistic technique.

Is Cézanne's concern to express himself, to give to art, that is, one more artist? He 'swore to die painting.' Was that just in order to live on? Does he sacrifice himself in this passion which knows no happiness simply so that his paintings might give form to the singular weather of his soul? This much no one can doubt: what he seeks has only one name. Painting. But painting can be found only in the work currently in progress, which demands that he himself exist only in it, and of which all his canvases are only traces, along an infinite road yet to be discovered.

Leonardo da Vinci is another example of this passion which wants to raise the work to the essence of art and which finally perceives in each work only an inconclusive step along the path of a search which we too recognize in the unfinished canvases, the pictures which seem open: this path is now the only essential work. We would certainly misconstrue Leonardo's destiny if we saw him as a painter who did not put his art above everything. He made painting an absolute. Yet it is not his judgments that reveal this to us, not even when he defines painting as 'the greatest spiritual process.' It is rather his anguish, that fright which seized him each time he put himself in front of a canvas. Because of conditions proper to the Renaissance, the search led Leonardo out of painting. But his was a search for art and art alone. The terror of having to realize the unrealizable, the anguish of painting, caused the search to evolve into forgetfulness of what was sought and into the exploration of a pure, useless knowledge in order that the frightful moment of realization become always more distant until the day when, in his notes, this revealing assertion was inscribed: 'One must not desire the impossible.' But why is the impossible what the work desires when it has become concern for its own origin?

Risk

In one of Rilke's letters, addressed to Clara Rilke, we find this answer: 'Works of art are always the products of a danger incurred, of an experience pursued to the end, to the point where man can no longer continue.' The work of art is linked to a risk; it is the affirmation of an extreme experience. But what is this risk? What is the nature of the bond that unites the work to risk?

From the point of view of the work (from the point of view of the requirements which characterize it and which we have described), we clearly see that it demands a sacrifice of him who makes it possible. The poet belongs to the poem; he belongs to it only insofar as he keeps to this free belonging. This relation is not simply the formal devotion which nineteenth-century writers stress. When it is said of the writer that he must live only in order to write well, or of the artist that he must sacrifice everything to the demands of his art, the perilous urgency, the prodigality of the risk which informs the artist's relation to the work is not expressed at all. The scholar too gives himself entirely to his scholarly task. And morality in general, the call of duty, pronounce the same fanatical decree, ultimately calling upon the individual to sacrifice himself and to perish. But the work is not such an unambiguous value demanding of us that we exhaust ourselves for its sake, for love of it, or out of fidelity to the goal it represents to us. If the artist runs a risk, it is because the work itself is essentially a risk. By belonging to the work, it is likewise to risk that he belongs.

In one of the *Sonnets to Orpheus*, Rilke summons us with these words:

> We, we infinitely risked.

Why infinitely? Man is the most precarious of all beings, for he jeopardizes himself. The construction of a world, the transformation of nature through productive activity, only succeeds because of a daring challenge in the course of which everything easy is discounted. However, the goal of a protected, a satisfied and secure life also finds expression in this audacity. Precise tasks and reasonable obligations also speak. Man risks his life, but he does so under the protection of the familiar light of day, in view of the useful, the beneficial, and the true. Sometimes, in revolution, in war, under the pressure of history's development he risks his world, but he always does so in the name of a greater possibility, in order to reduce what exceeds his grasp, protect what he is, ensure the values to which his power is attached – in a word, to domesticate the day and extend it or verify it insofar as is possible.

What is the risk proper to the work when the work has the essence of art for its task? But is such a question not surprising in itself? Doesn't the artist appear to be free of life's burdens, and to bear no responsibility for what he creates? Does he not seem to live at his pleasure in the imaginary where, were he to run a risk, it would still be nothing but an image?

Exile

This is true. When Saint-John Perse named one of his poems *Exile*, he named the poetic condition as well. The poet is in exile; he is exiled from the city, from regular occupations and limited obligations, from everything connected to results, substantive reality, power. The outward aspect of the risk to which the work exposes him is precisely its inoffensive appearance. The poem is inoffensive, which is to say that whoever submits to it is deprived of himself as power, consents to be cast out from his own capability and from all forms of possibility.

The poem is exile, and the poet who belongs to it belongs to the dissatisfaction of exile. He is always lost to himself, outside, far from home; he belongs to the foreign, to the outside which knows no intimacy or limit, and to the separation which Hölderlin names when in his madness he sees rhythm's infinite space.

Exile, the poem then, makes the poet a wanderer, the one always astray, he to whom the stability of presence is not granted and who is deprived of a true abode. And this must be understood in the gravest sense: the artist does not belong to truth because the work is itself what escapes the movement of the true. For always, whatever our perspective upon it, it revokes the true, eludes signification, designating that region where nothing subsists, where what takes place has nevertheless not taken place, where what begins over has never begun. It points into the realm of the most dangerous indecision, toward the confusion from which nothing emerges. This eternal outside is quite well evoked by the image of the *exterior* darkness where man withstands that which the true must negate in order to become possibility and progress.

Error is the risk which awaits the poet and which, behind him, awaits every man who writes dependent upon an essential work. Error means wandering, the inability to abide and stay. For where the wanderer is, the conditions of a definitive here are lacking. In this absence of here and now what happens does not clearly come to pass as an event based upon which something solid could be achieved. Consequently, what happens does not happen, but does not pass either, into the past; it is never passed. It happens and recurs without cease; it is the horror and the confusion and the uncertainty of eternal repetition. It is not one truth or another that lacks, or truth in general; nor is it doubt that leads us on or despair that immobilizes us. The wanderer's country is not truth, but exile; he lives outside, on the other side which is by no means a beyond, rather the contrary. He remains separated, where the deep of dissimulation reigns, that elemental obscurity through which no way can be made and which because of that makes its awful way through him.

What man risks when he belongs to the work and when the work is the search for art is, then, the most extreme thing he could risk: not just his life, not only the world where he dwells, but his essence, his right to truth, and, even more, his right to death. He departs; he becomes, as Hölderlin calls him, the migrator – he who, like the priests of Dionysos, wanders from country to country in the sacred night. This errant migration can sometimes lead him to insignificance, to the facile contentment of a life crowned with approval, the platitudes of honorific irresponsibility. Sometimes it leads him into wretched vagrancy which is only the instability of a life bereft of a work. And sometimes it takes him to the deep where everything wavers, where everything meaningful is undermined, destabilized, where this upheaval ruins the work and hides in forgetfulness.

In the poem it is not any particular individual who risks himself alone, or a particular mind that is exposed to the touch and the burn of darkness. The risk is more essential. It is the danger of dangers by which, each time, the essence of language is radically placed in doubt. To risk language: this is one of the forms of this risk. To risk being – the word uttered when absence is spoken, and which the work pronounces by pronouncing the word *beginning* – this is the other form of the risk. In the work of art, being is risked. For whereas in the world where beings repel it in order to be, being is always concealed, negated, and denied (and thus protected too), in dissimulation's realm that which is concealed tends, on the contrary, to emerge, deep down in appearance, and that which is negated becomes the excess in affirmation. But this appearance reveals nothing, nothing is affirmed by this affirmation which is only the unstable position from which, if the work succeeds in containing it, the true will be able to take *place*.

The work draws light from the dark; it is a relation with what admits of no relations; it encounters being before the encounter is possible and where truth lacks. This is the essential risk. Here we reach the abyss. Here we bind ourselves, with a bond which cannot be too strong, to the nontrue, and to it we seek to bind an essential form of authenticity. This is what Nietzsche suggests when he says, 'We have art so as not to go under [touch the bottom] on account of truth.'[1]

He does not mean, as a superficial interpretation would have it, that art is the illusion which protects us against the mortal truth. He says with more certainty: we have art in order that what makes us go all the way to the bottom not belong to the domain of truth. The very bottom, the bottomless abyss belongs to art. And art is that deep which is *sometimes* the absence of profundity, of the foundation, the pure void bereft of importance, and *sometimes* that upon which a foundation can be given, but it is also *always at the same time* one and the other, the intertwining of the Yes and of the No, the ebb and flow of the essential ambiguity. And that is why all works of art and all literary works seem to leave comprehension behind and yet seem never to reach it, so that it must be said of them that they are always understood too much and always too little.

Let us try to investigate with more precision what happens to us because 'we have art.' And what is necessary in order that we have art? What is the meaning of this possibility? We still barely glimpse the implications of such questions, which have arisen in the work only since it has had art's essence for its task. And do we have art? The question remains undecided from the moment, precisely, when what must speak in the work is its origin.

The radical reversal

When a contemporary philosopher names death as man's extreme possibility, the possibility absolutely proper to him, he shows that the origin of possibility is linked in man to the fact that he *can* die, that for him death is yet one possibility more, that the event by which man departs from the possible and belongs to the impossible is nevertheless within his mastery, that it is the extreme moment of his possibility. (And this the philosopher expresses precisely by saying of death that it is 'the possibility of impossibility.')[2] Hegel had already seen action, language, liberty, and death to be aspects of one and the same movement; he had shown that only man's constant and resolute proximity to death allows him to become active nothingness capable of negating and transforming natural reality – of combating, of laboring, of knowing, and of being historical. This is a magical force: it is the absolute power of the negative which becomes the action of truth in the world. It brings negation to reality, form to the formless, definition to the indefinite. We want to draw these limits, mark these ends, come to the finish. That is the principle behind civilization's demands, the essence of the purposeful will which seeks achievement, which demands accomplishment and attains universal mastery. Existence is authentic when it is capable of enduring possibility right up to its extreme point, able to stride toward death as toward possibility par excellence. It is to this movement that the essence of man in Western history owes its having become action, value, future, labor and truth. The affirmation that in man all is possibility requires that death itself be possible: death itself, without which man would not be able to form the notion of an 'all' or to exist in view of a totality, must be what makes all – what makes totality – possible.

But what is art, and what can we say of literature? The question returns now with a particular violence. If we have art – which is exile from truth, which is the risk of an inoffensive game, which affirms man's belonging to the limitless outside where intimacy is unknown, where he is banished from his capability and from all forms of possibility – how does this come about? How, if he is altogether possibility, can man allow himself anything resembling art? If he has art, does this not mean that, contrary to his apparently authentic definition – the requirement which is in harmony with the law of the day – he entertains with death a relation which is not that of possibility, which does not lead to mastery or to understanding or to the progressive achievements of time, but exposes him to a radical reversal? *This reversal*: would it not seem to be the *original experience* which the work must touch, upon which it closes and which constantly threatens to close in upon art and withhold it? The end, in this perspective, would no longer be that which gives man the power to end – to limit, separate, and thus to grasp – but the infinite: the dreadful infinitude on account of which the end can never be overcome. Death, then, would not be 'the possibility absolutely proper to man,' my own death, that unique event which answers Rilke's prayer: 'O Lord, grant to each his own death,' but on the contrary, that which never happens to me, so that never do I die, but rather 'they die.' Men die always other than themselves, at the level of the neutrality and the impersonality of the eternal They.

The characteristics of this reversal can only be recalled briefly here.

They die: this is not a reassuring formula designed to put off the fearsome moment. *They die*: he who dies is anonymous, and anonymity is the guise in which the ungraspable, the unlimited, the unsituated is most dangerously affirmed among us. Whoever experiences this suffers an anonymous, impersonal force, the force of an event which, being the dissolution of every event, is starting over not only now, but was in its very beginning a beginning again. And in its domain everything that happens happens over again. From the instant 'they die,' the instant is revoked. When someone dies, 'when' designates not a particular date but no matter what date. Likewise there is a level of this experience at which death reveals its nature by appearing no longer as the demise of a particular person, or as death in general, but in this neutral form: someone or other's death. Death is always nondescript. Hence the feeling that the special signs of affection which those who were close to a person recently departed still show him are out of place. For now there is no more distinction to be made between close and distant. The only appropriate tears are impersonal ones, the general sadness of official mourners delegated by the indifference of the They. Death is public. If this does not mean that it is the sheer exteriorization which the spectacular side of death as ceremony expresses, one feels nonetheless at such spectacles how much death becomes indistinct and unmasterable *error*, the shifty point from which indetermination condemns time to the exhausting futility of repetition.

The experience of art

To the poet, to the artist this summons makes itself heard: 'Be dead evermore in Eurydice.'[3] This dramatic command apparently implies a reassuring other half: Be dead evermore in Eurydice so as to be alive in Orpheus. Art brings duplicity with it. This duplicity allows it to escape its own risk. It can always extricate itself by transforming the risk into security. Then it partakes of the world – of the world's successes and advantages – without incurring its obligations. Thus does art plunge into the other risk, the one which is without danger, which signifies only the unperceived loss of art, brilliant insignificance, tranquil talk wreathed in honors.

The duplicity cannot be outdone. But it must be suffered in all its depth. The duplicity of the happy dream which invites us to die sadly in Eurydice so as to survive gloriously in Orpheus is concealment concealing itself; it is forgetfulness profoundly forgotten. Yet behind this facile forgetting which arranges for us to obtain the satisfactions of glory, the fundamental duplicity is at work as well. It detaches us from all power. Now the happy dream is not so happy: it turns into a nightmare, it falls away in confusion and misery. The inessential, the complacent lightness becomes the unbearable loss of essence; beauty withers into error, error opens onto exile – onto migration outside, where there is neither intimacy nor rest. *Be dead evermore in Eurydice.* Yes, such is the call, such the command. But deep in this order 'dead evermore' is echoed by 'alive forever,' and here 'alive' does not signify life, but – in the guise of a reassuring ambiguity – the loss of the power to die, the loss of death as power and possibility. It signifies the essential sacrifice: the radical reversal which Rilke, who perhaps always sought to outwit it, expresses without grasping all the implications of what he writes, in a letter of January 6, 1923. He asks to see no longer in death something negative, but 'das Wort Tod ohne Negation zu lesen.' To read the word death *without* negation is to withdraw from it the cutting edge of decision and the power to negate; it is to cut oneself off from possibility and the true, but also from death as true event. It is to surrender to the indistinct and the undetermined, to the emptiness anterior to events, where the end has all the heaviness of starting over.

This experience is the experience of art. Art – as images, as words, and as rhythm – indicates the menacing proximity of a vague and vacant outside, a neutral existence, nil and limitless; art points into a sordid absence, a suffocating condensation where being ceaselessly perpetuates itself as nothingness.

Art is originally linked to this fund of impotence where everything falls back when the possible is attenuated. In the world, decisive affirmation dependably serves truth as a basis and foundation, as the place from which it can arise. By comparison, art originally represents the scandalous intimation of absolute error: the premonition of something not true but whose 'not' does not have the decisive character of a limit, for it is, rather, brimming and endless indeterminacy with which the true cannot communicate. Nor does truth by any means have the power to reconquer it. The true cannot define itself vis-à-vis this 'not' except by becoming the violence of the negative.

If the essential task of the true is to negate, this is because error *affirms* in the profuse plenitude which is its preserve outside of time and in all times. This affirmation is the perpetuity of what admits neither of beginning nor of end. It is neither productive nor destructive but stagnant; it is that which has never come, which is neither staunched nor spurting forth but coming back – the eternal lapping of return. It is in this sense that in art's milieu there is a pact contracted with death, with repetition, and with failure. Beginning again, repetition, the fatal return – everything evoked by experiences where estrangement is allied with the strangely familiar, where the irremediable takes the form of an endless repetition, where the same is posed in the dizziness of redoubling, where there is no cognition but only *re*cognition – all this alludes to that initial error which might be expressed as follows: what is first is not beginning, but beginning over, and being is precisely the *impossibility* of being for the first time.

One could bring this movement more sharply into focus – but not explain it – by evoking those forms and those crises called 'complexes.' Their essence is that at the moment they come about they have already done so: they only ever return. This is their characteristic feature. They are the experience of beginning again. 'Again, again!' is the cry of anguish struggling with the irremediable, with being. Again, again, such is the closed wound of the complex. It takes place again, it recurs, yet another time. The basis of failure lies, not in the fact that an experience meets with no success, but in its beginning all over again. Everything begins again always – yes, one more time, again, again.

Some time ago now, Freud, surprised by the tendency to repeat, the powerful call of the anterior, recognized in it the call of death itself. But perhaps what must finally come out is this: he who seeks in death the meaning of repetition is also led to ruin death as possibility – to bind it in repetition's spell. Yes, we are tied to disaster, but when failure returns, it must be understood as nothing but the return. The power that begins everything over again is older than the beginning: this is the error of our death.

A return to the question

We come here to the point where the question which has been asked of us makes the contradiction, to which every answer returns, emerge in all its force. What the work says is the word *beginning*. But today the work is the work of art: art is its starting point. And it says 'the beginning' when it says 'art,' which is its origin and whose essence has become its task. But where has art led us? To a time before the world, before the beginning. It has cast us out of our power to begin and to end; it has turned us toward the outside where there is no intimacy, no place to rest. It has led us into the infinite migration of error. For we seek art's essence, and it lies where the nontrue admits of nothing essential. We appeal to art's sovereignty: it ruins the kingdom. It ruins the origin by returning to it the errant immensity of directionless eternity. The work says the word *beginning* from a starting point – art – which is complicit with the futility of starting over. The work declares being – and says choice, mastery, form – by announcing art which says the fatality of being, says passivity and formless prolixity. At the very moment of the choice art still holds us back in a primordial Yes and No. There, before any beginning, the somber ebb and flow of dissimulation rumbles.

Such is the question. It asks not to be overcome. That the work is able to pronounce the work *beginning* precisely because the origin attracts it to the place where it risks utter ruin, and because, precisely, it must escape *with a leap* the implacable insistence of something having neither beginning nor end: this might well be said. And likewise this: that the work is this leap and that it immobilizes itself mysteriously between the truth which does not belong to it and the prolixity of the unrevealable which would prevent it from belonging to itself – that it hovers between death as the possibility of understanding and death as the horror of impossibility. Moreover, the work's successful completion so close to the indefinite and the formless glorifies the proportion in it and makes its coherence, exactitude, and limit all the more impressive. Indeed, all this can be said. And it would all form the elements of an answer. But what does the answer mean as long as in it there remains this question: Do we have art? To this query there can be no decisive answer, at least not to the extent that the work's origin is its concern and that its task is the essence of what verges on the inessential.

We asked ourselves: 'Why, when history contests it, does art tend to become essential presence?' What does this presence mean? Is it only the artistic form of what contests art, the affirmation of art's poverty reversed? Or does the desolate voice which asks,

'What use are poets in time of distress?' – does the distress toward which this question points mysteriously – express the essence of art more profoundly, so that in such a presence art could no longer be anything, save its own absence? But what is the time of distress?

This expression is borrowed from the elegy *Bread and Wine* by Hölderlin:

> In these times, very often it seems to me
> Better to sleep than to be so without companions
> And to wait so; what is there to do in these times, what to say?
> I do not know; what use are poets in time of distress?[4]

What is this time during which, as René Char says as well, 'the sole certainty which we possess of tomorrow's reality . . . the perfected form of the secret where we come to refresh ourselves, take precautions and sleep'? What is this time when poetry can only say: *what use are poets*? The elegy answers us with these other lines which precede a bit those we have just cited:

> From time to time man bears the divine plenitude.
> A dream of these times, that is what life is afterwards. But error
> Helps, like sleep, and distress makes us strong as does night.

It seems that art owes the strangest of torments and the very grave passion that animate it to the disappearance of the historical forms of the divine. Art was the language of the gods. The gods having disappeared, it became the language in which their disappearance was expressed, then the language in which this disappearance itself ceased to appear. This forgetfulness now speaks all alone. The deeper the forgetfulness, the more the deep speaks in this language, and the more the abyss of this deepness can become the hearing of the word.

Forgetting, error, the unhappiness of erring can be linked to an historical period: to the time of distress when the gods are absent twice over, because they are no longer there, because they are not there yet. This vacant time is that of error, where we do nothing but err because we lack the certitude of presence and the conditions of a true here. And nevertheless error helps us, 'das Irrsal hilft.' Elsewhere, in the variant of the poem *Dichterberuf*, Hölderlin says likewise that God's lack, his default helps us: 'Gottes Fehl hilft.' What does this mean?

The force, the risk proper to the poet is to dwell in God's default, the region where truth lacks. *The time of distress* designates the time which in all times is proper to art. But when historically the gods lack and the world of truth wavers, the time of distress emerges in the work as concern – the concern in which the work finds its preserve – threatening it: making it present and visible. The time of art is the time before time. The collective presence of the divine evokes this time by hiding it; history and the productive movement of history revoke it by denying it, and the work shows it, in the distress of the *What use*? as that which hides deep down in appearance, reappears in the heart of disappearance, comes to pass in the proximity and under the threat of a radical reversal, the reversal at work when 'they die.' Perpetuating being in the form of nothingness, this reversal changes light into fascination, the object into the image, and it makes us into the empty center of eternal repetition.

And yet 'error helps us.' It is the intimation in waiting, the deep of sleep keeping watch, the silent void of sacred memory. The poet is the intimacy of distress. He alone profoundly lives the empty time of absence, and in him error becomes straying's profundity, night becomes the *other* night. But what does this mean? When René Char writes, 'May risk light your way'; when Georges Bataille, comparing fortune and poetry says, 'The absence of poetry is misfortune'; when Hölderlin calls the empty, distressful present 'bountiful suffering, bountiful happiness,' what is seeking to express itself in these words? Why should our light come from risk? Why should the time of distress be the fortunate time? When Hölderlin speaks of poets who, like the priests of Bacchus, go wandering from country to country in the sacred night, is this perpetual departure, the *sorrow of straying* which has no place to arrive, to rest, also the *fecund migration*, the movement which mediates, that which makes of rivers a language and of language the dwelling, the power by which day abides and is our abode?

So then, is the work really the marvel of the beginning, in which error's indefiniteness would preserve us from inauthenticity's fraud? And is the nontrue an essential form of authenticity?[5] In that case, we do, then, have the work? We have art?

To this question there can be no response. The poem is the answer's absence. The poet is one who, through his sacrifice, keeps the question open in his work. At every time he lives the time of distress, and his time is always the empty time when what he must live is the double infidelity: that of men, that of the gods – and also the double absence of the gods who are no longer *and* who are not yet. The poem's space is entirely represented by this *and*, which indicates the double absence, the separation at its most tragic instant. But as for whether it is the *and* that unites and binds together, the pure word in which the void of the past and the void of the future become true presence, the 'now' of dawn – this question is reserved in the work. It is that which reveals itself in the work by returning to concealment, to the distress of forgetting. That is why the poem is solitude's poverty. This solitude is a grasp of the future, but a powerless grasp: prophetic isolation which, before time, ever announces the beginning.

Translated by Ann Smock

Notes

1 'Wir haben die Kunst, damit wir nicht an der Wahrheit zu Grunde gehen.'
2 Emmanuel Levinas is the first to have brought out what was at stake in this expression (*Time and the Other*, Pittsburgh, Duquesne University Press, 1990).
3 Rilke, *Sonnets to Orpheus*, XII, Pt. 2.
4 *In dürftiger Zeit*. The German expression is tougher and drier than the French [*au temps de détresse*]. It announces that toughness, that rigor with which the late Hölderlin defends himself against his yearning for the gods who have withdrawn, and maintains the distinction between the spheres – the one above and the one here below. With this distinction, Hölderlin maintains the purity of the sacred realm left empty by the double infidelity of men and gods. For the sacred is this very void, the sheer void of the interval which must be kept pure and empty according to the ultimate requirement: 'Preserve God with the purity of what distinguishes.'
5 To present this question in a context closer to historical actuality, one might say: the more the world is affirmed as the future and the broad daylight of truth, where everything will have value, bear meaning, where the whole will be achieved under the mastery of man and for his use, the more it seems that art must descend toward that point where nothing has meaning yet, the more it matters that art maintain the movement, the insecurity and the grief of that which

escapes every grasp and all ends. The artist and the poet seem to have received this mission: to call us obstinately back to error, to turn us toward that space where everything we propose, everything we have acquired, everything we are, all that opens upon the earth and in the sky, returns to insignificance, and where what approaches is the nonserious and the nontrue, as if perhaps thence sprang the source of all authenticity.

22

ARTISTIC ILLUSION AS VISIBLE ANTICIPATORY ILLUMINATION

Ernst Bloch

It is said that the beautiful provides pleasure. It might even be enjoyed. But that is not reward enough, for art is not food. Art lasts after it is enjoyed, and even in the most delightful cases art continues to exhibit itself in a 'prepainted' landscape. The wish dream reaches out for the indisputable better, and while doing so, it is something beautifully *shaped*, in contrast to the wish dream that has already become mainly political and operatable (*werkhaft*). Yet, one must ask whether there is something more than some illusionary play in those beautifully shaped creations? Is there something that is extremely artistic, but that, in contrast to the childlike, does not prepare for anything serious and means something? Is there any face value in the aesthetic chimes or sounds, any message that can be endorsed? Paintings enter less into this question since color has only a sensual certainty, and besides, color makes much less a claim on truth than words. Indeed, words not only serve poetry but also truthful information, and language provides more sensitivity for the latter than color, even as a drawing. Of course, all good art shapes and finishes its subject matter in a beautiful way, depicts things, people, conflicts in beautiful illusion. But what are we *honestly* to say about the way things are ended, about their maturation, in which only things that are invented are allowed to mature? What can we say about an abundance of material that is communicated in an illusionary way, in appearances (*Augenschein*) and sound (*Ohrenschein*)? What is the significance of Schiller's remarkable prophetic statement that what has been felt as something beautiful will come toward us one day as the truth? What is the significance of Plotinus' statement and later Hegel's that beauty is the sensual appearance of the *idea*? In his positivist period, Nietzsche confronted that assertion with a decisively more massive one, that all poets lie. Or, the arts make the vision of life more bearable by covering it with the veil of impure thinking. Francis Bacon sees the golden apples in the silver bowl as closely connected to deception (*Blendwerk*). They belong to the traditional *Idola theatri*. He compares truth to bare, bright daylight where masks, masquerades, and festive processions of the world appear only half as beautiful and majestic as they do in the candlelight of the art. Accordingly, artists are devoted to illusion from beginning to end. They have no proclivity for the truth; rather, the opposite. Premises for this antithesis of truth versus art can be found throughout the Enlightenment, and these premises made the artistic imagination suspicious when confronting a sense for facts. They were the *empirical* objections against the melancholy and flattened features, against the golden mist of the arts, and they were not the only ones that emanated from the Enlightenment. Next to these empirical objections there were the *rational* objections, which initially belonged to the Platonic theory of concepts and its especially famous, especially radical hostility toward the arts. In the calculatory course of reason during the bourgeois modern age, these rational objections made themselves fashionable again. This happened at a time when, according to Marx, there was a specific hostility toward art by capitalism in the nineteenth century – with the *l'art pour l'art* and the declaration of war by the Goncourts against the 'public' as counterattacks – that was unable to leave its mark. But the ludicrous inquiry of that French mathematician, who asked, 'What does that prove?' after seeing Racine's *Iphegenie*, is appropriate here. This question may seem ludicrous and also narrow-minded. Yet, it is, as a *purely rational* question, in keeping with a specific and great tradition of alienation from the arts and in keeping with the empiricist tradition. It is significant that, in all great systems of reason in the rationalistic modern age, the aesthetic component is omitted. The ideas in the aesthetic component are not deemed worthy of scientific discussion. During the period of French classical rationalism, the most important theories of art were concerned with poetry and with art *techniques*. Descartes was only interested in the mathematical aspects of music. Otherwise, neither in Descartes nor in Spinoza could one get the idea that art was included in the system of ideas and objects. Even the universal Leibniz used very few examples from the arts. For instance, there is a reference about the harmony enhancing effects of shadows and dissonances, but he used this because it served him for matters of much greater importance, namely, to verify what was the best of all worlds. For Leibniz, the harmonic beauty is a kind of indication of the scientifically discernible harmony of the world, but it is only a confused allusion, and therefore the truth can do without it. Consequently, the aesthetics of rationalism originated very late in a strange way: it became a philsophical discipline in the hands of the Wolffian philosopher Baumgarten and began with clear contempt for its object, even with an apology for the existence of its object. The aesthetic object was the so-called inferior capacity of cognition that was effectual in sensual perception and its projections. And even if beauty represented perfection in this area, it was not comparable to the value of conceptual cognition and its comprehensive clarity. The *rationalistic* degradation of the arts was in keeping with the empirical positivist position. And yet, this is not all that is to be said about the groups hostile toward art. The hatred of art became really glaring when it was based not on reason, but on faith, in the belief in the establishment of a *spiritual* truth. Then the hatred of art moved in its attack from the golden mist of art, which was usually the target of the empiricists and rationalists, to superficiality; beauty succumbs completely to the insubstantial exterior and therefore diverts from the essence of things. 'What is good about imitating the shadows of shadows?' Plato asks and thus makes his theory of concepts intellectually almost blunt. On the other hand: 'Thou shalt not make unto thee a graven image, nor any manner of likeness, of any thing that is in heaven above, or that is in the earth beneath, or that is in the water under the earth' is what the fourth commandment in the Bible commands and gives the key word for the hostility toward art in regard to Jahweh's invisibility and the prohibition of all idolatry. Hence, art in general became glistening, ultimately Luciferian perfection, which hindered the truly non-glistening art, and which even repudiated it. This was *religious* and *spiritual* hostility toward the arts. The equivalent in morality was logically a rejection of the all too great visibility of the 'work' and a turn toward the invisible genuineness of their 'character' (*Gesinnung*). Puritanism in such a comprehensive sense – reaching back to Bernhard de Clairvaux – finally culminated in Tolstoy's monstrous hatred of Shakespeare, culminated in the hatred of the bastion of beauty in general. Even in Catholicism during the time of Pope Marcellus, a *horror pulchri* led to the planned prohibition of the rich church music. And this horror, applied to what was visible, gave Protestantism the bare God who, in a moral belief, wanted to be worshipped through the word that is the truth. Thus, the claim of truth against beauty occurred in various forms – empirical, rationalistic, spiritual, and religious. Although these different claims on truth – subjectively the spiritual claim was one too – were disunited and so contradictory, they found a basis for unity in their serious intention to combat the game of illusion.

This issue has always moved the artists as well, especially since they took themselves seriously. In particular those artists, who refrained from dabbling with the arts in an isolated or decadent manner, felt committed to the question of truth. In the descriptions and stories of great realistic writers something beautiful also wants to be graphically true in a sufficient manner. It wants to be graphically true not only on the level of sensuous certainty but also on the level of wide open social relations, of elementary processes. This is how legitimate Homer's realism is, which is a realism of such complete accuracy that almost all of the Mycenaean civilization can be brought to mind with it. And Alexander von Humboldt, the natural scientist, – not a French mathematician – concluded from the 37th chapter of *Book of Job* that

> the meteorological processes taking place in the clouds, the formation and dissolution of the mist with different directions of the wind, the play of colors, the generation of hail and rolling thunder are described with individual plasticity. Also many questions are posed which our present discipline of physics knows how to formulate in scientific terminology but which it cannot solve sufficiently.
>
> (*Kosmos III*, Cotta, p. 35)

This sort of precision and reality is certainly part and parcel of all great writing, often of expressly spiritual and religious writing as in the imagery of the psalms. And the demand of significant realism to counter all superficiality and also all extravagance has been acknowledged by art itself to the honor of Homer, Shakespeare, Goethe, Keller, and Tolstoy. In recent times it has been the novel that has satisfied this demand, rising to great heights as if there had never been a distrust of *magister ludi* and his games in the name of veracity. And yet, the artists, and even the most practical ones, have not *settled* the question of aesthetic truth. At most they have enlarged it and made it more precise in a desirable and significant manner, for a realistic work of art in particular reveals that it is as an *art work*, that it is somewhat different from a source of historical or scientific knowledge or even discoveries. Precious words are peculiar to the art work, and they compel what is so strikingly signified by them beyond its given position. Telling stories is peculiar to the art work acting between persons and events in a way extremely alien to science. It is the telling of stories and also the artistry (*Kunst-Fertigkeit*) through which the empty space between what has been concretely observed is filled with what has been invented and that gives the action a well-rounded shape. But a semblance of rounding things out, rounding them over (*Überrunden*), is quite obvious in even the most realistic art works, especially in literary prose. The great illusion has a total effect that cannot be 'outdone' in those art works that do not present themselves as primarily realistic, be it that they consciously romanticize along with or beyond the existing conditions (*Vorhandenheit*), be it that they fructify far beyond a mere 'subject' the myth, which is the oldest nutrient of the arts anyway. Giotto's *Raising Lazarus from the Dead*, Dante's *Paradiso*, heaven in the last act of *Faust*, how do they relate – beyond all realism in regard to details – to the question of philosophers concerning truth? These works are certainly not true in the sense that they are borne out by all the knowledge that we have gathered from the world. But what is the meaning of the enormous impact of these works in form and content in regard to the world and legitimate issues? Here the question by that French mathematician 'What does that prove?' reemerges surprisingly on another level and cannot be avoided even if we dispense with mathematicians and farce. To put it differently, the question about the truth of art becomes philosophically the question concerning the given reproductive potentiality of the beautiful illusion, concerning its degree of reality in a reality of the world that is not one-dimensional, concerning the place of its object correlate. Utopia as the determination of the object, with the degree of being (*Seinsgrad*) of the really possible (*Realmöglichen*), presents a particularly rich problem for corroboration in the light of the iridescent phenomenon of art. And the answer to the aesthetic question about truth is that artistic illusion is generally not only mere illusion but one wrapped in images, a meaning that only portrays in images what can be carried on, where *the exaggeration and the telling of stories* (*Ausfabelung*) *represent an anticipatory illumination of reality circulating and signifying in the active present* (*Bewegt-Vorhandenen*), in an anticipatory illumination, which portrays things in a specifically aesthetic immanent way. Here, individual, social, and also elemental events are illuminated that the usual or sharp senses can barely detect yet. It is due to the fact that the anticipatory illumination is attainable in this way, that art propels its subjects, figures, situations, actions, landscapes to the end, that it expresses these things in sorrow, in fortune as well as in meaning. Anticipatory illumination itself is attainable by virtue of the fact that the craft (*métier*) of *propelling something to the end takes place in a dialectically open space*, where all objects can be aesthetically portrayed. To portray aesthetically means to be more immanent and accomplished, to be more elaborate, more essential than in the direct and sensual or direct and historical presence of this object. This elaboration, as anticipatory illumination, also remains an outward appearance, but it does not remain fantasy. Rather, everything that appears in the art images is sharpened, condensed, or made more decisive, and this is rarely shown by reality that is experienced. This decisiveness is based in the subjects themselves, makes the art with a substantiated illusion recognizable when looked at in the theater as paradigmatic institution. This art remains virtual but in the same sense as a mirror image is virtual; i.e., it reproduces an object, outside of itself, in all its depth onto a plane of reflection. And the anticipatory illumination, in contrast to religious illusion, remains immanent in all transcendence. The anticipatory illumination expands, as Schiller defined aesthetic realism using Goethe's works as an example, it expands 'nature without going beyond it.' Beauty and even the sublime are thus representative for a not-yet-developed existence of things, representative for a totally formed world without external coincidence, without unessentials, without incompletion (*Unausgetragenheit*). Therefore, the program of the aesthetically attempted anticipatory illumination is, How *to make the world be made perfect without exploding the world and without letting it apocaly[p]tically vanish as in the Christian-religious anticipatory illumination* (see also Ernst Bloch, *The Spirit of Utopia*, 1923, p. 141). Art, which possesses various concrete figures at all times, seeks this perfection only in those figures, with totality as something special that is regarded in a penetrating way. In contrast, religion seeks the utopian perfection in the totality, and salvation places the individual case completely within the universal, places it into 'I will make everything anew.' The human being shall be born again here; society shall be transformed into the *Civitas dei*; nature shall be transfigured into the divine. Art is different because it remains rounded. As 'classical' art, it loves the sailing around the existing coasts. Even as Gothic art, which crossed all boundaries, it contained something balanced, something homogenized. Only music, performed in open spaces, has an explosive effect, and that is why the art of music has always something eccentric in regard to the other arts, as if music were only transposed to the level of beauty and sublimity. All the other arts pursue the depiction of the pure carat value in individual figures, situations, and activities in the world without blowing the world up. That is why there is the complete visibility of this anticipatory illumination. Thus, art is non-illusion, for it has its effect in an extension of what developed (*Gewordenen*), in its formed, more suitable realization (*Ausprägung*). This can be seen in the writing of Juvenal, who, in order to express all possible frightening elements of a tempest, called it 'poetica tempestas,' in Goethe's profound remarks on Diderot's *Essay on Painting*, in which he pitted concentration as realism against naturalism that merely reproduced things as they are: 'And so the artist, grateful to nature which also created him, returns a second nature to nature but one that is filled, one that is imagined, one that is humanly perfect.' But at the same time, this humanized nature is one that is more perfect within itself, not in the manner of the sensual appearance of a finished idea, as Hegel taught us, but in the sense that it moves toward an increasing entelechical realization, as Aristotle pointed out. Even this entelechical or, as Aristotle also said, that which is typical and brings about completion is recalled in Engels' statement that realistic art is the depiction of typical characters in typical situations. The typical in Engels' definition does not mean, of course, the average but that which is significantly characteristic, in brief, the essential image of an object that is decisively developed in exemplary stages. Thus, the solution to the question of aesthetic truth lies in this direction: *art is a laboratory and also a feast of accomplished possibilities* plus the experienced alternatives within it while the performance as well as the result take place in the manner of the substantiated illusion, i.e., of the worldly completed anticipatory illumination. In great art, exaggeration as well as telling stories are most visibly applied to tendentious consequence and concrete utopia. Whether, of course, the call for perfection – we could call it the godless prayer of poetry – becomes practical to some degree and not only remains within aesthetic anticipatory illumination is not for poetry to decide but for society. Only a mastered history with an intervening countermove against inhibitions, with a decisive promotion of the tendency can help the essential, within the distance of art, become more of a phenomenon in dealing with life. Of course, this is the same as properly developed iconoclasm, which does not mean the destruction of art works but the intrusion into them, in order to fructify what has been, not only typically but paradigmatically, therefore exemplarily preserved in the art works. Wherever art does not play into the hands of illusion, there beauty, even sublimity, is that which mediates a presentiment of future freedom. Often rounded, never closed, Goethe's maxim of life is also valid for the arts – with the accent of conscience and content placed ultimately on openness.

The false autarky; the anticipatory illumination as real fragment

Often rounded: it does not suit a beautiful picture to present itself unfinished. What is incomplete is external to the picture, does not belong to it, and the artist who does not finish his work becomes unhappy about this. That is completely right and self-evident insofar as we are dealing with the sufficient formative power. The source of artistry is skill, which understands its subject and thus wants totally to nurture it. Of course, for the sake of the intimate nurturing, we have to pay attention to the threat by that kind of artistry that does not stem from skill but from the component of *mere illusion*, which is inherent even in the anticipatory illumination. The temptation of satisfied contemplation and its portrayal is sufficient for mere illusion, whether that which is portrayed is as imaginary as it might be. The imaginary or what has become imaginary can lend a particularly decorative roundedness to the mere illusion, one in which the seriousness of the matter least disturbs or interrupts the beautifully coherent play. Due to the fact that mere illusion lets the image live together particularly easily in a particularly irreal way, it guarantees that pleasant superficial coherence, which does not display any interest and presence of an object beyond the blank illusion. Disbelief in the depicted object can even be an aid to the smooth illusion, more than skepticism. Renaissance paintings show that in their depiction of the ancient gods the painters did not have to be afraid of not having sufficiently dealt with the sacred. The same is evident not much later in mythologically rounded poetry. In the *Lusiads*, Camoëns lets his goddess Themis say very ironically and yet in the most flowery verses that she herself, as well as Saturn, Jupiter, and all the other gods who appear, are 'conceited fabulous creatures, who are conducted to the mortals by blind delusion and only serve to provide fascination for the songs.' Although, in this case, the mythological substance has been retained through the use of the beautiful illusion, which was added to the possible allegories of an anticipatory illumination. This was accomplished by means of that completed fullness invited particularly by the illusion that is continuous. And finally, here is another invitation that comes from the side of the *immanence without the explosive leap* (*sprengenden Sprung*), as it exists for all the arts, not only for antiquity or the ancient classical art. In particular, the art of the Middle Ages provides several examples for a rounded aesthetic satisfaction despite the religious transcendental conscience. The Gothic style contains this conscience, but within itself there was an equally peculiar harmony deriving from the Greek classical balance. In the early works of Lukács he quite perceptively, although in an exaggerated way, noted that

> the church became a new polis . . . the leap became the gradation of the earthly and heavenly hierarchies. And in Giotto and Dante, in Wolfram von Eschenbach and Pisano, in St. Thomas and St. Francis the world became round again, easy to survey. The abyss lost the threat inherent in its actual depth, but all of its darkness, without losing any of its black-shining power, became pure surface and thus fitted itself easily into a closed unity of colors. The cry for redemption turned into a dissonance within the perfect rhythmic system of the world and thus made possible a new equilibrium no less colorful and

> perfect than that of the Greeks: the equilibrium of inadequate, heterogeneous intensities.
>
> (*The Theory of the Novel*, pp. 37–38)

However, the German secessions of the Gothic style, like those of Grünewald, are not affected by this kind of perfection. But this hypostasis of the aesthetic looks at us, even if not in full classical strength, all the more consistently from the Middle Ages, which remained determined by the Mediterranean. And therein is a harmony and a completeness of coherence that is not only idealistic but that, according to its last origins, stems from the great Pan, the prototype of all roundness. Pan is the one and all of the world and had been honored as that wholeness that does not lack anything. Hence, the ultimate temptation to nothing else than roundness, but hence, Greek equilibrium as the secular manner of the entirely pagan, and thus *the conception of the world without a leap: the astral myth*. In that myth the cosmos was really 'decoration,' i.e., balanced beauty; it circled continuously and *hen kai pan* a circle itself and not an open parable. It was a sphere and not a process fragment. Therefore, there is a reason why art is very often pantheistically based on those far too rounding (*rundenden*) figures, and conversely there is a reason why a system that fits together completely has a pleasing effect even outside art. The pleasure in the sensual appearance, in the living attire of the god, certainly contributes to that pantheistic aspect, but the harmonic undisrupted nexus, the 'cosmos' even without 'universe,' entices one more strongly to that pantheistic aspect. All these are the different reasons why a veritable artistry, an autarky of the apparent completeness can live in the art work, an exaggerated immanent completeness that first conceals the anticipatory illumination. But it is also true – and that is the decisive other, the decisive truth – that all great art shows that which is satisfactory and homogeneous about its work-coherence and where it is ruptured, unsealed, unfolded by its own iconoclasm, wherever the immanence has not been pushed to formal and substantial completeness, wherever that great art presents itself as still being *fragmented*. There, an objective, a highly objective hollow space with an *un-rounded immanence*, is opened – totally incomparable with the sheer coincidence of the avoidable fragmentation. And particularly there, the *aesthetic utopian meanings* of the beautiful, even of the sublime, reveal their conditions. Only what is broken in the art work silenced by the tone of the gallery that has made it into a mere *objet d'art*, or, better yet, only the already formed openness in great art works, provides the material and the form for the great cipher of the actual (*Eigentlichen*).

Never being closed, it fits the all too beautiful particularly well when the veneer breaks – when the surface turns pale or becomes darker, as in the evening when the light shines obliquely and the mountains emerge. The shattering of the surface just as the shattering of the merely cultural and ideological circumstances in which the works had been situated uncovers the profundity wherever it is. What is meant here is not the sentimental ruins and also not the kind of torso that, as often in Greek statues, keeps the figures closer together, produces greater unity and sculptural rigidity. Although that kind is possibly an enhancement of form, it does not necessarily reinforce the cipher, which is what counts in this instance. The reinforcement of the cipher happens only through the cracks of decay in the very specific sense that the decay has in regard to the *objet d'art* and as the transformation of the *objet d'art*. In this way, a *belated* fragment develops instead of ruins or the torso, namely, a fragment that can do better justice to the substantial depth of art than completion (*Beendetheit*), a completion that the work might exhibit on the spot. Thus, all great art becomes a belated fragment in the course of decay toward the essential, even totally self-contained art as the Egyptian, for the utopian ground blossoms in which the art work was planted. If the appropriation of the cultural heritage must always be critical, then this appropriation contains the self-dissolution of the *objet d'art*, which has become a museum showpiece as a particularly important element, but also contains the self-dissolution of the false finality (*Abgeschlossenheit*), which wants to have the art work in the right place and which makes more of a museum piece out of it. Such insularity takes a leap, and a sequence of figures arises, full of open, seductive symbol formations. And it arises even more when the phenomenon of the belated fragment connects with the fragment that *is created in the art work itself*, i.e., not in the usual, even shallow sense of the fragmentary as something unskilled or completed at random, but in a concrete sense as that which is not concluded despite supreme skill, that which *is transformed through the utopian pressure*. This is the case with great Gothic art, sometimes also with Baroque art, which has with all its powerful works a hollow space and behind that a fruitful darkness. Thus, the fully developed Gothic art, despite the presence of Pan, conducts a fragment of the central incapacity-to-finish (*Nicht-Enden-Können*). It is fitting when fragments develop in the usual sense of discontinuation, but it is unusual when the *Ultimum* appears, implicitly even though this is the only legitimate sense. Thus, Michelangelo left more fragments than any other great master, and this should give us cause for thought because it was the métier in which he was most adept, in sculpture, not painting. In painting he finished all the things he had started, whereas in ornamented columns, also in his architecture, he had pushed aside many half-finished things, which he never pulled out again and which he bequeathed. Vasari alerted art history to ponder the small number of Michelangelo's completely finished works and to ponder even more so when one considers that the huge dimension of the intended goal totally corresponded with the strength and nature of this genius. But that which corresponded to the huge dimension in Michelangelo himself, his own understanding of his overpowering nature and how to overpower a task, resisted the roundness and perfection of art in such a way that nothing of what had been carried out could become adequate or even perfect. Thus, perfection is driven so deep into whatever there is that it becomes a fragment. Such a fragment then is nothing less than an ingredient of the non-temple-like (*Un-Tempelhaften*), of the nonharmonic cathedral-like (*Kathedralischen*). It is conscience: the Gothic style still exists *post festum*. The depth of aesthetic perfection itself sets the unfinished in motion. In this respect, the non-fragmentary in Michelangelo in the customary sense, the figures of the Medici tomb, and the dome of St. Peter's Cathedral extend into that immensity that is the standard for the ultimate in the arts. Here we find the legitimate basis of the objective fragmentary for all works of this ultimate kind, in the *Westöstliche Diwan*, in Beethoven's last quartets – in *Faust*, in short, wherever, the inability to finish produces something great. And if one searches for the ideological reason that continues to be effective for such an inner iconoclasm in great perfect art and particularly there, then this reason lies in the pathos of the process, in the eschatological conscience, which was brought to the world by the Bible. In the religion of the Exodus and the realm, totality is solely a totally transformed and explosive one, a utopian totality. And in the face of this totality, not only our knowledge but also our entire previous development, to which our conscience refers, appear as a patchwork – as patchwork or objective fragment especially in the most productive sense, not only in the sense of the limitation of the species or even in the sense of resignation. The phrase 'See, I will make everything anew' in the sense of the apocalyptic explosion reigns above all that and influences all great art with the spirit after which Dürer named his Gothic creation *Apocalypsis cum figuris*. The human being is still not pervious. The course of the world is still undecided, unended, and so is the depth in all aesthetic information: *this utopian element is the paradox in the aesthetic immanence. It is the most thoroughly immanent to itself.* The aesthetic imagination would have enough conception in the world without that potential for the fragment, more than any other apperception, but ultimately there would be no correlate. For the world itself, as it lies in malice, lies in incompleteness and in the experimental process away from malice. The figures that this process generates, the ciphers, the allegories, and the symbols, in which the process is so rich, are *altogether fragments, real-fragments themselves through which the process flows unevenly and through which the process proceeds dialectically toward further forms of fragments*. The fragmentary is also valid for the symbol, although the symbol does not relate to the process but to the *unum necessarium* within the process. But the symbol also contains the fragment especially through that relation and by the fact that it is only a relation and not an attainment. The real-symbol itself is only one because it is not yet manifest in itself and for itself instead of being concealed from the observer and entirely clear in itself and for itself. It is that which makes the importance of the fragment from the point of view of art and not only from the art. The fragment is part of the object itself. It belongs, *rebus sic imperfectis et fluentibus*, to the matter of the world. The concrete utopia as determination of the object (*Objektbestimmtheit*) presupposes the concrete fragment as determination of the object and involves it, even though it may undoubtedly be the ultimate sublation. All artistic and religious anticipatory illumination is concrete only to the degree and measure that the fragmentary ultimately provides the level and the material for this, to constitute itself as the anticipatory illumination.

The matter concerns realism, all that is real has a horizon

To stick to things, to skim through them, both are wrong. Both remain external, superficial and abstract – as something immediate they remain tied to the surface. The sticking adheres to that surface anyway. Skimming through things has the surface in its own open interior as well as in the other, the merely evaporated immediacy to which it escapes. Still, skimming through things is more typical of a superior type of human than taking things as they are. Above all, sticking to things, even as a conscious act, remains shallow, i.e., empiristic, whereas imagining things or dreaming can become restrained when it becomes conscious. The shallow empiricist like the effusive enthusiast is always surprised by the flow of the real that both do not comprehend. As a fetishist of the so-called facts, the empiricist remains obstinate, whereas the dreamer may be teachable. In the world, it is only reification that conforms to the empiricist's notions, the reification that captures individual elements and solidifies them as facts, and the empiricist is bound to it. In contrast, skimming through things is at least movement. Thus, it reveals a behavior that does not have to be fundamentally capable of being unmediated with real movement. In regard to the formation process, skimming through things involves art even though with a lot of illusion, with a lot of dubious escape toward an intentionally untrue dream-illusion. But the concrete adjustment of skimming opens pictures, insights, and tendencies in art and not only in art alone that happen simultaneously in human beings and in corresponding objects. In particular, that which is concrete does not derive from the groveling empiricism and the corresponding aesthetic naturalism that never moves forward from the establishment of what is factual to the exploration of what essentially happens. In contrast, the imagination, as soon as it emerges concretely, knows how to bring to mind not only sensual exuberance but equally the relations of mediation in the really experienced (*erlebniswirklichen*) immediacy as well as behind it. Instead of the isolated fact and the superficial coherence of abstract immediacy, equally isolated from the entirety, the appearances relate to the entirety of their epoch and to the utopian totality that is in process. Through this kind of imagination, art becomes knowledge, i.e., by means of striking individual images and total paintings (*Gesamtgemälde*) of a characteristic and typical kind. Art investigates the 'meaningfulness' of the appearances and brings it to realization. By means of such an imagination, science grasps the 'meaningfulness' of the appearances through concepts that never remain abstract, that never cause the phenomenon to fade or ever lose it. In art and also in science, 'meaningfulness' is the specific of the general, is the respective instance for the dialectically typical coherence. It is the respective characteristically typical figure of totality. And the actual totality, where also the comprehended epochal entirety of all epochal elements is again an element itself, reveals itself particularly in the broadly conveyed great works only on the horizon, not in a broadly developed reality. Everything vital, Goethe says, has an atmosphere around it; everything real by virtue of being life, being process, by possibly being the correlate of the objective imagination, has on the whole a horizon. There is an inner horizon, which stretches vertically so to speak in self-darkness (*Selbstdunkel*), and an outer horizon of large breadth in the light of the world (*Weltlicht*). Both horizons, in their background (*Dahinter*), are filled with the same utopia. Consequently, they are identical in the ultimate. Where the prospective horizon is omitted, reality appears there only as a has-been, as a dead one, and it is the dead, namely, the naturalists and empiricists, who bury their dead ones here. Where the prospective horizon is continuously kept in sight, reality appears there as what it is concretely: as a network of paths (*Wegegeflecht*) of dialectical processes that take place in an unfinished world, in a world that would be totally unchangeable without the enormous future, the real possibilities within it. This includes the totality, which does not represent the isolated entirety of each part of a process, but which represents the entirety of the matter that is pending in the process in general. Therefore, it is a matter that is still tendentious and latent. This alone is realism. To be sure, it is not accessible to schematism of any kind that knows everything in advance, and that considers its uniform and formalistic pattern to be reality. Reality without real possibilities is not complete. The world without future-bearing (*zukunftstragende*) qualities deserves as little regard, art, or science as the world of the philistine does. *The concrete utopia stands at the horizon of every reality; the real possibility encloses the open dialectical tendency–latency until the very last moment*. The unconcluded movement of the unconcluded matter – and movement is, according to the profound words of Aristotle, 'unfinished entelechy' – is ultra-realistically traversed by that dialectical tendency–latency.

Translated by Jack Zipes and Frank Mecklenburg

Part 5

POSTSTRUCTURALISM AND POSTMODERNISM

INTRODUCTION

Georges Bataille	Sanctity, Eroticism and Solitude
Roland Barthes	The Plates of the *Encyclopedia*
Michel Foucault	Las Meninas
Jacques Derrida	The Parergon
Paul de Man	The Resistance to Theory
Jean Baudrillard	The Evil Demon of Images
Jean-François Lyotard	The Sublime and the Avant-Garde
Gilles Deleuze and **Félix Guattari**	Percept, Affect, and Concept

The terms 'poststructuralism' and 'postmodernism' are often used interchangeably. They have distinct but related meanings. In some cases, when the context is general or unspecific, the distinction can be blurred; in others, however, it is important to observe their differences, especially when one bears in mind their antecedents, structuralism and modernism. As I indicate in my introduction to the 'Modernism' section above, the modern is characterized by man's self-image as an autonomous, rational being, distinct from God, who, through reason and sensory experience, is able to know and manipulate the world. Modernism – modern aesthetic practice and debate – is a facet of this: dependent upon the techniques and technologies which the manipulation and understanding of the world have brought, and preoccupied with the medium of representation (paint, sound, words) either as something expressive in its own right or as something which can open up a new, non-imitative perspective on the world.

'Postmodernism' refers to the ideas and beliefs which follow from or emerge in response to modern thought. More specifically, it is a reaction against the excesses of modernism. It contests the model of an absolute, all-seeing reason, distinct from the contingencies of its physical environment and incapable of accommodating diversity. As Horkheimer and Adorno argue in *The Dialectic of Enlightenment* (1947),[1] Stalin, Hitler, Auschwitz, and Hiroshima are all demonstrations of what happens when truth is conceived as the shaping of the world in accordance with a universal template. Postmodernism is, therefore, suspicious of all claims to universal truth. In response, through the various forms in which it is manifest, it promotes recognition of the contingent, historical, constructed aspects of cultural practice. For example, the Lloyds building in London and the Pompidou Centre in Paris are considered exemplars of postmodern architecture because vital elements of construction and orientation normally hidden or kept inside, such as joints, ducting, stairwells, are made prominent and placed outside.

However, while it represents the restoration of materiality to thought, intention, and design, the postmodern is not a complete rejection of the modern. Such 'start-from-scratch' strategies only amount to placing confidence once again in ahistorical, clear, and distinct perception, and thus represent a forgetting of the past and all that should be learned from it. In 'Answering the Question: What is Postmodernism?', Lyotard avows that postmodernism is most visible in the processes of critique and reassessment which have driven the revolutions in modernism. 'Postmodernism thus understood is not modernism at its end but in the nascent state, and this state is constant.'[2] A *modern* aesthetic, he suggests, promotes consistent, recognizable forms of representation, whereas a *postmodern* aesthetic 'denies itself the solace of good forms' and 'searches for new presentations' which can 'impart a stronger sense of the unpresentable'.[3] Thus, for Lyotard, the postmodern works within the modern to draw attention to the mechanisms which have served the will to truth as processes or forms in their own right. The aesthetic is a crucial category for postmodernism. Its history as a realm of experience which exceeds conceptualization means that it represents a source of resistance to universal, reductive generalizations. Although modern figures such as Kant, Hegel, and some phenomenologists might try to enlist the aesthetic as that which motivates or completes abstract thought, much postmodern theory sets out to problematize or undermine these attempts.

Structuralism and poststructuralism are decisive movements in the demonstration of the material, constructed nature of knowledge. Structuralism originates in the work of the Swiss linguist Ferdinand de Saussure (1857–1913) and, in particular, his *Course in General Linguistics*, compiled after his death by his students and published in 1916.[4] Saussure's theory acquires its name because he asks us to think of language as a web-like structure. His main concern is not language in use, what he refers to as *parole*, an on-going, evolving body of utterances, but the cross-sectional relationships which define language as a system at any one moment, what he calls *langue*.

Saussure is challenging the traditional nomenclature theory of language. This theory treats words as labels. In the history of ideas stretching from Platonic idealism, through the emergence of science in the seventeenth century, to nineteenth-century positivism, it is assumed that language has meaning because words hook onto things or experiences in a one-to-one relationship. In reply, Saussure argues that meaning is a property of the internal, structural relationships each word has with the others in the web. There is nothing tree-like about the word 'tree'. There is no necessary correspondence between a signifier (the physical property of a sign, e.g., the sound or ink-pattern 'tree') and a signified (the concept or meaning we associate with the signifier). Their relationship, he asserts, is purely arbitrary.[5] If this is the case, how do signs acquire meaning? Saussure offers his concept of 'linguistic value' in response: each word has meaning purely because it is distinct from the other possible words which could be used; each part of the web is defined in terms of the other sections. For example, in the case of the near-synonyms 'to dread', 'to fear', and 'to be afraid', 'to dread' has its particular meaning or value because it isn't 'to fear' or 'to be afraid'.

It is hard to overestimate the importance of these developments. Meaning is shown to be differential, that is, not to reside in single categories, and, because of its structural nature, to have an autonomy distinct from the intention of the author. One cannot touch one part of the web without causing vibrations in other parts and, therefore, creating associations beyond those that were originally intended. Furthermore, articulation in sound is linked with articulation in thought. Our capacity to handle the world conceptually and our capacity to utter different sounds or make different marks are correlated and enfolded. Thought, which, for Descartes, was clear and distinct and *distinct from matter,* is suddenly equated with matter. Language, Saussure claims, acts

> as intermediary between thought and sound, in such a way that the combination of both necessarily produces a mutually complementary delimitation of units. Thought, chaotic by nature, is made precise by this process of segmentation. But what happens is neither a transformation of thoughts into matter, nor a transformation of sounds into ideas. What takes place, is a somewhat mysterious process by which 'thought–sound' evolves divisions, and a language takes shape with its linguistic units in between those two amorphous masses. One might think of it as being like air in contact with water: changes in atmospheric pressure break up the surface of the water into series of divisions, i.e., waves. The correlation between thought and sound, and the union of the two, is like that.[6]

Regarding texts as autonomous and internally structured meant there was a whole new dimension of relationships to be explored. In the 1960s and 1970s, theorists working in other subjects realized that their own fields of enquiry could be analysed structurally, for example, Christian Metz in film theory, Claude Lévi-Strauss in anthropology, Michel Serres in the philosophy of science, and Roland Barthes in semiotics and cultural theory.

While structuralism shows that meaning is a consequence of relationships internal to the medium of signification, *post*structuralism builds upon this internalism to challenge traditional notions of authorship, intention, meaning, and truth. Poststructuralism can be regarded as an extension of the disturbing and destabilizing effects which structuralism has on the traditional (nomenclature) belief that words give us the world. It contributes to postmodernism's reconceptualization and materialization of knowledge by drawing attention to the way in which concepts and ideas, through their own internal thickness, create meanings and possibilities that divert intention or expectation and exceed any claim to final truth. This furthers the political project of establishing plural, multivocal forms of representation. The poststructuralist text is often performative: its impact or affectability will come not only from *what is stated* but also from the *way it is stated.* Language ceases to be the tool we wield in order to manipulate the world and becomes something we have to grapple with, which can surprise or resist us. This makes the text less a disinterested judgement 'from on high' and more an intervention 'at ground level'.

Postmodernism brings the understanding that conceptual frameworks impose contingent, rather than necessary, divisions on the world and that, therefore, any univocal claim to truth will exclude or leave unheard other forms of experience. It is this project of reconceptualization, of transforming the identity of an object through adopting a new perspective in relation to it, to which the excesses of poststructuralism belong. The nine authors in this section illustrate the diversity of ways in which language opens new possibilities through disruption. They also show that Paris is, without a doubt, the capital of postmodernist and poststructuralist thought, since eight of the nine writers are French. Paul de Man is the exception, from Belgium.

Georges Bataille

Through his writing, the theorist and critic Georges Bataille (1897–1962) commits transgression. Bataille's principal themes are the concept of 'boundary' and the way in which moral, political, and epistemological boundaries are constructed within society. These areas are explored by Bataille himself 'exceeding the limit' and transgressing certain boundaries, for example, working across a number of literary genres – fiction, autobiography, criticism, philosophy – and by dealing with images of horror, obscenity, and material baseness. The latter aspect has earned him considerable controversy, and prompted many, including André Breton, to place his sanity in doubt. The removal of a priest's eye and its insertion first in the anus and then in the vagina of one of the central characters is the end-point of a series of physical and sexual extremes in Bataille's first published work, the novel *Story of the Eye* (*Histoire de l'œil*), issued in 1928 under the pseudonym Lord Auch. Through transgression, Bataille seeks to disclose the conflicts and aporias which define human values and institutions. It is our reactions to images like these which make social norms tangible. Why we react the way we do, including our labels 'horrific' and 'obscene', is an expression of a value system. Insanity is not an explanation. Like chasing a bump in a carpet round the room, the charge of 'insanity' simply moves the issue to another area in the fabric of societal construction: from definitions of 'acceptable images' to definitions of 'acceptable forms of conduct'.

Questions regarding the obscene and the pornographic belong to a debate in aesthetics initiated by Plato. In Plato's *Republic*, imagery, morality, and the right to have a place within the state are all integrated on the understanding that there is a two-way relation of imitation between art and life: art imitates life, and life imitates art. Individuals responsible for representations which do *not* depict the true or the honourable life, e.g., painters, tragic poets, should be banished from the state, Plato argues, on the grounds that some might accept their work as templates for false or dishonourable existence.

The featured essay from Bataille, 'Sanctity, Eroticism and Solitude' (1955), offers a giddying display of transgression within transgression. On the one hand, there are claims to the effect that it is impossible for language, or any other organized system, to embrace its opposite while, on the other, there are passages demonstrating that transgression itself only reinstitutes the contradictions of the very system it is trying to evade. Both sanctity and eroticism, for Bataille, are forms of transgression. Sanctity is the ritualistic apprehension of a sacred reality which can overwhelm us, and eroticism is the solitary transgression of sexual taboos. However, they lead to an impasse. While eroticism frees us from social restraint, it is nevertheless a solitary activity and so can release us 'only by separating us from everybody else'. And with Christian sanctity, although the Crucifixion redeems us, it is also 'that which ought not to have taken place'. The impasse arises because 'permitted' and 'forbidden' are mutually defining terms. Any set of principles definitive of thought or behaviour, Bataille suggests, cannot avoid instituting against itself a region which it can never enter or to which it can never apply. Therefore, transgression, crossing into the region of unacceptability, is necessarily *invited* as a consequence and, as such, is complicit with the order it eludes. 'Christianity invented the only path of transgression that still permitted discussion.' Bataille, though, asks us to treat his words with caution, for his own writing cannot avoid these contradictions. He is writing a homage to silence, a plea among philosophers for solitude.

The essay is ahead of its time in anticipating the importance deconstruction will assign (fifteen or so years later) to the textual instabilities implicit in binary oppositions, such as '*within* limits, *without* limits'. The paper is also, in parts, a rejoinder to Hegel. Whereas Hegel's *Phenomenology of Spirit* reduces materiality to an opacity of thought which is eventually overcome by reason, Bataille insists that there is always a level of base, material existence which exceeds thought. The rigour and discipline which define philosophical method prevent it from embracing the extremes of human life. Consequently, although it might aspire to be 'the sum of *knowledge*', as Hegel envisages the subject, philosophy can never be 'the sum of *experiences*'. Sartre is also in evidence here with the admission, from Bataille, that the philosopher, despite leading a disciplined life, nevertheless faces an 'overflowing' of possible experiences to which no rational guidance is adequate.

Roland Barthes

The work of the writer and theorist Roland Barthes (1915–80) also covers a variety of styles: anecdotal, journalistic, critical, and theoretical. This is a reflection of Barthes' central, enduring interest in semiotics: showing how all aspects of life and all forms of representation hold meaning in virtue of being implicated within systems of thought and, in particular, how events and objects which pass for 'natural' or 'everyday' in cultural life are in fact constructed in accordance with certain ideological values.

Mythologies (1957) is a good example: a collection of short articles, originally published in the monthly magazine *Les Lettres Nouvelles* from 1954 to 1956, analysing corners of French life. In his reading of striptease, he demonstrates how the practice is 'nationalized' or made acceptable in France through a series of 'layerings' – theatricality, luxury (of the feathers, furs, and gloves), dance, professionalism – all of which 'exorcise' the signified 'sex'.[7] Another study draws attention to the Gothic, cathedralesque qualities of the new Citroën DS 19 car: 'conceived with passion by unknown artists, and consumed in image if not in usage by a whole population which appropriates them as a purely magical object'.[8] The dovetailing of the car's various sections is as seamless as Christ's robe, and its windows are 'vast walls of air and space'.[9]

The essay representing Barthes here is 'The Plates of the *Encyclopedia*'. Although written mid-career (1964), the article is more indicative of the later, poststructuralist Barthes in that it shows how the creation of meaning cannot take place without certain features coming to light which threaten to divert or undermine the original intention. More significantly, it forms a trilogy with the essays which follow, from Foucault and Derrida, assessing how the internal organization of images relates to the binary structures of thought. All three argue to the effect that the priorities which govern form and composition in an image can turn in upon themselves, with the consequence that the construction of the image acquires an autonomy which shapes or even overrides the intellectual order the image supposedly serves.

Barthes' essay examines the conventions of illustration in eighteenth-century encyclopedias. He concentrates on the plates which are made up of two images: the bottom half shows its object 'anthologically' in its essence, close up, isolated from any context, while the top half presents the same object 'anecdotally' as part of a situation, linked to other objects and people in a vignette. It is the relationship between object and representation which interests Barthes. The encyclopedism of the eighteenth century, he suggests, is a decisive period in the dividing up of the world into objects; the categories and compartments of Enlightenment thought tame and reduce the natural world, carve it up into things that exist for us. However, in this attempt to objectify, he affirms, 'the real is constantly overcome by *some other thing*'. In trying to make the monsters of nature tame and familiar to us, reason unleashes the 'monstrous' transgressions of poetic juxtaposition. The primary intention of giving a complete, anthological and anecdotal illustration of a category, Barthes shows, cannot take place without summoning poetic and metaphorical elements, without a flea becoming a dragon or a snowflake becoming a flower. This has implications for the epistemic status of the illustrations and for the status of the knowledge contained within the encyclopedia as a whole.

Michel Foucault

The philosopher Michel Foucault (1926–84) examines the structures of organization at work in historical practices and institutions in order to show how knowledge and belief systems are constructed. He pays particular attention to aspects of social life which are 'normally' marginalized or suppressed, e.g., sexuality, criminality, madness, for they can be read in terms of the historical and ideological eddies in thought which have located them as marginal.

The Order of Things (1966) is one of Foucault's early texts, and one of his most important, for it concentrates on the meta-historical problem of cultural ordering and raises the possibility of seeing ordering itself in operation. Just how and why the organization of particulars should be an issue Foucault illustrates with Borges' 'certain Chinese encyclopedia'. Here, animals are divided into 'natural' kinds such as: 'belonging to the Emperor', 'embalmed', 'tame', 'fabulous', 'drawn with a very fine camelhair brush', 'having just broken the water pitcher', and 'that from a long way off look like flies'.[10] The example makes the point that conceptual divisions are contingent rather than necessary; schemes of categorization other than our own, no matter how ludicrous, are available.

The organization of thought becomes visible, Foucault maintains, through the tension or 'middle ground' which exists between competing *epistemes* or belief systems, for example, between, on the one hand, the codes and understandings which make us feel at home in a culture – 'its language, its schemes of perception, its exchanges, its techniques, its values' – and, on the other, scientific theories explaining why the world is ordered. This tensional middle ground reveals the 'propinquity of things'[11] in the absence of any particular order, and thereby 'liberates order itself':

> It is here that [order] appears, according to the culture and the age in question, continuous and graduated or discontinuous and piecemeal, linked to space or constituted anew at each instant by the driving force of time, related to a series of variables or defined by separate systems of coherences, composed of resemblances which are either successive or corresponding, organized around increasing difficulties, etc. This middle region, then, in so far as it makes manifest the modes of being of order, can be posited as the most fundamental of all: anterior to words, perceptions, and gestures, which are then taken to be more or less exact, more or less happy, expressions of it (which is why this experience of order in its pure primary state always plays a critical role).[12]

'Las Meninas' is the first chapter from *The Order of Things.* It refers to the painting by Velázquez of the same name, and shows how Foucault's thesis in the book is enacted by elements of composition in the picture. The painting, Foucault declares, is the representation of representation; it lets us see not just order but *the possibility of* order. The painting was produced in 1656. The date is significant because it is the decade which ushers in the classical age, one of the greatest 'discontinuities in the *episteme* of Western culture'.[13] Through the positioning of characters, their lines of sight, the concealments of the canvas and the frame, and the disclosure of the mirror, a network of relationships is set up which ensures that complementary elements are always kept at a distance from one another. Representation 'can never be present without some residuum':

> the face reflected in the mirror is also the face that is contemplating it; what all the figures in the picture are looking at are the two figures to whose eyes they too present a scene to be observed. The entire picture is looking out at a scene for which it is itself a scene.

The painting is organized in such a way that proximities and distances occur, and it is in these epistemic gaps that the possibility of making one thing correspond to another becomes apparent.

Jacques Derrida

Deconstruction is one of the most prominent and distinctive strategies of critique within post-structuralism. It is a form of textual analysis which grew out of the work of literary theorists based at (or affiliated with) Yale University in Connecticut in the late 1960s, early 1970s. The five principal figures were Harold Bloom, Paul de Man, Jacques Derrida, Geoffrey Hartman, and J. Hillis Miller, collectively known as the Yale School of Literary Criticism, and, of these, Derrida (b. 1930) and de Man (1919–83) have become the most talked about.

Given the structuralist thesis that language is a web of autonomous, differential relationships, it follows that any piece of writing will inadvertently generate echoes and associations other than the ones planned or acknowledged by the author. Orthodox literary criticism in Britain and America before and after the Second World War was the 'New Criticism'. Structuralist in essence, it regarded texts as works which could be interpreted purely on their own terms, looking only at the words on the page, and not as historical artefacts or reflections on events or insights into the life of the writer. Deconstruction continues the New Critical practice of close-reading but shifts attention to the way in which metaphors, turns of phrase, and distinctions adopted by the author can turn around and thwart her intention. Metaphors are targeted because they admit unanticipated significations into the text. Nietzsche's influence is evident here. Recall 'On Truth and Lie in an Extra-Moral Sense' in which he argues for the fundamental metaphoricity of all concepts.

Special significance is attached to binary oppositions in language, such as inner–outer, speech–writing, mental–physical, literal–metaphorical, etc. On the one hand, these enable the formation of value judgements by allowing one term to be elevated at the expense of its opposite but, on the other, as deconstructive readings show, the author's forthright, univocal assertion is often undermined when the underplayed term inadvertently reasserts itself. For example, in 'Reading (Proust)', de Man deconstructs Proust's attempts to establish the priority of private, inner experience by showing that they rest upon concepts of public, exterior involvement.[14]

Deconstruction blurs the boundary between literature and philosophy. Under deconstruction, literary texts become sites of contradiction eligible for the kind of 'claim against counter-claim' analysis normally associated with philosophy. Philosophy is not left unaltered. Once again, if language is a structure with its own internal properties, then it will refract or resist any endeavour to view the world through it. By stressing the materiality of thought, structuralism challenges the traditional philosophical assumption that our categories grant us direct, transparent access to the nature of things. As a result, philosophy is robbed of its status as a means to truth and becomes, in Richard Rorty's words, just another 'kind of writing', a sub-section of literature.[15] Philosophy, on this account, is interesting not because it is a truthful, transparent account of the world but because it is a network of names, ideas, proposals, and rejections, like a novel. Any attempt by a philosopher to claim that his work is distinct from art and free from the seduction of literary language is, therefore, grist to the deconstructionist's mill. Take de Man's reading of John Locke in 'The Epistemology of Metaphor' as an example.[16] Locke, in his *Essay Concerning Human Understanding* (1690), accuses figurative language of impeding and deceiving philosophical thought, yet, as de Man points out, in order to argue this, Locke himself has to make use of figurative language: 'Locke speaks of language as a "conduit" that may "corrupt the fountains of knowledge which are in things themselves" and, even worse, "break or stop the pipes whereby it is distributed to public use".'[17]

Language's ability to refract or subvert meaning is in a significant way necessary or ineluctable. No matter how perceptive we are in identifying hidden contradictions in other authors' texts, we ourselves are always subject to our own, similar conceptual blindspots. This goes some way to explaining the double-bind, 'take-apart then put-back-together' feel which the term 'deconstruction' has. It is not an analytical, reductive breakdown or 'destruction' of a text into its constituent claims but a form of writing which tries to acknowledge that, although operative metaphors and binarisms can be identified, they and the differential web of which they are a part nevertheless remain intact to reconstruct the critic's own claims. Acknowledgement occurs most tangibly in the performative aspects of Derrida's and de Man's texts (in a comparable sense to Adorno, whose work would also sit quite happily here). Textuality is displayed through puns, word-plays, and the revivification of etymological roots, rather than offering declarative, subject–predicate propositions which give the impression that the writer is in a position to bring closure, to cast conclusive judgement. This sense of a tensional, ineluctable re-enactment draws on Heidegger and his 'destruction' of ancient Greek ontology in *Being and Time*: a hermeneutical 'working-with-and-against' the grammatical and ontological structures bequeathed to language by the Greeks in order to articulate a 'fundamental' ontology, a schema more amenable to the subject's prospective, constructive openness towards the world.[18] Furthermore, as Merleau-Ponty demonstrates in 'The Intertwining – The Chiasm', it is the existence of a blindspot in perception, the impossibility of an utterly transparent view, that brings perception into being in the first place. Deconstruction, on this account, becomes an encounter with the densities and slippages of language that are constitutive of our ability to speak at all.

Derrida's essay 'Parergon' (1978) is an impressive deconstruction of the textual instabilities created by the motifs of ornament and framing in Kant's *Critique of Judgment.* Ornaments, for Kant, are *parerga,* from the Greek, meaning 'what does not belong to the whole presentation of the object as an intrinsic constituent, but [is] only an extrinsic addition'.[19] Questions regarding what is intrinsic and what is extrinsic to a concept or body are paramount for Kant, since he is attempting to show how one order of being, the conceptual, can open onto another, sensibility; he needs to be clear on these terms in order to establish their interaction. Yet, as Derrida evinces, how we determine what can or cannot be embraced by a concept is bound up with the uncertainty of the frame: 'aesthetic judgement *must* properly bear upon intrinsic beauty, not on finery and surrounds. Hence one must know . . . how to determine the intrinsic – what is framed – and know what one is excluding as frame *and* outside-the-frame'. Depending upon the form in which it appears on or in a work, Kant argues, ornament can *contribute* to beautiful form, as in drapery on statues, or it can amount to nothing more than 'finery' and 'impair genuine beauty', as in a gold frame which is 'merely attached' to a painting. This means the possibility of the boundaries and oppositions within Kant's system being internally coherent – a clear working out of what is intrinsic or extrinsic to his terms – rests upon an aesthetic sense of what contributes to or detracts from genuine beauty. Kant's *theory of* aesthetic experience is therefore organized according to a structure which is explained by *analogy to* aesthetic experience. Once again, as with Barthes and Foucault, the boundaries we exercise in thought are shown to be indi*visible* from the kinds of boundary we encounter in visual experience and, therefore, are made subject to the same contingencies and indeterminacies as sensory life.

However, despite this ingenious display by Derrida of circularity in Kant, it is not the case, as Derrida suggests, that, without its frame, the structure 'collapses forthwith'. For Kant's point is precisely that aesthetic experience is a state of conceptual freeplay in which *object and concept are not identical* or, in a more Derridean idiom, where there is no clear frame. Aesthetic experience motivates us to find expressions that can begin to describe the experience, and this process is vital to the way in which we assign concepts in our cognitive and moral undertakings. The canvas Kant is working on, I suggest, is broader and more finely woven than Derrida suspects. Nevertheless, his essay is an excellent display of how metaphor and image can organize philosophical argument.

Paul de Man

The 'resistance' in de Man's essay 'The Resistance to Theory' (1982) refers both to the opposition literary theory receives from other traditional studies, such as literary history and criticism, and to the oppositions generated within theory itself by its emphasis on rhetoric. Literary theory begins, for de Man, when the role of language in literature is made problematic. Traditional literary history and criticism (within which he includes aesthetics) take language for granted, and interpret a text either in terms of non-linguistic effects, e.g., tone, organic form, allusion, historical situation, or as pure, self-referential verbalism, answerable to nothing but itself. In contrast, theory brings the recognition that 'language is fiction not because it somehow refuses to acknowledge "reality", but because it is not a priori certain that language functions according to principles which are those, or which are *like* those, of the phenomenal world'. Structuralism draws attention to the thickness of language, de Man observes, but the tensions are already present in the *trivium*: the classical division of the science of language into logic, grammar, and rhetoric. While the links between logic and grammar have been well established, rhetoric remains an 'unsettling' element, 'disrupting the inner balance of the model'. When we speak rhetorically, we employ figures of speech or tropes and these, de Man asserts, 'pertain primordially to language': 'they are text-producing functions that are not necessarily patterned on a non-verbal [worldly] entity, whereas grammar is by definition capable of extra-linguistic generalization'. The theoretical exposition of a text thus throws up resistance because it requires the reader to negotiate, if not enjoy, the suasions and indeterminacies of language which an otherwise univocal, 'grammatical' account suppresses.

De Man's arguments apply not just to the study of literature but to all texts, in the broadest sense of 'forms of cultural representation'. This is for two reasons. First, 'theory' is now a cross-disciplinary activity. Rhetoric disrupts established distinctions, including divisions between subject areas. The term on its own has become the byword in most Anglo-American humanities departments for the form of analysis which views the text – literary, philosophical, cultural – as an autonomous site of potentially transgressive signification. Second, literariness, for de Man, does not apply to a particular canon or institution but to an awareness of representation as something active in its own right, and to an appreciation of the dangers of accepting any form of representation as a given, reliable means of accessing the world.

Is it the case that deconstruction applies only to literary or verbal texts? The Heideggerian component of necessity, which maintains that we are bound to *conceptuality* and all the slippages it incurs, would seem to suggest so. Can we be tied to certain forms of visual representation in the same way that we are tied to certain conceptual distinctions? Are revolutions in art and design comparable to paradigm shifts in thought? There are, I suggest, good grounds for entertaining the possibility of a broader, aesthetic deconstruction. Architecture is a good example. If deconstruction is a realization of the way in which language as rhetoric and figuration exceeds and undermines direction, then, I propose, deconstructive moments in architecture might be when we are made to slow down in our passage through a space because the building is allowing the 'metaphorical' properties of matter to suggest possibilities over and above 'the shortest possible route'. Deconstruction contributes to postmodernism: awareness of how the necessity of form enables yet impedes movement inclines us to dwell upon the constructed, contingent aspects of our being. However, although a fair amount has been written on deconstructionist architecture, Derrida is not entirely convinced by the concept. In an interview with Eva Meyer, entitled 'Architecture Where the Desire May Live', Derrida admits that he can find no real connection between his philosophy and deconstructionist architecture other than a metaphorical one.[20] This in itself, though, is an important connection.

In visual art, any work which problematizes yet reinvokes a particular form of representation could be considered a deconstructive performance on the grounds that it carries the appearance of application while also elevating aspects which are novel yet disruptive. Paintings which borrow other forms of representation, such as photorealism, pop art, the diagrammatic works of, for example, Patrick Caulfield and Michael Craig-Martin, acknowledge an origin, problematize it out of context, but bring new properties to it. Borrowing like this makes the work overtly metaphorical, since it performs the metaphorical structure of comparison (between original and new contexts) which creates multiple meanings. The ready-made is also therefore a good contender for deconstructive art since it requires a split-focus: the object's original use is displayed and undermined and, as a result, transformed through its relocation in the gallery.[21]

Jean Baudrillard

In Baudrillard's writing, the play of language not only frustrates any attempt to refer to the real but also changes the real to the point where the distinction between representation and reality no longer applies. Jean Baudrillard (b. 1929) is *the* philosopher of the late twentieth-century digital media circus. Information-generation and hype, he asserts, have achieved self-reference and integration to the extent that it is no longer possible to talk about a 'real' world existing independently of representation. His interest in the ontology or 'shape' of contemporary Western culture arises from his early fusion of Marxism and structuralism in the theorization of sign-systems.[22] Here, the capacity of a sign to acquire a significance over and above its original role as a token of worldly, social interaction is related by Baudrillard to the autonomy an object acquires as a gift or a sellable commodity distinct from the labour which produced it. The transformation is ontological: from 'relationship' – working with materials – to 'object' – an independent item. As an autonomous thing, the sign or the image ceases to be subservient to a governing intention or reality and, instead, becomes an active, world-shaping entity.

Baudrillard's essay 'The Evil Demon of Images' (1984) draws out the interwoven nature of image and reality in relation to contemporary cinema. Experience has become saturated with media imagery to the point that we can say, for example, that the Vietnam war 'in itself' never happened. Baudrillard makes this claim in relation to Coppola's *Apocalypse Now*. (He similarly denies the existence of the Gulf War as 'an event' independent of frenzied news coverage seven years later.)[23] The war was 'staged' with 'the same exaggeration, the same excessive means, the same monstrous candour' as the production of the film. The primary motive for the war, he suggests, was not justice or the defeat of an enemy but 'the sacrificial, excessive deployment of a power already filming itself as it unfolds'. Thus, cause and effect become 'scrambled'. Representation, that which traditionally *follows* reality as its impression or after-image, begins to impinge upon and change the world. Our condition is one of 'hyperreality': representation creates the world or, rather, creates worlds. It gives us images and events with lives of their own which then become templates for new realities. We aspire to them or use them as filters to colour our own being. How often do we *picture* our situation as a scene from a film or have a soundtrack running in our heads? It is no longer the case that we have simulation (or representation) and reality; rather, there are now only 'simulacra': information-led events which give the impression of objective content through their own short-circuiting of reality, through their own logic of mutual reflection and imbrication.

Much of Baudrillard's polemic depends upon how novel one finds his treatment of the 'real'. Reality conceived as a mind-independent domain of things, unaltered by perception, is one of modern philosophy's most problematic concepts, and has been regularly challenged or reworked ever since Kant. Baudrillard's notion of a perception-soaked reality, or 'simulacrum', is already present in the Kantian thesis that human faculties shape the world. However, this is not to deny Baudrillard his contemporary relevance. Advances in information technology are constantly adding to and changing the forms representation can take, and Baudrillard's arguments stand as crucial, critical responses to these times of media saturation.

Jean-François Lyotard

Consonant with Baudrillard, Jean-François Lyotard (b. 1924) argues that as information generation becomes increasingly diverse and complex, knowledge can no longer be regarded as a universal, centred body of ideas. In *The Postmodern Condition: A Report on Knowledge* (1979), one of the seminal texts of postmodern thought, Lyotard challenges the concept of the 'grand narrative' or 'meta-narrative': an overarching belief or principle used by a certain group to confer unity upon and, thereby, to legitimize its knowledge claims, e.g., Christianity, (Renaissance) humanism, scientific truth. Instead, he argues, knowledge has to be recognized as a more 'local' affair: matters of right and wrong, truth and falsehood are determined within communities and, more precisely, by relationships between phrases internal to genres of discourse.

Whereas Baudrillard collapses the domains of representation and reality into the realm of simulacra, Lyotard is more preoccupied with the idea that reality and representation are incommensurable. That is to say, a fundamental incompatibility exists between the world and the images or judgements we make about it which, according to Lyotard, prevents our knowledge claims from ever being wholly identical or adequate to reality. The sublime is an important category for him in this regard, since it entails moments of indefinability which test the limits of representation. In *Lessons on the Analytic of the Sublime* (1991),[24] a close-reading of the sublime in the *Critique of Judgment* allows Lyotard to appraise the interrelationships and limitations Kant defines for the faculties of cognition, and to assess the boundaries he draws around the communicability of sublime experience.

The featured essay from Lyotard, 'The Sublime and the Avant-Garde' (1984), argues for the sublime as a concept of privation, with implications for the political and epistemological status of art. Edmund Burke's theory of the sublime, from his *Philosophical Inquiry into the Origin of our Ideas of the Sublime and the Beautiful* (1757), is more prominent here than Kant's. Sublime experience involves the contradictory feelings of terror and delight and Burke identifies these with a sense of loss – 'the threat of nothing further happening' – which is then withdrawn, allowing a normal sequence of experiences to return. Burke's removal of what is familiar, Lyotard argues, prepares the ground for the avant-garde's stripping away of established, conventional forms of representation. Avant-garde art, he avers, 'abandons the role of identification that the work previously played in relation to the community of addressees'. This supports Lyotard's position on art in 'What is Postmodernism?', noted above: postmodern artworks show the impossibility of complete knowledge *through their form*, rather than offering the idea as a subject for practised, stylized expression. However, he finds that the processes of revolution and renewal in modern art are worryingly consistent with capitalism, and observes that artists can be seduced by market-driven demand for the 'new'. The 'ambiguous, even perverse' correlation which exists between capitalism and the sublime leaves room for a reply though.

Gilles Deleuze and Félix Guattari

One of the ambitions linking the philosophers in this section is to restore a sense of contingency or incompleteness to the concept, thereby checking any modern, Enlightenment impulse to catalogue or manipulate the world. Gilles Deleuze (1925–95) shares this intention. He seeks to bring particularity to the concept: to transform the concept from being a principle of reduction or generalization, to being a generator of poetic and unexpected association. 'Plant' or 'growth' metaphors play an important role in plotting the course of Deleuze's ideas. Thought in the history of philosophy, he asserts, is 'tree-like': individuals are attached to a concept or ideas are attached to a central thesis, like branches to a trunk.[25] In contrast, he proposes a conception of thought based on the 'rhizome': an underground stem that grows horizontally and pushes up lateral shoots; claims are linked not by continuous, vertical progression, but through leaps of association and the relation of seemingly unconnected ideas. Once again, this has the effect of making the writing performative in a fashion comparable to Adorno or Bataille or Derrida. The writing style itself is used to *make a point* rather than just qualify the way the writer organizes his words to *describe the point.*

Deleuze's studies of Nietzsche and Kant – *Nietzsche and Philosophy* (1962) and *Kant's Critical Philosophy: The Doctrine of the Faculties* (1963) – pay special attention to the relationship between the concept and the particular. Although Kant takes the radical step of integrating concepts with the diversity of the sensible manifold, he nevertheless succumbs to the conceptual homogenization of the particular, according to Deleuze, by equating the pure concepts of the understanding with the concept of an *object in general.*[26] Nietzsche's influence is more positive, however, Deleuze thinks, for he removes altogether the distinction between concept and object and, in its place, introduces an irresolvable dynamic of forces. The essay 'On Truth and Lie in an Extra-Moral Sense' (1873) above is a good demonstration of how Nietzsche replaces order with play.

'Percept, Affect, and Concept' is from *What is Philosophy?* (1991), co-authored by Deleuze and the psychoanalyst Félix Guattari.[27] It is the fourth and final time they worked together before their respective deaths in 1995 and 1992.[28] Collaboration, as a method of enquiry, is appropriate for poststructuralism. It frees the author from the responsibility of exercising complete control over a text, and encourages a more discursive, conversational form of thought: each author can respond to asides and excursions from the other. Deleuze has said of his working relationship with Guattari that 'We don't work, we negotiate. We were never in the same rhythm, we were always out of step.'[29] Disjunction or a lack of co-ordination is sometimes to be desired.

As the penultimate chapter of *What is Philosophy?*, 'Percept, Affect, and Concept' evokes earlier discussion and draws together certain themes. However, given Deleuze and Guattari's 'rhizomic' style, and the fact that it is not the conclusion to the book, the chapter has enough internal coherence to be read independently. The book examines the nature of philosophy and its relationship with art and science. Philosophy, they argue, is the creation of concepts in the sense, for example, that Kant introduces a new concept of time.[30] Concepts have to be made: they are 'not waiting for us ready-made, like heavenly bodies. There is no heaven for concepts. They must be invented, fabricated, or rather created and would be nothing without their creator's signature.'[31]

Art, on the other hand, according to Deleuze and Guattari, is the formation of percepts and affects: it makes experience *stand on its own*, distinct from the artist and her original experience; perception is made to stand on its own, apart from its object, as 'percept', and affection is given form distinct from the moment as 'affect'. Art is 'a being of sensation and nothing else: it exists in itself'.

Art and philosophy, they claim, 'intersect and intertwine but without synthesis or identification'.[32] This is because concepts and sensations are overlapping regions. Deleuze and Guattari's definition of a concept is a crucial premise here. The concept, they affirm, is not an abstract, isolated entity but a principle of interrelationship. Each one not only contains 'bits or components that come from other concepts' but also links up with these others in a state or 'plane' of mutual support, co-ordination, and articulation. A concept is thus a 'heterogenesis':

> an ordering of its components by zones of neighbourhood. It is ordinal, an intension present in all the features that make it up. The concept is in a state of survey [*survol*] in relation to its components, endlessly traversing them according to an order without distance.[33]

Comparable with the essays from Blanchot and Vattimo above, Deleuze and Guattari conduct what amounts to a 'topography of thought': an examination of the correspondences and counterpoints which emerge when the shape and direction of thought are influenced by the spatial, material properties introduced by metaphors. In this instance, they explore the ideas and associations brought to light by conceiving of aesthetic experience as a plane: that which is made to intersect with other surfaces, and against which nuances and details are allowed to stand out. From the opening reference to a canvas, to the significance given by phenomenology to architectural surfaces, to the 'plane' as a frame for composition, Deleuze and Guattari create a conceptual structure which invites us to consider art as *the contrasts and connections made by the structure*. Through contrast and connection, art and philosophy are shown to interlock *yet maintain their non-identity*: 'sensation itself becomes sensation of concept' and 'concept becomes concept of sensation' yet these relationships cannot exist without there being an element which is 'still to come, still indeterminate or unknown'.

The essay is also notable for interweaving many different aspects of twentieth-century aesthetic theory. Adorno's theory of knowledge in *Negative Dialectics* (1966) would seem to be an influence. On this account, concepts exist in a constellational relationship around an object, giving us plural insights into its being while preserving a level of indeterminacy. Deleuze and Guattari actually describe their notion of the concept as 'the contour, the configuration, the constellation of an event to come'.[34] They also share phenomenology's interest in Cézanne. For Merleau-Ponty, the tessellated planes in Cézanne's paintings display the limits and possibilities of the artist's (and the viewer's) physical immersion in the world and, for Deleuze and Guattari, they become the 'sections' of a house – 'the pieces of differently oriented planes' – that 'provide flesh with its framework' and 'give sensation the power to stand on its own within autonomous *frames*'.[35] With the 'frame', we are reminded of Derrida's 'Parergon' and the question of what is inside and what is outside a concept. Overall, Deleuze and Guattari's 'aesthetics of the concept' is very close to the intuitionism proposed by the early twentieth-century Italian idealist philosopher Benedetto Croce

(1866–1952). Largely ignored by the Continental tradition, but receiving some attention from Anglo-American philosophy, Croce's *Aesthetic as the Science of Expression and the Linguistic in General* (1902) shows that the concept, as an event in thought, always presupposes an intuition, a picturing before the mind of a particular impression: 'this river, this lake, this brook, this rain, this glass of water'.[36] The aesthetic and the conceptual, he suggests, are 'certainly different' but 'not entirely detached'; they are like 'two forces, each pulling in its own direction'.[37]

The eight essays in this section illustrate the kinds of claims and strategies which are described as 'poststructuralist' or 'postmodern'. The writing is very much aware of itself as writing. At issue is the linguistic, conceptual order which we bring to the world. The aesthetic is relevant because it is the realm of experience which, in the history of philosophy, has been positioned beyond conceptual description, and so is the region whose edges and surfaces indicate the limits of thought. The move away from thought as universal, abstract surveillance to thought as contingent, material involvement means that many theories of knowledge are taking sensory, bodily, aesthetic experience as their foundation, e.g., reliance on sensory and spatial metaphors. Language comes not 'after the event' but constitutes the event; it is something to be played with, stretched, and teased.

Poststructuralism has its dissenters, however. Some would describe these texts as playful; some would say they are difficult; others might go so far as to call them nonsense. Contemporary French theory is sometimes criticized for its level of jargon and the often unfathomable prose which results. It is all very well making grand claims about pluralization and the exploration of limits, critics exclaim, but all we have ended up with are self-legitimizing discourses of buzz-words and free-for-all arguments which refuse to engage with or find themselves answerable to any form of realism.[38] The criticisms arise because the verbal and terminological freedom which often accompanies reconceptualization makes it hard to get a definite purchase on the material, and gives the impression that the grain of the real world is not impinging upon the theorist's claims.

My intention here is not to pursue the debate, but simply to point out that it exists. The relationship between understanding and writing style is itself a philosophical issue. We think about texts metaphorically: their 'accessibility', whether or not they are 'clear' or 'hard', their 'difficulty', having to work 'against them', and there are interesting arguments for and against the cultivation of 'obscure' prose. It is enough to say in conclusion that, in the twentieth century, the boundaries between art, literature, and philosophy are no longer solid. There can still be statements 'about' the world but just what this 'aboutness' involves cannot be neatly categorized and identified with one form of representation or another. We should not be in too much of a rush to 'see through' these texts, to reduce them to a thesis. This would be like equating a film with its synopsis. Reality surprises us the most when we bump up against it. These texts offer similar resistance.

Notes

1 Max Horkheimer and Theodor W. Adorno, *The Dialectic of Enlightenment*, trans. John Cumming, New York, Continuum, 1972.
2 Jean-François Lyotard, *The Postmodern Condition: A Report on Knowledge*, trans. Geoffrey Bennington and Brian Massumi, Minneapolis, Minnesota University Press; Manchester, Manchester University Press, 1984, p. 79.
3 Ibid., p. 81.
4 Ferdinand de Saussure, *Course in General Linguistics*, trans. Roy Harris, London, Duckworth, 1983.

5 Saussure is not the first to make this point. It is already present in Schopenhauer's *World as Will and Representation* (1818, 1844) and Nietzsche's 'On Truth and Lie in an Extra-Moral Sense' (1873).
6 Saussure, *Course in General Linguistics*, pp. 110–11.
7 Roland Barthes, *Mythologies*, trans. Annette Lavers, London, Jonathan Cape, 1974, p. 87.
8 Ibid., p. 88.
9 Ibid., p. 89.
10 Michel Foucault, *The Order of Things*, London, Routledge, 1994, p. xv.
11 Ibid., p. xxiv.
12 Ibid., p. xxi.
13 Ibid., p. xxii.
14 Paul de Man, *Allegories of Reading: Figural Language in Rousseau, Nietzsche, Rilke, and Proust*, New Haven, Yale University Press, 1979, pp. 58–59.
15 Richard Rorty, 'Philosophy as a Kind of Writing: An Essay on Derrida', *Consequences of Pragmatism*, Brighton, Harvester, 1982, pp. 90–109.
16 Paul de Man, 'The Epistemology of Metaphor', *Critical Inquiry*, 1978, vol. 5, pp. 13–30.
17 Ibid., p. 16.
18 See in particular Martin Heidegger, *Being and Time*, trans. John Macquarrie and Edward Robinson, Oxford, Blackwell, 1995, §6, pp. 41–49.
19 Immanuel Kant, *Critique of Judgment*, trans. Werner S. Pluhar, Indianapolis, Hackett Publishing Company, 1987, Ak. 226, p. 72.
20 Jacques Derrida, 'Architecture Where the Desire May Live', *Rethinking Architecture: A Reader in Cultural Theory*, ed. Neil Leach, London, Routledge, 1997, pp. 319–23.
21 Danto argues convincingly for the metaphorical status of the ready-made in *The Transfiguration of the Commonplace*, Cambridge, Massachusetts, Harvard University Press, 1981.
22 See, for example, Jean Baudrillard, *For a Critique of the Political Economy of the Sign*, trans. Charles Levin, St Louis, Telos Press, 1981, and *Symbolic Exchange and Death*, trans. Ian Grant, London, Sage, 1993.
23 See Jean Baudrillard, 'The Reality Gulf', *The Guardian*, 11 January 1991, and 'La guerre du Golfe n'a pas en lieu' ('The Gulf War Has Not Taken Place'), *Liberation*, 29 March 1991.
24 Jean-François Lyotard, *Lessons on the Analytic of the Sublime*, trans. Elizabeth Rottenberg, Stanford, Stanford University Press, 1994.
25 The 'tree-like' metaphor originally features in Deleuze and Guattari's critique of Freud but is nonetheless representative of Deleuze's stance with regard to philosophy's orthodox conception of thought. See Gilles Deleuze and Félix Guattari, *Anti-Oedipus: Capitalism and Schizophrenia 1*, trans. Robert Hurley, M. Seem, and H.R. Lane, New York, Viking Press, 1977.
26 This, it needs pointing out, is based upon a highly selective and deliberately 'associational' reading of Kant which ignores many of his explicit intentions and his arguments for the claim that generality anticipates particularity.
27 Gilles Deleuze and Félix Guattari, *What is Philosophy?*, trans. Hugh Tomlinson and Graham Burchill, London, Verso, 1996.
28 Their other three collaborations are: *Anti-Oedipus: Capitalism and Schizophrenia 1* (1972); *Kafka: Towards a Minor Literature*, trans. Dana Polan, Minneapolis, University of Minnesota Press, 1986; and *A Thousand Plateaus: Capitalism and Schizophrenia 2* (1980), trans. Brian Massumi, Minneapolis, University of Minnesota Press, 1987.
29 Gilles Deleuze and Claire Parnet, *Dialogues*, trans. Hugh Tomlinson and Barbara Habberjam, Minneapolis, University of Minnesota Press, 1987, p. 17, and quoted by Hugh Tomlinson and Graham Burchill in their 'Translators' Introduction' to *What is Philosophy?*, p. viii.
30 Instead of the Newtonian concept of a linear succession of episodes, Kant presents time as a threefold principle of anticipation, retention, and succession, fundamental to the organization of experience.
31 Deleuze and Guattari, *What is Philosophy?*, p. 5.
32 Ibid., pp. 198–99.
33 Ibid., p. 20.
34 Ibid., p. 32.
35 For Merleau-Ponty's interpretation of Cézanne, see Merleau-Ponty, 'Eye and Mind', *The Merleau-Ponty Aesthetics Reader*, ed. Galen A. Johnson, Evanston, Illinois, Northwestern University Press, 1996, pp. 121–60.

36 Benedetto Croce, *Aesthetic as the Science of Expression and the Linguistic in General*, trans. Colin Lyas, Cambridge, Cambridge University Press, 1997, p. 24.

37 Ibid., p. 24.

38 For a damning critique of many of the thinkers in this section and the next, see Alan Sokal and Jean Bricmont, *Intellectual Impostures*, London, Profile Books, 1998.

23

SANCTITY, EROTICISM AND SOLITUDE

Georges Bataille

Today I wish to discuss sanctity, eroticism and solitude.[1] Before I come to lay certain ideas coherently before you, let me say a word about my intention, which you may find surprising. The word 'eroticism' is ambiguously suggestive. I should like just to say why I have decided to discuss eroticism, sanctity and solitude in the same breath.

My starting point is that eroticism is a solitary activity. At the least it is a matter difficult to discuss. For not only conventional reasons, eroticism is defined by secrecy. It cannot be public. I might instance some exceptions but somehow eroticism is outside ordinary life. In our experience taken as a whole it is cut off from the normal communication of emotions. There is a taboo in force. Nothing is absolutely forbidden, for there are always transgressions. But the taboo is sufficiently active for me to be able to say by and large that eroticism, perhaps the most intense of emotions, is as if it did not exist as far as our existence is present for us in the form of speech and language. These days the taboo has been attenuated somewhat – otherwise I could not be talking to you today – but I think that just the same, since this hall belongs to the world of speech, eroticism must remain something exterior as far as we are concerned. Talk about it I shall, but as something beyond our present set of experiences, as a beyond accessible on one condition only, that we leave the world we now inhabit to shut ourselves up in solitude. Particularly it seems to me that to reach this beyond, we must renounce the philosophical attitude. The philosopher can speak of everything he feels. Erotic experience will commit us to silence.

This is not true of an experience possibly very close to it[:] the experience of sanctity. The emotions felt in that experience can be expressed in a speech or form the subject of a sermon. Yet erotic experience is possibly close to sanctity.

I do not mean that eroticism and sanctity are of the same nature, and anyway that subject falls outside my scope. All I mean is that both experiences have an extreme intensity. When I speak of sanctity I am referring to the life that the presence of a sacred reality within us informs, a reality that may completely overwhelm us. Just now I shall be content to look at the emotion of sanctity on the one hand and at the emotion of eroticism on the other, in so far as each has extreme intensity. My meaning is that with these two emotions one brings us closer to other men and the other cuts us off from them and leaves us in solitude.

That is the starting point of the argument I want to lay before you. I shall not speak from the philosophical standpoint as it is usually understood. Let me affirm here and now that the philosophical experience as such excludes both these emotions. I agree that the philosopher's experience is a separate one, untouched by other experiences – a specialist's experience, in fact. Emotions put it out of joint. I have long been struck by one thing. The true philosopher must devote his life to philosophy. In the practice of philosophy there is no serious reason why we should not find the weakness common to all cognitive activity – superiority in one field bought at the expense of relative ignorance in other fields. The situation gets worse every day; every day it becomes harder to acquire the sum of human knowledge since this sum is always and unendingly on the increase. The principle that philosophy should be this sum of knowledge treated not simply as a juxtaposition of facts in the memory but as a synthesising operation is still retained, but with great difficulty; every day philosophy becomes a little more of a specialised discipline like the others. It is not my purpose today to discuss the impossibility of constructing a philosophy independent of political experience, except to say that this is a characteristic orientation of contemporary philosophy. On this point philosophy has opened its doors to experience. But once this principle has been admitted, philosophy is still commonly studied in a vacuum. I mean that it is difficult to live and to philosophise simultaneously. I mean that humanity is made up of separate experiences and philosophy is only one experience among others. Philosophy finds it harder and harder to be the sum of knowledge, but it does not even aim at being the sum of experiences, in the specialist's peculiar narrow-mindedness. Yet what significance can the reflections of mankind upon himself and on being in general have, if they take no account of the intense emotional states? Obviously this implies the specialisation of something which by definition may on no account be allowed to be anything but total and universal. Obviously philosophy can only be the sum of the possibles in the sense of a synthesis, or nothing.

I repeat: philosophy is the sum of the possibles in the sense of a synthesis, or nothing.

This, I think, is what it was for Hegel. Erotic experience, at least in the first forms of his dialectic construction, had an overt share in the elaboration of the system, but it is not impossible to believe that it secretly had a deeper influence. Eroticism can only be envisaged dialectically, and conversely the dialectician, if he does not confine himself to formalism, necessarily has his eyes fixed on his own sexual experience. However that may be (and I do admit that one may hesitate faced with this somewhat obscure point), it seems that in part at least Hegel drew his peculiar dialectic from his theological knowledge as well as from his knowledge of Meister Eckhart and Jacob Boehme. But I have not brought Hegel into the discussion in order to insist on the value of his philosophy. On the contrary, in spite of my reservations I intend to assign Hegel deliberately to specialised philosophy. Besides, I only need to remind you how strongly he opposed that tendency of contemporary romantic philosophy to assert that anyone could be a philosopher with no special preparation. I do not say that he was wrong to blame improvisation in the sphere of philosophy; that would be out of the question. But Hegel's practically impenetrable system, even if it were the ultimate in philosophy, certainly has this quality of specialised discipline. It assembles ideas, but at the same time cuts those assembled ideas off from experience. That no doubt was his ambition, for in Hegel's mind the immediate is bad, and Hegel would certainly have identified what I call experience with the immediate. Nevertheless, without embarking on a philosophical discussion I should like to stress the fact that Hegel's argument rings like a specialised activity. I do not think that he can have helped feeling this himself. In order to counter objections in advance he contended that philosophy was a development in time, a speech delivered in successive phases. Everybody can agree with this, but it means making a special moment subordinate to the others out of each moment of philosophy. Thus we only abandon specialisation to slumber with the specialist, this time without recall.

I do not say that each of us, or anybody, is entitled to wake up. This sum of the possibles seen as a synthesis may exist only in my imagination. I feel quite free to fail. I am uneasy at the thought of taking a failure for a success. Above all I do not yet see the need for limiting the potentialities before me by imposing a specialised piece of work upon myself. What I have in mind is a choice which faces each one of us at each moment. At this very minute I have the choice between obedience to the theory I have undertaken to expound to you and a response to some whim or other that might seize me. I get out of this with some difficulty by telling myself that what I am saying coincides with the direction of the whim; I do not give in to the wish to yield to it but I recognise the greater value of the whim, the opposite of specialisation. Specialisation is the condition of efficiency, and the search for efficiency is characteristic of anyone who feels what he lacks. In this there is an admission of impotence, a humble submission to necessity.

True enough, there is a regrettable weakness in wanting such and such a result and not taking the steps that would bring it about. But there is a strength in not wanting this result and refusing to take the road that leads to it. At this intersection, sanctity is just as much of a possible choice as eroticism. Sanctity is at first on the side of caprice as far as specialised effort goes. The saint is not after efficiency. He is prompted by desire and desire alone and in this resembles the erotic man. The point is whether desire corresponds, better than the specialisation of a project, better than the specialisation that ensures a project's efficiency, with the essence of philosophy, if philosophy is first of all, as I contend it is, the sum of the possibles seen as an operation of synthesis. To put it another way: can that operation be thought of through the simple process of calculation ending in specialisation? Or again, can the sum of the possibles be thought of through the predominance of interest over whim, the other name for desire?

Before going any further I shall try now to make the essential point about eroticism in spite of the difficulty of talking about it.

In the very first place eroticism differs from animal sexuality in that human sexuality is limited by taboos and the domain of eroticism is that of the transgression of these taboos. Desire in eroticism is the desire that triumphs over the taboo. It presupposes man in conflict with himself. The taboos against human sexuality really have specialised forms; for example they affect incest or menstruation, but they can also be thought of in a general way, as for example a way which certainly did not exist in the earliest times (during the transition from the animal to the human), a way even now called into question – nakedness. In fact the taboo on nakedness is today simultaneously very strong and in question. Everybody realises the absurd relativity, the gratuitousness of the taboo on nakedness, the fact that it has been conditioned by historical events; everybody realises also that the taboo on nakedness and the transgression of that taboo make up the general stuff of eroticism, I mean sexuality turned into eroticism (the sexuality peculiar to man, the sexuality of a creature with the gift of tongues). With so-called neurotic complications and with vice of one sort or another, this notion is always significant. Vice can be thought of as the art of giving oneself the feeling of transgression in a more or less maniac way.

Perhaps I should remind you of the curious origin of the theory of taboo and transgression. We find it in the oral teaching of Marcel Mauss whose work is certainly the least questioned contribution to the French school of sociology, but it was followed up by nothing in print. Mauss had a certain distaste for formulating his ideas and giving them a definitive and printable shape. I can even quite believe that the most remarkable results must have been an embarrassment to him. The basis of the transgression theory does indeed appear in his written work, but only in the form of a brief indication; it is not dwelt upon. Thus in the *Essai sur le sacrifice* he says in a couple of sentences that the Greeks regarded the sacrifice of the Bouphonia as the crime of the sacrificer. He does not generalise. I myself did not follow his oral teaching, but as far as transgression is concerned Marcel Mauss' doctrine is set forth in a little book by one of his pupils, *L'Homme et le sacré*, by Roger Caillois. As luck would have it Roger Caillois, far from being a mere compiler, was himself capable not only of setting out the facts in a compelling fashion but of giving his arguments the strength of active and personal thinking. Caillois' theories may be summed up as follows. For the peoples with whom ethnography is concerned man's time is divided into profane time and sacred time, profane time being ordinary time, the time of work and of respect for the taboos, and sacred time being that of celebrations, that is in essence the time of transgressing the taboos. As far as eroticism goes, celebrations are often a time of sexual licence. As far as religion goes, it is particularly the time for sacrifice, for the transgression of the taboo on murder.

I have given a formal exposition of this doctrine with my personal elaborations in a work dealing with the Lascaux cave paintings, paintings made by the first men, that is, when art was born, when man had really made the step from animal to human.[2] I felt impelled to connect the taboo with work. Work certainly existed before the beginnings of art. We have traces of work in the shape of stone tools preserved in the earth whose relative dates we can ascertain. I decided that work must have implied from the beginning the existence of a world of work from which sexual life and murder and death in general were excluded. Sexual life on the one hand, murder, death and war on the other are grave if not overwhelming disturbances where work is concerned. I cannot see that there is any doubt that such moments must have been radically banished from working time, when men must soon have been co-operating with each other. When it was a question of work the creation and suppression of life must have been put aside, for work itself, in comparison with moments of intense emotion where life and death were at stake and asserting themselves, was a neutral time, a sort of annulment.

The point I am making must I think by now be plain enough. I do not say that non-specialised philosophy is possible. But philosophy in so far as it is a specialised undertaking is work. That is to say that it excludes without even deigning to notice them the moments of intense emotion I referred to earlier. Hence it is not that sum of the possibles seen as a synthesising operation that I take to be of cardinal value. It is not the sum of the possibles, the sum of possible experiences, but only the sum of certain well-defined experiences aimed at knowledge. It is only the sum of knowledge. With a clear conscience, even with a feeling of getting rid of a foreign body, getting rid of some muck, or at least of a source of error, it leaves out the intense emotion bound up with birth, with the creation of life as with death. I am not the first to feel surprised at this disappointing consequence of philosophy, the expression of average humanity become foreign to extreme humanity, that is to the convulsions of sex and death. It even seems to me as if a reaction against this cold and rigid aspect of philosophy is characteristic of modern philosophy as a whole from, say, leaving out Kierkegaard, Nietzsche to Heidegger. Naturally, or so it seems to me, philosophy is in a parlous condition. It has no common ground with a certain extravagant bohemianism of thought which I may well incarnate for some of you. In this it is fully justified. Philosophy is nothing if it is not an effort and hence a disciplined effort, but when it brings in concerted effort and discipline, does not philosophy also fail in its deepest purpose, at least if it is as I have said, 'the sum of the possibles seen as a synthesising operation'? The final point I want to make is that philosophy finds itself in an impasse; without discipline it could accomplish nothing and yet in that it cannot embrace the extremes of its subject, the extremes of the possible as I have called them, the outermost reaches of human life, it is doomed to failure. If it is to be fundamental even a philosophy of death must turn away from its subject. But this is not to say that philosophy is still possible if it becomes absorbed in it, losing itself in the final vertigo, or only if at the summit philosophy denies philosophy and sneers at philosophy. Supposing indeed that philosophy really sneered at philosophy; that would entail at once discipline and the abandonment of discipline; at such a moment the sum of the possibles is at stake in its entirety, and the sum is a synthesis, not merely an addition, since it ends in that synthetic view where human effort shows its impotence and relaxes in the feeling of its impotence with no regrets. Without discipline this point could not have been reached, but discipline itself can never go the whole road. This is the truth of experience. All the time the mind, the brain of man is reduced to the state of a container overflowing with, burst by its contents – like a suitcase into which objects keep being put which stops being a suitcase in the end, since it ceases to enclose the objects entrusted to it. And above all, extreme states bring an element that cannot be subjected to calm reflection into the sum of the possibles.

I will try to give an accurate description of this overflowing that we may experience.

We are faced with the necessity of making a choice. First we must make a quantitative choice. If we see them as homogeneous the possibles are too numerous. For example, given the limited span of life, we must forgo reading such and such a book in which we might perhaps have found fundamental principles and the answer to the question we are asking ourselves. Then we must tell ourselves that we cannot reach the possibles described in that book.

If the experience of extreme states of being is in question, this time the choice is a qualitative one. For such an experience dislocates us and excludes calm reflection, its essence being to put us 'beside ourselves'. It is difficult to imagine the life of a philosopher continually or at least fairly often beside himself. We come back to the essential human experience dividing time into working time and sacred time. The fact of remaining open to possibilities bordering on madness (which is what happens with any possibility concerned with eroticism, with the threat, or more often the presence, of death, or with sanctity) keeps the work of reflection continually subordinate to something else, and just here reflection comes to an end.

In practice we do not reach an absolute impasse, but what is the heart of the matter? More often than not we forget that philosophy is as competitive as any game. The idea is to get as far on as one can. Humiliatingly enough we are in the position of a man trying to set up a record. The palm may be awarded to developments in various directions according to various points of view. From the point of view of professorial philosophy, the palms obviously go to the man who works and holds aloof from the possibilities offered by transgression. I am deeply suspicious, I admit, of superiority in the opposite direction, where the winner would be the refuser, the ingenuous mouthpiece of laziness and pretension. In agreeing to compete I have personally felt it necessary to accept the difficulties of both paths, the path of transgression as well as the path of work. The limit occurs when it is plainly impossible to respond satisfactorily in both directions at the same time. It is no good persisting. I think the only answer to the question I have put is a feeling of oppression and impotence. We are obviously faced with the impossible. It is not necessary to be resigned but we must realise that the absence of resignation delivers us from nothing. One temptation I must admit to feeling, however. At least with transgression, coinciding as it does with laziness, I can see the advantage of apparent inferiority. But even that is a lie, I cannot deny it; the competition is open and I have entered my name. The fact that my participation is for me inevitably bound up with disputing the principles of the superiority in question has nothing to do with it. One must still advance as far as possible and my indifference is beside the point. Even if I refuse to be involved my refusal is not entire and that is enough. I am committed just the same. Today in any case here I am speaking to you, and that means that solitude is not enough for me.

Let us now push this enquiry to its logical conclusion and try to show the significance of Christianity in relation to the questions I have put forward. Not that I think that I ought to discuss specifically Christian sanctity when I refer to sanctity. But whatever my intentions are there is no practical difference in the minds of my hearers between sanctity and Christian sanctity, and I have not brought up this point in order to balk the issue. To return to the ideas I was trying to put over just now, I must emphasise the fact that in the Christian system what I call transgression is called sin. Sin is a fault, it is that which ought not to have happened. Take first the death on the Cross: it is a sacrifice, a sacrifice whose victim is God himself. But although the sacrifice redeems us, although the Church sings its paradoxical *Felix Culpa!* – happy error – to the underlying fault, that which redeems us is also that which ought not to have taken place. For Christianity the taboo is absolute and transgression of any kind is condemned out of hand. Yet the condemnation is relaxed because of the very fault most to be condemned, the worst transgression imaginable. The transition from eroticism to sanctity makes very good sense. It is the transition from that which is damned and rejected to that which is fortunate and blessed. On the one hand eroticism is the solitary fault, the thing which saves us only by separating us from everybody else, the thing that saves us only in the euphoria of an illusion, since when all is said and done that which in eroticism bears us to pinnacles of intensity also lays the curse of solitude upon us at the same time. On the other hand sanctity delivers us from solitude but on the condition that we accept the paradox of the happy error, the Felix Culpa! whose very extravagance redeems us. Under such circumstances we can only return to our fellow men by evading the issue. This evasion is doubtless worthy of the name 'renunciation' since in Christianity we cannot simultaneously perform a transgression and enjoy its fruits – only others can enjoy them in damnation and solitude. Harmony with his fellows is not recovered by the Christian unless he forgoes the enjoyment of the means of his redemption, of that which is still never anything but transgression and the violation of the taboos upon which civilisation is founded.

If we follow the path marked out by Christianity, it is true, we can not only escape from solitude but also achieve a kind of equilibrium which avoids the primary disequilibrium of my starting point, preventing us from reconciling discipline and work with the experience of the ultimate. Christian sanctity at any rate opens up the possibility of pushing as far as it will go the experience of that final convulsion ultimately leading to death. Sanctity and the transgression of the taboo concerning death are not to be completely identified. War particularly is the transgression of this taboo. But sanctity is none the less placed on a level with death; in this, sanctity resembles the heroism of the warrior lived out by the saint as if he were dying. What a bewildering twist of direction, though! He lives as though he were dying, but in order to achieve eternal life! Sanctity is always a project. Perhaps not in essence. St. Theresa used to say that even if Hell were to swallow her up she could not but persevere. Anyway, the intention to gain eternal life is connected with sanctity as if with its opposite. Just as if in sanctity only a compromise allowed the saint to make common ground with the mob, with the rest of humanity. With the mob and with philosophy, which comes to the same thing – common ideas, in fact.

The oddest thing is that agreement has been reached between deliberate transgression and the other kinds on the understanding that it shall be a tacit one. This agreement occurs in all forms of archaic religions. Christianity invented the only path of transgression that still permitted discussion. Here let us recognise simply that discussion freed from Christian principles tends to deny anything that looks like transgression and to deny at the same time anything that looks like a taboo. On the sexual level, take the aberration of nudism, which is a denial of the sexual taboo, a denial of the transgression which the taboo necessarily engenders. If you like, discussion is the denial of that which distinguishes the human as opposed to the animal.

As far as I am concerned – it seems to me – as I have been speaking – that I have paid a kind of homage – a rather clumsy one – to silence. A homage to eroticism, too – perhaps. But at this point I should like to counsel my hearers the most extreme caution. I am really speaking a dead language. This language, I believe, is the language of philosophy. I will go so far as to say that in my opinion philosophy is also the death of language. It is also a sacrifice. The operation I spoke of that synthesises all the possibles is the suppression of every contribution of language which substitutes a neutral and indifferent atmosphere for the experience of springing life. I have cautioned you about language. I must therefore caution you at the same time against my own words. Not that I want to end upon a note of farce, but I have been trying to talk a language that equals zero, a language equivalent to nothing at all, a language that returns to silence. I am not talking about nothingness, which sometimes looks to me like a pretext for adding a specialised chapter onto speech; I am talking about the suppression of whatever language may add to the world. I realise that this suppression cannot be rigorously applied. Anyway the point is not to bring in another sort of duty. But I owe it to myself to put you on guard against an unfortunate use of what I have said. From this point anything that does not take us out of the world (in the sense that through the Church or against the Church a sort of sanctity takes men out of the world) would betray my purpose. I said that discipline, committing us to the ways of work as it does, moves us away from the experience of extremes. Agreed, at least in a general sense, but this experience has its own discipline. At any rate this discipline is primarily contrary to any form of verbal apology of eroticism. Eroticism is silence, I have said; it is solitude. But not for people whose very presence in the world is a pure denial of silence, a chattering, a neglect of potential solitude.

Translated by Mary Dalwood

Notes

1 Lecture given to the Collège Philosophique, Spring 1955.

2 *Lascaux ou la naissance de l'art* ('Les grands siècles de la peinture'), Geneva, Skira, 1955. I say 'the first men', but only in so far as the men of Lascaux cannot have been so very different from the first men. The Lascaux cave paintings are obviously later than the date that can be assigned accurately enough to the 'birth of art'.

24

THE PLATES OF THE *ENCYCLOPEDIA*

Roland Barthes

Our literature has taken a long time to discover the object; we must wait till Balzac for the novel to be the space not only of pure human relations but also of substances and usages called upon to play their part in the story of passions: could Grandet have been a miser (literarily speaking) without his candle ends, his lumps of sugar, and his gold crucifix? Long before literature, the *Encyclopedia*, particularly in its plates, practices what we might call a certain philosophy of the object, i.e., reflects on its being, produces at once an inventory and a definition; technological purpose no doubt compelled the description of objects; but by separating image from text, the *Encyclopedia* committed itself to an autonomous iconography of the object whose power we enjoy today, since we no longer look at these illustrations with mere information in mind.

The plates of the *Encyclopedia* present the object, and this presentation already adds to the illustration's didactic purpose a more gratuitous justification, of an aesthetic or oneiric order: the imagery of the *Encyclopedia* can best be compared with one of those Great Expositions held the world over in the last century or so, and of which, in its period, the Encyclopedic illustration was a kind of ancestor: in both cases, we are concerned with a census and a spectacle: we consult the plates of the *Encyclopedia* as we would visit today's World's Fair in Brussels or New York. The objects presented are literally encyclopedic, i.e., they cover the entire sphere of substances shaped by man: clothes, vehicles, tools, weapons, instruments, furniture, all that man makes out of wood, metal, glass, or fiber is catalogued here, from the chisel to the statue, from the artificial flower to the ship. This Encyclopedic object is ordinarily apprehended by the image on three levels: anthological, since the object, isolated from any context, is presented *in itself*; anecdotic, when it is 'naturalized' by its insertion into a large-scale *tableau vivant* (which is what we call a vignette); genetic, when the image offers us the trajectory from raw substance to finished object: genesis, essence, praxis, the object is thus accounted for in all its categories: sometimes it *is*, sometimes it is *made*, sometimes it even *makes*. Of these three states, assigned here and there to the object-as-image, one is certainly favored by the *Encyclopedia*: that of birth: it is good to be able to show how we can produce things from their very nonexistence and thus to credit man with an extraordinary power of creation: here is a countryside; the plenitude of Nature (meadows, hills, trees) constitutes a kind of human void from which we cannot see what will emerge; yet the image moves, objects are born, precursors of humanity: lines are drawn on the earth, stakes are pounded in, holes dug; a cross-section shows us, beneath a desert Nature, the powerful network of galleries and lodes: a mine is born. This is a kind of symbol: Encyclopedic man *mines* all Nature with human signs; in the Encyclopedic landscape, we are never alone; however strong the elements, there is always a fraternal *product* of man: the object is the world's human signature.

We know that a simple substance can make a whole story legible: Brecht has rediscovered the wretched essence of the Thirty Years' War by the radical treatment of fabrics, wicker, and wood. The Encyclopedic object emerges from general substances which are still those of the artisanal era. If we visit a World's Fair today, we perceive in all the objects exhibited two or three dominant substances, glass, metal, plastic no doubt; the substance of the Encyclopedic object is of a more vegetal age: it is wood which dominates in this great catalogue; it produces a world of objects easy on the eyes, already human by their substance, resistant but not brittle, constructible but not plastic. Nothing shows wood's humanizing power better than the *Encyclopedia*'s machines; in this world of technology (which is still artisanal, for the industrial is as yet unborn), the machine is obviously a capital object; now most of the *Encyclopedia*'s machines are made out of wood; they are enormous, highly complicated scaffoldings in which metal frequently supplies only notched wheels. The wood which constitutes them keeps them subservient to a certain notion of *play*: these machines are (for us) like big toys; contrary to modern images, man, always present in some corner of the machine, does not accompany it in a simple relation of surveillance; turning a crank, pressing a pedal, spinning a thread, he participates in the machine in a manner that is both active and delicate; the engraver represents him for the most part dressed neatly as a gentleman; this is not a worker but a little lord who plays on a kind of technological organ, all of whose gears and wheels are exposed; what is striking about the Encyclopedic machine is its absence of secrecy; in it there is no hidden place (spring or housing) which would magically conceal energy, as is the case with our modern machines (it is the myth of electricity to be a self-generated, hence enclosed, power); the energy here is essentially transmission, amplification of a simple human movement; the Encyclopedic machine is never anything but an enormous relay; man is at one term, the object at the other; between the two, an architectural milieu, consisting of beams, ropes, and gears, through which, like a light, human strength is simultaneously developed, refined, focused, and enlarged: hence, in the gauze-loom, a little man in a jacket, sitting at the keyboard of a huge wooden machine, produces an extremely fine web, as if he were playing music; elsewhere, in a completely bare room, containing only a maze of wood and tarred ropes, a young woman sitting on a bench turns a crank, while her other hand rests gently on her knee[;] a *simpler* idea of technology is inconceivable.

An almost naïve simplicity, a kind of Golden Legend of artisanry (for there is no trace of social distress): the *Encyclopedia* identifies the simple, the elementary, the essential, and the causal. Encyclopedic technology is simple because it is reduced to a two-term space: the causal trajectory which proceeds from substance to object; hence all the plates which involve some technological operation (of transformation) mobilize an aesthetic of bareness: huge, empty, well-lighted rooms, in which man cohabits alone with his work: a space without parasites, walls bare, tables cleared; the simple, here, is nothing but the vital; this is made explicit in the bakery; as a primary element, bread implies an austere site; on the other hand, pastry, belonging to the order of the superfluous, proliferates in instruments, operations, products, whose fussy ensemble constitutes a certain *baroque*. In a general way, the object's *production* sweeps the image toward an almost sacred simplicity; its *use*, on the other hand (represented at the moment of sale, in the shop), authorizes an embellishment of the vignette, abounding in instruments, accessories, and attitudes: austerity of creation, luxury of commerce, such is the double regime of the Encyclopedic object: the density of the image and its ornamental charge always signifies that we are shifting from production to consumption.

Of course, the object's pre-eminence in this world derives from an inventorying effort, but inventory is never a neutral idea; to catalogue is not merely to ascertain, as it appears at first glance, but also to appropriate. The *Encyclopedia* is a huge ledger of ownership; Bernard Groetheuysen has noted an opposition between the *orbis pictus* of the Renaissance, animated by the spirit of an adventurous knowledge, and the encyclopedism of the eighteenth century, based on a learning of appropriation. Formally (this is apparent in the plates), ownership depends on a certain dividing up of things: to appropriate is to fragment the world, to divide it into finite objects subject to man in proportion to their very discontinuity: for we cannot separate without finally naming and classifying, and at that moment, property is born. In mythic terms, possession of the world began not with Genesis but at the Flood, when man was obliged to name each kind of animal and to house it, i.e., to separate it from its next of species; the *Encyclopedia*, moreover, takes an essentially pragmatic view of Noah's ark; for it, the ark is not a ship – an object always more or less *oneiric* – but a long floating crate, a goods locker; the only problem it appears to offer the *Encyclopedia* is certainly not theological: it is the problem of its construction, or even, in more technical terms, as is only right, of its framing, and even more specifically, of its fenestration, since each of its windows corresponds to a typical pair of animals, thus divided, named, domesticated (docilely sticking their heads out the opening).

Encyclopedic nomenclature, whatever its technological esotericism on occasion, actually establishes a familiar possession. This is remarkable, for nothing logically obliges the object to be invariably friendly to man. The object, quite the contrary, is humanly a very ambiguous thing; we have noted that for a long time our literature did not acknowledge it; later (which is to say, on the whole, today), the object has been endowed with an unfortunate opacity; assimilated to an inhuman state of nature, its proliferation cannot be noted without a sentiment of apocalypse or of alienation: the modern object is either asphyxiation (Ionesco) or nausea (Sartre). The Encyclopedic object is on the contrary subjugated (we might say that it is precisely pure *object* in the etymological sense of the term), for a very simple and constant reason: it is on each occasion *signed* by man; the image is the privileged means of this human presence, for it permits discreetly locating a permanent man on the object's horizon; the plates of the *Encyclopedia* are always populated (they afford thereby a close relationship with another 'progressive' or, to be more precise, bourgeois iconography: seventeenth-century Dutch painting); you can imagine the most naturally solitary, 'savage' object; be sure that man will nonetheless appear in a corner of the image; he will be considering the object, or measuring it, or surveying it, using it at least as a spectacle; take the Giant's Causeway, that mass of terrifying basalt composed by Nature at Antrim, in Ireland; this inhuman landscape is, one might say, stuffed with humanity; gentlemen in tricornes, lovely ladies contemplate the horrible landscape, chatting familiarly; farther on, men are fishing, scientists are weighing the mineral substance: analyzed into functions (spectacle, fishing, science), the basalt is *reduced*, tamed, familiarized, because it is *divided*; what is striking in the entire *Encyclopedia* (and especially in its images) is that it proposes a *world without fear* (we shall see in a moment that the monstrous is not excluded, but in a category much more 'surrealist' than terrifying). We can even specify more clearly what the man of the Encyclopedic image is reduced to – what is, in some sense, the very essence of his humanity: his hands. In many plates (and not the least beautiful), hands, severed from any body, flutter around the work (for their lightness is extreme); these hands are doubtless the symbol of an artisanal world (again we are concerned with traditional, virtually unmechanized trades, the steam engine is kept out of sight), as is seen by the importance of the tables (huge, flat, well lighted, often encircled by hands); but beyond artisanship, the hands are inevitably the inductive sign of the human essence: do we not see even today, in a less obvious fashion, that our advertising constantly returns to this mysterious motif, at once natural and supernatural, as if man could not get over having hands? It is not easy to be done with a civilization of the hand.

Hence in the immediate state of its representations, the *Encyclopedia* is constantly concerned to familiarize the world of objects (which is its primary substance) by adding to it the obsessive cipher of man. Yet beyond the letter of the image, this humanization implies an intellectual system of an extreme subtlety: the Encyclopedic image is human not only because man is represented in it but also because it constitutes a structure of *information*. This structure, though iconographic, is articulated in most instances like real language (the one which, in fact, we call *articulate*), whose two dimensions as revealed by structural linguistics it reproduces: we know, in fact, that all discourse involves signifying units and that these units are ordered according to two axes, one of substitution (paradigmatic), the other of contiguity (syntagmatic); each unit can thereby *vary* (potentially) with its parents, and *link* (in reality) with its neighbors. This is what happens, *grosso modo*, in an *Encyclopedia* plate. The majority of these plates are formed of two parts; in the lower part, the tool or the gesture (the object of the demonstration), isolated from any real context, is shown in its essence; it constitutes the informative unit, and this unit is generally *varied*: its aspects, elements, kinds are detailed; this part of the plate has the role of *declining* the object, of manifesting its paradigm; on the contrary, in the upper part or vignette, this same object (and its varieties) is apprehended in a lively scene (generally a scene of sale or manufacture, shop or workroom), linked to other objects within a real situation: here we rediscover the syntagmatic dimension of the message; and just as in oral discourse the system of the language, perceptible chiefly on the paradigmatic level, is somehow *hidden* behind the living stream of words, in the same way the Encyclopedic plate plays simultaneously on intellectual demonstration (by its objects) and on fictive life (by its scenes). Here is a trade plate (the pastrycook): down below, the ensemble of various instruments necessary to the profession; in this paradigmatic state, the instrument has no life: inert, frozen in its essence, it is merely a demonstrative schema, analogous to the quasi-academic form of a verbal or nominal paradigm; up above, on the contrary, the chopping board, the whisk (the pastrycooks were making *pâtés en croûte*), the sieve, the molds are arranged, linked together, 'enacted' in a *tableau vivant*, exactly as the 'cases' distinguished by grammar are ordinarily given without our thinking of them in real discourse, with this difference, that the Encyclopedic syntagm is of an extreme density of meaning; in informational language, we would say that the scene involves little 'noise' (see, for instance, the workshop in which the chief operations of engraving are gathered together).

Most of the objects from the lower paradigm are therefore reassembled in the vignette under the heading of signs; whereas the figured nomenclature of the instruments, utensils, products, and gestures involves by definition no secrecy, the vignette, charged with a disseminated meaning, always presents itself a little like a riddle: we must decipher it, locate in it the informative units. The vignette has the riddle's actual density: *all* the information must turn up in the experienced scene (whence, upon scrutiny, a certain exploration of meaning); in the plate devoted to cotton, a certain number of accidents must necessarily refer to the exoticism of the vegetal realm: the palm, the stubble, the island, the Chinaman's shaved head, his long pipe (impractical, it would seem, for working with cotton but which evokes the image of opium), none of this information is innocent: the image is crammed with demonstrative significations; analogously, Demosthenes' lantern is admirable *because* two men are discussing it and pointing to it; it is an antiquity *because* it adjoins a ruin; it is situated in Greece *because* there is the sea, a boat; we contemplate its present state *because* a band of men are dancing in a ring nearby, performing something like the *bouzouki*. Of this kind of cryptographic vocation of the image, there is no better symbol than the two plates dedicated to the hemispheres; a sphere, enclosed by a fine network of lines, makes legible the outline of its continents; but these lines and these contours are only a light transparency behind which float, like a meaning *from behind*, the figures of the constellations (the Wagoner, the Dolphin, the Scales, the Dog).

However, the vignette, a condensate of meaning, also offers a resistance to meaning, and we might say that it is in this resistance, paradoxically, that the plate's language becomes a complete, an adult language. It is, as a matter of fact, apparent that for a reader of the period the scene itself often involves very little new information: who had not seen a pastrycook's shop, a tilled field, a river fishery? The vignette's function is therefore elsewhere: the syntagm (since it is with it that we are concerned) tells us here, once again, that language (and *a fortiori*, iconic language) is not pure intellectual communication: meaning is completed only when it is somehow naturalized in a complete action of man; for the *Encyclopedia*, too, there is a message only *in situation*, whereby we see how ambiguous, finally, the *Encyclopedia*'s didacticism is: very strong in the lower (paradigmatic) part of the plate, it is diluted at its syntagmatic level, to join (without actually being lost) what we must, in fact, call the fictive truth of any human action. At its demonstrative stage, the Encyclopedic plate constitutes a *radical language*, consisting of pure concepts, with neither word tools nor syntax; at the higher stage, this radical language becomes a human *langue*, it deliberately loses in intelligibility what it gains in experience.

The vignette does not have only an existential function, but also, one might say, an *epic* one; it is entrusted to represent the glorious term of a great trajectory, that of substance, transformed, sublimated by man, through a series of episodes and stations: this is symbolized perfectly by the cross-section of the mill, where we see the grain proceed from story to story to be resolved into flour. The demonstration becomes even stronger when it is deliberately artificial: through the weapon shop's open door, we see two men dueling out in the street: the scene is unlikely, though logical if one wants to show the ultimate term of the operation (subject of the plate), which is small-arms supply: there is a trajectory of the object which must be honored to the end. This trajectory is often paradoxical (whence the interest in showing the terms clearly); an enormous mass of wood and cordage produces a delicate flowered carpet: the finished object, so different from the apparatus which has given birth to it, is placed in view; the effect and the cause, juxtaposed, form a figure of meaning by contiguity (what is called metonymy): the framing of the loom finally *signifies* the carpet. The paradox reaches its (delicious) apogee when we can no longer perceive any relation of substance between the initial substance and the object arrived at: at the card-maker's, the playing cards are generated out of a void, the hole in the cardboard; in the workshop of the artificial-flower maker, not only does nothing recall the flower, but even the operations which lead to it are constantly antipathetic to the idea of the flower: these are stampings, stencilings, hammer taps, punch-outs: what relation between such shows of strength and the anemone's fragile efflorescence? Precisely a human relation, the relation of the omnipotent praxis of man, which out of nothing can make everything.

Thus the *Encyclopedia* constantly testifies to a certain epic of substance, but this epic is also in a sense that of the mind: the trajectory of substance is nothing, for the Encyclopedist, but the progress of reason: the image has a logical function *as well.* Diderot says as much explicitly apropos of the machine for making stockings, whose image will reproduce structure:

> *We may regard it as a single and unique reasoning of which the work's fabrication is the conclusion; therefore there reigns among its parts so great a dependence that were we to remove even a single one, or to alter the form of those regarded as least important, we should destroy the entire mechanism.*

Here we find prophetically formulated the very principle of cybernetic ensembles; the plate, image of the machine, is indeed in its way a brain; we introduce substance into it and set up the 'program': the vignette (the syntagm) serves as a conclusion. This logical character of the image has another model, that of dialectics: the image analyzes, first enumerating the scattered elements of the object or of the operation and flinging them as on a table before the reader's eyes, then recomposing them, even adding to them the density of the scene, i.e., of life. The Encyclopedic mounting is based on reason: it descends into analysis as deeply as is necessary in order to '*perceive the elements without confusion*' (according to another phrase of Diderot's, precisely apropos of the drawings, results of investigations on the spot made by draughtsmen in the workshops): the image is a kind of rational synopsis: it illustrates not only the object or its trajectory but also the very mind which conceives it; this double movement corresponds to a double reading: if you read the plate from bottom to top, you obtain in a sense an experiential reading, you relive the object's epic trajectory, its flowering in the complex world of consumers; you proceed from Nature to sociality; but if you read the image from top to bottom, starting from the vignette, it is the progress of the analytic mind that you are reproducing; the world gives you the usual, the evident (the scene); with the Encyclopedist, you descend gradually to causes, to substances, to primary elements, you proceed from the experiential to the causal, you intellectualize the object. The privilege of the image – opposed in this to writing, which is linear – is to compel our reading to have no specific meaning: an image is always deprived of a logical vector (as certain modern experiences tend to prove); those of the *Encyclopedia* possess a precious circularity: we can read them starting from the experiential or, on the contrary, from the intelligible: the real world is not reduced, it is suspended between two great orders of reality, in truth, irreducible orders.

Such is the informative system of the Encyclopedic image. Yet the information does not end with what the image could say to the reader of its period: the modern reader also receives from this old image certain information which the Encyclopedist could not foresee: historical information, first of all: it is quite evident that the plates of the *Encyclopedia* are a mine of precious data as to the civilization of the eighteenth century (at least of its first half); oneiric information, if one may put it so, subsequently: the period object stirs in us certain strictly modern analogies; here is a phenomenon of connotation (connotation, a specific linguistic notion, is constituted by the development of a second meaning) which profoundly justifies the new edition of the old documents. Take, for example, the Lyons diligence; the *Encyclopedia* could aim at nothing but the objective – matte, one might say – reproduction of a certain means of transport; now it happens that this massive and closed trunk immediately wakens in us what we might call memories of the imagination: stories of bandits, kidnappings, ransoms, nocturnal transfers of mysterious prisoners, and, even closer to us, Westerns, the whole heroic and sinister myth of the mail coach is there, in this black object, innocently given, as a photograph of the period might have given it to us. There is a *depth* in the Encyclopedic image, the very depth of time which transforms the object into myth.

This leads to what we must call the Poetics of the Encyclopedic image, if we agree to define Poetics as the sphere of the infinite vibrations of meaning, at the center of which is placed the literal object. We can say that there is not one plate of the *Encyclopedia* which fails to vibrate well beyond its demonstrative intent. This singular vibration is above all an astonishment. Of course, the Encyclopedic image is always clear; but in a deeper region of ourselves, beyond the intellect, or at least in its profile, certain questions are born and exceed us. Consider the astonishing image of man reduced to his network of veins; here anatomical boldness unites with the great poetic and philosophic interrogation: *What is it*? What name to give it? How give a name? A thousand names rise up, dislodging each other: a tree, a bear, a monster, a hair shirt, a fabric, everything which overflows the human silhouette, distends it, draws it toward regions remote from itself, makes it overstep the divisions of Nature; yet, just as in the sketch of a master, the swarm of pencil strokes finally resolves into a pure and exact form, perfectly signifying, so here all the vibrations of meaning concur to impose upon us a certain idea of the object; in this initially human, then animal, then vegetal form we still recognize a kind of unique matter – vein, hair, or thread – and we accede to that great undifferentiated substance of which verbal or pictural poetry is the mode of knowledge: confronting the man of the *Encyclopedia* we must say *the fibrous*, as the ancient Greeks said *the moist* or *the warm* or *the round*: a certain essence of substance is here affirmed.

As a matter of fact, there cannot be anarchic poetry. The iconography of the *Encyclopedia* is poetic because its overflows of meaning always have a certain unity, suggest an ultimate meaning transcending all the *essays* of meaning. For example: the image of the womb is actually quite enigmatic; yet its metaphoric vibrations (as if it were a flayed ox, the interior of a body which dissolves and floats away) do not contradict the original traumatism attached to this object. There is a certain horror and a certain fascination common to some objects, which precisely establishes them in a homogeneous *class*, whose unity and identity is affirmed by Poetics. It is this profound order of metaphor which justifies – poetically – the recourse to a certain category of the *monstrous* (at least, according to the law of connotation, this is what we perceive in the presence of certain plates): anatomical monsters, as in the case of the enigmatic womb or that of the bust with the arms cut off, the breast opened, the face thrown back (meant to show the arteries of the thorax); surrealist monsters (those equestrian statues sheathed in wax and cords), huge and incomprehensible objects (halfway between the stocking and the wallet and which are neither one nor the other, in the stocking loom), subtler monsters (plates of poison with sharp, black crystals); all these transgressions of Nature make us understand that the poetic (for the monstrous can only be the poetic) is never established except by a displacement of the level of perception: it is one of the *Encyclopedia*'s great gifts to *vary* (in the musical sense of the term) the level on which one and the same object can be perceived, thereby liberating the very secrets of form: seen through the microscope, the flea becomes a horrible monster, caparisoned with plates of bronze, armed with steel spines, with the head of a wicked bird, and this monster achieves the strange sublimity of mythological dragons; elsewhere, and in another key, the snowflake, enlarged, becomes a complicated and harmonious flower. Is poetry not a certain power of *disproportion*, as Baudelaire saw so well, describing the effects of reduction and focusing that hashish induces?

Another exemplary category of the poetic (alongside the monstrous): a certain *immobility*. We always praise the movement of a drawing. Yet, by an inevitable paradox, the *image* of movement can only be arrested; in order to signify itself, movement must be immobilized at the extreme point of its course; it is this incredible, untenable repose that Baudelaire called the emphatic truth of gesture and that we find in demonstrative painting – that of Gros, for instance; to this suspended, oversignifying gesture we might give the name *numen*, for it is indeed the gesture of a god who silently creates man's fate, i.e., meaning. In the *Encyclopedia*, numinous gestures abound, for what man makes cannot be insignificant. In the chemical laboratory, for example, each character offers us *slightly* impossible actions, for in truth an action cannot be simultaneously effective and significant, a gesture cannot be altogether an action: the boy washing the pans, oddly, is not looking at what he is doing; his face, turned toward us, grants the operation he is performing a kind of demonstrative solitude; and if the two chemists are having a discussion, it is necessary that one of them raise a finger to signify by this emphatic gesture the learned character of the conversation. Similarly, in the drawing academy, the students are *caught* at the most improbable moment of their agitation. There is, in fact, a physical order in which Zeno's paradox is true, when the arrow flies and yet does not, flies by not flying, and this order is that of painting (here, of drawing).

As we see, Encyclopedic poetics are always defined as a certain unrealism. It is the *Encyclopedia*'s wager (in its plates) to be both a didactic work, based consequently on a severe demand for objectivity (for 'reality'), and a poetic work in which the real is constantly overcome by *some other thing* (the *other* is the sign of all mysteries). By purely graphic means, which never resort to the noble alibi of *art*, Encyclopedic drawing explodes the exact world it takes as its subject. We may specify the meaning of this subversion which affects not only ideology (and in this the *Encyclopedia*'s plates singularly enlarge the dimensions of the enterprise) but also, in a much more serious manner, human rationality. In its very order (described here in the form of the syntagm and the paradigm, the vignette and the bottom of the page), the Encyclopedic plate accomplishes this *risk* of reason. The vignette, a realistic representation of a simple, familiar world (shops, workshops, landscapes) is linked to a certain tranquil evidence of the world: the vignette is calm, reassuring; what can be more deliciously domestic than the kitchen garden with its enclosing walls, its espaliers in the sun? What can be happier, more docile, than the fisherman at his line, the tailor sitting at his window, the feather vendors and the child talking to them? In this Encyclopedic heaven (the upper part of the plates), evil is infrequent; scarcely a trace of discomfort over the hard labors of the glassworkers, armed with pathetic tools, poorly protected against the terrible heat; and when Nature darkens, there always remains a man somewhere to reassure us: a fisherman with a torch beside the night sea, a scientist discoursing before the black basalts of Antrim, the surgeon's light hand resting on the body he is cutting open, figures of knowledge inserted into the heart of the storm (in the engraving of water-spouts). Yet as soon as we leave the vignette for the more analytic plates or images, the world's peaceful order gives way to a certain *violence*. All the forces of reason and unreason concur in this poetic disquiet; first of all metaphor itself makes an infinitely ambiguous object out of a simple, literal object: the sea urchin is *also* a sun, a monstrance: the named world is never certain, constantly fascinated by divined and inaccessible essences; and then, above all (and this is the final interrogation raised by these plates), the analytic mind itself, armed with triumphant reason, can only double the explained world by a new world *to be explained*, according to a process of infinite circularity which is that of the dictionary itself, wherein the world can be defined only by other words; by 'entering' into details, by displacing the levels of perception, by revealing the hidden, by isolating the elements from their practical context, by giving objects an abstract essence, in short by 'opening up' nature, the Encyclopedic image can only, at a certain moment, transcend Nature, attaining to a supernature: it is by dint of didacticism that a kind of wild surrealism is generated here (a phenomenon which we also find in an ambiguous mode in the disturbing encyclopedia Flaubert gives us in *Bouvard and Pécuchet*): do we want to show how equestrian statues are cast? We must wrap them in an extravagant apparatus of wax, tapes, and supports: what madness could attain to this *limit* (not to mention the violent demystification which reduces a warrior Louis XIV to this monstrous doll)? In a general way, the *Encyclopedia* is fascinated, at reason's instance, by the *wrong side* of things: it cross-sections, it amputates, it turns inside out, it tries to get *behind* Nature. Now any 'wrong side' is disturbing: science and parascience are mixed, above all on the level of the image. The *Encyclopedia* constantly proceeds to an impious fragmentation of the world, but what it finds at the term of this fracture is not the fundamental state of pure causes; in most cases the image obliges it to recompose an object that is strictly *unreasonable*; once the first nature is dissolved, another nature appears, quite as formed as the first. In a word, the fracture of the world is impossible: a glance suffices – ours – for the world to be eternally complete.

Translated by Richard Howard

25

LAS MENINAS

Michel Foucault

I

The painter is standing a little back from his canvas. He is glancing at his model; perhaps he is considering whether to add some finishing touch, though it is also possible that the first stroke has not yet been made. The arm holding the brush is bent to the left, towards the palette; it is motionless, for an instant, between canvas and paints. The skilled hand is suspended in mid-air, arrested in rapt attention on the painter's gaze; and the gaze, in return, waits upon the arrested gesture. Between the fine point of the brush and the steely gaze, the scene is about to yield up its volume.

But not without a subtle system of feints. By standing back a little, the painter has placed himself to one side of the painting on which he is working. That is, for the spectator at present observing him he is to the right of his canvas, while the latter, the canvas, takes up the whole of the extreme left. And the canvas has its back turned to that spectator: he can see nothing of it but the reverse side, together with the huge frame on which it is stretched. The painter, on the other hand, is perfectly visible in his full height; or at any rate, he is not masked by the tall canvas which may soon absorb him, when, taking a step towards it again, he returns to his task; he has no doubt just appeared, at this very instant, before the eyes of the spectator, emerging from what is virtually a sort of vast cage projected backwards by the surface he is painting. Now he can be seen, caught in a moment of stillness, at the neutral centre of this oscillation. His dark torso and bright face are half-way between the visible and the invisible: emerging from that canvas beyond our view, he moves into our gaze; but when, in a moment, he makes a step to the right, removing himself from our gaze, he will be standing exactly in front of the canvas he is painting; he will enter that region where his painting, neglected for an instant, will, for him, become visible once more, free of shadow and free of reticence. As though the painter could not at the same time be seen on the picture where he is represented and also see that upon which he is representing something. He rules at the threshold of those two incompatible visibilities.

The painter is looking, his face turned slightly and his head leaning towards one shoulder. He is staring at a point to which, even though it is invisible, we, the spectators, can easily assign an object, since it is we, ourselves, who are that point: our bodies, our faces, our eyes. The spectacle he is observing is thus doubly invisible: first, because it is not represented within the space of the painting, and, second, because it is situated precisely in that blind point, in that essential hiding-place into which our gaze disappears from ourselves at the moment of our actual looking. And yet, how could we fail to see that invisibility, there in front of our eyes, since it has its own perceptible equivalent, its sealed-in figure, in the painting itself? We could, in effect, guess what it is the painter is looking at if it were possible for us to glance for a moment at the canvas he is working on; but all we can see of that canvas is its texture, the horizontal and vertical bars of the stretcher, and the obliquely rising foot of the easel. The tall, monotonous rectangle occupying the whole left portion of the real picture, and representing the back of the canvas within the picture, reconstitutes in the form of a surface the invisibility in depth of what the artist is observing: that space in which we are, and which we are. From the eyes of the painter to what he is observing there runs a compelling line that we, the onlookers, have no power of evading: it runs through the real picture and emerges from its surface to join the place from which we see the painter observing us; this dotted line reaches out to us ineluctably, and links us to the representation of the picture.

In appearance, this locus is a simple one; a matter of pure reciprocity: we are looking at a picture in which the painter is in turn looking out at us. A mere confrontation, eyes catching one another's glance, direct looks superimposing themselves upon one another as they cross. And yet this slender line of reciprocal visibility embraces a whole complex network of uncertainties, exchanges, and feints. The painter is turning his eyes towards us only in so far as we happen to occupy the same position as his subject. We, the spectators, are an additional factor. Though greeted by that gaze, we are also dismissed by it, replaced by that which was always there before we were: the model itself. But, inversely, the painter's gaze, addressed to the void confronting him outside the picture, accepts as many models as there are spectators; in this precise but neutral place, the observer and the observed take part in a ceaseless exchange. No gaze is stable, or rather, in the neutral furrow of the gaze piercing at a right angle through the canvas, subject and object, the spectator and the model, reverse their roles to infinity. And here the great canvas with its back to us on the extreme left of the picture exercises its second function: stubbornly invisible, it prevents the relation of these gazes from ever being discoverable or definitely established. The opaque fixity that it establishes on one side renders forever unstable the play of metamorphoses established in the centre between spectator and model. Because we can see only that reverse side, we do not know who we are, or what we are doing. Seen or seeing? The painter is observing a place which, from moment to moment, never ceases to change its content, its form, its face, its identity. But the attentive immobility of his eyes refers us back to another direction which they have often followed already, and which soon, there can be no doubt, they will take again: that of the motionless canvas upon which is being traced, has already been traced perhaps, for a long time and forever, a portrait that will never again be erased. So that the painter's sovereign gaze commands a virtual triangle whose outline defines this picture of a picture: at the top – the only visible corner – the painter's eyes; at one of the base angles, the invisible place occupied by the model; at the other base angle, the figure probably sketched out on the invisible surface of the canvas.

As soon as they place the spectator in the field of their gaze, the painter's eyes seize hold of him, force him to enter the picture, assign him a place at once privileged and inescapable, levy their luminous and visible tribute from him, and project it upon the inaccessible surface of the canvas within the picture. He sees his invisibility made visible to the painter and transposed into an image forever invisible to himself. A shock

Diego Rodríguez de Silva y Velázquez, *Las Meninas*. © Museo Nacional del Prado, Madrid

that is augmented and made more inevitable still by a marginal trap. At the extreme right, the picture is lit by a window represented in very sharp perspective; so sharp that we can see scarcely more than the embrasure; so that the flood of light streaming through it bathes at the same time, and with equal generosity, two neighbouring spaces, overlapping but irreducible: the surface of the painting, together with the volume it represents (which is to say, the painter's studio, or the salon in which his easel is now set up), and, in front of that surface, the real volume occupied by the spectator (or again, the unreal site of the model). And as it passes through the room from right to left, this vast flood of golden light carries both the spectator towards the painter and the model towards the canvas; it is this light too, which, washing over the painter, makes him visible to the spectator and turns into golden lines, in the model's eyes, the frame of that enigmatic canvas on which his image, once transported there, is to be imprisoned. This extreme, partial, scarcely indicated window frees a whole flow of daylight which serves as the common locus of the representation. It balances the invisible canvas on the other side of the picture: just as that canvas, by turning its back to the spectators, folds itself in against the picture representing it, and forms, by the superimposition of its reverse and visible side upon the surface of the picture depicting it, the ground, inaccessible to us, on which there shimmers the Image *par excellence*, so does the window, a pure aperture, establish a space as manifest as the other is hidden; as much the common ground of painter, figures, models, and spectators, as the other is solitary (for no one is looking at it, not even the painter). From the right, there streams in through an invisible window the pure volume of a light that renders all representation visible; to the left extends the surface that conceals, on the other side of its all too visible woven texture, the representation it bears. The light, by flooding the scene (I mean the room as well as the canvas, the room represented on the canvas, and the room in which the canvas stands), envelops the figures and the spectators and carries them with it, under the painter's gaze, towards the place where his brush will represent them. But that place is concealed from us. We are observing ourselves being observed by the painter, and made visible to his eyes by the same light that enables us to see him. And just as we are about to apprehend ourselves, transcribed by his hand as though in a mirror, we find that we can in fact apprehend nothing of that mirror but its lustreless back. The other side of a psyche.

Now, as it happens, exactly opposite the spectators – ourselves – on the wall forming the far end of the room, Velázquez has represented a series of pictures; and we see that among all those hanging canvases there is one that shines with particular brightness. Its frame is wider and darker than those of the others; yet there is a fine white line around its inner edge diffusing over its whole surface a light whose source is not easy to determine; for it comes from nowhere, unless it be from a space within itself. In this strange light, two silhouettes are apparent, while above them, and a little behind them, is a heavy purple curtain. The other pictures reveal little more than a few paler patches buried in a darkness without depth. This particular one, on the other hand, opens onto a perspective of space in which recognizable forms recede from us in a light that belongs only to itself. Among all these elements intended to provide representations, while impeding them, hiding them, concealing them because of their position or their distance from us, this is the only one that fulfils its function in all honesty and enables us to see what it is supposed to show. Despite its distance from us, despite the shadows all around it. But it isn't a picture: it is a mirror. It offers us at last that enchantment of the double that until now has been denied us, not only by the distant paintings but also by the light in the foreground with its ironic canvas.

Of all the representations represented in the picture this is the only one visible; but no one is looking at it. Upright beside his canvas, his attention entirely taken up by his model, the painter is unable to see this looking-glass shining so softly behind him. The other figures in the picture are also, for the most part, turned to face what must be taking place in front – towards the bright invisibility bordering the canvas, towards that balcony of light where their eyes can gaze at those who are gazing back at them, and not towards that dark recess which marks the far end of the room in which they are represented. There are, it is true, some heads turned away from us in profile: but not one of them is turned far enough to see, at the back of the room, that solitary mirror, that tiny glowing rectangle which is nothing other than visibility, yet without any gaze able to grasp it, to render it actual, and to enjoy the suddenly ripe fruit of the spectacle it offers.

It must be admitted that this indifference is equalled only by the mirror's own. It is reflecting nothing, in fact, of all that is there in the same space as itself: neither the painter with his back to it, nor the figures in the centre of the room. It is not the visible it reflects, in those bright depths. In Dutch painting it was traditional for mirrors to play a duplicating role: they repeated the original contents of the picture, only inside an unreal, modified, contracted, concave space. One saw in them the same things as one saw in the first instance in the painting, but decomposed and recomposed according to a different law. Here, the mirror is saying nothing that has already been said before. Yet its position is more or less completely central: its upper edge is exactly on an imaginary line running half-way between the top and the bottom of the painting, it hangs right in the middle of the far wall (or at least in the middle of the portion we can see); it ought, therefore, to be governed by the same lines of perspective as the picture itself; we might well expect the same studio, the same painter, the same canvas to be arranged within it according to an identical space; it could be the perfect duplication.

In fact, it shows us nothing of what is represented in the picture itself. Its motionless gaze extends out in front of the picture, into that necessarily invisible region which forms its exterior face, to apprehend the figures arranged in that space. Instead of surrounding visible objects, this mirror cuts straight through the whole field of the representation, ignoring all it might apprehend within that field, and restores visibility to that which resides outside all view. But the invisibility that it overcomes in this way is not the invisibility of what is hidden: it does not make its way around any obstacle, it is not distorting any perspective, it is addressing itself to what is invisible both because of the picture's structure and because of its existence as painting. What it is reflecting is that which all the figures within the painting are looking at so fixedly, or at least those who are looking straight ahead; it is therefore what the spectator would be able to see if the painting extended further forward, if its bottom edge were brought lower until it included the figures the painter is using as models. But it is also, since the picture does stop there, displaying only the painter and his studio, what is exterior to the picture, in so far as it is a picture – in other words, a rectangular fragment of lines and colours intended to represent something to the eyes of any possible spectator. At the far end of the room, ignored by all, the unexpected mirror holds in its glow the figures that the painter is looking at (the painter in his represented, objective reality, the reality of the painter at his work); but also the figures that are looking at the painter (in that material reality which the lines and the colours have laid out upon the canvas). These two groups of figures are both equally inaccessible, but in different ways: the first because of an effect of composition peculiar to the painting; the second because of the law that presides over the very existence of all pictures in general. Here, the action of representation consists in bringing one of these two forms of invisibility into the place of the other, in an unstable superimposition – and in rendering them both, at the same moment, at the other extremity of the picture – at that pole which is the very height of its representation: that of a reflected depth in the far recess of the painting's depth. The mirror provides a metathesis of visibility that affects both the space represented in the picture and its nature as representation; it allows us to see, in the centre of the canvas, what in the painting is of necessity doubly invisible.

A strangely literal, though inverted, application of the advice given, so it is said, to his pupil by the old Pachero when the former was working in his studio in Seville: 'The image should stand out from the frame.'

II

But perhaps it is time to give a name at last to that image which appears in the depths of the mirror, and which the painter is contemplating in front of the picture. Perhaps it would be better, once and for all, to determine the identities of all the figures presented or indicated here, so as to avoid embroiling ourselves forever in those vague, rather abstract designations, so constantly prone to misunderstanding and duplication, 'the painter', 'the characters', 'the models', 'the spectators', 'the images'. Rather than pursue to infinity a language inevitably inadequate to the visible fact, it would be better to say that Velázquez composed a picture; that in this picture he represented himself, in his studio or in a room of the Escurial, in the act of painting two figures whom the Infanta Margarita has come there to watch, together with an entourage of duennas, maids of honour, courtiers, and dwarfs; that we can attribute names to this group of people with great precision: tradition recognizes that here we have Doña Maria Agustina Sarmiente, over there Nieto, in the foreground Nicolaso Pertusato, an Italian jester. We could then add that the two personages serving as models to the painter are not visible, at least directly; but that we can see them in a mirror; and that they are, without any doubt, King Philip IV and his wife, Mariana.

These proper names would form useful landmarks and avoid ambiguous designations; they would tell us in any case what the painter is looking at, and the majority of the characters in the picture along with him. But the relation of language to painting is an infinite relation. It is not that words are imperfect, or that, when confronted by the visible, they prove insuperably inadequate. Neither can be reduced to the other's terms: it is in vain that we say what we see; what we see never resides in what we say. And it is in vain that we attempt to show, by the use of images, metaphors, or similes, what we are saying; the space where they achieve their splendour is not that deployed by our eyes but that defined by the sequential elements of syntax. And the proper name, in this particular context, is merely an artifice: it gives us a finger to point with, in other words, to pass surreptitiously from the space where one speaks to the space where one looks; in other words, to fold one over the other as though they were equivalents. But if one wishes to keep the relation of language to vision open, if one wishes to treat their incompatibility as a starting-point for speech instead of as an obstacle to be avoided, so as to stay as close as possible to both, then one must erase those proper names and preserve the infinity of the task. It is perhaps through the medium of this grey, anonymous language, always over-meticulous and repetitive because too broad, that the painting may, little by little, release its illuminations.

We must therefore pretend not to know who is to be reflected in the depths of that mirror, and interrogate that reflection in its own terms.

First, it is the reverse of the great canvas represented on the left. The reverse, or rather the right side, since it displays in full face what the canvas, by its position, is hiding from us. Furthermore, it is both in opposition to the window and a reinforcement of it. Like the window, it provides a ground which is common to the painting and to what lies outside it. But the window operates by the continuous movement of an effusion which, flowing from right to left, unites the attentive figures, the painter, and the canvas, with the spectacle they are observing; whereas the mirror, on the other hand, by means of a violent, instantaneous movement, a movement of pure surprise, leaps out from the picture in order to reach that which is observed yet invisible in front of it, and then, at the far end of its fictitious depth, to render it visible yet indifferent to every gaze. The compelling tracer line, joining the reflection to that which it is reflecting, cuts perpendicularly through the lateral flood of light. Lastly – and this is the mirror's third function – it stands adjacent to a doorway which forms an opening, like the mirror itself, in the far wall of the room. This doorway too forms a bright and sharply defined rectangle whose soft light does not shine through into the room. It would be nothing but a gilded panel if it were not recessed out from the room by means of one leaf of a carved door, the curve of a curtain, and the shadows of several steps. Beyond the steps, a corridor begins; but instead of losing itself in obscurity, it is dissipated in a yellow dazzle where the light, without coming in, whirls around on itself in dynamic repose. Against this background, at once near and limitless, a man stands out in full-length silhouette; he is seen in profile; with one hand he is holding back the weight of a curtain; his feet are placed on different steps; one knee is bent. He may be about to enter the room; or he may be merely observing what is going on inside it, content to surprise those within without being seen himself. Like the mirror, his eyes are directed towards the other side of the scene; nor is anyone paying any more attention to him than to the mirror. We do not know where he has come from: it could be that by following uncertain corridors he has just made his way around the outside of the room in which these characters are collected and the painter is at work; perhaps he too, a short while ago, was there in the forefront of the scene, in the invisible region still being contemplated by all those eyes in the picture. Like the images perceived in the looking-glass, it is possible that he too is an emissary from that evident yet hidden space. Even so, there is a difference: he is there in flesh and blood; he has appeared from the outside, on the threshold of the area represented; he is indubitable – not a probable reflection but an irruption. The mirror, by making visible, beyond even the walls of the studio itself, what is happening in front of the picture, creates, in its sagittal dimension, an oscillation between the interior and the exterior. One foot only on the lower step, his body entirely in profile, the ambiguous visitor is coming in and going out at the same time, like a pendulum caught at the bottom of its swing. He repeats on the spot, but in the dark reality of his body, the instantaneous movement of those images flashing across the room, plunging into the mirror, being reflected there, and springing out from it again like visible, new, and identical species. Pale, minuscule, those silhouetted figures in the mirror are challenged by the tall, solid stature of the man appearing in the doorway.

But we must move down again from the back of the picture towards the front of the stage; we must leave that periphery whose volute we have just been following. Starting from the painter's gaze, which constitutes an off-centre centre to the left, we perceive first of all the back of the canvas, then the paintings hung on the wall, with the mirror in their centre, then the open doorway, then more pictures, of which, because of the sharpness of the perspective, we can see no more than the edges of the frames, and finally, at the extreme right, the window, or rather the groove in the wall from which the light is pouring. This spiral shell presents us with the entire cycle of representation: the gaze, the palette and brush, the canvas innocent of signs (these are the material tools of representation), the paintings, the reflections, the real man (the completed representation, but as it were freed from its illusory or truthful contents, which are juxtaposed to it); then the representation dissolves again: we can see only the frames, and the light that is flooding the pictures from outside, but that they, in return, must reconstitute in their own kind, as though it were coming from elsewhere, passing through their dark wooden frames. And we do, in fact, see this light on the painting, apparently welling out from the crack of the frame; and from there it moves over to touch the brow, the cheekbones, the eyes, the gaze of the painter, who is holding a palette in one hand and in the other a fine brush . . . And so the spiral is closed, or rather, by means of that light, is opened.

This opening is not, like the one in the back wall, made by pulling back a door; it is the whole breadth of the picture itself, and the looks that pass across it are not those of a distant visitor. The frieze that occupies the foreground and the middle ground of the picture represents – if we include the painter – eight characters. Five of these, their heads more or less bent, turned or inclined, are looking straight out at right angles to the surface of the picture. The centre of the group is occupied by the little Infanta, with her flared pink and grey dress. The princess is turning her head towards the right side of the picture, while her torso and the big panniers of her dress slant away slightly towards the left; but her gaze is directed absolutely straight towards the spectator standing in front of the painting. A vertical line dividing the canvas into two equal halves would pass between the child's eyes. Her face is a third of the total height of the picture above the lower frame. So that here, beyond all question, resides the principal theme of the composition; this is the very object of this painting. As though to prove this and to emphasize it even more, Velázquez has made use of a traditional visual device: beside the principal figure he has placed a secondary one, kneeling and looking in towards the central one. Like a donor in prayer, like an angel greeting the Virgin, a maid of honour on her knees is stretching out her hands towards the princess. Her face stands out in perfect profile against the background. It is at the same height as that of the child. This attendant is looking at the princess and only at the princess. A little to the right, there stands another maid of honour, also turned towards the Infanta, leaning slightly over her, but with her eyes clearly directed towards the front, towards the same spot already being gazed at by the painter and the princess. Lastly, two other groups made up of two figures each: one of these groups is further away; the other, made up of the two dwarfs, is right in the foreground. One character in each of these pairs is looking straight out, the other to the left or the right. Because of their positions and their size, these two groups correspond and themselves form a pair: behind, the courtiers (the woman, to the left, looks to the right); in front, the dwarfs (the boy, who is at the extreme right, looks in towards the centre of the picture). This group of characters, arranged in this manner, can be taken to constitute, according to the way one looks at the picture and the centre of reference chosen, two different figures. The first would be a large X: the top left-hand point of this X would be the painter's eyes; the top right-hand one, the male courtier's eyes; at the bottom left-hand corner there is the corner of the canvas represented with its back towards us (or, more exactly, the foot of the easel); at the bottom right-hand corner, the dwarf (his foot on the dog's back). Where these two lines intersect, at the centre of the X, are the eyes of the Infanta. The second figure would be more that of a vast curve, its two ends determined by the painter on the left and the male courtier on the right – both these extremities occurring high up in the picture and set back from its surface; the centre of the curve, much nearer to us, would coincide with the princess's face and the look her maid of honour is directing towards her. This curve describes a shallow hollow across the centre of the picture which at once contains and sets off the position of the mirror at the back.

There are thus two centres around which the picture may be organized, according to whether the fluttering attention of the spectator decides to settle in this place or in that. The princess is standing upright in the centre of a St Andrew's cross, which is revolving around her with its eddies of courtiers, maids of honour, animals, and fools. But this pivoting movement is frozen. Frozen by a spectacle that would be absolutely invisible if those same characters, suddenly motionless, were not offering us, as though in the hollow of a goblet, the possibility of seeing in the depths of a mirror the unforeseen double of what they are observing. In depth, it is the princess who is superimposed on the mirror; vertically, it is the reflection that is superimposed on the face. But, because of the perspective, they are very close to one another. Moreover, from each of them there springs an ineluctable line: the line issuing from the mirror crosses the whole of the depth represented (and even more, since the mirror forms a hole in the back wall and brings a further space into being behind it); the other line is shorter: it comes from the child's eyes and crosses only the foreground. These two sagittal lines converge at a very sharp angle, and the point where they meet, springing out from the painted surface, occurs in front of the picture, more or less exactly at the spot from which we are observing it. It is an uncertain point because we cannot see it; yet it is an inevitable and perfectly defined point too, since it is determined by those two dominating figures and confirmed further by other, adjacent dotted lines which also have their origin inside the picture and emerge from it in a similar fashion.

What is there, then, we ask at last, in that place which is completely inaccessible because it is exterior to the picture, yet is prescribed by all the lines of its composition? What is the spectacle, what are the faces that are reflected first of all in the depths of the Infanta's eyes, then in the courtiers' and the painter's, and finally in the distant glow of the mirror? But the question immediately becomes a double one: the face reflected in the mirror is also the face that is contemplating it; what all the figures in the picture are looking at are the two figures to whose eyes they too present a scene to be observed. The entire picture is looking out at a scene for which it is itself a scene. A condition of pure reciprocity manifested by the observing and observed mirror, the two stages of which are uncoupled at the two lower corners of the picture: on the left the canvas with its back to us, by means of which the exterior point is made into pure spectacle; to the right the dog lying on the floor, the only element in the picture that is neither looking at anything nor moving, because it is not intended, with its deep reliefs and the light playing on its silky hair, to be anything but an object to be seen.

Our first glance at the painting told us what it is that creates this spectacle-as-observation. It is the two sovereigns. One can sense their presence already in the respectful gaze of the figures in the picture, in the astonishment of the child and the dwarfs. We recognize them, at the far end of the picture, in the two tiny silhouettes gleaming out from the looking-glass. In the midst of all those attentive faces, all those richly dressed bodies, they are the palest, the most unreal, the most compromised of all the painting's images: a movement, a little light, would be sufficient to eclipse them. Of all these figures represented before us, they are also the most ignored, since no one is paying the slightest attention to that reflection which has slipped into the room behind them all, silently occupying its unsuspected space; in so far as they are visible, they are the frailest and the most distant form of all reality. Inversely, in so far as they stand outside the picture and are therefore withdrawn from it in an essential invisibility, they provide the centre around which the entire representation is ordered: it is they who are being faced, it is towards them that everyone is turned, it is to their eyes that the princess is being presented in her holiday clothes; from the canvas with its back to us to the Infanta, and from the Infanta to the dwarf playing on the extreme right, there runs a curve (or again, the lower fork of the X opens) that orders the whole arrangement of the picture to their gaze and thus makes apparent the true centre of the composition, to which the Infanta's gaze and the image in the mirror are both finally subject.

In the realm of the anecdote, this centre is symbolically sovereign, since it is occupied by King Philip IV and his wife. But it is so above all because of the triple function it fulfils in relation to the picture. For in it there occurs an exact superimposition of the model's gaze as it is being painted, of the spectator's as he contemplates the painting, and of the painter's as he is composing his picture (not the one represented, but the one in front of us which we are discussing). These three 'observing' functions come together in a point exterior to the picture: that is, an ideal point in relation to what is represented, but a perfectly real one too, since it is also the starting-point that makes the representation possible. Within that reality itself, it cannot not be invisible. And yet, that reality is projected within the picture – projected and diffracted in three forms which correspond to the three functions of that ideal and real point. They are: on the left, the painter with his palette in his hand (a self-portrait of Velázquez); to the right, the visitor, one foot on the step, ready to enter the room; he is taking in the scene from the back, but he can see the royal couple, who are the spectacle itself, from the front; and lastly, in the centre, the reflection of the king and the queen, richly dressed, motionless, in the attitude of patient models.

A reflection that shows us quite simply, and in shadow, what all those in the foreground are looking at. It restores, as if by magic, what is lacking in every gaze: in the painter's, the model, which his represented double is duplicating over there in the picture; in the king's, his portrait, which is being finished off on that slope of the canvas that he cannot perceive from where he stands; in that of the spectator, the real centre of the scene, whose place he himself has taken as though by usurpation. But perhaps this generosity on the part of the mirror is feigned; perhaps it is hiding as much as and even more than it reveals. That space where the king and his wife hold sway belongs equally well to the artist and to the spectator: in the depths of the mirror there could also appear – there ought to appear – the anonymous face of the passer-by and that of Velázquez. For the function of that reflection is to draw into the interior of the picture what is intimately foreign to it: the gaze which has organized it and the gaze for which it is displayed. But because they are present within the picture, to the right and to the left, the artist and the visitor cannot be given a place in the mirror: just as the king appears in the depths of the looking-glass precisely because he does not belong to the picture.

In the great volute that runs around the perimeter of the studio, from the gaze of the painter, with his motionless hand and palette, right round to the finished paintings, representation came into being, reached completion, only to dissolve once more into the light; the cycle was complete. The lines that run through the depth of the picture, on the other hand, are not complete; they all lack a segment of their trajectories. This gap is caused by the absence of the king – an absence that is an artifice on the part of the painter. But this artifice both conceals and indicates another vacancy which is, on the contrary, immediate: that of the painter and the spectator when they are looking at or composing the picture. It may be that, in this picture, as in all the representations of which it is, as it were, the manifest essence, the profound invisibility of what one sees is inseparable from the invisibility of the person seeing – despite all mirrors, reflections, imitations, and portraits. Around the scene are arranged all the signs and successive forms of representation; but the double relation of the representation to its model and to its sovereign, to its author as well as to the person to whom it is being offered, this relation is necessarily interrupted. It can never be present without some residuum, even in a representation that offers itself as a spectacle. In the depth that traverses the picture, hollowing it into a fictitious recess and projecting it forward in front of itself, it is not possible for the pure felicity of the image ever to present in a full light both the master who is representing and the sovereign who is being represented.

Perhaps there exists, in this painting by Velázquez, the representation as it were, of Classical representation, and the definition of the space it opens up to us. And, indeed, representation undertakes to represent itself here in all its elements, with its images, the eyes to which it is offered, the faces it makes visible, the gestures that call it into being. But there, in the midst of this dispersion which it is simultaneously grouping together and spreading out before us, indicated compellingly from every side, is an essential void: the necessary disappearance of that which is its foundation – of the person it resembles and the person in whose eyes it is only a resemblance. This very subject – which is the same – has been elided. And representation, freed finally from the relation that was impeding it, can offer itself as representation in its pure form.

26

THE PARERGON[1]

Jacques Derrida

economize on the abyss: not only save oneself from falling into the bottomless depths by weaving and folding back the cloth to infinity, textual art of the reprise, multiplication of patches within patches, but also establish the laws of reappropriation, formalize the rules which constrain the logic of the abyss and which shuttle between the economic *and* the aneconomic, the raising [*la relève*][2] *and* the fall, the abyssal operation which can only work toward the *relève and* that in it which regularly reproduces collapse

what then is the object of the third *Critique*? The critique of pure theoretical reason assumes the exclusion (*Ausschliessung*) of all that is not theoretical knowledge: the affect (*Gefühl*) in its two principal values (pleasure/unpleasure) and the power to desire (*Begehrungsvermögen*). It cuts out its field only by cutting itself off from the interests of desire, by losing interest in desire. From the moment that understanding alone can give constitutive principles to knowledge, the exclusion bears simultaneously on reason which transgresses the limits of possible knowledge of nature. Now the a priori principles of reason, although regulative with regard to the faculty of knowing, are constitutive with regard to the faculty of desiring. The critique of pure theoretical reason thus excludes both reason *and* desire, desire's reason and reason's desire, the desire for reason.

What is it about, at bottom? The bottom.

The understanding and reason are not two disconnected faculties; they are articulated in a certain task and a certain number of operations which involve, precisely, articulation, i.e., discourse. For between the two faculties, an articulated member, a third faculty comes into play. This intermediary member which Kant names precisely *Mittelglied*, middle articulation, is judgment (*Ur-teil*). But what will be the nature of the a priori principles of the middle articulation? Will they be constitutive or regulative? Do they give a priori rules to pleasure and unpleasure? What is at stake in this question can be measured by the fact that regulative principles would not allow the demarcation of a *proper domain* (*eigenes Gebiet*).

Since the *Mittelglied* also forms the articulation of the theoretical and the practical (in the Kantian sense), we are plunging into a place that is *neither* theoretical *nor* practical or else *both* theoretical *and* practical. Art (in general), or rather the beautiful, if it takes place, is inscribed here. But this *here*, this place is announced as a place deprived of place. It runs the risk, in taking place, of not having its own proper domain. But this does not deprive it, for all that, of jurisdiction and foundation: what has no domain (*Gebiet*) or field (*Feld*) of its own, no 'field of objects' defining its 'domain,' can have a 'territory' and a 'ground' (*Boden*) possessing a 'proper legality' (*Introduction*, III).

The *Mittelglied*, intermediary member, must in effect be treated as a separable part, a particular part (*als ein besonderer Theil*). But also as a nonparticular, nondetachable part, since it forms the articulation between two others; one can even say, anticipating Hegel, an originary part (*Ur-teil*). It is indeed a question of judgment. The same paragraph recalls that a critique of pure reason, i.e., of our faculty of judging according to a priori principles, would be 'incomplete' (*unvollständig*) if a theory of judgment, of the *Mittelglied*, did not form a 'particular part' of it. But immediately after, in the following sentence, that in a pure philosophy the principles of judgment would not form a *detached* part, between the theoretical part and the practical part, but could be *attached, annexed* (*angeschlossen*) to each of the two. Kant thus seems to mean two contradictory things at the same time: that it is necessary to disengage the middle member as a detachable part, operate the partition of the part, but also that it is necessary to re-member the whole by re-forming the nexus, the connection, the re-annexation of the part to the two major columns of the corpus. Let us not forget that it is here a question of judgment (*Ur-teil*), of the function of the copula: does it play a separable role, its own part, or does it work in the orchestra of reason, in the concert of the practical and the theoretical?

Let us look more closely at this paragraph in the preface to the third *Critique*. It does not involve any contradiction. The separation of the part is not prescribed and forbidden from the same point of view. Within a critique of pure reason, of our faculty of judging according to a priori principles, the part must be detached and examined separately. But in a pure philosophy, in a 'system of pure philosophy,' everything must be sewn back together. The critique detaches because it is itself only a moment and a part of the system. It is in the critique that, precisely, the critical suspension is produced, the *krinein*, the in-between, the question of knowing whether the theory of judgment is theoretical *or* practical, and whether it is then referred to a regulatory *or* constitutive instance. But the system of pure philosophy *will have had to* include the critical within itself, and construct a general discourse which will get the better of the detachable and account for it. This system of pure philosophy is what Kant calls *metaphysics*. It is not yet possible. Only the critique can have a program that is currently possible.

The question of desire, of pleasure and of unpleasure is thus also the question of a *detachment* (neither the word nor the concept appears *as such* in the *Critique*) which will itself be specified, dismembered or re-membered: *detachment* – separation of a member –, *detachment* – delegation of a representative, sign or symbol on assignment (the beautiful as *symbol* of morality, problems of the hypotyposis, of the trace

(*Spur*), of 'cipher-script' (*Chiffreschrift*), of the intermittent sign (*Wink*); see for example sections 42 and 59), *detachment* – disinterested attitude as essence of aesthetic experience.

In order to express the relationship between the two possibles (the now-possible of the critique and the future-possible of metaphysics), Kant proposes another metaphor. He borrows it, already, from art, which has not yet been discussed, from the technique of architecture, architectonics: the pure philosopher, the metaphysician, will have to operate *like* a good architect, like a good *tekhnitēs* of edification. He will be a sort of artist. Now what does a good architect do, according to Kant? He must first of all be certain of the ground, the foundation, the fundament.

> A Critique of pure reason, i.e., of our faculty of judging on a priori principles, would be incomplete if the critical examination of judgment, which is a faculty of knowledge, and, as such, lays claim to independent principles, were not dealt with separately. Still, however, its principles cannot, in a system of pure philosophy, form a separate constituent part intermediate between the theoretical and practical divisions, but may when needful (*im Nothfalle*) be annexed (*angeschlossen*) to one or other as occasion requires (*gelegentlich*). For if such a system is some day worked out (*zu Stande kommen*) under the general name of Metaphysic . . . then the critical examination of the ground for this edifice must have been previously carried down to the very depths of the foundations (*Grundlage*) of the faculty of principles independent of experience, lest in some quarter (*an irgend einem Theile*) it might give way (collapse, *sinke*), and, sinking, inevitably bring with it the ruin (*Einsturz*) of all.
>
> (Meredith, pp. 4–5)[3]

The proper instance of the critique: the architect of reason searches, probes, prepares the ground. In search of the bedrock, the ultimate *Grund* on which to raise the whole of metaphysics. But also in search of roots, of the common root which then divides in the phenomenal light, and which never itself yields up to experience. Thus the critique as such attempts to descend to the *bythos*, to the *bottom* of the abyss, without knowing whether it exists.

It is still too early to interrogate the general functioning of metaphor and analogy in the third *Critique*. This functioning is perhaps not simply reflected by the theory which, in the book, both includes it and plunges into its abyss.

We have just encountered the first 'metaphor': beginning of the preface (*Vorrede*). Now at the end of the introduction which follows (*Einleitung*), and as if to frame the whole prolegomenon, will be the metaphor of the artificial work securing the passage over the natural gulf, the bridge (*Brücke*) projected over the great abyss (*grosse Kluft*). Philosophy, which in this book has to think art through – art in general and fine art – as a part of its field or of its edifice, is here *representing itself* as a part of its part: philosophy as an art of architecture. It represents itself, it *detaches itself*, detaches from itself a proxy, a part of itself beside itself in order to think the whole, to saturate or heal over the whole that suffers from detachment. The philosophy of art presupposes an art of philosophizing, a major art, but also a miner's art in its critical preliminaries, an architect's art in its edifying erection. And if, as will be said further on, fine art is always an art of genius, then the *Anthropology from the Pragmatic Point of View* would for preference delegate a German to the post of critique: the German genius shows itself best on the side of the root, the Italian on that of the crown of leaves, the French on that of the flower and the English on that of the fruit. Finally, if this pure philosophy or fundamental metaphysics here proposes to account for, among other things, desire, pleasure and unpleasure, it exposes itself and represents itself first of all in its own desire. The desire of reason would be a fundamental desire, a desire for the fundamental, a desire to go to the *bythos*. Not an empirical desire since it leads toward the unconditioned, and that which yields itself up in the currency of a determinate metaphor ought, as a metaphor of reason, to account for [*rendre raison de*] all other metaphors. It would figure the being-desire of desire, the desire of/for reason as desire for a grounded structure. Edifying desire would be produced as an art of philosophizing, commanding all the others and accounting for [*rendant raison de*] all rhetoric.

'Great difficulties' arise. A theory of judgment as *Mittelglied* must be constructed. But there will be 'great difficulties' (*grosse Schwierigkeiten*) in finding for judgment a priori principles which are proper to it and which would protect the theory from empiricism. One can find a priori concepts only in the understanding. The faculty of judgment uses them, it applies them, but it does not have at its disposal any concepts which belong to it or are specifically reserved for it. The only concept which it can produce is an empty concept, in a sense, and one which does not give anything to be known. By it, 'nothing is properly known.' It supplies a 'rule' of usage which comprises no objectivity, no relation to the object, no knowledge. The rule is subjective, the faculty of judgment gives itself its own norms, and it must do so, failing which it would be necessary to call upon another faculty or arbitration, *ad infinitum*. And yet this *subjective* rule is applied to judgments, to statements which by their structure lay claim to universal objectivity.

Such would be the difficulty, the constraint, the confusion, the *Verlegenheit*. It seems to confirm a certain Hegelian and subsequently Heideggerian verdict: this discourse on the beautiful and on art, because it remains at the stage of a theory of judgment, gets tangled up in the – derived – opposition of subject and object.

Of the beautiful and of art it has not yet been question. Nothing, up to this point, suggested that it should be a question of these. And now here is Kant declaring that this 'great difficulty' *of principle* (subjective or objective) 'is found' (*findet sich*), that it is met with 'principally' (*hauptsächlich*) in the judgments 'which are called aesthetic.' These could have constituted an example, however important, a major occurrence of the 'difficulty.' But in truth it is the principal example, the unique specimen which gives meaning and orients the multiplicity. The examination of this example, namely the aesthetic domain, forms the choice morsel, the 'most important piece' (*das wichtigste Stück*) of the critique of the faculty of judgment. Although they bring *nothing* to knowledge, aesthetic judgments, insofar as they are judgments, come under the faculty of knowing alone, a faculty which they put in relation with pleasure or unpleasure according to an a priori principle. This relationship of knowledge to pleasure reveals itself here in its purity since there is nothing to know, but such is precisely the enigma, the enigmatic (*das Rätselhafte*) at the heart of judgment. It is why a 'special section' (*besondere Abteilung*), a particular division, a cut-out sector, a detached part, form the object of the third *Critique*.

One must not expect from it what in principle it does not, in its declared intention, promise. This critique of taste does not concern production; it has in view neither 'education' nor 'culture,' which can very well do without it. And as the *Critique* will show that one cannot assign conceptual rules to the beautiful, it will not be a question of constituting an *aesthetic*, even a general one, but of analyzing the formal conditions of possibility of an aesthetic judgment in general, hence of an aesthetic objectivity in general.

With this transcendental aim, Kant demands to be read without indulgence. But for the rest, he admits the lacks, the lacunary character (*Mangelhaftigkeit*) of his work. This is the word Hegel uses too.

What does the lack depend on? What lack is it?

And what if it were the frame. What if the lack formed the frame of the theory. Not its accident but its frame. More or less still: what if the lack were not only the lack of a theory of the frame but the place of the lack in a theory of the frame.

Edge [*arête*]/lack

The 'lacunary character' of his work, according to Kant at least, hangs on the fact that nature has muddled up, complicated, tangled up (*verwickelt*) the problems. The author's excuses are limited to the first part of the work, to the critique of aesthetic judgment, and not to the critique of teleological judgment. It is only in the first part that the deduction will not have the clarity and distinctness (*Deutlichkeit*) which one would, however, be entitled to expect from a knowledge through concepts. After deploring that nature has mixed up the threads, at the moment when he is finishing his critical work (*Hiemit endige ich also mein ganzes kritisches Geschäft*), admitting the lacunae and projecting a bridge over the abyss of the other two critiques, Kant speaks of his age. He must gain time, not let the delay accumulate, hurry on toward the doctrine.

* * *

But a book. And a book of philosophy. If it is a book of metaphysics in the Kantian sense, hence a book of pure philosophy, one can in principle enter it from any point: it is a sort of architecture. In the third *Critique*, there is pure philosophy, there is talk of it and its plan is drawn. In terms of the analogy (but how to measure its terms) one ought to be able to begin anywhere and follow any order, although the quantity and the quality, the force of the reading may depend, as with a piece of architecture, on the point of view and on a certain relation to the ideal limit – which acts as a frame. There are only ever points of view: but the solidity, the existence, the structure of the edifice do not depend on them. Can one say the same, by analogy, of a book? One does not necessarily gain access to a piece of architecture by following the order of its production, starting at the foundations and arriving at the roof-ridge. And we must distinguish here between perception, analysis, penetration, utilization, even destruction. But does one read a book of pure philosophy if one does not begin with the foundations and follow the juridical order of its writing? What then is it to read philosophy and must one only read it? To be sure, the juridical order supported by the foundations does not coincide with the factual order: for example, Kant wrote his introduction after finishing the book and it is the most powerful effort to gather together the whole system of his philosophy, to give his whole discourse a *de jure* foundation, to articulate critique with philosophy. The introduction follows, the foundation comes after having come first. But even if it were established that in principle, in metaphysics in the Kantian sense, one must begin at the foundations, critique is not metaphysics: it is, *first, in search of* the foundation (and thus in fact comes *afterwards*), suspended like a crane or a dragline bucket above the pit, working to scrape, probe, clear, and open up a sure ground. In what order to read a critique? The *de facto* order or the *de jure* order? The *ordo inveniendi* or the *ordo exponendi*? All these questions differ/defer, each is subordinate to the others, and whatever their interminable breadth, they are valid in general for any critical text.

a supplementary complication constrains us to reconsider the way these questions fit together. The third *Critique* is not just one critique among others. Its specific object has the form of a certain type of judgment – the reflective judgment – which works (on) the example in a very singular way. The distinction between reflective and determinant judgment, a distinction that is both familiar and obscure, watches over all the internal divisions of the book. I recall it in its poorest generality. The faculty of judgment *in general* allows one to think the particular as contained under the general (rule, principle, law). When the generality is given first, the operation of judgment subsumes and *determines* the particular. It is determinant (*bestimmend*), it specifies, narrows down, comprehends, tightens. In the contrary hypothesis, the *reflective* judgment (*reflectirend*) has only the particular at its disposal and must climb back up to, return toward generality: the example (this is what matters to us here) is here given prior to the law and, in its very uniqueness as example, allows one to discover that law. Common scientific or logical discourse proceeds by determinant judgments, and the example follows in order to determine or, with a pedagogical intention, to illustrate. In art and in life, wherever one must, according to Kant, proceed to reflective judgments and assume (by analogy with art: we shall come to this rule further on) a finality[4] the concept of which we do not have, the *example precedes*. There follows a singular historicity and (counting the simulacrum-time) a certain (regulated, relative) ficture of the theoretical on the authority of this reflective hinge,[5] I begin my reading of the third *Critique* with some examples.

Is this docility perverse? Nothing yet permits a decision.

So I begin with some examples: not with the introduction, which gives the laws, nor with the beginning of the book (the analytic of the beautiful). Nor with the middle nor the end, but somewhere near the conclusion of the analytic of the beautiful, paragraph 14 [of the *Critique*]. It is entitled 'Clarification by Examples' (*Erlaüterung durch Beispiele*).

Its most obvious intention is to clarify the structure of 'the proper object of the pure judgment of taste' (*den eigentlichen Gegenstand des reinen Geschmacksurtheils*). I shall not even cite all the examples, but only some of them, and I shall provisionally leave to one side the very complicated theory of colors and sounds, of drawing and composition, which is unfolded between the two fragments I translate here. Unless it be broached at the same time. I shall in any case assume you have read it.

> Aesthetic, just like theoretical (logical) judgements, are divisible into empirical and pure. The first are those by which agreeableness or disagreeableness, the second those by which beauty, is predicated of an object or its mode of representation. The former are judgements of sense (material aesthetic judgements), the latter (as formal) alone judgements of taste proper (*allein eigentliche Geschmacksurtheile*).
>
> A judgement of taste, therefore, is only pure so far as its determining ground (*Bestimmungsgrunde*) is tainted with no merely empirical delight (*Wohlgefallen*). But such a taint is always present where charm (*Reiz*) or emotion (*Rührung*) have a share in the judgement (*einen Antheil an dem Urtheile haben*) by which something is to be described as beautiful . . .
>
> All form of objects of sense (both of external and also, mediately, of internal sense) is either *figure* (*Gestalt*) or *play* (*Spiel*). In the latter case it is either play of figures (in space: mimic and dance), or mere play of sensations (in time). The charm (*Reiz*) of colours, or of the agreeable tones of instruments, may be added (*hinzukommen*): but the *design* (*Zeichnung*) in the former and the composition (*Composition*) in the latter constitute the proper object of the pure judgement of taste. To say that the purity alike of colours and of tones, or their variety and contrast, seem to contribute (*beizutragen*) to beauty, is by no means to imply that, because in themselves agreeable, they therefore yield an addition (*einen . . . Zusatz*) to the delight in the form (*Wohlgefallen an der Form*) and one on a par with it (*gleichartigen*). The real meaning rather is that they make this form more clearly, definitely, and completely (*nur genauer, bestimmter und vollständiger*) intuitable (*anschaulich machen*), and besides stimulate the representation by their charm, as they excite and sustain the attention directed to the object itself.
>
> Even what is called *ornamentation* [*Zierathen*: decoration, adornment,

embellishment] (*Parerga*) i.e., what is only an adjunct, and not an intrinsic constituent in the complete representation of the object (*was nicht in die ganze Vorstellung des Gegenstandes als Bestandstück innerlich, sondern nur äusserlich als Zuthat gehört*), in augmenting the delight of taste does so only by means of its form. Thus it is with the frames (*Einfassungen*) of pictures or the drapery on statues, or the colonnades of palaces. But if the ornamentation does not itself enter into the composition of the beautiful form – if it is introduced (*angebracht*: fixed on) like a gold frame (*goldene Rahmen*) merely to win approval for the picture by means of its charm – it is then called *finery* [*parure*] (*Schmuck*) and takes away from the genuine beauty.

(Meredith, pp. 65, 67–68 [cf. Pluhar, pp. 69–72])

a theory which would run along as if on wheels

the clothes on statues – for example – would thus be ornaments: *parerga*.

Kant explains himself elsewhere on the necessity of having recourse to dead or scholarly languages. The Greek here confers a quasi-conceptual dignity to the notion of this *hors-d'œuvre* which however does not stand simply outside the work [*hors d'œuvre*], also acting alongside, right up against the work (*ergon*). Dictionaries most often give 'hors-d'œuvre,' which is the strictest translation, but also 'accessory, foreign or secondary object,' 'supplement,' 'aside,' 'remainder.' It is what the principal subject *must not become*, by being separated from itself: the education of children in legislation ([Plato,] *Laws* 766a) or the definition of science ([Plato,] *Theaetetus* 184a) *must not* be treated as *parerga*. In the search for the cause or the knowledge of principles, *one must avoid* letting the *parerga* get the upper hand over the essentials ([Aristotle,] *Nicomachean Ethics* 1098a 30). Philosophical discourse will always have been *against* the *parergon*. But what about this *against*?

A *parergon* comes against, beside, and in addition to the *ergon*, the work done [*fait*], the fact [*le fait*], the work, but it does not fall to one side, it touches and cooperates within the operation, from a certain outside. Neither simply outside nor simply inside. Like an accessory that one is obliged to welcome on the border, on board [*au bord, à bord*]. It is first of all the on (the) bo(a)rd(er) [*Il est d'abord l'à-bord*].

If we wanted to play a little – for the sake of poetics – at etymology, the *à-bord* would refer us to the Middle High German *bort* (table, plank, deck of a vessel).

> The *bord* is thus properly speaking a plank; and etymology allows us to grasp the way its meanings link together. The primary meaning is the deck of a vessel, i.e., a construction made of planks; then, by metonymy, that which borders, that which encloses, that which limits, that which is at the extremity.

Says Littré.

But the *etymon* will always have had, for whoever knows how to read, its border-effects.

Boats are never far away when one is handling figures of rhetoric.[6] Brothel [*bordel*] has the same etymology; it's an easy one, at first a little hut made of wood.

The *bord* is made of wood, and apparently indifferent like the frame of painting. Along with stone, better than stone, wood names matter (*hylē* means wood). These questions of wood, of matter, of the frame, of the limit between inside and outside, must, somewhere in the margins, be constituted together.

The *parergon*, this supplement outside the work, must, if it is to have the status of a philosophical quasi-concept, designate a formal and general predicative structure, which one can transport *intact* or deformed and reformed *according to certain rules*, into other fields, to submit new contents to it. Now Kant does use the word *parergon* elsewhere: the context is very different but the structure is analogous and just as problematical. It is to be found in a very long note added to the second edition of *Religion within the Limits of Reason Alone*. This place, the form of this place, is of great import.

To what is the 'Note' appended? To a 'General Remark' which closes the second part.

Now what is the *parergon*? It is the concept of the remark, of this 'General Remark,' insofar as it defines what comes to be added to *Religion within the Limits of Reason Alone* without being a part of it and yet without being absolutely extrinsic to it. Each part of the book comprises a 'General Remark' (*Allgemeine Anmerkung*), a *parergon* concerning a *parergon*. As there are four parts to *Religion*, then the book is in a manner of speaking *framed* [*cadrée*], but also squared up [*quadrillée*][7] by these four remarks on *parerga*, hors-d'œuvres, 'additives' which are neither inside nor outside.

The beginning of the note appended, in the second edition, to the first of the 'General Remarks,' defines the status of the remark as *parergon*:

> This general Remark is the first of four which have been added [*angehängt*: appended, like appendixes] to each piece of this text (*jedem Stück dieser Schrift*) and which might have as titles: (1) Of the effects of grace; (2) Of miracles; (3) Of mysteries; (4) Of the means of grace. They are in some measure *parerga* of religion within the limits of pure reason; they are not integral parts of it (*sie gehören nicht innerhalb dieselben*) but they verge on it [*aber stossen doch an sie an:* they touch it, push it, press it, press against it, seek contact, exert a pressure at the frontier]. Reason, conscious of its impotence (*Unvermögens*) to satisfy its moral need [the only need which should ground or should have grounded religion within the limits of reason alone], reaches as far as these transcendent ideas which are potentially able to make good the lack (*die jenen Mangel ergänzen*), without however appropriating them (*sich zuzueignen*) as extension of its domain (*Besitz*, possession). It contests neither the possibility nor the reality of the objects of these ideas but it cannot admit

> them into its maxims for thought and action. It even holds that if, in the unfathomable field of the supernatural, there is something more (*noch etwas mehr*) than what it can render intelligible to itself and which would however be necessary to supply [Gibelin's translation of *Ergänzung*] its moral insufficiency, this thing, even though unknown, will come to the aid (*zu statten kommen*) of its good will, thanks to a faith which one could call (as regards its possibility) *reflective* (*reflectirenden*) because the dogmatic faith which declares that it *knows* seems to it presumptuous and not very sincere; for to remove difficulties with regard to what is in itself (in practical terms) well established is only a secondary task (*parergon*) when those difficulties concern transcendent questions.

What is translated as 'secondary task' is *Nebengeschäfte*: incidental business or bustle, activity or operation which comes *beside* or *against*. The *parergon* inscribes something which comes as an extra, *exterior* to the proper field (here that of pure reason and of *Religion within the Limits of Reason Alone*) but whose transcendent exteriority comes to play, abut onto, brush against, rub, press against the limit itself and intervene in the inside only to the extent that the inside is lacking. It is lacking *in* something and it is lacking *from itself*. Because reason is 'conscious of its impotence to satisfy its moral need,' it has recourse to the *parergon*, to grace, to mystery, to miracles. It needs the supplementary work. This additive, to be sure, is threatening. Its use is critical. It involves a risk and exacts a price the theory of which is elaborated. To each *parergon* of *Religion* there is a corresponding damage, a detriment (*Nachteil*) and the four classes of dangers will correspond to the four types of *parergon*: (1) for the would-be internal experience (effects of grace), there is *fanaticism*; (2) for the would-be external experience (miracles), there is *superstition*; (3) for the would-be insight of the understanding into the supernatural order there is *illuminism*; (4) for the would-be actions on the supernatural (means of grace), there is *thaumaturgy*. These four aberrations or seductions of reason nevertheless also have in view a certain pleasing, pleasing-God (*gottgefälliger Absicht*).

So, as an example among examples, the clothing on statues (*Gewänder an Statuen*) would have the function of a *parergon* and an ornament. This means (*das heisst*), as Kant makes clear, that which is not internal or intrinsic (*innerlich*), as an integral part (*als Bestandstück*), to the total representation of the object (*in die ganze Vorstellung des Gegenstandes*) but which belongs to it only in an extrinsic way (*nur äusserlich*) as a surplus, an addition, an adjunct (*als Zuthat*), a supplement.

Hors-d'œuvres, then, the clothes of statues, which both decorate and veil their nudity. Hors-d'œuvres stuck onto the edging of the work nonetheless, and to the edging of the represented body to the extent that – such is the argument – they supposedly do not belong to the whole of the representation. What is represented in the representation would be the naked and natural body; the representative essence of the statue would be related to this, and the only beautiful thing in the statue would be that representation; it alone would be essentially, purely, and intrinsically beautiful, 'the proper object of a pure judgment of taste.'

This delimitation of the center and the integrity of the representation, of its inside and its outside, might already seem strange. One wonders, too, where to have clothing commence. Where does a *parergon* begin and end. Would any garment be a *parergon*. G-strings and the like. What to do with absolutely transparent veils. And how to

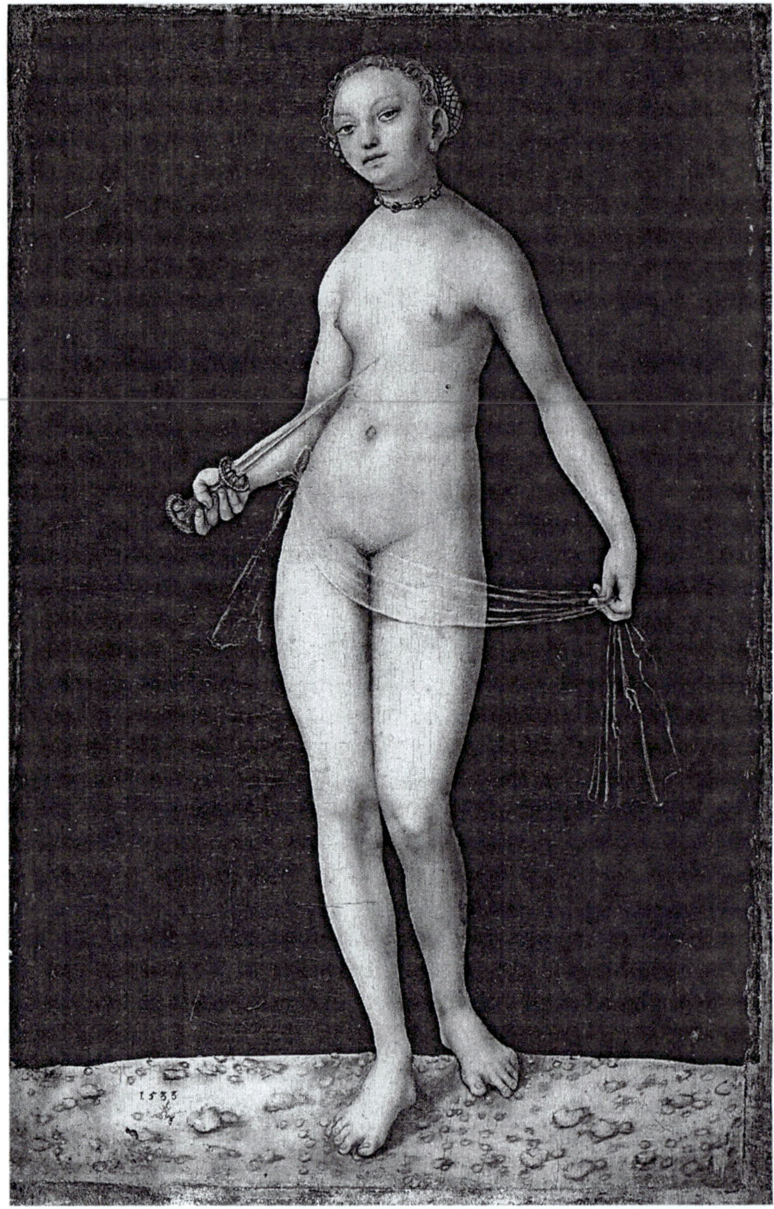

Lucas Cranach, *Lucretia*, 1533. © Gemäldegalerie, Staatliche Museen zu Berlin

transpose the statement to painting. For example, Cranach's Lucretia holds only a light band of transparent veil in front of her sex: where is the *parergon*? Should one regard as a *parergon* the dagger which is not part of her naked and natural body and whose point she holds turned toward herself, touching her skin (in that case only the point of the *parergon* would touch her body, in the middle of a triangle formed by her two breasts and her navel)? A *parergon*, the necklace that she wears around her neck?

The question of the representative and objectivizing essence, of its outside and its inside, of the criteria engaged in this delimitation, of the value of naturalness which is presupposed in it, and, secondarily or primarily, of the place of the human body or of its privilege in this whole problematic. If any *parergon* is only added on by virtue of an internal lack in the system to which it is added (as was verified in *Religion*), what is it that is lacking in the representation of the body so that the garment should come and supplement it? And what would art have to do with this? What would it give to be seen? Cause to be seen? Let us see? Let us cause to be seen? Or let itself be shown?

We are only at the beginning of our astonishment at this paragraph. (*Parergon* also means the exceptional, the strange, the extraordinary.) I have torn the 'garment' a little too hastily from the middle of a series of three examples, of three *parerga* which are no less strange. Each in itself, first of all, and then in their association. The example immediately following is that of the columns around sumptuous buildings (*Säulengänge um Prachtgebäude*). These columns are also, then, supplementary *parerga*. After the garment, the column? Why would the column be external to the building? Where does the criterion, the critical organ, the organum of discernment come from here? It is no less obscure than in the previous case. It even presents an extra difficulty: the *parergon* is added this time to a work which *does not represent anything* and which is itself already *added to* nature. We think we know what properly belongs or does not belong to the human body, what is detached or not detached from it – even though the *parergon* is precisely an ill-detachable detachment. But in a work of architecture, the *Vorstellung*, the representation is not structurally representational or else is so only through detours complicated enough, no doubt, to disconcert anyone who tried to discern, in a critical manner, the inside from the outside, the integral part and the detachable part. So as not to add to these complications, I shall leave to one side, provisionally, the case of columns in the form of the human body, those that support or represent the support of a window (and does a window form part of the inside of a building or not? And what about the window of a building in a painting?), and which can be naked or clothed, can represent a man or a woman, a distinction to which Kant makes no reference.

With this example of the columns is announced the whole problematic of inscription in a milieu, of the marking out of the work in a field of which it is always difficult to decide if it is natural or artificial and, in this latter case, if it is *parergon* or *ergon*. For not every milieu, even if it is contiguous with the work, constitutes a *parergon* in the Kantian sense. The natural site chosen for the erection of a temple is obviously not a *parergon*. Nor is an artificial site: neither the crossroads, nor the church, nor the museum, nor the other works around one or other. But the garment or the column is. Why? It is not because they are detached but on the contrary because they are more difficult to detach and above all because without them, without their quasi-detachment, the lack on the inside of the work would appear; or (which amounts to the same thing for a lack) would not appear. What constitutes them as *parerga* is not simply their exteriority as a surplus, it is the internal structural link which rivets them to the lack in the interior of the *ergon*. And this lack would be constitutive of the very unity of the *ergon*. Without this lack, the *ergon* would have no need of a *parergon*. The *ergon*'s lack is the lack of a *parergon*, of the garment or the column which nevertheless remains exterior to it. How to give *energeia* its due?

Can one attach the third example to this series of examples, to the question that they pose? It is in fact the first of the examples, and I have proceeded in reverse. In appearance it is difficult to associate it with the other two. It is to do with the frames for paintings (*Einfassungen der Gemälde*). The frame: a *parergon* like the others. The series might seem surprising. How can one assimilate the function of a frame to that of a garment on (in, around, or up against) a statue, and to that of columns around a building? And what about a frame framing a painting representing a building surrounded by columns in clothed human form? What is incomprehensible about the edge, about the *à-bord* appears not only at the internal limit, the one that passes between the frame and the painting, the clothing and the body, the column and the building, but also at the external limit. *Parerga* have a thickness, a surface which separates them not only (as Kant would have it) from the integral inside, from the body proper of the *ergon*, but also from the outside, from the wall on which the painting is hung, from the space in which statue or column is erected, then, step by step, from the whole field of historical, economic, political inscription in which the drive to signature is produced (an analogous problem . . .). No 'theory,' no 'practice,' no 'theoretical practice' can intervene effectively in this field if it does not weigh up and bear on the frame, which is the decisive structure of what is at stake, at the invisible limit to (between) the interiority of meaning (put under shelter by the whole hermeneuticist, semioticist, phenomenologicalist, and formalist tradition) *and* (to) all the empiricisms of the extrinsic which, incapable of either seeing or reading, miss the question completely.

The *parergon* stands out [*se détache*] both from the *ergon* (the work) and from the milieu, it stands out first of all like a figure on a ground. But it does not stand out in the same way as the work. The latter also stands out against a ground. But the parergonal frame stands out against two grounds [*fonds*], but with respect to each of those two grounds, it merges [*se fond*] into the other. With respect to the work which can serve as a ground for it, it merges into the wall, and then, gradually, into the general text. With respect to the background which the general text is, it merges into the work which stands out against the general background. There is always a form on a ground, but the *parergon* is a form which has as its traditional determination not that it stands out but that it disappears, buries itself, effaces itself, melts away at the moment it deploys its greatest energy. The frame is in no case a background in the way that the milieu or the work can be, but neither is its thickness as margin a figure. Or at least it is a figure which comes away of its own accord [*s'enlève d'elle-même*].

What would Kant have said about a frame framing a painting representing a building surrounded by columns (examples of this are numerous), columns in the form of clothed human bodies (the frescoes on the vault of the Sistine Chapel – what is its frame? – whose represented, painted object is a sculpted volume itself representing, for example to the right of Jonah, naked children forming a column which supports a ceiling, etc. Same implication around the Persian Sibyl or around Zachariah holding a book in his hand, or around Jeremiah, or the Libyan Sibyl; it is difficult to say whether the children-columns are clothed or unclothed: they are *bearing* clothes), the whole frame being placed on the easel of a painter who is himself represented by another painting.

It may appear that I am taking unfair advantage by persisting with two or three possibly fortuitous examples from a secondary subchapter; and that it would be better to go to less marginal places in the work, nearer to the center and the heart of the matter [*le fond*]. To be sure. The objection presupposes that one already knows what is the center or the heart of the third *Critique*, that one has already located its frame and the limit of its field. But nothing seems more difficult to determine. The *Critique* presents itself as a work (*ergon*) with several sides, and as such it ought to allow itself to be centered and framed, to have its ground delimited by being marked out, with a frame, against a general background. But this frame is problematical. I do not know what is essential and what is accessory in a work. And above all I do not know what this thing is, that is neither essential nor accessory, neither proper nor improper, and that Kant calls *parergon*, for example the frame. Where does the frame take place. Does it take place. Where does it begin. Where does it end. What is its internal limit. Its external limit. And its surface between the two limits. I do not know whether the passage in the third *Critique* where the *parergon* is defined is itself a *parergon*. Before deciding what is parergonal in a text which poses the question of the *parergon*, one has to know what a *parergon* is – at least, if there is any such thing.

To the impatient objector, if s/he insists on seeing the thing itself at last: the whole analytic of aesthetic judgment forever assumes that one can distinguish rigorously between the intrinsic and the extrinsic. Aesthetic judgment *must* properly bear upon intrinsic beauty, not on finery and surrounds. Hence one must know – this is a fundamental presupposition, presupposing what is fundamental – how to determine the intrinsic – what is framed – and know what one is excluding as frame *and* outside-the-frame. We are thus *already* at the unlocatable center of the problem. And when Kant replies to our question 'What is a frame?' by saying: it's a *parergon*, a hybrid of outside and inside, but a hybrid which is not a mixture or a half-measure, an outside which is called to the inside of the inside in order to constitute it as an inside; and when he gives as examples of the *parergon*, alongside the frame, clothing and column, we ask to see, we say to ourselves that there are 'great difficulties' here, and that the choice of examples, and their association, is not self-evident.

The more so because, according to the logic of the supplement, the *parergon* is divided in two. At the limit between work and absence of work, it divides in two. And this division gives rise to a sort of pathology of the *parergon*, the forms of which must be named and classified, just as *Religion* recognized four types of parergonal misdeeds or detriments. Kant is in the process of determining 'the proper object of the pure judgment of taste.' But he does not simply exclude from it the *parergon* as such and in general. Only in certain conditions. The criterion of exclusion is here a formality.

What must we understand by formality?

The *parergon* (frame, garment, column) can augment the pleasure of taste (*Wohlgefallen des Geschmacks*), contribute to the proper and intrinsically aesthetic representation if it intervenes *by its form* (*durch seine Form*) and only by its form. If it has a 'beautiful form,' it forms part of the judgment of taste properly speaking or in any case intervenes directly in it. This is, if you like, the normal *parergon*. But if on the other hand it is not beautiful, purely beautiful, i.e., of a formal beauty, it lapses into *adornment* (*Schmuck*) and harms the beauty of the work, it does it wrong and causes it detriment (*Abbruch*). This is analogous to the detriment or damage (*Nachteil*) of *Religion*.

Now the example of this degradation of the simple *parergon* into a seductive adornment is again a frame, this time the gilded frame (*goldene Rahmen*), the gilding of the frame done in order to recommend the painting to our attention by its attraction

(*Reiz*). What is bad, external to the pure object of taste, is thus what seduces by an attraction; and the example of what leads astray by its force of attraction is a color, the gilding, in as much as it is nonform, content, or sensory matter. The deterioration of the *parergon*, the perversion, the adornment, is the attraction of sensory matter. As design, organization of lines, forming of angles, the frame is not at all an adornment and one cannot do without it. But in its purity, it ought to remain colorless, deprived of all empirical sensory materiality.

This opposition form/matter governs, as we know, the whole *Critique* and inscribes it within a powerful tradition. According to *The Origin of the Work of Art*, it is one of the three determinations (*hypokeimenon/symbebekos; aistheton/noeton, eidos-morphē/hylē*) which fall violently upon the thing. It procures a 'conceptual schema' (*Begriffsschema*) for any theory of art. It suffices to associate the rational with the formal, the irrational with matter, the irrational with the illogical, the rational with the logical, to couple the whole lot to the subject/object pair, in order to have at one's disposal a *Begriffsmechanik* that nothing can resist. But from what region does this determination of the thing as formed matter come? Its wholesale usage by aesthetics allows us to conceive of it as a deportation from the domain of art. In any case, Christian creationism would, according to Heidegger, have brought with it a 'particular incitement,' a supplementary motivation for considering the form–matter complex as the structure of every entity, the *ens creatum* as the unity of *forma* and *materia*. Though faith has disappeared, the schemas of Christian philosophy remain effective.

> Thus it is that the interpretation of the thing in terms of matter and form, whether it remains medieval or becomes transcendental in the Kantian sense, has become common and self-evident. But this does not make it any less than the other interpretations of the thingness of the thing a superimposition fallen onto (*Überfall*) the being-thing of the thing. This situation reveals itself already in the fact of naming things properly speaking (*eigentlichen Dinge*) things pure and simple [*bloss Dinge*: naked things]. This 'naked' (*bloss*) does however mean the stripping (*Entblössung*) of the character of usefulness (*Dienlichkeit*) and of being made. The naked thing (*blosse Ding*) is a sort of product (*Zeug*) but a product divested (*entkleidete*) of its being-as-product. Being-thing then consists in what still remains (*was noch übrigbleibt*). But this remainder (*Rest*) is not properly (*eigens*) determined in itself . . .

and what if the *Überfall* had the structure of the *parergon*? The violent superimposition which falls aggressively upon the thing, the 'insult' as the French translator says for the *Überfall*, strangely but not without pertinence, which enslaves it and, literally, conjugates it, under matter/form – is this superimposition the contingency of a case, the fall of an accident, or a necessity which remains to be examined? And what if, like the *parergon*, it were neither the one nor the other? And what if the *remainder* could never, in its structure as remainder, be determined 'properly,' what if we must no longer even expect or question anything within that horizon

* * *

it will be said that not all frames are, or have been, or will be square, rectangular, or quadrangular figures, nor even simply angular. Tables and tableaux (*Tafel*) likewise not. This is true: a critical and systematic and typological history of framing seems possible and necessary.[8] But the angle in general, the quadrangular in particular will not be just one of its objects among others. Everything that is written here is valid for the logic of parergonal bordering *in general*, but the privilege of 'cadre' [*frame*], though it seems more fortunate in the Latin than in the Germanic languages, is not fortuitous

Kantian question: the relation of the concept to the nonconcept (up/down, left/right), to the body, to the signature which is placed 'on' the frame: in fact, sometimes; structurally, always. The prosthesis

which does not run along as though on wheels in the third *Critique* as soon as one looks a little more closely at the example, that example of an example which forms and is formed by the frame. If things run as though on wheels, this is perhaps because things aren't going so well, by reason of an internal infirmity in the thesis which demands to be supplemented by a prosthesis or only ensures the progress of the exposition with the aid of a wheelchair or a child's pushchair. Thus one pushes forward something which cannot stand up, does not erect itself by itself in its process. Framing always supports and contains that which, by itself, collapses forthwith, exc

Translated by Geoff Bennington and Ian McLeod

Notes

1 *Editor's note:* this chapter, called 'The Parergon', is the second in a series of four chapters with the umbrella title 'Parergon' in Derrida's book *The Truth in Painting*. The abrupt, mid-sentence opening is the original start to this chapter and is part of Derrida's strategy, together with the frame breaks that punctuate the text, of using the form and style of his writing to confront philosophical themes, in this case, notions of inside and outside, inclusion and exclusion. Unless followed by the author's initials, all subsequent notes to 'The Parergon' have been added by the translators.

2 *Relève*, from the verb *relever* [to stand up again, to raise, to relieve), is also Derrida's translation of Hegel's *Aufhebung*.

3 *Editor's note:* the longer passages from Kant are quoted from the English translation, *Kant's Critique of Aesthetic Judgement* by James Creed Meredith, Oxford, Clarendon Press, 1911, and page references to this work are given in brackets in the text. Cf. Werner S. Pluhar's translation of the *Critique of Judgment*, Indianapolis, Hackett, 1987, pp. 4–5.

4 'Finality' translates *finalité*, the received French translation of Kant's *Zweckmässigkeit*, traditionally rendered into English as 'purposiveness.' We have preferred to translate Derrida's 'finalité sans fin' literally as 'finality without end,' rather than revert to the standard 'purposiveness without purpose': this allows us to preserve a certain sense of Derrida's exploitation of different senses of the word *fin* ('end'), and to avoid certain traditional assumptions about Kant which Derrida's essay suspends at the very least. 'Purpose' would be more suitable for *but*, but we have tended to translate this as 'goal' to avoid confusion.

5 'Hinge' translates *brisure*, which carries connotations of both breaking and joining; see *De la grammatologie*, Paris, Minuit, 1967, p. 96; translated by Gayatri Chakravorty Spivak as *[Of] Grammatology*, Baltimore, Johns Hopkins University Press, 1976, pp. 65ff.

6 Perhaps referring to hackneyed examples of rhetorical figures, such as 'forty sails' for 'forty ships' in Dumarsais, Fontanier, etc. But *bateau* used adjectivally also *means* 'hackneyed.'

7 *Quadrillée* insists on the 'squareness' implied in *cadre*, but it also carries an important sense of coverage, control, surveillance.

8 When 'Parergon' was first published, I had not yet read Meyer Schapiro, 'Sur quelques problèmes de sémiotique de l'art visuel: champ et véhicule dans les signes iconiques,' translated into French by Jean-Claude Lebensztejn, *Critique* 315–16 [(1973), pp. 843–66; originally published in *Semiotica* I, no. 3 (1969): pp. 223–42].

The reader will find more than one indication concerning the 'history' of framing, its 'late invention,' the not very 'natural' character of the 'rectangular frame,' as well as 'the frame that bends and turns inward into the field of the picture to compress or entangle the figures (the trumeau of Souillac, the Imago Hominis in the Echternach Gospels . . .)' (p. 228).

I also refer, as goes without saying, to *all* of Lebensztejn's publications. – J.D.

27

THE RESISTANCE TO THEORY

Paul de Man

This essay was not originally intended to address the question of teaching directly, although it was supposed to have a didactic and an educational function – which it failed to achieve. It was written at the request of the Committee on the Research Activities of the Modern Language Association as a contribution to a collective volume entitled *Introduction to Scholarship in Modern Languages and Literatures*. I was asked to write the section on literary theory. Such essays are expected to follow a clearly determined program: they are supposed to provide the reader with a select but comprehensive list of the main trends and publications in the field, to synthesize and classify the main problematic areas and to lay out a critical and programmatic projection of the solutions which can be expected in the foreseeable future. All this with a keen awareness that, ten years later, someone will be asked to repeat the same exercise.

I found it difficult to live up, in minimal good faith, to the requirements of this program and could only try to explain, as concisely as possible, why the main theoretical interest of literary theory consists in the impossibility of its definition. The Committee rightly judged that this was an inauspicious way to achieve the pedagogical objectives of the volume and commissioned another article. I thought their decision altogether justified, as well as interesting in its implications for the teaching of literature.

I tell this for two reasons. First, to explain the traces in the article of the original assignment which account for the awkwardness of trying to be more retrospective and more general than one can legitimately hope to be. But secondly, because the predicament also reveals a question of general interest: that of the relationship between the scholarship (the key word in the title of the MLA volume), the theory, and the teaching of literature.

Overfacile opinion notwithstanding, teaching is not primarily an intersubjective relationship between people but a cognitive process in which self and other are only tangentially and contiguously involved. The only teaching worthy of the name is scholarly, not personal; analogies between teaching and various aspects of show business or guidance counselling are more often than not excuses for having abdicated the task. Scholarship has, in principle, to be eminently teachable. In the case of literature, such scholarship involves at least two complementary areas: historical and philological facts as the preparatory condition for understanding, and methods of reading or interpretation. The latter is admittedly an open discipline, which can, however, hope to evolve by rational means, despite internal crises, controversies and polemics. As a controlled reflection on the formation of method, theory rightly proves to be entirely compatible with teaching, and one can think of numerous important theoreticians who are or were also prominent scholars. A question arises only if a tension develops between methods and the knowledge which those methods allow one to reach. If there is indeed something about literature, as such, which allows for a discrepancy between truth and method, between *Wahrheit* and *Methode*, then scholarship and theory are no longer necessarily compatible; as a first casualty of this complication, the notion of 'literature as such' as well as the clear distinction between history and interpretation can no longer be taken for granted. For a method that cannot be made to suit the 'truth' of its object can only teach delusion. Various developments, not only in the contemporary scene but in the long and complicated history of literary and linguistic instruction, reveal symptoms that suggest that such a difficulty is an inherent focus of the discourse about literature. These uncertainties are manifest in the hostility directed at theory in the name of ethical and aesthetic values, as well as in the recuperative attempts of theoreticians to reassert their own subservience to these values. The most effective of these attacks will denounce theory as an obstacle to scholarship and, consequently, to teaching. It is worth examining whether, and why, this is the case. For if this is indeed so, then it is better to fail in teaching what should not be taught than to succeed in teaching what is not true.

A general statement about literary theory should not, in theory, start from pragmatic considerations. It should address such questions as the definition of literature (what is literature?) and discuss the distinction between literary and non-literary uses of language, as well as between literary and non-verbal forms of art. It should then proceed to the descriptive taxonomy of the various aspects and species of the literary genus and to the normative rules that are bound to follow from such a classification. Or, if one rejects a scholastic for a phenomenological model, one should attempt a phenomenology of the literary activity as writing, reading or both, or of the literary work as the product, the correlate of such an activity. Whatever the approach taken (and several other theoretically justifiable starting-points can be imagined) it is certain that considerable difficulties will arise at once, difficulties that cut so deep that even the most elementary task of scholarship, the delimitation of the corpus and the *état présent* of the question, is bound to end in confusion, not necessarily because the bibliography is so large but because it is impossible to fix its borderlines. Such predictable difficulties have not prevented many writers on literature from proceeding along theoretical rather than pragmatic lines, often with considerable success. It can be shown however that, in all cases, this success depends on the power of a system (philosophical, religious or ideological) that may well remain implicit but that determines an a priori conception of what is 'literary' by starting out from the premises of the system rather than from the literary thing itself – if such a 'thing' indeed exists. This last qualification is of course a real question which in fact accounts for the predictability of the difficulties just alluded to: if the condition of existence of an entity is itself particularly critical, then the theory of this entity is bound to fall back into the pragmatic. The difficult and inconclusive history of literary theory indicates that this is indeed the case for literature in an even more manifest manner than for other verbalized occurrences such as jokes, for example, or even dreams. The attempt to treat literature theoretically may as well resign itself to the fact that it has to start out from empirical considerations.

Pragmatically speaking, then, we know that there has been, over the last fifteen to twenty years, a strong interest in something called literary theory and that, in the United States, this interest has at times coincided with the importation and reception of foreign, mostly but not always continental influences. We also know that this wave of interest now seems to be receding as some satiation or disappointment sets in after the initial enthusiasm. Such an ebb and flow is natural enough, but it remains interesting, in this case, because it makes the depth of the resistance to literary theory so manifest. It is a recurrent strategy of any anxiety to defuse what it considers threatening by magnification or minimization, by attributing to it claims to power of which it is bound to fall short. If a cat is called a tiger it can easily be dismissed as a paper tiger; the question remains however why one was so scared of the cat in the first place. The same tactic works in reverse: calling the cat a mouse and then deriding it for its pretence to be mighty. Rather than being drawn into this polemical whirlpool, it might be better to try to call the cat a cat and to document, however briefly, the contemporary version of the resistance to theory in this country.

The predominant trends in North American literary criticism, before the 1960s, were certainly not averse to theory, if by theory one understands the rooting of literary exegesis and of critical evaluation in a system of some conceptual generality. Even the most intuitive, empirical and theoretically low-key writers on literature made use of a minimal set of concepts (tone, organic form, allusion, tradition, historical situation, etc.) of at least some general import. In several other cases, the interest in theory was publicly asserted and practised. A broadly shared methodology, more or less overtly proclaimed, links together such influential text books of the era as *Understanding Poetry* (Brooks and Warren), *Theory of Literature* (Wellek and Warren) and *The Fields of Light* (Reuben Brower) or such theoretically oriented works as *The Mirror and the Lamp*, *Language as Gesture*, and *The Verbal Icon*.

Yet, with the possible exception of Kenneth Burke and, in some respects, Northrop Frye, none of these authors would have considered themselves theoreticians in the post-1960 sense of the term, nor did their work provoke as strong reactions, positive or negative, as that of later theoreticians. There were polemics, no doubt, and differences in approach that cover a wide spectrum of divergencies, yet the fundamental curriculum of literary studies as well as the talent and training expected for them were not being seriously challenged. New Critical approaches experienced no difficulty fitting into the academic establishments without their practitioners having to betray their literary sensibilities in any way; several of its representatives pursued successful parallel careers as poets or novelists next to their academic functions. Nor did they experience difficulties with regard to a national tradition which, though certainly less tyrannical than its European counterparts, is nevertheless far from powerless. The perfect embodiment of the New Criticism remains, in many respects, the personality and the ideology of T.S. Eliot, a combination of original talent, traditional learning, verbal wit and moral earnestness, an Anglo-American blend of intellectual gentility not so repressed as not to afford tantalising glimpses of darker psychic and political depths, but without breaking the surface of an ambivalent decorum that has its own complacencies and seductions. The normative principles of such a literary ambiance are cultural and ideological rather than theoretical, oriented towards the integrity of a social and historical self rather than towards the impersonal consistency that theory requires. Culture allows for, indeed advocates, a degree of cosmopolitanism, and the literary spirit of the American Academy of the fifties was anything but provincial. It had no difficulty appreciating and assimilating outstanding products of a kindred spirit that originated in Europe: Curtius, Auerbach, Croce, Spitzer, Alonso, Valéry and also, with the exception of some of his works, J.P. Sartre. The inclusion of Sartre in this list is important, for it indicates that the dominant cultural code we are trying to evoke cannot simply be assimilated to a political polarity of the left and the right, of the academic and the non-academic, of Greenwich Village and Gambier, Ohio. Politically oriented and predominantly non-academic journals, of which the *Partisan Review* of the fifties remains the best example, did not (after due allowance is made for all proper reservations and distinctions) stand in any genuine opposition to the New Critical approaches. The broad, though negative, consensus that brings these extremely diverse trends and individuals together is their shared resistance to theory. This diagnosis is borne out by the arguments and complicities that have since come to light in a more articulate opposition to the common opponent.

The interest of these considerations would be at most anecdotal (the historical impact of twentieth-century literary discussion being so slight) if it were not for the theoretical implications of the resistance to theory. The local manifestations of this resistance are themselves systematic enough to warrant one's interest.

What is it that is being threatened by the approaches to literature that developed during the sixties and that now, under a variety of designations, make up the ill-defined and somewhat chaotic field of literary theory? These approaches cannot be simply equated with any particular method or country. Structuralism was not the only trend to dominate the stage, not even in France, and structuralism as well as semiology are inseparable from prior tendencies in the Slavic domain. In Germany, the main impulses have come from other directions, from the Frankfurt School and more orthodox Marxists, from post-Husserlian phenomenology and post-Heideggerian hermeneutics, with only minor inroads made by structural analysis. All these trends have had their share of influence in the United States, in more or less productive combinations with nationally rooted concerns. Only a nationally or personally competitive view of history would wish to hierarchize such hard-to-label movements. The possibility of doing literary theory, which is by no means to be taken for granted, has itself become a consciously reflected-upon question and those who have progressed furthest in this question are the most controversial but also the best sources of information. This certainly includes several of the names loosely connected with structuralism, broadly enough defined to include Saussure, Jakobson and Barthes as well as Greimas and Althusser, that is to say, so broadly defined as to be no longer of use as a meaningful historical term.

Literary theory can be said to come into being when the approach to literary texts is no longer based on non-linguistic, that is to say historical and aesthetic, considerations or, to put it somewhat less crudely, when the object of discussion is no longer the meaning or the value but the modalities of production and of reception of meaning and of value prior to their establishment – the implication being that this establishment is problematic enough to require an autonomous discipline of critical investigation to consider its possibility and its status. Literary history, even when considered at furthest remove from the platitudes of positivistic historicism, is still the history of an understanding of which the possibility is taken for granted. The question of the relationship between aesthetics and meaning is more complex, since aesthetics apparently has to do with the *effect* of meaning rather than with its content *per se*. But aesthetics is in fact, ever since its development just before and with Kant, a phenomenalism of a process of meaning and understanding, and it may be naive in that it postulates (as its name indicates) a phenomenology of art and of literature which may well be what is at issue. Aesthetics is part of a universal system of philosophy rather than a specific theory. In the nineteenth-century philosophical tradition, Nietzsche's challenge of the system erected by Kant, Hegel and their successors, is a version of the general question of philosophy. Nietzsche's critique of metaphysics includes, or starts out from, the aesthetic, and the same could be argued for Heidegger. The invocation of prestigious philosophical names does not intimate that the present-day development of literary theory is a by-product of larger philosophical speculations. In some rare cases, a direct link may exist between philosophy and literary theory. More frequently, however, contemporary literary theory is a relatively autonomous version of questions that also surface, in a different context, in philosophy, though not necessarily in a clearer and more rigorous form. Philosophy, in England as well as on the Continent, is less freed from traditional patterns than it sometimes pretends to believe and the prominent, though never dominant, place of aesthetics among the main components of the system is a constitutive part of this system. It is therefore not surprising that contemporary literary theory came into being from outside philosophy and sometimes in conscious rebellion against the weight of its tradition. Literary theory may now well have become a legitimate concern of philosophy but it cannot be assimilated to it, either factually or theoretically. It contains a necessarily pragmatic moment that certainly weakens it as theory but that adds a subversive element of unpredictability and makes it something of a wild card in the serious game of the theoretical disciplines.

The advent of theory, the break that is now so often being deplored and that sets it aside from literary history and from literary criticism, occurs with the introduction of linguistic terminology in the metalanguage about literature. By linguistic terminology is meant a terminology that designates reference prior to designating the referent and takes into account, in the consideration of the world, the referential function of language or, to be somewhat more specific, that considers reference as a function of language and not necessarily as an intuition. Intuition implies perception, consciousness, experience, and leads at once into the world of logic and of understanding with all its correlatives, among which aesthetics occupies a prominent place. The assumption that there can be a science of language which is not necessarily a logic leads to the development of a terminology which is not necessarily aesthetic. Contemporary literary theory comes into its own in such events as the application of Saussurian linguistics to literary texts.

The affinity between structural linguistics and literary texts is not as obvious as, with the hindsight of history, it now may seem. Peirce, Saussure, Sapir and Bloomfield were not originally concerned with literature at all but with the scientific foundations of linguistics. But the interest of philologists such as Roman Jakobson or literary critics such as Roland Barthes in semiology reveals the natural attraction of literature to a theory of linguistic signs. By considering language as a system of signs and of signification rather than as an established pattern of meanings, one displaces or even suspends the traditional barriers between literary and presumably non-literary uses of language and liberates the corpus from the secular weight of textual canonization. The results of the encounter between semiology and literature went considerably further than those of many other theoretical models – philological, psychological or classically epistemological – which writers on literature in quest of such models had tried out before. The responsiveness of literary texts to semiotic analysis is visible in that, whereas other approaches were unable to reach beyond observations that could be paraphrased or translated in terms of common knowledge, these analyses revealed patterns that could only be described in terms of their own, specifically linguistic, aspects. The linguistics of semiology and of literature apparently have something in common that only their shared perspective can detect and that pertains distinctively to them. The definition of this something, often referred to as literariness, has become the object of literary theory.

Literariness, however, is often misunderstood in a way that has provoked much of the confusion which dominates today's polemics. It is frequently assumed, for instance, that literariness is another word for, or another mode of, aesthetic response. The use, in conjunction with literariness, of such terms as style and stylistics, form or even 'poetry' (as in 'the poetry of grammar'), all of which carry strong aesthetic connotations, helps to foster this confusion, even among those who first put the term in circulation. Roland Barthes, for example, in an essay properly and revealingly dedicated to Roman Jakobson, speaks eloquently of the writer's quest for a perfect coincidence of the phonic properties of a word with its signifying function.

> We would also wish to insist on the Cratylism of the name (and of the sign) in Proust . . . Proust sees the relationship between signifier and signified as motivated, the one copying the other and representing in its material form the signified essence of the thing (and not the thing itself) . . . This realism (in the scholastic sense of the word), which conceives of names as the 'copy' of the ideas, has taken, in Proust, a radical form. But one may well ask whether it is not more or less consciously present in all writing and whether it is possible to be a writer without some sort of belief in the natural relationship between names and essences. The poetic function, in the widest sense of the word, would thus be defined by a Cratylian awareness of the sign, and the writer would be the conveyor of this secular myth which wants language to imitate the idea and which, contrary to the teachings of linguistic science, thinks of signs as motivated signs.[1]

To the extent that Cratylism assumes a convergence of the phenomenal aspects of language, as sound, with its signifying function as referent, it is an aesthetically oriented conception; one could, in fact, without distortion, consider aesthetic theory, including its most systematic formulation in Hegel, as the complete unfolding of the model of which the Cratylian conception of language is a version. Hegel's somewhat cryptic reference to Plato, in the *Aesthetics*, may well be interpreted in this sense. Barthes and Jakobson often seem to invite a purely aesthetic reading, yet there is a part of their statement that moves in the opposite direction. For the convergence of sound and meaning celebrated by Barthes in Proust and, as Gérard Genette has decisively shown,[2] later dismantled by Proust himself as a seductive temptation to mystified minds, is also considered here to be a mere *effect* which language can perfectly well achieve, but which bears no substantial relationship, by analogy or by ontologically grounded imitation, to anything beyond that particular effect. It is a rhetorical rather than an aesthetic function of language, an identifiable trope (paranomasis) that operates on the level of the signifier and contains no responsible pronouncement on the nature of the world – despite its powerful potential to create the opposite illusion. The phenomenality of the signifier, as sound, is unquestionably involved in the correspondence between the name and the thing named, but the link, the relationship between word and thing is not phenomenal but conventional.

This gives the language considerable freedom from referential restraint, but it makes it epistemologically highly suspect and volatile, since its use can no longer be said to be determined by considerations of truth and falsehood, good and evil, beauty and ugliness, or pleasure and pain. Whenever this autonomous potential of language can be revealed by analysis, we are dealing with literariness and, in fact, with literature as the place where this negative knowledge about reliability of linguistic utterance is made available. The ensuing foregrounding of material, phenomenal aspects of the signifier creates a strong illusion of aesthetic seduction at the very moment when the actual aesthetic function has been, at the very least, suspended. It is inevitable that semiology or similarly oriented methods be considered formalistic, in the sense of being aesthetically rather than semantically valorized, but the inevitability of such an interpretation does not make it less aberrant. Literature involves the voiding, rather than the affirmation, of aesthetic categories. One of the consequences of this is that, whereas we have traditionally been accustomed to reading literature by analogy with the plastic arts and with music, we now have to recognize the necessity of a non-perceptual, linguistic moment in painting and in music, and learn to *read* pictures rather than to *imagine* meaning.

If literariness is not an aesthetic quality, it is also not primarily mimetic. Mimesis becomes one trope among others, language choosing to imitate a non-verbal entity just as paranomasis 'imitates' a sound without any claim to identity (or reflection on difference) between the verbal and non-verbal elements. The most misleading representation of literariness, and also the most recurrent objection to contemporary literary theory, considers it as pure verbalism, as a denial of the reality principle in the name of absolute fictions, and for reasons that are said to be ethically and politically shameful. The attack reflects the anxiety of the aggressors rather than the guilt of the accused. By allowing for the necessity of a non-phenomenal linguistics, one frees the discourse on literature from naive oppositions between fiction and reality, which are themselves an offspring of an uncritically mimetic conception of art. In a genuine semiology as well as in other linguistically oriented theories, the referential function of language is not being denied – far from it; what is in question is its authority as a model for natural or phenomenal cognition. Literature is fiction not because it somehow refuses to acknowledge 'reality', but because it is not a priori certain that language functions according to principles which are those, or which are *like* those, of the phenomenal world. It is therefore not a priori certain that literature is a reliable source of information about anything but its own language.

It would be unfortunate, for example, to confuse the materiality of the signifier with the materiality of what it signifies. This may seem obvious enough on the level of light and sound, but it is less so with regard to the more general phenomenality of space, time or especially of the self: no one in his right mind will try to grow grapes by the luminosity of the word 'day', but it is very difficult not to conceive the pattern of one's past and future existence as in accordance with temporal and spatial schemes that belong to fictional narratives and not to the world. This does not mean that fictional narratives are not part of the world and of reality; their impact upon the world may well be all too strong for comfort. What we call ideology is precisely the confusion of linguistic with natural reality, of reference with phenomenalism. It follows that, more than any other mode of inquiry, including economics, the linguistics of literariness is a powerful and indispensable tool in the unmasking of ideological aberrations, as well as a determining factor in accounting for their occurrence. Those who reproach literary theory for being oblivious to social and historical (that is to say ideological) reality are merely stating their fear at having their own ideological mystifications exposed by the tool they are trying to discredit. They are, in short, very poor readers of Marx's *German Ideology*.

In these all too summary evocations of arguments that have been much more extensively and convincingly made by others, we begin to perceive some of the answers to the initial question: what is it about literary theory that is so threatening that it provokes such strong resistances and attacks? It upsets rooted ideologies by revealing the mechanics of their workings; it goes against a powerful philosophical tradition of which aesthetics is a prominent part; it upsets the established canon of literary works and blurs the borderlines between literary and non-literary discourse. By implication, it may also reveal the links between ideologies and philosophy. All this is ample enough reason for suspicion, but not a satisfying answer to the question. For it makes the tension between contemporary literary theory and the tradition of literary studies appear as a mere historical conflict between two modes of thought that happen to hold the stage at the same time. If the conflict is merely historical, in the literal sense, it is of limited theoretical interest, a passing squall in the intellectual weather of the world. As a matter of fact, the arguments in favor of the legitimacy of literary theory are so compelling that it seems useless to concern oneself with the conflict at all. Certainly, none of the objections to theory, presented again and again, always misinformed or based on crude misunderstandings of such terms as mimesis, fiction, reality, ideology, reference and, for that matter, relevance, can be said to be of genuine rhetorical interest.

It may well be, however, that the development of literary theory is itself overdetermined by complications inherent in its very project and unsettling with regard to its status as a scientific discipline. Resistance may be a built-in constituent of its discourse, in a manner that would be inconceivable in the natural sciences and unmentionable in the social sciences. It may well be, in other words, that the polemical opposition, the systematic non-understanding and misrepresentation, the insubstantial but eternally recurrent objections, are the displaced symptoms of a resistance inherent in the theoretical enterprise itself. To claim that this would be a sufficient reason not to envisage doing literary theory would be like rejecting anatomy because it has failed to cure mortality. The real debate of literary theory is not with its polemical opponents but rather with its own methodological assumptions and possibilities. Rather than asking why literary theory is threatening, we should perhaps ask why it has such difficulty going about its business and why it lapses so readily either into the language of self-justification and self-defence or else into the overcompensation of a programmatically euphoric utopianism. Such insecurity about its own project calls for self-analysis, if one is to understand the frustrations that attend upon its practitioners, even when they seem to dwell in serene methodological self-assurance. And if these difficulties are indeed an integral part of the problem, then they will have to be, to some extent, ahistorical in the temporal sense of the term. The way in which they are encountered on the present local literary scene as a resistance to the introduction of linguistic terminology in aesthetic and historical discourse about literature is only one particular version of a question that cannot be reduced to a specific historical situation and called modern, postmodern, post-classical or romantic (not even in Hegel's sense of the term), although its compulsive way of forcing itself upon us in the guise of a system of historical periodization is certainly part of its problematic nature. Such difficulties can be read in the text of literary theory at all times, at whatever historical moment one wishes to select. One of the main achievements of the present theoretical trends is to have restored some awareness of this fact. Classical, medieval and Renaissance literary theory is now often being read in a way that knows enough about what it is doing not to wish to call itself 'modern.'

We return, then, to the original question in an attempt to broaden the discussion enough to inscribe the polemics inside the question rather than having them determine it. The resistance to theory is a resistance to the use of language about language. It is therefore a resistance to language itself or to the possibility that language contains factors or functions that cannot be reduced to intuition. But we seem to assume all too readily that, when we refer to something called 'language', we know what it is we are talking about, although there is probably no word to be found in the language that is as overdetermined, self-evasive, disfigured and disfiguring as 'language'. Even if we choose to consider it at a safe remove from any theoretical model, in the pragmatic history of 'language', not as a concept, but as a didactic assignment that no human being can bypass, we soon find ourselves confronted by theoretical enigmas. The most familiar and general of all linguistic models, the classical *trivium*, which considers the sciences of language as consisting of grammar, rhetoric and logic (or dialectics), is in fact a set of unresolved tensions powerful enough to have generated an infinitely prolonged discourse of endless frustration of which contemporary literary theory, even at its most self-assured, is one more chapter. The difficulties extend to the internal articulations between the constituent parts as well as to the articulation of the field of language with the knowledge of the world in general, the link between the *trivium* and the *quadrivium*, which covers the non-verbal sciences of number (arithmetic), of space (geometry), of motion (astronomy), and of time (music). In the history of philosophy, this link is traditionally, as well as substantially, accomplished by way of logic, the area where the rigor of the linguistic discourse about itself matches up with the rigor of the mathematical discourse about the world. Seventeenth-century epistemology, for instance, at the moment when the relationship between philosophy and mathematics is particularly close, holds up the language of what it calls geometry (*mos geometricus*), and which in fact includes the homogeneous concatenation between space, time and number, as the sole model of coherence and economy. Reasoning *more geometrico* is said to be 'almost the only mode of reasoning that is infallible, because it is the only one to adhere to the true method, whereas all other ones are by natural necessity in a degree of confusion of which only geometrical minds can be aware'.[3] This is a clear instance of the interconnection between a science of the phenomenal world and a science of language conceived as definitional logic, the pre-condition for a correct axiomatic–deductive, synthetic reasoning. The possibility of thus circulating freely between logic and mathematics has its own complex and problematic history as well as its contemporary equivalences with a different logic and a different mathematics. What matters for our present argument is that this articulation of the sciences of language with the mathematical sciences represents a particularly compelling version of a continuity between a theory of language, as logic, and the knowledge of the phenomenal world to which mathematics give access. In such a system, the place of aesthetics is preordained and by no means alien, provided the priority of logic, in the model of the *trivium*, is not being questioned. For even if one assumes, for the sake of argument and against a great deal of historical evidence, that the link between logic and the natural sciences is secure, this leaves open the question, within the confines of the *trivium* itself, of the relationship between grammar, rhetoric and logic. And this is the point at which literariness, the use of language that foregrounds the rhetorical over the grammatical and the logical function, intervenes as a decisive but unsettling element which, in a variety of modes and aspects, disrupts the inner balance of the model and, consequently, its outward extension to the non-verbal world as well.

Logic and grammar seem to have a natural enough affinity for each other and, in the tradition of Cartesian linguistics, the grammarians of Port-Royal experienced little difficulty at being logicians as well. The same claim persists today in very different methods and terminologies that nevertheless maintain the same orientation toward the universality that logic shares with science. Replying to those who oppose the singularity of specific texts to the scientific generality of the semiotic project, A.J. Greimas disputes the right to use the dignity of 'grammar' to describe a reading that would not be committed to universality. Those who have doubts about the semiotic method, he writes, 'postulate the necessity of constructing a grammar for each particular text. But the essence (*le propre*) of a grammar is its ability to account for a large number of texts, and the metaphorical use of the term . . . fails to hide the fact that one has, in fact, given up on the semiotic project'.[4] There is no doubt that what is here prudently called 'a large number' implies the hope at least of a future model that would in fact be applicable to the generation of all texts. Again, it is not our present purpose to discuss the validity of this methodological optimism, but merely to offer it as an instance of the persistent symbiosis between grammar and logic. It is clear that, for Greimas as for the entire tradition to which he belongs, the grammatical and the logical function of language are co-extensive. Grammar is an isotope of logic.

It follows that, as long as it remains grounded in grammar, any theory of language, including a literary one, does not threaten what we hold to be the underlying principle of all cognitive and aesthetic linguistic systems. Grammar stands in the service of logic which, in turn, allows for the passage to the knowledge of the world. The study of grammar, the first of the *artes liberales*, is the necessary pre-condition for scientific and humanistic knowledge. As long as it leaves this principle intact, there is nothing threatening about literary theory. The continuity between theory and phenomenalism is asserted and preserved by the system itself. Difficulties occur only when it is no longer possible to ignore the epistemological thrust of the rhetorical dimension of discourse, that is, when it is no longer possible to keep it in its place as a mere adjunct, a mere ornament within the semantic function.

The uncertain relationship between grammar and rhetoric (as opposed to that between grammar and logic) is apparent, in the history of the *trivium*, in the uncertain status of figures of speech or tropes, a component of language that straddles the disputed borderlines between the two areas. Tropes used to be part of the study of grammar but were also considered to be the semantic agent of the specific function (or effect) that rhetoric performs as persuasion as well as meaning. Tropes, unlike grammar, pertain primordially to language. They are text-producing functions that are not necessarily patterned on a non-verbal entity, whereas grammar is by definition capable of extra-linguistic generalization. The latent tension between rhetoric and grammar precipitates out in the problem of reading, the process that necessarily partakes of both. It turns out that the resistance to theory is in fact a resistance to reading, a resistance that is perhaps at its more effective, in contemporary studies, in the methodologies that call themselves theories of reading but nevertheless avoid the function they claim as their object.

What is meant when we assert that the study of literary texts is necessarily dependent on an act of reading, or when we claim that this act is being systematically avoided? Certainly more than the tautology that one has to have read at least some parts, however small, of a text (or read some part, however small, of a text about this text) in order to be able to make a statement about it. Common as it may be, criticism by hearsay is only rarely held up as exemplary. To stress the by no means self-evident necessity of reading implies at least two things. First of all, it implies that literature is not a transparent message in which it can be taken for granted that the distinction between the message and the means of communication is clearly established. Second, and more problematically, it implies that the grammatical decoding of a text leaves a residue of indetermination that has to be, but cannot be, resolved by grammatical means, however extensively conceived. The extension of grammar to include para-figural dimensions is in fact the most remarkable and debatable strategy of contemporary semiology, especially in the study of syntagmatic and narrative structures. The codification of contextual elements well beyond the syntactical limits of the sentence leads to the systematic study of metaphrastic dimensions and has considerably refined and expanded the knowledge of textual codes. It is equally clear, however, that this extension is always strategically directed towards the replacement of rhetorical figures by grammatical codes. The tendency to replace a rhetorical by a grammatical terminology (to speak of hypotaxis, for instance, to designate anamorphic or metonymic tropes) is part of an explicit program, a program that is entirely admirable in its intent since it tends towards the mastering and the clarification of meaning. The replacement of a hermeneutic by a semiotic model, of interpretation by decoding, would represent, in view of the baffling historical instability of textual meanings (including, of course, those of canonical texts) a considerable progress. Much of the hesitation associated with 'reading' could thus be dispelled.

The argument can be made, however, that no grammatical decoding, however refined, could claim to reach the determining figural dimensions of a text. There are elements in all texts that are by no means ungrammatical, but whose semantic function is not grammatically definable, neither in themselves nor in context. Do we have to interpret the genitive in the title of Keats' unfinished epic *The Fall of Hyperion* as meaning 'Hyperion's fall', the case story of the defeat of an older by a newer power, the very recognizable story from which Keats indeed started out but from which he increasingly strayed away, or as 'Hyperion falling', the much less specific but more disquieting evocation of an actual process of falling, regardless of its beginning, its end or the identity of the entity to whom it befalls to be falling. This story is indeed told in the later fragment entitled *The Fall of Hyperion*, but it is told about a character who resembles Apollo rather than Hyperion, the same Apollo who, in the first version (called *Hyperion*), should definitely be triumphantly standing rather than falling if Keats had not been compelled to interrupt, for no apparent reason, the story of Apollo's triumph. Does the title tell us that Hyperion is fallen and that Apollo stands, or does it tell us that Hyperion and Apollo (and Keats, whom it is hard to distinguish, at times, from Apollo) are interchangeable in that all of them are necessarily and constantly falling? Both readings are grammatically correct, but it is impossible to decide from the context (the ensuring narrative) which version is the right one. The narrative context suits neither and both at the same time, and one is tempted to suggest that the fact that Keats was unable to complete either version manifests the impossibility, for him as for us, of reading his own title. One could then read the word 'Hyperion' in the title *The Fall of Hyperion* figurally, or, if one wishes, intertextually, as referring not to the historical or mythological character but as referring to the title of Keats' own earlier text (*Hyperion*). But are we then telling the story of the failure of the first text as the success of the second, the Fall of *Hyperion* as the Triumph of *The Fall of Hyperion*? Manifestly yes, but not quite, since the second text also fails to be concluded. Or are we telling the story of why all texts, as texts, can always be said to be falling? Manifestly yes, but not quite, either, since the story of the fall of the first version, as told in the second, applies to the first version only and could not legitimately be read as meaning also the fall of *The Fall of Hyperion*. The undecidability involves the figural or literal status of the proper name Hyperion as well as of the verb falling, and is, thus a matter of figuration and not of grammar. In 'Hyperion's Fall', the word 'fall' is plainly figural, the representation of a figural fall, and we, as readers, read this fall standing up. But in 'Hyperion falling', this is not so clearly the case, for if Hyperion can be Apollo and Apollo can be Keats, then he can also be us and his figural (or symbolic) fall becomes his and our literal falling as well. The difference between the two readings is itself structured as a trope. And it matters a great deal how we read the title, as an exercise not only in semantics, but in what the text actually does to us. Faced with the ineluctable necessity to come to a decision, no grammatical or logical analysis can help us out. Just as Keats had to break off his narrative, the reader has to break off his understanding at the very moment when he is most directly engaged and summoned by the text. One could hardly expect to find solace in this 'fearful symmetry' between the author's and the reader's plight since, at this point, the symmetry is no longer a formal but an actual trap, and the question no longer 'merely' theoretical.

This undoing of theory, this disturbance of the stable cognitive field that extends from grammar to logic to a general science of man and of the phenomenal world, can in its turn be made into a theoretical project of rhetorical analysis that will reveal the inadequacy of grammatical models of non-reading. Rhetoric, by its actively negative relationship to grammar and to logic, certainly undoes the claims of the *trivium* (and by extension, of language) to be an epistemologically stable construct. The resistance to theory is a resistance to the rhetorical or tropological dimension of language, a dimension which is perhaps more explicitly in the foreground in literature (broadly conceived) than in other verbal manifestations or – to be somewhat less vague – which can be revealed in any verbal event when it is read textually. Since grammar as well as figuration is an integral part of reading, it follows that reading will be a negative process in which the grammatical cognition is undone, at all times, by its rhetorical displacement. The model of the *trivium* contains within itself the pseudo-dialectic of its own undoing and its history tells the story of this dialectic.

This conclusion allows for a somewhat more systematic description of the contemporary theoretical scene. This scene is dominated by an increased stress on reading as a theoretical problem or, as it is sometimes erroneously phrased, by an increased stress on the reception rather than on the production of texts. It is in this area that the most fruitful exchanges have come about between writers and journals of various countries and that the most interesting dialogue has developed between literary theory and other disciplines, in the arts as well as in linguistics, philosophy and the social sciences. A straightforward *report* on the present state of literary theory in the United States would have to stress the emphasis on reading, a direction which is already present, moreover, in the New Critical tradition of the forties and the fifties. The methods are now more technical, but the contemporary interest in a poetics of literature is clearly linked, traditionally enough, to the problems of reading. And since the models that are being used certainly are no longer *simply* intentional and centered on an identifiable self, nor *simply* hermeneutic in the postulation of a single originary, pre-figural and absolute text, it would appear that this concentration on reading would lead to the rediscovery of the theoretical difficulties associated with rhetoric. This is indeed the case, to some extent; but not quite. Perhaps the most instructive aspect of contemporary theory is the refinement of the techniques by which the threat inherent in rhetorical analysis is being avoided at the very moment when the efficacy of these techniques has progressed so far that the rhetorical obstacles to understanding can no longer be mistranslated in thematic and phenomenal commonplaces. The resistance to theory which, as we saw, is a resistance to reading, appears in its most rigorous and theoretically elaborated form among the theoreticians of reading who dominate the contemporary theoretical scene.

It would be a relatively easy, though lengthy, process to show that this is so for theoreticians of reading who, like Greimas or, on a more refined level, Riffaterre or, in a very different mode, H.R. Jauss or Wolfgang Iser – all of whom have a definite, though sometimes occult, influence on literary theory in this country – are committed to the use of grammatical models or, in the case of *Rezeptionsaesthetik*, to traditional hermeneutic models that do not allow for the problematization of the phenomenalism of reading and therefore remain uncritically confined within a theory of literature rooted in aesthetics. Such an argument would be easy to make because, once a reader has become aware of the rhetorical dimensions of a text, he will not be amiss in finding textual instances that are irreducible to grammar or to historically determined meaning, provided only he is willing to acknowledge what he is bound to notice. The problem quickly becomes the more baffling one of having to account for the shared reluctance to acknowledge the obvious. But the argument would be lengthy because it has to involve a textual analysis that cannot avoid being somewhat elaborate; one can succinctly suggest the grammatical indetermination of a title such as *The Fall of Hyperion*, but to confront such an undecidable enigma with the critical reception and reading of Keats' text requires some space.

The demonstration is less easy (though perhaps less ponderous) in the case of theoreticians of reading whose avoidance of rhetoric takes another turn. We have witnessed, in recent years, a strong interest in certain elements in language whose function is not only not dependent on any form of phenomenalism but on any form of cognition as well, and which thus excludes, or postpones, the consideration of tropes, ideologies, etc., from a reading that would be primarily performative. In some cases, a link is reintroduced between performance, grammar, logic, and stable referential meaning, and the resulting theories (as in the case of Ohmann) are not in essence distinct from those of avowed grammarians or semioticians. But the most astute practitioners of a speech act theory of reading avoid this relapse and rightly insist on the necessity to keep the actual performance of speech acts, which is conventional rather than cognitive, separate from its causes and effects – to keep, in their terminology, the illocutionary force separate from its perlocutionary function. Rhetoric, understood as persuasion, is forcefully banished (like Coriolanus) from the performative moment and exiled in the affective area of perlocution. Stanley Fish, in a masterful essay, convincingly makes this point.[5] What awakens one's suspicion about this conclusion is that it relegates persuasion, which is indeed inseparable from rhetoric, to a purely affective and intentional realm and makes no allowance for modes of persuasion which are no less rhetorical and no less at work in literary texts, but which are of the order of persuasion by *proof* rather than persuasion by seduction. Thus to empty rhetoric of its epistemological impact is possible only because its tropological, figural functions are being bypassed. It is as if, to return for a moment to the model of the *trivium*, *rhetoric* could be isolated from the generality that grammar and logic have in common and considered as a mere correlative of an illocutionary power. The equation of rhetoric with psychology rather than with epistemology opens up dreary prospects of pragmatic banality, all the drearier if compared to the brilliance of the performative analysis. Speech act theories of reading in fact repeat, in a much more effective way, the grammatization of the *trivium* at the expense of rhetoric. For the characterization of the performative as sheer convention reduces it in effect to a grammatical code among others. The relationship between trope and performance is actually closer but more disruptive than what is here being proposed. Nor is this relationship properly captured by reference to a supposedly 'creative' aspect of performance, a notion with which Fish rightly takes issue. The performative power of language can be called positional, which differs considerably from conventional as well as from 'creatively' (or, in the technical sense, intentionally) constitutive. Speech act oriented theories of reading read only to the extent that they prepare the way for the rhetorical reading they avoid.

But the same is still true even if a 'truly' rhetorical reading that would stay clear of any undue phenomenalization or of any undue grammatical or performative codification of the text could be conceived – something which is not necessarily impossible and for which the aims and methods of literary theory should certainly strive. Such a reading would indeed appear as the methodical undoing of the grammatical construct and, in its systematic disarticulation of the *trivium*, will be theoretically sound as well as effective. Technically correct rhetorical readings may be boring, monotonous, predictable and unpleasant, but they are irrefutable. They are also totalizing (and potentially totalitarian) for since the structures and functions they expose do not lead to the knowledge of an entity (such as language) but are an unreliable process of knowledge production that prevents all entities, including linguistic entities, from coming into discourse as such, they are indeed universals, consistently defective models of language's impossibility to be a model language. They are, always in theory, the most elastic theoretical and dialectical model to end all models and they can rightly claim to contain within their own defective selves all the other defective models of reading-avoidance, referential, semiological, grammatical, performative, logical, or whatever. They are theory and not theory at the same time, the universal theory of the impossibility of theory. To the extent however that they are theory, that is to say teachable, generalizable and highly responsive to systematization, readings, like the other kinds, still avoid and resist the reading they advocate. Nothing can overcome the resistance to theory since theory is itself this resistance. The loftier the aims and the better the methods of literary theory, the less possible it becomes. Yet literary theory is not in danger of going under; it cannot help but flourish, and the more it is resisted, the more it flourishes, since the language it speaks is the language of self-resistance. What remains impossible to decide is whether this flourishing is a triumph or a fall.

Notes

1 Roland Barthes, 'Proust et les noms' in *To Honor Roman Jakobson*, The Hague, 1967, part I, pp. 157ff.
2 'Proust et le langage indirect' in *Figures II*, Paris, 1969.
3 Pascal, 'De l'esprit géométrique et de l'art de persuader', in *Œuvres complètes* presented by L. Lafuma, Paris, Editions du Seuil, 1963, pp. 349ff.
4 A.J. Greimas, *Du sens*, Paris, Editions du Seuil, 1970, p. 13.
5 Stanley Fish, 'How to do things with Austin and Searle: Speech Act Theory and Literary Criticism', *MLN* 91 (1976), pp. 983–1025. See especially p. 1008.

28

THE EVIL DEMON OF IMAGES

Jean Baudrillard

A propos the cinema and images in general (media images, technological images), I would like to conjure up the perversity of the relation between the image and its referent, the supposed real; the virtual and irreversible confusion of the sphere of images and the sphere of a reality whose nature we are less and less able to grasp. There are many modalities of this absorption, this confusion, this diabolical seduction of images. Above all, it is the reference principle of images which must be doubted, this strategy by means of which they always appear to refer to a real world, to real objects, and to reproduce something which is logically and chronologically anterior to themselves. None of this is true. As simulacra, images precede the real to the extent that they invert the causal and logical order of the real and its reproduction. Benjamin, in his essay 'The Work of Art in the Age of Mechanical Reproduction', already pointed out strongly this modern revolution in the order of production (of reality, of meaning) by the precession, the anticipation of its reproduction.

It is precisely when it appears most truthful, most faithful and most in conformity to reality that the image is most diabolical – and our technical images, whether they be from photography, cinema or television, are in the overwhelming majority much more 'figurative', 'realist', than all the images from past cultures. It is in its resemblance, not only analogical but technological, that the image is most immoral and most perverse.

The appearance of the mirror already introduced into the world of perception an ironical effect of *trompe-l'œil*, and we know what malefice was attached to the appearance of doubles. But this is also true of all the images which surround us: in general, they are analysed according to their value as representations, as media of presence and meaning. The immense majority of present day photographic, cinematic and television images are thought to bear witness to the world with a naive resemblance and a touching fidelity. We have spontaneous confidence in their realism. We are wrong. They only seem to resemble things, to resemble reality, events, faces. Or rather, they really do conform, but their conformity itself is diabolical.

We can find a sociological, historical and political equivalent to this diabolical conformity, to this evil demon of conformity, in the modern behaviour of the masses who are also very good at complying with the models offered to them, who are very good at reflecting the objectives imposed on them, thereby absorbing and annihilating them. There is in this conformity a force of seduction in the literal sense of the word, a force of diversion, distortion, capture and ironic fascination. There is a kind of fatal strategy of conformity.

A recent example may be found in Woody Allen's film, *Zelig*: in trying to be oneself, to cultivate difference and originality, one ends up resembling everyone and no longer seducing anyone. This is the logic of present day psychological conformity. Zelig, on the other hand, is launched on an adventure of total seduction, in an involuntary strategy of global seduction: he begins to resemble everything which approaches him, everything which surrounds him. Nor is this the mimetic violence of defiance or parody, it is the mimetic non-violence of seduction. To begin to resemble the other, to take on their appearance, is to seduce them, since it is to make them enter the realm of metamorphosis despite themselves.

This seductive force, this fatal strategy, is a kind of animal genie or talent – not simply that of the chameleon, which is only its anecdotal form. It is not the conformism of animals which delights us; on the contrary, animals are never conformist, they are seductive, they always appear to result from a metamorphosis. Precisely because they are not individuals, they pose the enigma of their resemblance. If an animal knows how to conform, it is not to its own being, its own individuality (banal strategy), but to appearances in the world. This is what Zelig does too with his animal genie – he is polymorphous (but not perverse); he is incapable of functional adaptation to contexts, which is true conformism, our conformism, but able to seduce by the *play* of resemblance. Savages do no less when they put on the successive masks of their gods, when they 'become' their successive divinities – this is also to seduce them. It is of course against this strategy of seduction that psychiatry struggles, and it is what gives rise to the magical infatuation of the crowds for Zelig (in German, *selig* means 'blessed').

The remarkable thing about this film is that it leads astray all possible interpretations. There is thus also a seduction of interpretation, with the complicity of certain intellectuals, as well as a polymorphous montage technique which allows it to ironically adapt to all possibilities.

More generally, the image is interesting not only in its role as reflection, mirror, representation of, or counterpart to, the real, but also when it begins to contaminate reality and to model it, when it only conforms to reality the better to distort it, or better still: when it appropriates reality for its own ends, when it anticipates it to the point that the real no longer has time to be produced as such.

It is not only daily life which has become cinematographic and televisual, but war as well. It has been said that war is the continuation of politics by other means; we can also say that images, media images, are the continuation of war by other means. Take *Apocalypse Now*. Coppola made his film the same way the Americans conducted the war – in this sense, it is the best possible testimony – with the same exaggeration, the same excessive means, the same monstrous candour . . . and the same success. War as a trip, a technological and psychedelic fantasy; war as a succession of special effects, the war become film well before it was shot; war replaced by technological testing. For the Americans, it was above all the latter: a test site, an enormous field on which to test their weapons, their methods, their power.

Coppola does the same thing: he tests the power of intervention of cinema, tests the impact of cinema become a vast machine of special effects. In this sense his film is very much the prolongation of war by other means, the completion of that incomplete war, its apotheosis. War becomes film, film becomes war, the two united by their mutual overflow of technology.

The real war was conducted by Coppola in the manner of Westmoreland. Leaving aside the clever irony of napalming Philippino forests and villages to recreate the hell of South Vietnam, everything is replayed, begun again through cinema: the Molochian joy of the shoot, the sacrificial joy of so many millions spent, of such a holocaust of means, of so many difficulties, and the dazzling paranoia in the mind of the creator who, from the beginning, conceived this film as a *world* historical event for which the Vietnam war would have been no more than a pretext, would ultimately not have existed – and we cannot deny it: 'in itself' the Vietnam war never happened, perhaps it was only a dream, a baroque dream of napalm and the tropics, a psychotropic dream in which the issue was not politics or victory but the sacrificial, excessive deployment of a power already filming itself as it unfolds, perhaps expecting nothing more than consecration by a superfilm, which perfects the war's function as a mass spectacle.

No real distance, no critical direction, no desire for any 'raised consciousness' in relation to the war: in a sense this is the brutal quality of the film, not to be undermined by any anti-war moral psychology. Coppola may very well dress up his helicopter captain in a cavalry hat and have him wipe out a Vietnamese village to the sound of Wagner – these are not critical, distant signs; they are immersed in the machinery, part of the special effect. Coppola makes films in the same manner, with the same nostalgic megalomania, with the same non-signifying fury, the same magnified Punch and Judy effect. One can ask, how is such a horror possible (not the war, properly speaking, but that of the film)? But there is no response, no possible judgement. The Vietnam war and the film are cut from the same cloth, nothing separates them: this film is part of the war. If the Americans (apparently) lost the other, they have certainly won this one. *Apocalypse Now* is a global victory. It has a cinematographic power equal and superior to that of the military and industrial complexes, of the Pentagon and governments. Nothing is understood in relation to war or cinema (at least the latter) unless one has grasped this indistinguishability – which is not the ideological or moral indistinguishability of good and evil, but that of the reversibility of destruction and production, of the immanence of something in its very revolution, of the organic metabolism of every technology, from carpet bombing to film stock . . .

As for the anticipation of reality by images, the precession of images and media in relation to events, such that the connection between cause and effect becomes scrambled and it becomes impossible to tell which is the effect of the other – what better example than the nuclear accident at Harrisburg, a 'real' incident which happened just after the release of *The China Syndrome*? This film is a fine example of the supremacy of the televised event over the nuclear event which itself remains improbable and in some sense imaginary.

Moreover, the film unintentionally shows this: it is the intrusion of TV into the reactor which as it were triggers the nuclear incident – because it is the anticipation and model of it in the day to day world: telefission of the real and of the real world – because TV and information in general are a kind of catastrophe in René Thom's formal, topological sense: a radical, qualitative change in an entire system. Or rather, TV and nuclear power are of the same kind: behind the 'hot' and negentropic concepts of energy and information, they have the same dissuasive force as cold systems. TV is also a nuclear, chain-reactive process, but implosive: it cools and neutralises the meaning and energy of events. Thus, behind the presumed risk of explosion, that is, of hot catastrophe, the nuclear conceals a long, cold catastrophe – the universalisation of a system of dissuasion, of deterrence.

The homology between nuclear power and television can be read directly in the images. Nothing resembles the command and control centre of the reactor more than the TV studios, and the nuclear consoles share the same imaginary as the recording and broadcasting studios. Everything happens between these two poles: the other core, that of the reactor, in principal the real core of the affair, remains concealed from us, like the real; buried and indecipherable, ultimately of no importance. The drama is acted out on the screens and nowhere else.

Harrisburg, Watergate and *Network* form the trilogy of *The China Syndrome* – an inextricable trilogy in which we cannot tell which is the effect or the symptom of the others: is the ideological argument (the Watergate effect) only the symptom of the nuclear (the Harrisburg effect) or the informational model (the *Network* effect)? – is the real (Harrisburg) only the symptom of the imaginary (*Network*, *The China Syndrome*) or vice versa? Marvellous indistinguishability, ideal constellation of simulation.

The conjunction of *The China Syndrome* and Harrisburg haunts us. But is it so involuntary? Without examining any magical links between simulacrum and reality, it is clear that *The China Syndrome* is not unrelated to the 'real' accident at Harrisburg, not by a causal logic but by those relations of contagion and unspoken analogy which link the real, models and simulacra: the induction of the nuclear incident at Harrisburg by the film corresponds, with disquieting obviousness, to the induction of the incident by TV in the film. A strange precession of a film before the real, the most astonishing we have seen: reality corresponding point by point to the simulacra, even down to the suspensive, incomplete character of the catastrophe, which is essential from the point of view of dissuasion: the real so arranged itself, in the image of the film, as to produce a *simulation* of catastrophe.

It is only a further step, which we should briskly take, to reverse our logical order and see *The China Syndrome* as the real event and Harrisburg its simulacrum. For it is by the same logic that the nuclear reality in the film follows from the television effect and Harrisburg in 'reality' follows from the cinema effect of *The China Syndrome*.

But the latter is not the original prototype of Harrisburg; one is not the simulacrum and the other the reality: there are only simulacra, and Harrisburg is a kind of simulation in the second degree. There is indeed a chain reaction; but *it is not the nuclear chain reaction but that of the simulacra* and of the simulation in which all the energy of the real is effectively engulfed, not in a spectacular nuclear explosion but in a secret and continuous implosion, which is perhaps taking a more deadly turn than all the explosions which presently lull us.

For an explosion is always a promise, it *is* our hope: see how much, in the film as well as at Harrisburg, everyone expects it to go up, that destruction speak its name and deliver us from this unnameable panic, from this invisible nuclear panic of dissuasion. Let the 'core' of the reactor expose at last its glowing power of destruction, let it reassure us as to the admittedly catastrophic presence of energy and gratify us with its spectacle. For the problem is that there is no nuclear spectacle, no spectacle of nuclear energy in itself (Hiroshima is past): it is for this reason that it is rejected – it would be perfectly accepted if it lent itself to spectacle like earlier forms of energy. Parousia of catastrophe: substantial boost to our messianic libido.

But that will never recur. What will happen will never be explosion but implosion.

Never again will we see energy in its spectacular and pathetic form – all the romanticism of explosion which had so much charm, since it was also that of revolution – but only the cold energy of simulacra and its distillation in homeopathic doses into the cold systems of information.

What else does the media dream of if not raising up events by its very presence? Everyone deplores it, but everyone is secretly fascinated by this eventuality. Such is the logic of simulacra: no longer divine predestination, but the precession of models, which is no less inexorable. And it is for this reason that events no longer have any meaning: not because they are insignificant in themselves, but because they have been preceded by models with which their own process can only coincide.

For some time now, in the dialectical relation between reality and images (that is, the relation that we wish to believe dialectical, readable from the real to the image and vice versa), the image has taken over and imposed its own immanent, ephemeral logic; an immoral logic without depth, beyond good and evil, beyond truth and falsity; a logic of the extermination of its own referent, a logic of the implosion of meaning in which the message disappears on the horizon of the medium. In this regard, we all remain incredibly naive: we always look for a good usage of the image, that is to say a moral, meaningful, pedagogic or informational usage, without seeing that the image in a sense revolts against this good usage, that it is the conductor neither of meaning nor good intentions, but on the contrary of an implosion, a denegation of meaning (of events, history, memory, etc.). I am reminded of *Holocaust*, the television series on the concentration camps . . .

Forgetting the extermination is part of the extermination itself. That forgetting, however, is still too dangerous and must be replaced by an artificial memory (everywhere, today, it is artificial memories which obliterate people's memories, which obliterate people from memory). This artificial memory replays the extermination – but too late for it to profoundly unsettle anything, and above all it does so via a medium which is itself cold, radiating oblivion, dissuasion and extermination in an even more systematic manner, if this is possible, than the camps themselves. TV, the veritable final solution to the historicity of every event. The Jews are recycled not through the crematory ovens or the gas chambers but through the sound track and images, through the cathode tube and the micro-chip. Forgetting, annihilation thereby achieves at last an aesthetic dimension – nostalgia gives them their final finish.

Henceforth, 'everyone knows', everyone has trembled before the extermination – a sure sign that 'it' will never happen again. But in effect what is thus exorcised so cheaply, at the cost of a few tears, will never recur because it is presently happening in the very form through which it is denounced, through the very medium of this supposed exorcism: television. The same process of forgetting, of liquidation, of extermination, the same annihilation of memories and of history, the same inverse, implosive radiation, the same absorption without trace, the same black hole as Auschwitz. They want us to believe that TV will remove the mortgage of Auschwitz by raising collective consciousness, whereas it is the perpetuation of it in a different guise, under the auspices not of a *site* of annihilation but a *medium* of dissuasion.

What everyone fails to understand is that *Holocaust* is above all (and exclusively) a *televised* event or rather object (McLuhan's fundamental rule which must not be forgotten). That is to say, it is an attempt to reheat a *cold* historical event – tragic but cold, the first great event of cold systems, those cooling systems of dissuasion and extermination which were subsequently deployed in other forms (including the Cold War, etc.) and in relation to the cold masses (the Jews no longer even concerned by their own death, eventually self-managing it, no longer even masses in revolt: dissuaded unto death, dissuaded even of their own death). To reheat this cold event via a cold medium, television, for masses who are themselves cold, who will only find in it the occasion for a tactile chill and a posthumous emotion, a dissuasive shiver, which sends them into oblivion with a kind of aesthetic good faith.

The cold light of television is inoffensive to the imagination (even that of children) since it no longer carries any imaginary, for the simple reason that *it is no longer an image*.

In this sense the TV image has to be placed in opposition to the cinema, which still carries an intense imaginary. Although it is contaminated more and more by TV, the cinema is still an image – that means not only a screen and a visual form but a myth, something that belongs to the sphere of the double, the phantasm, the mirror, the dream, etc. . . . Nothing of that in the TV image, which doesn't suggest anything and has a magnetic effect. The TV image is only a screen. More than that: a miniaturized terminal located in your head and *you* are the screen and the TV looks at you, goes through you like a magnetic tape – a tape, not an image.

Thus, properly speaking it is *Holocaust* the television film which constitutes the definitive holocaust event. Likewise, with *The Day After* it is not the atomic conflict depicted in the film but the film itself which is the catastrophic event.

This film should inspire a salutary terror, it should dissuade by the spectacle of terror. However, I don't see anything as a result of this film. The slides at the New York Museum of Natural History move me much more profoundly: you can shiver at the ice age and feel the charm of the prehistoric, but here I feel neither the shiver nor the charm of nuclear power, nor even suspense nor the final blinding flash.

Is it a bad film? Certainly. But isn't it rather that all this is unimaginable? Isn't it rather that, in our imaginary, nuclear conflict is a total event, without appeal and with no tomorrow, whereas here it simply brings about a regression of the human race according to the worst naive stereotypes of savagery? But we already know that state, indeed we have barely left it. Our desire is rather for something which no longer takes place on a human scale, for some anterior or ulterior mystery: what will the earth be like when we are no longer on it? In a word, we dream of our disappearance, and of seeing the world in its inhuman purity (which is precisely not the state of nature).

But these limits, these extremes that we imagine, this catastrophe – can it be metaphorised in images? It is not certain that its mythical evocation is possible, any more than that of our bio-molecular destiny or that of the genetic code, which is the other dimension, the corollary of the nuclear. We can no longer be affected by it – proof that we have already been irradiated! Already to our minds the catastrophe is no more than a comic strip. Its filmic projection is only a diversion from the real nuclearisation of our lives. The real nuclear catastrophe has already happened, it happens every day, and this film is part of it. It is *it* which *is* our catastrophe. It does not represent it, it does not evoke it, on the contrary it shows that it has already happened, that it is already here, since it is impossible to imagine.

For all these reasons I do not believe in a pedagogy of images, nor of cinema, nor *a fortiori* in one of television. I do not believe in a dialectic between image and reality, nor therefore, in respect of images, in a pedagogy of message and meaning. The secret of the image (we are still speaking of contemporary, technical images) must not be sought in its differentiation from reality, and hence in its representative value (aesthetic, critical or dialectical), but on the contrary in its 'telescoping' into reality, its short-circuit with reality, and finally, in the implosion of image and reality. For us there is an increasingly definitive lack of differentiation between image and reality which no longer leaves room for representation as such.

This collusion between images and life, between the screen and daily life, can be experienced every day in the most ordinary manner. Especially in America, not the least charm of which is that even outside the cinemas the whole country is cinematographic. You cross the desert as if in a western; the metropolis is a continual screen of signs and formulae. Life is a travelling shot, a kinetic, cinematic, cinematographic sweep. There is as much pleasure in this as in those Dutch or Italian towns where, upon leaving the museum, you rediscover a town in the very image of the paintings, as if it had stepped out of them. It is a kind of miracle which, even in a banal American way, gives rise to a sort of aesthetic form, to an ideal confusion which transfigures life, as in a dream. Here, cinema does not take on the exceptional form of a work of art, even a brilliant one, but invests the whole of life with a mythical ambience. Here it becomes truly exciting. This is why the idolatry of stars, the cult of Hollywood idols, is not a media pathology but a glorious form of the cinema, its mythical transfiguration, perhaps the last great myth of our modernity. Precisely to the extent that the idol no longer represents anything but reveals itself as a pure, impassioned, contagious image which effaces the difference between the real being and its assumption into the imaginary.

All these considerations are a bit wild, but that is because they correspond to the unrestrained film buff that I am and have always wished to remain – that is in a sense uncultured and fascinated. There is a kind of primal pleasure, of anthropological joy in images, a kind of brute fascination unencumbered by aesthetic, moral, social or political judgements. It is because of this that I suggest they are immoral, and that their fundamental power lies in this immorality.

This brute fascination for images, above and beyond all moral or social determination, is also not that of dreaming or the imaginary, understood in the traditional sense. Other images, such as those in painting, drawing, theatre or architecture, have been better able to make us dream or imagine; other modes of expression as well (undoubtedly language makes us dream better than the image). So there is something more than that which is peculiar to our modern media images: if they fascinate us so much it is not because they are sites of the production of meaning and representation – this would not be new – it is on the contrary because they are sites of the *disappearance* of meaning and representation, sites in which we are caught quite apart from any judgement of reality, thus sites of a fatal strategy of denegation of the real and of the reality principle.

We have arrived at a paradox regarding the image, our images, those which unfurl upon and invade our daily life – images whose proliferation, it should be noted, is potentially infinite, whereas the extension of meaning is always limited precisely by its end, by its finality: from the fact that images ultimately have no finality and proceed by total contiguity, infinitely multiplying themselves according to an irresistible epidemic process which no one today can control, our world has become truly infinite, or rather exponential by means of images. It is caught up in a mad pursuit of images, in an ever greater fascination which is only accentuated by video and digital images. We have thus come to the paradox that these images describe the equal impossibility of the real and of the imaginary.

For us the medium, the image medium, has imposed itself between the real and the imaginary, upsetting the balance between the two, with a kind of fatality which has its own logic. I call this a fatal process in the sense that there is a definitive immanence of the image, without any possible transcendent meaning, without any possible dialectic of history – fatal also in the sense not merely of an exponential, linear unfolding of images and messages but of an exponential enfolding of the medium around itself. The fatality lies in this endless enwrapping of images (literally: without end, without destination) which leaves images no other destiny than images. The same thing happens everywhere today, when production has no destiny apart from production – overdetermination of production by itself – when sex has no destiny other than sex – sexual overdetermination of sexuality. This process may be found everywhere today, for better and for worse. In the absence of rules of the game, things become caught up in their own game: images become more real than the real; cinema itself becomes more cinema than cinema, in a kind of vertigo in which (to return to our initial problem, that of resemblance) it does no more than resemble itself and escape in its own logic, in the very perfection of its own model.

I am thinking of those exact, scrupulous set-pieces such as *Chinatown*, *The Day of the Condor*, *Barry Lyndon*, *1900*, *All the President's Men*, the very perfection of which is disturbing. It is as if we were dealing with perfect remakes, with extraordinary montages which belong more to a combinatory process (or mosaic in the McLuhanesque sense), with large photo, kino or historio-synthetic machines, rather than with real films. Let us be clear: their quality is not in question. The problem is rather that they leave us somehow totally indifferent.

Take *The Last Picture Show*. You need only be sufficiently distracted, as I was, to see it as a 1950s original production: a good film of manners and the ambience of small town America, etc. A slight suspicion: it was a little too good, better adjusted, better than the others, without the sentimental, moral and psychological tics of the films of that period. Astonishment at the discovery that it is a 1970s film, perfectly nostalgic, brand new, retouched, a hyperrealist restitution of a '50s film. There is talk of remaking silent films, doubtless better than those of the period. A whole generation of films is appearing which will be to those we have known what the android is to man: marvellous, flawless artifacts, dazzling simulacra which lack only an imaginary and that particular hallucination which makes cinema what it is. Most of those that we see today (the best) are already of this order. *Barry Lyndon* is the best example: no better has been made, no better will be made, but *what* exactly? Evocation? No, not even evocation but *simulation*. All the toxic radiation has been filtered out, all the ingredients are present in precise doses, not a single mistake.

Cool, cold pleasure which is not even aesthetic properly speaking: functional pleasure, equational pleasure, pleasure of machination. We need only think of Visconti (*The Leopard*, *Senso*, etc., which recall *Barry Lyndon* in certain respects) in order to grasp the difference, not only in style but in the cinematographic act. With Visconti, there is meaning, history, a sensual rhetoric, dead moments, a passionate game, not only in the historical content but in the direction. None of that with Kubrick, who controls his film like a chessboard, and makes history an operational scenario. Nor does this refer back to the old opposition between finesse and geometry: there meaning was still in play, meaning was at stake. Whereas we are entering into an era of films which no longer have meaning properly speaking, large synthetic machines with variable geometry.

Is there already something of this in Sergio Leone's westerns? Perhaps. All registers tend in this direction. *Chinatown* is the detective story redesigned by laser. It is not really a question of perfection. Technical perfection can *belong* to the meaning, and in this case it is neither nostalgic nor hyperrealist; it is an effect of art. Here, it is an effect of model: it is one of the tactical reference values. In the absence of any real syntax of meaning there are only *tactical* values in a complex whole in which, for example, the CIA as an all-purpose mythological machine, Robert Redford as a polyvalent star, social relations as necessary references to history, and *technical virtuosity as a necessary reference to cinema* are all admirably combined.

Cinema and its trajectory: from the most fantastic or mythical to the realistic and hyperrealistic.

In its present endeavours cinema increasingly approaches, with ever increasing perfection, absolute reality: in its banality, in its veracity, in its starkness, in its tedium, and at the same time in its pretentiousness, in its pretension to be the real, the immediate, the unsignified, which is the maddest of enterprises (in the same way that the pretension of functionalist design to designate, as the highest degree of the object, the form in which it coincides with its function, its use-value, is properly an insane enterprise). No culture has ever had this naive and paranoiac, this puritanical and terrorist vision of signs. Terrorism is always of the real. Simultaneous with this attempt at absolute coincidence with the real, cinema also approaches an absolute coincidence with itself. This is not contradictory: it is the very definition of the hyperreal. Hypotyposis and specularity. Cinema plagiarises and copies itself, remakes its classics, retroactivates its original myths, remakes silent films more perfect than the originals, etc. All this is logical. *Cinema is fascinated by itself as a lost object just as it (and we) are fascinated by the real as a referential in perdition.* Previously there was a living, dialectical, full and dramatic relationship between cinema and the imaginary (that is, novelistic, mythical unreality, even down to the delirious use of its own technique). Today, there is an inverse negative relation between the cinema and reality: it results from the loss of specificity which both have suffered. Cold collage, cool promiscuity, asexual engagement of two cold media which evolve in asymptotic line towards one another: cinema attempting to abolish itself in the absolute of reality, the real already long absorbed in cinematographic (or televised) hyperreality.

Translated by Paul Patton and Paul Foss

29

THE SUBLIME AND THE AVANT-GARDE[1]

Jean-François Lyotard

I

In 1950–1, Barnett Baruch Newman painted a canvas measuring 2.42 m by 5.42 m which he called *Vir Heroicus Sublimis*. In the early sixties he entitled his first three sculptures *Here I, Here II, Here III*. Another painting was called *Not Over There, Here*, two paintings were called *Now*, and two others were entitled *Be*. In December 1948, Newman wrote an essay entitled *The Sublime is Now*.

How is one to understand the sublime, or let us say provisionally, the object of a sublime experience, as a 'here and now'? Quite to the contrary, isn't it essential to this feeling that it alludes to something which can't be shown, or presented (as Kant said, *dargestellt*)? In a short unfinished text dating from late 1949, *Prologue for a New Aesthetic*, Newman wrote that in his painting, he was not concerned with a 'manipulation of space nor with the image, but with a sensation of time'. He added that by this he did not mean time laden with feelings of nostalgia, or drama, or references and history, the usual subjects of painting. After this denial (*dénégation*) the text stops short.

So, what kind of time was Newman concerned with, what 'now' did he have in mind? Thomas Hess, his friend and commentator, felt justified in writing that Newman's time was the *Makom* or the *Hamakom* of Hebraic tradition – the *there*, the site, the place, which is one of the names given by the Torah to the Lord, the Unnameable. I do not know enough about *Makom* to know whether this was what Newman had in mind. But then again, who does know enough about *Now*? Newman can certainly not have been thinking of the 'present instant', the one that tries to hold itself between the future and the past, and gets devoured by them. This 'now' is one of the temporal 'ecstasies' that has been analysed since Augustine's day and since Edmund Husserl, according to a line of thought that has attempted to constitute time on the basis of consciousness. Newman's *now* which is no more than *now* is a stranger to consciousness and cannot be constituted by it. Rather, it is what dismantles consciousness, what deposes consciousness, it is what consciousness cannot formulate, and even what consciousness forgets in order to constitute itself. What we do not manage to formulate is that something happens, *dass etwas geschieht*. Or rather, and more simply, that it happens . . . *dass es geschieht*. Not a major event in the media sense, not even a small event. Just an occurrence.

This isn't a matter of sense or reality bearing upon *what* happens or *what* this might mean. Before asking questions about what it is and about its significance, before the *quid*, it must 'first' so to speak 'happen', *quod*. That it happens 'precedes', so to speak, the question pertaining to what happens. Or rather, the question precedes itself, because 'that it happens' is the question relevant as event, and it 'then' pertains to the event that has just happened. The event happens as a question mark 'before' happening as a question. *It happens* is rather 'in the first place', *is it happening, is this it, is it possible*? Only 'then' is any mark determined by the questioning: is this or that happening, is it this or something else, is it possible that this or that?

An event, an occurrence – what Martin Heidegger called *ein Ereignis* – is infinitely simple, but this simplicity can only be approached through a state of privation. That which we call thought must be disarmed. There is a tradition and an institution of philosophy, of painting, of politics, of literature. These 'disciplines' also have a future in the form of Schools, of programmes, projects, and 'trends'. Thought works over what is received, it seeks to reflect on it and overcome it. It seeks to determine what has already been thought, written, painted, or socialized in order to determine what hasn't been. We know this process well, it is our daily bread. It is the bread of war, soldiers' biscuit. But this agitation, in the most noble sense of the word (agitation is the word Kant gives to the activity of the mind that has judgement and exercises it), this agitation is only possible if something remains to be determined, something that hasn't yet been determined. One can strive to determine this something by setting up a system, a theory, a programme or a project – and indeed one has to, all the while anticipating that something. One can also inquire about the remainder, and allow the indeterminate to appear as a question mark.

What all intellectual disciplines and institutions presuppose is that not everything has been said, written down or recorded, that words already heard or pronounced are not the last words. 'After' a sentence, 'after' a colour, comes another sentence, another colour. One doesn't know which, but one thinks one knows if one relies on the rules that permit one sentence to link up with another, one colour with another, rules preserved in precisely those institutions of the past and future that I mentioned. The School, the programme, the project – all proclaim that after this sentence comes that sentence, or at least that kind of sentence is mandatory, that one kind of sentence is permitted, while another is forbidden. This holds true for painting as much as for the other activities of thought. After one pictorial work, another is necessary, permitted, or forbidden. After one colour, this other colour; after this line, that one. There isn't an enormous difference between an avant-grade manifesto and a curriculum at the Ecole des Beaux Arts, if one considers them in the light of this relationship to time. Both are options with respect to what they feel is a good thing to happen subsequently. But both also forget the possibility of nothing happening, of words, colours, forms or sounds not coming; of this sentence being the last, of bread not coming daily. This is the misery that the painter faces with a plastic surface, of the musician with the acoustic surface, the misery the thinker faces with a desert of thought, and so on. Not only faced with the empty canvas or the empty page, at the 'beginning' of the work, but every time something has to be waited for, and thus forms a question at every point of questioning (*point d'interrogation*), at every 'and what now?'

The possibility of nothing happening is often associated with a feeling of anxiety, a term with strong connotations in modern philosophies of existence and of the unconscious. It gives to waiting, if we really mean waiting, a predominantly negative value. But suspense can also be accompanied by pleasure, for instance pleasure in welcoming the unknown, and even by joy, to speak like Baruch Spinoza, the joy obtained by the intensification of being that the event brings with it. This is probably a contradictory feeling. It is at the very least a sign, the question mark itself, the way in which *it happens* is withheld and announced: *Is it happening*? The question can be modulated in any tone. But the mark of the question is 'now', *now* like the feeling that nothing might happen: the nothingness now.

Between the seventeenth and eighteenth centuries in Europe this contradictory feeling – pleasure and pain, joy and anxiety, exaltation and depression – was christened or re-christened by the name of the *sublime*. It is around this name that the destiny of classical poetics was hazarded and lost; it is in this name that aesthetics asserted its critical rights over art, and that romanticism, in other words, modernity, triumphed.

It remains to the art historian to explain how the word sublime reappeared in the language of a Jewish painter from New York during the forties. The word sublime is common currency today in colloquial French to suggest surprise and admiration, somewhat like America's 'great', but the idea connoted by it has belonged (for at least two centuries) to the most rigorous kind of reflection on art. Newman is not unaware of the aesthetic and philosophical stakes with which the word *sublime* is involved. He read Edmund Burke's *Inquiry* and criticized what he saw as Burke's over 'surrealist' description of the sublime work. Which is as much as to say that, conversely, Newman judged surrealism to be over-reliant on a pre-romantic or romantic approach to indeterminacy. Thus, when he seeks sublimity in the here and now he breaks with the eloquence of romantic art but he does not reject its fundamental task, that of bearing pictorial or otherwise expressive witness to the inexpressible. The inexpressible does not reside in an over there, in another words, or another time, but in this: in that (something) happens. In the determination of pictorial art, the indeterminate, the 'it happens' is the paint, the picture. The paint, the picture as occurrence or event, is not expressible, and it is to this that it has to witness.

To be true to this displacement in which consists perhaps the whole of the difference between romanticism and the 'modern' avant-garde, one would have to read *The Sublime is Now* not as *The Sublime is Now* but as *Now the Sublime is Like This*. Not elsewhere, not up there or over there, not earlier or later, not once upon a time. But as here, now, it happens that, . . . and it's this painting. Here and now there is this painting, rather than nothing, and that's what is sublime. Letting-go of all grasping intelligence and of its power, disarming it, recognizing that this occurrence of painting was not necessary and is scarcely foreseeable, a privation in the face of *Is it happening*? guarding the occurrence 'before' any defence, any illustration, and any commentary, guarding before being on one's guard, before 'looking' (*regarder*) under the aegis of *now*, this is the rigour of the avant-garde. In the determination of literary art this requirement with respect to the *Is it happening*? found one of its most rigorous realizations in Gertrude Stein's *How to Write*. It's still the sublime in the sense that Burke and Kant described and yet it isn't their sublime any more.

II

I have said that the contradictory feeling with which indeterminacy is both announced and missed was what was at stake in reflection on art from the end of the seventeenth to the end of the eighteenth centuries. The sublime is perhaps the only mode of artistic sensibility to characterize the modern. Paradoxically, it was introduced to literary discussion and vigorously defended by the French writer who has been classified in literary history as one of the most dogged advocates of ancient classicism. In 1674 Boileau published his *Art poètique*, but he also published *Du sublime*, his translation or transcription from the *Peri tou hupsou*. It is a treatise, or rather an essay, attributed to a certain Longinus about whose identity there has long been confusion, and whose life we now estimate as having begun towards the end of the first century of our era. The author was a rhetorician. Basically, he taught those oratorical devices with which a speaker can persuade or move (depending on the genre) his audience. The didactics of rhetoric had been traditional since Aristotle, Cicero, and Quintilian. They were linked to the republican institution; one had to know how to speak before assemblies and tribunals.

One might expect that Longinus' text would invoke the maxims and advice transmitted by this tradition by perpetuating the didactic form of *technē rhetorikē*. But surprisingly, the sublime, the indeterminate – were destabilizing the text's didactic intention. I cannot analyse this uncertainty here. Boileau himself and numerous other commentators, especially Fénélon, were aware of it and concluded that the sublime could only be discussed in sublime style. Longinus certainly tried to define sublimity in discourse, writing that it was unforgettable, irresistible, and most important, thought-provoking – '*il y a à partir d'elle beaucoup de réflexion*' (*hou polle anatheoresis*) (from the sublime springs a lot of reflection). He also tried to locate sources for the sublime in the ethos of rhetoric, in its pathos, in its techniques: figures of speech, diction, enunciation, composition. He sought in this way to bend himself to the rules of the genre of the 'treatise' (whether of rhetoric or poetics, or politics) destined to be a model for practitioners.

However, when it comes to the sublime, major obstacles get in the way of a regular exposition of rhetorical or poetic principles. There is, for example, wrote Longinus, a sublimity of thought sometimes recognizable in speech by its extreme simplicity of turn of phrase, at the precise point where the high character of the speaker makes one expect greater solemnity. It sometimes even takes the form of outright silence. I don't mind if this simplicity, this silence, is taken to be yet another rhetorical figure. But it must be granted that it constitutes the most indeterminate of figures. What can remain of rhetoric (or of poetics) when the rhetorician in Boileau's translation announces that to attain the sublime effect 'there is no better figure of speech than one which is completely hidden, that which we do not even recognize as a figure of speech'? Must we admit that there are techniques for hiding figures, that there are figures for the erasure of figures? How do we distinguish between a hidden figure and what is not a figure? And what is it, if it isn't a figure? And what about this, which seems to be a major blow to didactics: when it is sublime, discourse accommodates defects, lack of taste, and formal imperfections. Plato's style, for example, is full of bombast and bloated strained comparisons. Plato, in short, is a mannerist, or a baroque writer compared to Lysias, and so is Sophocles compared to an Ion or Pindar compared to a Bacchylides. The fact remains that, like those first named, he is sublime, whereas the second ones are merely perfect. Shortcomings in technique are therefore trifling matters if they are the price to be paid for 'true grandeur'. Grandeur in speech is true when it bears witness to the incommensurability between thought and the real world.

Is it Boileau's transcription that suggests this analogy, or is it the influence of early Christianity on Longinus? The fact that grandeur of spirit is not of this world cannot but suggest Pascal's hierarchy of orders. The kind of perfection that can be demanded in the domain of *technē* isn't necessarily a desirable attribute when it comes to sublime feeling. Longinus even goes so far as to propose inversions of reputedly natural and rational syntax as examples of sublime effect. As for Boileau, in the preface he wrote in 1674 for Longinus' text, in still further addenda made in 1683 and 1701 and also in the *Xth Réflexion* published in 1710 after his death he makes final the previous tentative break with the classical institution of *technē*. The sublime, he says, cannot be taught, and didactics are thus powerless in this respect; the sublime is not linked to rules that can be determined through poetics; the sublime only requires that the reader or listener have conceptual range, taste, and the ability 'to sense what everyone senses first'. Boileau therefore takes the same stand as Pêre Bouhours, when in 1671 the latter declared that beauty demands more than just a respect for rules, that it requires a further 'je ne sais quoi', also called *genius* or something 'incomprehensible and inexplicable', a 'gift from God', a fundamentally 'hidden' phenomenon that can be recognized only by its effects on the addressee. And in the polemic that set him against Pierre-Daniel Huet, over the issue of whether the Bible's *Fiat Lux, et Lux fuit* is sublime, as Longinus thought it was, Boileau refers to the opinion of the Messieurs de Port Royal and in particular to Silvestre de Saci: the Jansenists are masters when it comes to matters of hidden meaning, of eloquent silence, of feeling that transcends all reason and finally of openness to the *Is it happening*?

At stake in these poetic-theological debates is the status of works of art. Are they copies of some ideal model? Can reflection on the more 'perfect' examples yield rules of formation that determine their success in achieving what they want, that is, persuasiveness and pleasure? Can understanding suffice for this kind of reflection? By meditating on the theme of sublimity and of indeterminacy, meditation about works of art imposes a major change on *technē* and the institutions linked to it – Academies, Schools, masters and disciples, taste, the enlightened public made up of princes and courtiers. It is the very destination or destiny of works which is being questioned. The predominance of the idea of *technē* placed works under a multiple regulation, that of the model taught in the studios, Schools, and Academies, that of the taste shared by the aristocratic public, that of a purposiveness of art, which was to illustrate the glory of a name, divine or human, to which was linked the perfection of some cardinal virtue or other. The idea of the sublime disrupts this harmony. Let us magnify the features of – this disruption. Under Diderot's pen, *technē* becomes '*le petit technique*' (mere trivial technique). The artist ceases to be guided by a culture which made of him the sender and master of a message of glory: he becomes, insofar as he is a genius, the involuntary addressee of an inspiration come to him from an 'I know not what'. The public no longer judges according to the criteria of a taste ruled by the tradition of shared pleasure: individuals unknown to the artist (the 'people') read books, go through the galleries of the Salons, crowd into the theatres and the public concerts, they are prey to unforeseeable feelings: they are shocked, admiring, scornful, indifferent. The question is not that of pleasing them by leading them to identify with a name and to participate in the glorification of its virtue, but that of surprising them. 'The sublime', writes Boileau, 'is not strictly speaking something which is proven or demonstrated, but a marvel, which seizes one, strikes one, and makes one feel.' The very imperfections, the distortions of taste, even ugliness, have their share in the shock-effect. Art does not imitate nature, it creates a world apart, *eine Zwischenwelt*, as Paul Klee will say, *eine Nebenwelt*, one might say, in which the monstrous and the formless have their rights because they can be sublime.

You will (I hope) excuse such a simplification of the transformation which takes place with the modern development of the idea of the sublime. The trace of it could be found before modern times, in Medieval aesthetics – that of the Victorines for example. In any case, it explains why reflection on art should no longer bear essentially on the 'sender' instance/agency of works, but on the 'addressee' instance. And under the name 'genius' the latter instance is situated, not only on the side of the public, but also on the side of the artist, a feeling which he does not master. Henceforth it seems right to analyse the ways in which the subject is affected, its ways of receiving and experiencing feelings, its ways of judging works. This is how aesthetics, the analysis of the addressee's feelings, comes to supplant poetics and rhetoric, which are didactic forms, of and by the understanding, intended for the artist as sender. No longer 'How does one make a work of art?', but 'What is it to experience an affect proper to art?'. And indeterminacy returns, even within the analysis of this last question.

III

Baumgarten published his *Aesthetica*, the first aesthetics, in 1750. Kant will say of this work simply that it was based on an error. Baumgarten confuses judgement, in its determinant usage, when the understanding organizes phenomena according to categories, with judgement in its reflexive usage when, in the form of feeling, it relates to the indeterminate relationship between the faculties of the judging subject. Baumgarten's aesthetics remains dependent on a conceptually determined relationship to the work of art. The sense of beauty is for Kant, on the contrary, kindled by a free harmony between the function of images and the function of concepts occasioned by an object of art or nature. The aesthetics of the sublime is still more indeterminate: a pleasure mixed with pain, a pleasure that comes from pain. In the event of an absolutely large object – the desert, a mountain, a pyramid – or one that is absolutely powerful – a storm at sea, an erupting volcano – which like all absolutes can only be thought, without any sensible/sensory intuition, as an Idea of reason, the faculty of presentation, the imagination, fails to provide a representation corresponding to this Idea. This failure of expression gives rise to a pain, a kind of cleavage within the subject between what can be conceived and what can be imagined or presented. But this pain in turn engenders a pleasure, in fact a double pleasure: the impotence of the imagination attests *a contrario* to an imagination striving to figure even that which cannot be figured, and that imagination thus aims to harmonize its object with that of reason – and that furthermore the inadequacy of the images is a negative sign of the immense power of ideas. This dislocation of the faculties among themselves gives rise to the extreme tension (Kant calls it agitation) that characterizes the pathos of the sublime, as opposed to the calm feeling of beauty. At the edge of the break, infinity, or the absoluteness of the Idea can be revealed in what Kant calls a negative presentation, or even a non-presentation. He cites the Jewish law banning images as an eminent example of negative presentation: optical pleasure when reduced to near nothingness promotes an infinite contemplation of infinity. Even before romantic art had freed itself from classical and baroque figuration, the door had thus been opened to inquiries pointing towards abstract and Minimal art. Avant-gardism is thus present in germ in the Kantian aesthetic of the sublime. However, the art whose effects are analysed in that aesthetics is, of course, essentially made up of attempts to represent sublime objects. And the question of time, of the *Is it happening?*, does not form part – at least not explicitly – of Kant's problematic.

I do, however, believe that question to be at the centre of Edmund Burke's *Philosophical Inquiry into the Origin of our Ideas of the Sublime and Beautiful*, published in 1757. Kant may well reject Burke's thesis as empiricism and physiologism, he may well borrow from Burke the analysis of the characterizing contradiction of the feeling of the sublime, but he strips Burke's aesthetic of what I consider to be its major stake – to show that the sublime is kindled by the threat of nothing further happening. Beauty gives a positive pleasure. But there is another kind of pleasure that is bound to a passion stronger than satisfaction, and that is pain and impending death. In pain the body affects the soul. But the soul can also affect the body as though it were experiencing some externally induced pain, by the sole means of representations that are unconsciously associated with painful situation. This entirely spiritual passion, in Burke's lexicon, is called terror. Terrors are linked to privation: privation of light, terror of darkness; privation of others, terror of solitude; privation of language, terror of silence; privation of objects, terror of emptiness; privation of life, terror of death. What is terrifying is that the *It happens that* does not happen, that it stops happening.

Burke wrote that for this terror to mingle with pleasure and with it to produce the feeling of the sublime, it is also necessary that the terror-causing threat be suspended, kept at bay, held back. This suspense, this lessening of a threat or a danger, provokes a kind of pleasure that is certainly not that of a positive satisfaction, but is, rather, that of relief. This is still a privation, but it is privation at one remove: the soul is deprived of the threat of being deprived of light, language, life. Burke distinguishes this pleasure of secondary privation from positive pleasures, and he baptizes it with the name *delight*.

Here then is an account of the sublime feeling: a very big, very powerful object threatens to deprive the soul of any 'it happens', strikes it with 'astonishment' (at lower intensities the soul is seized with admiration, veneration, respect). The soul is thus dumb, immobilized, as good as dead. Art, by distancing this menace, procures a pleasure of relief, of delight. Thanks to art, the soul is returned to the agitated zone between life and death, and this agitation is its health and its life. For Burke, the sublime was no longer a matter of elevation (the category by which Aristotle defined tragedy), but a matter of intensification.

Another of Burke's observations merits attention because it heralds the possibility of emancipating works of art from the classical rule of imitation. In the long debate over the relative merits of painting and poetry, Burke sides with poetry. Painting is doomed to imitate models, and to figurative representations of them. But if the object of art is to create intense feelings in the addressee of works, figuration by means of images is a limiting constraint on the power of emotive expression since it works by recognition. In the arts of language, particularly in poetry, and particularly in poetry which Burke considered to be not a genre with rules, but the field where certain researches into language have free rein, the power to move is free from the verisimilitudes of figuration.

> What does one do when one wants to represent an angel in a painting? One paints a beautiful young man with wings: but will painting ever provide anything as great as the addition of this one word – the Angel of the *Lord*? and how does one go about painting, with equal strength of feeling, the words 'A universe of death' where ends the journey of the fallen angels in Milton's *Paradise Lost*?

Words enjoy several privileges when it comes to expressing feelings: they are themselves charged with passionate connotations; they can evoke matters of the soul without having to consider whether they are visible; finally, Burke adds, 'It is in our power to effect with words combinations that would be impossible by any other means.' The arts, whatever their materials, pressed forward by the aesthetics of the sublime in search of intense effects, can and must give up the imitation of models that are merely beautiful, and try out surprising, strange, shocking combinations. Shock is, *par excellence*, the evidence of (something) *happening*, rather than nothing, suspended privation.

Burke's analyses can easily, as you will have guessed, be resumed and elaborated in a Freudian–Lacanian problematic (as Pierre Kaufman and Baldine Saint-Girons have done). But I recall them in a different spirit, the one my subject – the avant-garde – demands. I have tried to suggest that at the dawn of romanticism, *Burke's* elaboration of the aesthetics of the sublime, and to a lesser degree *Kant*'s, *outlined a world of possibilities for artistic experiments in which the avant-gardes would later trace out their paths*. There are in general no direct influences, no empirically observable connections. Manet, Cézanne, Braque, and Picasso probably did not read Kant or Burke. It is more a matter of an irreversible deviation in the destination of art, a deviation affecting all the valencies of the artistic condition. The artist attempts combinations allowing the event. The art-lover does not experience a simple pleasure, or derive some ethical benefit from his contact with art, but expects an intensification of his conceptual and emotional capacity, an ambivalent enjoyment. Intensity is associated with an ontological dislocation. The art object no longer bends itself to models, but tries to present the fact that there is an unpresentable; it no longer imitates nature, but is, in Burke, the actualization of a figure potentially there in language. The social community no longer recognizes itself in art objects, but ignores them, rejects them as incomprehensible, and only later allows the intellectual avant-garde to preserve them in museums as the traces of offensives that bear witness to the power, and the privation, of the spirit.

IV

With the advent of the aesthetics of the sublime, the stake of art in the nineteenth and twentieth centuries was to be the witness to the fact that there is indeterminacy. For painting, the paradox that Burke signalled in his observations on the power of words is, that such testimony can only be achieved in a determined fashion. Support, frame, line, colour, space, the figure – were to remain, in romantic art, subject to the constraint of representation. But this contradiction of end and means had, as early as Manet and Cézanne, the effect of casting doubt on certain rules that had determined, since the Quattrocento, the representation of the figure in space and the organization of colours and values. Reading Cézanne's correspondence, one understands that his *œuvre* was not that of a talented painter finding his 'style', but that of an artist attempting to respond to the question: what is a painting? His work had at stake to inscribe on the supporting canvas only those 'colouristic sensations', those 'little sensations' that of themselves, according to Cézanne's hypothesis, constitute the entire pictorial existence of objects, fruit, mountain, face, flower, without consideration of either history or 'subject', or line, or space, or even light. These elementary sensations are hidden in ordinary perception which remains under the hegemony of habitual or classical ways of looking. They are only accessible to the painter, and can therefore only be re-established by him, at the expense of an interior ascesis that rids perceptual and mental fields of prejudices inscribed even in vision itself. If the viewer does not submit to a complementary ascesis, the painting will remain senseless and impenetrable to him. The painter must not hesitate to run the risk of being taken to be a mere dauber. 'One paints for very few people', writes Cézanne. Recognition from the regulatory institutions of painting – Academy, salons, criticism, taste – is of little importance compared to the judgement made by the painter-researcher and his peers on the success obtained by the work of art in relation to what is really at stake: to make seen what makes one see, and not what is visible.

Maurice Merleau-Ponty elaborated on what he rightly called 'Cézanne's doubt' as though what was at stake for the painter was indeed to grasp and render perception at its birth – perception 'before' perception. I would say: colour in its occurrence, the wonder that 'it happens' ('it', something: colour), at least to the eye. There is some credulity on the part of the phenomenologist in this trust he places in the 'originary' value of Cézanne's 'little sensations'. The painter himself, who often complained of their inadequacy, wrote that they were 'abstractions', that 'they did not suffice for covering the canvas'. But why should it be necessary to cover the canvas? Is it forbidden to be abstract?

The doubt which gnaws at the avant-gardes did not stop with Cézanne's 'colouristic sensations' as though they were indubitable, and, for that matter, no more did it stop with the abstractions they heralded. The task of having to bear witness to the indeterminate carries away, one after another, the barriers set up by the writings of theorists and by the manifestos of the painters themselves. A formalist definition of the pictorial object, such as that proposed in 1961 by Clement Greenberg when confronted with American 'post-plastic' abstraction, was soon overturned by the current of Minimalism. Do we have to have stretchers so that the canvas is taut? No. What about colours? Malevitch's black square on white had already answered this question in 1915. Is an object necessary? Body art and happenings went about proving that it is not. A space, at least, a space in which to display, as Duchamp's 'fountain' still suggested? Daniel Buren's work testifies to the fact that even this is subject to doubt.

Whether or not they belong to the current that art history calls Minimalism or Arte Povera, the investigations of the avant-gardes question one by one the constituents one might have thought 'elementary' or at the 'origin' of the art of painting. They operate *ex minimis*. One would have to confront the demand for rigour that animates them with the principle sketched out by Adorno at the end of *Negative Dialectics*, and that controls the writing of his *Aesthetic Theory*: the thought that 'accompanies metaphysics in its fall', he said, can only proceed in terms of 'micrologies'.

Micrology is not just metaphysics in crumbs, any more than Newman's painting is Delacroix in scraps. Micrology inscribes the occurrence of a thought as the unthought that remains to be thought in the decline of 'great' philosophical thought. The avant-gardist attempt inscribes the occurrence of a sensory now as what cannot be presented and which remains to be presented in the decline of great representational painting. Like micrology, the avant-garde is not concerned with what happens to the 'subject', but with: 'Does it happen?', with privation. This is the sense in which it still belongs to the aesthetics of the sublime.

In asking questions of the *It happens* that the work of art is, avant-garde art abandons the role of identification that the work previously played in relation to the community of addressees. Even when conceived, as it was by Kant, as a *de jure* horizon or presumption rather than a *de facto* reality, a *sensus communis* (which, moreover, Kant refers to only when writing about beauty, not the sublime) does not manage to achieve stability when it comes to interrogative works of art. It barely coalesces, too late, when these works, deposited in museums, are considered part of the community heritage and are made available for its culture and pleasure. And even here, they must be objects, or they must tolerate objectification, for example through photography.

In this situation of isolation and misunderstanding, avant-garde art is vulnerable and subject to repression. It seems only to aggravate the identity-crisis that communities went through during the long 'depression' that lasted from the thirties until the end of 'reconstruction' in the mid-fifties. It is impossible here even to suggest how the Party-states born of fear faced with the 'Who are we?', and the anxiety of the void, tried to convert this fear or anxiety into hatred of the avant-gardes. Hildegarde Brenner's study of artistic policy under Nazism, or the films of Hans-Jürgen Sylberberg do not merely analyse these repressive manoeuvres. They also explain how neo-romantic, neo-classical and symbolic forms imposed by the cultural commissars and collaborationist artists – painters and musicians especially – had to block the negative dialectic of the 'Is it happening?', by translating and betraying the question as a waiting for some fabulous subject or identity: 'Is the pure people coming?', 'Is the Führer coming?', 'Is Siegfried coming?'. The aesthetics of the sublime, thus neutralized and converted into a politics of myth, was able to come and build its architectures of human 'formations' on the Zeppelin Feld in Nürnberg.

Thanks to the 'crisis of overcapitalization' that most of today's so-called highly developed societies are going through, another attack on the avant-gardes is coming to light. The threat exerted against the avant-garde search for the artwork event, against attempts to welcome the *now*, no longer requires Party-states to be effective. It proceeds 'directly' out of market economics. The correlation between this and the aesthetics of the sublime is ambiguous, even perverse. The latter, no doubt, has been and continues to be a reaction against the matter-of-fact positivism and the calculated realism that governs the former, as writers on art such as Stendhal, Baudelaire, Mallarmé, Apollinaire and Breton all emphasize.

Yet there is a kind of collusion between capital and the avant-garde. The force of scepticism and even of destruction that capitalism has brought into play, and that Marx never ceased analysing and identifying, in some way encourages among artists a mistrust of established rules and a willingness to experiment with means of expression, with styles, with ever-new materials. There is something of the sublime in capitalist economy. It is not academic, it is not physiocratic, it admits of no nature. It is, in a sense, an economy regulated by an Idea – infinite wealth or power. It does not manage to present any example from reality to verify this Idea. In making science subordinate to itself through technologies, especially those of language, it only succeeds, on the contrary, in making reality increasingly ungraspable, subject to doubt, unsteady.

The experience of the human subject – individual and collective – and the aura that surrounds this experience, are being dissolved into the calculation of profitability, the satisfaction of needs, self-affirmation through success. Even the virtually theological depth of the worker's condition, and of work, that marked the socialist and union movements for over a century, is becoming devalorized, as work becomes a control and manipulation of information. These observations are banal, but what merits attention is the disappearance of the temporal continuum through which the experience of generations used to be transmitted. The availability of information is becoming the only criterion of social importance. Now information is by definition a short-lived element. As soon as it is transmitted and shared, it ceases to be information, it becomes an environmental given, and 'all is said', we 'know'. It is put into the machine memory. The length of time it occupies is, so to speak, instantaneous. Between two pieces of information, 'nothing happens', by definition. A confusion thereby becomes possible, between what is of interest to information and the director, and what is the question of the avant-gardes, between what happens – the new – and the 'Is it happening?', the *now*.

It is understandable that the art-market, subject like all markets to the rule of the new, can exert a kind of seduction on artists. This attraction is not due to corruption alone. It exerts itself thanks to a confusion between innovation and the *Ereignis*, a confusion maintained by the temporality specific to contemporary capitalism. 'Strong' information, if one can call it that, exists in inverse proportion to the meaning that can be attributed to it in the code available to its receiver. It is like 'noise'. It is easy for the public and for artists, advised by intermediaries – the diffusers of cultural merchandise – to draw from this observation the principle that a work of art is avant-garde in direct proportion to the extent that it is stripped of meaning. Is it not then like an event?

It is still necessary that its absurdity does not discourage buyers, just as the innovation introduced into a commodity must allow itself to be approached, appreciated and purchased by the consumers. The secret of an artistic success, like that of a commercial success, resides in the balance between what is surprising and what is 'well-known', between information and code. This is how innovation in art operates: one re-uses formulae confirmed by previous success, one throws them off balance by combining them with other, in principle incompatible, formulae, by amalgamations, quotations, ornamentations, pastiche. One can go as far as kitsch or the grotesque. One flatters the 'taste' of a public that can have no taste, and the eclecticism of a sensibility enfeebled by the multiplication of available forms and objects. In this way one thinks that one is expressing the spirit of the times, whereas one is merely reflecting the spirit of the market. Sublimity is no longer in art, but in speculation on art.

The enigma of the 'Is it happening?' is not dissolved for all this, nor is the task of painting, that there is something which is not determinable, the 'There is' (*Il y a*) itself, out of date. The occurrence, the *Ereignis*, has nothing to do with the *petit frisson*, the cheap thrill, the profitable pathos, that accompanies an innovation. Hidden in the cynicism of innovation is certainly the despair that nothing further will happen. But innovating means to behave as though lots of things happened, and to make them happen. Through innovation, the will affirms its hegemony over time. It thus conforms to the metaphysics of capital, which is a technology of time. The innovation 'works'. The question mark of the 'Is it happening?' stops. With the occurrence, the will is defeated. The avant-gardist task remains that of undoing the presumption of the mind with respect to time. The sublime feeling is the name of this privation.

Translated by Lisa Liebmann, with Geoff Bennington and Marian Hobson

Note

1 This text was first published in *Art Forum*, 22, part 8 (April 1984), pp. 36–43, in a translation by Lisa Liebmann, which is reproduced with kind permission. Alterations were made to the French text by Jean-François Lyotard when he gave the paper in Cambridge in March 1984, and these have been translated by Geoff Bennington and Marian Hobson and incorporated into the translation.

30

PERCEPT, AFFECT, AND CONCEPT

Gilles Deleuze and Félix Guattari

The young man will smile on the canvas for as long as the canvas lasts. Blood throbs under the skin of this woman's face, the wind shakes a branch, a group of men prepare to leave. In a novel or a film, the young man will stop smiling, but he will start to smile again when we turn to this page or that moment. Art preserves, and it is the only thing in the world that is preserved. It preserves and is preserved in itself (*quid juris?*), although actually it lasts no longer than its support and materials – stone, canvas, chemical color, and so on (*quid facti?*). The young girl maintains the pose that she has had for five thousand years, a gesture that no longer depends on whoever made it. The air still has the turbulence, the gust of wind, and the light that it had that day last year, and it no longer depends on whoever was breathing it that morning. If art preserves it does not do so like industry, by adding a substance to make the thing last. The thing became independent of its 'model' from the start, but it is also independent of other possible personae who are themselves artists-things, personae of painting breathing this air of painting. And it is no less independent of the viewer or hearer, who only experience it after, if they have the strength for it. What about the creator? It is independent of the creator through the self-positing of the created, which is preserved in itself. What is preserved – the thing or the work of art – is *a bloc of sensations, that is to say, a compound of percepts and affects.*

Percepts are no longer perceptions; they are independent of a state of those who experience them. Affects are no longer feelings or affections; they go beyond the strength of those who undergo them. Sensations, percepts, and affects are *beings* whose validity lies in themselves and exceeds any lived. They could be said to exist in the absence of man because man, as he is caught in stone, on the canvas, or by words, is himself a compound of percepts and affects. The work of art is a being of sensation and nothing else: it exists in itself.

Harmonies are affects. Consonance and dissonance, harmonies of tone or color, are affects of music or painting. Rameau emphasized the identity of harmony and affect. The artist creates blocs of percepts and affects, but the only law of creation is that the compound must stand up on its own. The artist's greatest difficulty is to make it *stand up on its own*. Sometimes this requires what is, from the viewpoint of an implicit model, from the viewpoint of lived perceptions and affections, great geometrical improbability, physical imperfection, and organic abnormality. But these sublime errors accede to the necessity of art if they are internal means of standing up (or sitting or lying). There is a pictorial possibility that has nothing to do with physical possibility and that endows the most acrobatic postures with the sense of balance. On the other hand, many works that claim to be art do not stand up for an instant. Standing up alone does not mean having a top and a bottom or being upright (for even houses are drunk and askew); it is only the act by which the compound of created sensations is preserved in itself – a monument, but one that may be contained in a few marks or a few lines, like a poem by Emily Dickinson. Of the sketch of an old, worn-out ass, 'How marvellous! It's done with two strokes, but set on immutable bases,' where the sensation bears witness all the more to years of 'persistent, tenacious, disdainful work.'[1] In music, the minor mode is a test that is especially essential since it sets the musician the challenge of wresting it from its ephemeral combinations in order to make it solid and durable, self-preserving, even in acrobatic positions. The sound must be held no less in its extinction than in its production and development. Through his admiration of Pissaro and Monet, what Cézanne had against the Impressionists was that the optical mixture of colors was not enough to create a compound sufficiently 'solid and lasting like the art of the museums,' like 'the perpetuity of blood' in Rubens.[2] This is a way of speaking, because Cézanne does not add something that would preserve Impressionism; he seeks instead a different solidity, other bases and other blocs.

The question of whether drugs help the artist to create these beings of sensation, whether they are part of art's internal means that really lead us to the 'doors of perception' and reveal to us percepts and affects, is given a general answer inasmuch as drug-induced compounds are usually extraordinarily flaky, unable to preserve themselves, and break up as soon as they are made or looked at. We may also admire children's drawings, or rather be moved by them, but they rarely stand up and only resemble Klee or Miró if we do not look at them for long. The paintings of the mad, on the contrary, often hold up, but on condition of being crammed full, with no empty space remaining. However, blocs need pockets of air and emptiness, because even the void is sensation. All sensation is composed with the void in composing itself with itself, and everything holds together on earth and in the air, and preserves the void, is preserved in the void by preserving itself. A canvas may be completely full to the point that even the air no longer gets through, but it is only a work of art if, as the Chinese painter says, it nonetheless saves enough empty space for horses to prance in (even if this is only through the variety of planes).[3]

We paint, sculpt, compose, and write with sensations. We paint, sculpt, compose, and write sensations. As percepts, sensations are not perceptions referring to an object (reference): if they resemble something it is with a resemblance produced with their own methods; and the smile on the canvas is made solely with colors, lines, shadow, and light. If resemblance haunts the work of art, it is because sensation refers only to its material: it is the percept or affect of the material itself, the smile of oil, the gesture of fired clay, the thrust of metal, the crouch of Romanesque stone, and the ascent of Gothic stone. The material is so varied in each case (canvas support, paintbrush or equivalent agent, color in the tube) that it is difficult to say where in fact the material ends and sensation begins; preparation of the canvas, the track of the brush's hair, and many other things besides are obviously part of the sensation. How could the sensation be preserved without a material capable of lasting? And however short the time it lasts, this time is considered as a duration. We will see how the plane of the material ascends irresistibly and invades the plane of composition of the sensations themselves to the point of being part of them or indiscernible from them. It is in this sense that the painter is said to be a painter and nothing but a painter, 'with color seized as if just pressed out of the tube, with the imprint of each hair of his brush,' with this blue that is not a water blue 'but a liquid paint blue.' And yet, in principle at least, sensation is not the same thing as the material. What is preserved by right is not the material, which constitutes only the *de facto* condition, but, insofar as this condition is satisfied (that is, that canvas, color, or stone does not crumble into dust), it is the percept or affect that is preserved in itself. Even if the material lasts for only a few seconds it will give sensation the power to exist and be preserved in itself *in the eternity that coexists with this short duration.* So long as the material lasts, the sensation enjoys an eternity in those very moments. Sensation is not realized in the material without the material passing completely into the sensation, into the percept or affect. All the material becomes expressive. It is the affect that is metallic, crystalline, stony, and so on; and the sensation is not colored but, as Cézanne said, coloring. That is why those who are nothing but painters are also more than painters, because they 'bring before us, in front of the fixed canvas,' not the resemblance but the pure sensation 'of a tortured flower, of a landscape slashed, pressed, and plowed,' giving back 'the water of the painting to nature.'[4] One material is exchanged for another, like the violin for the piano, one kind of brush for another, oil for pastel, only inasmuch as the compound of sensations requires it. And, however strong an artist's interest in science, a compound of sensations will never be mistaken for the 'mixtures' of material that science determines in states of affairs, as is clearly shown by the 'optical mixture' of the impressionists.

By means of the material, the aim of art is to wrest the percept from perceptions of objects and the states of a perceiving subject, to wrest the affect from affections as the transition from one state to another: to extract a bloc of sensations, a pure being of sensations. A method is needed, and this varies with every artist and forms part of the work: we need only compare Proust and Pessoa, who invent different procedures in the search for the sensation as being.[5] In this respect the writer's position is no different from that of the painter, musician, or architect. The writer's specific materials are words and syntax, the created syntax that ascends irresistibly into his work and passes into sensation. Memory, which summons forth only old perceptions, is obviously not enough to get away from lived perceptions; neither is an involuntary memory that adds reminiscence as the present's preserving factor. Memory plays a small part in art (even and especially in Proust). It is true that every work of art is a *monument*, but here the monument is not something commemorating a past, it is a bloc of present sensations that owe their preservation only to themselves and that provide the event with the compound that celebrates it. The monument's action is not memory but fabulation. We write not with childhood memories but through blocs of childhood that are the becoming-child of the present. Music is full of them. It is not memory that is needed but a complex material that is found not in memory but in words and sounds: 'Memory, I hate you.' We attain to the percept and the affect only as to autonomous and sufficient beings that no longer owe anything to those who experience or have experienced them: Combray like it never was, is, or will be lived; Combray as cathedral or monument.

If methods are very different, not only in the different arts but in different artists, we can nevertheless characterize some great monumental types, or 'varieties,' of compounds of sensations: *the vibration*, which characterizes the simple sensation (but it is already durable or compound, because it rises and falls, implies a constitutive difference of level, follows an invisible thread that is more nervous than cerebral); *the embrace or the clinch* (when two sensations resonate in each other by embracing each other so tightly in a clinch of what are no more than 'energies'); *withdrawal, division, distension* (when, on the contrary, two sensations draw apart, release themselves, but so as now to be brought together by the light, the air, or the void that sinks between them or into them, like a wedge that is at once so dense and so light that it extends in every direction as the distance grows, and forms a bloc that no longer needs a support). Vibrating sensation – coupling sensation – opening or splitting, hollowing out sensation. These types are displayed almost in their pure state in sculpture, with its sensations of stone, marble, or metal, which vibrate according to the order of strong and weak beats, projections and hollows, its powerful clinches that intertwine them, its development of large spaces between groups or within a single group where we no longer know whether it is the light or the air that sculpts or is sculpted.

The novel has often risen to the percept – not perception of the moor in Hardy but the moor as percept; oceanic percepts in Melville; urban percepts, or those of the mirror, in Virginia Woolf. The landscape *sees*. Generally speaking, what great writer has not been able to create these beings of sensation, which preserve in themselves the hour of a day, a moment's degree of warmth (Faulkner's hills, Tolstoy's or Chekhov's steppes)? The percept is the landscape before man, in the absence of man. But why do we say this, since in all these cases the landscape is not independent of the supposed perceptions of the characters and, through them, of the author's perceptions and memories? How could the town exist without or before man, or the mirror without the old woman it reflects, even if she does not look at herself in it? This is Cézanne's enigma, which has often been commented upon: 'Man absent from but entirely within the landscape.' Characters can only exist, and the author can only create them, because they do not perceive but have passed into the landscape and are themselves part of the compound of sensations. Ahab really does have perceptions of the sea, but only because he has entered into a relationship with Moby Dick that makes him a becoming-whale and forms a compound of sensations that no longer needs anyone: ocean. It is Mrs. Dalloway who perceives the town – but because she has passed into the town like 'a knife through everything' and becomes imperceptible herself. *Affects are precisely these nonhuman becomings of man*, just as percepts – including the town – are *nonhuman landscapes of nature*. Not a 'minute of the world passes,' says Cézanne, that we will preserve if we do not 'become that minute.'[6] We are not in the world, we become with the world; we become by contemplating it. Everything is vision, becoming. We become universes. Becoming animal, plant, molecular, becoming zero. Kleist is no doubt the author who most wrote with affects, using them like stones or weapons, seizing them in becomings of sudden petrification or infinite acceleration, in the becoming-bitch of Penthesilea and her hallucinated percepts. This is true of all the arts: what strange becomings unleash music across its 'melodic landscapes' and its 'rhythmic characters,' as Messiaen says, by combining the molecular and the cosmic, stars, atoms, and birds in the same being of sensation? What terror haunts Van Gogh's head, caught in a becoming-sunflower? In each case style is needed – the writer's syntax, the musician's modes and rhythms, the painter's lines and colors – to raise lived perceptions to the percept and lived affections to the affect.

We dwell on the art of the novel because it is the source of a misunderstanding: many people think that novels can be created with our perceptions and affections, our memories and archives, our travels and fantasies, our children and parents, with the interesting characters we have met and, above all, the interesting character who is inevitably oneself (who isn't interesting?), and finally with our opinions holding it all together. If need be, we can invoke great authors who have done nothing but recount their lives – Thomas Wolfe or Henry Miller. Generally we get composite works in which we move about a great deal but in search of a father who is found only in ourself: the journalist's novel. We are not spared the least detail, in the absence of any really artistic work. The cruelty we may have seen and the despair we have experienced do not need to be transformed a great deal in order to produce yet again the opinion that generally emerges about the difficulties of communication. Rossellini saw this as a reason for giving up art: art was allowing itself to be invaded too much by infantilism and cruelty, both cruel and doleful, whining and satisfied at the same time, so that it was better to abandon it.[7] More interestingly, Rosselini saw the same thing taking place in painting. But it is literature primarily that has constantly maintained an equivocal relationship with the lived. We may well have great powers of observation and much imagination, but is it possible to write with perceptions, affections, and opinions? Even in the least autobiographical novels we see the confrontation and intersection of the opinions of a multitude of characters, all in accordance with the perceptions and affections of each character with his social situation and individual adventures, and all of it swept up in the vast current of the author's opinion, which, however, divides itself so as to rebound on the characters, or which hides itself so that readers can form their own: this is indeed how Bakhtin's great theory of the novel begins (happily it does not end there; it is precisely the 'parodic' basis of the novel).

Creative fabulation has nothing to do with a memory, however exaggerated, or with a fantasy. In fact, the artist, including the novelist, goes beyond the perceptual states and affective transitions of the lived. The artist is a seer, a becomer. How would he recount what happened to him, or what he imagines, since he is a shadow? He has seen something in life that is too great, too unbearable also, and the mutual embrace of life with what threatens it, so that the corner of nature or districts of the town that he sees, along with their characters, accede to a vision that, through them, composes the percepts of that life, of that moment, shattering lived perceptions into a sort of cubism, a sort of simultaneism, of harsh or crepuscular light, of purple or blue, which have no other object or subject than themselves. 'What we call styles,' said Giacometti, 'are those visions fixed in time and space.' It is always a question of freeing life wherever it is imprisoned, or of tempting it into an uncertain combat. The death of the porcupine in Lawrence and the death of the mole in Kafka are almost unbearable acts of the novelist. Sometimes it is necessary to lie down on the earth, like the painter does also, in order to get to the 'motif,' that is to say, the percept. Percepts can be telescopic or microscopic, giving characters and landscapes giant dimensions as if they were swollen by a life that no lived perception can attain. Balzac's greatness. It is of little importance whether these characters *are* mediocre: they *become* giants, like Bouvard and Pecuchet, Bloom and Molly, Mercier and Camier, without ceasing to be what they are. It is by dint of mediocrity, even of stupidity or infamy, that they are able to become not simple (they are never simple) but gigantic. Even dwarves and cripples will do: all fabulation is the fabrication of giants.[8] Whether mediocre or grandiose, they are too alive to be livable or lived. Thomas Wolfe extracts a giant from his father, and Henry Miller extracts a dark planet from the city. Wolfe may describe the people of old Catawba through their stupid opinions and their mania for discussion, but what he does is set up the secret monument of their solitude, their desert, their eternal earth, and their forgotten, unnoticed lives. Faulkner may also cry out: oh, men of Yoknapatawpha. It is said that the monumental novelist is himself 'inspired' by the lived, and this is true: M. de Charlus closely resembles Montesquiou, but between Montesquiou and M. de Charlus there is ultimately roughly the same relationship as between the barking animal-dog and the celestial constellation-Dog.

How can a moment of the world be rendered durable or made to exist by itself? Virginia Woolf provides an answer that is as valid for painting and music as it is for writing: 'Saturate every atom,' 'eliminate all waste, deadness, superfluity,' everything that adheres to our current and lived perceptions, everything that nourishes the mediocre novelist; and keep only the saturation that gives us the percept. 'It must include nonsense, fact, sordidity: *but made transparent*'; 'I want to put practically everything in; yet to saturate.'[9] Through having reached the percept as 'the sacred source,' through having seen Life in the living or the Living in the lived, the novelist or painter returns breathless and with bloodshot eyes. They are athletes – not athletes who train their bodies and cultivate the lived, no matter how many writers have succumbed to the idea of sport as a way of heightening art and life, but bizarre athletes of the 'fasting-artist' type, or the 'great Swimmer' who does not know how to swim. It is not an organic or muscular athleticism but its inorganic double, 'an affective Athleticism,' an athleticism of becoming that reveals only forces that are not its own – 'plastic specter.'[10] In this respect artists are like philosophers. What little health they possess is often too fragile, not because of their illnesses or neuroses but because they have seen something in life that is too much for anyone, too much for themselves, and that has put on them the quiet mark of death. But this something is also the source or breath that supports them through the illnesses of the lived (what Nietzsche called health). 'Perhaps one day we will know that there wasn't any art but only medicine.'[11]

The affect goes beyond affections no less than the percept goes beyond perceptions. The affect is not the passage from one lived state to another but man's nonhuman becoming. Ahab does not imitate Moby Dick, and Penthesilea does not 'act' the bitch: becoming is neither an imitation nor an experienced sympathy, nor even an imaginary identification. It is not resemblance, although there is resemblance. But it is only a produced resemblance. Rather, becoming is an extreme contiguity within a coupling of two sensations without resemblance or, on the contrary, in the distance of a light that captures both of them in a single reflection. André Dhotel knew how to place his characters in strange plant-becomings, becoming tree or aster: this is not the transformation of one into the other, he says, but something passing from one to the other.[12] This something can be specified only as sensation. It is a zone of indetermination, of indiscernibility, as if things, beasts, and persons (Ahab and Moby Dick, Penthesilea and the bitch) endlessly reach that point that immediately precedes their natural differentiation. This is what is called an *affect*. In *Pierre; or, The Ambiguities*, Pierre reaches the zone in which he can no longer distinguish himself from his half-sister, Isabelle, and he becomes woman. Life alone creates such zones where living beings whirl around, and only art can reach and penetrate them in its enterprise of co-creation. This is because from the moment that the material passes into sensation, as in a Rodin sculpture, art itself lives on these zones of indetermination. They are blocs. Painting needs more than the skill of the draftsman who notes resemblances between human and animal forms and gets us to witness their transformation: on the contrary, it needs the power of a ground that can dissolve forms and impose the existence of a zone in which we no longer know which is animal and which human, because something like the triumph or monument of their nondistinction rises up – as in Goya or even Daumier or Redon. The artist must create the syntactical or plastic methods and materials necessary for such a great undertaking, which re-creates everywhere the primitive swamps of life (Goya's use of etching and aquatint). The affect certainly does not undertake a return to origins, as if beneath civilization we would rediscover, in terms of resemblance, the persistence of a bestial or primitive humanity. It is within our civilization's temperate surroundings that equatorial or glacial zones, which avoid the differentiation of genus, sex, orders, and kingdoms, currently function and prosper. It is a question only of ourselves, here and now; but what is animal, vegetable, mineral, or human in us is now indistinct – even though we ourselves will especially acquire distinction. The maximum determination comes from this bloc of neighborhood like a flash.

It is precisely because opinions are functions of lived experience that they claim to have a certain knowledge of affections. Opinions prevail on human passions and their eternity. But, as Bergson observed, one has the impression that opinion misjudges affective states and groups them together or separates them wrongly.[13] It is not even enough to do what psychoanalysis does and give forbidden objects to itemized affections or substitute simple ambivalences for zones of indetermination. A great novelist is above all an artist who invents unknown or unrecognized affects and brings them to light as the becoming of his characters: the crepuscular states of knights in the novels of Chrétien de Troyes (in relation to a possible concept of chivalry), the states of almost catatonic 'rest' that merge with duty according to Mme de Lafayette (in relation to a concept of quietism), on up to Beckett's state, as affects that are all the more imposing as they are poor in affections. When Zola suggests to his readers, 'take note; my characters do not suffer from remorse,' we should see not the expression of a physiologist's thesis but the ascription of new affects that arise with the creation of characters in naturalism: the Mediocre, the Pervert, the Beast (and what Zola calls instinct is inseparable from a becoming-animal). When Emily Brontë traces the bond between Heathcliff and Catherine, she invents a violent affect, like a kinship between two wolves, which above all should not be mistaken for love. When Proust seems to be describing jealousy in such minute detail, he is inventing an affect, because he constantly reverses the order in affections presupposed by opinion, according to which jealousy would be an unhappy consequence of love: for him, on the contrary, jealousy is finality, destination; and if we must love, it is so that we can be jealous, jealousy being the meaning of signs – affect as semiology. When Claude Simon describes the incredible passive love of the earth-woman, he sculpts an affect of clay. He may say, 'this is my mother,' and we believe him since he says it, but it is a mother who has passed into sensation and to whom he erects a monument so original that she no longer has an ascribable relationship with her real son but, more distantly, with another created character, Faulkner's Eula. It is in this way that, from one writer to another, great creative affects can link up or diverge, within compounds of sensations that transform themselves, vibrate, couple, or split apart: it is these beings of sensation that account for the artist's relationship with a public, for the relation between different works by the same artist, or even for a possible affinity between artists.[14] The artist is always adding new varieties to the world. Beings of sensation are varieties, just as the concept's beings are variations, and the function's beings are variables.

It should be said of all art that, in relation to the percepts or visions they give us, artists are presenters of affects, the inventors and creators of affects. They not only create them in their work, they give them to us and make us become with them, they draw us into the compound. Van Gogh's sunflowers are becomings, like Dürer's thistles or Bonnard's mimosas. Redon entitled a lithograph 'There was perhaps a first vision attempted in the flower.' The flower sees – pure and simple terror: 'And do you see that sunflower looking in through the bedroom window? It stares into my room all day.'[15] A floral history of painting is like the endlessly and continuously resumed creation of the percepts and affects of flowers. Whether through words, colors, sounds, or stone, art is the language of sensations. Art does not have opinions. Art undoes the triple organization of perceptions, affections, and opinions in order to substitute a monument composed of percepts, affects, and blocs of sensations that take the place of language. The writer uses words, but by creating a syntax that makes them pass into sensation that makes the standard language stammer, tremble, cry, or even sing: this is the style, the 'tone,' the language of sensations, or the foreign language within language that summons forth a people to come, 'Oh, people of old Catawba,' 'Oh, people of Yoknapatawpha.' The writer twists language, makes it vibrate, seizes hold of it, and rends it in order to wrest the percept from perceptions, the affect from affections, the sensation from opinion – in view, one hopes, of that still-missing people.

> I repeat – my memory is not loving but inimical, and it labors not to reproduce but to distance the past. What was it my family wished to say? I do not know. It was tongue-tied from birth – but it had, nevertheless, something that it might have said. Over my head and over the head of many of my contemporaries there hangs the congenital tongue-tie. We were not taught to speak but to babble – and only by listening to the swelling noise of the age and bleached by the foam on the crest of its wave did we acquire a language.[16]

This is, precisely, the task of all art and, from colors and sounds, both music and painting similarly extract new harmonies, new plastic or melodic landscapes, and new rhythmic characters that raise them to the height of the earth's song and the cry of humanity: that which constitutes tone, health, becoming, a visual and sonorous bloc. A monument does not commemorate or celebrate something that happened but confides to the ear of the future the persistent sensations that embody the event: the constantly renewed suffering of men and women, their re-created protestations, their constantly resumed struggle. Will this all be in vain because suffering is eternal and revolutions do not survive their victory? But the success of a revolution resides only in itself, precisely in the vibrations, clinches, and openings it gave to men and women at the moment of its making and that composes in itself a monument that is always in the process of becoming, like those tumuli to which each new traveler adds a stone. The victory of a revolution is immanent and consists in the new bonds it installs between people, even if these bonds last no longer than the revolution's fused material and quickly give way to division and betrayal.

Aesthetic figures, and the style that creates them, have nothing to do with rhetoric. They are sensations: percepts and affects, landscapes and faces, visions and becomings.

But is not the philosophical concept defined by becoming, and almost in the same terms? Still, aesthetic figures are not the same as conceptual personae. It may be that they pass into one another, in either direction, like Igitur or Zarathustra, but this is insofar as there are sensations of concepts and concepts of sensations. It is not the same becoming. Sensory becoming is the action by which something or someone is ceaselessly becoming-other (while continuing to be what they are), sunflower or Ahab, whereas conceptual becoming is the action by which the common event itself eludes what is. Conceptual becoming is heterogeneity grasped in an absolute form; sensory becoming is otherness caught in a matter of expression. The monument does not actualize the virtual event but incorporates or embodies it: it gives it a body, a life, a universe. This was how Proust defined the art-monument by that life higher than the 'lived,' by its 'qualitative differences,' its 'universes' that construct their own limits, their distances and proximities, their constellations and the blocs of sensations they put into motion – Rembrandt-universe or Debussy-universe. These universes are neither virtual nor actual; they are possibles, the possible as aesthetic category ('the possible or I shall suffocate'), the existence of the possible, whereas events are the reality of the virtual, forms of a thought-Nature that survey every possible universe. This is not to say that the concept precedes sensation in principle: even a concept of sensation must be created with its own means, and a sensation exists in its possible universe without the concept necessarily existing in its absolute form.

Can sensation be assimilated to an original opinion, to *Urdoxa* as the world's foundation or immutable basis? Phenomenology finds sensation in perceptual and affective 'a priori materials' that transcend the perceptions and affections of the lived: Van Gogh's yellow or Cézanne's innate sensations. As we have seen, phenomenology must become the phenomenology of art because the immanence of the lived to a transcendental subject must be expressed in transcendent functions that not only determine experience in general but traverse the lived itself here and now, and are embodied in it by constituting living sensations. The being of sensation, the bloc of percept and affect, will appear as the unity or reversibility of feeling and felt, their intimate intermingling like hands clasped together: it is the *flesh* that, at the same time, is freed from the lived body, the perceived world, and the intentionality of one toward the other that is still too tied to experience; whereas flesh gives us the being of sensation and bears the original opinion distinct from the judgment of experience – flesh of the world and flesh of the body that are exchanged as correlates, ideal coincidence.[17] A curious Fleshism inspires this final avatar of phenomenology and plunges it into the mystery of the incarnation. It is both a pious and a sensual notion, a mixture of sensuality and religion, without which, perhaps, flesh could not stand up by itself (it would slide down the bones, as in Bacon's figures). The question of whether flesh is adequate to art can be put in this way: can it support percept and affect, can it constitute the being of sensation, or must it not itself be supported and pass into other powers of life?

Flesh is not sensation, although it is involved in revealing it. We spoke too quickly when we said that sensation embodies. Sometimes flesh is painted with pink (superimpositions of red and white), and sometimes with broken tones [*tons rompus*[18]], a juxtaposition of complementaries in unequal proportions. But what constitutes sensation is the becoming animal or plant, which wells up like a flayed beast or peeled fruit beneath the bands of pink in the most graceful, delicate nude, Venus in the mirror; or which suddenly emerges in the fusion, firing, or casting of broken tones, like the zone of indiscernibility of beast and man. Perhaps it would be an interference or chaos, were there not a second element to make the flesh hold fast. Flesh is only the thermometer of a becoming. The flesh is too tender. The second element is not so much bone or skeletal structure as house or framework. The body blossoms in the house (or an equivalent, a spring, a grove). Now, what defines the house are 'sections,' that is to say, the pieces of differently oriented planes that provide flesh with its framework – foreground and background, horizontal and vertical sections, left and right, straight and oblique, rectilinear or curved.[19] These sections are walls but also floors, doors, windows, French windows, and mirrors, which give sensation the power to stand on its own within autonomous *frames*. They are the sides of the bloc of sensation. There are certainly two signs of the genius of great painters, as well as of their humility: the respect, almost dread, with which they approach and enter into color; and the care with which they join together the sections or planes on which the type of depth depends. Without this respect and care painting is nothing, lacking work and thought. The difficult part is not to join hands but to join planes – to produce bulging with joined planes or, on the contrary, to break them open or cut them off. The two problems, the architecture of planes and the regime of color, are often mixed up. As for the joining of horizontal and vertical planes in Cézanne, 'Planes in color, planes! The colored place where the heart of the planes is fused.' No two great painters, or even œuvres, work in the same way. However there are tendencies in a painter: in Giacometti, for example, the receding horizontal planes differ from right to left and seem to come together on the thing (the flesh of the small apple), but like a pincer that would pull it backward and make it disappear if a vertical plane, of which we see only the thread without thickness, did not fix it, checking it at the last moment, giving it a durable existence, in the form of a long pin passing through it and rendering it spindly in turn. The house takes part in an entire becoming. It is life, the 'nonorganic life of things.' In every way possible, the house-sensation is defined by the joining of planes in accordance with a thousand orientations. The house itself (or its equivalent) is the finite junction of colored planes.

The third element is the universe, the cosmos. Not only does the open house communicate with the landscape, through a window or a mirror, but the most shut-up house opens onto a universe. Monet's house finds itself endlessly caught up by the plant forces of an unrestrained garden, a cosmos of roses. A universe-cosmos is not flesh. Neither is it sections, joined up parts of planes, or differently oriented planes, although it may be constituted by the connection of every plane to infinity. But ultimately the universe appears as the area of plain, uniform color [*l'aplat*[20]], the single great plane, the colored void, the monochrome infinite. The French window, as in Matisse, now opens only onto an area of plain, uniform black. The flesh, or rather the figure, is no longer the inhabitant of the place, of the house, but of the universe that supports the house (becoming). *It is like a passage from the finite to the infinite*, but also from territory to deterritorialization. It is indeed the moment of the infinite: infinitely varied infinites. In Van Gogh, Gauguin, or, today, Bacon, we see the immediate tension between flesh and the area of plain, uniform color surging forth, between the flows of broken tones [*tons rompus*] and the infinite band of a pure, homogeneous, vivid, and saturated color ('instead of painting the ordinary wall of the mean room, I paint infinity, a plain background of the richest, intensest blue').[21] It is true that the monochrome area of plain color is something other than a background. And when painting wants to start again at zero, by constructing the percept as a minimum before the void, or by bringing it closer to the maximum of the concept, it works with monochrome freed from any house or flesh. Blue in particular takes on the infinite and turns the percept into a 'cosmic sensibility' or into that which is most conceptual or 'propositional' in nature – color in the absence of man, man who has passed into color. But if the blue (or black or white) is exactly the same within a picture, or from one picture to another, then it is the painter who becomes blue – 'Yves the monochrome' – in accordance with a pure affect that topples the universe into the void and leaves the painter above all with nothing to do.[22]

The colored or, rather, coloring void, is already force. Most of the great monochromes of modern painting no longer need to resort to little mural bouquets but present subtle imperceptible variations (which are constitutive of a percept nevertheless), either because they are cut off or edged on one side by a band, ribbon, or section of a different color or tone that, through proximity or distance, changes the intensity of the area of plain, uniform color or because they present almost virtual linear or circular figures, in matching tones, or because they are holed or slit: these are problems of junction, once again, but considerably expanded. In short, the area of plain, uniform color vibrates, clenches or cracks open because it is the bearer of glimpsed forces. And this, first of all, is what makes painting abstract: summoning forces, populating the area of plain, uniform color with the forces it bears, making the invisible forces visible in themselves, drawing up figures with a geometrical appearance but that are no more than forces – the forces of gravity, heaviness, rotation, the vortex, explosion, expansion, germination, and time (as music may be said to make the sonorous force of time audible, in Messiaen for example, or literature, with Proust, to make the illegible force of time legible and conceivable). Is this not the definition of the percept itself – to make perceptible the imperceptible forces that populate the world, affect us, and make us become? Mondrian achieves this by simple differences between the sides of a square, Kandinsky by linear 'tensions,' and Kupka by planes curved around the point. From the depths of time there comes to us what Worringer called the abstract and infinite northern line, the line of the universe that forms ribbons, strips, wheels, and turbines, an entire 'vitalized geometry,' *rising to the intuition of mechanical forces*, constituting a powerful nonorganic life.[23] Painting's eternal object is this: to paint forces, like Tintoretto.

Perhaps also we rediscover the house and the body? – because the infinite area of plain, uniform color is often that onto which the window or door opens; or it is the wall of the house itself, or the floor. Van Gogh and Gauguin sprinkle the area of plain, uniform color with little bunches of flowers so as to turn it into wallpaper on which the face stands out in broken tones. In fact, the house does not shelter us from cosmic forces; at most it filters and selects them. Sometimes it turns them into benevolent forces: Archimedes' force, the force of the water's pressure on a graceful body floating in the bath of the house, has never been made visible in painting in the way that Bonnard succeeded in doing in *Le Nu au bain*. But equally, the most baleful forces can come in through the half-open or closed door: cosmic forces themselves are what produce zones of indiscernibility in the broken tones of a face, slapping, scratching, and melting it in every way, and these zones of indiscernibility reveal the forces lurking in the area of plain, uniform color (Bacon). The clinch of forces as percepts and becomings as affects are completely complementary. According to Worringer, the abstract line of force is rich in animal motifs. Animal, plant, and molecular becomings correspond to cosmic or cosmogenetic forces: to the point that the body disappears into the plain color or becomes part of the wall or, conversely, the plain color buckles and whirls around in the body's zone of indiscernibility. In short, the being of sensation is not the flesh but the compound of nonhuman forces of the cosmos, of man's nonhuman becomings, and of the ambiguous house that exchanges and adjusts them, makes them whirl around like winds. Flesh is only the developer which disappears in what it develops: the compound of sensation. Like all painting, abstract painting is sensation, nothing but sensation. In Mondrian the room accedes to the being of sensation by dividing the infinite empty plane by colored sections that, in turn, give it an infinite openness.[24] In Kandinsky, houses are sources of abstraction that consist less in geometrical figures than in dynamic trajectories and errant lines, 'paths that go for a walk' in the surroundings. In Kupka it is first of all on the body that the painter cuts out colored ribbons or sections that will give, in the void, the curved planes that populate it by becoming cosmogenetic sensations. Is sensation spiritual, or already a living concept – the room, house, universe? Abstract art, and then conceptual art, directly pose the question that haunts all painting – that of its relation to the concept and the function.

Perhaps art begins with the animal, at least with the animal that carves out a territory and constructs a house (both are correlative, or even one and the same, in what is called a habitat). The territory–house system transforms a number of organic functions – sexuality, procreation, aggression, feeding. But this transformation does not explain the appearance of the territory and the house; rather it is the other way around: the territory implies the emergence of pure sensory qualities, of sensibilia that cease to be merely functional and become expressive features, making possible a transformation of functions.[25] No doubt this expressiveness is already diffused in life, and the simple field of lilies might be said to celebrate the glory of the skies. But with the territory and the house it becomes constructive and erects ritual monuments of an animal mass that celebrates qualities before extracting new causalities and finalities from them. This emergence of pure sensory qualities is already art, not only in the treatment of external materials but in the body's postures and colors, in the songs and cries that mark out the territory. It is an outpouring of features, colors, and sounds that are inseparable insofar as they become expressive (philosophical concept of territory). Every morning the *Scenopoetes dentirostris*, a bird of the Australian rain forests, cuts leaves, makes them fall to the ground, and turns them over so that the paler, internal side contrasts with the earth. In this way it constructs a stage for itself like a ready-made; and directly above, on a creeper or a branch, while fluffing out the feathers beneath its beak to reveal their yellow roots, it sings a complex song made up from its own notes and, at intervals, those of other birds that it imitates: it is a complete artist.[26] This is not synesthesia in the flesh but blocs of sensations in the territory – colors, postures, and sounds that sketch out a total work of art. These sonorous blocs are refrains; but there are also refrains of posture and color, and postures and colors are always being introduced into refrains: bowing low, straightening up, dancing in a circle and lines of colors. The whole of the refrain is the being of sensation. Monuments are refrains. In this respect art is continually haunted by the animal. Kafka's art is the most profound meditation on the territory and the house, the burrow, portrait-postures (the inhabitant's lowered head with chin sunk into their chest or, on the contrary,

'Shamefaced Lacky' whose angular head goes right through the ceiling); sounds-music (dogs who are musicians in their very postures; Josephine, the singing mouse, of whom it will never be known whether she sings; Gregor whose squeaking combines with his sister's violin in a complex bedroom–house–territory relationship). All that is needed to produce art is here: a house, some postures, colors, and songs – on condition that it all opens onto and launches itself on a mad vector as on a witch's broom, a line of the universe or of deterritorialization – *Perspective on a Room with Occupants* (Klee).

Every territory, every habitat, joins up not only its spatiotemporal but its qualitative planes or sections: a posture and a song for example, a song and a color, percepts and affects. And every territory encompasses or cuts across the territories of other species, or intercepts the trajectories of animals without territories, forming interspecies junction points. It is in this sense that, to start with, Uexkühl develops a melodic, polyphonic, and contrapuntal conception of Nature. Not only does birdsong have its own relationships of counterpoint but it can find these relationships in the song of other species, and it may even imitate these other songs as if it were a question of occupying a maximum of frequencies. The spider's web contains 'a very subtle portrait of the fly,' which serves as its counterpoint. On the death of the mollusk, the shell that serves as its house becomes the counterpoint of the hermit crab that turns it into its own habitat, thanks to its tail, which is not for swimming but is prehensile, enabling it to capture the empty shell. The tick is organically constructed in such a way that it finds its counterpoint in any mammal whatever that passes below its branch, as oak leaves arranged in the form of tiles find their counterpoint in the raindrops that stream over them. This is not a teleological conception but a melodic one in which we no longer know what is art and what nature ('natural technique'). There is counterpoint whenever a melody arises as a 'motif' within another melody, as in the marriage of bumblebee and snapdragon. These relationships of counterpoint join planes together, form compounds of sensations and blocs, and determine becomings. But it is not just these determinate *melodic compounds*, however generalized, that constitute nature; another aspect, an infinite *symphonic plane of composition*, is also required: from House to universe. From endosensation to exosensation. This is because the territory does not merely isolate and join but opens onto cosmic forces that arise from within or come from outside, and renders their effect on the inhabitant perceptible. The oak's plane of composition is what supports or includes the force of the acorn's development and the force of formation of raindrops, and the tick's plane of composition is what supports the force of light, which can attract the insect to the end of a branch to a sufficient height, and the force of weight with which it lets itself fall onto the passing mammal – and between them nothing, an alarming void that can last for years if no mammals pass by.[27] Sometimes forces blend into one another in subtle transitions, decompose hardly glimpsed; and sometimes they alternate or conflict with one another. Sometimes they allow themselves to be selected by the territory, and the most benevolent ones are those that enter the house. Sometimes they send out a mysterious call that draws the inhabitant from the territory and launches it on an irresistible voyage, like chaffinches that suddenly assemble in their millions or crayfish that set off in step on an immense pilgrimage to the bottom of the water. Sometimes they swoop down on the territory, turn it upside down, wickedly, restoring the chaos from which, with difficulty, the territory came. But if nature is like art, this is always because it combines these two living elements in every way: House and Universe, *Heimlich* and *Unheimlich*, territory and deterritorialization, finite melodic compounds and the great infinite plane of composition, the small and large refrain.

Art begins not with flesh but with the house. That is why architecture is the first of the arts. When Dubuffet tries to identify a certain condition of *art brut*, he turns first of all to the house, and all his work stands between architecture, sculpture, and painting. And, not going beyond form, the most scientific architecture endlessly produces and joins up planes and sections. That is why it can be defined by the 'frame,' by an interlocking of differently oriented frames, which will be imposed on the other arts, from painting to the cinema. The prehistory of the picture has been presented as passing through the fresco within the frame of the wall, stained glass within the frame of the window, and mosaic within the frame of the floor: 'The frame is the umbilicus that attaches the picture to the monument of which it is the reduction,' like the gothic frame, with small columns, diagonal ribs, and openwork spire.[28] By making architecture the first art of the frame, Bernard Cache is able to list a certain number of enframing forms that do not determine in advance any concrete content or function of the edifice: the wall that cuts off, the window that captures or selects (in direct contact with the territory), the ground-floor that wards off or rarefies ('rarefying the earth's relief so as to give a free path to human trajectories'), the roof that envelops the place's singularity ('the sloping roof puts the edifice on a hill'). Interlocking these frames or joining up all these planes – wall section, window section, floor section, slope section – is a composite system rich in points and counterpoints. The frames and their joins hold the compounds of sensations, hold up figures, and intermingle with their upholding, with their own appearance. These are the faces of a dice of sensation. Frames or sections are not coordinates; they belong to compounds of sensations whose faces, whose interfaces, they constitute. But however extendable this system may be, it still needs a vast plane of composition that carries out a kind of *deframing* following lines of flight that pass through the territory only in order to open it onto the universe, that go from house–territory to town–cosmos, and that now dissolve the identity of the place through variation of the earth, a town having not so much a place as vectors folding the abstract line of relief. On this plane of composition, as on 'an abstract vectorial space,' geometrical figures are laid out – cone, prism, dihedron, simple plane – which are no more than cosmic forces capable of merging, being transformed, confronting each other, and alternating; world before man yet produced by man.[29] The planes must now be taken apart in order to relate them to their intervals rather than to one another and in order to create new affects.[30] We have seen that painting pursued the same movement. The frame or the picture's edge is, in the first place, the external envelope of a series of frames or sections that join up by carrying out counterpoints of lines and colors, by determining compounds of sensations. But the picture is also traversed by a deframing power that opens it onto a plane of composition or an infinite field of forces. These processes may be very diverse, even at the level of the external frame: irregular forms, sides that do not meet, Seurat's painted or stippled frames, and Mondrian's squares standing on a corner, all of which give the picture the power to leave the canvas. The painter's action never stays within the frame; it leaves the frame and does not begin with it.

Literature, and especially the novel, seems to be in the same situation. What matters is not, as in bad novels, the opinions held by characters in accordance with their social type and characteristics but rather the relations of counterpoint into which they enter and the compounds of sensations that these characters either themselves experience or make felt in their becomings and their visions. Counterpoint serves not to report real or fictional conversations but to bring out the madness of all conversation and of all dialogue, even interior dialogue. Everything that novelists must extract from the perceptions, affections, and opinions of their psychosocial 'models' passes entirely into the percepts and affects to which the character must be raised without holding on to any other life. And this entails a vast plane of composition that is not abstractly preconceived but constructed as the work progresses, opening, mixing, dismantling, and reassembling increasingly unlimited compounds in accordance with the penetration of cosmic forces. Bakhtin's theory of the novel goes in this direction by showing, from Rabelais to Dostoyevsky, the coexistence of contrapuntal, polyphonic, and plurivocal compounds with an architectonic or symphonic plane of composition.[31] A novelist like Dos Passos achieves an extraordinary art of counterpoint in the compounds he forms with characters, current events, biographies, and camera eyes, at the same time as a plane of composition is expanded to infinity so as to sweep everything up into Life, into Death, the town cosmos. If we return to Proust, it is because he more than anyone else made the two elements, although present in each other, almost follow one another; the plane of composition, for life and for death, emerges gradually from compounds of sensation that he draws up in the course of lost time, until appearing in itself with time regained, the force, or rather the forces, of pure time that have now become perceptible. Everything begins with Houses, each of which must join up its sections and hold up compounds – Combray, the Guermantes' house, the Verdurins' salon – and the houses are themselves joined together according to interfaces, but a planetary Cosmos is already there, visible through the telescope, which ruins or transforms them and absorbs them into an infinity of the patch of uniform color. Everything begins with refrains, each of which, like the little phrase of Vinteuil's sonata, is composed not only in itself but with other, variable sensations, like that of an unknown passer-by, like Odette's face, like the leaves of the Bois de Boulogne – and everything comes to an end at infinity in the great Refrain, the phrase of the septet in perpetual metamorphosis, the song of the universe, the world before or after man. From every finite thing, Proust makes a being of sensation that is constantly preserved, but by vanishing on a plane of composition of Being: 'beings of flight.'

EXAMPLE 13

The situation of music seems no different and perhaps embodies the frame even more powerfully. Yet it is said that sound has no frame. But compounds of sensation, sonorous blocs, equally possess sections or framing forms each of which must join together to secure a certain closing-off. The simplest cases are the melodic *air*, which is a monophonic refrain; the *motif*, which is already polyphonic, an element of a melody entering into the development of another and creating counterpoint; and the *theme*, as the object of harmonic modifications through melodic lines. These three elementary forms construct the sonorous house and its territory. They correspond to the three modalities of a being of sensation, for the air is a vibration, the motif is a clinch, a coupling, whereas the theme does not close without also unclenching, splitting, and opening. In fact, the most important musical phenomenon that appears as the sonorous compounds of sensation become more complex is that their closure or shutting-off (through the joining of their frames, of their sections) is accompanied by a possibility of opening onto an ever more limitless plane of composition. According to Bergson, musical beings are like living beings that compensate for their individuating closure by an openness created by modulation, repetition, transposition, juxtaposition. If we consider the sonata we find a particularly rigid enframing form based upon a bithematism, and in which the first movement presents the following sections: exposition of the first theme, transition, exposition of the second theme, developments on the first or second, coda, development of the first with modulation, and so on. It is an entire house with its rooms. But it is the first movement, rather, that forms a cell in this way, and great musicians rarely follow the canonical form; the other movements can open out, especially the second, through theme and variation, until Liszt ensures a fusion of movements in the 'symphonic poem.' The sonata appears then rather like a crossroads form where the opening of a plane of composition is born from the joining of musical sections, from the closure of sonorous compounds.

In this respect, the old procedure of theme and variation, which maintains the harmonic frame of the theme, gives way to a sort of deframing when the piano generates *compositional studies* (Chopin, Schumann, Liszt): this is a new essential moment, because creative labor no longer bears on sonorous compounds, motifs, and themes, even if this may involve extracting a plane from them, but on the contrary bears directly on the plane of composition itself, so that it gives birth to much freer and deframed compounds, to almost incomplete or overloaded aggregates, in permanent disequilibrium. Increasingly, it is the 'color' of the sound that matters. We pass from the House to the Cosmos (according to a formula taken up by Stockhausen's work). The work of the plane of composition develops in two directions that involve a disaggregation of the tonal frame: the immense uniform areas [*aplats*] of continuous variation that couple and combine the forces that have become sonorous in Wagner, or the broken tones [*tons rompus*] that separate and disperse the forces by harmonizing their reversible passages in Debussy – Wagner-universe, Debussy-universe. All the tunes, all the little framing or framed refrains – childish, domestic, professional, national, territorial – are swept up in the great Refrain, a powerful song of the earth – the deterritorialized – which arises with Mahler, Berg, or Bartók. And no doubt in each case the plane of composition generates new closures, as in serial music. But, each time, the musician's action consists in deframing, in finding the opening, taking up the plane of composition once more, in accordance with the formula that obsesses Boulez: to plot a transversal, irreducible to both the harmonic vertical and melodic horizontal, that involves sonorous blocs of variable individuation but that also opens them up or splits them in a space-time that determines their density and their course over the plane.[32] The great refrain arises as we distance ourselves from the house, even if this is in order to return, since no one will recognize us any more when we come back.

Composition, composition is the sole definition of art. Composition is aesthetic, and what is not composed is not a work of art. However, technical composition, the work of the material that often calls on science (mathematics, physics, chemistry, anatomy), is not to be confused with aesthetic composition, which is the work of sensation. Only the latter fully deserves the name *composition*, and a work of art is never produced by or for the sake of technique. To be sure, technique includes many things that are individualized according to each artist and work: words and syntax in literature; not only the canvas but its preparation in painting, pigments, their mixtures, and methods of perspective; or the twelve tones of Western music, instruments, scales, and pitch. And the relationship between the two planes, between technical and aesthetic planes of composition, constantly varies historically. Take two states of oil painting that can be opposed to each other: in the first case, the picture is prepared with a white chalk background on which the outline is drawn and washed in (sketch), and finally color, light, and shade are put down. In the other case, the background becomes increasingly thick, opaque, and absorbent, so that it takes on a tinge with the wash and the work becomes impasted on a brown range, 'reworkings' [*repentirs*[33]] taking the place of the sketch: the painter paints on color, then color alongside color, increasingly the colors become accents, the architecture being assured by 'the contrast of complementaries and the agreement of analogues' (Van Gogh); it is through and in color that the architecture will be found, even if the accents must be given up in order to reconstitute large coloring units. It is true that Xavier de Langlais sees throughout this second case a long decline, a decadence that collapses into the ephemeral and fails to restore an architecture: the picture darkens, becomes dull, or quickly flakes.[34] And doubtless this remark raises the question, at least negatively, of progress in art, since Langlais judges decadence as beginning after Van Eyck (somewhat like those who see music coming to an end with the Gregorian chant, or philosophy with Thomas Aquinas). But it is a technical remark that concerns only the material: not only is the duration of the material quite relative but sensation belongs to a different order and possesses an existence in itself for as long as the material lasts. The relationship of sensation with the material must therefore be assessed within the limits of the duration, whatever this may be. If there is progress in art it is because art can live only by creating new percepts and affects as so many detours, returns, dividing lines, changes of level and scale. From this point of view, the distinction between two states of oil painting assumes a completely different, aesthetic and no longer technical aspect – this distinction clearly does not come down to 'representational or not,' since no art and no sensation have ever been representational.

In the first case *sensation is realized in the material* and does not exist outside of this realization. It could be said that sensation (the compound of sensations) is projected onto the well-prepared technical plane of composition, in such a way that the aesthetic plane of composition covers it up. The material itself must therefore include mechanisms of perspective as a result of which the projected sensation is realized not solely by covering up the picture but according to a depth. Art thus enjoys a semblance of transcendence that is expressed not in a thing to be represented but in the paradigmatic character of projection and in the 'symbolic' character of perspective. According to Bergson the Figure is like fabulation: it has a religious origin. But, when it becomes aesthetic, its sensory transcendence enters into a hidden or open opposition to the suprasensory transcendence of religion.

In the second case it is no longer sensation that is realized in the material *but the material that passes into sensation*. Of course, sensation no more exists outside of this passage, and the technical plane of composition has no more autonomy, than in the first case: it is never valid for itself. But now it might be said that it *ascends* into the aesthetic plane of composition and, as Damisch says, gives it a specific thickness independent of any perspective or depth. It is at this moment that the figures of art free themselves from an apparent transcendence or paradigmatic model and avow their innocent atheism, their paganism. Of course, between these two cases, between these two states of sensation and these two poles of technique, transitions, combinations, and coexistences are constantly being produced (the impasted work of Titian or Rubens, for example): the poles are more abstract than really distinct movements. Nonetheless, modern painting, even when it is satisfied with oil and medium,[35] turns increasingly toward the second pole and makes the material ascend and pass 'into the thickness' of the aesthetic plane of composition. That is why it is so wrong to define sensation in modern painting by the assumption of a pure visual flatness: the error is due perhaps to the fact that thickness does not need to be pronounced or deep. It could be said that Mondrian was a painter of thickness; and when Seurat defined painting as 'the art of ploughing a surface,' the only support he needs is the furrows and peaks of unglazed drawing paper. This is painting that no longer has any background because the 'underneath' comes through: the surface can be furrowed or the plane of composition can take on thickness insofar as the material rises up, independently of depth or perspective, independently of shadows and even of the chromatic order of color (the arbitrary colorist). One no longer covers over; one raises, accumulates, piles up, goes through, stirs up, folds. It is a promotion of the ground, and sculpture can become flat since the plane is stratified. One no longer paints 'on' but 'under.' These new powers of texture, that ascent of the ground with Dubuffet, have been pushed a long way by informal art, and by abstract expressionism and minimal art also, when they work with saturations, fibers, and layers, or when they use tarlatan or tulle in such a way that the painter can paint behind the picture in a state of blindness.[36] With Hantaï, foldings hide from the painter's sight what, once unfolded, they give up to the spectator's eye. In any case, and in all of these states, painting is thought: vision is through thought, and the eye thinks, even more than it listens.

Hubert Damisch turned the thickness of the plane into a genuine concept by showing that 'plaiting could well fulfil a role for future painting similar to that performed by perspective.' This is not peculiar to painting, since Damisch finds the same distinction at the level of the architectural plane when Scarpa, for example, suppresses the movement of projection and the mechanisms of perspective so as to inscribe volumes in the thickness of the plane itself.[37] From literature to music a material thickness is affirmed that does not allow itself to be reduced to any formal depth. It is characteristic of modern literature for words and syntax to rise up into the plane of composition and hollow it out rather than carry out the operation of putting it into perspective. It is also characteristic of modern music to relinquish projection and the perspectives that impose pitch, temperament, and chromatism, so as to give the sonorous plane a singular thickness to which very diverse elements bear witness: the development of studies for the piano, which cease being just technical and become 'compositional studies' (with the extension given to them by Debussy); the decisive importance assumed by the orchestra with Berlioz; the rise of timbre in Stravinsky and Boulez; the proliferation of percussive affects with metals, skins, and woods, and their combination with wind instruments to constitute blocs inseparable from the material (Varèse); the redefinition of the percept according to noise, to raw and complex sound (Cage); not only the enlargement of chromatism to other components of pitch but the tendency to a non-chromatic appearance of sound in an infinite continuum (electronic or electro-acoustic music).

There is only a single plane in the sense that art includes no other plane than that of aesthetic composition: in fact, the technical plane is necessarily covered up or absorbed by the aesthetic plane of composition. It is on this condition that matter becomes expressive: either the compound of sensations is realized in the material, or the material passes into the compound, but always in such a way as to be situated on a specifically aesthetic plane of composition. There are indeed technical problems in art, and science may contribute toward their solution, but they are posed only as a function of aesthetic problems of composition that concern compounds of sensation and the plane to which they and their materials are necessarily linked. Every sensation is a question, even if the only answer is silence. In art the problem is always that of finding what monument to erect on this plane, or what plane to slide under this monument, and both at the same time: hence, in Klee, the 'monument at the edge of the fertile country' and the 'monument in fertile country.' Are there not as many different planes as universes, authors, or even works? In fact, universes, from one art to another as much as in one and the same art, may derive from one another, or enter into relations of capture and form constellations of universes, independently of any derivation, but also scattering themselves into nebulae or different stellar systems, in accordance with qualitative distances that are no longer those of space and time. Universes are linked together or separated on their lines of flight, so that the plane may be single at the same time as universes are irreducibly multiple.

Everything (including technique) takes place between compounds of sensation and the aesthetic plane of composition. Now the latter does not come before, being neither intentional nor preconceived and having nothing to do with a program, but neither does it come afterward, although the awareness of it is formed progressively and often suddenly appears afterward. The town does not come after the house, nor the cosmos after the territory. The universe does not come after the figure, and the figure is an aptitude of a universe. We have gone from the composite sensation to the plane of composition, but only so as to recognize their strict coexistence or complementarity, neither of them advancing except through the other. The composite sensation, made up of percepts and affects, deterritorializes the system of opinion that brought together dominant perceptions and affections within a natural, historical, and social milieu. But the composite sensation is reterritorialized on the plane of composition, because it erects its houses there, because it appears there within interlocked frames or joined sections that surround its components; landscapes that have become pure percepts, and characters that become pure affects. At the same time the plane of composition involves sensation in a higher deterritorialization, making it pass through a sort of deframing which opens it up and breaks it open onto an infinite cosmos. As in Pessoa, a sensation does not occupy a place on the plane without extending it, distending it over the entire earth, and freeing all the sensations it contains: opening out or splitting open, *equaling infinity*. Perhaps the peculiarity of art is to pass through the finite in order to rediscover, to restore the infinite.

What defines thought in its three great forms – art, science, and philosophy – is always confronting chaos, laying out a plane, throwing a plane over chaos. But philosophy wants to save the infinite by giving it consistency: it lays out a plane of immanence that, through the action of conceptual personae, takes events or consistent concepts to infinity. Science, on the other hand, relinquishes the infinite in order to gain reference: it lays out a plane of simply undefined coordinates that each time, through the action of partial observers, defines states of affairs, functions, or referential propositions. Art wants to create the finite that restores the infinite: it lays out a plane of composition that, in turn, through the action of aesthetic figures, bears monuments or composite sensations. Damisch has analyzed accurately Klee's picture *Equals Infinity*. It is certainly not an allegory but the act of painting that appears as a painting. It seems to us that the brown blobs dancing in the margin and crossing the canvas are the infinite passage of chaos; the sowing of points on the canvas, divided by rods, is the finite composite sensation, but opening onto the plane of composition that restores the infinite to us, = ∞. However, art should not be thought to be like a synthesis of science and philosophy, of the finite and infinite routes. The three routes are specific, each as direct as the others, and they are distinguished by the nature of the plane and by what occupies it. Thinking is thought through concepts, or functions, or sensations and no one of these thoughts is better than another, or more fully, completely, or synthetically 'thought.' The frames of art are no more scientific coordinates than sensations are concepts, or vice versa. Abstract art and conceptual art are two recent attempts to bring art and philosophy together, but they do not substitute the concept for the sensation; rather they create sensations and not concepts. Abstract art seeks only to refine sensation, to dematerialize it by setting out an architectonic plane of composition in which it would become a purely spiritual being, a radiant thinking and thought matter, no longer a sensation of sea or tree, but a sensation of the concept of sea or concept of tree. Conceptual art seeks an opposite dematerialization through generalization, by installing a sufficiently neutralized plane of composition (the catalog that brings together works not displayed, the ground covered by its own map, disused spaces without architecture and the 'flatbed'[38] plane) so that everything takes on a value of sensation reproducible to infinity: things, images or clichés, propositions – a thing, its photograph on the same scale and in the same place, its dictionary definition. However, in the latter case it is not at all clear that this way leads either to the sensation or to the concept, because the plan of composition tends to become 'informative,' and the sensation depends upon the simple 'opinion' of a spectator who determines whether or not to 'materialize' the sensation, that is to say, decides whether or not it is art. This is a lot of effort to find ordinary perceptions and affections in the infinite and to reduce the concept to a *doxa* of the social body or great American metropolis.

The three thoughts intersect and intertwine but without synthesis or identification. With its concepts, philosophy brings forth events. Art erects monuments with its sensations. Science constructs states of affairs with its functions. A rich tissue of correspondences can be established between the planes. But the network has its culminating points, where sensation itself becomes sensation of concept or function, where the concept becomes concept of function or of sensation, and where the function becomes function of sensation or concept. And none of these elements can appear without the other being still to come, still indeterminate or unknown. Each created element on a plane calls on other heterogeneous elements, which are still to be created on other planes: thought as heterogenesis. It is true that these culminating points contain two extreme dangers: either leading us back to the opinion from which we wanted to escape or precipitating us into the chaos that we wanted to confront.

Translated by Hugh Tomlinson and Graham Burchill

Notes

1 Edith Wharton, *Les metteurs en scène*, Paris, 10–18, 1986, p. 263. It concerns an academic and worldly painter who gives up painting after seeing a little picture by one [of] his unrecognized contemporaries: 'And me, I have not created any of my works, I have simply adopted them.'

2 Joachim Gasquet, *Cézanne: A Memoir with Conversations*, trans. Christopher Pemberton, London, Thames and Hudson, 1991, p. 164.

3 See François Cheng, *Vide et plein*, Paris, Seuil, 1979, p. 63 (citation of the painter Huang Pin-Hung).

4 Antonin Artaud, 'Van Gogh: The Man Suicided by Society,' in *Artaud Anthology*, ed. Jack Hirschman, San Francisco: City Lights Books, 1965, pp. 156, 160 (translation modified):

> As a painter, and nothing else but a painter, Van Gogh adopted the methods of pure painting and never went beyond them . . . The marvelous thing is that this painter who was only a painter . . . among all the existing painters, is [also] the one who makes us forget that we are dealing with painting.
>
> (pp. 154–56)

5 José Gil devotes a chapter to the procedure by which Pessoa extracts the percept on the basis of lived perceptions, particularly in 'L'ode maritime.' *Fernando Pessoa ou la métaphysique des sensations*, Paris, La Différence, 1988, chap. 2.

6 Gasquet, *Cézanne*, p. 154. See Erwin Straus, *Du sens des sens*, Paris, Millon, n.d., p. 519:

> The great landscapes have a wholly visionary characteristic. Vision is what of the invisible becomes visible . . . The landscape is invisible because the more we conquer it, the more we lose ourselves in it. To reach the landscape we must sacrifice as much as we can all temporal, spatial, objective determination; but this abandon does not only attain the objective, it affects us ourselves to the same extent. In the landscape we cease to be historical beings, that is to say, beings who can themselves be objectified. We do not have any memory for the landscape, we no longer have any memory for ourselves in the landscape. We dream in daylight with open eyes. We are hidden to the objective world, but also to ourselves. This is feeling.

7 Roberto Rossellini, *Le Cinéma révélé*, Paris, Etoile-Cahiers du cinéma, 1984, pp. 80–82.

8 In the second chapter of *The Two Sources of Morality and Religion*, trans. T. Ashley Audra and Cloudesley Brereton with the assistance of W. Horsfall Carter (New York, Henry Holt, 1935), Bergson analyzes fabulation as a visionary faculty very different from the imagination and that consists in creating gods and giants, 'semi-personal powers or effective presences.' It is exercised first of all in religions, but it is freely developed in art and literature.

9 Virginia Woolf, *The Diary of Virginia Woolf*, ed. Anne Olivier Bell, London, Hogarth Press, 1980, vol. 3, pp. 209, 210.

10 Antonin Artaud, *The Theatre and Its Double*, trans. Mary Caroline Richards, New York, Grove Press, 1958, p. 134.

11 Jean-Marie Gustave Le Clézio, *HAI*, Paris, Flammarion, 1991 p. 7 ('I am an Indian' – although I do not know how to cultivate corn or make a dugout). In a famous text, Michaux spoke of the 'health' peculiar to art: postface to 'Mes propriétés' – in Henri Michaux, *La Nuit remue*, Paris, Gallimard, 1935, p. 193.

12 André Dhôtel, *Terres de mémoire*, Paris, Presses Universitaires de France, 1979, pp. 225–26.

13 Emile Bergson, *The Creative Mind*, trans. Mabelle L. Andison, Westport, Connecticut, Greenwood Press, 1946, pp. 59–60.

14 These three questions frequently recur in Proust, especially in 'Time Regained' in *Remembrance of Things Past*, trans. C.K. Scott Moncrieff and Terence Kilmartin; and by Andreas Mayor, London, Chatto and Windus, 1982, vol. 3, pp. 931–32 (on life, vision, and art as the creation of universes).

15 Malcolm Lowry, *Under the Volcano*, Harmondsworth, Penguin, 1963, p. 183.

16 Osip Mandelstam, *The Noise of Time: The Prose of Osip Mandelstam*, trans. with critical essays by Clarence Brown, San Francisco, North Point Press, 1986, pp. 109–10.

17 Mikel Dufrenne, in *Phénoménologie de l'expérience esthétique* (Paris, Presses Universitaires de France, 1953), produced a kind of analytic of perceptual and affective a priori, which founded sensation as a relationship of the body and the world. He stayed close to Erwin Straus. But is there a being of sensation that manifests itself in the flesh? Maurice Merleau-Ponty followed this path in *The Visible and the Invisible* (trans. A. Lingis, Evanston, Illinois, Northwestern University Press, 1969). Dufrenne emphasized a number of reservations concerning such an ontology of the flesh (see *L'Œil et l'oreille*, Montreal, Hexagone, 1987). Recently, Didier

Franck has again taken up Merleau-Ponty's theme by showing the decisive importance of the flesh in Heidegger and already in Husserl (see *Heidegger et le problème de l'espace*, Paris, Minuit, 1986, and *Chair et corps*, Paris, Minuit, 1981). This whole problem is at the center of a phenomenology of art. Perhaps Michel Foucault's still-unpublished book *Les Aveux de la chair* will teach us about the most general origins of the notion of the flesh and its significance in the Church Fathers.

18 There does not seem to be a standard equivalent technical term in English for the French *tons rompus*, which means colors or tones made up of several different colors or tones. Van Gogh's letters, which are a principal reference point for this notion, speak of colors that are 'broken' with other colors; following this we have translated the term as 'broken tones.'

19 As Georges Didi-Huberman demonstrates, the flesh gives rise to a 'doubt': it is too close to chaos. Hence the necessity of a complementarity between the 'pink' [*incarnat*] and the 'section' [*pan*], the essential theme of *La Peinture incarnée* (Paris, Minuit, 1985), which is taken up again and developed in *Devant l'image* (Paris, Minuit, 1990).

20 As with *tons rompus*, the term with which it is contrasted here, there does not seem to be a standard English equivalent for the French *aplat*. The noun has connotations of flatness, following the verb *aplatir* (to flatten or smooth out), but in painting it signifies areas of plain, uniform color. In the absence of a single English word we have decided to use the entire phrase 'area of plain, uniform color.'

21 Vincent Van Gogh, letter no. 520 to Theo, 11 August 1888, in *The Complete Letters of Vincent Van Gogh*, Greenwich, Connecticut, New York Graphic Society, 1958, vol. 3. Broken tones and their relationship with the area of plain, uniform color are a frequent theme of the correspondence. Similarly for Gauguin; see letter to Schuffenecker, 8 October 1888, in *Lettres*, Paris, Grasset, 1946, p. 140:

> I have done a self-portrait for Vincent . . . I think it is one of my best: absolutely incomprehensible (for example) it is so abstract . . . its drawing is completely special, complete abstraction . . . The color is a color far from nature; imagine a vague memory of pottery buckled by great heat. All the reds, the violets, scored by the fire's blaze like a furnace glowing to the eyes, seat of the struggles of the painter's thought. All on a chrome ground sprinkled with childish bunches of flowers. Room of pure young girl.

This is the idea of the 'arbitrary colorist' according to Van Gogh.

22 Cf. *Artstudio* (n.d.), no. 16, 'Monochromes' (Geneviève Monnier and Denys Riout on Klein, and Pierre Sterckx on the 'current avatars of monochrome').

23 Wilhelm Worringer, *Form in Gothic*, London, Putnam's and Sons, 1927.

24 Piet Mondrian, 'Réalité naturelle et réalité abstraite,' in Michel Seuphor, *Piet Mondrian, sa vie, sa œuvre*, Paris, Flammarion, n.d., on the room and its unfolding. Michel Butor has analyzed this unfolding of the room into squares or rectangles, and the opening onto an interior square, empty and white like the 'promise of a future room.' Michel Butor, 'Le carré et son habitant,' *Répertoire III*, Paris, Minuit, 1992, pp. 307–09, 314–15.

25 It seems to us that Lorenz's mistake is wanting to explain the territory by an evolution of functions: Konrad Lorenz, *On Aggression*, trans. Marjorie Kerr Wilson, New York, Harcourt, Brace and World, 1966.

26 Alan John Marshall, *Bower Birds*, Oxford, Clarendon Press, 1954; and E.T. Gilliard, *Birds of Paradise and Bower Birds*, London, Weidenfeld, 1969.

27 See Jakob von Uexküll's masterpiece, *Mondes animaux et monde humain, Théorie de la signification*, Paris, Gonthier, 1965, pp. 137–42: 'counterpoint, motif of development, and morphogenesis.'

28 Henry van de Velde, *Déblaiement d'art*, Brussels: Archives architecture moderne, 1979, p. 20.

29 On all these points, the analysis of enframing forms, and of the town–cosmos (the example of Lausanne), see Bernard Cache's forthcoming *L'Ameublement du territoire*.

30 Pascal Bonitzer formed the concept of deframing [*décadrage*] in order to highlight new relationships between the planes in cinema (*Cahiers du cinéma* 284, January 1978): 'disjointed, crushed or fragmented' planes, thanks to which cinema becomes an art by getting free from the commonest emotions, which were in danger of preventing its aesthetic development, and

by producing new affects. See Pascal Bonitzer, *Le Champ aveugle: essais sur le cinéma*, Paris, Gallimard – Cahiers du cinéma, 1982: 'system of the emotions.'

31 Mikhail Bakhtine, *Esthétique et théorie du roman*, trans. Daria Olivier, Paris, Gallimard, 1978.

32 Pierre Boulez, especially *Orientations*, trans. Martin Cooper, London, Faber, 1986, and *Boulez on Music Today*, trans. S. Bradshaw and Richard Rodney Bennett, London, Faber, 1971. The extension of the series into durations, intensities, and timbres is not an act of closure but, on the contrary, an opening of what is closed in the series of pitches [*hauteurs*].

33 We have translated *repentirs* as 'reworkings,' but the French also conveys the sense of 'corrections and revisions made while the painting is being executed,' that is to say, not a reworking of a completed painting.

34 Xavier de Langlais, *La Technique de la peinture à l'huile*, Paris, Flammarion, 1988; Johann Wolfgang von Goethe, *Theory of Colors*, Cambridge, Massachusetts, MIT Press, 1970, pp. 902–09.

35 *Médium* is the same in English – 'medium' – and signifies the liquid used to bind powdered color to produce paint, e.g., oil, size, egg yolk, gum arabic.

36 See Christian Bonnefoi, 'Interview et comment par Yves-Alain Bois,' *Macula* (n.d.), pp. 5–6.

37 Hubert Damisch, *Le Fenêtre jaune cadmium; ou Les dessous de la peinture*, Paris, Seuil, 1984, pp. 275–305 (and p. 80, on the thickness of the plane in Pollock). Damisch has insisted more than other writers on art-as-thought and painting-as-thought, such as Dubuffet in particular sought to institute. Mallarmé made the book's 'thickness' a dimension distinct from its depth; see Jacques Schérer, *Le Livre de Mallarmé*, Paris, Gallimard, 1978, p. 55. Boulez takes up this theme on his own account for music (*Orientations*).

38 In English in the original.

Part 6

PSYCHOANALYSIS AND FEMINISM

INTRODUCTION

Sigmund Freud

In a 1913 article, Sigmund Freud (1856–1939) defines psychoanalysis as 'a medical procedure which aims at the cure of certain forms of nervous disease (the neuroses) by a psychological technique'.[1] This modest definition does not do justice to the impact which his work has had on our understanding of the relationship between mental and physical life. His early studies of hypnotism, made while in Paris working under the innovative French neurologist Jean-Martin Charcot, showed that a patient's symptoms could be temporarily removed following suggestions made by the hypnotist. This implied there was a psychosomatic relation between mental ideas and physical behaviour. 'Psychosomatic' is often associated with medical cases where changes in behaviour occur because a patient *thinks* the medicine will help him, rather than because the medicine itself has a definite causal effect. It therefore carries with it an unfortunate sense of delusion. With Freud, however, the word is not used as a contrast term to causality. His concern lies with the influence which ideas have on physical reality. The process of thought, especially the act of interpreting images and events from the patient's mental life, he argues, affects and alters behaviour. Neuroses are created by civilization and the interests of respectability suppressing certain actions and desires. The pressure which these repressed events exert on our mental lives can be relieved through verbalization. However, it is not the accurate description of original meaning – as in the question 'Did this really happen?' – which relieves the pressure, Freud argues, but the free, metaphorical play of associations. Through examination of neuroses, dreams, and parapraxes (or slips of the tongue, now, of course, referred to as Freudian slips), Freud constructs a revolutionary theory of the human psyche as a structure of meaning or interpretation.

All this is in stark contrast to nineteenth-century psychology's commitment to positivism and knowledge through experimentation and observation: once the data of physical sensation had been exhaustively described, the positivists argued, there was nothing left to say about the world. Psychology prior to Freud had already acknowledged that there was more to the individual's mental life than the experiences of which she was consciously aware. 'What we are conscious of', the philosopher William Hamilton wrote in 1842, 'is constructed out of what we are not conscious of.'[2] A century earlier, Hume had announced that the self was something which eluded conscious, perceptual grasp.[3] From the 1770s, public displays of animal magnetism, mesmerism, and hypnotism were offered as evidence of the existence of unconscious mental activity. The problem was how to access and account for this dimension of experience. It takes the form of one of philosophy's oldest conundrums: how can one know that which is beyond knowability? How are we to arrive at conscious knowledge of the unconscious?

The physicalist or vitalist approach was to assume that unconsciously motivated experiences ultimately had a latent, conscious origin, usually a particular childhood event. This commitment to a unitary cause was analogous to the positivist thesis that mental states could be identified with particular events in the individual's nervous system, e.g., Bell and Magendie's law of specific nerve energies, and Comte's phrenology.[4] The vitalist programme of analysis maintained that the patient could be freed from the trauma if the analyst prompted him through talking and interpretation to remember the experience, that is, to allow a cathartic release of the experience into consciousness.

The problem with this view, Freud argues, is that it regards each experience to be meaningful in itself and assumes that the meaning of the experience, once released, is open and accessible to consciousness without restriction or reservation. It is a mistake, he asserts, to picture the unconscious as merely a second, albeit submerged consciousness. In his 1915 theoretical essay, 'The Unconscious', he argues:

> Just as Kant warned us not to overlook the fact that our perceptions are subjectively conditioned and must not be regarded as identical with what is perceived though unknowable, so psycho-analysis warns us not to equate perceptions by means of consciousness with the unconscious mental processes which are their object. Like the physical, the psychical is not necessarily in reality what it appears to us to be.[5]

This point develops Freud's allusion to Kant in *The Interpretation of Dreams* (1900) where he identifies the opacity of unconscious mental activity with the partial and transformative nature of sensory perception: the unconscious, he writes, '*is as incompletely presented by the data of consciousness as is the external world by the communications of our sense organs*'.[6]

Psychoanalysis encounters the opacity of experience in a variety of ways. For example, Freud discovered that a later event can alter the relevance which is ascribed to an earlier one, so that what was innocent as an event can become traumatic as a memory. The case of Emma is an example.[7] Having her genitalia felt through her clothes by a male shopkeeper when she was eight *only becomes traumatic* for her when, four years later, she encounters two shopping assistants in a store laughing together. Also, Freud judged the emergence of fantasy in patients' descriptions of events to be an important aspect of neuroses. Acts of sexual abuse recounted during analysis, directed against the patient when they were a child by an adult, had often never taken place; they were fantasies made up by the patient or suggested to them by Freud himself. It was not the case that the patients were 'simply' lying but, as Freud remarks, that 'there are no indications of reality in the unconscious, so that one cannot distinguish between the truth and fiction that is cathected with affect'.[8] This realization prompted him to conclude that, as regards neurosis, 'psychical reality was of more importance than material reality'.[9]

Perhaps the most well-known example of a psychological impulse which obscures and conceals is the concept of *Verdrängung* or 'defence' or 'repression'. The term was already in use in nineteenth-century psychology, for example, by Herbart, but is assigned a particular and central role in Freud's system. The essence of repression, Freud avers, '*lies simply in turning something away, and keeping it at a distance, from the conscious*'.[10] It is a form of 'psychical censorship' which operates both at large (where there is 'psychical equilibrium') in the formation of dreams and, more specifically, in the formation of neuroses (cases of 'psychical disturbance'), such as anxiety hysteria, where, for example, fear of an animal is the conscious manifestation of an unconscious, libidinal and fearful perception of the patient's father. The theory of repression is supported by the 'pleasure principle': the course of mental events 'takes a direction such that its final outcome coincides with . . . an avoidance of unpleasure or a production of pleasure'.[11] We forget so many facts of our external and internal lives, Freud suggests, because they are distressing or shameful or painful. However, it is possible for the analyst to make the patient translate and express them in some way. As he declares in his 'Autobiographical Study', in order to make an experience conscious again,

> it was necessary to overcome something that fought against one in the patient; it was necessary to make efforts on one's own part so as to urge and compel him to remember . . . The expenditure of force on the part of the physician was evidently the measure of a resistance on the part of the patient. It was only necessary to translate into words what I myself had observed, and I was in possession of the theory of repression.[12]

The text representing Freud is an abridged version of 'The Unconscious'. It is the clearest and most forthright exposition of both his concept of 'the unconscious' and his understanding of the relation between repression and language. The essay is one of the five surviving metapsychological papers from 1915. Studies of Freud's correspondence suggest that a further seven were completed during the year but later destroyed by him.[13] The difference between conscious and unconscious presentations, and 'what it is that repression denies to the rejected presentation in the transference neuroses', Freud argues, is 'translation into words which shall remain attached to the object. A presentation which is not put into words, or a psychical act which is not hypercathected, remains thereafter in the [unconscious] in a state of repression.' At issue here are 'considerations of representability': the way in which a word or phrase might find expression and re-presentation in an image or vice versa, and, most importantly, the shifts in emphasis and meaning which occur with the transition from one medium to another. 'Displacement' refers to the process of conversion which leads from one idea to another, and 'condensation' acknowledges that it is the very 'pouring of the content of a thought into another mould' which creates connections that 'might not otherwise have been present'.[14] The relationship between word and thing or concept and image is thus the axis of exchange between the conscious and the unconscious in Freud's system.

The technical term 'cathexis' is prominent in the final section of 'The Unconscious' and requires explanation. It is an important word for Freud: it reflects the shift in his thought from positivist neurology to a more interpretive psychology, and is vital to his theory of repression. 'Cathexis' is a translation, invented by Strachey (the overseeing editor of the English *Standard Edition* of Freud's works), of the original German *Besetzung*, meaning 'filling' or 'occupation' (as by troops) or 'charge' (as in electrical charge). Strachey's translation is derived from the Greek *catechein*, meaning 'to occupy'. The introduction of the concept in pyschology follows the positivist neurological discovery that the nervous system consists of chains of neurones and the inference that mental processes correspond to material quanta.

Freud grew up and worked in positivist Vienna, and so could not help but be influenced by the philosophy. As Strachey notes, Freud often relies on phrases such as '*mit Energie ausgestattet*' ('supplied with energy') and '*mit einer Erregungssumme behaftet*' ('loaded with a sum of excitation').[15] In 'The Neuro-Psychoses of Defence' (1894), Freud suggests that 'in mental functioning something is to be distinguished – a quota of affect or sum of excitation – which possesses all the characteristics of a quantity (though we have no means of measuring it), which is . . . spread over the memory-traces of ideas somewhat as an electric charge is spread over the surface of a body'.[16] However, as Freud's research led him away from identifying traumas with particular neurological events to associating them with structures of meaning around events, so his use of terms such as 'cathexis' and 'cathectic energy' became more theoretical or even metaphorical; they became, in effect, abstract ways of describing the extent to which ideas *occupy* the mind. Thus, in *The Interpretation of Dreams*, a *neglected* line of thought is one which has '*not received*' cathectic energy, a *repressed* idea is one from which cathexis 'has been *withdrawn*', and a 'purposive cathexis' is a particular idea which 'is capable of attracting the attention of consciousness to itself'.[17] This 'drawing attention to oneself' or 'becoming prominent', Freud terms 'hypercathexis'. We might understand 'cathexis' in general then to refer to the propensity of an idea to appear before consciousness.

Here, Freud shares phenomenology's interest in intentionality or object-directedness: consciousness is necessarily consciousness of something. Enfolded within every moment of consciousness are the binary elements of subjective awareness and *the something* which that awareness is awareness of. Although normally ascribed to Brentano, the concept of intentionality has its roots in Kant's Transcendental Deduction and his attempt to show how the experiential divide between subject and object originally opens. The conditions of possibility of subjectivity, Kant asserts, are, at one and the same time, the conditions of possibility of objectivity. Compare this with Freud's suggestion that 'we form the idea of there being an original libidinal cathexis of the ego, from which some is later given off to objects, but which fundamentally persists and is related to the object-cathexes much as the body of an amoeba is related to the pseudopodia which it puts out'.[18] Freud ultimately identifies cathexis with his concept of libido, the energy of the sexual instincts present, he maintains, from the beginning in every individual's life.[19] This is on the basis that sexual instinct is itself a form of object-directedness, the highest form of which is 'the state of being in love, when the subject seems to give up his own personality in favour of an object-cathexis'.[20]

Is it the case that Freud relies too heavily on the free association of ideas? Every idea can be associated with something, so how can psychoanalysis claim to be the objective assessment of a latent, original content? Freud does consider this objection. Association is never free in the sense that it is random or arbitrary. We can only ever exclude ideas 'that are *known* to us'.[21] Once we have done this, 'unknown' or 'unconscious' ideas take over. It is through apparently superficial or easy-going associations that 'the resistance of censorship' is made manifest. The jump from one idea to another is a thick and complex transformation, comparable to 'the problem of representing in pictures a leading article from a political newspaper' (Freud's analogy)[22] or to giving an aesthetic description of an artwork. Through association and conceptual translation, we test the recalcitrance of ideas, and it is these textures of meaning which define the psyche for Freud.

It is the importance Freud assigns to interpretation which has made his theory of the self so influential in the arts: the meanings we attach to events are generated when experiences are brought into relation or undergo transformation through representation. To appreciate this point, one only has to consider how placing two objects side by side creates a network of similarities and differences which affects how each of the two objects is perceived. Art and literature therefore become paradigm forms of experience for psychoanalysis, since they are discourses which create significance through juxtaposition and which require interpretation.

Jacques Lacan

Freud's work was brought to a wider audience and subject to radical interpretation through the seminars of Jacques Lacan (1901–81), France's most controversial psychoanalyst. Lacan never held an academic post and, until 1966, had published only one book – his doctoral thesis of 1932 – but achieved prominence through the weekly public seminars he began in Paris in 1953. Reluctantly, he published a selection of seminar transcripts in 1966, entitled *Écrits*, and five thousand copies were sold within a fortnight. His popularity, however, cannot be divorced from his notoriety. The flouting of conventions established by the Société Psychoanalytique de Paris, his staunch opposition to orthodox ego psychology, and the frequent opacity of his prose were all causes of friction between Lacan and other members of the psychoanalytic community.

Lacan 'returns to Freud' in order to revitalize his key concepts, including the unconscious. Recognition of the subversive and revolutionary nature of Freud's ideas, Lacan asserts, has been inhibited by American ego psychology's emphasis on the self as a unified and homogeneous whole. Lacan reinvigorates Freud to present the self as a necessarily divided entity: an opening onto or an intertwinement with that which is other than itself.

Two major influences on Lacan are Hegel and structuralism. The anthropologist Claude Lévi-Strauss, in his *Elementary Structures of Kinship* (1949),[23] showed how Saussure's structural theory of relations applied not just to language but also to broader patterns of social behaviour and organization. This had the effect of making structuralism a very attractive theoretical position across the humanities. What, to conventional, empirical methods of analysis, appeared as an external form masking internal, unexplained organization, for example, sexual taboos, the unconscious, could be represented by structuralism as a series of differences and relationships which held explanatory potential for an individual's or community's entire behaviour.

Hegel's philosophy was also prevalent in post-war France, following the seminars given in Paris during the 1930s by the Russian philosopher Alexandre Kojève on his *Phenomenology of Spirit*. His interpretation emphasized the master–slave analogy (or lordship–bondage in the Miller translation) used by Hegel to illustrate the dependence relations which exist between consciousness (master) and its object (slave) in the dialectic. The dialectical relationship which Hegel draws between consciousness and its object means that, as consciousness works towards the *telos* of Absolute Spirit, it is perpetually defining itself against its object. However, a moment of otherness is created by perception, he argues, when it realizes that the object is other than consciousness has judged it to be, giving self-consciousness the structure of Desire: desire for an otherness which is opposite to it but which, given the dynamic nature of the dialectic, necessarily eludes it. 'Self-consciousness', Hegel writes, 'is Desire' since it is 'certain of itself only by superseding this other that presents itself to self-consciousness as an independent life', but the very act of supersession only generates a new otherness.[24]

Desire is a vital category for Lacan. It plays an ontological role, signifying the necessarily split, transitive order of the subject, as opposed to a state of need which can be readily satisfied. His synthesis of structuralism and Hegelian dialectic creates a psychoanalysis which theorizes subjectivity as an event – a dynamic or a series of transformations – which takes place within a framework of differences, and which is motivated by an insatiable appetite for otherness. A good demonstration of this is the thinking behind Lacan's claim that 'what the psychoanalytic experience discovers in the unconscious is the whole structure of language'.[25] Metaphor and metonymy, Lacan argues, exemplify the Hegelian–structuralist thesis that meaning is not the stable relationship between a signifier and a signified but the condition of play whereby one signifier always summons another, and in 'The Agency of the Letter in the Unconscious or Reason since Freud', he identifies metaphor and metonymy with Freud's concepts of condensation and displacement respectively.[26] Metaphor is the linguistic device which describes one thing in the terms of another, for example, 'love is a battlefield', 'time is a river', and corresponds to the image of pouring one content into the mould of another which Freud used to define the condensation of ideas. The process of displacement, where one idea leads to another, Lacan suggests, can be likened to metonymy, whereby the name of part of a thing is substituted for the name of the whole, or vice versa, for example, 'crown' for 'monarch' (part for whole) or the name of a country given as the name of its football team (whole for part). It is the continual metaphoric and metonymic transformation from one idea to the next, without the possibility of a resting place or a 'home' concept, which prompts Lacan to situate the unconscious as a linguistic faculty of desire.

The emphasis on 'being as transformation' goes some way towards explaining the density of Lacan's prose. Writing, in contrast to the 'vitality' – the flow, interruptions, and digressions – of the spoken seminar, he maintains, introduces 'the kind of tightening up that I like in order to leave the reader no other way out than the way in, which I prefer to be difficult'.[27] Difficulty is cultivated because the reader is compelled to endure the action of constraint which, it is claimed, represents the passage to understanding and new interpretation. 'Passage' can be taken in its spatial, architectural sense here, especially given the 'corridor' metaphor ('no other way out than the way in') implicit in the quotation. We might picture new meaning sparking from the surface-to-surface friction created as we edge our way along the walls of a confined space. The sexual nature of this imagery is considered by Luce Irigaray below.

Two observations can also be made with regard to the metaphorical properties of art, in the name of an aesthetics of the unconscious. First, surrealism is a highly metaphorical form of composition: the placing of incompatible objects side by side or the conversion of one object into something else. Vanguard surrealists included, in painting, René Magritte, Giorgio de Chirico, and Salvador Dali and, in literature, André Breton, Louis Aragon, and Paul Eluard. They drew on Freud for inspiration and, in turn, were themselves admired by the young Lacan. However, Freud himself dismissed them as 'complete fools'.[28] Second, art's *fundamentally* metaphorical nature is demonstrated by Nietzsche in 'On Truth and Lie in an Extra-Moral Sense'. For Nietzsche, art is metaphorical not just in terms of the juxtaposition of images, but through the substitution of media involved in the creative process, for example, the transition from object, to gesture, to mark in the action of drawing. Nietzsche's claim is part of a larger argument to establish art as the truest from of knowledge. The relation between perception and the world, he declares, is itself metaphorical, as there is no one-to-one correspondence between the world as it is and the world as we experience it to be. Metaphoricity makes art one of the activities through which the subject negotiates her position (with Nietzsche) in a world without preordained truth and (with Lacan) in a world whose otherness, in part, defines her.

The featured essay from Lacan, 'Of the Gaze as *Objet Petit a*', is from *Four Fundamental Concepts of Psychoanalysis.* First published in 1973, the book is the transcript of the seminar he gave at the École Normale Supérieure in Paris between January and June 1964. 'Of the Gaze' does not focus on any one of the four concepts in particular (the drive, repetition, transference, and the unconscious) but implicates them all in its analysis of vision. The essay shows how painting and the gaze have desire as their basic structure, and draws on the phenomenology of Merleau-Ponty to situate vision as a decentred opening onto the world, in opposition to the Renaissance and Cartesian concept of vision as the distant, objective surveillance conducted by a centred, autonomous ego. Lacan in fact acknowledges the 'happy coincidence' (*tuchē*) of receiving 'a copy of the newly published, posthumous work of [his] friend Maurice Merleau-Ponty', *The Visible and the Invisible*, in the same week as he was giving the seminar.[29]

Lacan does not define the term '*objet petit a*'. By remaining untranslated, he believes, it acquires the status of an algebraic sign or 'matheme'. This reflects the conviction, held in the last decade of his life, that the fundamental claims of psychoanalysis could be formalized mathematically. A definition is possible, however. '*Objet petit a*' denotes any specific thing which can become an object of desire. The '*a*' stands for '*autre*' (other) and '*petit a*' (small 'a') distinguishes the particular other from the '*Autre*' or '*grand Autre*' (the capitalized Other) which denotes the Hegelian, ontological condition of otherness in general. 'The gaze' (or 'the look') is a concept from Sartre's existentialism which attaches significance to the fact that, in Lacan's words, 'I see only from one point, but in my existence I am looked at from all sides'.[30] The concept, for Sartre, refers principally to the reproachful glance which another person gives me and which makes me aware of myself as an object for the other person. The notion holds wider significance in that it displays the 'that which sees is also seen' structure used by phenomenology to unfold subjectivity and objectivity from the singular, intentional fabric of experience.

Vision introduces the question of how our desire interacts with the desire of others and how we recognize their desire. By having my being defined through my relation with otherness and, therefore, other people and things, I myself am implicated in the order which, in turn, gives definition to those people and things. As Lacan puts it, 'man's desire is the desire of the Other'.[31] Any account, whether structural or dialectical, which makes subjectivity and objectivity poles in a relationship needs to include a component of resistance or texture in order to maintain some difference between them, to prevent them from collapsing into one another. If, Lacan asks,

> it is merely at the level of the desire of the Other that man can recognize his desire, as desire of the Other, is there not something here that must appear to him to be an obstacle to his fading, which is a point at which his desire can never be recognized? This obstacle is never lifted, nor ever to be lifted, for analytic experience shows us that it is in seeing a whole chain come into play at the level of the desire of the Other that the subject's desire is constituted.[32]

To extend the analogy: the *objet petit a*, Lacan will argue in 'Of the Gaze', is a link in the chain. Vision is a part of desire since it is an opening onto otherness, and '*objet petit a*' denotes those items in experience and in art which let us see the moment when objects *give themselves to vision* (*le donner-à-voir*), as illustrated, for example, by *trompe l'œil* (deceiving the eye) paintings and, from Lacan's anecdote, a gleam of light off a sardine can floating in the sea. What has to be recognized is that this 'giving itself to vision' is not a singular act of generosity but one of many which perpetuate a dependence relation between consciousness and the other; it does not satiate the appetite of the eye but, rather, creates the tension which ensures that vision cannot collapse into itself.

There are, as Lacan admits, clear parallels between his and Merleau-Ponty's accounts of vision. Sight is not a window onto a ready-made world, Merleau-Ponty avers, but a 'resistance' or 'thickness' which manifests the disclosive, intentional structure of experience. However, his friend withdraws from his enquiry, Lacan suggests, and takes refuge in the concept of 'the flesh of the world' as an 'original point of vision', whereas the psychoanalyst wants to maintain a sense of rupture or loss as the foundation of his epistemology. But this criticism is unfair. The remainder of Lacan's study adheres quite closely to Merleau-Ponty's revised phenomenological dictum, 'that which sees *cannot be seen*', even down to using one of his most distinctive metaphors for perception: 'the point of the gaze always participates in the ambiguity of the jewel'.[33] These themes are developed below in Luce Irigaray's feminist critique of vision in Merleau-Ponty's philosophy.

Julia Kristeva

Feminist philosophy plays a vital role in Continental aesthetics' challenging of traditional conceptual boundaries. It proposes new forms of thought within, and sometimes against, the horizons of experience opened up by psychoanalysis, phenomenology, and poststructuralism. Psychoanalysis occupies a key position in the evolution of feminism. First, it provides feminism with a revolutionary theory of subjectivity, where meaning is shown not to reside in certain privileged terms (i.e., patriarchal) but to occur through material, metaphorical transformation. And second, it identifies fundamental aspects of our being, for example, language and our general openness to the world, with sexuality. For example, the Oedipus complex, identified by Freud, is transformed by Lacan into a theory of language. In the Oedipus complex, the original, intimate relationship between boy-child and mother is broken when the child realizes that it has to compete with the father for his mother's affections. The three-way relationship between father, mother, and child, Lacan suggests, is the order of language or, to give it Lacan's technical phrase, the 'symbolic order'. Since the subject (the child) now has to negotiate with and through a third term (the father and, by analogy, the word) to achieve contact with what was once directly and reciprocally in front of him (the mother and, by analogy, external reality), a situation with a linguistic structure comes into being.

There are various kinds of feminism: liberal, Marxist, socialist, psychoanalytic, existentialist, and radical. One of the main distinctions which can be drawn is between those feminists who demand equality with men and those who challenge the structures of thought which frame the debate. The former is the liberal feminist viewpoint, whereas the latter is shared by different positions, e.g., existentialist, psychoanalytic, for which 'radical feminism' often serves as the collective noun. To seek equality, the radicals claim against the liberals, is to seek equality *on male terms*. Addressing the role and the identity of women as issues in isolation, they continue, fails to acknowledge that positions in the debate have been determined by a history of thought which is male-dominated, i.e., patriarchal. It is this order which must be addressed if the concept of 'woman' is to become something more than the obverse of 'man'.

Julia Kristeva, Luce Irigaray, and Hélène Cixous are leading figures in contemporary French radical feminism. Within this, however, they work from different and, at times, diametrically opposed viewpoints. Both Irigaray and Cixous entertain the notion of an *écriture feminine* or 'feminine writing' which embodies a new, differential and tactile approach to language. The importance given to the body by psychoanalysis as an object under interpretation is used by Irigaray to turn texts in the history of philosophy against themselves, drawing organic, textured language from arguments which outwardly try to suppress the epistemological significance of the body. The form and status of writing are also paramount for Cixous. Of the three, her style conforms the least to the conventions of the philosophy essay. Primarily a novelist, she experiments with literary style and subverts the accepted conventions of narrative to restore materiality to the text and to generate new ways of representing physical, bodily experience. Kristeva, though, avoids the notion of a feminine writing: it reaffirms the binary division between the masculine and the feminine, she claims, and, as such, only serves to reinforce patriarchy's commitment to essentialist, categorial thought. Instead, she offers a way of glimpsing an order of signification that is unconscious and therefore anterior to patriarchy by examining Lacan's Oedipal theory of meaning through the lens of structuralist linguistics.

Julia Kristeva (b. 1941) came to Paris from Bulgaria as a student in 1965, and straight away became involved in the city's intellectual life, attending the seminars of Roland Barthes and mixing with the literary avant-garde. Her interest in the ideas of Barthes and Lacan is synthesized in her structuralist interpretation of Lacan's claim that the unconscious is organized like a language. She draws on Lacan's distinction between the pre-Oedipal 'imaginary' and the post-Oedipal 'symbolic' stages in the development of a child's awareness. The imaginary is the period of transition from the child's not being able to distinguish where he ends and his mother begins to the realization that he is an object in the world among others. This shift in perception is brought about by the child recognizing a divide between the openness or incompleteness of his subjectivity and the outlined wholeness of his image in a mirror (the 'mirror stage'). However, the imaginary is not something which is over and done with in a matter of months. Instead, it remains with the individual throughout adulthood as the principle of wanting to identify oneself with an image. Because it is prior to the symbolic, the imaginary represents a domain of potential meaning that is prior to any knowledge of linguistic division and gender specificity. It is the manner in which the imaginary breaks through and disrupts the symbolic which interests Kristeva. She adopts the term 'semiotic' to refer to the prelinguistic, generative aspect of the imaginary. Rather than propose a category of writing peculiar to the feminine, Kristeva directs our attention to the occasions in writing when meaning or a particular theme breaks down, for these are the moments, she argues, when the binary divisions, including the division between the masculine and the feminine, are contravened. In all of this, *biological differences between the sexes are not denied.* Rather, it is the values and associations which are used to make sense of the distinction – 'What is a man? What is a woman?' – and the larger network of concepts and beliefs to which they belong that are being challenged.

In her later work, Kristeva considers the interplay between the semiotic and the symbolic by looking at different kinds of personal and aesthetic experience. *Powers of Horror* (1980) focuses on the abject: the experience of being repelled or disgusted by the thing in front of us, for example, the smell of rotting flesh or our lips touching the skin on the surface of milk. Abjection lets us see how everyday, symbolic understanding intersects with those experiences which have been deleted from acceptability. 'Approaching Abjection', the opening chapter of *Powers of Horror*, gives tasters of the essays on avant-garde, modernist literature which make up the greater part of the book. The texts of Dostoyevsky, Proust, Joyce, Artaud, and Céline, through their content and style, Kristeva claims, skirt 'the boundary of what is assimilable, thinkable: abject'. They show how conventional, symbolic representation can retrace 'the fragile limits of the speaking being, closest to its [semiotic] dawn'.

Comparisons can be drawn between the abject and the Kantian sublime. Both, as extreme forms of experience, overwhelm us and temporarily remove our identity, remove the distinction between subject and object. The sublime in Kant is a moment of excess which allows the imagination to become aware of its own power to organize experience, and the abject, in Kristeva's analysis, is experienced at its strongest when the subject is thrown back from its object to the 'impossibility within' which constitutes desire, the basis of the subject's relationship with all objects. Perception, as desire, gives the object (the *objet a* in Lacan's terminology) to the subject but the subject, who wants to identify itself with the object, doesn't find itself there and, instead, loses itself. Repugnance, Kristeva declares, 'keeps the subject from floundering'.

Luce Irigaray

Whereas Kristeva accepts the Oedipal structure given to language by Lacan, Luce Irigaray (b. 1930) argues that Freud's and Lacan's positions are themselves products of patriarchal thought. As she observes, the Oedipus complex applies first and foremost to the *boy*-child's relationship with the mother, and the penis is the organ which co-ordinates sexuality for both men and women in the works of Freud and Lacan. In the sense that a sign stands for something which is absent, the penis or 'phallus' (the term used in this wider, linguistic context) is seen by Lacan as the sign that stands for the child's pre-Oedipal relationship with the mother which has been lost and, therefore, becomes representative of language in general. Language, including Freudian and Lacanian psychoanalysis, Irigaray asserts, is 'phallocentric'. The reflexive nature of Irigaray's argument – that the charge of language's male-centredness itself rests upon the male-centred Oedipus complex – is in keeping with her interest in deconstruction. A deconstructive reading of a text searches out those moments when images or distinctions turn against or contradict themselves and, in a similar fashion, Irigaray applies the principles and methods of psychoanalysis to philosophical texts in order to subvert their meaning. Arguments, and the images they rely upon, are subject to metaphorical interpretation in order to disclose repressed, unconscious orders of signification which can begin to constitute a feminine writing. Irigaray and Lacan had worked closely together at the University of Paris at Vincennes, but her charge of phallocentrism against psychoanalysis, made in *Speculum of the Other Woman* (1974), prompted Lacan to terminate her lectureship. Shunned also by the other major universities, she nevertheless retained her position and received support from the students at the Centre National de la Recherche Scientifique.

The main claim made by radical feminism against patriarchal knowledge is that it takes truth to be a one-to-one correspondence between statement and world. In any situation, it is assumed, there can be only one true description, and the fit between object and description will be independent of subjective and historical perspectives. Against this, radical feminist philosophy argues for a form of knowledge which accommodates difference. Knowledge, it is argued, is necessarily made from a perspective and thus there will be different accounts of a situation dependent upon the various speakers' points of view. Kant's claim that the possibility of objective description is created by subjective conditions of possibility is evident here. Furthermore, in a hermeneutic vein, knowledge can be generated through the dialogue which occurs between the different positions. In this regard, the body is a vital object for radical feminist thought because it is always an object under interpretation. There are biological differences between the male and female body but the differences are not meaningful in themselves. Rather, they are constructed and appointed (either positive or negative) relative to a culture and its value system. Thus, the body, as a network of differences in need of evaluation and description, becomes a model for a theory which seeks to show how a respect for difference can be accommodated in the construction of knowledge.

The body is a prominent theme in Irigaray's writing for this reason, and also for the importance she attaches to the epistemological value of the different senses. Sight, she claims, is consistent with patriarchal forms of knowledge in that it is the sense which gives the impression that everything is transparently open to inspection and can be grasped in an instant. In *This Sex Which Is Not One* (1977), she asserts that the penis, although sensitive to touch, is primarily a visual object – erect, upright, clearly open to view – and, as such, stands as the Platonic ideal of the one, true object of knowledge. The vagina, in contrast, is an immanently tactile organ: it 'represents *the horror of nothing to see*' but 'this incompleteness of form . . . allows her organ to touch itself over and over again' and 'no one can forbid her to do so, for her genitals are formed of two lips in continuous contact'.[34] Touch becomes a metaphor for the kind of writing which, on Irigaray's terms, is feminine. The writing of women, she argues, does not 'privilege sight' but takes 'each figure back to its source, which is among other things *tactile*. It comes back in touch with itself in that origin without ever constituting in it, constituting itself in it, as some sort of unity.'[35] Whereas phallocentric structures of thought treat concepts as unities which can grasp and fix their objects in a singular, definitional fashion, Irigaray urges us to regard concepts as fluid and textural: 'those rubbings between two infinitely near neighbours that create a dynamics'.[36] Metaphor, as the transformation or *passage* from one concept to another and as a disrupter of proper, definitional usage, is a paradigm form of feminine discourse. In this respect, the radical feminist project can be allied with the phenomenological assault made on established conceptual hierarchies in the name of metaphor by Nietzsche and Heidegger.

Two surfaces in contact – the toucher and the touched – is a crucial image in Merleau-Ponty's phenomenology. It illustrates the thick yet folded materiality which makes the body the original 'opening' of the intentional structure of experience. There is a lot in Merleau-Ponty's work which supports Irigaray's writing, for example, he redefines the body as a form of access to the world which challenges traditional, object-centred categories. The contest between sight and touch in his 'The Intertwining – The Chiasm' is the focus of Irigaray's study in 'The Invisible of the Flesh', one of a series of lectures given at the Erasmus University in Rotterdam in 1982. She draws attention to some of the tensions in his writing, where he is working against the 'divisionary' tendencies in subject–object language, and rewords them as 'performances' of radical feminist epistemology. For example, Merleau-Ponty's description of one hand touching another is transformed by Irigaray into a situation where there is no object or subject:

> With no passive or active, or even middle-passive. A sort of fourth mode? Neither active, nor passive, nor middle-passive. Always more passive than the passive. And nevertheless active. The hands joined, palms together, fingers outstretched, constitute a very particular touching. A gesture often reserved for women (at least in the West) and which evokes, doubles, the *touching of the lips* silently applied upon one another.

The status of Irigaray's article in relation to Merleau-Ponty's is interesting. On the one hand, it could be objected that a close-reading of a Merleau-Ponty essay is not really representative of Irigaray's own thought or, worse still, places her in a subordinate position. On the other, integrated, contact-driven discussion – speaking directly to others as opposed to being a single voice – is a paradigm form of feminist 'tactile' writing. Is she criticizing his thesis, upbraiding him for gaps and oversights in his argument, or providing a much more conversational, excursive response, a meditation that refrains from binary 'for or against' judgement? She does claim that he 'accords an exorbitant privilege to vision' but, in Merleau-Ponty's favour, this is because, of all the senses, sight is the one which does the most to divide up the world into individual, external objects and, therefore, is the hardest to redescribe in phenomenological, pre-objective terms. Ultimately, Irigaray's position in relation to Merleau-Ponty is not to be decided here, other than to say that the way we, as interpreters, assess how ideas emerge with or against or from others becomes an important contribution in a climate where the very status of thought and verbal exchange are at issue.

Hélène Cixous

Radical feminism already makes us wary of using categories such as 'linguist' or 'psychoanalyst' to sum up its authors, but the writings of Hélène Cixous (b. 1937) make the task of classification especially difficult. Cixous' *écriture feminine* takes a variety of forms: novels, stories, fictions, theatre, essays, theory, and criticism. She uses the style and format of writing to transgress the binary distinctions of Western, phallocentric thought: by making the form of her work as significant as its content, her texts acquire a contingency and a particularity which eludes existent conceptual divisions. Professionalism and the culture of the expert dictate that you become adept *at one thing* but Cixous shrugs this off, cultivating instead the innocence of marking, scribbling, jotting down in an attempt to achieve a state of 'knowing how not to know', knowing how not to know in phallocentric terms.

The insight that comes from employing different media and styles itself becomes the object of speculation in 'The Last Painting or the Portrait of God'. The 1986 essay, one of Cixous' more discursive pieces, compares painting and writing as forms of representation. 'I would like to write like a painter. I would like to write like painting,' she announces at the start. Fidelity is her principal concern: 'fidelity to what exists . . . In painting as in writing, there is no other "beauty" than fidelity to what is.' Painting, she claims, can submit us to process, 'can let things come through' whereas language is 'troubled by phrases already heard a thousand times'. What ensures fidelity, she argues, is a sense of dissatisfaction and primarily, for the artist or writer, dissatisfaction with her medium. The 'last painting' in Cixous' title is based on a quotation from the expressionist painter and writer Oskar Kokoschka and refers to the level of perception that is achieved in the last painting of a long series: the repetition the artist has to go through before the representation of water lilies ceases to be mere representation and the distinction between subject and object, perceiver and perceived, disappears, leaving only 'the day's atom on the canvas'. But this moment will always elude us; the painting will always be *the next one*. There is the rule, Cixous observes, that repetition in writing is bad form, but it is the right to repeat that she wants to claim for writing: 'to repeat the word until it becomes dry orange-skin'. This would approach a portrait of God, a portrait 'of what escapes us and makes us wonder'.

On the one hand, Cixous' account of painting is somewhat idealized or romanticized. A lot of what she writes comes from the fact that, as she admits, she is not a painter: 'I can't nourish your eyes with mimosa light. So I beg you: please, see the mimosas that I see. Imagine the mimosas. See what you don't see, out of love for me'. Painting, though, is not as direct and immediate as Cixous assumes. Every medium has its own materiality – its structures of possibility and resistance – which cannot help but alter and redirect the moment. Even the task of recreating a colour throws the painter into a complex state of negotiation with her medium. On the other hand, Cixous' essay is an expression of the desire for fulfilment which an artist from one background feels in response to the work of an artist from another. It is the hope or promise which an artist sees in another way of working that intrigues her. 'Would I love this way', Cixous asks, 'if I were a painter?' She transforms the incompleteness of her medium (the written word) into a plea for greater attentiveness to our own incompleteness and to the 'hope for the impossible' which arises from dissatisfaction.

Comparisons can be drawn between Cixous' essay and Sartre's 'What is Writing?' above.

Cixous' initial assertion of the immediacy of painting stands in direct contrast to Sartre's claim for its obstructive materiality; the visual image, he avows, possesses a thinghood which distracts the viewer from their commitment to worldly activity, whereas language is transparent and passes the reader onto the world. However, with the equivocation that appears later in Cixous' paper, when both painting and writing are shown as incomplete, the two thinkers' ideas are, for a time, parallel. As Roquentin realizes at the end of Sartre's novel *Nausea*, the impossibility of full and final description is not an indication of the futility of language but, rather, a dynamic which motivates the author to generate new forms of expression.

Notes

1 Sigmund Freud, 'The Claims of Psycho-Analysis to Scientific Interest', *Totem and Taboo, Standard Edition of the Complete Psychological Works of Sigmund Freud* XIII, ed. James Strachey, London, Hogarth Press, 1974, p. 165. All further references to this edition of Freud's works abbreviated to *SE*.
2 Quoted by Jonathan Miller, 'Going Unconscious', *Hidden Histories of Science*, ed. Robert B. Silvers, London, Granta, 1997, p. 19.
3 For example, Hume writes: 'When my perceptions are remov'd for any time, as by sound sleep; so long am I insensible of myself, and may truly be said not to exist'; David Hume, *A Treatise of Human Nature* (1739), ed. L.A. Selby-Bigge, Oxford, Clarendon Press, 1978, p. 252.
4 See Daniel N. Robinson, *An Intellectual History of Psychology*, New York, Macmillan, 1981, pp. 326–42.
5 Freud, 'The Unconscious', *Papers on Metapsychology*, *SE* XIV, p. 171.
6 Freud, *The Interpretation of Dreams, Part 2*, *SE* V, p. 613, original emphasis.
7 A full account is given in 'Project for a Scientific Psychology' (1895), *SE* I, pp. 353–56.
8 Freud, 'Fliess Papers: Letter 69, September 21, 1897', *SE* I, p. 260.
9 Freud, 'Autobiographical Study', *SE* XX, p. 34.
10 Freud, 'Repression', *SE* XIV, p. 147.
11 Freud, *Beyond the Pleasure Principle*, *SE* XVIII, p. 7. See also 'Instincts and Their Vicissitudes', *SE* XIV, p. 121 n. and 'Repression', pp. 146–53.
12 Freud, 'Autobiographical Study', p. 29.
13 Strachey recounts this at *SE* XIV, pp. 105–06.
14 Freud, *The Interpretation of Dreams, Part 2*, p. 344.
15 Strachey, 'Editor's Introduction', *SE* II, p. xxiii.
16 Freud, *SE* III, p. 60.
17 Freud, *The Interpretation of Dreams, Part 2*, p. 594.
18 Freud, *SE* XIV, pp. 75–79.
19 See, for example, 'On Narcissism: An Introduction', *SE* XIV, p. 75, and 'Repression', p. 152.
20 Freud, 'On Narcissism', p. 76.
21 Freud, *The Interpretation of Dreams, Part 2*, p. 528.
22 Different versions of the analogy can be found at ibid., p. 340 and 'A Metapsychological Supplement to the Theory of Dreams', *SE* XIV, p. 228 n.
23 Claude Lévi-Strauss, *The Elementary Structures of Kinship*, trans. J.H. Bell and John von Sturmer, Boston, Beacon Press, 1969.
24 G.W.F. Hegel, *Phenomenology of Spirit*, trans. A.V. Miller, Oxford, Oxford University Press, 1977, para. 174, p. 108.
25 Jacques Lacan, 'The Agency of the Letter in the Unconscious or Reason since Freud', *Écrits: A Selection*, trans. Alan Sheridan, London, Tavistock, 1977, p. 147.
26 Ibid., p. 160.
27 Ibid., p. 146.
28 Sigmund Freud, letter of 20 July 1938 to Stefan Zweig, *Letters of Sigmund Freud 1873–1939*, ed. Ernest L. Freud, trans. Tania and James Stern, London, Hogarth Press, 1961, p. 444, and quoted by David

Macey in his Introduction to *Four Fundamental Concepts of Psychoanalysis*, trans. Alan Sheridan, London, Vintage, 1977, p. xv.

29 Jacques Lacan, 'The Eye and the Gaze', *Four Fundamental Concepts*, p. 71. This first section from 'Of the Gaze as *Objet Petit a*' has not been included.

30 Ibid., p. 72.

31 Lacan, *Four Fundamental Concepts*, p. 38.

32 Ibid., p. 235.

33 Merleau-Ponty writes:

> All knowledge takes its place within the horizons opened up by perception. There can be no question of describing perception itself as one of the facts thrown up in the world, since we can never fill up, in the picture of the world, that gap which we ourselves are, and by which it comes into existence for someone, since perception is the 'flaw' in this 'great diamond'.

See *Phenomenology of Perception*, trans. Colin Smith, London, Routledge, 1978, p. 207.

34 Luce Irigaray, *This Sex Which Is Not One*, trans. Catherine Porter, Ithaca, New York, Cornell University Press, 1985, pp. 24, 26.

35 Ibid., p. 79.

36 Ibid., p. 79.

31

THE UNCONSCIOUS

Sigmund Freud

We have learnt from psycho-analysis that the essence of the process of repression lies, not in putting an end to, in annihilating, the idea which represents an instinct, but in preventing it from becoming conscious. When this happens we say of the idea that it is in a state of being 'unconscious',[1] and we can produce good evidence to show that even when it is unconscious it can produce effects, even including some which finally reach consciousness. Everything that is repressed must remain unconscious; but let us state at the very outset that the repressed does not cover everything that is unconscious. The unconscious has the wider compass: the repressed is a part of the unconscious.

How are we to arrive at a knowledge of the unconscious? It is of course only as something conscious that we know it, after it has undergone transformation or translation into something conscious. Psycho-analytic work shows us every day that translation of this kind is possible. In order that this should come about, the person under analysis must overcome certain resistances – the same resistances as those which, earlier, made the material concerned into something repressed by rejecting it from the conscious.

I Justification for the concept of the unconscious

Our right to assume the existence of something mental that is unconscious and to employ that assumption for the purposes of scientific work is disputed in many quarters. To this we can reply that our assumption of the unconscious is *necessary* and *legitimate*, and that we possess numerous proofs of its existence.

It is *necessary* because the data of consciousness have a very large number of gaps in them; both in healthy and in sick people psychical acts often occur which can be explained only by presupposing other acts, of which, nevertheless, consciousness affords no evidence. These not only include parapraxes and dreams in healthy people, and everything described as a psychical symptom or an obsession in the sick; our most personal daily experience acquaints us with ideas that come into our head we do not know from where, and with intellectual conclusions arrived at we do not know how. All these conscious acts remain disconnected and unintelligible if we insist upon claiming that every mental act that occurs in us must also necessarily be experienced by us through consciousness; on the other hand, they fall into a demonstrable connection if we interpolate between them the unconscious acts which we have inferred. A gain in meaning is a perfectly justifiable ground for going beyond the limits of direct experience. When, in addition, it turns out that the assumption of there being an unconscious enables us to construct a successful procedure by which we can exert an effective influence upon the course of conscious processes, this success will have given us an incontrovertible proof of the existence of what we have assumed. This being so, we must adopt the position that to require that whatever goes on in the mind must also be known to consciousness is to make an untenable claim.

We can go further and argue, in support of there being an unconscious psychical state, that at any given moment consciousness includes only a small content, so that the greater part of what we call conscious knowledge must in any case be for very considerable periods of time in a state of latency, that is to say, of being psychically unconscious. When all our latent memories are taken into consideration it becomes totally incomprehensible how the existence of the unconscious can be denied. But here we encounter the objection that these latent recollections can no longer be described as psychical, but that they correspond to residues of somatic processes from which what is psychical can once more arise. The obvious answer to this is that a latent memory is, on the contrary, an unquestionable residuum of a *psychical* process. But it is more important to realize clearly that this objection is based on the equation – not, it is true, explicitly stated but taken as axiomatic – of what is conscious with what is mental. This equation is either a *petitio principii* which begs the question whether everything that is psychical is also necessarily conscious; or else it is a matter of convention, of nomenclature. In this latter case it is, of course, like any other convention, not open to refutation. The question remains, however, whether the convention is so expedient that we are bound to adopt it. To this we may reply that the conventional equation of the psychical with the conscious is totally inexpedient. It disrupts psychical continuities, plunges us into the insoluble difficulties of psycho-physical parallelism,[2] is open to the reproach that for no obvious reason it over-estimates the part played by consciousness, and that it forces us prematurely to abandon the field of psychological research without being able to offer us any compensation from other fields.

It is clear in any case that this question – whether the latent states of mental life, whose existence is undeniable, are to be conceived of as conscious mental states or as physical ones – threatens to resolve itself into a verbal dispute. We shall therefore be better advised to focus our attention on what we know with certainty of the nature of these debatable states. As far as their physical characteristics are concerned, they are totally inaccessible to us: no physiological concept or chemical process can give us any notion of their nature. On the other hand, we know for certain that they have abundant points of contact with conscious mental processes; with the help of a certain amount of work they can be transformed into, or replaced by, conscious mental processes, and all the categories which we employ to describe conscious mental acts, such as ideas, purposes, resolutions and so on, can be applied to them. Indeed, we are obliged to say of some of these latent states that the only respect in which they differ from conscious ones is precisely in the absence of consciousness. Thus we shall not hesitate to treat them as objects of psychological research, and to deal with them in the most intimate connection with conscious mental acts.

The stubborn denial of a psychical character to latent mental acts is accounted for by the circumstance that most of the phenomena concerned have not been the subject of study outside psycho-analysis. Anyone who is ignorant of pathological facts, who regards the parapraxes of normal people as accidental, and who is content with the old saw that dreams are froth [*'Träume sind Schäume'*][3] has only to ignore a few more problems of the psychology of consciousness in order to spare himself any need to assume an unconscious mental activity. Incidentally, even before the time of psycho-analysis, hypnotic experiments, and especially post-hypnotic suggestion, had tangibly demonstrated the existence and mode of operation of the mental unconscious.[4]

The assumption of an unconscious is, moreover, a perfectly *legitimate* one, inasmuch as in postulating it we are not departing a single step from our customary and generally accepted mode of thinking. Consciousness makes each of us aware only of his own states of mind; that other people, too, possess a consciousness is an inference which we draw by analogy from their observable utterances and actions, in order to make this behaviour of theirs intelligible to us. (It would no doubt be psychologically more correct to put it in this way: that without any special reflection we attribute to everyone else our own constitution and therefore our consciousness as well, and that this identification is a *sine qua non* of our understanding.) This inference (or this identification) was formerly extended by the ego to other human beings, to animals, plants, inanimate objects and to the world at large, and proved serviceable so long as their similarity to the individual ego was overwhelmingly great; but it became more untrustworthy in proportion as the difference between the ego and these 'others' widened. To-day, our critical judgement is already in doubt on the question of consciousness in animals; we refuse to admit it in plants and we regard the assumption of its existence in inanimate matter as mysticism. But even where the original inclination to identification has withstood criticism – that is, when the 'others' are our fellow-men – the assumption of a consciousness in them rests upon an inference and cannot share the immediate certainty which we have of our own consciousness.

Psycho-analysis demands nothing more than that we should apply this process of inference to ourselves also – a proceeding to which, it is true, we are not constitutionally inclined. If we do this, we must say: all the acts and manifestations which I notice in myself and do not know how to link up with the rest of my mental life must be judged as if they belonged to someone else: they are to be explained by a mental life ascribed to this other person. Furthermore, experience shows that we understand very well how to interpret in other people (that is, how to fit into their chain of mental events) the same acts which we refuse to acknowledge as being mental in ourselves. Here some special hindrance evidently deflects our investigations from our own self and prevents our obtaining a true knowledge of it.

This process of inference, when applied to oneself in spite of internal opposition, does not, however, lead to the disclosure of an unconscious; it leads logically to the assumption of another, second consciousness which is united in one's self with the consciousness one knows. But at this point, certain criticisms may fairly be made. In the first place, a consciousness of which its own possessor knows nothing is something very different from a consciousness belonging to another person, and it is questionable whether such a consciousness, lacking, as it does, its most important characteristic, deserves any discussion at all. Those who have resisted the assumption of an unconscious *psychical* are not likely to be ready to exchange it for an unconscious *consciousness*. In the second place, analysis shows that the different latent mental processes inferred by us enjoy a high degree of mutual independence, as though they had no connection with one another, and knew nothing of one another. We must be prepared, if so, to assume the existence in us not only of a second consciousness, but of a third, fourth, perhaps of an unlimited number of states of consciousness, all unknown to us and to one another. In the third place – and this is the most weighty argument of all – we have to take into account the fact that analytic investigation reveals some of these latent processes as having characteristics and peculiarities which seem alien to us, or even incredible, and which run directly counter to the attributes of consciousness with which we are familiar. Thus we have grounds for modifying our inference about ourselves and saying that what is proved is not the existence of a second consciousness in us, but the existence of psychical acts which lack consciousness. We shall also be right in rejecting the term 'subconsciousness' as incorrect and misleading.[5] The well-known cases of '*double conscience*'[6] (splitting of consciousness) prove nothing against our view. We may most aptly describe them as cases of a splitting of the mental activities into two groups, and say that the same consciousness turns to one or the other of these groups alternately.

In psycho-analysis there is no choice for us but to assert that mental processes are in themselves unconscious, and to liken the perception of them by means of consciousness to the perception of the external world by means of the sense-organs.[7] We can even hope to gain fresh knowledge from the comparison. The psycho-analytic assumption of unconscious mental activity appears to us, on the one hand, as a further expansion of the primitive animism which caused us to see copies of our own consciousness all around us, and, on the other hand, as an extension of the corrections undertaken by Kant of our views on external perception. Just as Kant warned us not to overlook the fact that our perceptions are subjectively conditioned and must not be regarded as identical with what is perceived though unknowable, so psycho-analysis warns us not to equate perceptions by means of consciousness with the unconscious mental processes which are their object. Like the physical, the psychical is not necessarily in reality what it appears to us to be. We shall be glad to learn, however, that the correction of internal perception will turn out not to offer such great difficulties as the correction of external perception – that internal objects are less unknowable than the external world.

II Various meanings of 'the unconscious' – the topographical point of view

Before going any further, let us state the important, though inconvenient, fact that the attribute of being unconscious is only one feature that is found in the psychical and is by no means sufficient fully to characterize it. There are psychical acts of very varying value which yet agree in possessing the characteristic of being unconscious. The unconscious comprises, on the one hand, acts which are merely latent, temporarily unconscious, but which differ in no other respect from conscious ones and, on the other hand, processes such as repressed ones, which if they were to become conscious would be bound to stand out in the crudest contrast to the rest of the conscious processes. It would put an end to all misunderstandings if, from now on, in describing the various kinds of psychical acts we were to disregard the question of whether they were conscious or unconscious, and were to classify and correlate them only according to their relation to instincts and aims, according to their composition and according to which of the hierarchy of psychical systems they belong to. This, however, is for various reasons impracticable, so that we cannot escape the ambiguity of using the words 'conscious' and 'unconscious' sometimes in a descriptive and sometimes in a systematic sense, in which latter they signify inclusion in particular systems and possession of certain characteristics. We might attempt to avoid confusion by giving the psychical systems which we have distinguished certain arbitrarily chosen names which have no reference to the attribute of being conscious. Only we should first have to specify what the grounds are on which we distinguish the systems, and in doing this we should not be able to evade the attribute of being conscious, seeing that it forms the point of departure for all our investigations. Perhaps we may look for some assistance from the proposal to employ, at any rate in writing, the abbreviation *Cs.* for consciousness and *Ucs.* for what is unconscious, when we are using the two words in the systematic sense.[8]

Proceeding now to an account of the positive findings of psycho-analysis, we may say that in general a psychical act goes through two phases as regards its state, between which is interposed a kind of testing (censorship). In the first phase the psychical act is unconscious and belongs to the system *Ucs.*; if, on testing, it is rejected by the censorship, it is not allowed to pass into the second phase; it is then said to be 'repressed' and must remain unconscious. If, however, it passes this testing, it enters the second phase and thenceforth belongs to the second system, which we will call the system *Cs*. But the fact that it belongs to that system does not yet unequivocally determine its relation to consciousness. It is not yet conscious, but it is certainly capable of becoming conscious (to use Breuer's expression)[9] – that is, it can now, given certain conditions, become an object of consciousness without any special resistance. In consideration of this capacity for becoming conscious we also call the system *Cs.* the 'preconscious'. If it should turn out that a certain censorship also plays a part in determining whether the preconscious becomes conscious, we shall discriminate more sharply between the systems *Pcs.* and *Cs*. For the present let it suffice us to bear in mind that the system *Pcs.* shares the characteristics of the system *Cs.* and that the rigorous censorship exercises its office at the point of transition from the *Ucs.* to the *Pcs.* (or *Cs.*).

By accepting the existence of these two (or three) psychical systems, psycho-analysis has departed a step further from the descriptive 'psychology of consciousness' and has raised new problems and acquired a new content. Up till now, it has differed from that psychology mainly by reason of its *dynamic* view of mental processes; now in addition it seems to take account of psychical *topography* as well, and to indicate in respect of any given mental act within what system or between what systems it takes place. On account of this attempt, too, it has been given the name of 'depth-psychology'.[10] We shall hear that it can be further enriched by taking yet another point of view into account.

If we are to take the topography of mental acts seriously we must direct our interest to a doubt which arises at this point. When a psychical act (let us confine ourselves here to one which is in the nature of an idea[11]) is transposed from the system *Ucs.* into the system *Cs.* (or *Pcs.*), are we to suppose that this transposition involves a fresh record – as it were, a second registration – of the idea in question, which may thus be situated as well in a fresh psychical locality, and alongside of which the original unconscious registration continues to exist?[12] Or are we rather to believe that the transposition consists in a change in the state of the idea, a change involving the same material and occurring in the same locality? This question may appear abstruse, but it must be raised if we wish to form a more definite conception of psychical topography, of the dimension of depth in the mind. It is a difficult one because it goes beyond pure psychology and touches on the relations of the mental apparatus to anatomy. We know that in the very roughest sense such relations exist. Research has given irrefutable proof that mental activity is bound up with the function of the brain as it is with no other organ. We are taken a step further – we do not know how much – by the discovery of the unequal importance of the different parts of the brain and their special relations to particular parts of the body and to particular mental activities. But every attempt to go on from there to discover a localization of mental processes, every endeavour to think of ideas as stored up in nerve-cells and of excitations as travelling along nerve-fibres, has miscarried completely.[13] The same fate would await any theory which attempted to recognize, let us say, the anatomical position of the system *Cs.* – conscious mental activity – as being in the cortex, and to localize the unconscious processes in the sub-cortical parts of the brain.[14] There is a hiatus here which at present cannot be filled, nor is it one of the tasks of psychology to fill it. Our psychical topography has *for the present* nothing to do with anatomy; it has reference not to anatomical localities, but to regions in the mental apparatus, wherever they may be situated in the body.

In this respect, then, our work is untrammelled and may proceed according to its own requirements. It will, however, be useful to remind ourselves that as things stand our hypotheses set out to be no more than graphic illustrations. The first of the two possibilities which we considered – namely, that the *Cs.* phase of an idea implies a fresh registration of it, which is situated in another place – is doubtless the cruder but also the more convenient. The second hypothesis – that of a merely *functional* change of state – is a priori more probable, but it is less plastic, less easy to manipulate. With the first, or topographical, hypothesis is bound up that of a topographical separation of the systems *Ucs.* and *Cs.* and also the possibility that an idea may exist simultaneously in two places in the mental apparatus – indeed, that if it is not inhibited by the censorship, it regularly advances from the one position to the other, possibly without losing its first location or registration.

This view may seem odd, but it can be supported by observations from psycho-analytic practice. If we communicate to a patient some idea which he has at one time repressed but which we have discovered in him, our telling him makes at first no change in his mental condition. Above all, it does not remove the repression nor undo its effects, as might perhaps be expected from the fact that the previously unconscious idea has now become conscious. On the contrary, all that we shall achieve at first will be a fresh rejection of the repressed idea. But now the patient has in actual fact the same idea in two forms in different places in his mental apparatus: first, he has the conscious memory of the auditory trace of the idea, conveyed in what we told him; and secondly, he also has – as we know for certain – the unconscious memory of his experience as it was in its earlier form.[15] Actually there is no lifting of the repression until the conscious idea, after the resistances have been overcome, has entered into connection with the unconscious memory-trace. It is only through the making conscious of the latter itself that success is achieved. On superficial consideration this would seem to show that conscious and unconscious ideas are distinct registrations, topographically separated, of the same content. But a moment's reflection shows that the identity of the information given to the patient with his repressed memory is only apparent. To have heard something and to have experienced something are in their psychological nature two quite different things, even though the content of both is the same.

So for the moment we are not in a position to decide between the two possibilities that we have discussed. Perhaps later on we shall come upon factors which may turn the balance in favour of one or the other. Perhaps we shall make the discovery that our question was inadequately framed and that the difference between an unconscious and a conscious idea has to be defined in quite another way.

* * *

VII Assessment of the unconscious

What we have put together in the preceding discussions is probably as much as we can say about the *Ucs.* so long as we only draw upon our knowledge of dream-life and the transference neuroses. It is certainly not much, and at some points it gives an impression of obscurity and confusion; and above all it offers us no possibility of co-ordinating or subsuming the *Ucs.* into any context with which we are already familiar. It is only the analysis of one of the affections which we call narcissistic psychoneuroses that promises to furnish us with conceptions through which the enigmatic *Ucs.* will be brought more within our reach and, as it were, made tangible.

Since the publication of a work by Abraham (1908) – which that conscientious author has attributed to my instigation – we have tried to base our characterization of Kraepelin's 'dementia praecox' (Bleuler's 'schizophrenia') on its position with reference to the antithesis between ego and object. In the transference neuroses (anxiety hysteria, conversion hysteria and obsessional neurosis) there was nothing to give special prominence to this antithesis. We knew, indeed, that frustration in regard to the object brings on the outbreak of the neurosis and that the neurosis involves a renunciation of the real object; we knew too that the libido that is withdrawn from the real object reverts first to a phantasied object and then to one that had been repressed (introversion).[16] But in these disorders object-cathexis in general is retained with great energy, and more detailed examination of the process of repression has obliged us to assume that object-cathexis persists in the system *Ucs.* in spite of – or rather in consequence of – repression. Indeed, the capacity for transference, of which we make use for therapeutic purposes in these affections, presupposes an unimpaired object-cathexis.

In the case of schizophrenia, on the other hand, we have been driven to the assumption that after the process of repression the libido that has been withdrawn does not seek a new object, but retreats into the ego; that is to say, that here the object-cathexes are given up and a primitive objectless condition of narcissism is re-established. The incapacity of these patients for transference (so far as the pathological process extends), their consequent inaccessibility to therapeutic efforts, their characteristic repudiation of the external world, the appearance of signs of a hypercathexis of their own ego, the final outcome in complete apathy – all these clinical features seem to agree excellently with the assumption that their object-cathexes have been given up. As regards the relation of the two psychical systems to each other, all observers have been struck by the fact that in schizophrenia a great deal is expressed as being conscious which in the transference neuroses can only be shown to be present in the *Ucs.* by psycho-analysis. But to begin with we were not able to establish any intelligible connection between the ego–object relation and the relationships of consciousness.

What we are seeking seems to present itself in the following unexpected way. In schizophrenics we observe – especially in the initial stages, which are so instructive – a number of changes in *speech*, some of which deserve to be regarded from a particular point of view. The patient often devotes peculiar care to his way of expressing himself, which becomes 'stilted' and 'precious'. The construction of his sentences undergoes a peculiar disorganization, making them so incomprehensible to us that his remarks seem nonsensical. Some reference to bodily organs or innervations is often given prominence in the content of these remarks. To this may be added the fact that in such symptoms of schizophrenia as are comparable with the substitutive formations of hysteria or obsessional neurosis, the relation between the substitute and the repressed material nevertheless displays peculiarities which would surprise us in these two forms of neurosis.

Dr. Victor Tausk of Vienna has placed at my disposal some observations that he has made in the initial stages of schizophrenia in a female patient, which are particularly valuable in that the patient was ready to explain her utterances herself.[17] I will take two of his examples to illustrate the view I wish to put forward, and I have no doubt that every observer could easily produce plenty of such material.

A patient of Tausk's, a girl who was brought to the clinic after a quarrel with her lover, complained that *her eyes were not right, they were twisted.* This she herself explained by bringing forward a series of reproaches against her lover in coherent language. 'She could not understand him at all, he looked different every time; he was a hypocrite, an eye-twister,[18] he had twisted her eyes; now she had twisted eyes; they were not her eyes any more; now she saw the world with different eyes.'

The patient's comments on her unintelligible remark have the value of an analysis, for they contain the equivalent of the remark expressed in a generally comprehensible form. They throw light at the same time on the meaning and the genesis of schizophrenic word-formation. I agree with Tausk in stressing in this example the point that the patient's relation to a bodily organ (the eye) has arrogated to itself the representation of the whole content [of her thoughts]. Here the schizophrenic utterance exhibits a hypochondriac trait: it has become '*organ-speech*'.[19]

A second communication by the same patient was as follows: 'She was standing in church. Suddenly she felt a jerk; she had to *change her position, as though somebody was putting her into a position, as though she was being put in a certain position.*'

Now came the analysis of this through a fresh series of reproaches against her lover.

> He was common, he had made her common, too, though she was naturally refined. He had made her like himself by making her think that he was superior to her; now she had become like him, because she thought she would be better if she were like him. He had *given a false impression of his position*; now she was just like him [by identification,] he had *put her in a false position.*

The physical movement of 'changing her position', Tausk remarks, depicted the words 'putting her in a false position' and her identification with her lover. I would call attention once more to the fact that the whole train of thought is dominated by the element which has for its content a bodily innervation (or, rather, the sensation of it). Furthermore, a hysterical woman would, in the first example, have *in fact* convulsively twisted her eyes, and, in the second, have given actual jerks, instead of having the *impulse* to do so or the *sensation* of doing so: and in neither example would she have any accompanying conscious thoughts, nor would she have been able to express any such thoughts afterwards.

These two observations, then, argue in favour of what we have called hypochondriacal speech or 'organ-speech'. But, what seems to us more important, they also point to something else, of which we have innumerable instances (for example, in the cases collected in Bleuler's monograph [1911]) and which may be reduced to a definite formula. In schizophrenia *words* are subjected to the same process as that which makes the dream-images out of latent dream-thoughts – to what we have called the primary psychical process. They undergo condensation, and by means of displacement transfer their cathexes to one another in their entirety. The process may go so far that a single word, if it is specially suitable on account of its numerous connections, takes over the representation of a whole train of thought.[20] The works of Bleuler, Jung and their pupils offer a quantity of material which particularly supports this assertion.[21]

Before we draw any conclusion from impressions such as these, let us consider further the distinctions between the formation of substitutes in schizophrenia on the one hand, and in hysteria and obsessional neurosis on the other – subtle distinctions which nevertheless make a strange impression. A patient whom I have at present under observation has allowed himself to be withdrawn from all the interests of life on account of a bad condition of the skin of his face. He declares that he has blackheads and deep holes in his face which everyone notices. Analysis shows that he is playing out his castration complex upon his skin. At first he worked at these blackheads remorselessly; and it gave him great satisfaction to squeeze them out, because, as he said, something spurted out when he did so. Then he began to think that a deep cavity appeared wherever he had got rid of a blackhead, and he reproached himself most vehemently with having ruined his skin for ever by 'constantly fiddling about with his hand'. Pressing out the content of the blackheads is clearly to him a substitute for masturbation. The cavity which then appears owing to his fault is the female genital, i.e. the fulfilment of the threat of castration (or the phantasy representing that threat) provoked by his masturbating. This substitutive formation has, in spite of its hypochondriacal character, considerable resemblance to a hysterical conversion; and yet, we have a feeling that something different must be going on here, that a substitutive formation such as this cannot be attributed to hysteria, even before we can say in what the difference consists. A tiny little cavity such as a pore of the skin would hardly be used by a hysteric as a symbol for the vagina, which he is otherwise ready to compare with every imaginable object that encloses a hollow space. Besides, we should expect the multiplicity of these little cavities to prevent him from using them as a substitute for the female genital. The same applies to the case of a young patient reported by Tausk some years ago to the Vienna Psycho-Analytical Society. This patient behaved in other respects exactly as though he were suffering from an obsessional neurosis; he took hours to wash and dress, and so on. It was noticeable, however, that he was able to give the meaning of his inhibitions without any resistance. In putting on his stockings, for instance, he was disturbed by the idea that he must pull apart the stitches in the knitting, i.e. the holes, and to him every hole was a symbol of the female genital aperture. This again is a thing which we cannot attribute to an obsessional neurotic. Reitler observed a patient of the latter sort, who also suffered from having to take a long time over putting on his stockings; this man, after overcoming his resistances, found as the explanation that his foot symbolized a penis, that putting on the stocking stood for a masturbatory act, and that he had to keep on pulling the stocking on and off, partly in order to complete the picture of masturbation, and partly in order to undo that act.

If we ask ourselves what it is that gives the character of strangeness to the substitutive formation and the symptom in schizophrenia, we eventually come to realize that it is the predominance of what has to do with words over what has to do with things. As far as the thing goes, there is only a very slight similarity between squeezing out a blackhead and an emission from the penis, and still less similarity between the innumerable shallow pores of the skin and the vagina; but in the former case there is, in both instances, a 'spurting out', while in the latter the cynical saying, 'a hole is a hole', is true verbally. What has dictated the substitution is not the resemblance between the things denoted but the sameness of the words used to express them. Where the two – word and thing – do not coincide, the formation of substitutes in schizophrenia deviates from that in the transference neuroses.

If now we put this finding alongside the hypothesis that in schizophrenia object-cathexes are given up, we shall be obliged to modify the hypothesis by adding that the cathexis of the *word*-presentations of objects is retained. What we have permissibly called the conscious presentation[22] of the object can now be split up into the presentation of the *word* and the presentation of the *thing*; the latter consists in the cathexis, if not of the direct memory-images of the thing, at least of remoter memory-traces derived from these. We now seem to know all at once what the difference is between a conscious and an unconscious presentation [see pp. 511–12]. The two are not, as we supposed, different registrations of the same content in different psychical localities, nor yet different functional states of cathexis in the same locality; but the conscious presentation comprises the presentation of the thing plus the presentation of the word belonging to it, while the unconscious presentation is the presentation of the thing alone. The system *Ucs.* contains the thing-cathexes of the objects, the first and true object-cathexes; the system *Pcs.* comes about by this thing-presentation being hypercathected through being linked with the word-presentations corresponding to it. It is these hypercathexes, we may suppose, that bring about a higher psychical organization and make it possible for the primary process to be succeeded by the secondary process which is dominant in the *Pcs.* Now, too, we are in a position to state precisely what it is that repression denies to the rejected presentation in the transference neuroses: what it denies to the presentation is translation into words which shall remain attached to the object. A presentation which is not put into words, or a psychical act which is not hypercathected, remains thereafter in the *Ucs.* in a state of repression.

I should like to point out at what an early date we already possessed the insight which to-day enables us to understand one of the most striking characteristics of schizophrenia. In the last few pages of *The Interpretation of Dreams*, which was published in 1900, the view was developed that thought-processes, i.e. those acts of cathexis which are comparatively remote from perception, are in themselves without quality and unconscious, and that they attain their capacity to become conscious only through being linked with the residues of perceptions of *words*.[23] But word-presentations, for their part too, are derived from sense-perceptions, in the same way as thing-presentations are; the question might therefore be raised why presentations of objects cannot become conscious through the medium of their *own* perceptual residues. Probably, however, thought proceeds in systems so far remote from the original perceptual residues that they have no longer retained anything of the qualities of those residues, and, in order to become conscious, need to be reinforced by new qualities. Moreover, by being linked with words, cathexes can be provided with quality even when they represent only *relations* between presentations of objects and are thus unable to derive any quality from perceptions. Such relations, which become comprehensible only through words, form a major part of our thought-processes. As we can see, being linked with word-presentations is not yet the same thing as becoming conscious, but only makes it possible to become so; it is therefore characteristic of the system *Pcs.* and of that system alone.[24] With these discussions, however, we have evidently departed from our subject proper and find ourselves plunged into problems concerning the preconscious and the conscious, which for good reasons we are reserving for separate treatment.[25]

As regards schizophrenia, which we only touch on here so far as seems indispensable for a general understanding of the *Ucs.*, a doubt must occur to us whether the process here termed repression has anything at all in common with the repression which takes place in the transference neuroses. The formula that repression is a process which occurs between the systems *Ucs.* and *Pcs.* (or *Cs.*), and results in keeping something at a distance from consciousness, must in any event be modified, in order that it may also be able to include the case of dementia praecox and other narcissistic affections. But the ego's attempt at flight, which expresses itself in the withdrawal of the conscious cathexis, nevertheless remains a factor common [to the two classes of neurosis]. The most superficial reflection shows us how much more radically and profoundly this attempt at flight, this flight of the ego, is put into operation in the narcissistic neuroses.

If, in schizophrenia, this flight consists in withdrawal of instinctual cathexis from the points which represent the *unconscious* presentation of the object, it may seem strange that the part of the presentation of this object which belongs to the system *Pcs.* – namely, the word-presentations corresponding to it – should, on the contrary, receive a more intense cathexis. We might rather expect that the word-presentation, being the preconscious part, would have to sustain the first impact of repression and that it would be totally uncathectable after repression had proceeded as far as the unconscious thing-presentations. This, it is true, is difficult to understand. It turns out that the cathexis of the word-presentation is not part of the act of repression, but represents the first of the attempts at recovery or cure which so conspicuously dominate the clinical picture of schizophrenia.[26] These endeavours are directed towards regaining the lost object, and it may well be that to achieve this purpose they set off on a path that leads to the object *via* the verbal part of it, but then find themselves obliged to be content with words instead of things. It is a general truth that our mental activity moves in two opposite directions: either it starts from the instincts and passes through the system *Ucs.* to conscious thought-activity; or, beginning with an instigation from outside, it passes through the system *Cs.* and *Pcs.* till it reaches the *Ucs.* cathexes of the ego and objects. This second path must, in spite of the repression which has taken place, remain traversable, and it lies open to some extent to the endeavours made by the neurosis to regain its objects. When we think in abstractions there is a danger that we may neglect the relations of words to unconscious thing-presentations, and it must be confessed that the expression and content of our philosophizing then begins to acquire an unwelcome resemblance to the mode of operation of schizophrenics.[27] We may, on the other hand, attempt a characterization of the schizophrenic's mode of thought by saying that he treats concrete things as though they were abstract.

If we have made a true assessment of the nature of the *Ucs.* and have correctly defined the difference between an unconscious and a preconscious presentation, then our researches will inevitably bring us back from many other points to this same piece of insight.

Translated by James Strachey et al.

Notes

1 [Editor's note (James Strachey).] For English readers, it must be observed, there is a further ambiguity in the word 'unconscious' which is scarcely present in the German. The German words '*bewusst*' and '*unbewusst*' have the grammatical form of passive participles, and their usual sense is something like 'consciously known' and 'not consciously known'. The English 'conscious', though it *can* be used in the same way, is also used, and perhaps more commonly, in an *active* sense: 'he was conscious of the sound' and 'he lay there unconscious'. The German terms do not often have this active meaning, and it is important to bear in mind that 'conscious' is in general to be understood in a passive sense in what follows. The German word '*Bewusstsein*', on the other hand (which is here translated 'consciousness'), *does* have an active sense. Thus, for instance, on page 510 Freud speaks of a psychical act becoming 'an object of consciousness'; again, in the last paragraph of the first section of the paper (page 509) he speaks of 'the perception [of mental processes] by means of consciousness'; and in general, when he uses such phrases as 'our consciousness' he is referring to our consciousness *of* something. When he wishes to speak of a mental state's consciousness in the *passive* sense, he uses the word '*Bewusstheit*', which is translated here 'the attribute of being conscious', 'the fact of being conscious' or simply 'being conscious' – where the English 'conscious' is, as almost always in these papers, to be taken in the passive sense.

2 Freud seems himself at one time to have been inclined to accept this theory, as is suggested by a passage in his book on aphasia, *Zur Auffassung der Aphasien*, Vienna, 1891, pp. 56ff. The passage can be found translated at *SE* XIV, pp. 206–08. [*Editor:* all references to Freud's works are to the *Standard Edition of the Complete Psychological Works of Sigmund Freud*, ed. James Strachey, London, Hogarth Press, 1974, abbreviated to *SE*, followed by the volume number in Roman numerals.]

3 Cf. *The Interpretation of Dreams* (1900), *SE* IV, p. 133.

4 In his very last discussion of the subject, in the unfinished fragment 'Some Elementary Lessons in Psycho-Analysis' (1940), *SE* XXII, pp. 279–86, Freud entered at some length into the evidence afforded by post-hypnotic suggestion.

5 In some of his very early writings, Freud himself used the term 'subconscious', e.g. in his French paper on hysterical paralyses [translated as 'Some Points for a Comparative Study of Organic and Hysterical Motor Paralyses', *SE* I, pp. 157–59] and in *Studies on Hysteria* (1895), *SE* II, p. 69n. But he disrecommends the term as early as in *The Interpretation of Dreams, SE* V, p. 615. He alludes to the point again in 'Resistance and Repression', Lecture XIX of his *Introductory Lectures* (1916–17), *SE* XVI, pp. 286–302, and argues it a little more fully near the end of Chapter II of *The Question of Lay Analysis* (1926), *SE* XX, pp. 191–99.

6 The French term for 'dual consciousness'.

7 This idea had already been dealt with at some length in Chapter VII (F) of *The Interpretation of Dreams*, *SE* V, pp. 615–17.

8 Freud had already introduced these abbreviations in *The Interpretation of Dreams*, *SE* V, pp. 540ff.

9 See *Studies on Hysteria*, Breuer and Freud (1895), *SE* II, p. 225.

10 By Bleuler (1914). See the 'History of the Psycho-Analytic Movement' (1914), *SE* XIV, p. 41.

11 The German word here is '*Vorstellung*', which covers the English terms 'idea', 'image' and 'presentation'.

12 The conception of an idea being present in the mind in more than one 'registration' was first put forward by Freud in a letter to Fliess of December 6, 1896 (Letter 52, *SE* I, pp. 233–39). It is used in connection with the theory of memory in Chapter VII (Section B) of *The*

Interpretation of Dreams (1900*a*), *SE* V, p. 539; and it is alluded to again in Section F of the same chapter (ibid., p. 610) in an argument which foreshadows the present one.

13 Freud had himself been much concerned with the question of the localization of cerebral functions in his work on aphasia, *Zur Auffassung der Aphasien*.

14 Freud had insisted on this as early as in his preface to his translation of Bernheim's *De la suggestion* (Freud, 1888–89).

15 The topographical picture of the distinction between conscious and unconscious ideas is presented in Freud's discussion of the case of 'Little Hans' (1909), *SE* X, pp. 120f., and at greater length in the closing paragraphs of his technical paper 'On Beginning the Treatment' (1913), *SE* XII, pp. 121–44.

16 The process is described in detail in Section (*a*) of Freud's paper on 'Types of Onset of Neurosis' (1912), *SE* XII, pp. 227–38.

17 A paper referring to the same patient was later published by Tausk (1919).

18 The German '*Augenverdreher*' has the figurative meaning of 'deceiver'.

19 Cf. Freud's discussion of hypochondria in the second part of 'On Narcissism' (1914), *SE* XIV, pp. 82–91.

20 *The Interpretation of Dreams*, *SE* V, p. 595.

21 The dream-work, too, occasionally treats words like things, and so creates very similar 'schizophrenic' utterances or neologisms. See *The Interpretation of Dreams*, *SE* IV, pp. 295ff. A distinction between what happens in dreams and in schizophrenia is drawn, however, in 'A Metapsychological Supplement to the Theory of Dreams', p. 229.

22 '*Vorstellung*.' This word has as a rule been translated above by 'idea'. [See p. 510 and note 11 above.] From this point till the end of the paper, '*Vorstellung*' is uniformly translated by 'presentation' – '*Wortvorstellung*' 'presentation of the word' or 'word-presentation'; '*Sachvorstellung*' 'presentation of the thing' or 'thing-presentation'. These words were formerly translated by the somewhat misleading 'verbal idea' and 'concrete idea'. In 'Mourning and Melancholia' (*SE* XIV, p. 256) Freud replaced '*Sachvorstellung*' by the synonymous '*Dingvorstellung*'; and he had used this second version earlier, in *The Interpretation of Dreams*, *SE* IV, pp. 295–6, and near the beginning of Chapter IV of his book on jokes (1905). – The distinction between 'word-presentations' and 'thing-presentations' was already in his mind when he wrote these earlier works, and it no doubt derives from his studies on the aphasias. The matter was discussed at some length in *Zur Auffassung der Aphasien*, and the relevant passage has been translated in *SE* XIV, pp. 209–15.

23 *The Interpretation of Dreams*, *SE* V, p. 617. See also ibid., p. 574. This hypothesis had in fact been put forward (though not published) by Freud even earlier, in his 'Project for a Scientific Psychology' of 1895 (towards the beginning of Section 1 of Part III, *SE* I, pp. 388–91). It had also been mentioned by him more recently, in his paper 'Formulation on the Two Principles of Mental Functioning' (1911), *SE* XII, pp. 213–26.

24 Freud took up this subject again at the beginning of Chapter II of *The Ego and the Id* (1923).

25 This seems likely to be a reference to a missing paper on consciousness.

26 See Part III of Freud's Schreber analysis in 'Psycho-Analytic Notes on an Autobiographical Account of a Case of Paranoia', *SE* XII, pp. 3–82.

27 Freud had already made this point at the end of the second essay in *Totem and Taboo* (1912–13), *SE* XIII, p. 73.

32

OF THE GAZE AS *OBJET PETIT A*

Jacques Lacan

Anamorphosis

Of the foundation of consciousness · *The privilege of the gaze as* objet a · *The optics of the blind* · *The phallus in the picture*

Vainement ton image arrive à ma rencontre
Et ne m'entre où je suis qui seulement la montre
Toi te tournant vers moi tu ne saurais trouver
Au mur de mon regard que ton ombre rêvée.

Je suis ce malheureux comparable aux miroirs
Qui peuvent réfléchir mais ne peuvent pas voir
Comme eux mon oeil est vide et comme eux habité
De l'absence de toi qui fait sa cécité.[1]

You may remember that, in one of my earlier lectures, I began by quoting the poem, 'Contrechant', from Aragon's *Le Fou d'Elsa*. I did not realize at the time that I would be developing the subject of the gaze to such an extent. I was diverted into doing so by the way in which I presented the concept of repetition in Freud.

We cannot deny that it is within the explanation of repetition that this digression on the scopic function is situated – no doubt by Maurice Merleau-Ponty's recently published work, *Le Visible et l'invisible*. Moreover, it seemed to me that, if an encounter were to be found there, it was a happy one, one destined to stress, as I shall try to do today, how, in the perspective of the unconscious, we can situate consciousness.

You know that some shadow, or, to use another term, some 'resist' – in the sense one speaks of 'resist' in the dying of material – marks the fact of consciousness in Freud's very discourse.

But, before taking things up again at the point we left them last time, I must first clear up a misunderstanding that appears to have arisen in the minds of certain members of the audience concerning a term I used last time. Some of you seem to have been perplexed by a word that is simple enough, and which I commented on, namely, the *tychic*. Apparently, it sounded to some of you like a sneeze. Yet I made it quite clear that it was the adjective formed from *tuchē* just as *psychique* (psychical) is the adjective corresponding to *psuchē* (psyche). I used this analogy at the heart of the experience of repetition quite intentionally, because for any conception of the psychical development as elucidated by psycho-analysis, the fact of the tychic is central. It is in relation to the eye, in relation to the *eutuchia* or the *dustuchia*, the happy encounter and the unhappy encounter, that my lecture today will be ordered.

1

I saw myself seeing myself, young Parque says somewhere. Certainly, this statement has rich and complex implications in relation to the theme developed in *La Jeune Parque*, that of femininity – but we haven't got there yet. We are dealing with the philosopher, who apprehends something that is one of the essential correlates of consciousness in its relation to representation, and which is designated as *I see myself seeing myself*. What evidence can we really attach to this formula? How is it that it remains, in fact, correlative with that fundamental mode to which we referred in the Cartesian *cogito*, by which the subject apprehends himself as thought?

What isolates this apprehension of thought by itself is a sort of doubt, which has been called methodological doubt, which concerns whatever might give support to thought in representation. How is it, then, that the *I see myself seeing myself* remains its envelope and base, and, perhaps more than one thinks, grounds its certainty? For, *I warm myself by warming myself* is a reference to the body as body – I feel that sensation of warmth which, from some point inside me, is diffused and locates me as body. Whereas in the *I see myself seeing myself*, there is no such sensation of being absorbed by vision.

Furthermore, the phenomenologists have succeeded in articulating with precision, and in the most disconcerting way, that it is quite clear that I see *outside*, that perception is not in me, that it is on the objects that it apprehends. And yet I apprehend the world in a perception that seems to concern the immanence of the *I see myself seeing myself*. The privilege of the subject seems to be established here from that bipolar reflexive relation by which, as soon as I perceive, my representations belong to me.

This is how the world is struck with a presumption of idealization, of the suspicion of yielding me only my representations. Serious practice does not really weigh very heavy, but, on the other hand, the philosopher, the idealist, is placed there, as much in confrontation with himself as in confrontation with those who are listening to him, in an embarrassing position. How can one deny that nothing of the world appears to me except in my representations? This is the irreducible method of Bishop Berkeley, about whose subjective position much might be said – including something that may have eluded you in passing, namely, this *belong to me* aspect of representations, so reminiscent of property. When carried to the limit, the process of this meditation, of this reflecting reflection, goes so far as to reduce the subject apprehended by the Cartesian meditation to a power of annihilation.

The mode of my presence in the world is the subject in so far as by reducing itself solely to this certainty of being a subject, it becomes active annihilation. In fact, the process of the philosophical meditation throws the subject towards the transforming historical action, and, around this point, orders the configured modes of active self-consciousness through its metamorphoses in history. As for the meditation on being that reaches its culmination in the thought of Heidegger, it restores to being itself that power of annihilation – or at least poses the question of how it may be related to it.

This is also the point to which Maurice Merleau-Ponty leads us. But, if you refer to his text, you will see that it is at this point that he chooses to withdraw, in order to propose a return to the sources of intuition concerning the visible and the invisible, to come back to that which is prior to all reflection, thetic or non-thetic, in order to locate the emergence of vision itself. For him, it is a question of restoring – for, he tells us, it can only be a question of a reconstruction or a restoration, not of a path traversed in the opposite direction – of reconstituting the way by which, not from the body, but from something that he calls the flesh of the world, the original point of vision was able to emerge. It would seem that in this way one sees, in this unfinished work, the emergence of something like the search for an unnamed substance from which I, the seer, extract myself. From the toils (*rets*), or rays (*rais*), if you prefer, of an iridescence of which I am at first a part, I emerge as eye, assuming, in a way, emergence from what I would like to call the function of *seeingness (voyure)*.

A wild odour emanates from it, providing a glimpse on the horizon of the hunt of Artemis – whose touch seems to be associated at this moment of tragic failure in which we lost him who speaks.

Yet is this really the way he wished to take? The traces that remain of the part to come from his meditation permits us to doubt it. The reference-points that are provided in it, more particularly for the strictly psycho-analytic unconscious, allow us to perceive that he may have been directed towards some search, original in relation to the philosophical tradition, towards that new dimension of meditation on the subject that analysis enables us to trace.

Personally, I cannot but be struck by certain of these notes, which are for me less enigmatic than they may seem to other readers, because they correspond very exactly to the schemata – with one of them, in particular – that I shall be dealing with here. Read, for example, the note concerning what he calls the turning inside-out of the finger of a glove, in as much as it seems to appear there – note the way in which the leather envelops the fur in a winter glove – that consciousness, in its illusion of *seeing itself seeing itself*, finds its basis in the inside-out structure of the gaze.

2

But what is the gaze?

I shall set out from this first point of annihilation in which is marked, in the field of the reduction of the subject, a break – which warns us of the need to introduce another reference, that which analysis assumes in reducing the privileges of the consciousness.

Psycho-analysis regards the consciousness as irremediably limited, and institutes it as a principle, not only of idealization, but of *méconnaissance*, as – using a term that takes on new value by being referred to a visible domain – *scotoma*. The term was introduced into the psycho-analytic vocabulary by the French School. Is it simply a metaphor? We find here once again the ambiguity that affects anything that is inscribed in the register of the scopic drive.

For us, consciousness matters only in its relation to what, for propaedeutic reasons, I have tried to show you in the fiction of the incomplete text – on the basis of which it is a question of recentring the subject as speaking in the very lacunae of that in which, at first sight, it presents itself as speaking. But I am stating here only the relation of the pre-conscious to the unconscious. The dynamic that is attached to the consciousness as such, the attention the subject brings to his own text, remains up to this point, as Freud has stressed, outside theory and, strictly speaking, not yet articulated.

It is here that I propose that the interest the subject takes in his own split is bound up with that which determines it – namely, a privileged object, which has emerged from some primal separation, from some self-mutilation induced by the very approach of the real, whose name, in our algebra, is the *objet a*.

In the scopic relation, the object on which depends the phantasy from which the subject is suspended in an essential vacillation is the gaze. Its privilege – and also that by which the subject for so long has been misunderstood as being in its dependence – derives from its very structure.

Let us schematize at once what we mean. From the moment that this gaze appears, the subject tries to adapt himself to it, he becomes that punctiform object, that point of vanishing being with which the subject confuses his own failure. Furthermore, of all the objects in which the subject may recognize his dependence in the register of desire, the gaze is specified as unapprehensible. That is why it is, more than any other object, misunderstood (*méconnu*), and it is perhaps for this reason, too, that the subject manages, fortunately, to symbolize his own vanishing and punctiform bar (*trait*) in the illusion of the consciousness of *seeing oneself see oneself*, in which the gaze is elided.

If, then, the gaze is that underside of consciousness, how shall we try to imagine it?

The expression is not inapt, for we can give body to the gaze. Sartre, in one of the most brilliant passages of *L'Etre et le néant*, brings it into function in the dimension of the existence of others. Others would remain suspended in the same, partially derealizing, conditions that are, in Sartre's definition, those of objectivity, were it not for the gaze. The gaze, as conceived by Sartre, is the gaze by which I am surprised – surprised in so far as it changes all the perspectives, the lines of force, of my world, orders it, from the point of nothingness where I am, in a sort of radiated reticulation of the organisms. As the locus of the relation between me, the annihilating subject, and that which surrounds me, the gaze seems to possess such a privilege that it goes so far as to have me scotomized, I who look, the eye of him who sees me as object. In so far as I am under the gaze, Sartre writes, I no longer see the eye that looks at me and, if I see the eye, the gaze disappears.

Is this a correct phenomenological analysis? No. It is not true that, when I am under the gaze, when I solicit a gaze, when I obtain it, I do not see it as a gaze. Painters, above all, have grasped this gaze as such in the mask and I have only to remind you of Goya, for example, for you to realize this.

The gaze sees itself – to be precise, the gaze of which Sartre speaks, the gaze that surprises me and reduces me to shame, since this is the feeling he regards as the most dominant. The gaze I encounter – you can find this in Sartre's own writing – is, not a seen gaze, but a gaze imagined by me in the field of the Other.

If you turn to Sartre's own text, you will see that, far from speaking of the emergence of this gaze as of something that concerns the organ of sight, he refers to the sound of rustling leaves, suddenly heard while out hunting, to a footstep heard in a corridor. And when are these sounds heard? At the moment when he has presented himself in the action of looking through a keyhole. A gaze surprises him in the function of voyeur, disturbs him, overwhelms him and reduces him to a feeling of shame. The gaze in question is certainly the presence of others as such. But does this mean that originally it is in the relation of subject to subject, in the function of the existence of others as looking at me, that we apprehend what the gaze really is? Is it not clear that the gaze intervenes here only in as much as it is not the annihilating subject, correlative of the world of objectivity, who feels himself surprised, but the subject sustaining himself in a function of desire?

Is it not precisely because desire is established here in the domain of seeing that we can make it vanish?

3

We can apprehend this privilege of the gaze in the function of desire, by pouring ourselves, as it were, along the veins through which the domain of vision has been integrated into the field of desire.

It is not for nothing that it was at the very period when the Cartesian meditation inaugurated in all its purity the function of the subject that the dimension of optics that I shall distinguish here by calling 'geometral' or 'flat' (as opposed to perspective) optics was developed.

I shall illustrate for you, by one object among others, what seems to me exemplary in a function that so curiously attracted so much reflection at the time.

One reference, for those who would like to carry further what I tried to convey to you today, is Baltrusaïtis' book, *Anamorphoses*.

In my seminar, I have made great use of the function of anamorphosis, in so far as it is an exemplary structure. What does a simple, non-cylindrical anamorphosis consist of? Suppose there is a portrait on this flat piece of paper that I am holding. By chance, you see the blackboard, in an oblique position in relation to the piece of paper. Suppose that, by means of a series of ideal threads or lines, I reproduce on the oblique surface each point of the image drawn on my sheet of paper. You can easily imagine what the result would be – you would obtain a figure enlarged and distorted according to the lines of what may be called a perspective. One supposes that – if I take away that which has helped in the construction, namely, the image placed in my own visual field – the impression I will retain, while remaining in that place, will be more or less the same. At least, I will recognize the general outlines of the image – at best, I will have an identical impression.

I will now pass around something that dates from a hundred years earlier, from 1533, a reproduction of a painting that, I think, you all know – Hans Holbein's *The Ambassadors*. It will serve to refresh the memories of those who know the picture well. Those who do not should examine it attentively. I shall come back to it shortly.

Vision is ordered according to a mode that may generally be called the function of images. This function is defined by a point-by-point correspondence of two unities in space. Whatever optical intermediaries may be used to establish their relation, whether their image is virtual, or real, the point-by-point correspondence is essential. That which is of the mode of the image in the field of vision is therefore reducible to the simple schema that enables us to establish anamorphosis, that is to say, to the relation of an image, in so far as it is linked to a surface, with a certain point that we shall call the 'geometral' point. Anything that is determined by this method, in which the straight line plays its role of being the path of light, can be called an image.

Art is mingled with science here. Leonardo da Vinci is both a scientist, on account of his dioptric constructions, and an artist. Vitruvius's treatise on architecture is not far away. It is in Vignola and in Alberti that we find the progressive interrogation of the geometral laws of perspective, and it is around research on perspective that is centred a privileged interest for the domain of vision – whose relation with the institution of the Cartesian subject, which is itself a sort of geometral point, a point of perspective, we cannot fail to see. And, around the geometral perspective, the picture – this is a very important function to which we shall return – is organized in a way that is quite new in the history of painting.

I should now like to refer you to Diderot. The *Lettre sur les aveugles à l'usage de ceux qui voient* (Letter on the Blind for the use of those who see) will show you that this construction allows that which concerns vision to escape totally. For the geometral space of vision – even if we include those imaginary parts in the virtual space of the mirror, of which, as you know, I have spoken at length – is perfectly reconstructible, imaginable, by a blind man.

What is at issue in geometral perspective is simply the mapping of space, not sight. The blind man may perfectly well conceive that the field of space that he knows, and which he knows as real, may be perceived at a distance, and as a simultaneous act. For him, it is a question of apprehending a temporal function, instantaneity. In Descartes, dioptrics, the action of the eyes, is represented as the conjugated action of two sticks. The geometral dimension of vision does not exhaust, therefore, far from it, what the field of vision as such offers us as the original subjectifying relation.

This is why it is so important to acknowledge the inverted use of perspective in the structure of anamorphosis.

It was Dürer himself who invented the apparatus to establish perspective. Dürer's 'lucinda' is comparable to what, a little while ago, I placed between that blackboard and myself, namely, a certain image, or more exactly a canvas, a trellis that will be traversed by straight lines – which are not necessarily rays, but also threads – which will link each point that I have to see in the world to a point at which the canvas will, by this line, be traversed.

It was to establish a correct perspective image, therefore, that the *lucinda* was introduced. If I reverse its use, I will have the pleasure of obtaining not the restoration of the world that lies at the end, but the distortion, on another surface, of the image that I would have obtained on the first, and I will dwell, as on some delicious game, on this method that makes anything appear at will in a particular stretching.

I would ask you to believe that such an enchantment took place in its time. Baltrusaïtis' book will tell you of the furious polemics that these practices gave rise to, and which culminated in works of considerable length. The convent of the Minims, now destroyed, which once stood near the rue des Tournelles, carried on the very long wall of one of its galleries and representing as if by chance St John at Patmos a picture that had to be looked at through a hole, so that its distorting value could be appreciated to its full extent.

Distortion may lend itself – this was not the case for this particular fresco – to all the paranoiac ambiguities, and every possible use has been made of it, from Arcimboldi to Salvador Dali. I will go so far as to say that this fascination complements what geometral researches into perspective allow to escape from vision.

How is it that nobody has ever thought of connecting this with . . . the effect of an erection? Imagine a tattoo traced on the sexual organ *ad hoc* in the state of repose and assuming its, if I may say so, developed form in another state.

How can we not see here, immanent in the geometral dimension – a partial dimension in the field of the gaze, a dimension that has nothing to do with vision as such – something symbolic of the function of the lack, of the appearance of the phallic ghost?

Now, in *The Ambassadors* – I hope everyone has had time now to look at the reproduction – what do you see? What is this strange, suspended, oblique object in the foreground in front of these two figures?

The two figures are frozen, stiffened in their showy adornments. Between them is a series of objects that represent in the painting of the period the symbols of *vanitas*. At the same period, Cornelius Agrippa wrote his *De Vanitate scientiarum*, aimed as much at the arts as the sciences, and these objects are all symbolic of the sciences and arts as they were grouped at the time in the *trivium* and *quadrivium*. What, then, before this display of the domain of appearance in all its most fascinating forms, is this object, which from some angles appears to be flying through the air, at others to be tilted? You cannot know – for you turn away, thus escaping the fascination of the picture.

Begin by walking out of the room in which no doubt it has long held your attention. It is then that, turning round as you leave – as the author of the *Anamorphoses* describes it – you apprehend in this form . . . What? A skull.

This is not how it is presented at first – that figure, which the author compares to a

Hans Holbein, *The Ambassadors*. © National Gallery, London

cuttlebone and which for me suggests rather that loaf composed of two books which Dali was once pleased to place on the head of an old woman, chosen deliberately for her wretched, filthy appearance and, indeed, because she seems to be unaware of the fact, or, again, Dali's soft watches, whose signification is obviously less phallic than that of the object depicted in a flying position in the foreground of this picture.

All this shows that at the very heart of the period in which the subject emerged and geometral optics was an object of research, Holbein makes visible for us here something that is simply the subject as annihilated – annihilated in the form that is, strictly speaking, the imaged embodiment of the *minus-phi* [(– φ)] of castration, which for us, centres the whole organization of the desires through the framework of the fundamental drives.

But it is further still that we must seek the function of vision. We shall then see emerging on the basis of vision, not the phallic symbol, the anamorphic ghost, but the gaze as such, in its pulsatile, dazzling and spread out function, as it is in this picture.

This picture is simply what any picture is, a trap for the gaze. In any picture, it is precisely in seeking the gaze in each of its points that you will see it disappear. I shall try to develop this further next time.

* * *

The line and light

Desire and the picture · The story of a sardine can · The screen · Mimicry · The organ · You never look at me from the place I see you

The function of the eye may lead someone who is trying to enlighten you to distant explorations. When, for example, did the function of the organ and, to begin with, its very presence, appear in the evolution of living beings?

The relation of the subject with the organ is at the heart of our experience. Among all the organs with which we deal, the breast, the faeces, etc., there is the eye, and it is

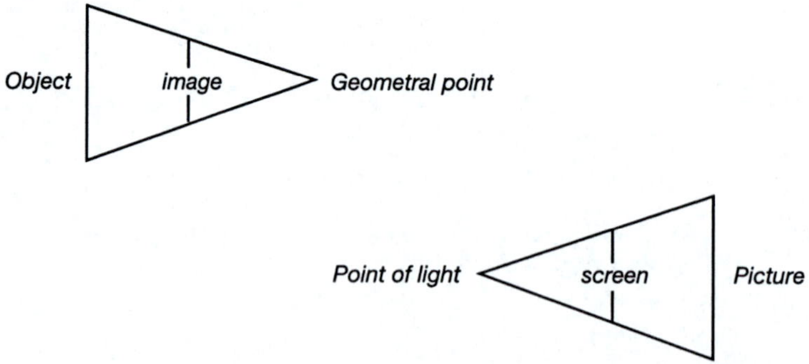

striking to see that it goes back as far as the species that represent the appearance of life. You no doubt eat oysters, innocently enough, without knowing that at this level in the animal kingdom the eye has already appeared. Such discoveries teach us, it should be said, all manner of things. Yet we must choose from among these things those that are most relative to our search.

Last time, I think I said enough to enable you to grasp the interest of this small, very simple triangular schema that I have reproduced at the top of the blackboard.

It is there simply to remind you in three terms of the optics used in this operational montage that bears witness to the inverted use of perspective, which came to dominate the technique of painting, in particular, between the end of the fifteenth and the end of the seventeenth centuries. Anamorphosis shows us that it is not a question in painting of a realistic reproduction of the things of space – a term about which one could have many reservations.

The little schema also allows me to remark that certain optics allow that which concerns vision to escape. Such optics are within the grasp of the blind. I have already referred you to Diderot's *Lettre*, which shows to what extent the blind man is capable of taking account of, reconstructing, imagining, speaking about everything that vision yields to us of space. No doubt, on this possibility, Diderot constructs a permanent equivocation with metaphysical implications, but this ambiguity animates his text and gives it its mordant character.

For us, the geometral dimension enables us to glimpse how the subject who concerns us is caught, manipulated, captured, in the field of vision.

In Holbein's picture I showed you at once – without hiding any more than usual – the singular object floating in the foreground, which is there to be looked at, in order to catch, I would almost say, *to catch in its trap*, the observer, that is to say, us. It is, in short, an obvious way, no doubt an exceptional one, and one due to some moment of reflection on the part of the painter, of showing us that, as subjects, we are literally called into the picture, and represented here as caught. For the secret of this picture, whose implications I have pointed out to you, the kinships with the *vanitas*, the way this fascinating picture presents, between the two splendidly dressed and immobile figures, everything that recalls, in the perspective of the period, the vanity of the arts and sciences – the secret of this picture is given at the moment when, moving slightly away, little by little, to the left, then turning around, we see what the magical floating object signifies. It reflects our own nothingness, in the figure of the death's head. It is a use, therefore, of the geometral dimension of vision in order to capture the subject, an obvious relation with desire which, nevertheless, remains enigmatic.

What is the desire which is caught, fixed in the picture, but which also urges the artist to put something into operation? And what is that something? This is the path along which we shall try to move today.

1

In this matter of the visible, everything is a trap, and in a strange way – as is very well shown by Maurice Merleau-Ponty in the title of one of the chapters of *Le Visible et l'invisible* – *entrelacs* (interlacing, intertwining). There is not a single one of the divisions, a single one of the double sides that the function of vision presents, that is not manifested to us as a labyrinth. As we begin to distinguish its various fields, we always perceive more and more the extent to which they intersect.

In the domain that I have called that of the geometral, it seems at first that it is light that gives us, as it were, the thread. In effect, you saw this thread last time linking us to each point of the object and, in the place where it crosses the network in the form of a screen on which we are going to map the image, functioning quite definitely as a thread. Now, the light is propagated, as one says, in a straight line, this much is certain. It would seem, then, that it is light that gives us the thread.

Yet, reflect that this thread has no need of light – all that is needed is a stretched thread. This is why the blind man would be able to follow all our demonstrations, providing we took some trouble in their presentation. We would get him, for example, to finger an object of a certain height, then follow the stretched thread. We would teach him to distinguish, by the sense of touch in his finger-ends, on a surface, a certain configuration that reproduces the mapping of the images – in the same way that we imagine, in pure optics, the variously proportioned and fundamentally homological relations, the correspondences from one point to another in space, which always, in the end, amounts to situating two points on a single thread. This construction does not, therefore, particularly enable us to apprehend what is provided by light.

How can we try to apprehend that which seems to elude us in this way in the optical structuring of space? It is always on this question that the traditional argument bears. Philosophers, going back from Alain, the last to have concerned himself with it, and quite brilliantly, to Kant, and even to Plato, all expatiate on the supposed deceptiveness of perception – and, at the same time, they all find themselves once again masters of the exercise, by stressing the fact that perception finds the object where it is, and that the appearance of the cube as a parallelogram is precisely, owing to the rupture of space that underlies our very perception, what makes us perceive it as a cube. The whole trick, the hey presto!, of the classic dialectic around perception, derives from the fact that it deals with geometral vision, that is to say, with vision in so far as it is situated in a space that is not in its essence the visual.

The essence of the relation between appearance and being, which the philosopher, conquering the field of vision, so easily masters, lies elsewhere. It is not in the straight line, but in the point of light – the point of irradiation, the play of light, fire, the source from which reflections pour forth. Light may travel in a straight line, but it is refracted, diffused, it floods, it fills – the eye is a sort of bowl – it flows over, too, it necessitates, around the ocular bowl, a whole series of organs, mechanisms, defences. The iris reacts not only to distance, but also to light, and it has to protect what takes place at the bottom of the bowl, which might, in certain circumstances, be damaged by it. The eyelid, too, when confronted with too bright a light, first blinks, that is, it screws itself up in a well-known grimace.

Furthermore, it is not that the eye has to be photo-sensitive – we know this. The whole surface of the tegument – no doubt for various reasons that are not visual – may be photo-sensitive, and this dimension can in no way be reduced to the functioning of vision. There is a certain adumbration of photo-sensitive organs in the pigmentary spots. In the eye, the pigment functions fully, in a way, of course, that the phenomenon shows to be infinitely complex. It functions within the cones, for example, in the form of a rhodopsin. It also functions inside the various layers of the retina. This pigment comes and goes in functions that are not all, nor always immediately discoverable and clear, but which suggest the depth, the complexity and, at the same time, the unity of the mechanisms concerned with light.

The relation of the subject with that which is strictly concerned with light seems, then, to be already somewhat ambiguous. Indeed, you see this on the schema of the two triangles, which are inverted at the same time as they must be placed one upon the other. What you have here is the first example of this functioning of interlacing, intersection, chiasma, which I pointed out above, and which structures the whole of this domain.

In order to give you some idea of the question posed by this relation between the subject and light, in order to show you that its place is something other than the place of the geometral point defined by geometric optics, I will now tell you a little story.

It's a true story. I was in my early twenties or thereabouts – and at that time, of course, being a young intellectual, I wanted desperately to get away, see something different, throw myself into something practical, something physical, in the country say, or at the sea. One day, I was on a small boat, with a few people from a family of fishermen in a small port. At that time, Brittany was not industrialized as it is now. There were no trawlers. The fisherman went out in his frail craft at his own risk. It was this risk, this danger, that I loved to share. But it wasn't all danger and excitement – there were also fine days. One day, then, as we were waiting for the moment to pull in the nets, an individual known as Petit-Jean, that's what we called him – like all his family, he died very young from tuberculosis, which at that time was a constant threat to the whole of that social class – this Petit-Jean pointed out to me something floating on the surface of the waves. It was a small can, a sardine can. It floated there in the sun, a witness to the canning industry, which we, in fact, were supposed to supply. It glittered in the sun. And Petit-Jean said to me – *You see that can? Do you see it? Well, it doesn't see you!*

He found this incident highly amusing – I less so. I thought about it. Why did I find it less amusing than he? It's an interesting question.

To begin with, if what Petit-Jean said to me, namely, that the can did not see me, had any meaning, it was because in a sense, it was looking at me, all the same. It was looking at me at the level of the point of light, the point at which everything that looks at me is situated – and I am not speaking metaphorically.

The point of this little story, as it had occurred to my partner, the fact that he found it so funny and I less so, derives from the fact that, if I am told a story like that one, it is because I, at that moment – as I appeared to those fellows who were earning their livings with great difficulty, in the struggle with what for them was a pitiless nature – looked like nothing on earth. In short, I was rather out of place in the picture. And it was because I felt this that I was not terribly amused at hearing myself addressed in this humorous, ironical way.

I am taking the structure at the level of the subject here, and it reflects something that is already to be found in the natural relation that the eye inscribes with regard to light. I am not simply that punctiform being located at the geometral point from which the perspective is grasped. No doubt, in the depths of my eye, the picture is painted. The picture, certainly, is in my eye. But I am not in the picture.

That which is light looks at me, and by means of that light in the depths of my eye, something is painted – something that is not simply a constructed relation, the object on which the philosopher lingers – but something that is an impression, the shimmering of a surface that is not, in advance, situated for me in its distance. This is something that introduces what was elided in the geometral relation – the depth of field, with all its ambiguity and variability, which is in no way mastered by me. It is rather it that grasps me, solicits me at every moment, and makes of the landscape something other than a landscape, something other than what I have called the picture.

The correlative of the picture, to be situated in the same place as it, that is to say, outside, is the point of gaze, while that which forms the mediation from the one to the other, that which is between the two, is something of another nature than geometral, optical space, something that plays an exactly reverse role, which operates, not because it can be traversed, but on the contrary because it is opaque – I mean the screen.

In what is presented to me as space of light, that which is gaze is always a play of light and opacity. It is always that gleam of light – it lay at the heart of my little story – it is always this which prevents me, at each point, from being a screen, from making the light appear as an iridescence that overflows it. In short, the point of gaze always participates in the ambiguity of the jewel.

And if I am anything in the picture, it is always in the form of the screen, which I earlier called the stain, the spot.

2

This is the relation of the subject with the domain of vision. The word subject must not be understood here in the usual sense of the word, in the subjective sense – this relation is not an idealist relation. This overview, which I call the subject, and which I regard as giving consistency to the picture, is not simply a representative overview.

There are many ways of being wrong about this function of the subject in the domain of the spectacle.

Certainly, there are plenty of examples in *La Phénoménologie de la perception* of what happens behind the retina. Merleau-Ponty cleverly extracts from a mass of writing some very remarkable facts, showing, for example, that simply the fact of masking, by means of a screen, part of a field functioning as a source of composite colours – produced, for example, by two wheels, two screens, which, one revolving behind the other, must compose a certain tone of light – that this intervention alone reveals in a quite different way the composition in question. Indeed, here we grasp the purely subjective function, in the ordinary sense of the word, the note of central mechanism that intervenes, for the play of light arranged in the experiment, all the elements of which we know, is distinct from what is perceived by the subject.

Perceiving the effects of reflection of a field or a colour is quite different – it does have a subjective side to it, but one arranged quite differently. Let us, for example, place a yellow field beside a blue field – by receiving the light reflected on the yellow field, the blue field will undergo some change. But, certainly, everything that is colour is merely subjective – there is no objective correlative in the spectrum to enable us to attach the quality of colour to the wavelength, or to the relevant frequency at this level of light vibration. There is something objective here, but it is situated differently.

Is that all there is to it? Is that what I am talking about when I speak of the relation between the subject and what I have called the picture? Certainly not.

The relation between the subject and the picture has been approached by certain philosophers, but they have, if I may say so, missed the point. Read the book by Raymond Ruyer called *Néo-finalisme*, and see how, in order to situate perception in a teleological perspective, he is forced to situate the subject in an absolute overview. There is no need, except in the most abstract way, to posit the subject in absolute overview, when, in the example he gives, it is merely a question of getting us to grasp what the perception of a draught-board is – a draught-board belongs essentially to that geometral optics that I was careful to distinguish at the outset. We are here in space *partes extra partes*, which always provides such an objection to the apprehension to the object. In this direction, the thing is irreducible.

Yet there is a phenomenal domain – infinitely more extended than the privileged points at which it appears – that enables us to apprehend, in its true nature, the subject in absolute overview. Even if we cannot give it being, it is nonetheless necessary. There are facts that can be articulated only in the phenomenal dimension of the overview by which I situate myself in the picture as stain – these are the facts of mimicry.

This is not the place to go into all the more or less complex problems posed by the question of mimicry. I would refer you to the specialized works on the subject – they are not only fascinating in themselves, but they provide ample material for reflexion. I shall content myself with stressing what has not, perhaps, been sufficiently brought out. To begin with, I shall ask a question – how important is the function of adaptation in mimicry?

In certain phenomena of mimicry one may speak perhaps of an adaptive or adapted coloration and realize, for example – as Cuénot has shown, probably with some relevance in certain cases – that coloration, in so far as it is adapted completely, is simply a way of defending oneself against light. In an environment in which, because of what is immediately around, the colour green predominates, as at the bottom of a pool containing green plants, an animalcule – there are innumerable ones that might serve as examples – becomes green for as long as the light may do it harm. It becomes green, therefore, in order to reflect the light *qua* green, thus protecting itself, by adaptation, from its effects.

But, in mimicry, we are dealing with something quite different. Let us take an example chosen almost at random – it is not a privileged case – that of the small crustacean known as *caprella*, to which is added the adjective *acanthifera*. When such a crustacean settles in the midst of those animals, scarcely animals, known as briozoaires, what does it imitate? It imitates what, in that quasi-plant animal known as the briozoaires, is a stain – at a particular phase of the briozoaires, an intestinal loop forms a stain, at another phase, there functions something like a coloured centre. It is to this stain shape that the crustacean adapts itself. It becomes a stain, it becomes a picture, it is inscribed in the picture. This, strictly speaking, is the origin of mimicry. And, on this basis, the fundamental dimensions of the inscription of the subject in the picture appear infinitely more justified than a more hesitant guess might suggest at first sight.

I have already referred to what Caillois says about this in his little book *Méduse et compagnie*, with that unquestionable penetration that is sometimes found in the non-specialist – his very distance may enable him to grasp certain implications in what the specialist has merely stated.

Certain scientists claim to see in the register of coloration merely more or less successful facts of adaptation. But the facts show that practically nothing that can be called adaptation – in the sense in which the term is usually understood, that is to say, as behaviour bound up with the needs of survival – practically nothing of this is to be found in mimicry, which, in most cases, proves to be inoperant, or operating strictly in the opposite direction from that which the adaptive result might be presumed to demand. On the other hand, Caillois brings out the three headings that are in effect the major dimensions in which the mimetic activity is deployed – travesty, camouflage, intimidation.

Indeed, it is in this domain that the dimension by which the subject is to be inserted in the picture is presented. Mimicry reveals something in so far as it is distinct from what might be called an *itself* that is behind. The effect of mimicry is camouflage, in the strictly technical sense. It is not a question of harmonizing with the background but, against a mottled background, of becoming mottled – exactly like the technique of camouflage practised in human warfare.

In the case of travesty, a certain sexual finality is intended. Nature shows us that this sexual aim is produced by all kinds of effects that are essentially disguise, masquerade. A level is constituted here quite distinct from the sexual aim itself, which is found to play an essential role in it, and which must not be distinguished too hastily as being that of deception. The function of the lure, in this instance, is something else, something before which we should suspend judgement before we have properly measured its effects.

Finally, the phenomenon known as intimidation also involves this over-valuation that the subject always tries to attain in his appearance. Here too, we should not be too hasty in introducing some kind of inter-subjectivity. Whenever we are dealing with imitation, we should be very careful not to think too quickly of the other who is being imitated. To imitate is no doubt to reproduce an image. But at bottom, it is, for the subject, to be inserted in a function whose exercise grasps it. It is here that we should pause for a moment.

Let us now see what the unconscious function as such tells us, in so far as it is the field which, for us, offers itself to the conquest of the subject.

3

In this direction, a remark of Caillois' should guide us. Caillois assures us that the facts of mimicry are similar, at the animal level, to what, in the human being is manifested as art, or painting. The only objection one might make to this is that it seems to indicate, for René Caillois, that the notion of painting is itself so clear that one can refer to it in order to explain something else.

What is painting? It is obviously not for nothing that we have referred to as picture the function in which the subject has to map himself as such. But when a human subject is engaged in making a picture of himself, in putting into operation that something that has as its centre the gaze, what is taking place? In the picture, the artist, we are told by some, wishes to be a subject, and the art of painting is to be distinguished from all others in that, in the work, it is as subject, as gaze, that the artist intends to impose himself on us. To this, others reply by stressing the object-like side of the art product. In both these directions, something more or less appropriate is manifested, which certainly does not exhaust the question.

I shall advance the following thesis – certainly, in the picture, something of the gaze is always manifested. The painter knows this very well – his morality, his search, his quest, his practice is that he should sustain and vary the selection of a certain kind of gaze. Looking at pictures, even those most lacking in what is usually called the gaze, and which is constituted by a pair of eyes, pictures in which any representation of the human figure is absent, like a landscape by a Dutch or a Flemish painter, you will see in the end, as in filigree, something so specific to each of the painters that you will feel the presence of the gaze. But this is merely an object of research and perhaps merely illusion.

The function of the picture – in relation to the person to whom the painter, literally, offers his picture to be seen – has a relation with the gaze. This relation is not, as it might at first seem, that of being a trap for the gaze. It might be thought that, like the actor, the painter wishes to be looked at. I do not think so. I think there is a relation with the gaze of the spectator, but that it is more complex. The painter gives something to the person who must stand in front of his painting which, in part, at least, of the painting, might be summed up thus – *You want to see? Well, take a look at this!* He gives something for the eye to feed on, but he invites the person to whom this picture is presented to lay down his gaze there as one lays down one's weapons. This is the pacifying, Apollonian effect of painting. Something is given not so much to the gaze as to the eye, something that involves the abandonment, the *laying down*, of the gaze.

The problem is that a whole side of painting – expressionism – is separated from this field. Expressionist painting, and this is its distinguishing feature, provides something by way of a certain satisfaction – in the sense in which Freud uses the term in relation to the drive – of a certain satisfaction of what is demanded by the gaze.

In other words, we must now pose the question as to the exact status of the eye as organ. The function, it is said, creates the organ. This is quite absurd – function does not even explain the organ. Whatever appears in the organism as an organ is always presented with a large multiplicity of functions. In the eye, it is clear that various functions come together. The discriminatory function is isolated to the maximum degree at the level of the *fovea*, the chosen point of distinct vision. Something quite different occurs over the rest of the surface of the retina, incorrectly distinguished by specialists as the locus of the scotopic function. But here, too, chiasma is to be found, since it is this last field, supposedly created to perceive things in diminished lighting, which provides the maximum possibility of perceiving the effects of light. If you wish to see a star of the fifth or sixth size, do not look straight at it – this is known as the Arago phenomenon. You will be able to see it only if you fix your eye to one side.

These functions of the eye do not exhaust the character of the organ in so far as it emerges on the couch, and in so far as the eye determines there what every organ determines, namely, duties. What is wrong about the reference to instinct, a reference that is so confused, is that one does not realize that instinct is the way which an organism has of extricating itself in the best possible way from an organ. There are many examples, in the animal kingdom, of cases in which the organism succumbs to an excess, a hyper-development of an organ. The supposed function of instinct in the relation between organism and organ certainly seems to have been defined as a kind of morality. We are astonished by the so-called pre-adaptations of instinct. The extraordinary thing is that the organism can do anything with its organ at all.

In my reference to the unconscious, I am dealing with the relation to the organ. It is not a question of the relation to sexuality, or even to the sex, if it is possible to give any specific reference to this term. It is a question rather of the relation to the phallus, in as much as it is lacking in the real that might be attained in the sexual goal.

It is in as much as, at the heart of the experience of the unconscious, we are dealing with that organ – determined in the subject by the inadequacy organized in the castration complex – that we can grasp to what extent the eye is caught up in a similar dialectic.

From the outset, we see, in the dialectic of the eye and the gaze, that there is no coincidence, but, on the contrary, a lure. When, in love, I solicit a look, what is profoundly unsatisfying and always missing is that – *You never look at me from the place from which I see you.*

Conversely, *what I look at is never what I wish to see*. And the relation that I mentioned earlier, between the painter and the spectator, is a play, a play of *trompe-l'œil*, whatever one says. There is no reference here to what is incorrectly called figurative, if by this you mean some reference or other to a subjacent reality.

In the classical tale of Zeuxis and Parrhasios, Zeuxis has the advantage of having made grapes that attracted the birds. The stress is placed not on the fact that these grapes were in any way perfect grapes, but on the fact that even the eye of the birds was taken in by them. This is proved by the fact that his friend Parrhasios triumphs over him for having painted on the wall a veil, a veil so lifelike that Zeuxis, turning towards him said, *Well, and now show us what you have painted behind it*. By this he showed that what was at issue was certainly deceiving the eye (*tromper l'œil*). A triumph of the gaze over the eye.

Next time, we shall return to this function of the eye and the gaze.

* * *

What is a picture?

Being and its semblance · *The lure of the screen* · Dompte-regard *and* trompe-l'œil ·[2]
The backward glance · *Gesture and touch* · Le donner-à-voir *and* invidia[3]

Today, then, I must keep to the wager to which I committed myself in choosing the terrain in which the *objet a* is most evanescent in its function of symbolizing the central lack of desire, which I have always indicated in a univocal way by the algorithm $(-\varphi)$.

I don't know whether you can see the blackboard, but as usual I have marked out a few reference-points. *The* objet a *in the field of the visible is the gaze*. After which, enclosed in a chain bracket, I have written:

$$\begin{cases} \textit{in nature} \\ \textit{as} = (-\varphi) \end{cases}$$

We can grasp in effect something which, already in nature, appropriates the gaze to the function to which it may be put in the symbolic relation in man.

Below this, I have drawn the two triangular systems that I have already introduced – the first is that which, in the geometral field, puts in our place the subject of the representation, and the second is that which turns *me* into a picture. On the right-hand line is situated, then, the apex of the first triangle, the point of the geometral subject, and it is on that line that I, too, turn myself into a picture under the gaze, which is inscribed at the apex of the second triangle. The two triangles are here superimposed, as in fact they are in the functioning of the scopic register.

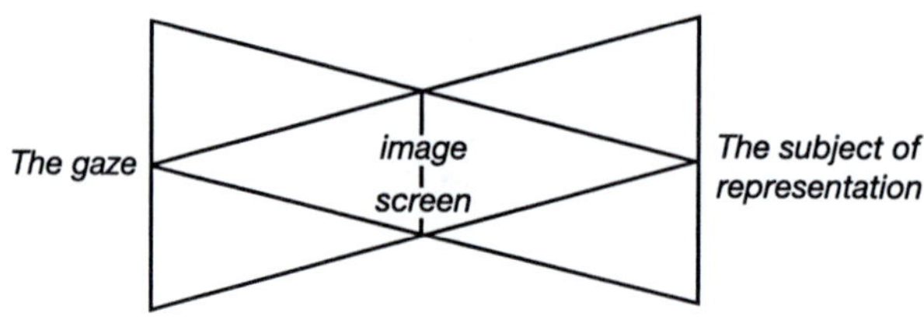

1

I must, to begin with, insist on the following: in the scopic field, the gaze is outside, I am looked at, that is to say, I am a picture.

This is the function that is found at the heart of the institution of the subject in the visible. What determines me, at the most profound level, in the visible, is the gaze that is outside. It is through the gaze that I enter light and it is from the gaze that I receive its effects. Hence it comes about that the gaze is the instrument through which light is embodied and through which – if you will allow me to use a word, as I often do, in a fragmented form – I am *photo-graphed.*

What is at issue here is not the philosophical problem of representation. From that point of view, when I am presented with a representation, I assure myself that I know quite a lot about it, I assure myself as a consciousness that knows that it is only representation, and that there is, beyond, the thing, the thing itself. Behind the phenomenon, there is the noumenon, for example. I may not be able to do anything about it, because my *transcendental categories*, as Kant would say, do just as they please and force me to take the thing in their way. But, then, that's all right, really – everything works out for the best.

In my opinion, it is not in this dialectic between the surface and that which is beyond that things are suspended. For my part, I set out from the fact that there is something that establishes a fracture, a bi-partition, a splitting of the being to which the being accommodates itself, even in the natural world.

This fact is observable in the variously modulated scale of what may be included, ultimately, under the general heading of mimicry. It is this that comes into play, quite obviously, both in sexual union and in the struggle to the death. In both situations, the being breaks up, in an extraordinary way, between its being and its semblance, between itself and that paper tiger it shows to the other. In the case of display, usually on the part of the male animal, or in the case of grimacing swelling by which the animal enters the play of combat in the form of intimidation, the being gives of himself, or receives from the other, something that is like a mask, a double, an envelope, a thrown-off skin, thrown off in order to cover the frame of a shield. It is through this separated form of himself that the being comes into play in his effects of life and death, and it might be said that it is with the help of this doubling of the other, or of oneself, that is realized the conjunction from which proceeds the renewal of beings in reproduction.

The lure plays an essential function therefore. It is not something else that seizes us at the very level of clinical experience, when, in relation to what one might imagine of the attraction to the other pole as conjoining masculine and feminine, we apprehend the prevalence of that which is presented as *travesty*. It is no doubt through the mediation of masks that the masculine and the feminine meet in the most acute, most intense way.

Only the subject – the human subject, the subject of the desire that is the essence of man – is not, unlike the animal, entirely caught up in this imaginary capture. He maps himself in it. How? In so far as he isolates the function of the screen and plays with it. Man, in effect, knows how to play with the mask as that beyond which there is the gaze. The screen is here the locus of mediation.

Last time, I alluded to the reference given by Maurice Merleau-Ponty in *La Phénoménologie de la perception* in which, from well-chosen examples based on the experiments of Gelb and Goldstein, one can already see, simply at the perceptual level, how the screen re-establishes things, in their status as real. If, by being isolated, an effect of lighting dominates us, if, for example, a beam of light directing our gaze so captivates us that it appears as a milky cone and prevents us from seeing what it illuminates, the mere fact of introducing into this field a small screen, which cuts into that which is illuminated without being seen, makes the milky light retreat, as it were, into the shadow, and allows the object it concealed to emerge.

At the perceptual level, this is the phenomenon of a relation that is to be taken in a more essential function, namely, that in its relation to desire, reality appears only as marginal.

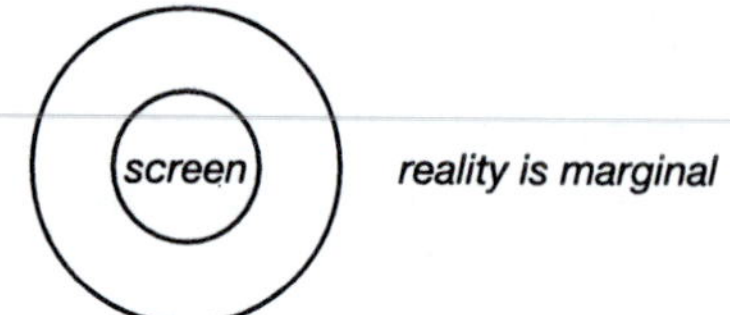

This is certainly one of the features that scarcely seems to have been noticed in pictorial creation. Yet rediscovering in the picture what is, strictly speaking, composition, the lines dividing the surfaces created by the painter, vanishing traces, lines of force, frames (*bâtis*) in which the image finds its status is a fascinating game – but I am astonished that in one very remarkable book they are called *frameworks* (*charpentes*). For this term eliminates their principal effect. By a sort of irony, on the back of this book, there nevertheless figures, as being more exemplary than any other, a picture by Rouault on which is traced a circular line to enable us to grasp the main point.

Indeed, there is something whose absence can always be observed in a picture – which is not the case in perception. This is the central field, where the separating power of the eye is exercised to the maximum in vision. In every picture, this central field cannot but be absent, and replaced by a hole – a reflection, in short, of the pupil behind which is situated the gaze. Consequently, and in as much as the picture enters into a relation to desire, the place of a central screen is always marked, which is precisely that by which, in front of the picture, I am elided as subject of the geometral plane.

This is why the picture does not come into play in the field of representation. Its end and effect are elsewhere.

2

In the scopic field, everything is articulated between two terms that act in an antinomic way – on the side of things, there is the gaze, that is to say, things look at me, and yet I see them. This is how one should understand those words, so strongly stressed, in the Gospel, *They have eyes that they might not see*. That they might not see what? Precisely, that things are looking at them.

This is why I have introduced painting into our field of exploration by the narrow door offered by us by Roger Caillois – everyone noticed last time that I made a slip of the tongue in calling him René, heaven knows why – in observing that mimicry is no doubt the equivalent of the function which, in man, is exercised in painting.

This is not the occasion to begin a psycho-analysis of the painter, which is always such a tricky matter, and which always produces a shocked reaction on the part of the listener. Nor is it a question of art criticism, and yet someone who is close to me, and whose views count for a great deal with me, told me that he was very troubled when I embarked on something very like art criticism. Of course, that is the danger, and I shall try to avoid any such confusion.

If one considers all the modulations imposed on painting by the variations of the subjectifying structure that have occurred in history, it is clear that no formula can possibly embrace those aims, those ruses, those infinitely varied tricks. Indeed, you saw clearly enough last time that after declaring that there is in painting a certain *dompte-regard*, a taming of the gaze, that is to say, that he who looks is always led by the painting to lay down his gaze, I immediately introduced the corrective that it is nevertheless in a quite direct appeal to the gaze that expressionism is situated. For those who remain unconvinced, I will explain what I mean. I am thinking of the work of such painters as Munch, James Ensor, Kubin, or even of that painting which, curiously enough, one might situate in a geographical way as laying siege to that which in our time is concentrated in painting in Paris. When will we see the limits of this siege lifted? That, if I am to believe the painter André Masson, with whom I was talking recently, is the most immediate question. Well! To point out references like these, is not to enter into the shifting, historical game of criticism, which tries to grasp what is the function of painting at a particular moment, for a particular author at a particular time. For me, it is at the radical principle of the function of this fine art that I am trying to place myself.

To begin with, I would stress that it is in setting out from painting that Maurice Merleau-Ponty was particularly led to overthrow the relation, which has always been made by thought, between the eye and the mind. What he has shown in a quite admirable way, beginning with what he calls, with Cézanne himself, *those little blues, those little browns, those little whites*, those touches that fall like rain from the painter's brush, is that the function of the painter is something quite different from the organization of the field of representation in which the philosopher held us in our status as subjects.

And what is that? Where does that get us? It already gives form and embodiment to the field in which the psycho-analyst has advanced since Freud, with what, in Freud, is crazy daring, and what, in those who follow him, soon becomes imprudence.

Freud always stressed with infinite respect that he did not intend to settle the question of what it was in artistic creation that gave it its true value. When he is dealing with painters and poets, there is a point at which his appreciation stops. He cannot say, he does not know, what, for everybody, for those who look or hear, is the value of artistic creation. Nevertheless, when he studies Leonardo, let us say, roughly speaking, that he tries to find the function that the artist's original phantasy played in his creation – his relation to those two mothers Freud sees represented in the painting in the Louvre or in the cartoon in London, by that double body, branching at the level of the waist, which seems to blossom from the entwined legs at the base. Is it in this direction that we must look?

Or should we see the principle of artistic creation in the fact that it seems to extract – remember how I translated *Vorstellungsrepräsentanz* – that something that stands for representation? Was it to this that I was leading you when I made a distinction between the picture and representation?

Certainly not – except in very rare works, except in a painting that sometimes emerges, a dream painting, so rare that it can scarcely be situated in the function of painting. Indeed, perhaps this is the limit at which we would have to designate what is called psychopathological art.

That which is the creation of the painter is structured in a quite different way. Precisely to the extent that we restore the point of view of structure in the libidinal relation, perhaps the time has come when we may question to advantage – because our new algorithms allow us to articulate the answer better – what is involved in artistic creation. For me, it is a question of creation as Freud designated it, that is to say, as sublimation, and of the value it assumes in a social field.

In a way that is at once vague and precise, and which concerns only the success of the work, Freud declares that if a creation of desire, which is pure at the level of the painter, takes on commercial value – a gratification that may, all the same, be termed secondary – it is because its effect has something profitable for society, for that part of society that comes under its influence. Broadly speaking, one can say that the work calms people, comforts them, by showing them that at least some of them can live from the exploitation of their desire. But for this to satisfy them so much, there must also be that other effect, namely, that *their* desire to contemplate finds some satisfaction in it. It elevates the mind, as one says, that is to say, it encourages renunciation. Don't you see that there is something here that indicates the function I called *dompte-regard*?

As I said last time, *dompte-regard* is also presented in the form of *trompe-l'œil*. In this sense, I appear to be moving in the opposite direction from tradition, which situates its function as being very distinct from that of painting. Yet I did not hesitate to end my last talk by observing, in the opposition of the works of Zeuxis and Parrhasios, the ambiguity of two levels, that of the natural function of the lure and that of *trompe-l'œil*.

If the birds rushed to the surface on which Zeuxis had deposited his dabs of colour, taking the picture for edible grapes, let us observe that the success of such an undertaking does not imply in the least that the grapes were admirably reproduced, like those we can see in the basket held by Caravaggio's *Bacchus* in the Uffizi. If the grapes had been painted in this way, it is not very likely that the birds would have been deceived, for why should the birds see grapes portrayed with such extraordinary verisimilitude? There would have to be something more reduced, something closer to the sign, in something representing grapes for the birds. But the opposite example of Parrhasios makes it clear that if one wishes to deceive a man, what one presents to him is the painting of a veil, that is to say, something that incites him to ask what is behind it.

It is here that this little story becomes useful in showing us why Plato protests against the illusion of painting. The point is not that painting gives an illusory equivalence to the object, even if Plato seems to be saying this. The point is that the *trompe-l'œil* of painting pretends to be something other than what it is.

What is it that attracts and satisfies us in *trompe-l'œil*? When is it that it captures our attention and delights us? At the moment when, by a mere shift of our gaze, we are able to realize that the representation does not move with the gaze and that it is merely a *trompe-l'œil*. For it appears at that moment as something other than it seemed, or rather it now seems to be that something else. The picture does not compete with appearance, it competes with what Plato designates for us beyond appearance as being the Idea. It is because the picture is the appearance that says it is that which gives the appearance that Plato attacks painting, as if it were an activity competing with his own.

This other thing is the *petit a*, around which there revolves a combat of which *trompe-l'œil* is the soul.

If one tries to represent the position of the painter concretely in history, one realizes that he is the source of something that may pass into the real and on which, at all times, one might say, one takes a lease. The painter, it is said, no longer depends on aristocratic patrons. But the situation is not fundamentally changed with the advent of the picture dealer. He, too, is a patron, and a patron of the same stamp. Before the aristocratic patron, it was the religious institution, with the holy image, that gave artists a living. The artist always has some financial body behind him and it is always a question of the *objet á*, or rather a question of reducing it – which may, at a certain level, strike you as being rather mythical – to an *a* with which – this is true in the last resort – it is the painter as creator who sets up a dialogue.

But it is much more instructive to see how the *a* functions in its social repercussions.

Icons – the Christ in triumph in the vault at Daphnis or the admirable Byzantine mosaics – undoubtedly have the effect of holding us under their gaze. We might stop there, but were we to do so we would not really grasp the motive that made the painter set about making this icon, or the motive it satisfies in being presented to us. It is something to do with the gaze, of course, but there is more to it than that. What makes the value of the icon is that the god it represents is also looking at it. It is intended to please God. At this level, the artist is operating on the sacrificial plane – he is playing with those things, in this case images, that may arouse the desire of God.

Indeed, God is the creator of certain images – we see this in Genesis, with the *Zelem Elohim*. And iconoclastic thought itself still preserves this when it declares there is a god that does not care for this. He is certainly alone in this. But I do not want to go too far today in a direction that would take us right to the heart of one of the most essential elements of the province of the Names-of-the-Father: a certain pact may be signed beyond every image. Where we are, the image remains a go-between with the divinity – if Javeh forbids the Jews to make idols, it is because they give pleasure to the other gods. In a certain register it is not God who is not anthropomorphic, it is man who is begged not to be so. But that's enough of that.

Let us pass now to the next stage, which I shall call *communal*. Let us go to the great hall of the Doges' Palace in which are painted all kinds of battles, such as the battle of Lepanto, etc. The social function, which was already emerging at the religious level, is now becoming clear. Who comes here? Those who form what Retz calls '*les peuples*', the audiences. And what do the audiences see in these vast compositions? They see the gaze of those persons who, when the audience are not there, deliberate in this hall. Behind the picture, it is their gaze that is there.

You see, one can say that there are always lots of gazes behind. Nothing new is introduced in this respect by the epoch that André Malraux distinguishes as the modern, that which comes to be dominated by what he calls '*the incomparable monster*', namely, the gaze of the painter, which claims to impose itself as being the only gaze. There always was a gaze behind. But – this is the most subtle point – where does this gaze come from?

3

We now come back to the *little blues, little whites, little browns* of Cézanne, or again to the delightful example that Maurice Merleau-Ponty gives in passing in his *Signes*, namely, that strange slow-motion film in which one sees Matisse painting. The important point is that Matisse himself was overwhelmed by the film. Maurice Merleau-Ponty draws attention to the paradox of this gesture which, enlarged by the distension of time, enables us to imagine the most perfect deliberation in each of these brush strokes. This is an illusion, he says. What occurs as these strokes, which go to make up the miracle of the picture, fall like rain from the painter's brush is not choice, but something else. Can we not try to formulate what this something else is?

Should not the question be brought closer to what I called the rain of the brush? If a bird were to paint would it not be by letting fall its feathers, a snake by casting off its scales, a tree by letting fall its leaves? What it amounts to is the first act in the laying down of the gaze. A sovereign act, no doubt, since it passes into something that is materialized and which, from this sovereignty, will render obsolete, excluded, inoperant, whatever, coming from elsewhere, will be presented before this product.

Let us not forget that the painter's brushstroke is something in which a movement is terminated. We are faced here with something that gives a new and different meaning to the term regression – we are faced with the element of motive in the sense of response, in so far as it produces, behind it, its own stimulus.

There, that by which the original temporality in which the relation to the other is situated as distinct is here, in the scopic dimension, that of the terminal moment. That which in the identificatory dialectic of the signifier and the spoken will be projected forward as haste, is here, on the contrary, the end, that which, at the outset of any new intelligence, will be called the moment of seeing.

This terminal moment is that which enables us to distinguish between a gesture and an act. It is by means of the gesture that the brushstroke is applied to the canvas. And so true is it that the gesture is always present there that there can be no doubt that the picture is first felt by us, as the terms *impression* or *impressionism* imply, as having more affinity with the gesture than with any other type of movement. All action represented in a picture appears to us as a battle scene, that is to say, as something theatrical, necessarily created for the gesture. And, again, it is this insertion in the gesture that means that one cannot turn it upside down – whether or not it is figurative. If you turn a transparency around, you realize at once if it is being shown to you with the left in the place of the right. The direction of the gesture of the hand indicates sufficiently this lateral symmetry.

What we see here, then, is that the gaze operates in a certain descent, a descent of desire, no doubt. But how can we express this? The subject is not completely aware of it – he operates by remote control. Modifying the formula I have of desire as unconscious – *man's desire is the desire of the Other* – I would say that it is a question of a sort of desire *on the part of* the Other, at the end of which is the *showing* (*le donner-à-voir*).

How could this *showing* satisfy something, if there is not some appetite of the eye on the part of the person looking? This appetite of the eye that must be fed produces the hypnotic value of painting. For me, this value is to be sought on a much less elevated plane than might be supposed, namely, in that which is the true function of the organ of the eye, the eye filled with voracity, the evil eye.

It is striking, when one thinks of the universality of the function of the evil eye, that there is no trace anywhere of a good eye, of an eye that blesses. What can this mean, except that the eye carries with it the fatal function of being in itself endowed – if you will allow me to play on several registers at once – with a power to separate. But this power to separate goes much further than distinct vision. The powers that are attributed to it, of drying up the milk of an animal on which it falls – a belief as widespread in our time as in any other, and in the most civilized countries – of bringing with it disease or misfortune – where can we better picture this power than in *invidia*?

Invidia comes from *videre*. The most exemplary *invidia*, for us analysts, is the one I found long ago in Augustine, in which he sums up his entire fate, namely, that of the little child seeing his brother at his mother's breast, looking at him *amare conspectu*, with a bitter look, which seems to tear him to pieces and has on himself the effect of a poison.

In order to understand what *invidia* is in its function as gaze it must not be confused with jealousy. What the small child, or whoever, *envies* is not at all necessarily what he might want – *avoir envie*, as one improperly puts it. Who can say that the child who looks at his younger brother still needs to be at the breast? Everyone knows that envy is usually aroused by the possession of goods which would be of no use to the person who is envious of them, and about the true nature of which he does not have the least idea.

Such is true envy – the envy that makes the subject pale before the image of a completeness closed upon itself, before the idea that the *petit a*, the separated *a* from which he is hanging, may be for another the possession that gives satisfaction, *Befriedigung*.

It is to this register of the eye as made desperate by the gaze that we must go if we are to grasp the taming, civilizing and fascinating power of the function of the picture. The profound relation between the *a* and desire will serve as an example when I introduce the subject of the transference.

Translated by Alan Sheridan

Notes

1

In vain your image comes to meet me
And does not enter me where I am who only shows it
Turning towards me you can find
On the wall of my gaze only your dreamt-of shadow.

I am that wretch comparable with mirrors
That can reflect but cannot see
Like them my eye is empty and like them inhabited
By your absence which makes them blind.

2 The sense of the verb *dompter* is 'to tame', 'to subdue'. The reference, then, is to a situation in which the gaze is tamed by some object, such as a picture. Lacan has invented the phrase *dompte-regard* as a counterpart to the notion of *trompe-l'œil*, which has of course passed into the English language. – Translator.

3 *Donner-à-voir* means literally 'to give to be seen' and, therefore, 'to offer to the view'. The Latin *invidia*, translated as 'envy', derives, as Lacan points out, from *videre*, to see.

33

APPROACHING ABJECTION

Julia Kristeva

No Beast is there without glimmer of infinity,
No eye so vile nor abject that brushes not
Against lightning from on high, now tender, now fierce.
(Victor Hugo, *La Légende des siècles*)

Neither subject nor object

There looms, within abjection, one of those violent, dark revolts of being, directed against a threat that seems to emanate from an exorbitant outside or inside, ejected beyond the scope of the possible, the tolerable, the thinkable. It lies there, quite close, but it cannot be assimilated. It beseeches, worries, and fascinates desire, which, nevertheless, does not let itself be seduced. Apprehensive, desire turns aside; sickened, it rejects. A certainty protects it from the shameful – a certainty of which it is proud holds on to it. But simultaneously, just the same, that impetus, that spasm, that leap is drawn toward an elsewhere as tempting as it is condemned. Unflaggingly, like an inescapable boomerang, a vortex of summons and repulsion places the one haunted by it literally beside himself.

When I am beset by abjection, the twisted braid of affects and thoughts I call by such a name does not have, properly speaking, a definable *object*. The abject is not an ob-ject facing me, which I name or imagine. Nor is it an ob-jest, an otherness ceaselessly fleeing in a systematic quest of desire. What is abject is not my correlative, which, providing me with someone or something else as support, would allow me to be more or less detached and autonomous. The abject has only one quality of the object – that of being opposed to *I*. If the object, however, through its opposition, settles me within the fragile texture of a desire for meaning, which, as a matter of fact, makes me ceaselessly and infinitely homologous to it, what is *abject*, on the contrary, the jettisoned object, is radically excluded and draws me toward the place where meaning collapses. A certain 'ego' that merged with its master, a superego, has flatly driven it away. It lies outside, beyond the set, and does not seem to agree to the latter's rules of the game. And yet, from its place of banishment, the abject does not cease challenging its master. Without a sign (for him), it beseeches a discharge, a convulsion, a crying out. To each ego its object, to each superego its abject. It is not the white expanse or slack boredom of repression, not the translations and transformations of desire that wrench bodies, nights, and discourse; rather it is a brutish suffering that 'I' puts up with, sublime and devastated, for 'I' deposits it to the father's account [*verse au père – père-version*]: I endure it, for I imagine that such is the desire of the other. A massive and sudden emergence of uncanniness, which, familiar as it might have been in an opaque and forgotten life, now harries me as radically separate, loathsome. Not me. Not that. But not nothing, either. A 'something' that I do not recognize as a thing. A weight of meaninglessness, about which there is nothing insignificant, and which crushes me. On the edge of nonexistence and hallucination, of a reality that, if I acknowledge it, annihilates me. There, abject and abjection are my safeguards. The primers of my culture.

The improper/unclean

Loathing an item of food, a piece of filth, waste, or dung. The spasms and vomiting that protect me. The repugnance, the retching that thrusts me to the side and turns me away from defilement, sewage, and muck. The shame of compromise, of being in the middle of treachery. The fascinated start that leads me toward and separates me from them.

Food loathing is perhaps the most elementary and most archaic form of abjection. When the eyes see or the lips touch that skin on the surface of milk – harmless, thin as a sheet of cigarette paper, pitiful as a nail paring – I experience a gagging sensation and, still farther down, spasms in the stomach, the belly; and all the organs shrivel up the body, provoke tears and bile, increase heartbeat, cause forehead and hands to perspire. Along with sight-clouding dizziness, *nausea* makes me balk at that milk cream, separates me from the mother and father who proffer it. 'I' want none of that element, sign of their desire; 'I' do not want to listen, 'I' do not assimilate it, 'I' expel it. But since the food is not an 'other' for 'me,' who am only in their desire, I expel *myself*, I spit *myself* out, I abject *myself* within the same motion through which 'I' claim to establish *myself*. That detail, perhaps an insignificant one, but one that they ferret out, emphasize, evaluate, that trifle turns me inside out, guts sprawling; it is thus that *they* see that 'I' am in the process of becoming an other at the expense of my own death. During that course in which 'I' become, I give birth to myself amid the violence of sobs, of vomit. Mute protest of the symptom, shattering violence of a convulsion that, to be sure, is inscribed in a symbolic system, but in which, without either wanting or being able to become integrated in order to answer to it, it reacts, it abreacts. It abjects.

The corpse (or cadaver: *cadere*, to fall), that which has irremediably come a cropper, is cesspool, and death; it upsets even more violently the one who confronts it as fragile and fallacious chance. A wound with blood and pus, or the sickly, acrid smell of sweat, of decay, does not *signify* death. In the presence of signified death – a flat encephalograph, for instance – I would understand, react, or accept. No, as in true theater, without makeup or masks, refuse and corpses *show me* what I permanently thrust aside in order to live. These body fluids, this defilement, this shit are what life withstands, hardly and with difficulty, on the part of death. There, I am at the border of my condition as a living being. My body extricates itself, as being alive, from that border. Such wastes drop so that I might live, until, from loss to loss, nothing remains in me and my entire body falls beyond the limit – *cadere*, cadaver. If dung signifies the other side of the border, the place where I am not and which permits me to be, the corpse, the most sickening of wastes, is a border that has encroached upon everything. It is no longer I who expel, 'I' is expelled. The border has become an object. How can I be without border? That elsewhere that I imagine beyond the present, or that I hallucinate so that I might, in a present time, speak to you, conceive of you – it is now here, jetted, abjected, into 'my' world. Deprived of world, therefore, I *fall in a faint*. In that compelling, raw, insolent thing in the morgue's full sunlight, in that thing that no longer matches and therefore no longer signifies anything, I behold the breaking down of a world that has erased its borders: fainting away. The corpse, seen without God and outside of science, is the utmost of abjection. It is death infecting life. Abject. It is something rejected from which one does not part, from which one does not protect oneself as from an object. Imaginary uncanniness and real threat, it beckons to us and ends up engulfing us.

It is thus not lack of cleanliness or health that causes abjection but what disturbs identity, system, order. What does not respect borders, positions, rules. The in-between, the ambiguous, the composite. The traitor, the liar, the criminal with a good conscience, the shameless rapist, the killer who claims he is a savior . . . Any crime, because it draws attention to the fragility of the law, is abject, but premeditated crime, cunning murder, hypocritical revenge are even more so because they heighten the display of such fragility. He who denies morality is not abject; there can be grandeur in amorality and even in crime that flaunts its disrespect for the law – rebellious, liberating, and suicidal crime. Abjection, on the other hand, is immoral, sinister, scheming, and shady: a terror that dissembles, a hatred that smiles, a passion that uses the body for barter instead of inflaming it, a debtor who sells you up, a friend who stabs you . . .

In the dark halls of the museum that is now what remains of Auschwitz, I see a heap of children's shoes, or something like that, something I have already seen elsewhere, under a Christmas tree, for instance, dolls I believe. The abjection of Nazi crime reaches its apex when death, which, in any case, kills me, interferes with what, in my living universe, is supposed to save me from death: childhood, science, among other things.

The abjection of self

If it be true that the abject simultaneously beseeches and pulverizes the subject, one can understand that it is experienced at the peak of its strength when that subject, weary of fruitless attempts to identify with something on the outside, finds the impossible within; when it finds that the impossible constitutes its very *being*, that it *is* none other than abject. The abjection of self would be the culminating form of that experience of the subject to which it is revealed that all its objects are based merely on the inaugural loss that laid the foundations of its own being. There is nothing like the abjection of self to show that all abjection is in fact recognition of the want on which any being, meaning, language, or desire is founded. One always passes too quickly over this word, 'want,' and today psychoanalysts are finally taking into account only its more or less fetishized product, the 'object of want.' But if one imagines (and imagine one must, for it is the working of imagination whose foundations are being laid here) the experience of *want* itself as logically preliminary to being and object – to the being of the object – then one understands that abjection, and even more so abjection of self, is its only signified. Its signifier, then, is none but literature. Mystical Christendom turned this abjection of self into the ultimate proof of humility before God, witness

Elizabeth of Hungary who 'though a great princess, delighted in nothing so much as in abasing herself.'[1]

The question remains as to the ordeal, a secular one this time, that abjection can constitute for someone who, in what is termed knowledge of castration, turning away from perverse dodges, presents himself with his own body and ego as the most precious non-objects; they are no longer seen in their own right but forfeited, abject. The termination of analysis can lead us there, as we shall see. Such are the pangs and delights of masochism.

Essentially different from 'uncanniness,' more violent, too, abjection is elaborated through a failure to recognize its kin; nothing is familiar, not even the shadow of a memory. I imagine a child who has swallowed up his parents too soon, who frightens himself on that account, 'all by himself,' and, to save himself, rejects and throws up everything that is given to him – all gifts, all objects. He has, he could have, a sense of the abject. Even before things for him *are* – hence before they are signifiable – he drives them out, dominated by drive as he is, and constitutes his own territory, edged by the abject. A sacred configuration. Fear cements his compound, conjoined to another world, thrown up, driven out, forfeited. What he has swallowed up instead of maternal love is an emptiness, or rather a maternal hatred without a word for the words of the father; that is what he tries to cleanse himself of, tirelessly. What solace does he come upon within such loathing? Perhaps a father, existing but unsettled, loving but unsteady, merely an apparition but an apparition that remains. Without him the holy brat would probably have no sense of the sacred; a blank subject, he would remain, discomfited, at the dump for non-objects that are always forfeited, from which, on the contrary, fortified by abjection, he tries to extricate himself. For he is not mad, he through whom the abject exists. Out of the daze that has petrified him before the untouchable, impossible, absent body of the mother, a daze that has cut off his impulses from their objects, that is, from their representations, out of such daze he causes, along with loathing, one word to crop up – fear. The phobic has no other object than the abject. But that word, 'fear' – a fluid haze, an elusive clamminess – no sooner has it cropped up than it shades off like a mirage and permeates all words of the language with nonexistence, with a hallucinatory, ghostly glimmer. Thus, fear having been bracketed, discourse will seem tenable only if it ceaselessly confront that otherness, a burden both repellent and repelled, a deep well of memory that is unapproachable and intimate: the abject.

Beyond the unconscious

Put another way, it means that there are lives not sustained by *desire*, as desire is always for objects. Such lives are based on *exclusion*. They are clearly distinguishable from those understood as neurotic or psychotic, articulated by *negation* and its modalities, *transgression*, *denial*, and *repudiation*. Their dynamics challenges the theory of the unconscious, seeing that the latter is dependent upon a dialectic of negativity.

The theory of the unconscious, as is well known, presupposes a repression of contents (affects and presentations) that, thereby, do not have access to consciousness but effect within the subject modifications, either of speech (parapraxes, etc.), or of the body (symptoms), or both (hallucinations, etc.). As correlative to the notion of *repression*, Freud put forward that of *denial* as a means of figuring out neurosis, that of *rejection* (*repudiation*) as a means of situating psychosis. The asymmetry of the two repressions becomes more marked owing to denial's bearing on the object whereas repudiation affects desire itself (Lacan, in perfect keeping with Freud's thought, interprets that as 'repudiation of the Name of the Father').

Yet, facing the ab-ject and more specifically phobia and the splitting of the ego (a point I shall return to), one might ask if those articulations of negativity germane to the unconscious (inherited by Freud from philosophy and psychology) have not become inoperative. The 'unconscious' contents remain here *excluded* but in strange fashion: not radically enough to allow for a secure differentiation between subject and object, and yet clearly enough for a defensive *position* to be established – one that implies a refusal but also a sublimating elaboration. As if the fundamental opposition were between I and Other or, in more archaic fashion, between Inside and Outside. As if such an opposition subsumed the one between Conscious and Unconscious, elaborated on the basis of neuroses.

Owing to the ambiguous opposition I/Other, Inside/Outside – an opposition that is vigorous but previous, violent but uncertain – there are contents, 'normally' unconscious in neurotics, that become explicit if not conscious in 'borderline' patients' speeches and behaviour. Such contents are often openly manifested through symbolic practices, without by the same token being integrated into the judging consciousness of those particular subjects. Since they make the conscious/unconscious distinction irrelevant, borderline subjects and their speech constitute propitious ground for a sublimating discourse ('aesthetic' or 'mystical,' etc.), rather than a scientific or rationalist one.

An exile who asks, 'Where?'

The one by whom the abject exists is thus a *deject* who places (himself), *separates* (himself), situates (himself), and therefore *strays* instead of getting his bearings, desiring, belonging, or refusing. Situationist in a sense, and not without laughter – since laughing is a way of placing or displacing abjection. Necessarily dichotomous, somewhat Manichaean, he divides, excludes, and without, properly speaking, wishing to know his abjections is not at all unaware of them. Often, moreover, he includes himself among them, thus casting within himself the scalpel that carries out his separations.

Instead of sounding himself as to his 'being,' he does so concerning his place: '*Where* am I?' instead of '*Who* am I?' For the space that engrosses the deject, the excluded, is never *one*, nor *homogeneous*, nor *totalizable*, but essentially divisible, foldable, and catastrophic. A deviser of territories, languages, works, the *deject* never stops demarcating his universe whose fluid confines – for they are constituted of a non-object, the abject – constantly question his solidity and impel him to start afresh. A tireless builder, the deject is in short a *stray*. He is on a journey, during the night, the end of which keeps receding. He has a sense of the danger, of the loss that the pseudo-object attracting him represents for him, but he cannot help taking the risk at the very moment he sets himself apart. And the more he strays, the more he is saved.

Time: forgetfulness and thunder

For it is out of such straying on excluded ground that he draws his jouissance. The abject from which he does not cease separating is for him, in short, a *land of oblivion* that is constantly remembered. Once upon blotted-out time, the abject must have been a magnetized pole of covetousness. But the ashes of oblivion now serve as a screen and reflect aversion, repugnance. The clean and proper (in the sense of incorporated and incorporable) becomes filthy, the sought-after turns into the banished, fascination into shame. Then, forgotten time crops up suddenly and condenses into a flash of lightning an operation that, if it were thought out, would involve bringing together the two opposite terms but, on account of that flash, is discharged like thunder. The time of abjection is double: a time of oblivion and thunder, of veiled infinity and the moment when revelation bursts forth.

Jouissance and affect

Jouissance, in short. For the stray considers himself as equivalent to a Third Party. He secures the latter's judgment, he acts on the strength of its power in order to condemn, he grounds himself on its law to tear the veil of oblivion but also to set up its object as inoperative. As jettisoned. Parachuted by the Other. A ternary structure, if you wish, held in keystone position by the Other, but a 'structure' that is skewed, a topology of catastrophe. For, having provided itself with an *alter ego*, the Other no longer has a grip on the three apices of the triangle where subjective homogeneity resides; and so, it jettisons the object into an abominable real, inaccessible except through jouissance. It follows that jouissance alone causes the abject to exist as such. One does not know it, one does not desire it, one joys in it [*on en jouit*]. Violently and painfully. A passion. And, as in jouissance where the object of desire, known as object *a* [in Lacan's terminology], bursts with the shattered mirror where the ego gives up its image in order to contemplate itself in the Other, there is nothing either objective or objectal to the abject. It is simply a frontier, a repulsive gift that the Other, having become *alter ego*, drops so that 'I' does not disappear in it but finds, in that sublime alienation, a forfeited existence. Hence a jouissance in which the subject is swallowed up but in which the Other, in return, keeps the subject from foundering by making it repugnant. One thus understands why so many victims of the abject are its fascinated victims – if not its submissive and willing ones.

We may call it a border; abjection is above all ambiguity. Because, while releasing a hold, it does not radically cut off the subject from what threatens it – on the contrary, abjection acknowledges it to be in perpetual danger. But also because abjection itself is a composite of judgment and affect, of condemnation and yearning, of signs and drives. Abjection preserves what existed in the archaism of pre-objectal relationship, in the immemorial violence with which a body becomes separated from another body in order to be – maintaining that night in which the outline of the signified thing vanishes and where only the imponderable affect is carried out. To be sure, if I am affected by what does not yet appear to me as a thing, it is because laws, connections, and even structures of meaning govern and condition me. That order, that glance, that voice, that gesture, which enact the law for my frightened body, constitute and bring about an effect and not yet a sign. I speak to it in vain in order to exclude it from what will no longer be, for myself, a world that can be assimilated. Obviously, *I am* only *like* someone else: mimetic logic of the advent of the ego, objects, and signs. But when I *seek* (myself), *lose* (myself), or experience *jouissance* – then 'I' is *heterogeneous*. Discomfort, unease, dizziness stemming from an ambiguity that, through the violence of a revolt *against*, demarcates a space out of which signs and objects arise. Thus braided, woven, ambivalent, a heterogeneous flux marks out a territory that I can call my own because the Other, having dwelt in me as *alter ego*, points it out to me through loathing.

This means once more that the heterogeneous flow, which portions the abject and sends back abjection, already dwells in a human animal that has been highly altered. I experience abjection only if an Other has settled in place and stead of what will be 'me.' Not at all an other with whom I identify and incorporate, but an Other who precedes and possesses me, and through such possession causes me to be. A possession previous to my advent: a being-there of the symbolic that a father might or might not embody. Significance is indeed inherent in the human body.

At the limit of primal repression

If, on account of that Other, a space becomes demarcated, separating the abject from what will be a subject and its objects, it is because a repression that one might call 'primal' has been effected prior to the springing forth of the ego, of its objects and representations. The latter, in turn, as they depend on another repression, the 'secondary' one, arrive only a posteriori on an enigmatic foundation that has already been marked off; its return, in a phobic, obsessional, psychotic guise, or more generally and in more imaginary fashion in the shape of *abjection*, notifies us of the limits of the human universe.

On such limits and at the limit one could say that there is no unconscious, which is elaborated when representations and affects (whether or not tied to representations) shape a logic. Here, on the contrary, consciousness has not assumed its rights and transformed into signifiers those fluid demarcations of yet unstable territories where an 'I' that is taking shape is ceaselessly straying. We are no longer within the sphere of the unconscious but at the limit of primal repression that, nevertheless, has discovered an intrinsically corporeal and already signifying brand, symptom, and sign: repugnance, disgust, abjection. There is an effervescence of object and sign – not of desire but of intolerable significance; they tumble over into non-sense or the impossible real, but they appear even so in spite of 'myself' (which is not) as abjection.

Premises of the sign, linings of the sublime

Let us pause a while at this juncture. If the abject is already a wellspring of sign for a non-object, on the edges of primal repression, one can understand its skirting the somatic symptom on the one hand and sublimation on the other. The *symptom*: a language that gives up, a structure within the body, a non-assimilable alien, a monster, a tumor, a cancer that the listening devices of the unconscious do not hear, for its strayed subject is huddled outside the paths of desire. *Sublimation*, on the contrary, is nothing else than the possibility of naming the pre-nominal, the pre-objectal, which are in fact only a trans-nominal, a trans-objectal. In the symptom, the abject permeates me, I become abject. Through sublimation, I keep it under control. The abject is edged with the sublime. It is not the same moment on the journey, but the same subject and speech bring them into being.

For the sublime has no object either. When the starry sky, a vista of open seas or a stained glass window shedding purple beams fascinate me, there is a cluster of meaning, of colors, of words, of caresses, there are light touches, scents, sighs, cadences that arise, shroud me, carry me away, and sweep me beyond the things that I see, hear, or think. The 'sublime' object dissolves in the raptures of a bottomless memory. It is such a memory, which, from stopping point to stopping point, remembrance to remembrance, love to love, transfers that object to the refulgent point of the dazzlement in which I stray in order to be. As soon as I perceive it, as soon as I name it, the sublime triggers – it has always already triggered – a spree of perceptions and words that expands memory boundlessly. I then forget the point of departure and find myself removed to a secondary universe, set off from the one where 'I' am – delight and loss. Not at all short of but always with and through perception and words, the sublime is a *something added* that expands us, overstrains us, and causes us to be both *here*, as dejects, and *there*, as others and sparkling. A divergence, an impossible bounding. Everything missed, joy – fascination.

Before the beginning: separation

The abject might then appear as the most *fragile* (from a synchronic point of view), the most *archaic* (from a diachronic one) sublimation of an 'object' still inseparable from drives. The abject is that pseudo-object that is made up *before* but appears only *within* the gaps of secondary repression. *The abject would thus be the 'object' of primal repression.*

But what is primal repression? Let us call it the ability of the speaking being, always already haunted by the Other, to divide, reject, repeat. Without *one* division, *one* separation, *one* subject/object having been constituted (not yet, or no longer yet). Why? Perhaps because of maternal anguish, unable to be satiated within the encompassing symbolic.

The abject confronts us, on the one hand, with those fragile states where man strays on the territories of *animal*. Thus, by way of abjection, primitive societies have marked out a precise area of their culture in order to remove it from the threatening world of animals or animalism, which were imagined as representatives of sex and murder.

The abject confronts us, on the other hand, and this time within our personal archeology, with our earliest attempts to release the hold of *maternal* entity even before ex-isting outside of her, thanks to the autonomy of language. It is a violent, clumsy breaking away, with the constant risk of falling back under the sway of a power as securing as it is stifling. The difficulty a mother has in acknowledging (or being acknowledged by) the symbolic realm – in other words, the problem she has with the phallus that her father or her husband stands for – is not such as to help the future subject leave the natural mansion. The child can serve its mother as token of her own authentication; there is, however, hardly any reason for her to serve as go-between for it to become autonomous and authentic in its turn. In such close combat, the symbolic light that a third party, eventually the father, can contribute helps the future subject, the more so if it happens to be endowed with a robust supply of drive energy, in pursuing a reluctant struggle against what, having been the mother, will turn into an abject. Repelling, rejecting; repelling itself, rejecting itself. Ab-jecting.

In this struggle, which fashions the human beings, the *mimesis*, by means of which he becomes homologous to another in order to become himself, is in short logically and chronologically secondary. Even before being *like*, 'I' am not but do *separate, reject, ab-ject*. Abjection, with a meaning broadened to take in subjective diachrony, *is a precondition to narcissism*. It is coexistent with it and causes it to be permanently brittle. The more or less beautiful image in which I behold or recognize myself rests upon an abjection that sunders it as soon as repression, the constant watchman, is relaxed.

The 'chora,' receptacle of narcissism

Let us enter, for a moment, into that Freudian aporia called primal repression. Curious primacy, where what is repressed cannot really be held down, and where what represses always already borrows its strength and authority from what is apparently very secondary: language. Let us therefore not speak of primacy but of the instability of the symbolic function in its most significant aspect – the prohibition placed on the maternal body (as a defense against autoeroticism and incest taboo). Here, drives hold sway and constitute a strange space that I shall name, after Plato (*Timeus*, 48–53), a *chora*, a receptacle.

For the benefit of the ego or its detriment, drives, whether life drives or death drives, serve to correlate that 'not yet' ego with an 'object' in order to establish both of them. Such a process, while dichotomous (inside/outside, ego/not ego) and repetitive, has nevertheless something centripetal about it: it aims to settle the ego as center of a solar system of objects. If, by dint of coming back towards the center, the drive's motion should eventually become centrifugal, hence fasten on the Other and come into being as sign so as to produce meaning – that is, literally speaking, exorbitant.

But from that moment on, while I recognize my image as sign and change in order to signify, another economy is instituted. The sign represses the *chora* and its eternal return. Desire alone will henceforth be witness to that 'primal' pulsation. But desire ex-patriates the *ego* toward an *other* subject and accepts the exactness of the ego only as narcissistic. Narcissism then appears as a regression to a position set back from the other, a return to a self-contemplative, conservative, self-sufficient haven. Actually, such narcissism never is the wrinkleless image of the Greek youth in a quiet fountain. The conflicts of drives muddle its bed, cloud its water, and bring forth everything that, by not becoming integrated with a given system of signs, is abjection for it.

Abjection is therefore a kind of *narcissistic crisis*: it is witness to the ephemeral aspect of the state called 'narcissism' with reproachful jealousy, heaven knows why; what is more, abjection gives narcissism (the thing and the concept) its classification as 'seeming.'

Nevertheless, it is enough that a prohibition, which can be a superego, block the desire craving an other – or that this other, as its role demands, not fulfill it – for desire and its signifiers to turn back toward the 'same,' thus clouding the waters of Narcissus. It is precisely at the moment of narcissistic perturbation (all things considered, the permanent state of the speaking being, if he would only hear himself speak) that secondary repression, with its reserve of symbolic means, attempts to transfer to its own account, which has thus been overdrawn, the resources of primal repression. The archaic economy is brought into full light of day, signified, verbalized. Its strategies (rejecting, separating, repeating/abjecting) hence find a symbolic existence, and the very logic of the symbolic – arguments, demonstrations, proofs, etc. – must conform to it. It is then that the object ceases to be circumscribed, reasoned with, thrust aside: it appears as abject.

Two seemingly contradictory causes bring about the narcissistic crisis that provides, along with its truth, a view of the abject. *Too much strictness on the part of the Other*, confused with the One and the Law. The *lapse of the Other*, which shows through the breakdown of objects of desire. In both instances, the abject appears in order to uphold 'I' within the Other. The abject is the violence of mourning for an 'object' that has always already been lost. The abject shatters the wall of repression and its judgments. It takes the ego back to its source on the abominable limits from which, in order to be, the ego has broken away – it assigns it a source in the non-ego, drive, and death. Abjection is a resurrection that has gone through death (of the ego). It is an alchemy that transforms death drive into a start of life, of new signifi[c]ance.

Perverse or artistic

The abject is related to perversion. The sense of abjection that I experience is anchored in the superego. The abject is perverse because it neither gives up nor assumes a prohibition, a rule, or a law; but turns them aside, misleads, corrupts; uses them, takes advantage of them, the better to deny them. It kills in the name of life – a progressive despot; it lives at the behest of death – an operator in genetic experimentations; it curbs the other's suffering for its own profit – a cynic (and a psychoanalyst); it establishes narcissistic power while pretending to reveal the abyss – an artist who practices his art as a 'business.' Corruption is its most common, most obvious appearance. That is the socialized appearance of the abject.

An unshakable adherence to Prohibition and Law is necessary if that perverse interspace of abjection is to be hemmed in and thrust aside. Religion, Morality, Law. Obviously always arbitrary, more or less; unfailingly oppressive, rather more than less; laboriously prevailing, more and more so.

Contemporary literature does not take their place. Rather, it seems to be written out of the untenable aspects of perverse or superego positions. It acknowledges the impossibility of Religion, Morality, and Law – their power play, their necessary and absurd seeming. Like perversion, it takes advantage of them, gets round them, and makes sport of them. Nevertheless, it maintains a distance where the abject is concerned. The writer, fascinated by the abject, imagines its logic, projects himself into it, introjects it, and as a consequence perverts language – style and content. But on the other hand, as the sense of abjection is both the abject's judge and accomplice, this is also true of the literature that confronts it. One might thus say that with such a literature there takes place a crossing over of the dichotomous categories of Pure and Impure, Prohibition and Sin, Morality and Immorality.

For the subject firmly settled in its superego, a writing of this sort is necessarily implicated in the interspace that characterizes perversion; and for that reason, it gives rises in turn to abjection. And yet, such texts call for a softening of the superego. Writing them implies an ability to imagine the abject, that is, to see oneself in its place and to thrust it aside only by means of the displacements of verbal play. It is only after his death, eventually, that the writer of abjection will escape his condition of waste, reject, abject. Then, he will either sink into oblivion or attain the rank of incommensurate ideal. Death would thus be the chief curator of our imaginary museum; it would protect us in the last resort from the abjection that contemporary literature claims to expend while uttering it. Such a protection, which gives its quietus to abjection, but also perhaps to the bothersome, incandescent stake of the literary phenomenon itself, which, raised to the status of the sacred, is severed from its specificity. Death thus keeps house in our contemporary universe. By purifying (us from) literature, it establishes our secular religion.

As abjection – so the sacred

Abjection accompanies all religious structurings and reappears, to be worked out in a new guise, at the time of their collapse. Several structurations of abjection should be distinguished, each one determining a specific form of the sacred.

Abjection appears as a rite of defilement and pollution in the paganism that accompanies societies with a dominant or surviving matrilinear character. It takes on the form of the *exclusion* of a substance (nutritive or linked to sexuality), the execution of which coincides with the sacred since it sets it up.

Abjection persists as *exclusion* or taboo (dietary or other) in monotheistic religions, Judaism in particular, but drifts over to more 'secondary' forms such as *transgression* (of the Law) within the same monotheistic economy. It finally encounters, with Christian sin, a dialectic elaboration, as it becomes integrated in the Christian Word as a threatening otherness – but always nameable, always totalizable.

The various means of *purifying* the abject – the various catharses – make up the history of religions, and end up with that catharsis *par excellence* called art, both on the far and near side of religion. Seen from that standpoint, the artistic experience, which is rooted in the abject it utters and by the same token purifies, appears as the essential component of religiosity. That is perhaps why it is destined to survive the collapse of the historical forms of religions.

Outside of the sacred, the abject is written

In the contemporary practice of the West and owing to the crisis in Christianity, abjection elicits more archaic resonances that are culturally prior to sin; through them it again assumes its biblical status, and beyond it that of defilement in primitive societies. In a world in which the Other has collapsed, the aesthetic task – a descent into the foundations of the symbolic construct – amounts to retracing the fragile limits of the speaking being, closest to its dawn, to the bottomless 'primacy' constituted by primal repression. Through that experience, which is nevertheless managed by the Other, 'subject' and 'object' push each other away, confront each other, collapse, and start again – inseparable, contaminated, condemned, at the boundary of what is assimilable, thinkable: abject. Great modern literature unfolds over that terrain: Dostoyevsky, Lautréamont, Proust, Artaud, Kafka, Céline.

Dostoyevsky

The abject is, for Dostoyevsky, the 'object' of *The Possessed*: it is the aim and motive of an existence whose meaning is lost in absolute degradation because it absolutely rejected the moral *limit* (a social, religious, familial, and individual one) as absolute – God. Abjection then wavers between the *fading away* of all meaning and all humanity, burnt as by the flames of a conflagration, and the *ecstasy* of an ego that, having lost its Other and its objects, reaches, at the precise moment of this suicide, the height of harmony with the promised land. Equally abject are Verkhovensky and Kirilov, murder and suicide.

> A big fire at night always produces an exciting and exhilarating effect; this explains the attraction of fireworks; but in the case of fireworks, the graceful and regular shape of the flames and the complete immunity from danger produce a light and playful effect comparable to the effect of a glass of champagne. A real fire is quite another matter: there the horror and a certain sense of personal danger, combined with the well-known exhilarating effect of a fire at night, produce in the spectator (not, of course, in one whose house has burnt down) a certain shock to the brain and, as it were, a challenge to his own destructive instincts, which, alas, lie buried in the soul of even the meekest and most domesticated official of the lowest grade. This grim sensation is almost always delightful. 'I really don't know if it is possible to watch a fire without some enjoyment.'[2]

> There are seconds – they come five or six at a time – when you suddenly feel the presence of eternal harmony in all its fullness. It is nothing earthly. I don't mean that it is heavenly, but a man in his earthly semblance can't endure it. He has to undergo a physical change or die. This feeling is clear and unmistakable. It is as though you suddenly apprehended all nature and suddenly said: 'Yes, it is true – it is good.' . . . What is so terrifying about it is that it is so terribly clear and such gladness. If it went on for more than five seconds, the soul could not endure it and must perish. In those five seconds I live through a lifetime, and I am ready to give my life for them, for it's worth it. To be able to endure it for ten seconds, you would have to undergo a physical change. I think man ought to stop begetting children. What do you want children for, what do you want mental development, if your goal has been attained? It is said in the gospel that in the resurrection they neither marry nor are given in marriage, but are the angels of God in heaven. It's a hint. Is your wife giving birth to a baby?[3]

Verkhovensky is abject because of his clammy, cunning appeal to ideals that no longer exist, from the moment when Prohibition (call it God) is lacking. Stavrogin is perhaps less so, for his immoralism admits of laughter and refusal, something artistic, a cynical and gratuitous expenditure that obviously becomes capitalized for the benefit of private narcissism but does not serve an arbitrary, exterminating power. It is possible to be cynical without being irremediably abject; abjection, on the other hand, is always brought about by that which attempts to get along with trampled-down law.

> He's got everything perfect in his note-book, Verkhovensky went on. Spying. Every member of the society spies on the others, and he is obliged to inform against them. Everyone belongs to all the others, and all belong to everyone. All are slaves and equals in slavery. In extreme cases slander and murder, but, above all, equality. To begin with, the level of education, science, and accomplishment is lowered. A high level of scientific thought and accomplishment is open only to men of the highest abilities! Men of the highest ability have always seized the power and become autocrats. Such men cannot help being autocrats, and they've always done more harm than good; they are either banished or executed. A Cicero will have his tongue cut out, Copernicus will have his eyes gouged out, a Shakespeare will be stoned – there you have Shigalyov's doctrine! Slaves must be equal: without despotism there never has been any freedom or equality, but in a herd there is bound to be equality – there's the Shigalyov doctrine for you! Ha, ha, ha! You think it strange? I am for the Shigalyov doctrine![4]

Dostoyevsky has X-rayed sexual, moral, and religious abjection, displaying it as collapse of paternal laws. Is not the world of *The Possessed* a world of fathers, who are either repudiated, bogus, or dead, where matriarchs lusting for power hold sway – ferocious fetishes but nonetheless phantomlike? And by symbolizing the abject, through a masterful delivery of the jouissance produced by uttering it, Dostoyevsky delivered himself of that ruthless maternal burden.

But it is with Proust that we find the most immediately erotic, sexual, and desiring mainspring of abjection; and it is with Joyce that we shall discover that the feminine body, the maternal body, in its most un-signifiable, un-symbolizable aspect, shores up, in the individual, the fantasy of the loss in which he is engulfed or becomes inebriated, for want of the ability to name an object of desire.

Proust

Abjection, recognized as inherent in the mellow and impossible alteration of the ego, hence recognized as welded to narcissism, has, in Proust, something domesticated about it; without belonging to the realm of 'one's own clean and proper' or of the 'self evident,' it constitutes a scandal of which one has to acknowledge if not the banality at least the secrets of a telltale snob. Abjection, with Proust, is fashionable, if not social; it is the foul lining of society. That may be why he furnishes the only modern example, certified by dictionaries, of the use of the word 'abject' with the weak meaning it has (in French) at the end of the eighteenth century:

> In those regions that were almost slums, what a modest existence, abject, if you please, but delightful, nourished by tranquillity and happiness, he would have consented to lead indefinitely.[5]

Proust writes that if the object of desire is real it can only rest upon the abject, which is impossible to fulfill. The object of love then becomes unmentionable, a double of the subject, similar to it, but improper, because inseparable from an impossible identity. Loving desire is thus felt as an inner fold within that impossible identity, as an accident of narcissism, ob-ject, painful alteration, delightfully and dramatically condemned to find the other in the same sex only. As if one acceded to the truth, to the abject truth of sexuality, only through homosexuality – Sodom and Gomorrah, the *Cities of the Plain*.

> I had not even cause to regret my not having arrived in the shop until several minutes had elapsed. For from what I heard first at Jupien's shop, which was only a series of inarticulate sounds, I imagine that few words had been exchanged. It is true that these sounds were so violent that, if one set had not always been taken up an octave higher by a parallel plaint, I might have thought that one person was strangling another within a few feet of me, and that subsequently the murderer and his resuscitated victim were taking a bath to wash away the traces of the crime. I concluded from this later on that there is another thing as vociferous as pain, namely pleasure, especially when there is added to it – failing the fear of an eventual parturition, which could not be present in this case, despite the hardly convincing example in the *Golden Legend* – an immediate afterthought of cleanliness.[6]

Compared to this one, the orgy in Sade, meshing with a gigantic philosophy, be it that of the boudoir, had nothing abject about it. Methodical, rhetorical, and, from that point of view, regular, it broadens Meaning, Body, and Universe but is not at all exorbitant: everything is nameable for it, the whole is nameable. Sade's scene integrates: it allows for no other, no unthinkable, nothing heterogeneous. Rational and optimistic, it does not exclude. That means that it does not recognize a sacred, and in that sense it is the anthropological and rhetorical acme of atheism. Proustian writing, to the contrary, never gives up a judging prerogative, perhaps a biblical one, which splits, banishes, shares out, or condemns; and it is in relation to it, with it and against it, that the web of Proust's sentence, memory, sexuality, and morality is elaborated – infinitely spinning together differences (sexes, classes, races) into a homogeneity that consists only in signs, a fragile net stretched out over an abyss of incompatibilities, rejections, and abjections. Desire and signs, with Proust, weave the infinite cloth that does not hide but causes the subdued foulness to appear. As lapse, discomfort, shame, or blunder. As permanent threat, in short, to the homogenizing rhetoric that the writer composes against and with the abject.

Joyce

How dazzling, unending, eternal – and so weak, so insignificant, so sickly – is the rhetoric of Joycean language. Far from preserving us from the abject, Joyce causes it to break out in what he sees as prototype of literary utterance: Molly's monologue. If that monologue spreads out the abject, it is not because there is a woman speaking. But because, *from afar*, the writer approaches the hysterical body so that it might speak, so that he might speak, using it as springboard, of what eludes speech and turns out to be the hand to hand struggle of one woman with another, her mother of course, the absolute because primeval seat of the impossible – of the excluded, the outside-of-meaning, the abject. Atopia.

> the woman hides it not to give all the trouble they do yes he came somewhere Im sure by his appetite anyway love its not or hed be off his feed thinking of her so either it was one of those night women if it was down there he was really and the hotel story he made up a pack of lies to hide it planning it Hynes kept me who did I meet ah yes I met do you remember Menton and who else who let me see that big babbyface I saw him and he not long married flirting with a young girl at Pooles Myriorama and turned my back on him when he slinked out looking quite conscious what harm but he had the impudence to make up to me one time well done to him mouth almighty and his boiled eyes of all the big stupoes I ever met and thats called a solicitor only for I hate having a long wrangle in bed or else if its not that its some little bitch or other he got in with somewhere or picked up on the sly if they only knew him as well as I do yes because the day before yesterday he was scribbling something a letter when I came into the front room for the matches to show him Dignam's death.[7]

The abject here does not reside in the thematic of masculine sexuality as Molly might see it. Not even in the fascinated horror that the other women, sketched out in back of the men, imbue the speaker with. The abject lies, beyond the themes, and for Joyce generally, in the way one speaks; it is verbal communication, it is the Word that discloses the abject. But at the same time, the Word alone purifies from the abject, and that is what Joyce seems to say when he gives back to the masterly rhetoric that his *Work in progress* constitutes full powers against abjection. A single catharsis: the rhetoric of the pure signifier, of music in letters – *Finnegans Wake*.

Céline's journey, to the end of his night, will also encounter rhythm and music as being the only way out, the ultimate sublimation of the unsignifiable. Contrary to Joyce, however, Céline will not find salvation in it. Again carrying out a rejection, without redemption, himself forfeited, Céline will become, body and tongue, the apogee of that moral, political, and stylistic revulsion that brands our time. A time that seems to have, for a century now, gone into unending labor pains. The enchantment will have to wait for some other time, always and forever.

Borges

According to Borges the 'object' of literature is in any case vertiginous and hallucinatory. It is the Aleph, which appears, in its transfinite truth, at the time of a descent, worthy of Mallarmé's *Igitur*, into the cellar of the native house, condemned to destruction – by definition. A literature that dares to relate the dizzying pangs of such a descent is no more than mediocre mockery of an archaic memory that language lays out as much as it betrays it. The Aleph is exorbitant to the extent that, within the narrative, nothing could tap its power other than the narration of *infamy*. That is, of rampancy, boundlessness, the unthinkable, the untenable, the unsymbolizable. But what is it? Unless it be the untiring repetition of a drive, which, propelled by an initial loss, does not cease wandering, unsated, deceived, warped, until it finds its only stable object – death. Handling that repetition, staging it, cultivating it until it releases, beyond its eternal return, its sublime destiny of being a struggle with death – is it not that which characterizes writing? And yet, dealing with death in that manner, making sport of it, is that not infamy itself? The literary narrative that utters the workings of repetition must necessarily become, beyond fantastic tales, detective stories, and murder mysteries, a narrative of the infamous (*A Universal History of Infamy*). And the writer cannot but recognize himself, derisive and forfeited, in that abject character, Lazarus Morell, the frightful redeemer, who raises his slaves from the dead only to have them die more fully, but not until they have been circulated – and have brought in a return – like currency. Does that mean that literary objects, our fictional objects, like the slaves of Lazarus Morell, are merely ephemeral resurrections of that elusive Aleph? Does this Aleph, this impossible 'object,' this impossible imagination, sustain the work of writing, even though the latter is merely a temporary halt in the Borgesian race toward death, which is contained in the chasm of the maternal cave?

> The stealing of horses in one state and selling them in another were barely more than a digression in Morell's criminal career, but they foreshadowed the method that now assures him his rightful place in a Universal History of Infamy. This method is unique not only for the popular circumstances that distinguished it but also for the sordidness it required, for its deadly manipulation of hope, and for its step by step development, so like the hideous unfolding of a nightmare . . .
>
> Flashing rings on their fingers to inspire respect, they traveled up and down the vast plantations of the South. They would pick out a wretched black and offer him freedom. They would tell him that if he ran away from his master and allowed them to sell him, he would receive a portion of the money paid for him, and they would then help him escape again, this second time sending him to a free state. Money and freedom, the jingle of silver dollars together with his liberty – what greater temptation could they offer him? The slave became emboldened for his first escape.
>
> The river provided the natural route. A canoe; the hold of a steamboat; a scow; a great raft as big as the sky, with a cabin at the point or three or four wigwams – the means mattered little, what counted was feeling the movement and the safety of the unceasing river. The black would be sold on some other plantation, then run away again to the canebrakes or the morasses. There his terrible benefactors (about whom he now began to have serious misgivings) cited obscure expenses and told him they had to sell him one final time. On his return, they said, they would give him his part of both sales and his freedom. The man let himself be sold, worked for a while, and on his final escape defied the hounds and the whip. He then made his way back bloodied, sweaty, desperate, and sleepy . . .
>
> The runaway expected his freedom. Lazarus Morell's shadowy mulattoes would give out an order among themselves that was sometimes barely more than a nod of the head, and the slave would be freed from sight, hearing, touch, day, infamy, time, his benefactors, pity, the air, the hound packs, the world, hope, sweat, and himself. A bullet, a knife, or a blow, and the Mississippi turtles and catfish would receive the last evidence.[8]

Just imagine that imaginary machine transformed into a social institution – and what you get is the infamy of fascism.

Artaud

An 'I' overcome by the corpse – such is often the abject in Artaud's text. For it is death that most violently represents the strange state in which a non-subject, a stray, having lost its non-objects, imagines nothingness through the ordeal of abjection. The death that 'I' am provokes horror, there is a choking sensation that does not separate inside from outside but draws them the one into the other, indefinitely. Artaud is the inescapable witness of that torture – of that truth.

> The dead little girl says, I am the one who guffaws in horror inside the lungs of the live one. Get me out of there at once.[9]

> Once dead, however, my corpse was thrown out on the dunghill, and I remember having been macerated I don't know how many days or how many hours while waiting to awaken. For I did not know at first that I was dead: I had to make up my mind to understand that before I could succeed in raising myself. A few friends, then, who had completely forsaken me at first, decided to come and embalm my corpse and were joylessly surprised at seeing me again, alive.[10]

> I have no business going to bed with you, things, for I stink more than you do, god, and going to bed does not mean getting soiled but, to the contrary, clearing myself, from you.[11]

At that level of downfall in subject and object, the abject is the equivalent of death. And writing, which allows one to recover, is equal to a resurrection. The writer, then, finds himself marked out for identification with Christ, if only in order for him, too, to be rejected, ab-jected:

> For, as ball-breaking as this may seem, I am that Artaud crucified on Golgotha, not as christ but as Artaud, in other words as complete atheist. I am that body persecuted by erotic golosity, the obscene sexual erotic golosity of mankind, for which pain is a humus, the liquid from a fertile mucus, a serum worth sipping by one who has never on his own gained by being a man while knowing that he was becoming one.[12]

These different literary texts name types of abjects that are answerable to, this goes without saying, different psychic structures. The types of articulation (narrative and syntactic structures, prosodic processes, etc. in the different texts) also vary. Thus the abject, depending on the writer, turns out to be named differently when it is not merely suggested by linguistic modifications that are always somewhat elliptic. In the final part of this essay I shall examine in detail a specific articulation of the abject – that of Céline. Let me just say at this point, as an introduction, that contemporary literature, in its multiple variants, and when it is written as the language, possible at last, of that impossible constituted either by a-subjectivity or by non-objectivity, propounds, as a matter of fact, a sublimation of abjection. Thus it becomes a substitute for the role formerly played by the sacred, at the limits of social and subjective identity. But we are dealing here with a sublimation without consecration. Forfeited.

Catharsis and analysis

That *abjection*, which modernity has learned to repress, dodge, or fake, appears fundamental once the analytic point of view is assumed. Lacan says so when he links that word to the *saintliness* of the analyst, a linkage in which the only aspect of humor that remains is blackness.[13]

One must keep open the wound where he or she who enters into the analytic adventure is located – a wound that the professional establishment, along with the cynicism of the times and of institutions, will soon manage to close up. There is nothing initiatory in that rite, if one understands by 'initiation' the accession to a purity that the posture of *death* guaranteed (as in Plato's *Phaedo*) or the unadulterated treasure of the 'pure signifier' (as is the gold of truth in *The Republic*, or the pure separatism of the statesman in the *Statesman*). It is rather a heterogeneous, corporeal, and verbal ordeal of fundamental incompleteness: a 'gaping,' 'less One.' For the unstabilized subject who comes out of that – like a crucified person opening up the stigmata of its desiring body to a speech that structures only on condition that it let go – any signifying or human phenomenon, insofar as it *is*, appears in its being as abjection. For what impossible *catharsis*? Freud, early in his career, used the same word to refer to a therapeutics, the rigor of which was to come out later.

With Plato and Aristotle

The analyst is thus and forever sent back to the question that already haunted Plato when he wanted to take over where Apollonian or Dionysiac religion left off.[14] Purification is something only the Logos is capable of. But is that to be done in the manner of the *Phaedo*, stoically separating oneself from a body whose substance and passions are sources of impurity? Or rather, as in the *Sophist*, after having sorted out the worst from the best; or after the fashion of the *Philebus* by leaving the doors wide open to impurity, provided the eyes of the mind remain focused on truth? In such a case, pleasure, having become pure and true through the harmony of color and form as in the case of accurate and beautiful geometric form, has nothing in common, as the philosopher says, with 'the pleasures of scratching' (*Philebus* 51).

Catharsis seems to be a concern that is intrinsic to philosophy, insofar as the latter is an ethics and unable to forget Plato. Even if the *mixture* seems inevitable towards the end of the Platonic course, it is the mind alone, as harmonious wisdom, that insures purity: catharsis has been transformed, where transcendental idealism is concerned, into philosophy. Of the cathartic incantation peculiar to mysteries, Plato has kept only, as we all know, the very uncertain role of poets whose frenzy would be useful to the state only after having been evaluated, sorted out, and purified in its turn by wise men.

Aristotelian catharsis is closer to sacred incantation. It is the one that has bequeathed its name to the common, esthetic concept of catharsis. Through the mimesis of passions – ranging from enthusiasm to suffering – in 'language with pleasurable accessories,' the most important of which being *rhythm* and *song* (see the *Poetics*), the soul reaches *orgy* and *purity* at the same time. What is involved is a purification of body and soul by means of a heterogeneous and complex circuit, going from 'bile' to 'fire,' from 'manly warmth' to the 'enthusiasm' of the 'mind.' Rhythm and song hence arouse the impure, the other of mind, the passionate-corporeal-sexual-virile, but they harmonize it, arrange it differently than the wise man's knowledge does. They thus soothe frenzied outbursts (Plato, in the *Laws*, allowed such use of rhythm and meter only to the mother rocking her child), by contributing an *external* rule, a poetic one, which fills the gap, inherited from Plato, between body and soul. To Platonic *death*, which owned, so to speak, the state of purity, Aristotle opposed the act of *poetic purification* – in itself an impure process that protects from the abject only by dint of being immersed in it. The abject, mimed through sound and meaning, is *repeated*. Getting rid of it is out of the question – the final Platonic lesson has been understood, one does not get rid of the impure; one can, however, bring it into being a second time, and differently from the original impurity. It is a repetition through rhythm and song, therefore through what is not yet, or no longer is 'meaning,' but arranges, defers, differentiates and organizes, harmonizes pathos, bile, warmth, and enthusiasm. Benveniste translates 'rhythm' by 'trace' and 'concatenation' [*enchaînement*]. Prometheus is 'rhythmical,' and we call him 'bound' [*enchaîné*]. An attachment on the near and far side of language. Aristotle seems to say that there is a discourse of sex and that is not the discourse of knowledge – it is the only possible catharsis. That discourse is audible, and through the speech that it mimics it repeats on another register what the latter does not say.

Philosophical sadness and the spoken disaster of the analyst

Poetic catharsis, which for more than two thousand years behaved as an underage sister of philosophy, face to face and incompatible with it, takes us away from purity, hence from Kantian ethics, which has long governed modern codes and remains more faithful to a certain Platonic stoicism. By means of the 'universalizing of maxims,' as is well known, the Kant of the *Foundations of the Metaphysics of Ethics* or of the *Metaphysical Principles of Virtue* advocated an 'ethical gymnastics' in order to give us, by means of consciousness, control over our defilements and, through that very consciousness, making us free and joyous.

More skeptical and, from a certain point of view, more Aristotelian, Hegel, on the contrary, rejects a 'calculation' that claims to eliminate defilement, for the latter seems *fundamental* to him. Probably echoing the Greek polis, he conceives of no other ethics than that of the *act*. Also distrustful, however, of those fine aestheticizing souls who find purity in the elaboration of empty forms, he obviously does not hold to the mimetic and orgiastic catharsis of Aristotle. It is in the *historical* act that Hegel sees fundamental impurity being expended; as a matter of fact, the latter is a sexual impurity whose historical achievement consists in marriage. But – and this is where transcendental idealism, too, sadly comes to an end – here it is that desire (*Lust*), thus normalized in order to escape abject concupiscence (*Begierde*), sinks into a banality that is sadness and silence. How come? Hegel does not condemn impurity because it is exterior to ideal consciousness; more profoundly – but also more craftily – he thinks that it can and should get rid of itself through the historico-social act. If he thereby differs from Kant, he nevertheless shares his condemnation of (sexual) impurity. He agrees with his aim to keep consciousness apart from defilement, which, nevertheless, dialectically constitutes it. Reabsorbed into the trajectory of the Idea, what can defilement become if not the negative side of consciousness – that is, lack of communication and speech? In other words, defilement as reabsorbed in marriage becomes sadness. In so doing, it has not strayed too far from its logic, according to which it is a border of discourse – a silence.[15]

It is obvious that the analyst, from the abyss of his silence, brushes against the ghost of the sadness Hegel saw in sexual normalization. Such sadness is the more obvious to him as his ethics is rigorous – founded, as it must be in the West, on the remains of transcendental idealism. But one can also argue that the Freudian stance, which is dualistic and dissolving, unsettles those foundations. In that sense, it causes the sad, analytic silence to hover above a strange, foreign discourse, which, strictly speaking, shatters verbal communication (made up of a knowledge and a truth that are nevertheless heard) by means of a device that mimics terror, enthusiasm, or orgy, and is more closely related to rhythm and song than it is to the World. There is mimesis (some say identification) in the analytic passage through castration. And yet it is necessary that the analyst's interpretative speech (and not only his literary or theoretical bilingualism) be affected by it in order to be analytical. As counterpoise to a purity that found its bearings in disillusioned sadness, it is the 'poetic' unsettlement of analytic utterance that testifies to its closeness to, cohabitation with, and 'knowledge' of abjection.

I am thinking, in short, of the completely mimetic *identification* (transference and countertransference) of the analyst with respect to analysands. That identification allows for securing in their place what, when parcelled out, makes them suffering and barren. It allows one to regress back to the affects that can be heard in the breaks in discourse, to provide rhythm, too, to concatenate (is that what 'to become conscious' means?) the gaps of a speech saddened because it turned its back on its abject meaning. If there is analytic jouissance it is there, in the thoroughly poetic mimesis that runs through the architecture of speech and extends from coenesthetic image to logical and phantasmatic articulations. Without for that matter biologizing language, and while breaking away from identification by means of interpretation, analytic speech is one that becomes 'incarnate' in the full sense of the term. On that condition only, it is 'cathartic' – meaning thereby that it is the equivalent, for the analyst as well as for the analysand, not of purification but of rebirth with and against abjection.

This preliminary survey of abjection, phenomenological on the whole, will now lead me to a more straightforward consideration of analytic theory on the one hand, of the history of religions on the other, and finally of contemporary literary experience.

Translated by Leon S. Roudiez

Notes

1 Francis de Sales, *Introduction to a Devout Life*, trans. Thomas S. Kepler, New York, World, 1952, p. 125. (Modified to conform to the French text, which reads, 'l'abjection de soy-mesme.')
2 Fyodor Dostoyevsky, *The Devils*, trans. David Magarshack, London, Penguin Books, 1953, p. 512.
3 Ibid., pp. 586–87.
4 Ibid., pp. 418–19.
5 Marcel Proust, *Swann's Way*, trans. C.K. Scott-Moncrieff, New York, Random House, 1922, vol. 2, p. 141.
6 Proust, *Cities of the Plain*, trans. Frederick A. Blossom, New York, Random House, 1934, p. 9.
7 James Joyce, *Ulysses*, New York, Vintage Books, 1961, pp. 738–39.

8 Jorge Luis Borges, *A Universal History of Infamy*, trans. Norman Thomas Di Giovanni, New York, Dutton, 1979, pp. 23–25.
9 Antonin Artaud, 'Suppôts et supplications', in *Œuvres Complètes*, Paris, Gallimard, 1978, vol. 14, p. 14.
10 Ibid., p. 72.
11 Ibid., p. 203.
12 Ibid., p. 155.
13 Jacques Lacan, *Télévision*, Paris, Seuil, 1974, p. 28.
14 In connection with catharsis in the Greek world, see Louis Molinier, *Le Pur et l'impur dans la pensée des Grecs*, Paris, Klincksieck, 1952.
15 See A. Philonenko, 'Note sur les concepts de souillure et de pureté dans l'idéalisme allemand', *Les Etudes Philosophiques* 4 (1972), pp. 481–93.

34

THE INVISIBLE OF THE FLESH

A reading of Merleau-Ponty, 'The Intertwining – The Chiasm'

Luce Irigaray

> *If it is true that as soon as philosophy declares itself to be reflection or coincidence it prejudges what it will find, then once again it must recommence everything, reject the instruments reflection and intuition had provided themselves, and install itself in a locus where they have not yet been distinguished, in experiences that have not yet been 'worked over,' that offer us all at once, pell-mell, both 'subject' and 'object,' both existence and essence, and hence give philosophy resources to redefine them.*
>
> (Maurice Merleau-Ponty, 'The Intertwining – The Chiasm', p. 164).[1]

Up to this point, my reading and my interpretation of the history of philosophy agree with Merleau-Ponty: we must go back to a moment of prediscursive experience, recommence everything, all the categories by which we understand things, the world, subject–object divisions, recommence everything and pause at the 'mystery, as familiar as it is unexplained, of a light which, illuminating the rest, remains at its source in obscurity.'

> *If we could rediscover within the exercise of seeing and speaking some of the living references that assign themselves such a destiny in a language, perhaps they would teach us how to form our new instruments, and first of all to understand our research, our interrogation themselves.*
>
> (p. 164)

This operation is absolutely necessary in order to bring the maternal-feminine into language: at the level of theme, motif, subject, articulation, syntax, and so on. Which requires passage through the night, a light that remains in obscurity.

> *The visible about us seems to rest in itself. It is as though our vision were formed in the heart of the visible, or as though there were between it and us an intimacy as close as between the sea and the strand.*
>
> (p. 164)

If it were not the visible that was in question, it would be possible to believe that Merleau-Ponty is alluding here to intrauterine life. Moreover, he uses 'images' of the sea and the strand. Of immersion and emergence? And he speaks of the risk of the disappearance of the seer and the visible. Which corresponds doubly to a reality in intrauterine nesting: one who is still in this night does not see and remains without a visible (as far as we know); but the other seer cannot see him. The other does not see him, he is not visible for the other, who nevertheless sees the world, but without him. And if everything, the totality, is organized around him, then the other, one could almost say, sees nothing? A disorganized world? If the mother, or the woman, sees the world only from the perspective of the maternal function, she sees nothing. Except from this zero of the infant's nocturnal abode? The invisible of its prenatal life. This intimate secret of its-their birth and shared knowledge [*connaissance*]. What-had-not-yet-been-seen of and by its-their look. Seeing the universe in function of or beginning with that – which will never appear as something seen within the field of the visible.

Perhaps it comes about that, out of his nostalgia, man wishes to see that which she does not see? Her own invisible? His return would also be the search for this night of hers. Wanting to appropriate two invisibles, two positions of the one in relation to the other where they touch without the possibility of seeing each other, and without for all that finding the one behind the other. A look forever organized, or disorganized, around an impossibility of seeing [*un impossible à voir*]. Insurmountable other of the visible, not reducible to its invisible other side. It is a question of another world, another landscape, a *topos* or a locus of the irreversible.

The next sentence can be understood in the open field through this interpretive gesture: if we based ourselves in this visible, or rather in its resting place [*repos*], its heart, and if it passed into us, vision would vanish at the moment of its formation through the disappearance of either the seer or the visible.

Thus: there is either no more seer, or subject, or no more world, or visible. Either the one or the other at opposite poles, antagonistic, adverse. Although he dismisses the subject and the object, Merleau-Ponty nevertheless retains this polarity: seer/visible, which presupposes, here in particular, that the visible, still invisible in its resting place, would have vision and could give it to or take it away from the seer. Later on, he says that the seer and the visible are reversible, that in a way they come back to the same thing, but after having set up this dissociation from the start: the risk of the disappearance of the one *or* the other.

What follows returns the privilege to the *seer's* look. But of a vision in between the diurnal and the nocturnal in its touch. A look that is too close to make use of a certain perspective, of discrimination, distancing, or mastery? A carnal look, which becomes that which gives perspective to 'things': shelters them, gives birth to them, wraps them in the touch of a visibility that is one with them, keeps them from ever being naked, envelops them in a conjunctive tissue of visibility, an exterior–interior horizon in which, henceforth, they appear without being able to be distinguished, separated, or torn away from it.

> *Whence does it happen that in so doing it leaves them in their place, that the vision we acquire of them seems to us to come from them, and that to be seen is for them but a degradation of their eminent being?*
>
> (p. 164)

Enveloping things with his look, the seer would give birth to them, and/yet the mystery of his own birth would subsist in them. For now they contain this mystery of the prenatal night where he was palpated without seeing. A passive forever lacking an active. More passive than any passivity taken in a passive–active couple. A passivity that tries to turn itself into activity by sculpting, moving the totality of the world into a reversion of the intrauterine abode. Between these two extremes, *there is* a breach: the place of the other. The seer tries to put back together the most passive and the most active, to overcome the invisible of/in the other insofar as it would constitute a night that his look needed to reduce in order to organize his field of vision. He tries to establish a *continuum*, a duration, between the most passive and the most active. But he cannot manage it. Especially without memory of that first event where he is enveloped–touched by a tangible invisible of which his eyes are also formed, but which he will never see: with no seer, neither visible nor visibility in that place.

Perhaps there exists, there is, a *foreseeing* where the maternal is concerned? Something that would make the child believe it is seen before it sees? That the invisible looks at it? And, if the mother foresees her child, imagines it, she foresees it also in this sense that the feeling of it within herself is sometimes transformed into vision: a clairvoyance of, and within, the flesh. Could it be that he uses this clairvoyance to surround things? Constituting them as things, or reduplicating them as things, with that encompassing look with which he envelops them.

Whence does it happen that 'to be seen is for them [but] a degradation of their eminent being'? Sight reduces the invisible of things and of the look, their tissue, their clothing of seeing flesh, that nostalgia for a first abode lodged in and on them, which will be twice lost: in the coming to being of the seer and, even more, in the look's becoming vision; in the envelopment of things in names and in a network of names, a language, from this point, this axis, where their 'soul,' their cloak of invisibility, their immiscion in a fleshly layering [*feuilleté*] is degraded, flattened? Which happens through their appearing only from a vantage point, a sort of photograph that puts them into the world while wrenching them from their surroundings, the thickness of their gestures, which are also visual. But once there, opened up to the contemplation of their unfolding?

> *What is this talisman of color, this singular virtue of the visible that makes it, held at the end of the gaze, nonetheless much more than a correlative of my vision, such that it imposes my vision upon me as a continuation of its own sovereign existence?*
>
> (p. 164)

At this point, the talisman of color appears, with its 'atmospheric' properties, which are irreducible to the form that seeing defines. Color? The symptom and aftereffect of our incarnation, our genetic fate, our identity prior to any proper form perceivable from outside, to any visible, which will nevertheless appear but without ever encompassing itself in its growth. Color? That by which I (male or female) am moreover affronted as if by a genealogical heritage that I cannot change: I can change neither the color of my eyes nor my vision of things or of the atmosphere that results from this color. Correlatively (?), from without, color signals to me that it holds sovereignty over the purchase or the influence of my gaze. That it allows me to see rather than that I make it conform to my decisions? That it pours itself out, extends itself, escapes, imposes itself upon me as the reminder of what is most archaic in me, the *fluid*. Through which I (male or female) received life and was enveloped in my prenatal sojourn, by which I have been surrounded, clothed, nourished, in another body. Thanks to which I could also see the light, be born, and even see: air, light . . . Color resuscitates in me all of that prior life, the preconceptual, preobjective, presubjective, this *ground* of the visible where seeing and seen are not yet distinguished, where they reflect each other without any position having been established between them. Color bathes my gaze, which sees it, perceives it more or less well, changes it in its visibility, but can never delimit it, create it, bend it to its decisions. Color constitutes a given that escapes from the subjective realm and that still and always immerses the subject in an invisible sojourn of the visible, a sojourn that cannot be mastered: whether infernal or celestial, preceding or following a determinate incarnation into subject–object duality. This color, the correlative of my vision, of vision, far from being able to yield to my decisions, obliges me to see.

> *How does it happen that my look, enveloping them [things], does not hide them, and, finally, that, veiling them, it unveils them?*
>
> (pp. 164–65)

Following this detour by way of color, his sentence links up without a transition to what was being said about the vision of things. As if this passage on color had been only a parenthesis, whereas it will be developed at length. How should this construction be understood? What is its relation to the note at the bottom of the page? Not only is it a question of course notes here, and not really of a text, but the passage demonstrates an astonishing reversal: my gaze, which would receive itself from the visible, envelops things without hiding them and unveils them while veiling them. My gaze would be a connective tissue between the interior and the exterior. But formed inside (through 'the incorporation of the seer into the visible'), even if it is perfected outside. Formed within the living tissue of my body. On the inside prior to the constitution of its interior horizon. How do the inside of conception-organization and the inside of internal horizons mingle? Two leaves of my body and two leaves of the world seem to make it impossible for another flesh to be visible and seeing, between the one and the other. The subtlety of what is said of the visible and of its relation to the flesh does not rule out the solipsistic character of this touch(ing) between the world and the subject, of this touch(ing) of the visible and the seer in the subject itself.

Merleau-Ponty's whole analysis is marked by this labyrinthine solipsism. Without the other, and above all the other of sexual difference, isn't it impossible to find a way out of this description of the visible, doubled with that of the tactile of the touching hands? But unless we are to remain within the confines of this rigorous and luxuriant approach, we must ask the question of the other as touched and touching. And of an other whose body's ontological status would differ from my own.

> *We must first understand that this red under my eyes is not, as is always said, a* quale, *a pellicle of being without any thickness, a message at the same time indecipherable and evident, which one has or has not received, but of which, if one has received it, one knows all there is to know, and of which in the end there is*

> *nothing to say. It requires a focusing, however brief: it emerges from a less precise, more general redness, in which my gaze was caught, into which it sank, before – as we put it so aptly – fixing it. And, now that I have fixed it, if my eyes penetrate into it, into its fixed structure, or if they start to wander round about again, the* quale *resumes its atmospheric existence. Its precise form is bound up with a certain wooly, metallic, or porous (?) configuration or texture, and the* quale *itself counts for very little compared with these participations.*
>
> (p. 165)

Color is never a pellicle of being without thickness, in contradistinction to certain spectacles. Color is not deciphered without focusing, without taking into account its surroundings, the texture of the support in which it appears. A red is red in accord with or in function of its material ground, from which it cannot be separated. Also the concept of red is impossible. One could go so far as to say that it has no meaning. Color cannot be abstracted from its material ground, but it also cannot be seen except in contrast to other colors. Red is only red when it is joined with other colors which it dominates or which dominate it, which it attracts or which attract it, which it repels or which repel it. In short, it is a certain node in the weave of the simultaneous and the successive. 'It is a concretion of visibility, it is not an atom.' There would be no 'moment' of redness? Nevertheless, color is linked to the transient much more than to other visibles. But this transcience is more that of the flesh of the visible, which is recalled with difficulty, than of the precision of form (and) of the concept. Red, any color, is more in the mode of *participation* than of the solitary emergence of the concept.

> *A naked color, and in general a visible, is not a chunk of absolutely hard, indivisible being, offered all naked to a vision which could be only total or null, but is rather a sort of straits between exterior horizons and interior horizons ever gaping open.*
>
> (p. 165)

What is perceived would be not so much the color and the thing but the difference between things and colors. Sensation would have neither an object nor a moment, but it would take place only in the intervals *between*, through difference, succession. A sort of silent scale?

Ferdinand de Saussure describes the meaning [*sens*] of language thus, at least its organization. For Merleau-Ponty, is sensation already structured like a language? There would be no place for this bath in which my gaze is immersed, nor for this contemplation which touches on eternity, or which joins the moment and eternity. The gaze on or of the flesh of the visible is still modulated in the manner of a demiurgic possession . . . Which reverses values somewhat? Sensation is without doubt what we feel as most naively instantaneous. All the more reason to remember this, and that it is not a simple reserve for the appearance of the concept.

> *Between the alleged colors and the visible, we would find anew the tissue that lines them, sustains them, nourishes them, and which, for its part is not a thing, but a possibility, a latency, and a* flesh *of things.*
>
> (p. 165)

Where does this tissue come from? How is it nourished? Who or what gives it consistency? My body? My flesh? Or a maternal, materializing flesh, reproduction, subsistence there of the amniotic, placental tissue, which enveloped subject and things prior to birth, or of tenderness and the milieu that constituted the atmosphere of the nursling, the infant, still of the adult.

Here, Merleau-Ponty makes flesh go over to the realm of things and as if to their place of emergence, their prenatal ground, their nourishing soil . . . Indefinitely, he has exchanged seer and visible, touching and tangible, 'subject' and 'things' in an alternation, a fluctuation that would take place in a mil[i]eu that makes possible their passage from one or the other 'side.' An archaic fleshly atmosphere, a sojourn that it is difficult not to compare once again to the intrauterine or to the still barely differentiated symbiosis of infancy. Whence come *eyes*? Only eyes? But also *in the world*. Things would look at us. Above all where color or colors are concerned, things would recall all that they keep of the flesh of the world and notably of visibility.

According to Merleau-Ponty, the look would be a variant of touch. It palpates, envelops, espouses things. It discovers them as if it already knew them, 'as though it knew them before knowing them.' And no one knows who commands this secret complicity between things and the 'subject,' this 'prepossession of the visible.' No one knows, but the relationship of touching and being touched, which is very close to that of interrogating and being interrogated, perhaps indicates the secret of this still 'obscure' alliance between looking and being looked at. If my hands can quickly and with deft movement perceive the textures of matter – for example, of what is smooth or rough – this is a function of their kinship with the tactile world.

> *This can happen only if my hand, while it is felt from within, is also accessible from without, itself tangible, for my other hand, for example, if it takes its place among the things it touches, is in a sense one of them, opens finally upon a tangible being of which it is also a part. Through this crisscrossing within it of the touching and the tangible, its own movements incorporate themselves into the universe they interrogate, are recorded on the same map as it.*
>
> (p. 166)

This is only possible, if my hand, felt from within, is accessible from without, itself tangible to another hand. If it takes its place among the things it touches, opens onto the tangible of which it is a part, and if there occurs within it the crisscrossing of the touching and the tangible. Thus, 'its own movements incorporate themselves into the universe they interrogate, are recorded on the same map as it; the two systems are applied upon one another, as the two halves of an orange' (p. 166).

My movements *incorporate* themselves in the universe they interrogate. Two introjections, introspections cross. Two passages from within to without, from without to within, would be recorded on the same map. My hand and its 'other side,' and the universe and its 'other side' would be inscribed on the same horizon, would mingle their knowledge, their assimilations, in the same cycle or orbit, each one putting the other within–without, without–within? Which is impossible? Neither my hand nor the world is a 'glove,' nor can either be reduced to its clothing. Neither my hand nor the world is thus reversible. They are not pure actual phenomena, pure pellicles that are graspable one by the other, even empathetically. They have their roots, which are not reducible to the visible moment. Their roots and their atmospheres. To reverse them thus, the one in the other, would amount to destroying them in their own lives.

My hand feels itself from within and it is felt from without. These two 'systems are applied [u]pon one another, as the two halves of an orange. It is no different for the vision.'

This comparison with the orange seems strange. Is it still 'valid,' if the *two hands* are *joined*? Which brings about something very particular in the relation feeling–felt. With no object or subject. With no passive or active, or even middle-passive. A sort of fourth mode? Neither active, nor passive, nor middle-passive. Always more passive than the passive. And nevertheless active. The hands joined, palms together, fingers outstretched, constitute a very particular touching. A gesture often reserved for women (at least in the West) and which evokes, doubles, the *touching of the lips* silently applied upon one another. A touching more intimate than that of one hand taking hold of the other. A phenomenology of the passage between interior and exterior. A phenomenon that remains in the interior, does not appear in the light of day, speaks of itself only in gestures, remains always on the edge of speech, gathering the edges without sealing them. This gesture, reserved for prayer (?), could represent that of the two halves of the universe applied one upon the other at different times of their becoming. It can also be performed with the gaze: the eyes meet in a sort of silence of vision, a screen of resting before and after seeing, a reserve for new landscapes, new lights, a punctuation in which the eyes reconstitute for themselves the frame, the screen, the horizon of a vision.

> *There is double and crossed situating of the visible in the tangible and of the tangible in the visible; the two maps are complete, and yet they do not merge into one. The two parts are total parts and yet are not superposable.*
>
> (p. 166)

Of course there is a relation of the visible and the tangible. Is the doubling redoubled and crisscrossed? This is less certain. The look cannot take up the tangible. Thus I never see that *in which* I touch or am touched. What is at play in the caress does not see itself. The in-between, the middle, the *medium* of the caress does not see itself. In the same way and differently, I do not see that which allows me to see, that which touches me with light and air so that I see some 'thing.' This is perhaps, as far as I am concerned, what Merleau-Ponty calls the site of flesh in which things bathe? They begin to appear in a fog or a mist of invisibility. And it is still possible that my look – the most developed of all the senses? – disturbs the intelligence of my hand, of my touching. That it makes a screen which freezes the tactile nuptials, paralyzing the flow, turning it to ice, precipitating it, undoing its rhythm. The visible and the tactile do not obey the same laws or rhythms of the flesh. And if I can no doubt unite their powers, I cannot reduce the one to the other. I cannot situate the visible and the tangible in a chiasmus. Perhaps the visible needs the tangible but this need is not reciprocal?

Besides, if this doubled and crisscrossed situating of which Merleau-Ponty speaks neglects the sensible *medium*, then it also neglects the *mucous* of the carnal. We can agree that there is a situating of the visible in the tangible and of the tangible in the visible. But the two maps are incomplete and do not overlap: *the tangible is, and remains, primary in its opening*. Its touching on, of, and by means of the other. The dereliction of its ever touching this first touching. Which is true of the visible. And which opens up the question of 'God' but in a certain forgetfulness of the primary maternal-feminine. Which entails the fact that God is always entrusted to the look and never sufficiently imagined as tactile bliss. Who imagines the beyond as an infinitely blissful touching? Being touched by God, for example. Which is impossible to imagine insofar as God is the counterweight to immersion in intrauterine touching?

Deprived of this bliss, God will always be thought of as a God who touches in suffering but not in joy or bliss. A God who wounds in order to reopen the way to primary nostalgia? Never a God who envelops me, surrounds me, cradles me . . . Who loves me carnally, erotically. Why not? What kind of God is this? One who corresponds to a transcendental that is metaphysical but not physical (except prior to the first sin?). A God who would have created me as man or woman to make me guilty of my *body*? Who would have made us male and female to make the fulfillment of his creation sinful, forbidden, or impossible? Who is this God? And who has, since the beginning, committed the sin of simony *vis-à-vis* God? While speculating on the text of the law? But above all while exploiting (consciously or unconsciously) the meaning of the word. This is a difficult question; but more and more it seems to me that God has always been a victim of simony. Were it otherwise, would grace come to pass more easily? Whoever writes a truth or makes a pronouncement, above all concerning God, should always add: *open* [*ouvert(e)*].

Thus there is a crossing of the tangible in the visible and of the visible in the tangible, according to Merleau-Ponty. In this situating can be understood a desire for mastery that denies the opening of each of the maps.

But,

— I do not see the source of light that allows me to see. I sense it, often when I forget about it.
— I do not see the sound source that allows me to hear; I sense it.
— I do not see my body, or only a little.
— I do not see that *in which* I caress; the caress always takes place in a milieu which is its 'proper' milieu, which remains invisible; the most tangible of the tangible or the tangible 'itself' does not see itself.

Moreover, the chiasmus of the visible and the tangible is inversed in time. Is this what is at stake in the first sin? The tangible is primary and the visible claimed to equal it, even to surpass it. A tangible should remain intangible to figure as a blank space of the tangible in the visible: thou shalt not *touch* the tree of the *knowledge* of *good* and *evil*. The fact of having *touched* the fruit of that tree, of having tasted it, turned the tangible into something forbidden (you shall not touch each other, except to reproduce), and especially in the flesh of the visible: they saw that they were naked and they were obliged to cover themselves. The tangible represented a divine happiness, an 'earthly paradise,' until the moment when it entered into the perspective of the knowledge of good and evil. Of black and white? Of dichotomous oppositions that break into its tissue, riddle it with judgments, that transform touch into something other than itself while destroying palpation in disembodied, abstract forms of the sensible, cutting it up according to alternatives that respect neither its thresholds, its approaches, nor its mouths.

What is more, this transgression of the limits of the flesh, and of its visible, to have access to knowledge, or another knowledge, resulted in exile from the threshold of the earthly paradise, where the door of the garden and the entryways of the flesh overlapped according to the destiny that God had given us. For having wanted access to a knowledge that was alienated from carnal happiness, a knowledge that situated the tangible in the visible and the visible in the tangible according to the usual mode of our *episteme*, man was condemned to labor, suffering, carnal exile, the quest for God, the exploitation of nature for his nourishment . . .

The two maps of the visible and the tangible are not completely situated the one in the other and the other in the one. If one were to 'situate' [*relever*], it would be the tangible. But it remains instead the ground that is available for all the senses. A landscape much vaster but never enclosed in a map, the tangible is the matter and memory for all of the sensible. Which remembers without remembering thematically? It constitutes the very flesh of all things that will be sculpted, sketched, painted, felt, and so on, out of it.

First of all, the tangible is received, perceived prior to the dichotomies of active and passive. It is received like a bath that affects without and within, in fluidity. It is never completely situated in the visible. And, furthermore, in the tangible itself, it is not sure that it can transform itself into act.

With regard to the look, perhaps it is acquired later, even though it is received from and in the flesh, and it would or could take up that which can not be taken up? Can I live in the visible independent of touch? I can certainly go quite far. I distance myself, for the greater part, from my sensible body. And it remains that I see only by the touch of the light, and my eyes are situated in my body. I am touched and enveloped by the felt even before seeing it.

The question is perhaps that of the 'situating' or of the translation into my interior landscape. It is the felt that should conduct me there. Can I transform, transmute the sensible into some inwardness? How so? What will be lacking from this intimate landscape? It will always be incomplete.

With regard to the movements of my eyes, they do not take place uniquely within the visible universe: they also happen in the living crypt of my body and my flesh.

> *Without even entering into the implications proper to the seer and the visible, we know that, since vision is a palpation with the look, it must also be inscribed in the order of being that it discloses to us; he who looks must not himself be foreign to the world that he looks at. As soon as I see, it is necessary that the vision (as is so well indicated by the double meaning of the word) be doubled with a complementary vision or with another vision.*
>
> (pp. 166–67)

Someone must see me, so that I can be possessed by whoever sees me.

Without examining how far this identity of the seer and the visible may go, two questions can be put to him:

— that of the *prenatal sojourn* which is always invisible, in any case to my eyes, and in a way that another seer can see me seeing and I can see him: in this sense none of us can be substituted for his (or her) mother from the perspective of the gaze, the daughter being able to palpate the invisible 'as' her mother does (the 'as' is meaningful only through its difference from the impossibility of one who never carries an infant in her womb);

— that of the place of an *other sex* which sees me without my being able to see it too, and vice versa, especially in the name of the tangible and of an irreversible inversion of the gaze into a flesh for which no other can be substituted.

> *The body unites us directly with things through its own ontogenesis, by welding to one another the two outlines of which it is made, its two lips: the sensible mass it is and the mass of the sensible where it is born by segregation and upon which, as seer, it remains open.*
>
> (p. 167; translation modified)[2]

Two lips, a strange comparison: one on its side (the sensible mass it is), one on the side of the other (mass where it is born through segregation), to which, as a *seer*, it remains open. One lip that remains in or of its own sensible, another from which it will emerge, which it will see, and to which it will stay tied as seer. One that remains more on the side of touch? The other with the flesh of the visible? Two lips that do not touch each other in the same sensible realm, that, rigorously speaking, do not touch at all, unlike the lips of our 'body.'

The singularity of the body and the flesh of the feminine comes:

— both from the fact that the lips are doubled there: those above and those below;
— and from the fact that the sensible which is the feminine touches the sensible from which he or she emerges. The woman being woman and potentially mother, the two lips of which Merleau-Ponty speaks can touch themselves in her, between women, without having recourse to seeing. These two dimensions of which Merleau-Ponty speaks are *in* her body. And hence she experiences it as volume in a different way?

And this would be one of the differences between men and women, that these lips do not re-join each other according to the same economy. Whereas one needs the mother or her substitute, the other suffices within herself to be two, being mother and woman. The two being in the same already and still in the invisible?

> *Ideas are the other side of language and calculus. When I think they animate my interior speech, they haunt it as the 'little phrase' possesses the violinist, and they remain beyond the words as it remains beyond the notes – not in the sense that under the light of another sun hidden from us they would shine forth but because they are that certain divergence, that never-finished differentiation, that openness ever to be reopened between the sign and the sign, as the flesh is, we said, the dehiscence of the seer into the visible and of the visible into the seer.*
>
> (p. 178; translation modified)

This never-finished differentiation might be the symptom, the secret recollection of a sexual difference that has never been achieved in language. Something would always sing 'behind' words, like the trace of the resistance of an other that is irreducible to myself, that would require the unceasing practice of openness between signs. Letting the flesh appear between the sign and the sign. Dehiscence of the seer in the visible and of the visible in the seer which is insurmountable between these two 'signs': masculine and feminine, living signs that, as seer and visible, will never see each other. That in which their differences consist is experienced in touch but is never 'seen.' Not even in the meeting of their flesh. Flesh, the flesh of each one is not substitutable for the other. It is – prior to any God – transcendence here and now. While God can help to arrange space, space-time, he never takes 'the place of.' He lets difference be achieved, even invites it to happen. He does not fulfill it.

> *And just as my body sees only because it is a part of the visible in which it opens forth, the sense upon which the arrangement of the sounds opens reflects back upon that arrangement.*
>
> (p. 178)

'My body sees only because it is part of the visible.' If I cannot see the other in his alterity, and if he cannot see me, my body no longer sees anything in difference. I become blind as soon as it is a question of a differently sexed body. I may barely perceive some exterior phenomenon that reveals a little of the flesh of the visible. Where this is concerned, I remain in darkness, operating on 'premonitions,' 'tact,' 'radar,' 'wavelengths'? And the abundance of vestimentary compensation [*suppléance*] hardly makes up for this nudity, this dereliction? of my sexed body, devoid of carnal visibility.

Not seeing that '*because it is part of the visible in which it opens forth, the sense upon which the arrangement of the sounds opens*' reflects back on my body.

In utero, I see nothing (except darkness?), but I hear. Music comes before meaning. A sort of preliminary to meaning, coming after warmth, moisture, softness, kinesthesia. Do I hear first of all? After touch. But I cannot hear without touching; nor see, moreover. I hear, and what I hear is sexually differentiated. Voice is differentiated.

Do meaning and language inverse the order of hearing? Thus, first of all, I hear something of the feminine, some vocalizing in the feminine. However, language is said, is ordered in the masculine, except when it is a case of what linguists call a mark. The feminine follows the masculine grammatical norm, which is supposedly neuter or neutral, by adding to it a mark: *e*.[3] The feminine precedes and follows the masculine in language. The first music and the first meaning are perceived differently from what will or will not result from them as felt. Only rarely does the first music return to the subject (cf. Nietzsche's nostalgia on this subject, for example). When meaning does return, it is normally marked 'grave,' in the different senses of the word, while the first music is on the light, acute side. This vocalism is the most memorable, and/but it is not repeated in the weave of language. Which would come into being to take its place?

> *For the linguist language is an ideal system, a fragment of the intelligible world.*
>
> (p. 178)

Language is an ideal system not only for the linguist but for every speaking subject. In our language, we are always basically idealists. Cut off from mother nature, where, whence, we are born, from our archaic state, our archives of flesh. Twisted 'upon ourselves,' but starting from a primary part of the self that is abandoned 'with the other' – another feminine for both sexes. A part of the self does not come back to us in its primary-perception-reception. A part of our vitality that is buried, forgotten with the other, sometimes in the other, and which we receive with an other 'voice,' that of an ideal order (?) which covers us over. And which lacks voice, moreover. The text of the law, of codes, no longer has a voice. Even if it is in some way built upon the 'model' of the voice.

> *But, just as for me to see it is not enough that my look be visible for X, it is necessary that it be visible for itself, through a sort of torsion, reversal, or specular phenomenon, which is given from the sole fact that I am born.*
>
> (p. 178)

Why does birth imply this solipsism? It is true that it implies solitude. But can solitude be represented as this 'torsion on oneself,' notably through a specular phenomenon? Do the specular and the carnal belong to the same or to different orders? How do they articulate with each other, exclude each other? And, even though I can touch myself in a number of parts of my body, it is not possible for me to see myself in some of these. Notably it is impossible for me to see my look. I can see myself, partially, by narrowing my field of vision. I see certain parts of my body. But my *face* is never visible to me – naturally. I need a mirror to see it, and I never see it during the activities that constitute its carnal visibility. Does my face represent what is at stake in the passage from nature to culture, the stakes of representation? My back is difficult for me to see as well. And I am always being veiled, unveiled, violated by the other in this face. And the parts of my body that I cannot protect from my look.

Nor will I ever see the *mucous*, that most intimate interior of my flesh, neither the touch of the outside of the skin of my fingers nor the perception of the inside of these same fingers, but another threshold of the passage from outside to inside, from inside to outside, between inside and outside, between outside and inside: I will always feel veiled, unveiled, violated, often by the other in this dimension which I cannot protect with my look. These mucous membranes evade my mastery, just as my face does, yet differently. The joined hands, not those that take hold one of the other, grasp each other, but the hands that touch without taking hold – like the lips. The joined hands perhaps represent this memory of the intimacy of the mucous.

As for mirrors, they give access to another order of the visible. Cold, icy, frozen-freezing, and with no respect for the vital, operative qualities of laterality. I see myself in the mirror as if I were an other. I put that other that I am in the mirror between the other and myself, which disconcerts this experience of the inversed laterality of the other. The other whose left hand can seize my right hand, for example. Making me more passive than any passivity of and within my own touch. Forcing me into the within and the beyond of my horizon. Of all possible mastery. Whether it's an event or an accident, that depends . . . Between the other in the mirror and the other who inverts me, there is also the other of the same, at once closer and more distant. Also a phenomenon of visibility, given that without realizing it, the other detains my look as it sees him, and that he sees that which I cannot see of myself. A mutual dereliction in which we constitute, each for the other, holes in the invisible other than intrauterine life or carnal relations in the strict sense. The black hole of that into which we disappear, each into the other, continually.

Traditionally, man claims to be the one who sees, the one whose horizon would not be pierced from one end to the other both by his 'own' vision and by the look of the other who sees him. This belief, this will for mastery, probably constitutes one of the the most fundamental illusions of the flesh. The screen or armor that places an interdiction on loving relations. And the postulate of a God who is both invisible and who sees all, which makes up for the blind gaze of the other.

My face is always in darkness. It is never born. This is probably why it is at stake in a metaphysics that wants to bring into the light that which is not yet clear. And that maintains the most radical *polemos* with the maternal, the intrauterine: irreducible darkness.

(It is odd that when Jacques Lacan theorized the entrance into the specular world, he described the infant and its mother seeing themselves and each other in the same mirror. If the infant does not see himself alone in the mirror, how can he differentiate himself from his mother? He runs the risk of reduplicating, or creating, a confusing fusion with her if he enters into this other world with her.

Moreover, it does not seem that he needs a mirror to look at his mother and perceive her as *you*. The mirror functions as the sword of differentiation, the passage to a world other than that of the living, but not as that which would give the child access to the way out of the mother's world. To affirm this would be to say that he lacks the ability to use his eyes, including as a mirror, and that he needs a mirror to see the other.)

> *So also, if my words have a meaning, it is not because they present the systematic organization the linguist will disclose, it is because that organization, like the look, refers back to itself: the operative Word is the obscure region whence comes the instituted light, as the muted reflection of the body upon itself is what we call natural light.*
>
> (p. 178)

If my words have meaning, it is because they touch the other from the starting point of my perception, and having touched me and touching the other, they organize a possible dwelling for these perceptions. When the other understands, he gives and returns to me my dwelling. So long as he or she inhabits and relates to himself or herself in a habitable way. And so long as my words carry the meaning of a dwelling. Whence comes the necessity of 'organization,' a sort of 'house' that does not cut itself off from perceptions but shelters them and allows them to inhabit, cohabit, socially as well as politically.

> *The operative Word is the obscure region whence comes the instituted light.*
>
> (p. 178)

That which is operative in the word remains obscure once light is instituted. Thus light and its norms are based on an efficacy or an effectivity that is not very clear. Is the maternal-feminine engaged, enacted, while remaining in obscurity, especially where its social impact is concerned?

> *As there is a reversibility of the seeing and the visible, and as at the point where the two metamorphoses cross what we call perception is born . . .*
>
> (p. 178)

This reversibility is Merleau-Ponty's hypothesis. As if the *seen* enveloped me in its vision? Isn't this a sort of animism in which the visible becomes another living being?

In his view, are the seeing and the visible two aspects of himself? Two metamorphoses of himself that intersect in a closed system? Perception takes place in this crisscrossing of the seeing and the visible, of the look and the visible, of the one who looks and the world, things that are already enveloped, surrounded, 'layered' by looks. Does the seer see-perceive because of the fact that the visible is already clairvoyance? I would not be able to receive the visible world if there were no kinship between what I see there and my vision. This reversibility of the *world* and the *I* (which Merleau-Ponty refuses to dissociate, to separate into two) suggests some repetition of a prenatal sojourn where the universe and I form a closed economy, which is partly reversible (but only in the opposite direction, if reversibility can have meaning: the in utero *providing* it, the *hypokeimenon*, is more on the side of the maternal-feminine, the future 'subject' or seer on the side of the world or of things), or some anticipation of a heavenly sojourn, unless it is an alliance or a love pact between the world and things. In this indivisibility of the seer in relation to the visible, does some trace of animism remain as a sort of enveloping by the maternal power that is still present following birth, or as an anticipation of the presence of God? Or both? In this idea, something is said about the fact that no mourning has been performed for the birth process, nor for the cutting of reversibility through some umbilical cord. Although a pertinent analysis of the way I form a weave of sensations with the world, it is one that excludes solitude even though its own systemization is solipsistic. This seer is never alone, he dwells unceasingly in *his* world. Eventually he finds some accomplices there, but he never meets others. His universe represents, or re-creates, a vast intertwining of umbilical cords or passages. Perception would take place at each crossing of placental tissue with an embryo-nurseling that is always in direct connection with it (her).

If I wanted to apply some terms here which I do not really like to use outside of their strictly clinical setting – where, moreover, I do not use them as such – I might say that Merleau-Ponty's seer remains in an incestuous prenatal situation with the whole. This mode of existence or of being is probably that of all men, at least in the West. Also, given the historic period when Merleau-Ponty was writing, he would have been one of the few or one of the first people to have felt this. Is it still true that the perception of this situation remains veiled, an obscure light which illuminates the whole? Still without changing the movement or the dimension of 'things' or of the relations between them.

> *So also there is a reversibility of the speech and what it signifies; the signification is what comes to seal, to close, to gather up the multiplicity of the physical, physiological linguistic means of elocution, to contract them into one sole act.*
>
> (p. 178)

Speech, too, would form a sort of tissue with that which it signifies, signification coming to seal up each act, a crossroads of speech acts. Like a weaving stitch that holds the threads in a given space-time, fulfills their potentialities, their powers in a realization which, for this moment, completes the work, its virtualities.

> *As vision comes to complete the aesthesiological body . . .*
>
> (p. 178)

Merleau-Ponty accords an exorbitant privilege to vision. Or else, once again, he expresses the exorbitant privileging of vision in our culture. Must my aesthesiological body be completed by vision? Why completed? Why vision? Does it represent the sense which is the most capable of completing? The most unveiling/reveiling? That which covers? Especially gaps, depths, abysses? That which finishes, finishes me in relation to the other? In particular the other who is touching and being touched. The look by which I touch also creates a spectacle that allows me to approach the other without immediately being open to his, or her, senses. At least I may think so. And think of myself as autonomous, completed by my visual construction. It becomes the power and the fault in my aesthesiological body. Equally because in a certain way nothing is as sensitive, especially to touch, as my sight. But it can give me the illusion of a closed world, one that is closed because of the fact that I, male or female, was born of, issued from, an other, woman-mother.

What Merleau-Ponty seeks is something that closes the circuit of my relations with the universe in all its dimensions, and that allows me to perceive in the place where it is closed up. Vision is effectively a sense that can totalize, enclose, in its own way. More than the other senses, it is likely to construct a landscape, a horizon. Up to a certain point. It happens that movement is a more adequate way of building myself an aesthesiological body. And that, moving through the world, across the universe, or dancing, I construct more of a dwelling for myself than through vision. Merleau-Ponty would want it to be vision which closes – and works – my body, including the reversibility of the visible. And for the horizon to perfect me in a network, a garment, a skin, which we give ourselves, which we weave unceasingly in order to live, to be born. And to dwell, also, in a certain darkness, enveloped, also, in the visible, which is never pure transparency but carries in it, with it, the opacity, the weight, the thickness of the flesh. His analysis of vision becomes even more detailed, more beautiful, as it accords him the privilege over the other senses, as it takes back a great deal of the phenomenology of the tactile. Of course, vision is a mode of the tactile, but by giving it the privilege of closing up the aesthesiological body, Merleau-Ponty says of it what he could have said of the skin, the mucous, of their contacts. His phenomenology of vision almost mistakes itself for a phenomenology of painting or of the art of painting. On occasion, he speaks of it with the lyricism of one who loves art rather than with the rigor of a philosopher, as if one must give oneself over to its weights and measures. It is simply a question of signifying that this privilege accorded to vision indeed gives it some dimensions that metaphysics neglects, but there still remains the *privilege* of this sense over the others. Reduction of the tactile into the visible, to begin with. Fulfillment of the idea, of idealism, under its material, carnal aspects. A way of talking about the flesh that already cancels its most powerful components, those that are moreover creative in their power. At least there is a great risk of perpetuating this state of things when the relation to the world is 'closed' or directed by the visible (or by that tactility between the hands which is at issue in this text).

> *And, as the visible takes hold of the look which has unveiled it and which forms a part of it, the signification rebounds upon its own means, it annexes to itself the speech that becomes an object of science, it antedates itself by a retrograde movement which is never completely belied – because already, in opening the horizon of the nameable and of the sayable, the speech acknowledged that it has its place in that horizon; because no locutor speaks without making himself in advance allocutary*, be it only for himself; *because with one sole gesture he closes*

> *the circuit of his relation to himself and that of his relation to the others, and, with the same stroke, also sets himself up as* delocutary, *speech of which one speaks: he offers himself and offers every word to a universal Word.*
>
> (pp. 178–79)

Signification is in language. It antedates itself in language, the expectation of speech as well as the look in the visible. The movement (since it is a question here of aesthesiology) does not seem the same in each case. Language would be more of the order of a temporal bridge between retroaction and anticipation. The 'subject' keeping itself always in this endless crisscrossing of an anticipation and a recurrence [*effet de retour*], a reversal [*effet de rebours*] to that which is said and which becomes available for another saying. There again, the circle is closed by the sedimentations of its comings and goings.

Two points may be noted, among others:

1. The circularity of these speech patterns explains why it is so difficult to effect any changes. The entire speaking body of the subject is in some way archaeologically structured by an already spoken language. To signify to him that this language must or can be modified amounts to asking him to modify body, his flesh. Which cannot be done in a day. Or in a year. Resistance to all the discoveries that convulse language can be understood in this way. Also the impossibility of accepting, without a detachment that is truly difficult to conceive for one who does not feel its carnal necessity, the idea that discourse is *monosexual* and that it is necessary to make room, leave a place, for another discourse, one that is put together differently. This resistance shows itself to be at least as strong, if not stronger, where psychoanalysts are concerned, insofar as they deal with a store of conscious language. They do not accept for all that that this store, this *background*,[4] might be interpretable, might unfold itself like a language, the repressed-censored of another sex that asks to come into being.

2. These sedimentations of language weave between past and future, and my present speech is rooted in what has already been said and closes up the circularity between the subject and his speech. Language, languages find themselves constituted like another ground, or rather like another circular matrix, with which the subject maintains permanent exchanges, from which he receives himself without always being able or willing to modify it. Moreover, he calls his language his 'mother tongue,' which is the sign of a substitution rather than a reality. His language is in no way created by a mother or mothers, except insofar as it sometimes reduplicates the dwelling in the mother and in nature. But this reproduction is not a maternal creation.

This language and these languages, therefore, are firmly rooted, and undoubtedly there is nothing more difficult than changing their culture. Especially since the subject also anticipates his interlocutor, his allocutor, since he creates his own allocutor, since 'with one sole gesture he closes the circuit of his relation to himself and that of his relation to the others, and, with the same stroke, also sets himself up as *delocutary*, speech of which one speaks: he offers himself and offers every word to a universal Word' (pp. 178–79). In his speech acts but also in his linguistic relation with the other, the subject closes his circle, his bubble.

Speech is not used to communicate, to encounter, but to talk to oneself, to duplicate and reduplicate oneself, to surround, even to inter oneself. There is no becoming, except that which is already closed off. No air, except that which would exhale words already spoken, already brought into existence? Nothing new, nothing being born in this *universal word* which amounts to the most solipsistic construction, constitution of a subject who would no longer know, or not know, the event. Who, in a certain way, would always have been there, turning in circles from the beginning, in a language that has been determined in this way. Like a present that would move around while remaining the same? A sort of puncture in the tissue of the world, between the tissue of the world and that of the subject, between the tissue of language and the thread of the subject, as both are transposed and exchanged with each other, like a machine that puts or sews things together by making a forward stitch backward, a backward stitch forward, and so on, indefinitely. Without any creation, invention, event, or randomness except for this interminable operation.

No new speech is possible here. One cannot imagine any allocutor, any other of either sex. No other description tells so rigorously of incarceration in a 'universal Word.' This Word which would not give place to the unforeseeability of God, the universe, the other. A Word of 'perpetual repetition'? A Word that no longer has an *open* future and consequently shuts out certain enunciatory practices: cries for help, announcements, demands, expressions of gratitude, prophecy, poetry, and so on. Necessarily, an other is present in these practices, but not that allocutor for whom I can substitute myself, whom I can anticipate. The circuit is open. Meaning does not function like the circularity of something already given and received. It is still in the process of making itself. And the superior overview of a metalanguage is and will always be partial where this is concerned. It is not possible to overhang or encircle such a production of speech. Ceaselessly engaged in seeking its rhythm, its measure, its poetry, its house, its country, its passages, its shortcuts, toward itself, toward the other, others – the same or foreign – its ethics. A speech that is always at risk, stable and unstable, like a step that is discovering itself, inventing itself at each instant, also in function of the newness of the landscape. A speech in which there is nothing of the universal. Even if occasionally it expresses the universe better than an unchanging, eternal speech. A neutral speech, about the neuter? The speech of a subject who tries unceasingly to compensate for his incarnation in his language, his tongue, and who elaborates moreover a technically powerful machine, a sort of mechanical miming of parturition, but one that is not a 'sublimation of the flesh.' Hardly even a mechanism of solipsistic survival. A kind of duplication or stand-in for the constitution of the flesh? A reversal of the maternal gift of flesh, in the autarchy of the subject of and in language.

For a sublimation of the flesh, what is lacking is a passage through silence and solitude which leads to the existence, the emergence of a speech of one who is born in a space still to be defined by him, to be marked by him, so that, when speaking of himself, he can also speak of himself to the other, and hear him.

> *We shall have to follow more closely this transition from the mute world to the speaking world. For the moment we want only to suggest that one can speak neither of a destruction nor of a conservation of silence (and still less of a destruction that conserves or of a realization that destroys – which is not to solve but to pose the problem). When the silent vision falls into speech, and when the speech in turn, opening up a field of the nameable and the sayable, inscribes itself in that field, in its place, according to its truth – in short, when it metamorphoses the structures of the visible world and makes itself a gaze of the mind,* intuitus

> mentis – *this is always in virtue of the same fundamental phenomenon of reversibility which sustains both the mute perception and the speech and which manifests itself by an almost carnal existence of the idea, as well as by a sublimation of the flesh.*
>
> (p. 179)

There is no silence for Merleau-Ponty. The structure of a mute world is such that all the possibilities of language are already given there. Nothing therefore about the dereliction of the lack in language or about the creative virtualities that would inscribe themselves in this silence. Speech is or is not actualized, but its field and its means and their possible realizations are already there. Nothing new can be said. No way to say it can be invented. Everything is there and is unceasingly reversible. Just as in the case of the visible. Speech has, among other functions, that of bearing the silence of the visible into sonority, of metamorphosing it and itself into a gaze of the mind, 'always in virtue of the same fundamental phenomenon of reversibility which sustains both the mute perception and the speech and which manifests itself by an almost carnal existence of the idea, as well as by a sublimation of the flesh' (p. 179).

The almost carnal existence of the idea and the sublimation of the flesh are seductive utterances and hypotheses, yet puzzling ones insofar as their permanences, their cycles or rotations are always already there, where the work that would make the idea become carnal and sublimate the flesh is never accomplished. It would be enough to remain in a state of reversibility – 'the ultimate truth' – for these operations or these conditions to take place. Whereas it is the opposite. If reversibility is not interrupted, the sublimation of the flesh cannot be achieved.

In other words: if the cord is not cut and there is no end to the osmotic exchanges with the maternal world and its substitutes, how can the sublimation of the flesh take place? It keeps on becoming in a closed circuit, in a sort of nourishing relationship with the other. Is it sublimated in order to accede to union with the other? It seems that this is not the case. Does it perpetuate a condition, maintain it with its permanence, amortize its cuts and shocks? What is called reversibility here is perhaps that by means of which the subject produces some mucous on the outside and is reenveloped by it. Some elaboration of the carnal undoubtedly takes place there. But always in its solipsistic relation to the maternal. There is *no trace of any carnal idea of the other woman nor of any sublimation of the flesh with the other*. At best an alchemy of substitution of a placental nourishment. A sort of layering that represents the archaeology of the subject, of the world, of their exchanges. But this archaeology already existed. The subject and the world would be already completed even when they were engaged in making themselves. Would they elaborate themselves in relation to an unchanging ground and horizon? In order to change the subject, his language, his world, everything would have to be undone and remade, including what is called the possibilities of language. Its grounds and foundations. And this postulate of a universal speech in which we exchanged, as in some unchanging, pregiven, presupposed exchange, would have to be brought into question.

> *In a sense, if we were to make completely explicit the architectonics of the human body, its ontological framework, and how it sees itself and hears itself, we would see that the structure of its mute world is such that all the possibilities of*

> *language are already given in it. Already our existence as seers (that is, we said, as beings who turn the world back upon itself and who pass over to the other side, who see one another with eyes).*
>
> (p. 179)

In Merleau-Ponty's view, the world turns back on itself. The seer does not open his eyes to the world or the other in a contemplation that seeks and respects their different horizons. Does he turn over the world as he turns his hand, his plaything, his creation? Could he plumb the structure of the world to its depths or manage to encompass it? But what gesture, what quality of gesture could make him believe that he has encompassed the world? Is it an intuition or a belief that Merleau-Ponty needs in order to think? A ground that he must give himself? A ground or thought that circles back to the same point while it progresses. In order to progress. Like the sun of the earth moving around the sun and around itself? We would perceive, encounter the world, look at the other at the crossing-points of these circles? Catching sight of each other, seeing each through the other.

Catching sight of each other, if we find ourselves on the course at the crisscrossing of the circles that make this possible? Which does not seem to be a matter of course given the reversibility between the visible and the seer, the closed world that reversibility entails for the *I* or the *you*. Within this world, movement is such that it would take extraordinary luck for two seers to catch sight of each other, find each other on the track of the same circle and cross paths, or look at each other as they walk in parallel lines. Or might it happen that they see each other's eyes? Another possibility which is highly unlikely. For this to come about, it would have to happen that two *seers* assimilated the 'universal Word,' its effects, the world, in exactly the same way, and that they found each other at the same point in space and time. An unlikely stroke of luck or chance? Or of grace? Which makes us identical at a given moment.

But Merleau-Ponty does not speak of this. The rest can only be an illusion of the flesh. We never catch sight of each other, and we do not see each other's eyes. No matter how universal speech may be, a world, *our* world separates us, a world from which we are never separated – in any case according to the kind of relations we entertain in Merleau-Ponty's analysis. We 'turn the world back on itself' and 'pass over to the other side' because we are seers? Undoubtedly, at each instant, for a pellicle of the horizon of visibility, not for the whole world. The world would have to be completed. Which is possible if the explanation of the architectonics of the body, 'its ontological framework,' shows that all the possibilities of language are given in the mute world. The world cannot be perceived without language, yet all of language exists virtually in silence. All that remains to be said is that the world is isomorphic with the subject and vice versa, and the whole is sealed up in a circle. Nothing new happens, only this permanent weaving between the world and the subject. Which supposes that the subject sees the whole, that he is the clairvoyant seeing of everything, with nothing left over – neither of the world nor of himself. If all of language already resides in the silence of the subject and of the world, like their ontological tissue, then I can turn the world back on itself and return to myself after having passed to the other side. Am I playing at hoops with the world (of) language? What do I add? Or what do I take away? It is always the same. I revolve around the 'center,' the point of anchorage, without getting closer. I keep on repeating a gesture which perhaps digs me in, deepens me? Digs in and deepens the world? Unites us? According to Merleau-Ponty, energy plays itself out in the backward-and-forward motion of a loom. But weaving the visible and my look in this way, I could just as well say that I close them off from myself. The texture becomes increasingly tight, taking me into it, sheltering me there but imprisoning me as well.

In a certain way, this subject never enters the world. He never emerges from an osmosis that allows him to say to the other, 'Who art thou?' But also, 'Who am I?' What sort of event do we represent for each other when together? Irreversible events except where death is concerned. The phenomenology of the flesh that Merleau-Ponty attempts is without question(s). It has no spacing or interval for the freedom of questioning between two. No other or Other to keep the world open. No genesis. No grace. Having become a god, man works and plays with the world until it is worn out? Very carefully. But not without a certain ennui? By himself.

> *And, in a sense, to understand a phrase is nothing else than to fully welcome it in its sonorous being, or, as we put it so well, to* hear what it says.
>
> (p. 179)

Here, meaning is mixed with sound, the totality of the chain of what is said, which is integral in all differentiations of the verbal chain. It is given with the words for those who have ears to hear, and who are situated in a landscape overrun with words, which is henceforth but a variant of speech. Everything is given, inside and outside. It remains only to welcome, decode, interpret, and hear.

> *In a sense the whole of philosophy, as Husserl says, consists in restoring a power to signify, a birth of meaning, or a wild meaning, an expression of experience by language, which in particular clarifies the special domain of language.*
>
> (p. 179)

Everything is given, and yet the function of philosophy is to restore a power to signify, a birth of meaning, or a wild meaning. The question is: can this be possible for it without changing the foundations of language? Without lifting the hypothesis that *reversibility* is the final truth? A hypothesis that must be questioned and 'opened up' if a meaning which has not yet been heard is to come into existence, that of a language which is sexuate and which encounters through speech and in the world a sex which is *irreducible* to it, and with which it is impossible to have relations of reversibility without remainder.

Translated by Carolyn Burke and Gillian C. Gill

Notes

1 *Editor's note:* page references following the quotations from Maurice Merleau-Ponty are to 'The Intertwining – The Chiasm', reproduced as chapter 9 in this volume.
2 At this point in Lingis's English translation, 'laps' is substituted for 'lips,' a typographical error that seems to mime what Irigaray calls the invisibility of the feminine. – Translator.
3 In French, an *e* is the mark of feminine gender. – Translator.
4 In English in the original text. – Translator.

35

THE LAST PAINTING OR THE PORTRAIT OF GOD

Hélène Cixous

I would like to write like a painter. I would like to write like painting.

The way I would like to live. Maybe the way I manage to live, sometimes. Or rather: the way it is sometimes given to me to live, in the present absolute.

In the happening of the instant.

Just at the moment of the instant, in what unfurls it, I touch down then let myself slip into the depth of the instant itself.

This is how I live, this is how I try to write. The best company for me is she or he who is in touch with the instant, in writing.

And what is a painter? A bird-catcher of instants.

'I will have to work very hard to render what I am looking for: the instantaneous impression, particularly the envelope of things, the same all-pervading light.'[1]

Monet, in 1890, is the one who said that: what I am looking for, instantaneousness . . . the same light spread throughout, the same light, the same light.

There is a literary *œuvre* which is dear to me, the work of Clarice Lispector. She wrote *Agua Viva*. This book aims to write-paint, aims to work on the gesture of writing as a gesture of painting. I say 'aims': one can always ask oneself the question of the reality of the thing. What brings this book closer to a painter's gesture is that it is a book of instants, a book from which each page could be taken out like a picture. Clarice says: 'Each thing has an instant in which it is. I want to take possession of the thing's *is*.'[2]

I want to take hold of the third person of the present. For me, that is what painting is, the chance to take hold of the third person of the present, the present itself.

But in life, it is

> only in the act of love – by the clear, starlike abstraction of what one feels [that] we capture the unknown quality of the instant, which is hard and crystalline and vibrant in the air, and life is that incalculable instant, greater than the event itself.

Who could write: 'Is my theme the instant? my life theme. I try to keep up with it, I divide myself thousands of times, into as many times as the seconds that pass away, fragmentary as I am and precarious the moments.'[3] It may be Clarice Lispector, it may be Monet.

I would like to write to what is living in life; I would like to be in the sea and render it in words. Which is impossible. I would like to write the rose-colored beach and the pearly ocean. And it is February. Completely impossible. My words can't tell you the simultaneously infinite and yet finite beach rolled out like a[n] immense carpet of rosy sands. My words are colorless. Barely sonorous? What I can tell you, a painter would show you.

I would like to break your heart with the magnificent calm of a beach safe from man. But I can't do it, I can only tell it. All I can do is tell the desire. But the painter can break your heart with the epiphany of a sea. There's a recipe: 'To really paint the sea, you have to see it everyday, at every hour and in the same place, to come to know the life in this location.'[4]

That's Monet. Monet who knows how to paint the sea: how to paint the sameness of the sea.

It's in vain that I say to you: Côte Rocheuse, Lion's Rock, Belle-Ile. And the green sea and the black lion don't fall on your heart over and over. I tell you of the rocks at Belle-Ile. But eternity doesn't suddenly stream forth and enter, weeping, through your eyes into the depths of your body.

With a haystack, I tell you 'haystack,' I don't reveal the setting sun to you, I don't intoxicate you with the discovery of the colors in the light, I don't make you laugh, I don't make you cry. I write.

I love paintings the way the blind must love the sun: feeling it, breathing it in, hearing it pass through the trees, adoring it with regret and pain, knowing it through the skin, seeing it with the heart. I don't paint. I need painting. I write in the direction of painting. I position myself toward the sun. Toward the light. Toward painting.

The blind don't see the sun? They see the sun in a different way. And perhaps I, in writing, paint in a different way. I paint in the dark. But this is my blind way of calling forth light.

I'm calling.

There are mimosas in the garden. I want so much to give them to you to see.

I am only a poet, I am only a poor painter without canvas without brush without palette.

But not without God; being only a poet, I am really obligated to count on God, or on you, or on someone.

I'm calling: Mimosa! I'm calling you.

I tell you on the telephone: I want so much for you to see the mimosas. I send you the word 'mimosa'; I hope that once delivered to your breast, it will transform itself into a vision of mimosa. I am a being who paints mimosas by phone.

If I were a painter! I would give you each mimosa-cluster whole. I would give you my mimosa-soul, down to the most minute quivering of the yellow spheres.

I would put my mimosoul on the canvas, before your eyes. But I don't paint. I can only speak to you of mimosas. I can sing the word 'mimosa.' I can make the magic name ring out, the mimosa word: I can give you the music of the mimosa. I can swear to you that (the) mimosa is a synonym for alleluia.

And still, how fortunate that there is the word 'mimosa'! I can tell you that the mimosa mimes. I can tell you, too, that the mimosa originates in Brazil.

But I can't nourish your eyes with mimosa light. So I beg you: please, see the mimosas that I see. Imagine the mimosas. See what you don't see, out of love for me. The mimosa is the painter's nymph.

I am the awkward sorceress of the invisible: my sorcery is powerless to evoke, without the help of your sorcery. Everything I evoke depends on you, depends on your trust, on your faith.

I gather words to make a great straw-yellow fire, but if you don't put in your own flame, my fire won't take, my words won't burst into pale yellow sparks. My words will remain dead words. Without your breath on my words, there will be no mimosas.

Ah! If I were Monet. I would fill your house with mimosas, with wisteria, with poppies. With palm trees. With straw. Only their fragrance would be missing.

I write. But I need the painter to give a face to my words. First of all, I write; then you must paint what I've said to you.

Am I jealous of the painter's power? Yes. No. I sense the terrific beating of the painter's heart, the vertigo, the urgency. It is perhaps what I like the most in painting: the beating of the heart. If I were a painter, what pain! what passion! What incessant jealousy of the sky, of the air, what torturous adoration of the light! If I were a painter I would see, I would see, I would see, I would see, I would be panic-stricken, I would run incessantly toward the potato fields, toward the pollard willows. If I were a painter I would know immediately that America is in the heath.

Since I am not a painter, I make detours and go through texts:

> Do come and paint with me on the heath, in the potato field, come and walk with me behind the plough and the shepherd – come and sit with me, looking into the fire – let the storm that blows across the heath blow through you.
>
> Break loose from your bonds. I do not know the future, in what way it might be different if everything should go smoothly with us, but I cannot speak differently: Don't seek it in Paris, don't seek it in America; it is always the same, forever and ever exactly the same. Change, if you will, but it is in the heath you must look.[5]

That was Van Gogh.

I would roll around in desire and pain if I were a painter beneath the stars; if I were a painter I would die endlessly of wonder. I would live in ecstasy until it was at last granted to me to *no longer* see the stars, to no longer see the silk of gray-silver water crossed through and through by a fine strip of sun from my feet to the infinite, in the water, to no longer see the magnificence of sun-powder, until it was at last granted to me to stretch myself out in the dust, to rest among the marvelous powders of the earth. If I were a painter I would live in the fire, I would want to take up the fire in my hands. I would want to catch fire. I would end up losing my sight, and I would thank God. It's fitting that Monet painted with eyes closed, at the end of his life.

I am nearsighted. And even if I have often blamed God for this, I often thank him for it. It's a relief. My nearsightedness spares me the agony of those who see the secrets of the sky. I write because I am nearsighted: it's also, I think, through nearsightedness, thanks to my nearsightedness, that I love:

I am someone who looks at things from very, very close up. Seen through my eyes, little things are very big. Details are my kingdoms. Some people survey. Some people who are far-seeing don't see what is very near. I am someone who sees the smallest letters of the earth. Flat on my stomach in the garden, I see the ants, I see each of the ants' feet. Insects become my heroes. Am I not a little bit right? Human beings are divine insects.

What is beautiful is that such little creatures can be so big.

Such are the benefits of my nearsightedness. This is how I console myself for not being a painter. Would I love this way if I were a painter?

How do I sense what I don't know – the painter's agony? The paintings are what tell me about the painter's passion. Not just *one* singular painting. But rather a series, a sheaf of paintings, a herd of paintings, a flock, a tribe of paintings. I see Monet's twenty-six cathedrals. I don't know if *one* cathedral would carry me away. Twenty-six cathedrals is a full gallop.

And I sense the struggle. I see the race of speed with the light. I see the challenge. I see the audacity.

The painter is the combatant of enigma.

The painter, the true painter, doesn't know how to paint. He looks for the secret. He will put his life into it. The painter is always Percival. He sets off, he leaves the forest, but in order to come back, on his way around the world, to the forest. I sense the painter's superhuman task: to capture the hundred cathedrals that are born in one day from the cathedral of Rouen. To see them being born. To see them succeeding one another. To see the cathedral in all its lights in one hour. It's to die for.

So he attacks the cathedral and the cathedral attacks him.

This is the struggle with the cathedral: 'It's killing, and for this I give up everything, you, my garden . . . And something which never happens, my sleep was filled with nightmares: the cathedral fell down on top of me, it appeared either blue, pink or yellow.'[6] And Julie Manet tells us:

> Mr. Monet showed us his cathedrals. There are twenty-six of them, and they are magnificent. Some are entirely violet, others white and yellow, with a blue sky, or pink with a slightly green sky. Then there is one in the fog . . . You discover every detail in them; they are as if suspended in mid-air.[7]

Seeing the cathedral's truth which is twenty-six, and noting it, means seeing time. Painting time. Painting the marriage of time with light. Painting the works of time and light.

That's what I would like to do if I were a painter.

The sun moves so quickly. The cathedral changes so often. It was pink a short time ago. Now look at it, violet and flying low.

And we are so slow.

Life is so rapid.

'I doggedly keep exploring a series of different effects (of haystacks), but at this time of year the sun goes down so quickly that I cannot follow it.'[8]

Following the sun, painting the differences. I see Monet attacking his poppy field, mounted on four easels. The paintbrushes fly about. Monet is racing.

And even as I have been writing this page, the sun has disappeared. We who write are so slow. And I think of the painter's magic swiftness.

Writing this, I said to myself that perhaps what I like about painting is its mad speed. And people will tell me, there are also slow painters. I don't know. I know nothing about it. I only imagine. But only those who are fast, those who pursue haystacks on four easels, matter to me.

And I think of the rapidity and fatality of desire: vying with light. 'You need a Japanese swiftness.' No, that wasn't Hokusai, but Van Gogh.

While I was writing this, I prudently held myself back from going out into all the fields that surround me, in order to avoid a too-great vertigo, and it was only when this brief reflection was over that I rewarded myself and wanted to reread Van Gogh's letters. I had been convinced that Van Gogh was a slow painter. Here is what I found:

> The Japanese draw quickly, very quickly, like a lightning flash, because their nerves are finer, their feeling simpler.
>
> . . . I have only been here a few months, but tell me this – could I, in Paris, have done the drawing of the boats *in an hour*? Even without the perspective frame, I do it now without measuring, just by letting my pen go.[9]

It is great that Claude Monet managed to paint those ten pictures between February and May. Quick work doesn't mean less serious work, it depends on one's self-confidence and experience.[10]

> I must warn you that everyone will think that I work too fast.
>
> Don't you believe a word of it.
>
> Is it not emotion, the sincerity of one's feeling for nature, that draws us, and if the emotions are sometimes so strong that one works without knowing one works, when sometimes the strokes come with a continuity and a coherence like words in a speech or a letter, then one must remember that it has not always been so, and that in time to come there will again be hard days, empty of inspiration.
>
> So one must strike while the iron is hot, and put the forged bars on one side.
>
> I have not yet done half the 50 canvases fit to be shown in public, and I must do them all this year.
>
> I know beforehand that they will be criticized as *hasty*.
>
> . . . If my health doesn't betray me, I shall polish off my canvases, and there will be some that will do among them.[11]

And to do that, what lightness must have been achieved!

For that, one has to have broken off with everything that holds one back: calculations, backward or sideways glances, hidden motives, acquired, accumulated, hardened knowledge. And especially all the fears: fear of the unknown, fear of criticism, fear of not knowing, fear of the evil eye: 'They will say I am mad' (that's Monet). Fears, one shakes them off. One plays with them. One paints quicker than they take hold.

One does not paint yesterday, one does not even paint today, one paints tomorrow, one paints what will be, one paints 'the imminence of.'

And to do that, letting go of all ties, one flings oneself beyond the ego. This is perhaps the greatest lesson painting gives us: flinging oneself beyond the ego. For the ego is the last root preventing flight. Or the last anchor. One has to unfasten oneself the best one can, with a snap, or by slowly filing away the soul-ring of lead.

I imagine it's easier for a landscape painter than for a writer to get free; the charm of the visible world is so powerful. At times, the painter's ego is no more attached than a milk tooth. A pull, and straight away, with a leap, in the middle of creation. We are born together. It's raining. We know nothing. We are part of everything.

> Under this fine rain I breathe in the innocence of the world. I feel coloured by the nuances of infinity. At this moment I am at one with my picture. We are an iridescent chaos . . . The sun penetrates me soundlessly like a distant friend that stirs up my laziness, fertilises it. We bring forth life.[12]

That was Cézanne.

At that moment, when the ego no longer weighs him down, the painter becomes permeable, becomes immense and virgin, and becomes woman. He lets light work in him. Submission to the process. He becomes tender, he becomes plant, he becomes earth, the sun impregnates him. *Tanta mansidão*, such gentleness . . . [13]

But how do we obtain this lightness, this active passivity, this capacity to let things come through, this submission to the process? We who are so heavy, so obstinately activist, so impatient. How could we become virgin and young and innocent? How could we come all the way from our over-furnished memories and our museums of words to the garden of beginnings and rustlings?

This is our problem as writers. We who must paint with brushes all sticky with words. We who must swim in language as if it were pure and transparent, though it is troubled by phrases already heard a thousand times. We who must clear a new path with each thought through thickets of clichés. We who are threatened at every metaphor, as I am at this moment, with false steps and false words.

But there is a path. It makes us go around the world to regain the second innocence. It's a long path. Only at the end of the path can we regain the force of simplicity or of nudity. Only at the end of life, I believe, will we be able to understand life's secret. One must have traveled a great deal to discover the obvious. One must have thoroughly rubbed and exhausted one's eyes in order to get rid of the thousands of scales we start with from making up our eyes.

There are poets who have strived to do this. I call 'poet' any writing being who sets out on this path, in quest of what I call the second innocence, the one that comes after knowing, the one that no longer knows, the one that knows how not to know.

I call 'poet' any writer, philosopher, author of plays, dreamer, producer of dreams, who uses life as a time of 'approaching.' Fortunately, we have inherited rigorous accounts of their adventures. There are poet-painters, like Van Gogh. There are poet-painters like Clarice Lispector. Whoever would like to know how to go about clearing the gaze should read *The Passion According to G.H.*,[14] by Clarice Lispector.

One must have gone a long way in order to finally leave behind our need to veil, or lie, or gild. Leaving behind the need to gild: this would be the passion according to Rembrandt.

In his very beautiful texts on Rembrandt, Genet says (still remaining within the tradition of reading Rembrandt) that the trajectory of Rembrandt's works began by gilding, by covering over with gold, and then by burning the gold, consuming it, to attain the gold-ash with which the last paintings are painted.

It is only at the end of a superhuman human-going-to-the-depths-of-the-fathomingof-life-and-back that one will be able to cease gilding everything (Rimbaud and Clarice also knew this). And then one can begin to adore.

This is when one will be allowed to arrive at what I have called, in a text entitled *Lemonade Everything Was So Infinite*, 'the last phrase,' the one that holds on to the book or the author with no more than a breath. I have allowed myself to adventure toward the canvas partly because I had written this text, *Lemonade Everything Was So Infinite*. Because, in order to work on what is, for me, the very treasure of writing – in other words, ultimate phrases that are full of being, both so heavy and so light that they are more precious to me than an entire book; in order to work on the mystery of these phrases, I have been led to help myself with painting. I have not found any other more helpful example than some of the long journeys undertaken by painters, by Rembrandt in particular. And, arbitrarily or not, I had made a distinction between what I had called 'works of art' and 'works of being.' For me, works of art are works of seduction, works that can be magnificent, works that are really destined to make themselves seen. Where I am arbitrary is in classifying this or that painter in this or that category. For example, for me, da Vinci's works are only works of art. This may be a mistake. But I will put forward a hypothesis: let us look at a painting by da Vinci and a painting by Rembrandt. We will see da Vinci's painting search us out with its eyes, not take its eyes off us, catch hold of us: these are eye-catching paintings.

In Rembrandt, what is overwhelming is the extent to which in the most intense presence, the people he had looked at are alone, have the absence of intimacy, do not feel themselves looked at; they are looking inside their hearts in the direction of the infinite. By going along this double path, I am now able to tell myself that what matters to me most, in art, are works of being: works which no longer need to proclaim their glory, or their magisterial origin, to be signed, to return, to make a return to celebrate the author. This was why, in the text where I dealt with that topic, I inscribed like a precious stone the phrase: 'Lemonade everything was so infinite . . . ,' a phrase that signified everything to me, the beginning and the end, the whole of life, enjoyment, nostalgia, desire, hope – an *unsigned* phrase by Kafka, a phrase that fell from his hand, from his man's hand at the moment he was not striving to be a writer, the moment he was Franz Kafka himself, beyond books. If these phrases have been collected and printed in spite of everything, it is because it was God's will that, deprived of his voice, as he was dying, Kafka scribbled down, on scraps of paper, what was passing through his mind: and those who were with him at the moment of his passing collected those scraps of paper that are for me the most beautiful books in the world. Perhaps these so very delicate phrases, these phrases of a dying man, are the equivalent, extremely rare in writing, of what is much more frequent in painting: the last paintings. It's at the end, at the moment when one has attained the period of relinquishing, of adoration, and no longer of gilding, that miracles happen.

A magnificent thing happened to Hokusai:

> In loving the pretentious style of He-ma-mu-sho-Niūdō, the painter Yamamizu Tengu, of Noshi-Koshiyama, appropriated for himself the incomprehensible art of his drawings. Now, I who have studied this style for almost a hundred years, without understanding any more of it than he, nevertheless had this strange thing happen to me: I notice that my characters, my animals, my

> insects, my fish, look as if they are escaping from the paper. Is this not truly extraordinary? And a publisher, who was informed of this fact, asked for these drawings, in such a way that I could not refuse him. Fortunately the engraver Ko-Izumi, a very skilled woodcutter, with his very sharp knife, took care to cut the veins and nerves of the beings I drew, and was able to deprive them of the liberty of escaping.[15]

What we have, when Hokusai was over two hundred years old, at the time when he was finally five or six years old, is a collection of drawings that scarcely hold back the beings, fish, insects, or men within their narrow limits.

In what way can I feel close to the painter (the one I love, the madman of painting, of drawing, the unworldly, the celestial, the airborne, the burning)?

First of all, in the need not to lie, not to veil in writing. Which doesn't mean I manage not to lie. It's so difficult not to lie when one writes. And maybe even in the need to write in order to lie less, to scrape the scales away, the too-rich words, to undecorate, unveil. In the need not to submit the subject of writing, of painting, to the laws of cultural cowardice and habit.

In the need, which doesn't mean its execution, not to make things pretty, not to make things clean, when they are not; not to do the right thing. But, whatever the price, to do the true thing.

Rembrandt, who is said not to have had particularly audacious tendencies, but who as a painter was absolutely free, drew and painted nude women I find admirably beautiful, although not everyone has been of this opinion. Here is what a contemporary, A. Houbraken, said in 1710:

> Rembrandt . . . refused to conform to the rules of other artists, and still less to follow the illustrious examples of those who had covered themselves with glory by taking beauty as a model; he contented himself with representing life as it offered itself to him, without making a choice. This is why the great poet Andries Pels very wittily said of him in his *Use and Abuse of the Stage* (page 36): 'Whenever he had to paint a nude woman, he took as a model not a Greek Venus but rather a washerwoman or servant girl from an inn: he called this deviation the imitation of nature and treated all the rest as vain decoration. From the sagging breasts and the deformed hands, to the frayed lace of the bodice opening across the stomach, to the garters around the legs – everything had to be shown, in order to remain faithful to nature. He did not want to listen to any of the rules of moderation that recommended the representation of only certain parts of the body.'
>
> I greatly appreciate Pels's frankness and I ask the reader not to misinterpret my sincere opinion: I do not hate the work of this man, but I wish to compare the different conceptions and methods of art, and to incite those who desire to learn to follow the best way. Apart from this, I join the same poet in saying: 'What a loss for art that such a skilled hand did not use its gifts better! For who would have surpassed him? But the greater the genius, the more he can stray when he does not yield to any principles or to any traditional rule, and when he thinks he can find everything within himself.'[16]

And to think that today, in our time, people think like this self-righteous biographer, but with a slight difference: painters are allowed to contemplate a woman's real nudity. But in writing, this is not yet entirely allowed.

What does my gesture of writing have in common with the gesture of the one who paints?

The concern with fidelity. Fidelity to what exists. To everything that exists. And fidelity is equal respect for what *seems* beautiful to us and what *seems* ugly to us. I stress *seems*.

But under the paintbrush, before the gaze, in the light of respect, there is nothing ugly which does not seem equally beautiful.

Painting does not know the ugly.

It isn't the beautiful that is true. It's the true that is . . . I don't want to say beautiful. The ugly looked at with respect and without hatred and without disgust is equal to the 'beautiful.' The nonbeautiful is also beautiful.

Or rather, there is no beautiful more beautiful than the ugly. In painting as in writing, there is no other 'beauty' than fidelity to what is. Painting renders – but what it renders is justice. Everything that is: the cathedral, the haystack, the sunflowers, the vermin, the peasants, the chair, the skinned ox, the flayed man, the cockroach.

Because everything that is loved, everything that finds grace, is equal to the 'beautiful.' Everything we don't reject.

We are the ones who decide that this is beautiful, that this is ugly. With our selfish tastes and distastes.

But everything is equal to God and to the painter. And this lesson is often given to the poet by painting. To love the ugly with an equal-to-equal love.

Everything that is (looked at justly) is good. Is exciting. Is 'terrible.' Life is terrible. Terribly beautiful, terribly cruel. Everything is marvelously terrible, to whoever looks at things as they are.

> I am toiling away at the rate of six paintings a day. I find it *terribly* difficult to catch all the colours of this country; at times, I am *appalled* at the kind of colours I have to use, I'm afraid my colours will seem *terrible* and yet I have considerably toned them down: this place is *drenched in light* . . . But how happy I am here because each day I can find the same effect again, *catch it and come to grips with it*.[17]

That was Monet.

Seeing the world as it is demands strengths, virtues. Which ones? Patience and courage.

The patience one has to have to approach the nonostensible, the minute, the insignificant, to discover the worm as a star without luster. To discover the grasshopper's worth.

The patience one must have to see the egg. The egg that might bore us at first glance the way a stone would. One needs patience to contemplate the egg, to brood on it, to see the hen in the egg, to see the history of the world in this shell. One needs another patience to see the absolute egg, the egg without the hen, the egg without signs, the naked egg, the egg egg. And it is with this patience that we can hope to see God.

And the kind of courage?

The greatest kind of courage. The courage to be afraid. To have the two fears. First we have to have the courage to be afraid of being hurt. We have to not defend ourselves. The world has to be suffered. Only through suffering will we know certain faces of the world, certain events of life: the courage to tremble and sweat and cry is as necessary for Rembrandt as for Genet. And it is necessary for Clarice Lispector to have the courage to feel disgust and love for the beggar with the amputated leg, disgust and love for the stump, horror at the rat which is also acceptance of the rat. For whoever writes, accepting the rat demands a far greater effort than for whoever has accepted the rat in advance, has begun to paint it. Whoever writes can easily hide her eyes.

And there is also the other fear, the least dazzling, the most burning: the fear of reaching joy, acute joy, the fear of allowing oneself to be carried away by exaltation, the fear of adoring. We must not be afraid of feeling this fear scalding the blood in our veins.

I am talking about what we are given to see, the spectacle of the world. Maybe it's easier for a painter than for someone who writes not to create hierarchies.

Painting may be more adept at not forgetting turtles than writing is. Writing is terribly human. Perhaps the word causes more fear and more hurt? . . . I don't know.

We can say joy. Can we paint it?

I'm talking about fidelity.

But perhaps the rarest, the most magnanimous fidelity, is the one we could have with regard to the reality of the human soul. It is so hard not to hate! Not to be the wolf for the other. To have for the traitor or the villain, the executioner, Rembrandt's calm and tender eyes for those who loved him, for those who betrayed him. Could Rembrandt be Shakespeare? I thought about it, thinking it was an impertinence. Van Gogh had thought about it before me.

> I have already read *Richard II*, *Henry IV* and half of *Henry V*. I read without wondering if the ideas of the people of those times were different from our own, or what would become of them if you confronted them with republican and socialist beliefs and so on. But what touches me, as in some novelists of our day, is that the voices of these people, which in Shakespeare's case reach us from a distance of several centuries, do not seem unfamiliar to us. It is so much alive that you think you know them and see the thing.
>
> And so what Rembrandt has alone or almost alone among painters, that tenderness of gaze which we see, whether it's in the 'Men of Emmaus' or in the 'Jewish Bride' or in some strange angelic figure as the picture you have had the good fortune to see, that brokenhearted tenderness, that glimpse of a superhuman infinitude that seems so natural there – in many places you come upon it in Shakespeare too. And then above all he is full of portraits, grave or gay, like 'Six' and the 'Traveler,' and like 'Saskia.'[18]

That was Van Gogh shortly before his death.

To be faithful as Shakespeare was to Lady Macbeth, to King Lear, to Shylock.

To create without commentary, without condemnation, without interpretation.

With respect for the shadows as for the light. Without knowing more or better.

I envy the painter: humility, in other words the justice of the look, is more easily granted to him than to the one who writes; because the painter is always defeated. He sees himself defeated. He always emerges out of breath from the combat that throws him on the world. Doesn't he always have before him the painting he hasn't done? The twenty-seventh cathedral, to remind him that one cathedral will always have escaped him?

Doesn't he have before his eyes the painting he will not do, the one that slips by his brush? The one he will do tomorrow, tomorrow if God wills it, or never?

There are painters who for me are voyagers of truth. They have given me lessons.

Whom do I call the voyagers of truth?

The one who painted water lilies for the last ten years of his life. The one who painted water lilies up until the last painting. Until his death. And then: 'The sea: I should like to always be before it or above it, and when I am dead, to be buried in a buoy.'[19] That is Monet's wish – to become seagull, water lily.

The one who painted a hundred Fujiyamas. The one who signed the map of China: 'Old man Manji crazy about painting, voyager from Katsushika, eighty-one years old.'

The one who searches until the last painting.

The one who paints with his right hand, his left hand, with his nails. This is Hokusai.

The one who knows that he will not find, because he knows that if he found, he would have nothing else to do except continue to search for the new mystery. The one who knows he must continue to search.

The one who does not become discouraged, does not tire.

I love the one who dares to stalk the secrets of light with the help of a single subject, armed with only a few water lilies.

And the lesson is: one does not paint ideas. One does not paint 'a subject.' One does not paint water lilies. And in the same way: no writing ideas. There is no subject. There are only mysteries. There are only questions.

Kandinsky sees the haystacks: 'And suddenly, for the first time, my eyes were drawn to a painting . . . I had the confused feeling that the subject was lacking in this picture . . . The subject, as the necessary element of paintings, lost all credit to my eyes.'[20]

What a struggle to no longer 'paint water lilies,' while *painting* water lilies. I mean: in order not to do the portrait of the water lilies, what a number of water lilies he will have had to paint before the representation of the water lilies wears itself out, before the water lilies are no longer the cause, before they are no longer the object, the aim, but the occasion, the everyday water lily, the day itself, the day's atom on the canvas.

Until they are no more, these water lilies, than Hokusai's everyday lion. In 1843, at the age of eighty-three, Hokusai tells himself that it is time he did his lions, and every morning he does his karashishi: 'I continue to draw hoping for a peaceful day' – that was the way he did two hundred and nineteen of them, until the lions were no more than the water lilies' path toward infinity.

And how I love the one who dared to paint the painter, again and again, until at the hundredth 'self-portrait' he succeeded in painting the painter impersonally; and yet ever so humanly; so nakedly human. Until we no longer think, 'This is a portrait of Rembrandt by himself.' Until at the hundredth portrait the name is so worn out that it no longer hides the man at all. And this man is as he is. He is old and absent-minded and, without proclaiming it and perhaps without knowing it, full of the mystery of age, time, and death.

I was in England during the Second World War, without any money and

> unhappy. My wife, who is younger and more courageous than I, said to me: 'Let's go and look for consolation in a museum.' Ruins were accumulating on the face of the earth. Not only was London being bombed – which was of little importance – but we learned every day of the annihilation of a new city. Devastation, destruction: the annihilation of a world becoming poorer and sadder. What bitterness. I looked at the last self-portrait of Rembrandt: ugly and broken, dreadful and full of despair; and so marvelously painted. And suddenly I understood: being capable of looking at oneself disappearing into the mirror – no longer seeing anything – and painting oneself as 'nothingness,' the negation of man. What a miracle, what a symbol. I drew courage and a new youth from this.[21]

That was Kokoschka.

How much patience, how much time in order for Rembrandt to cease resembling Rembrandt, to cease clinging to Rembrandt, and little by little to let himself slide, without being frightened, into the resemblance of someone, of no one.

How much greater a love for painting than for oneself! To come as far as the portraits of a man who allows himself to look, who allows himself to paint, who gives himself to be painted, by renouncing himself, who gives himself to painting as others do to God. And as the dead man does to science. So that it can advance on his body.

Perhaps Rembrandt dreamed of doing the last portrait of the painter? The one that only Rembrandt, at the end of his life, could have done? I dream of it.

The portrait of Rembrandt on his deathbed? For it is at this moment that he would have perceived the most anonymous, the most present, the most immediate, the most ephemeral, the essential, the mystery of human being. And if almost dead or already dead, in other words entirely freed from the rest of the Rembrandt he had painted, then he would have painted painting itself. He would truly have painted like no one.

I dream of this purity. I dream of this power of freedom. To paint the enigma. The enigmatic in painting. I think of the last Rembrandt. A man? Or a painting? I think of the last Hokusai. What is the name of the person who painted the last Hokusai?

I think of Hokusai's series of names like the series of water lilies. He had a hundred and one names. First he was called Shunro. Then, expelled from school, took the name Kusamara. Took the name Sori in '95. Hokusai Sori-ga, which means Studio of the North Star, Source of Truth; also called himself Toito, Litsu, Zen Hokusai, Gakyojin Hokusai, then Tawaraya, Hyakurin, Kanchi, and Sori.

Then abandoned the name Sori to his pupil. And called himself Tatsumasa, Sorobeku, Tokitaro, Gayojin Totogako Zen Hokusai, Sensei Kutsushika Taito, Zen Hokusai Tasmeitsu Gakyorojin Manji. All these names had a meaning. Not one was Hokusai.

Following himself without turning back. One after the other letting himself go.

Always being the future. Being the follower. The next one. Being one's own next one. The unknown one. Surpassing oneself. And yet not preceding the self. Abandoning oneself. In words. In curves. Abandoning one's names. One's signatures. Giving oneself entirely to rediscovery.

And so, in the course of time, what does this produce? What does this produce in the end?

A possibly mad purity.

One can tell the facts. One can invent some. It is more difficult to tell than to invent. Inventing is easy.

But the most difficult is fidelity to what one feels, there, at the extremity of life, at the nerve endings, around the heart.

And for that, there are no words. For what one feels, there are no words. For the reality of the soul, there are no words. But there are tears. One can allude to the divine. But the word 'god' is only a subterfuge.

Words are our accomplices, our traitors, our allies. We have to make use of them, spy on them, we should be able to purify them.

This is the dream of philosophers and poets. Words drive us mad. 'By repeating a word over and over again, it loses its meaning and becomes a hollow and redundant thing, and attains its own hard, enigmatic body.'[22]

Clarice amused herself by saying, 'Spirit, spirit, spirit.' And in the end, spirit flew. In the end, what is spirit?

'It is a sparkling and audacious word, like a flight of sparrows. Sometimes the repeated word becomes the dry orange-skin of itself, and no longer glows with even a sound.'[23]

What happens at the end of two hundred and nineteen lions? What happens at the end of ten thousand or a hundred thousand water lilies?

I claim the right to repeat the word until it becomes dry orange-skin, or until it becomes fragrance. I want to repeat the words 'I love you' until they become spirit.

But repetition, in those who write, is very badly received. The painter has the right to repeat until water lilies become divine sparrows.

To practice abandoning oneself to the water lilies.

Perhaps in the end that would give the portrait of God, or the self-portrait of God by Hokusai.

When Hokusai produced the hundred views of Mount Fuji, this is what he said:

> From the age of six, I had a passion for drawing the form of objects. By the age of about fifty, I had published an infinity of drawings, but nothing I produced before the age of seventy is worth counting. It was at the age of seventy-three that I more or less understood the structure of true nature, of animals, grasses, birds, fish, and insects.
>
> Consequently, by the age of eighty, I will have made even more progress; at ninety I will penetrate the mystery of things; at a hundred I will definitely have reached a degree of wonder, and when I am a hundred and ten, for my part, be it a dot, be it a line, everything will be alive.
>
> I ask those who will live as long as I do to see if I keep my word.
>
> Written at the age of seventy-five by myself, formerly Hokusai, today Gwakiō Rōjin, the old man crazy about drawing.[24]

This is truly the message of hope. It gives me a great deal of hope; I tell myself that when I am a hundred and ten, I will likewise know how to write a book that will be a dot.

Painting and writing – they are just that, hoping absolutely, they are what we might call *sunflower life*, to borrow an image from Van Gogh or from Clarice Lispector: 'Almost all lives are small. What enlarges a life is the inner life, are the thoughts, are the sensations, are the useless hopes . . . Hope is like a sunflower which turns aimlessly toward the sun. But it is not "aimless."'[25]

What enlarges a person's life are the impossible dreams, the unrealizable desires. The one that has not yet come true. And these hopes, these desires are so strong that at times one falls, and when a person falls, she sees, she is once again turned toward the inaccessible sun. Why does the flower have a fragrance that is not for anyone, and for nothing . . . ?

Like hope. Hope aims at hope itself.

And the painter? Paints from hope to hope. And between the two? Is there despair? Nonhope. Between-hope. But straightaway, hope arises. What I love is the painter's dissatisfaction, what a wonder: a furious Monet burning thirty canvases. Destroying his 'overworked' canvases.

Seen by us, these canvases were 'beautiful.' Seen by him, they are obstacles on the path to the last one.

His dissatisfaction is hope. Hope for the impossible. To turn oneself once again toward the sun is an act of faith. Writing the sun is as impossible as painting the air. This is what I want to do.

When I have finished writing, when I am a hundred and ten, all I will have done will have been to attempt a portrait of God. Of the God. Of what escapes us and makes us wonder. Of what we do not know but feel. Of what makes us live. I mean our own divinity, awkward, twisted, throbbing, our own mystery – we who are lords of this earth and do not know it, we who are touches of vermilion and yellow cadmium in the haystack and do not see it, we who are the eyes of this world and so often do not even look at it, we who could be the painters, the poets, the artists of life if only we wanted to; we who could be the lovers of the universe, if we really wanted to use our hands with mansuetude, we who so often use our booted feet to trample the world's belly.

We who are bits of sun, drops of ocean, atoms of the god, and who so often forget this, or are unaware of it, and so we take ourselves for employees. We who forget we could also be as luminous, as light, as the swallow that crosses the summit of the incomparable hill Fuji, so intensely radiant that we could ourselves be the painter's models, the heroes of human presence and the painter's gaze. But what we forget, the painter, who sees God each day in the process of changing, does not forget . . .

In what way do I feel different from these painters I love? In my way of loving an interior apple as much as an exterior apple.

> I received today a splendid apple, sent by Mr. Bellio; by its size and colours it is quite a phenomenon: he tells me that amidst so many orange trees I might feel like biting into a big apple from Normandy, hence his nice present.
>
> I did not dare to bite into it and offered it to Mr. Moreno.[26]

That was Monet.

Myself, I would have eaten it. In this way, I am different from those I would like to resemble. In my need to touch the apple without seeing it. To know it in the dark. With my fingers, with my lips, with my tongue.

In my need to share with you the food, the bread, the words, the painted food and also the not-painted food.

In my need to make use of my right hand to hold the pen and write, and of my two hands to hold nothing, to caress and to pray.

I am going to finish . . .

I have a postscript, Hokusai's address. In case, having reached the age of a hundred and ten, we are looking for him here it is:

> When you come, do not ask for Hokusai; they will not know how to answer you. Ask for the priest who draws and who recently moved into the building, ask the owner Gorobei for the beggar-priest in the courtyard of the Meio-in temple, in the middle of the bush.[27]

May I have merited such an address . . . by the time I am ninety years old . . .

Translated by Sarah Cornell et al.

Notes

1 Claude Monet, letter to Gustave Geffroy, in *Claude Monet at the Time of Giverny*, ed. Jacqueline and Maurice Guillaud, Paris, Guillaud, 1983, p. 80.
2 Clarice Lispector, *The Stream of Life*, trans. Elizabeth Lowe and Earl Fitz, Minneapolis, University of Minnesota Press, 1989, p. 3.
3 Ibid., p. 4.
4 Monet, letter to Alice Hoschedé, in *At the Time of Giverny*, p. 27.
5 *The Complete Letters of Vincent Van Gogh*, vol. 2, Greenwich, New York Graphic Society, n.d., p. 204. Cixous has slightly modified this translation. – Editor.
6 Monet, letter to Alice Hoschedé, in *At the Time of Giverny*, p. 36.
7 Journal of Julie Manet, in ibid., p. 36.
8 Monet, letter to Gustave Geffroy, in ibid., p. 80.
9 *The Complete Letters of Vincent Van Gogh*, vol. 2, p. 590.
10 Ibid., p. 596.
11 Ibid., pp. 598–99.
12 Paul Cézanne, quoted by Joachim Gasquet, in *At the Time of Giverny*, p. 208.
13 See Clarice Lispector, 'Such Gentleness,' in *Soulstorm: Stories by Clarice Lispector*, trans. Alexis Levitin, New York, New Directions, 1989, pp. 160–61.
14 See Clarice Lispector, *The Passion According to G.H.*, trans. Ronald W. Sousa, Minneapolis, University of Minnesota Press, 1988.
15 *Le Fou de peinture: Hokusai et son temps*, exhibition catalog, Centre Culturel du Marais, Paris, CRES, 1980, p. 217.
16 A. Houbraken, in Horst Gerson, *Rembrandt et son œuvre*, Paris, Hachette, 1968, p. 466.
17 Monet, letter to Alice Hoschedé, in *At the Time of Giverny*, p. 33, emphasis added.
18 *The Complete Letters of Vincent Van Gogh*, vol. 3, p. 187.
19 Monet, in *At the Time of Giverny*, p. 198.
20 Wassily Kandinsky, in ibid., p. 80.
21 Oskar Kokoschka, in Gerson, *Rembrandt et son œuvre*, p. 478.
22 Unpublished notebooks by Clarice Lispector, cited in Olga Borelli, *Clarice Lispector: Esboço para um possível retrato*, Rio de Janeiro, Editora Nova Fronteira, 1981, p. 77.
23 Ibid., p. 77.
24 *Le Fou de peinture*, p. 376.
25 Clarice Lispector, in Borelli, *Clarice Lispector*, p. 21.
26 Monet, letter to Alice Hoschedé, in *At the Time of Giverny*, p. 31.
27 *Le Fou de peinture*, p. 361.

SELECT BIBLIOGRAPHY OF MAJOR WORKS IN ENGLISH

Nineteenth-century German aesthetics

Immanuel Kant

Theoretical Philosophy, 1755–1770, ed. and trans. David Walford with Ralf Meerbote, Cambridge, Cambridge University Press, 1992.
Critique of Pure Reason (1781, 1787), trans. Norman Kemp Smith, London, Macmillan, 1990.
Critique of Pure Reason (1781, 1787), trans. Werner S. Pluhar, Indianapolis, Hackett, 1987.
Critique of Pure Reason (1781, 1787), trans. Paul Guyer and Allen W. Wood, Cambridge, Cambridge University Press, 1999.
Prolegomena to Any Future Metaphysics (1783), trans. Lewis White Beck, Indianapolis, Bobbs-Merrill, 1950 [now Macmillian].
Critique of Practical Reason (1788), trans. Lewis White Beck, Indianapolis, Bobbs-Merrill, 1956 [now Macmillan].
Practical Philosophy, ed. Mary Gregor, Cambridge, Cambridge University Press, 1999.
Critique of Judgement (1790), trans. James Creed Meredith, Oxford, Clarendon Press, 1952.
Critique of Judgment (1790), trans. Werner S. Pluhar, Indianapolis, Hackett, 1987.
Critique of the Power of Judgement (1790), trans. and ed. Paul Guyer and Eric Matthews, Cambridge, Cambridge University Press, 2000.

G.W.F. Hegel

Phenomenology of Mind (1807), trans. J.B. Baillie, New York, Harper and Row, 1967.
Phenomenology of Spirit (1807), trans. A.V. Miller, Oxford University Press, 1977.
Logic. Part One of the Encyclopaedia of the Philosophical Sciences (1830), trans. William Wallace, Oxford, Clarendon Press, 1975.
Philosophy of Nature. Part Two of the Encyclopaedia of the Philosophical Sciences (1830), trans. A.V. Miller, Oxford, Clarendon Press, 1970.
Philosophy of Nature. Part Two of the Encyclopaedia of the Philosophical Sciences (1830), trans. M.J. Petry, London, Allen and Unwin, 1970.
Philosophy of Mind. Part Three of the Encyclopaedia of the Philosophical Sciences (1830), trans. William Wallace, Oxford, Clarendon Press, 1971.
Aesthetics: Lectures on Fine Art (1835, 1842) vols I and II, trans. T.M. Knox, Oxford, Clarendon Press, 1975.
Introductory Lectures on Aesthetics, trans. B. Bosanquet, London, Penguin, 1993.
The Hegel Reader, ed. Stephen Houlgate, Oxford, Blackwell, 1998.

Friedrich Nietzsche

The Birth of Tragedy (1872), trans. Walter Kaufmann, New York, Vintage, 1967.
Human, All Too Human (1878), trans. Marion Faber with Stephen Lehmann, London, Penguin, 1994.
The Gay Science (1882), trans. Walter Kaufmann, New York, Vintage, 1974.
Thus Spoke Zarathustra (1883–92), trans. R.J. Hollingdale, London, Penguin, 1969.
Beyond Good and Evil (1886), trans. R.J. Hollingdale, London, Penguin, 1990.
On the Genealogy of Morals (1887), trans. Walter Kaufmann and R.J. Hollingdale, New York, Vintage, 1967.
The Case of Wagner (1888) [with *The Birth of Tragedy*], trans. Walter Kaufmann, New York, Vintage, 1967.
Twilight of the Idols (1888), trans. R.J. Hollingdale, London, Penguin, 1969.
Ecce Homo (1888), trans. Walter Kaufmann, New York, Vintage, 1967.
The Will to Power (from the *Nachgelassene Fragmente*, edited by Nietzsche's sister, Elisabeth Förster-Nietzsche), trans. Walter Kaufmann and R.J. Hollingdale, New York, Vintage, 1968.
The Portable Nietzsche, ed. and trans. Walter Kaufmann, New York, Viking, 1976.
A Nietzsche Reader, ed. and trans. R.J. Hollingdale, London, Penguin, 1977.
Philosophy and Truth: Selections from Nietzsche's Notebooks of the Early 1870s, ed. Daniel Breazeale, Atlantic Highlands, New Jersey, Humanities Press, 1990.

Phenomenology and hermeneutics

Martin Heidegger

History of the Concept of Time: Prolegomena (1925), trans. Theodore Kisiel, Bloomington, Indiana University Press, 1985.
Basic Problems of Phenomenology (1927), trans. Albert Hofstadter, Bloomington, Indiana University Press, 1982.
Being and Time (1927), trans. John Macquarrie and Edward Robinson, Oxford, Blackwell, 1995.
Being and Time (1927), trans. Joan Stambaugh, New York, State University of New York, 1996.
Kant and the Problem of Metaphysics (1929), trans. James S. Churchill, Bloomington, Indiana University Press, 1962.
Kant and the Problem of Metaphysics (1929), trans. Richard Taft, Bloomington, Indiana University Press, 1990.
An Introduction to Metaphysics (1953), trans. Ralph Manheim, New Haven, Yale University Press, 1959.
What is Called Thinking? (1954), trans. Fred D. Wieck and J. Glenn Gray, New York, Harper and Row, 1968.
The Principle of Reason (1957), trans. Reginald Lilly, Bloomington, Indiana University Press, 1991.
On the Way to Language (1959), trans. Peter D. Hertz and Joan Stambaugh, New York, Harper and Row, 1971.
What is a Thing? (1962), trans. W.B. Barton, Jr. and Vera Deutsch, Chicago, Henry Regnery Company, 1967.
Poetry, Language, Thought, trans. Albert Hofstadter, New York, Harper and Row, 1971.
Basic Writings, ed. David Farrell Krell, New York, Harper and Row, 1993.

Jean-Paul Sartre

The Transcendence of the Ego (1936), trans. Forrest Williams and Robert Kirkpatrick, New York, Noonday Press, 1962.

Nausea (1938), trans. Robert Baldick, London, Penguin, 1988.

Sketch for a Theory of the Emotions (1939), trans. Philip Mairet, London, Routledge, 1971.

The Psychology of the Imagination (1940), trans. Bernard Frechtman, London, Routledge, 1995.

Being and Nothingness (1943), trans. Hazel Barnes, London, Routledge, 1990.

Huis Clos (1945), ed. Keith Gore, London, Routledge, 1987.

Existentialism and Humanism (1946), trans. Philip Mairet, London, Methuen, 1997.

What is Literature? (1947), trans. Bernard Frechtman, London, Routledge, 1998.

Truth and Existence (written 1948, published posthumously in 1989), trans. Adrian van den Hoven, Chicago, University of Chicago Press, 1992.

Critique of Dialectical Reason (1960), trans. Alan Sheridan-Smith, London, New Left Books, 1976. Atlantic Highlands, New Jersey, Humanities Press, 1976.

The Words (1963), trans. Bernard Frechtman, New York, Braziller, 1964.

Essays in Existentialism, ed. Wade Baskin, New York, Citadel, 1995.

Emmanuel Levinas

The Theory of Intuition in Husserl's Phenomenology (1930), trans. Andre Orianne, Evanston, Northwestern University Press, 1985.

Existence and Existents (1947), trans. Alphonso Lingis, The Hague, Martinus Nijhoff, 1978.

Time and the Other (1948), trans. Richard Cohen, Pittsburgh, Duquesne University Press, 1990.

Totality and Infinity (1961), trans. Alphonso Lingis, Pittsburgh, Duquesne University Press, 1987.

Difficult Freedom: Essays on Judaism (1963), trans, Seán Hand, Baltimore, Johns Hopkins University Press, 1991.

Otherwise than Being, or Beyond Essence (1974), trans. Alphonso Lingis, The Hague, Martinus Nijhoff, 1981.

Ethics and Infinity (1982), trans. Richard Cohen, Pittsburgh, Duquesne University Press, 1985.

Collected Philosophical Papers, trans. Alphonso Lingis, Dordrecht, Martinus Nijhoff, 1987.

The Levinas Reader, ed. Seán Hand, Oxford, Blackwell, 1996.

Mikel Dufrenne

The Phenomenology of Aesthetic Experience (1953), trans. Edward S. Casey, Albert A. Anderson, Willis Domingo, and Leon Jacobson, Evanston, Northwestern University Press, 1973.

The Notion of the A Priori (1959), trans. Edward S. Casey, Evanston, Northwestern University Press, 1966.

In the Presence of the Sensuous (1967, 1976, 1981) 3 vols, trans. and ed. M.S. Roberts and D. Gallagher, Atlantic Highlands, New Jersey, Humanities Press, 1987.

Gaston Bachelard

The New Scientific Spirit (1934), trans. Arthur Goldhammer, Boston, Beacon Press, 1984.

The Psychoanalysis of Fire (1938), trans. Alan C.M. Ross, Boston, Beacon Press, 1964; and London, Routledge and Kegan Paul, 1964.

The Philosophy of No. A Philosophy of the New Scientific Mind (1940), trans. G.C. Waterston, New York, Orion Press, 1968.

Water and Dreams. An Essay on the Imagination of Matter (1942), trans. Edith Farrell, Dallas, Dallas Institute of Humanities and Cultural Publications, 1983.

Air and Dreams. An Essay on the Imagination of Movement (1943), trans. Edith and Frederick Farrell, Dallas, Dallas Institute of Humanities and Cultural Publications, 1988.
The Poetics of Space (1957), trans. Maria Jolas, New York, Orion Press, 1964.
The Flame of a Candle (1961), trans. Joni Caldwell, Dallas, Dallas Institute of Humanities and Cultural Publications, 1990.
The Right to Dream (1970), trans. J.A. Underwood, Dallas, Dallas Institute of Humanities and Cultural Publications, 1988.
On Poetic Imagination and Reverie: Selections from the Works of Gaston Bachelard, trans. Colette Gaudin, Indianapolis, Bobbs-Merrill, 1971.

Maurice Merleau-Ponty

The Structure of Behaviour (1942), trans. Alden L. Fisher, Boston, Beacon Press, 1963.
The Phenomenology of Perception (1945), trans. Colin Smith, London, Routledge, 1978.
Sense and Non-Sense (1948), trans. Hubert L. Dreyfus and Patricia Allen Dreyfus, Evanston, Northwestern University Press, 1964.
Consciousness and the Acquisition of Language (1950), trans. Hugh J. Silverman, Evanston, Northwestern University Press, 1973.
Signs (1960), trans. Richard C. McCleary, Evanston, Northwestern University Press, 1964.
The Visible and the Invisible (1964), ed. Claude Lefort, trans. Alphonso Lingis, Evanston, Northwestern University Press, 1968.
The Primacy of Perception, ed. James M. Edie, Evanston, Northwestern University Press, 1964.
The Prose of the World (1967), ed. Claude Lefort, trans. John O'Neill, London, Heinemann, 1974.
The Merleau-Ponty Aesthetics Reader, ed. Galen A. Johnson, Evanston, Northwestern University Press, 1993.

Hans-Georg Gadamer

Truth and Method (1960), trans. Joel Weinsheimer and Donald G. Marshall, London, Sheed and Ward, 1993.
Philosophical Hermeneutics, ed. David E. Linge, Berkeley, University of California Press, 1976.
Dialogue and Dialectic: Eight Hermeneutical Studies on Plato, New Haven, Yale University Press, 1980.
Reason in the Age of Science, Cambridge, Massachusetts, MIT Press, 1981.
Hegel's Dialectic: Five Hermeneutical Studies, New Haven, Yale University Press, 1982.
The Idea of the Good in Platonic–Aristotelian Philosophy, New Haven, Yale University Press, 1986.
The Relevance of the Beautiful and Other Essays, ed. Robert Bernasconi, Cambridge, Cambridge University Press, 1986.
Plato's Dialectical Ethics: Phenomenological Interpretations Relating to the Philebus, New Haven, Yale University Press, 1991.
Heidegger's Ways, Albany, State University of New York Press, 1994.
Literature and Philosophy in Dialogue, Albany, State University of New York Press, 1994.

Gianni Vattimo

The End of Modernity, trans. Jon R. Snyder, Cambridge, Polity Press, 1988.
The Transparent Society, trans. David Webb, Cambridge, Polity Press, 1992.
The Adventure of Difference: Philosophy after Nietzsche and Heidegger, trans. Cyprian Blamires with Thomas Harrison, Cambridge, Polity Press, 1993.

Marxism and critical theory

Karl Marx

Collected Works, Karl Marx, Friedrich Engels, Moscow, Progress, 1996 and London, Lawrence and Wishart, 1996.

Early Writings, trans. Rodney Livingstone and Gregor Benton, London, Penguin, 1992. This volume contains the full text of the extant *Economic and Philosophical Manuscripts* (1844).

Marx: Selected Writings, ed. David McLellan, Oxford, Oxford University Press, 1975. This volume contains extracts from the *Economic and Philosophical Manuscripts* (1844).

The German Ideology (1845–46), ed. C. Arthur, London, Lawrence and Wishart, 1970.

The Communist Manifesto (1848, with Friedrich Engels), ed. David McLellan, Oxford, Oxford University Press, 1998.

Grundrisse: Foundations of the Critique of Political Economy (1859), trans. Martin Nicolaus, London, Penguin, 1993.

Capital: A Critique of Political Economy. Vol. 1: The Process of Production of Capital (1867), trans. Ben Fowkes, London, Penguin, 1990.

Capital: A Critique of Political Economy. Vol. 2: The Process of Circulation of Capital (1867), trans. David Fernbach, London, Penguin, 1992.

Capital: A Critique of Political Economy. Vol. 3: The Process of Capitalist Production as a Whole (1867), trans. David Fernbach, London, Penguin, 1991.

Georg Lukács

Theory of the Novel: A Historico-Philosophical Essay on the Forms of Great Literature (1920), trans. Anna Bostock, Cambridge, Massachusetts, MIT Press, 1971.

History and Class Consciousness: Studies in Marxist Dialectics (1923), trans. Rodney Livingstone, London, Merlin Press, 1971.

The Historical Novel (1936), trans. Hannah and Stanley Mitchell, London, Merlin Press, 1962.

The Meaning of Contemporary Realism (1958), trans. John and Necke Mander, London, Merlin Press, 1963.

Studies in European Realism (1964), trans. E. Bone, New York, Grosset and Dunlap, 1964.

Essays on Thomas Mann (1964), trans. Stanley Mitchell, London, Merlin Press, 1964.

Goethe and His Age (1964), trans. Robert Anchor, London, Merlin Press, 1968.

Writer and Critic and Other Essays, trans. Arthur Kahn, London, Merlin Press, 1970. Selections from Lukács' literary criticism.

The Ontology of Social Being (1971–73) 3 vols, London, Merlin Press, 1978–80.

Marxism and Human Liberation: Essays on History, Culture and Revolution, New York, Delta Books, 1973.

Theodor W. Adorno

Dialectic of Enlightenment (1947, with Max Horkheimer), trans. John Cumming, New York, Continuum, 1972.

Minima Moralia: Reflections from Damaged Life (1951), trans. E.F.N. Jephcott, London, Verso, 1978.

Notes to Literature (1958, 1961) 2 vols, trans. Shierry Weber Nicholsen, New York, Columbia University Press, 1991.

Introduction to the Sociology of Music (1962), trans. E.B. Ashton, New York, Continuum, 1989.

Kierkegaard: The Construction of the Aesthetic (1962), trans. Robert Hullot-Kentor, Minneapolis, University of Minnesota Press, 1989.

The Jargon of Authenticity (1964), trans. Knut Tarnowski, London, Routledge, 1973.
Negative Dialectics (1966), trans. E.B. Ashton, London, Routledge, 1973.
Prisms (1967), trans. Samuel and Shierry Weber, Cambridge, Massachusetts, MIT Press, 1981.
Aesthetic Theory (1970), trans. C. Lenhardt, London, Routledge, 1984.
Aesthetic Theory (1970), trans. Robert Hullot-Kentor, Minneapolis, University of Minnesota Press, 1997.
The Philosophy of Modern Music, trans. A. Mitchell and W. Blomster, New York, Seabury Press, 1973.
The Culture Industry. Selected Essays on Mass Culture, London, Routledge, 1991.
Quasi una Fantasia: Essays on Modern Music, trans. Rodney Livingstone, London, Verso, 1992.

Herbert Marcuse

Reason and Revolution: Hegel and the Rise of Social Theory, Oxford, Oxford University Press, 1941.
Eros and Civilization: A Philosophical Enquiry into Freud, Boston, Beacon Press, 1955.
One-Dimensional Man: Studies in the Ideology of Advanced Industrial Society, Boston, Beacon Press, 1964.
Negation: Essays in Critical Theory, Boston, Beacon Press, 1968.
An Essay in Liberation, Boston, Beacon Press, 1969.
Five Lectures, Boston, Beacon Press, 1970.
Counterrevolution and Revolt, Boston, Beacon Press, 1972.
Studies in Critical Philosophy, Boston, Beacon Press, 1973.
Revolution or Reform: A Confrontation (with Karl Popper), ed. A. Ferguson, Chicago, University of Chicago Press, 1976.
The Aesthetic Dimension: Toward a Critique of Marxist Aesthetics, trans. Herbert Marcuse and Erica Sherover, Boston, Beacon Press, 1977.
Hegel's Ontology, Cambridge, Massachusetts, MIT Press, 1987.

Jürgen Habermas

The Structural Transformation of the Public Sphere: An Inquiry into a Category of Bourgeois Society (1962), trans. Thomas Burger with Frederick Lawrence, Cambridge, Polity Press, 1989.
Theory and Practice (1963), trans. John Viertel, Boston, Beacon Press, 1973.
Knowledge and Human Interests (1968), trans. Jeremy J. Shapiro, Boston, Beacon Press, 1971.
On the Logic of the Social Sciences (1970), trans. Shierry W. Nicholsen and Jerry Stark, Cambridge, Massachusetts, MIT Press, 1988.
Legitimation Crisis (1973), trans. Thomas McCarthy, Boston, Beacon Press, 1975.
Communication and the Evolution of Society (1976), trans. Thomas McCarthy, London, Heinemann, 1979.
The Theory of Communicative Action (1981) 2 vols, trans. Thomas McCarthy, Boston, Beacon Press, 1984, 1987.
The Philosophical Discourse of Modernity (1985), trans. Frederick Lawrence, Cambridge, Polity Press, 1987.
Moral Consciousness and Communicative Action, trans. Christian Lenhardt and Shierry Weber Nicholsen, Cambridge, Massachusetts, MIT Press, 1990.
Postmetaphysical Thinking, trans. William Mark Hohengarten, Cambridge, Massachusetts, MIT Press, 1992.
On the Pragmatics of Communication, ed. Maeve Cooke, Cambridge, Polity Press, 1999.

Fredric Jameson

Marxism and Form, Princeton, Princeton University Press, 1971.
The Prison-House of Language, Princeton, Princeton University Press, 1972.
The Political Unconscious: Narrative as a Socially Symbolic Act, London, Methuen, 1981.
Late Marxism: Adorno and the Persistence of the Dialectic, London, Verso, 1990.
Signatures of the Visible, London, Routledge, 1990.
Postmodernism, or the Cultural Logic of Late Capitalism, London, Verso, 1991.
The Geopolitical Aesthetic: Cinema and Space in the World System, Bloomington, Indiana University Press, 1992.
The Seeds of Time, New York, Columbia University Press, 1994.
The Cultural Turn: Selected Writings on the Postmodern, 1983–1998, London, Verso, 1998.

Modernism

Georg Simmel

The Philosophy of Money (1900), trans. Tom Bottomore and David Frisby, London, Routledge, 1990.
Conflict and the Web of Group Affiliations (1908), trans. Kurt H. Wolff and R. Bendix Hughes, Glencoe, Illinois, Free Press, 1955.
The Conflict in Modern Culture and Other Essays (1918), trans. D.E. Jenkinson *et al.*, New York, Barnes and Noble, 1968.
The Problems of the Philosophy of History, trans. G. Oakes, New York, Free Press, 1977.

Walter Benjamin

Illuminations, trans. Harry Zohn, London, Fontana, 1973.
Understanding Brecht, trans. Anna Bostock, London, Verso, 1973.
Charles Baudelaire: A Lyric Poet in the Era of High Capitalism, trans. Harry Zohn and Quinton Hoare, London, Verso, 1983.
One-Way Street and Other Writings, trans. Edmund Jephcott and Kingsley Shorter, London, Verso, 1985.
The Origin of German Tragic Drama, trans. John Osborne, London, Verso, 1985.
Reflections. Essays, Aphorisms, Autobiographical Writings, trans. Edmund Jephcott, New York, Schocken Books, 1986.
The Correspondence of Walter Benjamin, 1910–1940, ed. Gershom Scholem and Theodor W. Adorno, trans. Manfred R. Jacobsen and Evelyn M. Jacobsen, Chicago, University of Chicago Press, 1994.
Selected Writings, Vol. 1: 1913–1926, ed. Marcus Bullock and Michael W. Jennings, Cambridge, Massachusetts, Harvard University Press, 1996.
Selected Writings, Vol. 2: 1927–1940, ed. Marcus Bullock and Michael W. Jennings, Cambridge, Massachusetts, Harvard University Press, 1999.
The Arcades Project, trans. Howard Eiland and Kevin McLaughlin, Cambridge, Massachusetts, Harvard University Press, 1999.

Maurice Blanchot

Death Sentence (1948), trans. Lydia Davis, New York, Station Hill, 1978.
Thomas the Obscure (1950), trans. Robert Lemerton, New York, Station Hill, 1988.
When the Time Comes (1951), trans. Lydia Davis, New York, Station Hill, 1985.

The One Who Was Standing Apart From Me (1953), trans. Lydia Davis, New York, Station Hill, 1989.

The Space of Literature (1955), trans. Ann Smock, Lincoln, University of Nebraska Press, 1982.

The Last Man (1957), trans. Lydia Davis, New York, Columbia University Press, 1987.

The Infinite Conversation (1969), trans. Susan Hanson, Minneapolis, University of Minnesota Press, 1992.

The Madness of the Day (1973), trans. Lydia Davis, New York, Station Hill, 1981.

The Step Not Beyond (1973), trans. Lycette Nelson, Albany, State University of New York, 1992.

The Writing of the Disaster (1980), trans. Ann Smock, Lincoln, University of Nebraska Press, 1982.

The Unavowable Community (1983), trans. Pierre Joris, New York, Station Hill, 1988.

The Gaze of Orpheus and Other Literary Essays, ed. P. Adams Sitney, trans. Lydia Davis, New York, Station Hill, 1981.

The Sirens' Song: Selected Essays, ed. Gabriel Josipovici, trans. Sacha Rabinovitch, Bloomington, Indiana University Press, 1982, and Brighton, Harvester Press, 1982.

Vicious Circles, trans. Paul Auster, New York, Station Hill, 1985.

The Blanchot Reader, ed. Michael Holland, Oxford, Blackwell, 1995.

The Station Hill Blanchot Reader: Fiction and Literary Essays, ed. George Quasha, New York, Station Hill, 1998.

Ernst Bloch

The Principle of Hope, trans. Neville Plaice, Stephen Plaice, and Paul Knight, 3 vols, Cambridge, Massachusetts, MIT Press, 1986.

The Utopian Function of Art and Literature, trans. Jack Zipes and Frank Mecklenburg, Cambridge, Massachusetts, MIT Press, 1996.

Poststructuralism and postmodernism

Georges Bataille

The Story of the Eye by Lord Auch (1928), trans. Joachim Neugroschal, London, Penguin, 1982.

Inner Experience (1943), trans. Leslie Anne Boldt, Albany, State University of New York Press, 1988.

Guilty (1944), trans. Bruce Boone, Venice, Lapis Press, 1988.

The Accursed Share (1949), vol. 1, trans. Robert Hurley, New York, Zone Books, 1988.

Erotism (1957), trans. Mary Dalwood, London and New York, Marion Boyars, 1987.

Literature and Evil (1957), trans. Alastair Hamilton, London, Marion Boyars, 1986.

The Tears of Eros (1961), trans. Peter Connor, San Francisco, City Lights Books, 1989.

Visions of Excess: Selected Writings, 1927–1939, ed. Alan Stoekl, trans. Alan Stoekl, Carl R. Lovitt, and Donald M. Leslie Jr, Minneapolis, University of Minnesota Press, 1985.

Theory of Religion, trans. Robert Hurley, New York, Zone Books, 1989.

Roland Barthes

Writing Degree Zero (1953), trans. Annette Lavers and Colin Smith, New York, Hill and Wang, 1977.

Mythologies (1957), trans. Annette Lavers, London, Jonathan Cape, 1974.

Elements of Semiology (1964), trans. Annette Lavers and Colin Smith, New York, Hill and Wang, 1977.

The Fashion System (1967), trans. Matthew Ward and Richard Howard, New York, Hill and Wang, 1983.

S/Z (1970), trans. Richard Miller, New York, Hill and Wang, 1974.

The Empire of the Sign (1970), trans. Richard Howard, New York, Hill and Wang, 1982.

The Pleasure of the Text (1973), trans. Richard Miller, New York, Hill and Wang, 1975.

A Lover's Discourse: Fragments (1977), trans. Richard Howard, New York, Hill and Wang, 1984.

Image, Music, Text, trans. Stephen Heath, London, Fontana, 1977.

Camera Lucida: Reflections on Photography (1980), trans. Richard Howard, London, Vintage, 1993.

The Grain of the Voice: Interviews 1962–1980 (1981), trans. Linda Coverdale, New York, Hill and Wang, 1985.

The Responsibility of Forms, trans. Richard Howard, Berkeley, University of California Press, 1991.

Michel Foucault

Madness and Civilization: A History of Insanity in the Age of Reason (1961), trans. Richard Howard, New York, Vintage, 1973.

The Birth of the Clinic: An Archaeology of Medical Perception (1963), trans. Alan Sheridan, New York, Vintage, 1975.

The Order of Things: An Archaeology of Human Sciences (1966), London, Routledge, 1994.

An Archaeology of Knowledge (1969), trans. Alan Sheridan, London, Tavistock, 1974.

Discipline and Punish: The Birth of the Prison (1975), trans. Alan Sheridan, London, Penguin, 1977.

The History of Sexuality, Volume 1: An Introduction (1976), trans. Robert Hurley, London, Allen Lane, 1979.

The History of Sexuality, Volume 2: The Use of Pleasure (1984), trans. Robert Hurley, New York, Pantheon, 1985.

The History of Sexuality, Volume 3: The Care of the Self (1984), trans. Robert Hurley, New York, Pantheon, 1986.

The Foucault Reader, ed. Paul Rainbow, New York, Pantheon, 1984.

Essential Works of Foucault, 1954–1984, Volume 2: Aesthetics, Method, and Epistemology, ed. James Faubion, London, Penguin, 1998.

Jacques Derrida

Speech and Phenomena and Other Essays on Husserl's Theory of Signs (1967), trans. David B. Allinson, Evanston, Northwestern University Press, 1973.

Of Grammatology (1967), trans. Gayatari Spivak, Baltimore and London, Johns Hopkins University Press, 1976.

Writing and Difference (1967), trans. Alan Bass, Chicago, University of Chicago Press, 1978.

Margins of Philosophy (1972), trans. Alan Bass, Chicago, University of Chicago Press, 1982.

Positions (1972), trans. Alan Bass, Chicago, University of Chicago Press, 1982.

Dissemination (1972), trans. Barbara Johnson, Chicago, University of Chicago Press, 1981.

Glas (1974), trans. John P. Leavey Jr and Richard Rand, Lincoln, University of Nebraska Press, 1986.

The Truth in Painting (1978), trans. Geoff Bennington and Ian McLeod, Chicago, University of Chicago Press, 1987.

Spurs: Nietzsche's Styles (1978), trans. Barbara Harlow, Chicago, University of Chicago Press, 1979.

The Post Card: From Socrates to Freud and Beyond (1980), trans. Alan Bass, Chicago, University of Chicago Press, 1987.
Limited Inc., Evanston, Northwestern University Press, 1988.
Of Spirit: Heidegger and the Question, trans. Geoffrey Bennington and Rachel Bowlby, Chicago, University of Chicago Press, 1989.
Acts of Literature, ed. Derek Attridge, London, Routledge, 1992.
Memoirs of the Blind: The Self-Portrait and Other Ruins, trans. Pascale-Anne Brault and Michael Naas, Chicago, University of Chicago Press, 1993.
Spectres of Marx (1993), trans. Peggy Kamuf, London, Routledge, 1994.
Points: Interviews, 1974–1994, ed. Elisabeth Weber, trans. Peggy Kamuf *et al.*, Stanford, Stanford University Press, 1995.
On the Name, ed. Thomas Dutoit, Stanford, Stanford University Press, 1995.
The Derrida Reader: Between the Blinds, ed. Peggy Kamuf, London, Harvester Wheatsheaf, 1991.

Paul de Man

Allegories of Reading: Figural Language in Rousseau, Nietzsche, Rilke, and Proust, New Haven, Yale University Press, 1979.
Blindness and Insight: Essays in the Rhetoric of Contemporary Criticism, London, Methuen, 1983.
The Rhetoric of Romanticism, New York, Columbia University Press, 1984.

Jean Baudrillard

The System of Objects (1968), trans. James Benedict, London, Verso, 1996.
For a Critique of the Political Economy of the Sign (1972), trans. Charles Levin, St Louis, Telos Press, 1981.
The Mirror of Production (1973), trans. Mark Poster, St Louis, Telos Press, 1975.
Symbolic Exchange and Death (1976), trans. Ian Grant, London, Sage, 1993.
Seduction (1979), trans. Brian Singer, London, Macmillan, 1990.
Simulacra and Simulation (1981), trans. Sheila Faria Glaser, Ann Arbor, University of Michigan Press, 1984.
Fatal Strategies: Crystal Revenge (1983), trans. Philip Beitchman and W.G.J. Niesluchowski, London, Pluto, 1990.
America (1986), trans. Charles Turner, London, Verso, 1989.
Cool Memories (1987), trans. Charles Turner, London, Verso, 1990.
The Transparency of Evil: Essays in Extreme Phenomena (1990), trans. John J. St John, London, Verso, 1993.
The Illusion of the End, trans. Charles Turner, Cambridge, Polity Press, 1994.
Selected Writings, ed. Mark Poster, Cambridge, Polity Press, 1988.

Jean-François Lyotard

Libidinal Economy (1974), trans. Iain Hamilton Grant, Bloomington, Indiana University Press, 1993.
Just Gaming (1979) (with Jean-Loup Thébaud), trans. Wlad Godzich, Minneapolis, Minnesota University Press; Manchester, Manchester University Press, 1984.
The Postmodern Condition: A Report on Knowledge (1979), trans. Geoffrey Bennington and Brian Massumi, Minneapolis, Minnesota University Press; Manchester, Manchester University Press, 1984.

The Differend: Phrases in Dispute (1983), trans. George ven den Abeele, Minneapolis, Minnesota University Press; Manchester, Manchester University Press, 1984.

Peregrinations: Law, Form, Event, New York, Columbia University Press, 1988.

Heidegger and 'The Jews' (1988), trans. Andreas Michel and Mark Roberts, Minneapolis, Minnesota University Press, 1990.

The Inhuman: Reflections on Time (1988), trans. Geoffrey Bennington and Rachel Bowlby, Cambridge, Polity Press, 1991.

The Postmodern Explained to Children: Correspondence 1982–1985 (1988), trans. Julian Pefanis and Morgan Thomas, Sydney, Power Publications, 1992.

Lessons on the Analytic of the Sublime, trans. Elizabeth Rottenberg, Stanford, Stanford University Press, 1994.

The Lyotard Reader, ed. Andrew Benjamin, Oxford, Blackwell, 1989.

Gilles Deleuze and Félix Guattari

Empiricism and Subjectivity: An Essay on Hume's Theory of Human Nature (1953), trans. Constantin V. Boundas, New York, Columbia University Press, 1991.

Nietzsche and Philosophy (1962), trans. Hugh Tomlinson, New York, Columbia University Press, 1983.

Kant's Critical Philosophy: The Doctrine of the Faculties (1963), trans. Hugh Tomlinson and Barbara Habberjam, Minneapolis, University of Minnesota Press, 1984.

Expressionism in Philosophy: Spinoza (1968), trans. Martin Joughin, New York, Zone Books, 1990.

Difference and Repetition (1969), trans. Paul Patton, London, Athlone Press, 1994.

The Logic of Sense (1969), trans. Mark Lester, ed. Constantin V. Boundas, New York, Columbia University Press, 1990.

Anti-Oedipus: Capitalism and Schizophrenia 1 (1972) (with Félix Guattari), trans. Robert Hurley, M. Seem, and H.R. Lane, New York, Viking Press and Richard Sever, 1977.

Kafka: Toward a Minor Literature (1975) (with Félix Guattari), trans. Dana Polan, Minneapolis, University of Minnesota Press, 1986.

A Thousand Plateaus: Capitalism and Schizophrenia 2 (1980) (with Félix Guattari), trans. Brian Massumi, Minneapolis, University of Minnesota Press, 1987.

Spinoza: Practical Philosophy (1981), trans. Robert Hurley, San Francisco, City Lights Books, 1988.

Cinema 1: The Movement-Image (1983), trans. Hugh Tomlinson and Barbara Habberjam, Minneapolis, University of Minnesota Press, 1986.

Cinema 2: The Time-Image (1985), trans. Hugh Tomlinson and Roberts Galeta, Minneapolis, University of Minnesota Press, 1989.

The Fold: Leibniz and the Baroque (1988), trans. Tom Conley, Minneapolis, University of Minnesota Press, 1992.

Negotiations (1990), trans. Martin Joughin, New York, Columbia University Press, 1995.

What is Philosophy? (1991) (with Félix Guattari), trans. Hugh Tomlinson and Graham Burchell, London, Verso, 1994.

The Deleuze Reader, ed. Constantin Boundas, New York, Columbia University Press, 1993.

Psychoanalysis and feminism

Sigmund Freud

Letters of Sigmund Freud 1873–1939, ed. Ernest L. Freud, trans. Tania and James Stern, London, Hogarth Press, 1961.

Standard Edition of the Complete Psychological Works of Sigmund Freud, ed. James Strachey, London, Hogarth Press, 1974.
The Interpretation of Dreams (1900) (vols IV and V of *Complete Works*), trans. James Strachey, London, Penguin, 1991.
Art and Literature, trans. James Strachey, London, Penguin, 1991.
On Sexuality: Three Essays on the Theory of Sexuality, ed. Angela Richards, trans. James Strachey, London, Penguin, 1991.
Essentials of Psychoanalysis, ed. Anna Freud, Harmondsworth, Penguin, 1986.
The Freud Reader, ed. Peter Gay, London, Vintage, 1995.

Jacques Lacan

Écrits: A Selection (1966), trans. Alan Sheridan, London, Tavistock, 1977.
Television: A Challenge to the Psychoanalytic Establishment (1973), trans. Denis Hollier, Rosalind Krauss, and Annette Michelson, New York, Norton, 1990.
Four Fundamental Concepts of Psychoanalysis (1973), trans. Alan Sheridan, London, Vintage, 1977.
The Seminar of Jacques Lacan, 1953–1954, Book 1. Freud's Papers on Technique (1975), trans. John Forrester and Sylvana Tomaselli, Cambridge, Cambridge University Press, 1988.
The Seminar of Jacques Lacan, 1954–1955, Book 2. The Ego in Freud's Theory and in the Technique of Psychoanalysis (1978), ed. Jacques-Allain Miller, trans. Sylvana Tomaselli, Cambridge, Cambridge University Press, 1988.
The Seminar of Jacques Lacan, Book 3. The Psychoses (1981), trans. Russell Grigg, London, Routledge, 1993.
The Ethics of Psychoanalysis, 1959–1960, trans. Dennis Porter, London, Routledge, 1992.
The Seminar of Jacques Lacan, 1972–1973, Book 20. Encore (1975), ed. Jacques-Allain Miller, trans. Bruce Fink, New York, Norton, 1998.

Julia Kristeva

About Chinese Women (1974), trans. Anita Barrows, New York and London, Marion Boyars, 1986.
Revolution in Poetic Language (1974), trans. Margaret Waller, New York, Columbia University Press, 1984.
Desire in Language: A Semiotic Approach to Literature and Art (1977), trans. Thomas S. Gora, Alice Jardine, and Leon S. Roudiez, Oxford, Blackwell, 1984.
Powers of Horror: An Essay on Abjection (1980), trans. Leon S. Roudiez, New York, Columbia University Press, 1982.
Tales of Love (1983), trans. Leon S. Roudiez, New York, Columbia University Press, 1987.
Black Sun (1987), trans. Leon S. Roudiez, New York, Columbia University Press, 1989.
Strangers to Ourselves (1988), trans. Leon S. Roudiez, New York, Columbia University Press, 1991.
The Kristeva Reader, ed. Toril Moi, Oxford, Blackwell, 1986.

Luce Irigaray

Speculum of the Other Woman (1974), trans. Gillian C. Gill, New York, Cornell University Press, 1985.
This Sex Which Is Not One (1977), trans. Catherine Porter with Carolyn Burke, New York, Cornell University Press, 1985.
Marine Lover of Friedrich Nietzsche (1980), trans. Gillian C. Gill, New York, Columbia University Press, 1991.

Elemental Passions (1982), ed. Joanne Collier and Judith Still, New York, Routledge, 1992.
An Ethics of Sexual Difference (1984), trans. Carolyn Burke and Gillian C. Gill, New York, Cornell University Press, 1993.
Culture of Difference (1990), trans. Alison Martin, New York, Routledge, 1992.
The Irigaray Reader, ed. Margaret Whitford, Oxford, Blackwell, 1991.

Hélène Cixous

The Newly Born Woman (with Catherine Clément), trans. Betsy Wing, Manchester, Manchester University Press, 1986.
'Coming to Writing' and Other Essays, trans. Sarah Cornell *et al.*, Cambridge, Massachusetts, Harvard University Press, 1991.
Readings: The Poetics of Blanchot, Joyce, Kafka, Kleist, Lispector and Tsvetayeva, trans. Verena Andermatt Conley, Hemel Hempstead, Harvester Wheatsheaf, 1992.
The Hélène Cixous Reader, ed. Susan Sellers, London, Routledge, 1994.
Hélène Cixous, Rootprints: Memory and Life Writing (with Mireille Calle-Gruber), trans. Eric Prenowitz, London, Routledge, 1997.
Stigmata: Escaping Texts, London, Routledge, 1998.

INDEX

Book Shelves
BH201 .C59 2000
The continental aesthetics reader

CANISIUS COLLEGE LIBRARY
BUFFALO, NY